PUNK DIARY:
1970–1979

It would be difficult to find anyone more in touch with punk music than George Gimarc. Early in 1977, he originated one of America's first new wave radio programs, The Rock & Roll Alternative. It ran continuously for fourteen years and was heard on various stations in England, Ireland, Belgium, Italy, Australia and New Zealand, as well as at home in Texas. Since hitting the air in 1975, George has remained on the forefront of music, discovering new talent and breaking cutting edge sounds. He's interviewed hundreds of the scene's movers & shakers, making careers and setting trends. He was the driving force behind KDGE radio in Dallas; one of the nation's leading new rock stations with an audience in the hundreds of thousands. Always looking for the next big thing, he now runs an independent record company that releases CDs twice a year of unsigned bands from around America. His passion for music explains his collecting some 65,000 records, and knowing something about each and every one of them. There are few that can put a work like this together working from real life experience and their own resources.

George first started writing *Punk Diary: 1970–1979* because he needed a reference book on the period and there wasn't one to be found. Even now, a decade later, there is little except *England's Dreaming* which takes an accurate and detailed look at the entirety of the punk boom. *Punk Diary* changes all that. Not only accurate with the resources used to compile it, it has also been fact checked by many of the major musicians of the period, each giving it a resounding thumbs up.

more interesting than a 20 page punk fanzine

THE LIVE PAGE HEADLINE!

No Boring old farts on this pa
Except Brian.B

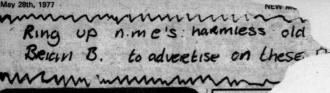

PUNK DIARY: 1970–1979

George Gimarc

VINTAGE

Published by Vintage 1994

2 4 6 8 10 9 7 5 3 1

First published in the United States of America by St. Martin's Press, 1994

Vintage
Random House, 20 Vauxhall Bridge Road,
London SW1V 2SA

Random House Australia (Pty) Limited
20 Alfred Street, Milsons Point, Sydney
New South Wales 2061, Australia

Random House New Zealand Limited
18 Poland Road, Glenfield,
Auckland 10, New Zealand

Random House South Africa (Pty) Limited
PO Box 337, Bergvlei, South Africa

Random House UK Limited Reg. No. 954009

A CIP catalogue record for this book
is available from the British Library

ISBN 0 09 952211 X

Printed and bound in Great Britain by
Clays Ltd, St Ives plc

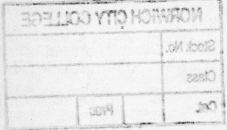

To Donna, who put up
with "that racket" from
the next room.

INTRODUCTION

"God, it must have taken you years!" That's the first thing people usually say when they pick up this book. It's true. Like a literary stalagmite, it's been growing bit by bit over the course of a decade or more. Mountains of newspapers, record company bios, tapes of personal interviews and recollections, and of course, just plain living the music. I was personally disappointed that there wasn't a comprehensive book on the punk movement. In the rock scene, this is important stuff. The punk movement was a frontal attack on rock stars the media held up to the heavens, mindless disco, and that tarted-up over-produced shit that ruled the radio. It brought music back to the streets.

The '70s punk movement, with it's trappings of safety pins, leather and bondage wear, seems like it happened a millennia ago. Yet the bands that emerged out of this clique shaped music with the same certainty and depth as the Beatles changed their generation. If it weren't for the musical enema that groups like the Stooges and the Damned gave to the establishment, we would probably have never heard of the Police, REM, The Cure, Depeche Mode, Pearl Jam or U2.

In the mid seventies, corporate rockers like The Eagles, Bob Seger and Queen were setting up dynasties and distancing themselves from their fans. If music were the world's cuisine, they were the white bread. Kids in garage bands setting out to copy their heroes could not even begin to come close to what was on those records. They were too polished, too packaged, too produced. What sixteen-year old could even begin to relate to Genesis? A corporate philosophy had taken over. Rock music had become a safe, packaged commodity, with consultants in control.

Then came the punks. Troublemakers. Attitude incarnate. They had nothing but disrespect for those before them. They distrusted anyone who wasn't one of them (and that was just about everyone). They set out to be a boil on the backside of the music world. They were homely, unkempt and generally couldn't play worth a damn. But that wasn't the point. They were a '70s rock hero's worst nightmare and this new sound was growing like an out of control fungus in every town and city in England and America. A radical change was in the wind. The late seventies saw a new movement sweep the world. Music was brought back to the street level, and a new generation of disfranchised kids found voice. Punk was labeled a fad, but this upstart escape from the treadmill of mediocrity was what saved rock and roll.

The punk movement is shrouded in mystery and misconception. Serious writers have never given serious thought to this upstart movement. Punks had no need for written approval! Fifteen years later, there is still no authoritative source book on the movement.

"PUNK DIARY: 1970 -'79" covers the first riotous decade of punk in England. The story begins in 1970, and lurches through an incredible cast of characters and unlikely role models. Although generally centered on the scene in Britain, there are some American groups included, those that had an impact on the UK scene.

What makes this unlike any other rock book is that it treats the scene on a day to day basis, diary style, the way it actually happened. The only way that this tangled web can make sense. Each entry details record releases, bands getting together or breaking up, riots, arrests, and revealing quotes from the personalities of the day. There's even a "Live Tonight" gig guide of who was playing where each night. The sources include a decades worth of music newspapers, front room fanzines, a towering stack of records, magazines, in-depth personal interviews and copious notes. There are over 2,200 music news entries and 1,000 recordings detailed.

Going through the book from beginning to end, you will experience what it was like to watch the scene unfold, without having to change wardrobe. This is not a book of record reviews. In "PUNK DIARY: 1970-'79" there are no foregone conclusions, no value judgments. Make your own connections between the people and events and see who influenced who, what was real and what was contrived. There will be myths shattered and forgotten heroes found.

If you have any additions, corrections or questions about "Punk Diary: 1970-'79" you can reach me at PO Box 280173, Dallas, Texas 75228.

George Gimarc
August 1994

1970/1971

"Each successive pop explosion has come roaring out of the clubs in which it was born like an angry young bull. Watching from the other side of the gate, the current establishment has proclaimed it as dangerous, subversive, a menace to youth and demanded that something be done about it...."

— George Melly, *Revolt Into Style* 1970

August 1970.............................

THE STOOGES release their second LP, "Fun House," for Elektra. The album sees the band drifting into longer and longer jams, like "Fun House" which clocks in at 7:46 and "Dirt" at 7:00. They've added saxophonist Steve MacKay who helps the Stooges realize the jazz style freakouts that echo their new fascination with John Coltrane. Other "Funhouse" tracks are "Down On The Street," "Loose," "1970," "L.A. Blues" and "T.V. Eye." A single of "Down On The Street" with the non-LP track "I Feel Alright" is also issued. Although the Stooges now have new guitarist James Williamson, the old band is on the LP, which is Iggy Pop on vocals, Dave Alexander on bass, Ron Asheton on guitar, Scott Asheton on drums and Steven Mackay on tenor sax. *Rolling Stones'* Charlie Burton reviews the LP "Funhouse" as, "...do you long to have your mind blow open so wide that it will take weeks for you to pick up the little, bitty pieces?...Then by all means you simply must visit us at the Stooges' Funhouse."

STIFF BEACH are a new power trio modeled after Cream, with influences spanning Django Reinhardt, Sun Ra and Capt. Beeheart. A few years ago, aspiring musician Andy Partridge bought a second hand tape recorder with £10 he won in a "Draw Your Favorite Monkee" contest. He's putting the tape deck to good use recording his new group Stiff Beach. Andy's on guitar and vocals, Michael "Spud" Taylor is on bass and Tony Climpson is the drummer. They've played two gigs so far, one at a W.H. Smith staff party and another at the British Legion club at Stratton. They're still pretty green, but Stiff Beach is just the root of the tree that will eventually grow into the trio called XTC.

BEANS It's a long way down the road to the Talking Heads. Along the way, Chris Frantz has been getting a little bored with music. He's been playing for a little over a year in an all cover band called the Beans, in a New York residency at the Electric Circus in St. Marks' Place. Now he's left the group and told his friends he's off to the Rhode Island School of Design.

February 1971.............................

BIZADI are a Baltimore-based duo of David Byrne and Mark Kehoe. They turn out versions of Frank Sinatra standards, showtunes and '50s pop songs, occasionally goofing on something like The ? and The Mysterians relic "96 Tears." You're most likely to see them playing in restaurants or on the streets. David plays violin, ukulele and guitar. It's still a few years before the Talking Heads get together.

February 10th, 1971 - Wednesday.............

PATTI SMITH moved to New York from New Jersey in '67. She got involved with the artistic community in New York City, making money where she could writing for rock magazines like *Creem, Rock Scene* and *Rolling Stone*. Some of her other writings are a little more private. It was in New York that Patti met Andy Warhol/Velvet Underground follower Gerard Malanga, who set up a debut performance for Patti reading some of her poems. With the help of a new acquaintance, Bobby Neuwirth, Patti Smith reads at St. Mark's Place in NYC select poems from her writings titled "Seventh Heaven." Through Bobby, the "right" selection of musicians and writers attend and Patti is instantly the new thing in the underground/hip/avant guarde sect. Among the poems selected for the evening was "Oath" which begins "Christ died for somebody's sins, but not mine." Years later Patti would use that as the opening to her groundbreaking version of "Gloria."

June 3rd, 1971 - Thursday.............

U2's future lead singer Paul Hewson is watching Middle Of The Road sing their #1 UK hit song "Chirpy Chirpy Cheep Cheep" on *Top Of The Pops*. He's captivated. A decade later Paul, who had since become Bono of U2, told *NME's* Robert Sharp "I must have been eleven at the time and thought, "Wow! This is what pop music is all about. You just sing like that and you get paid for it."

July 1971.............................

STIFF BEACH loses its drummer Tony Climpson, who is replaced by Tony Hill. "Spud" moves from bass to alto sax and Andy Partridge remains on guitar and vocals. The new group adopts the name Tongue. They change style from a "Cream" sound to more experimental

OCTOBER 1971

free form jazz. They plan to improvise around some of their better riffs when they play live, a big city move that is suicidal in a small town like Swindon. As is the nature of begining bands, Stiff Beach goes its separate ways and a new group comes together. Andy's new band is called Clark Kent. The group is Andy Partridge on guitar and vocals, Dave Cartner on guitar, Frank Bradbury on drums, Barry Archer on organ and Pete Cousens (aka T.F. Much) sitting in on bass for the gig at Headland's School dance. Peeking in the window from a soccer practice is future XTC collaborator Colin Moulding. Clark Kent are so bad, they drive everyone from the room. By early '72 the band will have changed again with a new drummer Paul Wilson and the new bassist "Nervous Steve." The band is re-named once again as Star Park.

October 10th, 1971 - Sunday..........................

ACTRESS are rehearsing in the back of a bicycle shop on Columbus near 82nd in New York. They got together early this year with guitarist Rick Rivets and Arthur Kane and drummer Billy Murcia. They were joined by bassist Johnny Volume (aka John Gezale Jr.) who then changed his stagename to Johnny Thunders, switched to guitar (as Arthur changed to bass) and took over. With Thunder's arrival, Rick Rivets was soon replaced with Sylvain Sylvain (aka Ronald Misrahi). The rehearsal tonight is being taped, capturing originals "Why Am I Alone," "I Need Your Love," "Human Race," "That's Poison," "When I Get Back Home" and "Talk To Me."

December 5th, 1971 - Sunday..........................

KILBURN & THE HIGH ROADS are a new group that began by rehearsing at the Jubilee Studio in Covent Garden (London) back in November of last year and worked enough of a set together to get a gig (their first) at the Croydon School of Art. They're fronted by 29-year-old Ian Dury, an Essex painter who loves American music from the late '50s, as well as writers like Hoagy Carmichael and Cole Porter. They do covers of "Lucille," The Walk," "Tallahassee Lassie," "I'm Walking" and "I'm In Love Again." The band is Ian Dury on vocals, Russell Hardy on piano, Ian Smith on bass, Terry Day on drums, Davey Dayne on sax and Ted Speight on guitar. They take their name from Kilburn High Road in North West London.

January 21st, 1972 Friday................

ELVIS COSTELLO meets another Liverpool musician at a New Year's party. Alan Mayes and Declan McManus (later known as Elvis Costello), found common ground in musicians like Neil Young, Van Morrison and Bob Dylan. Mayes is 18 and has been playing in bands for two years, McManus is 17 and has virtually no live experience, except when he would occasionally play rhythm guitar in his father's (Ross McManus) showband. Declan was invited to join Allan's group Rusty. The four piece folk rock band is Allan Mayes on vocals and guitar, Declan McManus on vocals and guitar, Dave Jago on vocals and Alan Brown on bass. Tonight the band play their first gig since Declan joined. The concert at the Lamplight Folk Club in Wallasey included a few originals like "The Lady Holds Out Her Hand," "Wisdom In The Basement" and "She's Almost Human." The covers were "Dance, Dance, Dance" by Neil Young, Dylan's "Mighty Quinn" and "I Been Working" by Van Morrison. Declan even brought along a song called "Warm House."

RUSTY ....Wallasey, The Lamplight

MEDIUM THEATRE and RUSTY

IN CONCERT

at LYNWOOD HALL, RICE LANE

SATURDAY, FEBRUARY 12th 1972

COMMENCE 7-30   TICKETS 25p

March 1972..................

THE NEW YORK DOLLS came from Actress, being joined by their new singer David JoHansen. He got together with the band last November and was quickly worked into the songs. Digging into his past you'll find bands like Vagabond Missionaries and a soulish cover band called Fast Eddie & The Electric Japs. David JoHansen joined Actress late last year. Their first appearance together was at a Christmas party where they played a load of covers to welfare pensioners. They've been rehearsing and honing their act. Their "real" debut is in the Palm Beach Room of the Diplomat Hotel on West 43rd.

May 1972.........................

GENETIC BREAKDOWN is the front room band that's the very root to the tree from which the Damned will sprout in three years. The band's lineup is variable, but generally includes Phil Burns on bass, his brother Ray Burns (the future Capt. Sensible of the Damned) on guitar, Xerxes on guitar, Dave Berk on drums and Paul Halford on vocals. The band will play on and off for two years before mutating into an early version of The Johnny Moped Band.

ROADSTAR is a new band put together by 11-year-old Matt Johnson. They're playing birthday parties, youth halls and the sort with glitter in their hair, stack heels and loon pants. Their set includes songs from Led Zeppelin, David Bowie, The Beatles, Marc Bolan and Deep Purple. They also have a few originals in the set. With Matt on vocals in the band is Nick Freeston on drums, Bret Giddings on guitar and Mart Bratby on bass. They've even tried their hand at making a few home recordings of themselves. It will be another seven years before Matt puts together his hit band The The.

June 13th, 1972 Tuesday..................

THE NEW YORK DOLLS begin a seventeen-week Tuesday residency at the Mercer Arts Center. The catacomb of rooms, in the

JUNE 1972

crumbling building, houses tiny spaces that feature new bands, art exhibits, videos, avant guarde films and plays. The owner of the Mercer had heard about the Dolls from Eric Emerson. The sad part is that due to a slight misunderstanding, they're billed as the "Dolls Of New York" for the first six shows. They're crowded into the Oscar Wilde Room, which only holds about one hundred people.

THE DOLLS OF NEW YORK ....New York City, Mercer Arts Center

July 13th, 1972 - Thursday.........................

RUSTY/ELVIS COSTELLO Liverpool folk group Rusty have undergone some changes over the spring. The former four piece band has been trimmed to just the duo of Allan Mayes and Declan McManus. Beginning June 6th, the duo had their own weekly folk club concerts at the Temple Bar in Liverpool, where they play, sometimes booking someone else too, and have an open mic. The Tuesday night bookings are a weekly event that stretch through the end of December. These regular events shouldn't make you think that Allan and Declan are getting rich. Nothing of the kind. The usual pay for one of their gigs is £10 to split two ways. Not much really. Rusty has also managed to get a gig outside of the Liverpool-Walton-Wallasey area they seem to always travel in. They've been booked to be the opening act for three London concerts with Ralph McTell ("Streets Of London") and Bridget St. John. Tonight they play at New Bards Folk Club, tomorrow the Half Moon in Putney and then on to the Troubadour in South Kensington.

August 8th, 1972 - Tuesday.........................

THE NEW YORK DOLLS are playing the Mercer Arts Center in New York and there's an influential member of the audience taking notes. Paul Nelson, A&M for Mercury Records loves what he's seeing. He's determined to sign the Dolls to the label. They're gaining a reputation in the music community as well. Among the faces at their concerts you might see John Cale, Lou Reed, Bette Midler, Todd Rundgren, and even David Bowie. Marty Thau has come on board as their manager, leaving a job at Paramount Records. There's a cassette tape of the Dolls that they recently recorded. This nine songs tape captures studio versions of "Bad Girl," "Looking For A Kiss," "Don't Start Me Talking," "Don't Mess With Cupid," "Human Being," "Personality Crisis," "Pills," "Jet Boy" and "Frankenstein." It would remain unissued and largley unheard until ROIR issued it twenty years later.

NEW YORK DOLLS ....New York City, Mercer Arts Center

Tuesday, August 8 10:30 PM
New York Dolls
Mercer Arts Center · 240 Mercer St.
Oscar Wilde Room · $2.50
"the best new young band I've ever seen!" MELODY MAKER

August 22nd, 1972 - Tuesday.........................

NEW YORK DOLLS *Melody Maker's* Roy Hollingworth files a report this week from New York writing, "The New York Dolls are certainly attracting much attention. Apart from Alice Cooper down to see them in Greenwich Village last week, one John Cale also popped in, as did an enormous video-tape crew. Still waiting in the wings is Paul Nelson from Mercury. The band has told him that they want a $250,000 deal. The label is sending in some of their other scouts to see what is so special. Label or not, it now appears that the band will be coming to London very shortly to cut their album and also do live dates."

RUSTY ....Liverpool, Temple Bar   NEW YORK DOLLS....................New York City, Mercer Arts Center

October 1st, 1972 - Sunday.........................

NEW YORK DOLLS Three Sunday nights in a row, Mercury A&M Paul Brown talks his label executives into checking out the Dolls. On the 24th, Vice-President Charlie Fach was prodded into going to the Mercer Arts Center to see the Dolls. Paul is nervous because the band is running late and is keeping them waiting. Fach waits and waits and waits. It's three hours before the band finally walks onstage. Fach watches for finteen minutes and leaves unimpressed. The next Sunday, Paul has coaxed Lou Simon in from Chicago. After waiting two hours, he sees a band he really enjoys, but is cautious because of the label's position on the band back in Chicago. Then tonight another A&R man, Robin McBride has flown in to see the Dolls. As usual, they're an hour late and play an anarchistic set. He is not impressed.

NEW YORK DOLLS ....New York City, Mercer Arts Center

October 19th, 1972 - Thursday.........................

WAYNE COUNTY/SUICIDE Roy Hollingworth is in New York City on assignment for *Melody Maker*. He's out to catch the newest and most outrageous and has stumbled onto Wayne County. It's 1:30 in the afternoon and Wayne is playing a short set during the lunch break at Loeb College in Greenwich Village. Roy describes him as, "...sporting lipstick and eyeshadow, carrying a handbag and wearing wobbling high-heeled ladies shoes...A feather hat topped a lush brunette wig which fell abundantly over a pinkish baby-doll nightdress, which in turn barely covered a lovely pair of legs encased in ruddy-coloured stockings atop a pair of dainty high heels." The show was attended by fifty or so students, most of whom were working on assignments between bites at their tables. He sang a few songs which included every naughty word he could think of, squirted members of the audience with a water pistol shaped like a dildo and got into a shouting match with the leader of the New York University Gay Liberation Front. Wayne left the stage to go change into another outrageous set of clothes while the band played on. When he emerged again it was in "a natty set of ragged crepe longjohn underpants and a saucy top." He was about to do another number that involved sitting on a toilet that had been brought out when the power was cut.

Later on in the same evening, Suicide were onstage in the Oscar Wilde room at the Mercer Arts Center in an evening self-described as "Punk, Funk and Sewer Music by Suicide." It's only $1 to enter the maze of concert rooms and theatres in a decaying

OCTOBER 1972

Greenwich Village setting. Suicide are two people, one mic and three keyboards. Roy notes that. "...one is dressed lazily in casual clothes, the other is dressed to kill. His face is covered in glitter, his clothes are shoddy and black and on the back of his leather jacket is jewelled "Suicide." The music is stark and simple. The vocalist shouts above the two chord droning. "It's like having a claw rip down your back. It lurks onwards and the singer jumps offstage and crawls over the floor." As the band played on, the small crowd dwindled. "It was fascinating. How two people could create such a thick wall of sound and atmosphere was an unbelievable achievement. It roared and groaned and the singer smacked himself on the head with the mic a couple of times and then fell in a heap in a corner and whimpered. What has rock created?"

October 29th, 1972 - Sunday....................

THE NEW YORK DOLLS are in London for the first time. Before their first concert they'll be doing some experimental recordings in a studio that the promoter Roy Fisher owned. Also, they go shopping for clothes and meet self styled culturist Malcolm McLaren when they visit his "Let It Rock" clothing shop. Malcolm loves the outrageous Dolls, too. Their UK debut show tonight is a charity concert with Rod Stewart and the Faces at Wembley Auditorium, playing between the Faces and opening act, the Pink Fairies. They play the same set they play back in New York to a much larger audience than they've ever faced. Where they usually play to a few hundred people, they're now in front of 13,000. The set is a combination of their own original material, as well as covers like Otis Redding's "Don't Mess With Cupid," Gary U.S. Bonds' "Seven Day Party" and Chuck Berry's "Back In The USA." In the audience is the persistent A&R man for Mercury, Paul Brown, with Mercury's president in tow. He thinks the band is the worst he's ever seen and he's not alone. *Melody Maker's* Mark Plummer reviewed the concert, writing, "The New York Dolls played what was possibly the worst sets I've seen. Their glamour bit brought wolf whistles and shouts to go before a note had been played and by the time a string had broken on Johnny Thunders' plexiglass guitar, they had lost what audience sympathy they had. Musically their set was dire and failed to gel, their two guitarists play all the old tired licks. And who really wants to know about "Pill City?" Wembley didn't, that's for sure." Brits will have another opportunity to see what the talk is all about for themselves at the Manchester Hard Rock on November 9th.

November 4th, 1972 - Sunday....................

THE NEWCASTLE BIG BAND are a sixteen-piece band that have a following growing to the extent that they've been given a Sunday afternoon residency at the Guildhall in Newcastle. Among their members is bassist and vocalist Gordon "Sting" Sumner. Meanwhile, Sting is also involved with the Phoenix Jazzmen who have just begun a weekly session at the Hawthorn Inn in Benwell Village, Newcastle. They also appear regularly at the Metro Club in Liverpool. Sting's jazz days will continue even after the Police are together until early 1977.

November 5th, 1972 - Monday....................

PATTI SMITH is onstage reading poetry tonight at the Mercer Arts Center. She's bottom of a Monday night bill featuring Teenage Lust and Eight Ball.

November 6th, 1972 - Monday........

THE NEW YORK DOLLS are stuck with tragedy on their first visit to the UK. Nineteen-year-old New York Dolls drummer Billy Murcia had been with some new found friends and was taking "Mandys" (Mandrax- a barbiturate) all afternoon. Finally he fell asleep and his "friends" panicked. They couldn't wake him. Someone thought the best way to counteract the downers was to get him into an ice cold bathtub of water and get some coffee into him, awake or not. He aspirated the coffee and nearly unconcious from the drugs anyway, choked and died. Those responsible fled. The band is flying back to the States immediately. The negotiations that the Dolls management were having with Track Records for the band in the UK are halted. In the days that followed, Sylvain Sylvain told the *Village Voice* that, "Billy lived a lot for his age. Of course we're still going to carry on as a group. We're looking for another drummer and we hope to come out strong in the new year." The Dolls had been in the UK for a few weeks, playing a charity gig with Rod Stewart and The Faces at Wembley. There was also supposed to be a gig with fellow New Yorker Lou Reed, but they got taken off bill after the band had already gone up to Liverpool for the show. Lou Reed was unhappy with the choice of the Dolls as an opening act for his UK tour and told the promoters that it was either the him or the Dolls. They're no fools when it comes to an audience draw and will have Lou Reed onstage while the Dolls look for other opportunities. While Reed has disposed of the Dolls, David Bowie is beginning to show interest in them. This has not been a good tour.

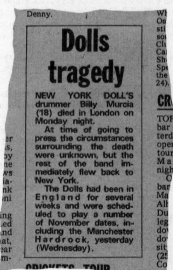

Denny.

Dolls tragedy

NEW YORK DOLL'S drummer Billy Murcia (18) died in London on Monday night.

At time of going to press the circumstances surrounding the death were unknown, but the rest of the band immediately flew back to New York.

The Dolls had been in England for several weeks and were scheduled to play a number of November dates, including the Manchester Hardrock, yesterday (Wednesday).

December 1972..............

PRE-SEX PISTOLS Steve Jones (14), Paul Cook (15) and Warwick "Wally" Nightingale (15) have a front-room band they play in together. They all sporadically attend the Christopher Wren School in Shepherd's Bush. Steve aspires someday to be a rock star just like Rod Stewart, but lacks the funds to buy the gear. Over the next three years he and Paul break into a variety of pop star's houses and backstage areas to accumulate musical instruments and PA. They practice a variety of cover songs.

DECEMBER 1972

December 19th, 1972 - Tuesday.....

THE NEW YORK DOLLS have taken on new drummer Jerry Nolan. He's been following the band since the begining and always thought he could play those songs better, faster, louder. Now he's got his chance. At his audition he played like he'd been a member all along and impressed the group. He'll make his first appearance with the New York Dolls tonight at the Mercer Arts Center.

December 25, 1972 - Monday........

ROBERT SMITH, future lead singer for the Cure, gets his first electric guitar. He's currently a student at Notre Dame Middle School for eleven to thirteen-year-olds.

February 11th, 1973 - Sunday.....

THE NEW YORK DOLLS' show tonight is billed as "The New York Dolls and all their friends." It's a triple bill tonight at the Mercer Arts Centre in New York City. The three bands involved are all a little bit left of center, all new groups. Opening the show are a New York based duo called Suicide. They're based around Alan Vega and Martin Rev and serve up very unusual fare. Next up is Bostonian Jonathan Richman and the Modern Lovers and a set from music critic Wayne County. Headlining the gig is the New York Dolls, a glam-rock outfit that are beginning to make people turn their heads with their make up, stack heel shoes and loud, fast approach to music. The party is from 10pm till dawn and tickets are only $5.

February 17th, 1973 - Saturday.....

RUSTY/ELVIS COSTELLO Earlier in the month, Declan McManus quit Rusty, to move to London. Now he's back with Allan Mayes and is playing one more gig at Warwick University, opening up for Cockney Rebel. During his time in Rusty, Declan had written over a dozen songs that he played publicly. Among them were "Warm House," "For Miles I See," "Dull Echoes," "Sweet Convincer," "Daybreaks," "Goodbye Florence," "Morning Changes," "Are You Afraid Of Your Children," "Two Days Rain," "The Show Must Go On," "Sleeper At The Wheel" and "Sunflower Lancers."

March 20th, 1973 - Tuesday.....

THE NEW YORK DOLLS have signed with Mercury Records. After supposedly seeing the group eighty times, A&R man Paul Nelson took a chance on the group and signed them. He's going to get Todd Rundgren to produce the album. There's a mixture of excitement and puzzled looks around Mercury Records concerning the Dolls. Some think that this is the most exciting, original new band in years, others think that they're the worst band they've ever heard.

March 23rd, 1973 - Friday.....

KRAFTWERK make their UK debut with a double LP combining their first two German releases. The futuristic tracks frequently venture past the seven-minute mark with rambling epics like "Stratovarius," "Vim Himmel Hoch," "Klingklang" and "Wellenlange." Kraftwerk are an all electronic duet of Ralf Hutter and Florian Schneider-Esleben. They met three years ago while at the Duseldorf Conservatory. They began together in a band called Organization, released one album in '70 called "Tone Float" and soon split up to start a new duo, Kraftwerk. Their two German-only LP's, "Highrail" and "Var," have been combined into the double release for the UK. The package is bargain priced at only £3.

KILBURN & THE HIGH ROADS ......London, Hope & Anchor   ENGLAND'S GLORY ....Anerly Town Hall

April 1973.....

THE NEON BOYS are Richard Meyers and Tom Miller. They had known each other since their boarding school days in New York. Myers and Miller were both into music and poetry. They went their separate ways in the late ''60s and eventually met up again in New York City in 1971. Richard Myers was busy hustling his poetry pamphlets around the streets and Tom Miller was already playing some in NYC as a folk-oriented solo act, as well as taking odd jobs doing whatever would pay the rent. The two got together and wanted a change in direction for themselves and to start a band together. They call themselves The Neon Boys and have been rehearsing and rehearsing since last fall. Filling out the trio is Billy Ficca, a school friend from Delaware, on drums. This combo actually recorded four Miller-Meyers compositions "Love Comes In Spurts," "High-Heeled Wheels," "Hot Dog" and "That's All I Know (Right Now)," although the songs would remain unreleased for almost a decade. Over the next few years, the pair would change their names to Tom Verlaine and Richard Hell. They would change the sound of the New York underground and be more important as influences than as hit acts. While looking for another guitarist for the Neon Boys, Tom Miller auditoned a number of people. One of them was Doug Colvin, who would later find fame as Dee Dee Ramone. In an *NME* interview Verlaine recalled, "One of those guys, his name's Dee Dee, actually came down to audition for the Neon Boys…and the guy didn't know a 'G' chord from an 'A' chord. We had two songs with just three straight forward chords apiece and he couldn't figure out where the hell they were! I mean, how can people call me hard to work with?"

APRIL 1973

April 18th, 1973 - Wednesday.........

DECLAN COSTELLO has gone solo, playing tonight in Twickenham (Southwest London) at the Barmy Arms pub. It's right across from Eel Pie Island and on the bill tonight is a mixture of covers as well as several songs Declan had written. He's changed his name from McManus to Costello, his grandmother's maiden surname.

DECLAN COSTELLO ....Riverside, Barmy Arms

May 1973 ....

STAR PARK (Mk II) is the newest name by the Swindon band previously known as Stiff Beach, Clark Kent and Tongue. They're ever-changing line-up now finds them with Colin Moulding on bass, Andy Partridge and Dave Cartner on guitar and Terry Chambers on drums. They're very influenced by American rock bands the MC 5 and the New York Dolls. Their big break is supporting Irish superstars Thin Lizzy at their concert at Swindon College. To prepare for the event they all adopt new "stage names." In deference to his long hair, Colin becomes "Curtains." Terry is "Blackhand" because of the black leather riding gloves he wears, Dave becomes "Dino Salvador" and Andy is nicknamed "Rocky." The stage is being set for them to become XTC. Three of the four members are present.

IGGY & THE STOOGES surprise everyone by getting back together. In August of '71 Iggy split the group up, moved to Florida and worked on his golf game while mowing lawns. He turned down offers to put the Stooges back together from Elektra. It was a chance meeting with David Bowie last year that sent Iggy back into the musical world. Iggy signed up with Bowie's management company and reformed the Stooges with Ron and Scott Asheton and James Williamson on guitar. The group flew to England and recorded this new album, the first of a two record deal with Columbia Records. Disagreements over the mixing of the LP delayed its release for almost a year but it's finally out now. It's called "Raw Power" and among the titles are "Search & Destroy," "Gimmie Danger," "I Need Somebody," "Shake Appeal" and "Death Trip." Columbia Records describes it as, "...a menacing wall of sound behind our hero's own brand of affirmative body-odour boogie. Praise Lucifer and pass the crushed glass in aspic." Iggy & The Stooges have out their latest LP "Raw Power." A single from the LP is released of "Search & Destroy" b/w "Shake Appeal."

May 26th, 1973 - Saturday....................

JETS OF AIR are a new band in the town of Leigh, just to the west of Manchester. It's school friends Pete Shelley, Garth Smith, Steve Cristy and others. They've called it the "Jets Of Air" after they heard the phrase in a school physics experiment. They play some originals such as Shelley's "Telephone Operator" as well as some covers like the Velvet Underground's "White Light White Heat," and some assorted Bowie and Roxy Music songs. The band hires the church halls and stages their own gig with tickets at a reasonable 15p. The Jets Of Air will become the Buzzcocks in another three years time and the song "Telephone Operator" will be dusted off by Pete Shelley a decade from now and become his solo hit after the Buzzcocks split up.

June 30th, 1973 - Saturday....................

PHOENIX JAZZMEN play a high profile gig today at Newcastle University. The trad-jazz group are Ronnie Young on trumpet, Gordon Solomon on trombone, Graham Shepherd on clarinet, John Hedley on guitar, Don Eddy on drums and Gordon Sumner on bass. Besides the date today, they also are regulars at four other clubs in the city. Gordon can also be found playing with the Newcastle Big Band and the River City Jazzmen. It's still four years until Gordon "Sting" Sumner will be a household name, but he's already getting quite a reputation as an in-demand bassist around Newcastle jazz circles.

CHRISSIE HYNDE is an American who's in love with England. Only a few weeks ago she came over with little more than a few items of clothing (including a a jacket with the name "Bernice" across it's back in fake snakeskin) and her Iggy Pop records. She's found some work at an architects firm in the day and is trying to get involved in the musicians scene in London by night. She attends parties and begins to meet the movers and shakers of the London rock scene. By the middle of January of '74, she'll get her first byline reviewing records for the *New Musical Express*. Her first review is of Neil Diamond's LP "Jonathan Livingston Seagull."

July 4th, 1973 - Wednesday....................

PRE-SEX PISTOLS Steve Jones and Paul Cook arrange one of their biggest and best thefts of musical gear yet. David Bowie played the Hammersmith Odeon in London the last two nights capping off his final tour of '73. It's such an important concert that D.A. Pennebaker filmed and RCA recorded the event. This evening, while the hall is half assembled and the crew is gone, Steve and Paul slip in and make off with all the expensive microphones and PA gear. They slipped into the hall and hid out until night, then worked around a sleeping guard. The whole lot is carted off in a "borrowed" minivan that Steve had arranged. The group that is utilizing the fruits of these illegal acquisitions are calling themselves The Strand, just like the Roxy Music song. Steve Jones is the singer with his friend Paul Cook on drums. Warwick "Wally" Nightingale in on guitar, Steve Hayes on bass and Jimmy Mackin on organ. The group rehearses a load of covers with a generous helping of Rod Stewart songs.

JULY 1973

July 13th, 1973- Friday......................................

KILBURN & THE HIGH ROADS are having a bit of luck come their way. First they found a manager, Dave Robinson and secondly, they've just signed up with Raft Records, a subsidiary of Warner Brothers. They're still playing fifties covers, but there are also some originals like "You're More Than Fair" and "Rough Kids," making their way into the live shows. Geoff Brown caught the Kilburns at the Kensington Pub tonight and reviewed the gig for the *Melody Maker*. He began his review this way; "Either he (Ian Dury) was propping the mike stand up or it was keeping him upright, but the guy certainly had style and the pose was clearly Gene Vincent's. Ian Dury is rather like a modern Vincent with maybe a touch of Beefheart's growl and a hint of Bryan Ferry's mannered delivery. You've guessed it, Dury is really an original." This is the second gig that the Kilburns have had in the last few months, since they've been in the studio lately working on some recordings for their debut single.

        KILBURN & THE HIGH ROADS ......London, The Kensington

July 21st, 1973 - Saturday.........................

BRIAN ENO keyboard player for Roxy Music since 1970, quits the group after what some see as a jealousy of Eno's crowd appeal by lead singer Bryan Ferry. About the split Bryan Ferry told the *Melody Maker* "I was cramping Eno's style. Two non-musicians in a band is one too many. I think he'll do very well by himself." Eno himself said "putting it as euphemistically as possible, Bryan felt the focus was divided by me being on stage and that wasn't what he wanted." Eno has already started on his separate career with a new song he's just written called "Baby's On Fire." He's also telling the press that his new band will be called "Loana and the Little Girls."

July 27th, 1973 - Friday............

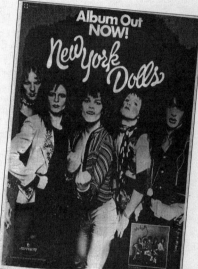

THE NEW YORK DOLLS' outrageous debut album is out in America. It won't be released in the UK until October 19th. It's self titled "The New York Dolls" and encompasses ten originals and one cover. The sessions were produced by Todd Rundgren who JoHansen refered to as, "...an expert on second rate rock 'n' roll." The mixing session took less than half a day. Titles include "Personality Crisis," "Looking For A Kiss," "Vietnamese Baby," "Trash," "Bad Girl," "Private World," and the Bo Diddley song "Pills." The album was produced by Todd Rundgren and is dedicated to Billy Doll (aka Billy Murcia) the band's original drummer. The controversial cover of the LP features the band all dressed in the most outrageous drag imaginable. High wigs, trowled on make up and high heels and garters. This is not the way the band appeared onstage, it was only a photo calculated to shock. On the back of the album, the band is photographed in their stage wear, budlging at tight seams and frequently held together with obvious safety pins. The scene growing in New York City seems centered on the Dolls and their potential for success. Venues like the Mercer Arts Center and Max's Kansas City are becoming the hip hangouts for those in the know. Other up-and-coming bands that are playing Greenwich Village include the Modern Lovers, The Harlots of 42nd Street, Teenage Lust, The Planets, Wayne County and Kiss.

October 5th, 1973 - Friday........

THE NEW YORK SCENE is featured in a *Melody Maker* two-page spread. They even put DJ/singer/transvestite Wayne County on the cover. The report by Dave Marsh gives descriptions of the hip clubs where the music is centered, like Max's Kansas City, The Coventry, Kenny's Castaways, the Diplomat Hotel, My Father's Place and the recently collapsed Mercer Arts Center. The New York Dolls get the most attention on the scene, since they've just had a major label record released, but other bands are surfacing that are developing a following as well. Wayne County him/herself is a regular scenemaker, his/her band now calling themselves Queen Elizabeth (featuring Wayne County). He's cleaned up his act a little, but it still falls under an "X" rating. The Dynomiters are three New Jersey kids who are somewhat like the Raspberries. The Harlots Of 42nd Street are described as "Acid-rockers discover the Doll's audience, decide to dress up and catch on. Only thing is they forgot to change the music." Teenage Lust is headed by two ex-David Peel & the Lower East Side members and are more in the vein of satire rather than the cutting edge. Marsh describes Kiss as, "...if they just stepped out of the underground movie "Pink Flamingos," leading me to believe I was right all along in thinking that the glitter craze was an ugliness contest."

THE STILETTOS are a new girl group floating around New York City. They're best described as a dance group with choreography that plays mostly covers. They're fronted by Debbie Harry, who used to be in Wind In The Willows back in 1969. Sharing vocals are Elda Gentile and Rosie Ross. They are also occasionally joined by guitarist Chris Stein, who also plays from time to time with Eric Emerson & the Magic Tramps. The majority of their set is along a Supremes meet the Shangri-La's vein. They'll make their debut at the Bobern Tavern later this month. It'll be Debbie Harry's big step to becoming Blondie.

October 20th, 1973 - Saturday.......................

THE ARTISTICS are a new college band practicing at the Rhode Island School Of Design in Providence. It's built around students David Byrne and Chris Frantz. The two had actually met there in 1970 as entering freshmen. Now their band has grown to include some other friends as well. David Anderson is on guitar, Hank Stahler plays bass and Tim Beale plays sax. Among their circle of friends was bassist

OCTOBER 1973

Martina Weymouth. She actually helped Chris and Dave to write the band's first original song, "Psycho Killer." Other original compositions at the time were "Sick Boy," "Spin Spin" and "I'm Not In Love." The rest of their set were '60s covers of songs like "96 Tears" "The Love I Saw In You Was Just A Mirage," "My Baby Must Be A Magician," "Psychotic Reaction," or the Knickerbocker's "Lies." The Artistics (their friends call them the Autistics) have played a few live gigs at parties. Onstage they're into the Mondo aesthetic and dress all in black. Byrne has a leopard skin guitar. After almost a year together, the Artistics felt stifled by their surroundings. "The only people who ever got famous in Providence were people in sports or people who committed some sort of hideous crime," mused Chris Frantz. They arrived in New York in September of 1974 and will in the next few months rename the group The Talking Heads.

JETS OF AIR............................Manchester, Bolton School Of Technology

October 31st, 1973 - Wednesday.....................

THE NEW YORK DOLLS are playing a special Halloween Bash at the plush Waldorf Astoria Grand Ballroom. The heavily hyped gig had several hundred gatecrashers who pushed into the ballroom already filled with about 1,500 celebrants. A costume contest was held, the prize being a "a bottle of Taylor New York State Champagne, a night on the town with the New York Dolls and a weekend for two at a lovely motel close by the Newark Airport." It was won by a pair dressed in silver lamé.

NEW YORK DOLLS ....New York City, Astoria Hotel

November 1973.................................

ALEX HARVEY, of the Sensational Alex Harvey Band, senses the stagnation in the music scene. He told the *NME* that, "Someone's got to come along and say to all of us 'all your ideas about rock and roll, all your ideas about sound, all your ideas about guitars, all your ideas about this and that are a load of wank!' This is where it is…someones' got to come along and say fuck you!"

TOM MILLER (the future Tom Verlaine) takes his place behind the mic on audition night at Reno Sweeney's, a New York nightclub. His friend Richard Myers (the future Richard Hell) is acting as his manager. Verlaine's constant supporter, Terry Ork, introduces him to Richard Lloyd who had only recently arrived in New York after bumming around the country for the last year.

THE STRAND is the root band for the Sex Pistols. It's the fall of '73 and Steve Jones regularly stopping by the clothing stores on Kings Road, checking out what is portable and easy to hide. He stops by "Too Fast To Live, Too Young To Die" and, looking for genuine help, asks its manager Malcolm McLaren if he knows where he can rent a rehearsal space for his band. McLaren not only found a room at the Covent Garden Community Center, but he paid for it as well. These days The Strand is a trio of Steve Jones, Paul Cook and Wally Nightingale, with Glen Matlock, a part time shop assistant at of Malcolm's joining in on bass. The group begins rehearsing, working up Rod Stewart tunes, as well as Mod pop songs suggested by Glen.

November 4th, 1973 - Sunday...........

PATTI SMITH and Lenny Kaye make their second live appearance. The first one was almost two years ago. The event is "Rocking Rimbaud" in Le Jardin, in the Diplomat Hotel. Patti does some of her poetry readings, as well as a few songs with Lenny Kaye, some originals and some R & B covers.

PATTI SMITH............................New York City, Diplomat Hotel (Le Jardin)

November 22nd, 1973 - Thursday.......

THE NEW YORK DOLLS arrive in the UK to play a few concerts. They start at Warwick University tonight, move on to York University on the 23rd, play Leeds University on the 24th, then follow on the 26th and 27th when they play the opening night of London's Biba store in the sixth floor Rainbow Restaurant. There will only be 600 tickets available for both of the Biba dates and Writing On The Wall will open the show. They'll be taping two TV shows as well on their visit, starting with the Russel Harty program tonight and their appearance on the *Old Grey Whistle Test* will be taped on November 26th. While across the Atlantic, the Dolls plan to tour in France, Denmark, Switzerland, Germany and Holland. They also have a single out tomorrow, "Jet Boy," taken from their eponymous album. Just in case you think rock is a high paying business, each member of the Dolls are being paid £75 a week for the three weeks of the tour. Don't spend it all at once.

PATTI SMITH

RIMBAUD/RIMBAUD/RIMBAUD

PERFORMS
★
AT LE JARDIN
108 West 43rd Street
SUNDAY EVENING
NOVEMBER 4, 7:00
★ ☆ ★
ONE PERFORMANCE
★ ☆ ☆ ★
Reservations: 245-5588 - $3.00

November 28th, 1973 - Wednesday......

THE NEW YORK DOLLS are in Paris. Arriving drunk at Orly Airport, Johnny Thunders got sick in the airport lounge after arriving. The press draw great attention to it and Malcolm McLaren (future manager of the Sex Pistols) is taking notes as he joins the band on the trip. He will later duplicate the incident with the Pistols for the benefit of the press. The New York Dolls' recorded performance is aired on the staid BBC 2 television program *Old Grey Whistle Test*. This prompts a comment about the band referring to them as "mock rock." On the program they sing their new single "Jet Boy" and "Looking For A Kiss." Letters begin pouring into the BBC about the outrageous group. There are those who see this as something worthwhile. Watching TV in Manchester is a very impressionable fourteen-year old Steven Patrick Morrissey. He is ASTOUNDED by the Dolls and sets out to find out everything he can about them.

Melody Maker's Steve Lake catches up with the Dolls in Leeds and gets a brief interview for the paper. Lead singer David JoHansen wants to put an end to the imitation Stones tag that the papers have hung on the band. "We're a bit bored with hearing about the

NOVEMBER 1973

Stones. I personally don't care, it doesn't bother me. A lot of times we tend to parodize on things that happened in the mid-sixties and not only the Stones, but a whole bunch of other people. We're especially into the old girl groups, they're more of an influence than anybody else." Later in the conversation David reveals that he was once lead singer with a band called Fast Eddie and the Electric Gaps that played all Japanese gear. Michael Watts caught up with the band at Biba's and stated clearly that, "…they're a great kick in the ass to the corpus of rock and roll…The Dolls, with their crude musicality and exaggerated posturing, are the new children of pop, mimicking their elders and blowing rude noises; generally letting out the stuffiness…Maybe in a couple of years time the musicologists will be having their say, but it doesn't even matter if the Dolls are around then. What counts is what they're speaking for now. That's how it used to be. Remember?"

December 1973.............................

TELEVISION, in some respects, started two years ago when Tom Miller and Richard Meyers had a group called The Neon Boys. They've been out of the scene for the last year and are now getting back together. Names they've considered are Goo-Goo and the Liberteens. The suggestion of "Television" by Richard Hell is a good one. With the new guitar playing friend Richard Lloyd that they met last month and with the retrieval of their old drummer Billy Ficca from Boston, a new band is born. To go with the new band the principles have to come up with new names as well. Richard Myers became Richard Hell, Tom Miller adopted the European surname Verlaine. They start writing material as well as practicing covers. Songs from this period include originals like "The Arms Of Venus de Milo," "Marquee Moon," "Double Exposure," as well as some covers of 13th Floor Elevators' tracks and Count Five's "Psychotic Reaction."

December 31st, 1973 - Monday.............

THE SYMPTOMS are playing their last-ever gig. Tonight's farewell show is opening up for Chilli Will & The Red Hot Peppers at the London, British Council. They've been playing together for about two years under various names. For a while they were The Plums, their drummer Patrick "Patch" Fisher had them appear as "Patchwork Quilt" once, their drummer Simon suggested "Four Ascetic Young Gentlemen," and their bassist Martin Stanway-Mayers came up with the Symptoms. The only problem is that at their farewell appearance their name is spelled incorrectly as the "Symptons." The guitarist/vocalist Robyn Hitchcock will later front the influential band the Soft Boys and later have a solo career of some repute in the '80s and '90s.

January 17th, 1974 - Thursday..

JOHNNY SOX are a band that have recently moved to England from Sweden, although they're not Swedish per se. It is fronted by Englishman Hugh Cornwell, as well as two Americans and two Swedes. The group arrived and got three gigs at three pubs. Last Saturday they played the Brecknock in London, followed by a gig at the Lord Nelson Pub. The third night they're at the Newlands Tavern. After that, the group goes their separate ways, with Cornwell moving on, beginning the Guildford Stranglers.

> THE NEWLANDS TAVERN, 40 Stuart Road, Peckham, SE15
> Thursday, January 17th
> # JOHNNY SOX
> Free admission

      JOHNNY SOX ....London, Newlands Tavern

January 27th, 1974 - Sunday.................

THE RAMONES are born. Just last Wednesday, with fifty dollars burning a hole in each of their pockets, Johnny (John Cummings) and Dee Dee (Douglas Colvin) stopped by Manny's Guitar Center on 48th Street in New York City and each bought a guitar. Johnny buys a blue Mosrite and Dee Dee gets a DanElectro Bass. Now they're getting together with Joey (Jeff Hyman) who plays drums to start a new band. Their first rehearsal is tonight. The three used to be in a high school band called the Tangerine Puppets and Joey had formerly played more recently with a glam outfit called Sniper.

      MODERN LOVERS ....New York City, The Townhouse Theatre

February 2nd, 1974 - Saturday.................

THE HELIUM KIDZ are the Swindon-based band on their way to becoming XTC. They're about to record their first set of semi-professional demos. They recently met a singer named Steve Hutchins who has a studio of sorts in a rented house in Morden, South London. They'll soon travel to London and begin recording six originals. Included in the session are "In Love With The Hurt," "Shark In The Pool," "Cafe," "Private Eye," "Adrenalin" and "Saturn Boy." They've also recently changed the name of the band AGAIN from Star Park (Mk II) to the Zip Code & The Helium Kidz (shortened quickly to just "Helium Kidz). It will take renaming the group once more to XTC before the band finds any real success.

      IGGY & STOOGES/GOOD RATS/
      TEEN LUST ....MY FATHER'S PLACE

February 15th, 1974 - Friday.................

THE RESIDENTS' first LP "Meet The Resident" is released on Ralph Records. 1,000 copies are pressed and sold in a jacket that appears to be "Meet The Beatles" with the Beatles' faces disfigured with crossed eyes, scars, etc. Bizarre songs on the album include "Numb Erone," "Guylum Bardot," "Consuelo's Departure," "Smelly Tongues" and "Skratz." This follows the band's '72 release "Santa Dog."

THE CARPENTERS are "On Top Of The World" in the pop music field, but they don't have a clue about rock and roll. In this week's

MARCH 1974

Melody Maker, Karen Carpenter says, "Music covers so many different areas. It's fine that Bowie is something new and original. I liked 'Space Oddity' but no, I wouldn't go out and buy one of his albums…And as for the New York Dolls they're just a bunch of amateurs and I don't think they even compare…Awful…screaming at the top of their lungs."

SUICIDE................................New York City, Brandy II   NEW YORK DOLLS/ELLIOT MURPHY...New York City, Academy Of Music

March 2nd, 1974 - Saturday..........................

TELEVISION play their first ever gig and win over the audience at the eighty-eight seat Townhouse Theatre on 46th Street in New York. The roots of the group actually extend back as far as 1971 when Tom Miller (aka Tom Verlaine), Richard Myers (aka Richard Hell) and Billy Ficca had a trio going for a few weeks under the name "The Neon Boys." The band Television came together in December of 1973 with the Neon Boys line-up reuniting, as well as the addition of Richard Lloyd on guitar.

THE NEW YORK DOLLS are back from their UK tour and are already in the studio working on their second LP with legendary producer Shadow Morton, who helped create '60s classics by bands like The Dixie Cups and The Vanilla Fudge. David admires his work with the Shangri-Las. Guitarist Johnny Thunders is even going to get his first ever vocal recording of a song he wrote called "Chatterbox."

PETE SHELLEY is an electrical engineering student at the Bolton Intsitute of Technology, who's also interested in songwriting. He's built a homemade oscillator and has started composing songs on it. A few months ago, a friend at college sold Pete a reel-to-reel tape deck that would allow tracks to be bounced and stacked. Pete experiments with recording some of his ideas at home. Some of his compositions include "Sky Yen" and "Telephone Operator."

TELEVISION ....New York, The Townhouse Theatre   ENO ....Manchester, Free Trade Hall

March 30th, 1974 - Saturday..........................

THE RAMONES are a trio of friends from the Forest Hills area of New York City. They're all around twenty-two or twenty-three years old. The line-up is Johnny on guitar, Joey on drums and Dee Dee on bass. This trio made their stage debut at the Performance Studio on E. 23rd Street in New York today. They got the space because their friend Tommy Erdelyi and a partner owned the studios. Johnny and neighbor Tommy Erdelyi met back in 1970 when they were in a Forest Hills High School and started a short lived band called the "Tangerine Puppets." Tommy's the one in the group with credible experience and he wants to be their manager. Tommy was working as an assistant engineer at the Record Plant in Manhattan on sessions with the famous and not so famous. The Ramones music can best be described as minimalist, buzzsaw pop. Tonight's show is in front of about thirty friends and curious people who saw the band's fliers.

THE RAMONES ....New York, The Performance Studio

April 5th, 1974 - Friday..........................

ENGLAND'S GLORY submits their demo tape to EMI. The group's demo sounds uncannily like the Velvet Underground. It's clear from listening to it that the singer, Peter Perrett, styles his own vocals after Lou Reed. Also in the group is Mick Kemp who is supposed to be "England's answer to Jonathan Richman." EMI doesn't sign the band, but wants to keep an eye on them. They'll perhaps regret that decision when England's Glory change into The Only Ones and sign with CBS.

DORIAN + ZERO/TELEVISION........New York City, Hotel Diplomat

April 7th, 1974 - Sunday..........................

JOHN LYDON & SIMON BEVERLY are new friends at Hackney College. They're both sixteen. John's a long haired lad interested in being different. He sometimes colors his hair blue, he takes the piss out of anyone he wants and won't be bothered with. Simon is enamored with David Bowie and likewise has dyed his hair red at the top and wears the most unusual clothes he can find, making his own cobbled together versions of the latest trend of fashion on the rock scene. This odd appearance marks him as a misfit in the special school. The two become inseparable. John nicknames his new friend "Sid" after a pet hamster that he has at home.

HOLLY WOODLAWN/
PATTI SMITH............................New York City, Reno Sweeney

April 14th, 1974 - Sunday..........................

THE NEW YORK DOLLS are on the air live on WBAB-FM on Long Island. Their concert from My Father's Place is being broadcast as an Easter surprise from the rock radio station. You can catch it tonight on the radio from ten p.m. till eleven if you're not at the show.

NEW YORK DOLLS/THE MIAMIS/
DAVID STEINBERG/ALLEE WILLS...New York City, My Father's Place   TELEVISION............................ New York City, CBGB's

April 21st, 1974 - Sunday..........................

GORDON "STING" SUMNER could be considered one of the most in-demand bass players around Newcastle. For the last two years, he's been a member of three different bands simultaneously, playing with each one on a different night. The Phoenix Jazzmen play standard New Orleans-style jazz, but most importantly, it's where Gordon gets his nickname "Sting". Gordon Solomon the trombone player in the band christened him "Sting" after seeing him in a yellow and black hooped sweatshirt. He thought Gordon looked like a giant bee. He also plays in The River City Jazz Band, fiddled around with Earthrise and settled into the Newcastle Big Band. Make no mistake, it is a

APRIL 1974

TELEVISION plus the STILLETTOES
about TELEVISION "The great thing about this band is they have absolutely no musical or socially redeeming characteristics and they know it...the next big break-through group coming out of New York." —John Felgenbaum, SOHO WEEKLY NEWS "The golden apple at the top of the tree." —Lenny Kaye, CAVALIER

appearing at C.B.G.B.
315 Bowery at Bleecker
Sunday May 5 10PM
food and drinks
available 982-4052

big band, sixteen pieces strong with several professionals in the group. They play at the University Theatre bar and easily mix Duke Ellington with the Beatles. He's also had the chance to make his first recording, a live LP called "Newcastle Big Band" recorded live on one of their excursions to Pau, France. It's filled with Neil Hefti type arrangements of classics like "C Jam Blues" and "Love For Sale."

NEW YORK DOLLS/SUZI QUATRO ..New York City, The Bottom Line
TELEVISION ....New York City, CBGB's

May 10th, 1974 - Friday.............................

THE NEW YORK DOLLS' album "Too Much, Too Soon" couldn't be a more aptly titled second album. The band has been rising on a comet of critical acclaim, even Rolling Stone Magazine refers to them as "the best hard rock band in America." Heady stuff. The second LP was recorded with producer Shadow Morton, who did nothing short of catching the raw power of the live show in a studio. Tracks include the stage hit "Babylon," as well as "Who Are The Mystery Girls," "Puss 'N' Boots," and the Johnny Thunders vocal track "Chatterbox." Covers on the album are the Cadets' '56 hit "Stranded In The Jungle," Archie Bell's 1969 hit "There's Gonna Be A Showdown," and Sonny Boy Williamson's "Don't Start Me Talkin." The front cover pic has the band in a mock live shot in far less of the drag style than their previous album. For full shock value, Thunders has a doll by the arm, as if he's about to use it to strike his guitar.

May 23rd, 1974 - Thursday.............................

JOHNNY MOPED has assembled a band which calls themselves "Johnny Moped and the 5 Arrogant Superstars." It's Johnny Moped on vocals, Xerxes on vocals and sax, Phil Burns on bass, Fred Mills on piano, Ray Burns on guitar and Dave Berk on drums. They'll change into Assault and Buggery by August, again changing names to the Commercial Band and slimming to a quartet in January.

TELEVISION ....New York City, Coventry

June 1974.............................

THE ARTISTICS have split up. The Rhode Island School of Design-based band has split when guitarist and vocalist David Byrne left school. He'll start up another band that plays more originals and depends less on '60s covers. They'll become the Talking Heads.

WANTED: FOUR GIRLS Kim Fowley and *Who Put The Bomp* magazine are sponsoring a contest to put together "the female Beatles, Stones, Who, Shangri-Las of the '70s!" A full page ad in the magazine reads "We're looking for the girls who will take up where Suzi Quatro and Fanny leave off, the kind of girls who always dreamed they were in a Phil Spector group, girls with the desire and ability to carve out a place for women in, "'70s rock as significant as that they held in the '60s." The search is on...the ultimate goal? The group that will become The Runaways.

WANTED: FOUR GIRLS
JOB: to play pop music.
PURPOSE: to find the female Beatles, Stones, Who, Shangri-las of the 70s!

THIS COULD BE YOU!

June 1st, 1974 - Saturday.............

MORRISSEY & SPARKS Fifteen-year-old Morrissey writes a zealous letter to the *New Musical Express* after seeing Sparks on *Top Of The Pop's* singing "This Town Ain't Big Enough For Both Of Us." He wrote, "Today I bought the album of the year, I feel I can say this without expecting several letters saying I'm talking rubbish. The album is 'Kimono My House' by Sparks. I bought it on the strength of the single. Every track is brilliant- although I must name 'Equator,' 'Complaints,' 'Amateur Hour,' and 'Here In Heaven' as the best tracks and in that order. Steven Morrissey, Manchester."

HELIUM KIDZ ....London, Fulham Greyhound

June 5th, 1974 - Wednesday.............................

THE PATTI SMITH GROUP, formerly a duo of Patti Smith and Lenny Kaye, was recently augmented by the addition of Richard Sohl on keyboards. The new group plus their friend Tom Verlaine (of Television), go into the legendary Electric Ladyland Studios in NYC to record tonight. The choice of studios is important to Patti, who feels a kinship to Jimi Hendrix, its former owner. She rented three hours of studio time to record her version of the '60s classic "Hey Joe" as a tribute to Patty Hearst. After mixing and finishing the song, there was a little time left over, so Patti did a reading of a poem she wrote called "Piss Factory." It was inspired by a job she held at a South Jersey factory where she was fired for writing poetry at work. The band just vamped along behind her while she recited. The session marks the first for everyone in the group except Lenny Kaye, who had "Crazy Like A Fox" released under the name Link Cromwell back in 1966. The quartets efforts are to be pressed up and released 1,000 copies as a private pressing on Robert Mapplethorpe's Mer Records, #601. It will be available at various Greenwich Village book and record stores.

TELEVISION/STILETTOS..............New York City, CBGB's

June 16th, 1974 - Sunday.............................

ROCKET FROM THE TOMBS are a new garage band in Cleveland that are playing at the Viking Saloon. Under the comic heading "The

JUNE 1974

World's Only Dumb-Metal Mind-Death Rock and Roll Band" they pound out songs that betray their heavy influence from the Stooges, Velvets and Troggs. The twist is that this band has a sense of humor. With a nod to Frank Zappa, Rocket From The Tombs play some covers that are rewritten with new comic lyrics, and some originals. Founders of the group are two local fanzine writers David Thomas (aka Crocus Behemoth) and Peter Laughner. Also present are Gene O'Connor and John Madansky. David and Peter will grow out of the group into one of their own called Pere Ubu. Gene O'Connor would become Cheetah Chrome and find fame in the Dead Boys. Along with the Electric Eels, and The Mirrors, they are the beginnings of a fruitful Cleveland underground.

July 3rd, 1974 - Wednesday.........................

SQUEEZE are an old band under a new name. Difford & Tilbrook first got together when fifteen-year-old Glenn Tilbrook saw an advert that Chris Difford put into a shop window in Blackheath Village. It read something like "Lead guitarist wanted for band. Recording soon." The two dubbed their band Cum, and were among the hundred bands who played at the Windsor Free Festival last August. They felt the chances of a band called Cum getting on "Top Of The Pops" were pretty slim, so they became Captain Trundlow's Sky Co. (Skyco for short). Now the pair have reinvented themselves into a combo called Squeeze. Membership in this exclusive club includes guitarists Glenn Tilbrook and Chris Difford, pianist Julian Holland and bassist Harry Kakoulli. Not too long ago, Jools and Glenn used to busk in local pubs (on piano and acoustic guitar) for beer money.

TELEVISION/SISTERS.................New York City, Club 82

July 6th, 1974 - Saturday.........................

STILETTOS New York's tacky side is revealed in a double page spread in this week's *Melody Maker*. Chris Charlesworth guides you through the scruffy underside of New York to clubs like the 82 Club, C.B.G.B's and The Mushroom. "Shock and outrage is the name of the game. The more freakish, the more outlandish the fetishes of the personnel and the more bizarre their clothes the better. It's not much more than grabbing a guitar, learning a few chords, applying lipstick and bingo!" He concedes that top of the genre are the New York

Dolls, then moves through the list of Teenage Lust, The Fast, Television, Jet Black, The Stilettos, Another Pretty Face and the Brats. The audiences at the concerts are as interesting as anything onstage and frequently the line between the observer and the observed is blurred. "Female impersonators, transvestites and their ilk, make the 82 their home and even today the element of bisexuality runs strong." Chris gives a pocket review of a Wednesday night show where a resident transvestite was upstaged by the opening band the Stilettos who "had more potential but less rehearsal. Fronted by a cuddly platinum blonde called Debbi, they're a girl vocal trio with a male guitar/bass/drums back up band. The three chicks take turns to sing solo while the other two chant away behind and some of the songs were well worth putting on vinyl."

FLIP CITY are a new rhythm & blues band fronted by vocalist, guitar player Declan McManus (aka Declan Costello). They're playing tonight at the Kensington Pub in London. It's going to be a few years before Declan McManus makes his mark on the music scene in a big way under the name Elvis Costello.

FLIP CITY...............................London, The Kensington Pub

July 20th, 1974 - Saturday.........................

THE RAMONES reflect a fundamental change that would shape the band from now on. Tommy Erdleyi, acting as the band's manager coaxed Joey and the rest of the group into the notion that Joey needed to be out front. Since Joey was going to be singing instead of drumming, they also needed to hold auditions for a replacement drummer. They went through so many auditions. Tommy would find himself sitting behind the kit and showing them what the band was looking for. Finally, after trying to teach drummers for the soon to be quartet, Tommy left his job at the studio and joined the Ramones as their new drummer. They're trying to find just the right material for the group, some covers like "I Fought The Law" and even a few songs they're writing themselves. Some of the originals are "I Don't Wanna Get Involved With You," (which would later change into "I Don't Wanna Walk Around With You"), "Blitzkrieg Bop," "Now I Wanna Sniff Some Glue," "I Don't Wanna Go Down To The Basement" and "Babysitter"

KILBURN & THE HIGH ROADS ......Egham Hythe, Social Center   FLIP CITY ....London, Hope & Anchor

July 21st, 1974 - Sunday.........................

CHRISSIE HYNDE came over in 1973 and bummed around a while, briefly writing some reviews for the *New Musical Express*. She even worked for a while in Malcolm McLaren's clothing shop "Sex." Recently she met a French guy on the street who's come up with an intriguing invitation. She's been invited to come to France to be join his band as a singer. She's interested in being in a band and takes the offer. She makes the rounds at the record labels posing as a *NME* music reviewer and gathers up some freebie albums that she sells for £40 down at Cheapo-Cheapo Records. That's gives her the money to get to France where she fronts the band Avec And The Alors who play the majority of their gigs are in a converted morgue turned dancehall.

FLIP CITY ....London, Newlands Tavern   TELEVISION...........................New York City, CBGB's
KILBURN & THE HIGH ROADS ......London, Fulham Greyhound

AUGUST 1974

August 16th, 1974 - Friday.........................

THE RAMONES/ANGEL AND THE SNAKES are playing together tonight in New York. Less than a month after getting their first UK press mention in a *Melody Maker* article, New York girl group the Stilettos have split up. The group was going more in the direction of Elda Gentile and less the way that Debbie Harry and Chris Stein wanted it. The group remains basically the same, with the band of Chris Stein, Fred Smith and Billy O'Connor. The difference behind the mic is that Elda and Amanda are being replaced by two more cooperative singers, Jackie and Julie. Debbie has assumed the position as lead singer. The new band play the first of two consecutive nights at the long, dark closet called C.B.G.B.'s in New York City under the new name Angel and The Snakes. Also on the bill is the Ramones.

When the Ramones take the tiny ten square foot stage, a set flies by so fast, that the ten songs only lasts about fifteen or twenty minutes. By now the Ramones have grown to a quartet with the addition of Tommy Ramone on drums and Joey switching over to vocals exclusively. There had also been a Ritchie Ramone and a George Ramone in the last six months, but they didn't last long. These gigs are played to a nearly empty club. Not a stellar beginning, but a start nevertheless.

TIGER LILY is a lucky new band getting its big break. It's been about six months since Tiger Lily got together, struggling along trying to get support slots and being ignored by the press, until now. Karl Dallas, writing for the *Melody Maker*, reviews the band performance tonight for the "Caught In The Act" column. Tiger Lily are the opening act at the Marquee for the Heavy Metal Kids. The audience is not the most receptive and Tiger Lily are not a guitar-heavy band. Even through the heckling and apathy, Karl sees the band as somewhere between David Bowie and the Velvet Underground and a welcome change to the usual fare at the Marquee these days. He also is pleasantly surprised that, "…you can actually hear the lyrics he is singing, which makes a change. And the words are actually worth hearing, which makes an even greater change, being something of a cut above the 'Diamond Dogs' technically, if running along the same rather predictably apocalyptic groove. The band, who are Steve Shears playing the incredible bending Gibson guitar, Chris Allen, bass and the Canadian Warren Cann on drums, are loose and enjoyable and even their out of tuneness (on their second gig together) seems to contribute something to the overall atmosphere." Tiger Lily is only the first step on the road to the band becoming the group called Ultravox that will hit the UK charts in the early '80s.

HEAVY METAL KIDS/TIGER LILY....London, The Marquee · ANGEL & THE SNAKES/THE RAMONES...New York City, CBGB's

September 7th, 1974 - Saturday.......................

THE 101'ERS make their debut at the Telegraph in Brixton, a not-so-charming part of South London. The R&B/boogie band got together in May when Joe Strummer returned from a brief stay in Wales where he fronted a band called The Vultures. The 101'ers take their name from their squat at 101 Walterton Road near Kilburn and Paddington. The group is "Mole" on bass, "Evil" Clive Timperley on lead guitar and vocals, Richard "Snakehips" Dudansky on drums and vocals, "Big John" Cassell on alto sax, Alvaro Pena on tenor sax, Jules on harmonica and future Clash vocalist Joe "Woody" Strummer on rhythm guitar and vocals.

THE 101'ERS..........................London, The Telegraph

September 10th, 1974 - Tuesday......................

CHRISSIE HYNDE is back in Ohio. She left the French band she was playing with when things just weren't working out. She's a rock and roller and wants to discover her roots. She winds up in Cleveland where she has joined a band called Jack Rabbit that plays mostly covers like "Fight The Power" by the Isleys. Also in the group are Duane Verh and a local "guitar hero" called Donny Baker. Chrissie attracts some unusual looks onstage at the Celler Door when she wears her rubber skirt and SKUM manifesto T-shirt she got from Malcolm's Sex clothing shop. She's even written new songs like "Thin Line Between Love & Hate," but Jack Rabbit haven't gotten around to learning it yet. While in Cleveland, she's teaching herself to sing with more confidence and learning her craft. She's also recently received a letter from her old employer, Malcolm McLaren, who has an idea for a new band for her to be part of. It's basically going to be her on guitar, NY Doll guitarist Sylvain Sylvain and Television bassist Richard Hell. She declines the offer and remains in Ohio, for the time being.

FLIP CITY..............................London, The Kensington

October 1974.......................................

THE HELIUM KIDZ were recently offered an audition session for Decca Records on the strength of their demo session from last February. They went to London and recorded, but nothing came of the sessions. They had even hoped that their new name "Skyscraper" would work better. Now they're back in the studio auditioning for Pye Records at Pye's Bryanston Place Studios. During the session they record four songs, two of which are new: "It's About Time We Had Some Rock & Roll" and "Teenage Planet." They've also changed their name back to the Helium Kidz.

November 1st, 1974 - Friday........................

CHRISSIE HYNDE is on the move. She had left Jack Rabbit in Ohio and taken a short trip with a girlfriend down to Tuscon, unhappy and aghast that everyone seemed to be into C&W music. After six days of this living hell, she gets telegram from Michael Memmi in Paris who wants her to come to be the singer in a new band. He sends her an air ticket and she leaves to join a group called The Frenchies. Tonight the Frenchies make their live debut at L'Olympia, opening up for the Flaming Groovies.

RAMONES..............................CBGB'S

NOVEMBER 1974

November 23rd, 1974 - Saturday......................

KILBURN & THE HIGH ROADS make their debut with the can-kicking "Rough Kids" coupled with "Billy Bentley." Recordings of the Kilburns have been anxiously awaited. They had a full LP set for release on Warners' subsidiary Raft Records, but Raft sunk back in April, taking the Kilburn's hopes with it. Now they're signed to Dawn Records (a Pye subsidiary). Reviews of the single in the music press express disappointment. So much had been expected of this wonderful live act and it didn't seem to translate to vinyl.

December 8th, 1974 - Sunday......................

THE STRANGLERS are a new trio that have only been together for about three months, but they're already feeling confident enough to get onstage. When Hugh Cornwell split Johnny Sox, he started a new group called the Guildford Stranglers, but has now shortened their name, dropping the Guildford. The trio includes bassist John (Jean Jacques) Burnel (London born son of French parents) and drummer Jet Black (aka Brian Duffy). It's going to be three years before the band will have their first single out. Tonight they're at the Brecknock and they have another gig scheduled for the Western Counties on the 30th.

THE STRANGLERS ....London, The Brecknock

January 17th - Friday......................

THE TALKING HEADS are the resurrected remnants of the Artistics and they're having rehearsals in a loft in the lower east side of NYC. David Byrne and drummer Chris Frantz have been joined by Martina Weymouth on bass. Their set includes a lot of originals as well as covers of "96 Tears," "1-2-3 Red Light," "I Can't Control Myself" and "Love Is All Around."

LIVE TONIGHT!

NEW YORK DOLLS/AGE & SNIPER
TELEVISION/BLONDIE................New York City, CBGB'S
THE DICTATORS ....New York City, Coventry

January 24th - Friday......................

BASTARD, a garage band in Crawley, Sussex begins making a bit of noise with music described as "pub rock with a hell of an edge to it." They've been playing since August of last year and have a set including covers of Stooges, Alice Cooper and several originals. Members include future Damned guitarist Brian James, Dez Potter on bass, Nobby France on drums and Alan Timms on vocals. The band plays around Crawley before taking in a tour of Belgium clubs. Brian James will leave the group to join a new band called the Damned next year.

FLIP CITY ....London, The Brecknock
TELEVISION/
BLONDIE & THE BANZAI BABIES.... New York City, CBGB'S

NEW YORK DOLLS/
WAYNE COUNTY ....New York City, Coventry

January 25th - Saturday......................

BLONDIE & THE BANZAI BABIES is the new name for Angel and The Snakes. It's all part of the long road to fame for Debbie Harry and Chris Stein, who has christened the group's new backing singer Tish and Snooky as "The Banzai Babies." They're picking up more and more gigs and are playing frequently at both CBGB's and the Performance Studio. You're just as likely to hear a psyched out version of "Goldfinger" a discofied "Lady Marmalade" or some of the band's originals. A song called "Giant Bats" would later appear as "Invasion Of The Giant Ants" on their debut album, as would the song "In The Flesh."

GRETA GARBAGE & THE TRASH CANS are the new band emerging in the front rooms of Dublin, that will eventually evolve into the Radiators From Space. They're called Greta Garbage and the Trash Cans and are the idea of Stephen Rapid (aka Steve Averill). He'd had the idea for a band for the last four years and now has done something about it. Like the Boomtown Rats, they're not considered as a punk band per se. They're just a high energy rock and roll band, with a little bit of glam, playing original songs in a currently unorthodox manner in Ireland.

NEW YORK DOLLS/
WAYNE COUNTY ....New York City, Coventry

TELEVISION/
BLONDIE & THE BANZAI BABIES......New York City, CBGB'S

January 26th - Sunday......................

ANDY SUMMERS is the subject of speculation in *Melody Maker*, that he might be picked as Mick Taylor's replacement in the Rolling Stones. They say he, "...would contrast with the hungry, debauched Keith Richards image and avoid upstaging Mick. A sturdy, reliable and experienced musician, he would be able to supple the required mixture of intuition and feeling." Andy has previously played with Zoot Money, The Animals, David Essex, Neil Sedaka and the cast of the *Rocky Horror Picture Show*. Sturdy or not, he doesn't get the job. His true fame awaits him in late '77 when he joins a new group called The Police.

TELEVISION/
BLONDIE & THE BANZAI BABIES....New York City, CBGB'S

FEBRUARY 1975

February 21st - Friday.....................................

KILBURN & THE HIGH ROADS have their latest single released by Dawn Records. It's the soulful "Crippled With Nerves" flipped with "Huffety Puff." Reviewers for the most part see it as a much better effort than their previous single, but still not indicative of the Kilburns' live charm. *Sounds* magazine hangs the band with "sounds as though the band aspire to be Britains' Dr. Hook."

THE HELIUM KIDZ are somewhat disappointed with their previous two auditions for Pye and Decca, so they record more demos, on their own time and money at T.W. Studios on Fulham Place Road in London. Titles they're working on include "Yabber Yabber Yabber," "Walking Across The Ceiling," "Star Park," "Shark In The Pool," and a new one, "Neon Shuffle."

AL STEWART/	TELEVISION/MUMPS (3 nights) ....New York City, CBGB'S
BRINSLEY SCHWARTZ ....Birmingham, Town Hall	NEW YORK DOLLS....................My Father's Place

February 28th - Friday.....................................

THE BRINSLEY SCHWARTZ press office announces that although the band will not continue as a touring band they may occasionally record together when time permits. Nick Lowe and Ian Gomm plan to continue song writing and have hopes of selling some of their songs to other bands. Brinsley has become a part-time member of Ducks Deluxe and Bob and Billy are keeping busy with some session work. Their spokesman also revealed that they "also plan to tour abroad now and then, provided their various individual activities enable all of them to be available simultaneously." There is some speculation that the remaining Brinsleys will be joining up with the remnants of Chilli Willi & The Red Hot Peppers, who have also just gone through a similar devastating personnel loss.

THE NEW YORK DOLLS are playing a set of three shows at the Little Hippodrome. They'll be onstage at midnight on Friday, play two shows on Saturday and play a "kiddie show" Sunday at 5pm. In anticipation of the event, Robert Cristagau wrote in the *Village Voice,* "Reports from the proving ground in Roslyn is that the new songs are great- David Doll says he's interesed in love- and the band's spirits are up despite setbacks. If they really have their second wind, this could be amazing." They debut their new look and it's a shocking new look at that. Gone are the stack heels and glitter. They've been replaced with red vinyl pants, high heeled Sex boots, red cire' T-Shirts and a hammer and sickle backdrop. This remake of the band's image was assembled by Malcolm McLaren and Vivien Westwood. A press release that McLaren sent around reads "What are the politics of boredom? Better Red Than Dead. Contrary to the vicious lies, The New York Dolls have not disbanded, and after having completed the first Red, 3-D Rock 'n' Roll movie entitled *Trash,* have in fact, assumed the role of the 'People's Information Collective' in direct association with the Red Guard." This show is in coordination with The Dolls' very special 'entente cordiale' with the Peoples Republic Of China." The new "Red" look was not well received by the audience. Even rock journalists who were normally prepared to see the New York Dolls do outrageous things, weren't prepared for this faux Communist look.

Opening the shows are Television. Malcolm McLaren is over for the Doll's shows in his new outfits and is impressed with Television bassist Richard Hell. He really loves his look with torn T-shirt, safety pins and razored hair. He wants to take him back to England to manage and promote, but Hell turns him down to remain with his band. Hell has other things in mind. He's leaving Television after tomorrow night's show.

NEW YORK DOLLS/TELEVISION	
STEVE LYONS EYESHOW ....New York City, Little Hippodrome	

March 14th - Friday.....................................

TIGER LILY's debut single "Ain't Misbehavin'" is released by Gull Records. The song is a cover of a Fats Waller song and was recorded to capitalize on the just rereleased X-rated movie of the same name. The other side is "Monkey Jive" and is a Tiger Lily original. The band are paid a total of £300 to record the song for the movie. They use the money to buy a synthesizer for the band. Tiger Lily are Warren Cann, Stevie Shears, Billy Curry, Chris St. John and Dennis Leigh.

March 23rd - Sunday.....................................

RICHARD HELL shocks the New York avant garde scene with the announcement that he's quitting Television. It's shocking because Television are the most highly thought-of new rock band on the NY scene and Hell's writing and playing were half of the reason. They consistently draw big crowds and there is record company interest, as well as endorsements from rock luminaries like David Bowie and Iggy Pop. Over the past few months there has been a subtle change in Television. They've been growing closer and closer to cutting a deal with Island Records and in the live shows Hell's songs have become increasingly rare. In the begining, both Hell and Verlaine shared the songs evenly. Lately Hell had been getting squeezed out. He sees opportunity elsewhere and he's been talking about teaming up with New York Dolls guitarist Johnny Thunders (real name Johnny Gonzales) and Dolls' drummer Jerry Nolan. Thunders and Nolan have been playing around since November, writing songs and working out a new set apart from the Dolls. Hell would be a brilliant addition to their group. They are currently looking for a keyboard/guitar player.

PATTI SMITH/TELEVISION ....New York City, CBGB'S

MARCH 1975

March 29th - Saturday...........

THE HELIUM KIDZ are featured in the *New Musical Express'* "Roadrunners" feature, spotlighting "new and/or local bands on the way up…or something." Today's feature is on Swindon-based Helium Kidz. The group is made up of Andy J. Partridge (21) on vocals, Dave D.C. Cartner (21) on guitar, Colin "Curtains" Moulding (19) on bass and Terry Chambers (19) on drums. The Helium Kidz are willing to "work themselves stupid if someone is willing to give them the opportunity to prove themselves…They aspire to attain the impossible dream of being able to throw a TV or two out of the window of an American hotel and have no one complain." They've been playing a few irregular dates at the Fulham Greyhound, in Wales and in their hometown of Swindon. Even on the £40-50 that they split up for the evenings entertainment, they've managed to pay off all of their old equipment and have started buying some new pieces. The band plays "a mixed program of hard rock." Original songs in their glam-pop set include, "Saturn Boy," "Little Gold Runner," "Shark In The Pool" and "Neon Shuffle."

HELIUM KIDZ: uphill struggle

PATTI SMITH/TELEVISION ....New York City, CBGB'S

April 2nd - Wednesday.....................

ALEHOUSE are a five piece Swindon band who play a few originals and loads of covers by groups like Thin Lizzy, Robin Trower, Steely Dan and Queen. This week they auditioned for Island Records and EMI. They've been around about two years now and play University gigs, pubs and whatever else they can manage to get. Alehouse are Rod Goodway on vocals, Larry "Mole" Williams on lead guitar, Dave Gregory on lead guitar, Tony Green on bass and Tony Macondach on drums. Dave Gregory will play with several bands before finding lasting success with XTC. It's ironic that they're featured in the *NME's* "Roadrunners" section the week after the Helium Kidz. In a few years, three of the Helium Kidz and Dave Gregory of Alehouse will become the XTC that is familiar to fans of the band in the '80s and '90s.

April 24th - Thursday......................

THE NEW YORK DOLLS have come to another crisis point. While on tour in Miami Florida, guitarist Johnny Thunders and drummer Jerry Nolan quit the New York Dolls. There seemed to be little direction in the group, the new image with the red suits wasn't going down well in the south and both Thunders and Nolan had drug habits that were sapping the creativity from the band. Combine that with the long drives and poor reception and something had to give. Will the group survive the loss? It's doubtful, but Syl, David, Arthur and a fill-in drummer named Blackie complete the Florida dates before finding their own ways home. Arthur and Blackie stayed in Florida, David flew back to New York and Syl and Malcolm point their battered green station wagon toward New Orleans.

THE 101'ERS' regular "Charlie Pig Dog" nights have come to a close. Almost every Wednesday since December they've staged their own gigs, charging 10p to get in. The pub owner has shut them down. They'll move their residency down the road to the Elgin Pub where they'll be for the next nine months. They are mentioned in *Melody Maker's* "Hot Licks" column with the complimentary, "…there go a really exciting rock and roll band like the 101'ers with a stack of AC 30's playing gigs like the Charlie Pigdog Club for a packet of peanuts and half a bitter."

THE SUBTERRANEANS are a short-lived band that are another step toward the Damned. The line up is almost complete. Chris Millar (aka Rat Scabies) has joined Ray Burns (aka Capt. Sensible) and Brian James. That's two thirds of the Damned right there. The other Subterraneans are Eyno on vocals, Hermine on vocals and writer Nick Kent on guitar and vocals. Nick has just left from a brief encounter playing with the future Sex Pistols. The Subterraneans only played two gigs.

THE COUNT BISHOPS COUNT ....London, The Kensington

April 30th - Wednesday.....................

THE HEARTBREAKERS is the group-in-waiting that combines ex-New York Dolls members Thunders and Nolan, with ex-Television Richard Hell. They make their live debut tonight opening up for Wayne County at NY Club 82. Although they have been searching for a fourth member, they have to go onstage as a trio. In the audience tonight is a very impressed Andrew Jakeman (aka Jake Riveria) who has just completed a US tour managing the affairs of Dr. Feelgood.

May 1975.......................

CABARET VOLTAIRE are a Sheffield-based, electronic, dadist trio who have just taken that next step up the career ladder by playing live. They take their name from a 1916 Dadist club in Zurich. It all started last year when Chris Watson bought a tape recorder and an oscillator. Chris, along with Stephen Mallinder and Richard Kirk recorded an accapella version of Bowie's "Five Years." They played around a bit more with electronic gear and soon found themselves being asked to play for tonight's "Science For People" show. The band presented their "Rock and Electronic Music" program and the evening ended up in a fight. Chris Watson from the band showed the *NME* just how easy-going Cabaret Voltaire was when he said, "I don't think any of us has any worries, artistically, because we don't have any intentions artistically. We've never set ourselves up to state anything."

THE STRANGLERS are a Guildford based trio searching for a keyboard player to round out their band. The group is comprised of two old friends, guitarist Hugh Cornwell and drummer Jet Black, as well as their newest member, bassist Jean Jacques Burnel. They search and find their new member with a *Melody Maker* musicians advert. He's keyboardist Dave Greenfield. There is also a sax player that answers the ad, but only lasts a few days in the group.

16

MAY 1975

May 17th - Saturday...............................

BLONDIE have more changes in their modular lineup. Drummer Billy O'Connor is quitting to go to law school and is being replaced by Clem Burke. Fred Smith quits to fill Richard Hell's hole in Television. They're down to a three-piece band and the two backing singers are splitting because they think the band is finished. They would eventually put together a band called the Sick Fucks. Debbie and Chris are very frustrated. Things seemed to be moving in the right direction and now they have to start again. Some demos are cut of songs from the Blondie set. There's the Shangri La's cover of "Out In The Streets" and originals like "Platinum Blonde," "Puerto Rico" and "Thin Line." There's also a comedy number they call "The Disco Song" that would surface in '79 as "Heart Of Glass" and be a massive world-wide hit.

EDDIE & THE HOT RODS are a Southend band that come from the same breeding ground as Dr. Feelgood and Mickey Jupp, but they're trying to distance themselves from the pub rock crowd. They've just come up to London for six weeks and have gotten a big break with a Saturday night residency at the Kensington in London. They're trying to make the change from playing pubs where teds throw glasses at them when they don't play old Bill Haley numbers, up to small clubs where they can play their own material without fear of being hit. With their own songs like "Writing On The Wall" and "Cruising In The Lincoln," they mix in some oldies by Sam The Sham ("Wooly Bully"), The Who ("The Kids Are Alright,") and some appropriate new material (Seger's "Get Out Of Denver"). Eddie & The Hot Rods don't have an Eddie in the group. They are lead by Barrie Masters, Steve Nichols on drums, Dave Higgs on guitar, Paul Gray on bass and Lou on harmonica. They've been compared to the early Stones but are developing their own style quickly.

        EDDIE & THE HOT RODS ....London, The Kensington

May 23rd - Friday...............................

KILBURN & THE HIGH ROADS have their debut album released by Dawn Records in the UK. It's titled "Handsome." This will be a "timepiece" representing the old Kilburns as they have recently added much new material and changed personnel in the band. The LP starts off with "The Roadett's Song." Among others are "Pam's Moods," "Crippled With Nerves," "Broken Skin," "Upminster Kid," "Patience," "So What," "The Call Up," "The Mambo Rumble and the Cocktail Rock" and a re-recorded version of "Rough Kids." The album was originally to be titled "No Hand Signals," but the other band members felt that was too distasteful. Two weeks ago the Kilburns lost their drummer David Rohaman, who has left the band to pursue a solo career. His place is being filled by Malcolm Mortimer who is a former member of G.T. Moore and the Reggae Guitars. The Kilburns are also planning to augment their act with two girl vocalists and are currently holding auditions.

        POODLES ....London, Camberwell School Of Art

May 24th - Saturday...............................

THE ELECTRIC EELS release their anti-music indie single "Cyclotron" and "Agitated." They are Dave "E" McManus on vocals, John Morton on lead guitar, Brian McMahon on rhythm guitar and Nick Knox on drums. This single is extremely raw and distorted and is in reality one of the first punk records ever. They've been playing together since '72 and their music is just as likely to include a guitar as it is a piece of sheet metal and a sledge hammer. They are based in Cleveland and described their music as "art terrorism." Onstage, as well as off, they wear safety pins and ripped T-shirts with rude slogans on them. They confront and confound.

        EDDIE & THE HOT RODS ....London, The Kensington

June 20th - Friday...............

THE RAMONES & THE TALKING HEADS share the bill tonight down at C.B.G.B's. The Ramones are hometown heroes and get the major space in the advertising. The Talking Heads get just a small line of print at the bottom. The Ramones press kit contains many amusing bits, including this description. "Their songs are brief, to the point and every one a potential hit single…The Ramones all originate from Forest Hills and kids who grew up there, became either musicians, degenerates or dentists. The Ramones are a little of each. Their sound is not unlike a fast drill on a rear molar." They have just been offered a single deal for indie Sire Records and have declined. They want an album. Still searching, they're going to audition for Rick Derringer and Sky Records on July 11. They'll have a chance to impress the producer when opening for Johnny Winter in concert at Waterbury, Conn.

        The Talking Heads show tonight is their live debut. The trio is led by David Byrne who built the band out of the split of an earlier predecessor called the Artistics.

        RAMONES/TALKING HEADS ....New York City, C.B.G.B's

July 7th - Monday...............................

THE HELIUM KIDZ (formerly Star Park, Skyscraper and Stiff Beach) change their name once again. Fat Fruit is suggested and declined. The Dukes Of Stratosphere is a strong front runner, but is a little too psychedelic sounding and fluffy. The name XTC is the winner, inspired by Jimmy Durante looking for the lost chord and exclaiming, "Dat's it, I'm in ecstasy," when he finds it. Besides that, it'll be easy to spot in the music newspapers, something the band is anxious to do since their mention in *NME's* "Roadrunner" a few weeks back. With the name change comes another personnel change too. They've added Jon Perkins on keyboards.

JULY 1975

July 16th - Wednesday..................................

BLONDIE has just made it under the wire. Only days ago they met a friend of Clem Burke's named Gary Valentine. He passed the audition and is the newest member of Blondie. It's just under the wire because Blondie are onstage tonight as part of the CBGB's Festival Of Unsigned Bands. Their set is being recorded for a CBGB's live album (their songs are never used on the final LP) as are the other bands.

LIVE TONIGHT!

RAMONES/TUFF DARTS/
BLONDIE/TALKING HEADS/
WHITE LIGHTNING ....New York, CBGB's (Festival)

July 22nd - Tuesday..................................

101'ERS have a rapidly growing following around London and the word is spreading across the channel as well. Skydog Records, the indie label responsible for the Flaming Groovies "Grease" EP, has made an offer to do a single with the band. No contracts have been inked yet. They continue to play whenever and wherever they can. Just last Saturday they played a free concert at Harlequin Records.

DEAD BOYS ....New York, CBGB's

July 26th - Saturday..................................

THE LONDON SS are looking for a singer and a drummer. The group is based around Tony James and Mick Jones. They're being helped with finding rehearsal space in Paddington and shaping the group by Bernard Rhodes, who himself wants a pop group to manage like his friend Malcolm McLaren. Jones and James have already refused to change the name of the group, but have taken the suggestion to start advertising and auditioning potential new members. The new players must fit into the London SS mold that is somewhere in the middle ground between the NY Dolls, MC5 and the Stooges. This band will be the starting place for many other bands. Tony James will find fame in Generation X and Mick Jones will begin the Clash and eventually start anew in Big Audio Dynamite.

POODLES ....London, The Marquee
101'ERS ....London, The Clarendon

HEARTBREAKERS/SHIRTS/
STAGGER LEE/MAD BROOK.........New York City, CBGB's (Festival)

August 1975..................................

THE SEX PISTOLS' future is made much clearer when Malcolm McLaren's assistant, Bernie Rhodes, sees green-haired Johnny Lydon wearing a Pink Floyd t-shirt with "I Hate" written over the top of it. He thought it was brilliant, what a display of attitude. Bernie invites Johnny to come back to the Roebuck Pub in King's Road to meet Malcolm, Glen Matlock, Steve Jones and Paul Cook. Johnny shows up and is invited to audition for the singers' spot in the new band. He was positioned before the jukebox, where he was prodded into singing. Not content to sing one of the '50s oldies on the juke, Lydon ripped though a totally over-the-top version of Alice Cooper's "Schools Out." He acted as ridiculous as he could because he was in a totally ridiculous situation. Malcolm saw something and invited Johnny to come round to a rehearsal next week at a pub called the Crunchie Frog in Rotherhithe. Johnny showed up, the band didn't. They didn't like him. Johnny calls Malcolm the next day and tells him to fuck off.

FRANKENSTEIN are the new band in Cleveland that would become the Dead Boys over the next year. When Rocket From The Tombs split last month, two members, Gene O'Connor (now calling himself Cheetah Chrome) and John Madansky (under the new name of Johnny Blitz) form a new group with a friend called Stiv Bators. They intend to rock out in an over the top glam-without-the-glitter band. They play some originals, as well as covers of songs from Kiss and Mott The Hoople. The next big break for the band will be in July of '76 when they finally make it to the stage of CBGB's in New York. After two albums, the Dead Boys will break up and Stiv Bators will start a new band called Lords Of The New Church with an ex-member of the Damned, Sham 69 and the Barracudas.

August 2nd - Saturday..................................

MALCOLM McLAREN's new Sex T-shirts are not only getting noticed, they're getting people arrested. Just today, Alan Jones had bought one of the new cowboy designs and was stopped on King's Road by two policemen, taken to the Vine Street Station and charged with public indecency. The shirt portrays two cowboys facing each other. Both have cowboy hats, vests, boots and no pants whatsoever. Their flaccid penises are almost touching while one straightens the others' collar. The pink shirt is printed in brown and is a new favorite around the Sex shop. Malcolm and Vivien will have to answer the charges in November.

EDDIE & THE HOT RODS ....London, Newlands Tavern
COUNT BISHOPS ....London, Harlequin Records (free)

TELEVISION/MARBLES/
TALKING HEADS/RUBY & REDNECKS/
MAD BROOK/ UNEASY SLEEPER ...New York City, CBGB's

August 15th - Friday..................................

THE 101'ERS have their live performance at the Hope & Anchor in London reviewed by Chas DeWhalley for the *New Musical Express*. They're rapidly becoming one of the best of the up-and-coming new bands around the London pub rock circuit. With the breakup of the Ducks DeLuxe and Brinsley Schwartz, there is a keen eye out for the new leaders of the pack. The band's set featured many '60s rock and R&B classics. Just a few of the songs that night were the Beatles' "Day Tripper," Eddie Cochran's "Summertime Blues," Van Morrison's hit "Gloria," "Shotgun Wedding," by Roy C, Slim Harpo's "Hip Shake." and loads of Chuck Berry standards. They also had some original

AUGUST 1975

songs like "Steam Gauge 99" and "Motor Boys Motor."

HEARTBREAKERS/
TALKING HEADS/BLONDIE...........New York City, C.B.G.B.'s

August 18th - Monday...............

TELEVISION's 45 of "Little Johnny Jewel" on NYC's Ork Records shows up in various record shops in Greenwich Village. Its flipside is "Part 2," the whole of the song was too long to fit on one side. You can find it at Village Oldies Record shop or mail order it direct from Ork Records for only $2. This little 45 is causing quite a buzz in New York. The *Village Voice* writes that the record is, "...characteristically dynamic and spooky. Tom Verlaine sings as if a knife were being held to his throat. The record doesn't capture Verlain's Texas-Chainsaw intensity (his live performances are thick with tension) but it's dissolute aura isn't easy to shake off." In the UK, its magic eludes *Melody Maker's* Steve Lake who wrote that it, "...promises to do for 1975 what Patti Smith's 'Hey Joe' did for 1974-absolutely nothing." Upset with the choice of song for the single, Richard Lloyd has quit the group. He'll stew for a few weeks and then come back into the fold.

THE HEARTBREAKERS don't live up to their hype, according to *Melody Maker's* Steve Lake, as he files his report of the scene raging around C.B.G.B.'s in New York City. His fave new unsigned band is The Shirts, but he finds time to name check several others like Stagger Lee, Second Wind, The Ramones, The Talking Heads and Blondie. Of all the positive things he's seeing, he's quite disappointed with the Heartbreakers. They've got a great stage look, but he feels they have no ability, "...an unlikely looking mess of black hair inside a baggy grey suit and a buttoned to the neck dark shirt erupts in a violent paroxysm, arms and legs hail wildly, a mouthful of snaggleteeth chews a lower lip into all sorts of preposterous pouts and an unfortunate electric guitar is savagely raped. This is Johnny Thunders, a failed New York Doll trying once again to make image pass as a substitute for playing chops. He almost gets away with it too. The Heartbreakers are awful, There's no two ways about it. They genuinely do not know how to play their chosen instruments."

EDDIE & THE HOT RODS ....London, Dingwalls

September 6th - Saturday........................

PATTI SMITH is in the studio working on her debut LP with former Velvet Underground keyboardist John Cale producing the sessions. They're recording at Jimi Hendrix's historic Electric Ladyland studios. The working title for the album is "Horses." The group is Patti Smith, Lenny Kaye, Richard Sohl, Ivan Kral and newest addition J.D. Daugherty.

MORRISSEY vs. AEROSMITH What has Aerosmith done to get under Morrissey's skin? Ever aspiring to be a rock writer, he puts pen to paper and writes to the *Melody Maker* again. His letter appears in this week's issue as such, "Aerosmith are one of those American dance-a-rama scenic bands with enough punch to see the Stones on pensions and enough make-up to last them through the winter. Their music is that of confused struggle, with vocalist Steven Tyler sounding as though he is using the microphone to brush his teeth. They are as original as a bar of soap and have as much to offer seventies rock as Ena Sharples. Aerosmith are just another street-corner rock 'n' roll band, using notorious Zeppelin riffs in an effort to steal out love and devotion. But when one ruminates over the fact that 'Toys In The Attic' is the band's third album. Thanks, but no thanks Aerosmith. I'll stick with the New York Dolls for my rock 'n' thrills. STEVE MORRISSEY, Kings Road, Stretford, Manchester."

September 13th - Saturday........................

THE DIVERSIONS are a Funk-Soul-R&B band, who have their debut single out today on Gull Records. It's a cover version of Carl Malcolm's "Fattie Bum Bum," flipped with an original called "Jamaica." This combo is most noteworthy for its vocalist and sax player Lene Lovich, who commands a striking presence in her leopard skin outfit and will have many hits on her own in the early '80s.

EDDIE & THE HOT RODS ....London, Newlands Tavern
RAMONES/BLONDIE ....New York City, Performance Studio

September 17th - Wednesday........

SQUEEZE are now under contract with RCA Records. The show tonight at the Fulham Greyhound will probably be a great one, the band is in a celebratory mood. They've been playing three nights a week at the Bricklayer's Arms in Greenwich, as well as some other scattered gigs and are now on their way to stardom. They'll soon be recording some tracks for the mega-label at Rockfield Studios.

SQUEEZE ....London, Fulham Greyhound

September 19th, - Friday........................

THE RAMONES are in a demo session again. This time they're recording for Marty Tau, former manager of the New York Dolls. Songs taped are "I Wanna Be Your Boyfriend" and "Judy Is A Punk." Tau was asked to manage the band but prefers the role of producer. He'll take the tapes over to Seymour Stein of Sire Records. Sire had offered the band a single deal back in June, but the Ramones are holding out for an LP.

SEPTEMBER 1975

September 26th - Friday..........

SEX PISTOLS' drummer Paul Cook is trying to buy time. He's finishing an electricians' apprenticeship and is saying that he's unhappy with Steve's guitar playing. Malcolm follows through by placing an ad in the *Melody Maker* in search of a strong guitar player for the group. He asked specifically for a "Whizz kid guitarist. Not older than 20, not worse looking than Johnny Thunders." Several called up, showed up and played. All were just not right, or simply dreadful. They actually do find a fifth "Sex Pistol." A fifteen-year-old named (future Rich Kid) Steve New joins the band as a result of the ad. He lasts a few weeks until they realize they didn't need another guitarist. It is a difficult time for Paul. He is being encouraged to give up a career he's worked at for years (and might not be able to return to), to take on a more serious role in a rock band that might not amount to anything.

COUNT BISHOPS ....London, Harlequin Records (free)

October 7th - Tuesday.............................

EDDIE & THE HOT RODS/THE 101'ERS are undoubtedly two of the more promising new "pub rock" bands. They've been paired for a Tuesday night residency at the Nashville beginning tonight. The bands are on equal footing with the headlining slot alternating from week to week. The 101'ers are picking up a lot of work, finding gigs at the University of London, Windsor Castle and other rooms that can afford the £10 or so a night the band usually gets.

October 10th - Friday.............................

SEX PISTOLS are rehearsing almost every day now, working up their own twisted versions of some of their favorite songs. In their list these days are the Small Faces' songs "My Mind's Eye" and "All Or Nothing," Count Five's "Psychotic Reaction," The Who's "Substitute," and Dave Berry's "Don't Give Me No Lip Child." They are also working on some songs of their own including one of Johnny's called "Scarface." Johnny has been so secretive with the rest of the band that they still don't know his last name. They have noticed his preoccupation with his rotting teeth and nickname him "Rotten," Johnny Rotten. There are also some last minute thoughts about the group name. Although they have been operation under the assumption that they are the Sex Pistols, this hasn't been formally agreed upon. The "Sex" comes in from Malcolm trying to promote his clothing shop Sex. The "Pistols" is just the opposite, a wonderful contrast to Sex.

CURVED AIR/SQUEEZE ....Guildford, Surrey Univ. 101'ERS ....London, Windsor Castle

October 15th - Wednesday.............................

THE RAMONES have just completed a series of dates at Mother's in Manhattan. Sire A&R assistant Craig Leon had seen the band and got Linda Stein down to see them. She was impressed enough that she got her husband Seymour to audition the band a few days later. Now the band is signed to Sire, with the deal they wanted all along, an album contract. The faltering label will have to get together the money to take the band into the studio soon.

October 18th - Saturday.............................

THE NEW YORK DOLLS in a new version of the group, are on stage tomorrow night at Max's Kansas City. Since the split of the original band, the remaining members (vocalist David JoHansen and guitarist Sylvain Sylvain) have decided to patch the band back together to come up with some "easy money." Fill-in Dolls, that JoHansen refers to as the "Dollettes," are drummer Tony Machine, Peter Jordan on bass and Chris Robinson adding keyboards to the line-up. More than that, they're talking about just returning from a successful tour of Japan where they played at Tokyo's Korakuen Stadium supporting Jeff Beck. This new line up cut a few demos, among which is a new JoHansen track called "Funky But Chic," just the way he would describe the band to others.

101'ERS ....London, Windsor Castle GRAHAM PARKER & RUMOUR.....London, Newlands Tavern

October 28th - Tuesday.............................

THE 101'ERS/EDDIE & THE HOT RODS gig at the Nashville tonight is reviewed by Fred Rath for *Sounds*. He's impressed with the two bands as being original, down-to-earth rock n roll. In fact he says, "Eddie & The Hot Rods look like those before-they-were-famous pics you get of the Stones, Yardbirds, etc." Likewise the 101'ers are complemented on, "...their lead vocalist (Joe Strummer), playing rhythm on a battered Fender, has all the aggressive qualities of a Chuck Berry/Eddie Cochran amalgam."

101'ERS/EDDIE & HOT RODS ....London, The Nashville GRAHAM PARKER & RUMOUR .....London, Hope & Anchor

October 31st - Friday.............................

BOOMTOWN RATS hail from Dun Laoghaire (near Dublin) and have just been booked for their first public performance at the South Bolton Street Technical School in Dublin. They have to decide on a name so that the gig can be advertised by the school. They have been jokingly calling themselves Mark Skid and the Y-Fronts, but that won't do. Lead singer Bob Geldof is in favor of the Darkside Demons. Others were pushing for the Nightlife Thugs. The night before the gig Geldof was reading the Woody Guthrie story "Bound For Glory." In it he discovered that Woody had belonged to an oiltown gang as a child, called "The Boomtown Rats." What a perfect name.

OCTOBER 1975

DEVO are onstage at the Crypt, opening up for improvisational jazz artist Sun Ra. It's an invitation-only concert for Radio station WHK, the AM half of WMMS-FM in Cleveland. Devo at this time are Mark Mothersbaugh, Bob Mothersbaugh, Jim Mothersbaugh and Gerald Casale. The group are far from what the station expected. They come out in their costumes as Booji Boy, The Clown, Jungle Jim and The Chinaman. In the liner notes to the 1992 Ryko CD release "The Mongoloid Years," Mark remembers, "using homemade electronic drums, and a mini-moog, a clavinet, a customized lobotomized Hagstrom guitar, and bass, we proceed to torture stoned urban hippies with 'performance art' way before that label even existed. Playing 'Jocko Homo' here for the first time, we incite members of the hideously costumed audience to invade the stage. They threaten to 'beat the shit out of you assholes.' We, of course, decide it is our duty to keep going. By the time Sun Ra opens his set with '25 Years to The 21st Century,' Devo has managed to clear the entire auditorium." Songs used to berate the stunned audience include "Subhuman Woman," "Bamboo Bimbo," "Beulah," "I Need A Chick" and "Jocko Homo" with it's familiar refrain "Are We Not Men? We Are Devo!"

BOOMTOWN RATS ....Dublin, Bolton St. Technical   RATBITES FROM HELL...............London, Dingwalls

November 1st - Saturday.....................................

CAFE SOCIETY are a trio of three singers, three acoustic guitars and loads of harmonies. Tom Robinson and Raphael Doyle had first met back in '68. They wrote a few songs together and drifted apart. By 1973, Raphael and Hereward Kaye had gotten together and Tom rejoined his old friend. They became Cafe Society and made their debut at the Troubadour Club in Earls Court. Since then, they've written a satchel full of songs and have come to the attention of Kinks headman Ray Davies who's signed the trio up on his new Konk Records label. Cafe Society now have 6,000 copies of their full length album "Cafe Society" released. Songs include "Poor Old Sailor," "Give Us A Break," "Such A Night," "The Old Man And The Child" and a song that Tom and Raphael wrote in '69 called "The Family Song." Tom Robinson will find fame on his own in 1977 with the Tom Robinson Band.

BARCLAY JAMES HARVEST/   KILBURN & THE HIGH ROADS ......London, Hope & Anchor
CAFE SOCIETY ....Liverpool, The Empire   DEAF SCHOOL.........................London, The Nashville

November 6th - Thursday..................

THE SEX PISTOLS play their first ever gig at St. Martins Art College, very near their cramped rehearsal space. The gig is arranged by bassist Glen Matlock who attends school there. Five songs into a blistering (should that be blustering?) set the plug is pulled on the band. They play their covers of the Who's "Substitute" and the Small Faces'"Whatcha Gonna Do About It?" On the latter song, they changed the lyric to sing "I want you to know that I HATE you baby, want you to know I DON'T care!" Headlining the bill that night are Bazooka Joe, a Hornsey Art College band that follow the fifties rock nostalgia trend in the wake of the film *American Graffiti*. Bazooka Joe centers around the talents of Danny Kleinman and Stuart Goddard (the future Adam Ant). Stuart is so impressed with the over-the-top nature of the band that he leaves Bazooka Joe the next day to begin planning another group.

BAZOOKA JOE/SEX PISTOLS ....London, St Martins Art College
THE 101er's ....London, The Elgin

November 7th - Friday...................

THE SEX PISTOLS get another gig arranged. A friend of Matlock's got the booking and the band are allowed to finally finish a prepared set of music, at the Central School Of Art and Design in Holborn in central London. It's total chaos onstage. The band is barely rehearsed, loose, and even frightened. They crash their way through a set. Although it's only thirty minutes worth of songs, the band has finally finished a live performance...without being interrupted.

CHAPMAN WHITNEY STREETWALKERS/
SQUEEZE ....Brighton, Sussex Univ.   EDDIE & THE HOT RODS...........London, The Red Cow
STRANGLERS......................London, Windsor Castle   ROOGALATOR/SEX PISTOLS......London, Central School Of Art

November 9th - Sunday.....................................

BLONDIE gets what could be their first critical review in the UK music press as part of a review of a triple bill at the Performance Studio in New York City. Among the curious attendants is *NME* writer Charles Murray. His report includes bits about The Ramones, Johnny Thunders and The Heartbreakers and "...supporting them, on that epic night at the Performance Studio, was Blondie (formerly of the decadent Ladybirds type vocal group The Stilettoes). She's this cute little bundle of platinum hair with a voice like a squeaky bath toy and quite the crudiest garage type garage band I've seen...Sadly, Blondie will never be a star simply because she ain't good enough. But, for the time being, I hope she's having fun."

FLIP CITY (2 shows) ....London, The Red Cow   THE POODLES ....London, The Marquee

November 10th - Monday.....................................

UNDERTONES Groups spring up like weeds everywhere and Northern Ireland is no exception. The newest group in Londonderry is the Undertones. The five members are starting out playing pop covers with inordinate volumes of youthful vigor. Throughout his childhood, lead singer Feargal Sharkey was constantly being pushed into various talent competitions, where he would sing traditional Irish songs and

NOVEMBER 1975

constantly win first prize. At the same time, a trio of brothers, John, Damien and Vincent O'Neill are putting together a rock band. They were joined by Billy Doherty and Mickey Bradley. When Mickey lost interest in the band, the others decided that Feargal (who was in Billy's class at school) would be a great singer. He's invited over to a rehearsal and it clicks. He's in. Together with Michael Bradley they call themselves the Undertones and start rehearsing a dozen or so of their favorite pop songs. The Undertones will become one of Ireland's top new rock acts in 1978, rivaled only by the Boomtown Rats, until upstarts U2 surpass them both in the early '80s.

THE 101er's ....London, Hope & Anchor

November 21st - Friday............................

PATTI SMITH's debut LP "Horses" has begun to leak out of the Arista offices. Although it's slated for release next week in the US and overseas in January, already the praise-filled reviews are pouring in. *The New York Times'* John Rockwell called it an, "...extraordinary disk...it will shake you and move you as little else can do." Writing for *Sounds*, John Ingham called it the, "Record of the year. Quite simply one of the most stunning, commanding, engrossing platters to come down the turnpike since John Lennon's 'Plastic Ono Band.'" The *NME* described it as having an amazing "depth and level of maturity" saying it was a better first album than those debut discs of the Beatles, Stones and Dylan. Only the *Melody Maker* seemed to differ in opinion when their reviewer stated, "...precisely what's wrong with rock and roll right now is that there's too many academics pretending to be cretins and too many cretins pretending to be academics... There's no way the contrived and affected amateurism of 'Horses' constitutes good rock & roll. 'Horses' is just bad. Period." The controversial album was produced by John Cale and also features Tom Verlaine of Television on one track ("Break It Up"). Patti's band on the LP is cohort Lenny Kaye, Ivan Kral, Jay Dee Daughtery and Richard Sohl. Included on the album are "Free Money," "Kimberly," "Redondo Beach," "Birdland," "Land" and "Elegie." Also included is an odd mixture of Gloria (in excelsious deo) and Gloria (Van Morrison). Even with such a late-in-the-year release, it is certain that this will be included on many top-album-of-the-year lists. The cover for the LP was shot by Patti's friend and sometimes roommate Robert Mapplethorpe.

STAGGER LEE/		EDDIE & THE HOT RODS.............London, The Red Cow
THE 101er's ....London, Acklam Hall		MOBIAS/SEX PISTOLS/FACTORY...London, Westfield College
STRANGLERS ....London, Cart & Horses		RAMONES...............................CBGB'S

November 27th - Thursday............................

EDDIE & THE HOT RODS are the budding young pub band from Canvey Island that have just signed to Island Records in the UK. No definite date is set for their first venture into the studio, but a live album would ideally suit their talents. By the way, they're all now given a salary by Island Records of a staggering £20 a week! Along with Dr. Feelgood they will become one of the leading bands in the "pub rock boom" that will be cut short when the punk movement takes over in '76.

THE 101er's ....London, The Elgin	JOHN CALE/NASTY POP ....Manchester, Free Trade Hall
EDDIE & THE HOT RODS ....London, The Kensington Hotel	WALLY/SQUEEZE ....York, College Of Art

November 28th - Friday............................

THE 101'ERS are in Jackson's Studios recording some demos. They cut four tracks including "Lets-a-git-a-bit-a-rockin," "Silent Telephone," "Motor Boys Motor" and "Sweety Of The St. North."

PERE UBU are proof positive that Cleveland must be an odd city. Pere Ubu has their debut single out in the US on their own Hearthan Records label. The "A" side (if you can call it that) is "30 Seconds Over Tokyo." It's a six minute track about a suicide bombing mission. The song was supposed to be the debut single from lead singer David Thomas' last band Rocket From The Tombs, but they split up before they could release it. Now Dave's new band Pere Ubu gets the chance. The flip side is "Heart Of Darkness." The group is very influenced by Capt. Beefheart and Frank Zappa. The roots of Pere Ubu lie in a comedy cover band called Rocket From The Tombs that David Thomas (aka Crocus Beheomoth) and Peter Laughner were in with members of what are now known as the Dead Boys. Also in Pere Ubu is Tom Herman on guitar and bass, Tim Wright on bass and guitar, Allen Ravenstine on synthesizer and R. Scott Kraus on drums. These days you can find the band playing regularly, every Thursday night at the Pirates Cove in Cleveland.

EDDIE & THE HOT RODS ....London, College Of Printing	
STRANGLERS ....Reading, Target Club	
SEX PISTOLS........................London, Queen Elizabeth College	
THE POODLES ....London, Bettina's	

December 5th - Friday............

THE SEX PISTOLS confuse another "hippy" audience. Malcolm McLaren, their manager, is beginning to see the difficulty in booking a band with a name like the Sex Pistols. He's started calling up a minor college official and claiming to be the support group, just to get onstage and get a reaction. Tonight is the band's fifth gig.

KRAFTWERK have their new album "Radio-Activity" released in the UK. It's the German futurists' follow up to their hit LP "Autobahn" and is also thematic. The general feel is that the tunes slide by, one after another, while in between you hear snippets of radio interference. Sounds trapped in the ether that have wound up in the bits between the

DECEMBER 1975

grooves. The effect is that the album is a continuous program, not a continuous composition as with "Autobahn." The simple black & white cover recalls European radios of the '40s.

THE 101ER'S	Hereford, The Flamingo	STRANGLERS	Turnford, New River Arms
SEX PISTOLS	London, Chelsea School Of Art	KILBURN & THE HIGH ROADS	London, Newlands Tavern

December 9th - Tuesday.......................

THE SEX PISTOLS play at Ravensbourne Art College, just twenty minutes outside of London. When the Sex Pistols take the stage, the room clears. Only a few curious and intrigued stragglers stay behind. One is Simon Barker, who is impressed and quickly spreads the word about this new group to his friends. He tells schoolmate Steve Bailey, who is now referring to himself as Steve Severin (or Spunka, or Two-Tone Steve). Also on the grapevine are Bill Broad (soon to be Billy Idol) who also goes to school in Bromley and Sue Ballion, (aka Suzie Sue). The inseparable unit grows and soon also includes Debbie Juvenile (Debbie Wilson), Sue Catwoman (Sue Lucas) and Sid Vicious (Simon Beverley). This group of oddly dressed teenagers would become fixtures at Sex Pistols' gigs and written up in a few of the music weeklies as being almost as famous as the band itself, and becoming dubbed the "Bromley contingent."

SEX PISTOLS/FOGG	Bromley, Ravensbourne Art College	SNAKES	London, Lord Westbury
DEE CLARK/FLIP CITY	London, The 100 Club	EDDIE & THE HOT RODS	London, The Red Cow

December 13th - Saturday.......................

CHRISSIE HYNDE is back in England after a breif time as lead singer for a group called the Frenchies. They played a couple of gigs, but she was disappointed with the group. Back to England, where she's met with Malcolm McLaren. He's putting together more musicians, something he loves to do. Two people he's met at parties that look promising are Chris Millar (the future Rat Scabies of the Damned) and his friend Ray Burns (the future Capt. Sensible of the Damned). Malcolm wants Chrissie to dress as a boy and play guitar in his new band, acting the part of a very effeminate boy. To add to the image, Malcolm also wants her to carry a cane. They're to be the Masters Of The Backside. There's also a guy they met at the Nashville called David Zero (the future Dave Vanian of the Damned) and David White. They rehearse a few times playing things like Spencer Davis' "Gimmie Some Lovin'" and the Troggs' "I Can't Control Myself." It only lasts for a few days and then the group start to do their own thing without Malcolm or Chrissie. Rat, Vanian and Sensible go off to work with a friend named Brian James in another new band called the Damned. Again, she's left out in the cold. Everyone's getting a band together but her. Chrissie is unsure of her guitar playing and wants to get better. While in the band, her bandmates wanted her to be the singer for the new group, but she refuses, wanting to be able to play and sing at the same time. So, she has to first master the guitar and she's only adequate on it now. They've seen her busking at tube stations and bus stops and know she's a talented singer.

THE JAM	London, Fulham Greyhound

December 24th - Wednesday.......................

PUNK MAGAZINE is a new magazine based out of New York that is designed to cater to the crowd that feels total disenfranchised by *Rolling Stone*, *Circus* and *Creem*. In the debut issue is an interview with the Ramones and a wicked cartoon of Lou Reed on the cover, portraying the artist in the mindset of his new LP "Metal Machine Music."

THE 101er's	London, Hope & Anchor	EDDIE & THE HOT RODS	London, The Red Cow

December 29th - Monday.......................

SLIK has just been signed to a deal with Bell Records. They hail from Scotland and had begun as "Salvation" where they are already selling out venues such as the Glasgow Apollo before they were renamed Slik. Their first single for Bell will be the original composition "Forever and Ever." The group is a four piece consisting of Midge Ure, Billy McIsaac, Jim McGinlay and Kenny Hyslop. Malcolm McLaren and Bernie Rhodes had recently been in Scotland looking for fabric for their shop and selling some equipment too hot to sell down south. Malcolm met Midge when trying to sell an amp and took down his name. Glen Matlock called up Midge to see if he was interested in being the band's vocalist, but he explained he'd already signed a deal with Slik. Glen and Midge would meet up again years later when Glen put together his post-Pistols band the Rich Kids.

MORRISSEY appears on the *Sounds* letter page with another bout of praise for the New York Dolls. He mourns the fact that both the Dolls and Jobriath were not appreciated as much as they deserved to be and concludes with his view of their legacy. "It's often forgotten that the Dolls were the beginning of a whole new music scene in America which has produced such rarities as Kiss, Aerosmith, The Tubes, Wayne Country, The Dictators and the current genius Bruce Springsteen- names which wouldn't stop the show, but have been the topic of much enthusiastic journalism. Not to mention the truck loads of amateur bands which, as I pen this epistle, will no doubt be screeching away at unrecognizable chords after bathing in the latest brands of cosmetics." - Steve Morrissey, Kings Road, Stretford, Manchester."

The New York Dolls' David and Syl, reform one more time for New Years.

JANUARY 1976

15th - Thursday..

THE LONDON SS has a constantly changing membership, that now includes Brady (aka Mick Jones, future Clash guitarist) and a friend of his from school Paul Simonon (future Clash bassist). Since the departure of Brian James who left to begin a band called the Damned, they've been joined by another guitarist, Chrissie Hynde. Chris Spedding has loaned her a Japanese Les Paul copy (a "Res Paw") and a little amp. When first considering the gig with the London SS, Chrissie was told that their manager Bernard Rhodes' idea was to have her play guitar in the new band "School Girl's Underwear." The name didn't play well with Chrissie. The new name is now the rude pun "Mike Hunt's Honorable Discharge." It's still a few years before Chrissie will have her first taste of success with a group called The Pretenders.

LIVE TONIGHT! DIVERSIONS/
KILBURN & THE HIGH ROADS ......London, Dingwalls

SNAKES ....London, Hope & Anchor

23rd - Friday..

MALICE have their first real band rehearsal at the hall in St. Edwards Church in Crawley. The group is school friends Marc Ceccagno on guitar, Michael Dempsey on bass, a drummer named Graham and Robert Smith on guitar. Graham's brother had a mic and an amp so he got to be the singer. They're planning on having rehearsals every Thursday night from now on. It takes practice if you want to be The Cure.

THE SWELL MAPS are a group of some friends who all happened to be sitting around their Solihull homes looking for something to do. The principle instigators, Nikki Sudden (aka Nikki Mattress, aka Nikki Thrush) and Epic Soundtracks, started playing together back in '72 when they were just kids. Jowe Head joined the group and took up guitar, Biggles Books also strapped on a guitar making the band a four piece. They're writing dozens of songs, but any public appearance would be way off.

HEARTBREAKERS have recorded some demos at SBS Studios in Yonkers. Among the songs are "Love Comes In Spurts," (a song Richard Hell wrote when in Television), Johnny Thunder's "I Want To Be Loved," and Hell's "I Belong To The Blank Generation."

WAYNE COUNTY & THE BACKSTREET BOYS are disappointed that their debut album has been canceled. Recorded by ESP Records, the LP featured originals such as "If You Don't Want To Fuck Me, Baby Fuck Off," "Brainwashed," "Man Enough To Be A Woman," and the Barbarians song "Are You A Boy Or Are You A Girl." Wayne is trying to find another label to release the LP.

STRANGLERS ....London, The Red Cow

TELEVISION/TALKING HEADS.......New York City, CBGB'S

February 12th - Thursday................................

SEX PISTOLS play their first proper London date opening up for Pub rockers Eddie & The Hot Rods at the legendary Marquee Club. The Marquee was the setting for the Mod movement in the '60s focusing on bands like the Who and the Yardbirds. The Hot Rods are doing an Island Records showcase and have booked the Pistols because of their notorious reputation. The Pistols are without doubt in unfriendly territory. The show is more than the audience expected. The Sex Pistols erupt onstage. Johnny throws Jordan across the floor, they leap into the fighting audience to have a little fun themselves. The band also have been promised stage monitors, but they're not on. Johnny sends a mic stand through one and things begin to domino. A destructive frenzy eventually leaves very little equipment for the headlining band as they smash up the Hot Rod's gear. Astonished that the opening band would trash their stage set, Eddie & The Hot Rods throw the Pistols off the tour after only one show. The press is there to check out the Sex Pistols, too, and they get their first mention from *NME* writer Neil Spencer, who writes up the concert under the headline "Don't Look Over Your Shoulder, But The Sex Pistols Are Coming." He writes "a chair arching gracefully through the air…to the obvious nonchalance of the bass, drums and guitar. Well, I didn't think they sounded that bad on first earful- then I saw it was the singer who'd done the throwing. He was stalking around the front rows…baring his teeth at the audience and stopping to chat to members of the band's retinue. He's called Johnny Rotten and the moniker fits…(the Sex Pistols are) a quartet of spiky teenage misfits from the wrong end of London roads, playing '60s styled white punk rock. Punks? Bruce Springsteen and the rest of 'em would get shredded if they went up against these boys." When interviewed about the incident, Hot Rods' Dave Higgs said, "They can't play or nuffink. They just insult the audience. They wrecked our PA. We waited for them to apologize, but they had fucked off." Guitarist Steve Jones confided to Neil afterwards, "Actually, we're not into music, we're into chaos."

EDDIE & HOT RODS/
SEX PISTOLS ....London, The Marquee

CAFE SOCIETY.........................London, The Golden Lion
DIVERSIONS...........................London, The Nashville

13th - Friday..

D.P. COSTELLO is the new name being used by Declan McManus, now on his own after breaking up R&B/rock band Flip City. Back in '74 he played briefly solo as Declan Costello. Tonight he's at the Half Moon in Putney, where he'll be every Friday this month. The only thing that remains from Flip City are a collection of demos recorded at the Hope & Anchor Studios last year. In the sessions Costello recorded original songs like "Radio Soul," "Living In Paradise," "Pay It Back," "Imagination Is A Powerful Deceiver," "I'm Packing Up" and "Don't Stop The Band." There were also some covers like the Amazing Rhythm Aces song "Third Rate Romance" and Dylan's "Knocking On Heaven's Door."

KILBURN & THE HIGH ROADS ......High Wycombe, The Nags Head
VIVIAN STANSHALL/D.P. COSTELLO .Putney, The Half Moon
THE 101 ER'S ....London, Hampstead Town Hall
STRANGLERS ....London, Red Cow

...mission free.

Friday

HALF MOON, Lower Richmond Road, Putney.

SINGERS WELCOME
DP COSTELLO

5. CECIL SHARP ... ALBION

FEBRUARY 1976

14th - Saturday..

THE SEX PISTOLS play a self styled "Valentine's Ball" at artist Andrew Logan's studio in Butler's Wharf. The showcase was staged by McLaren and Westwood to expose influential people, the "right people" in the underground fashion world to their new group. The Pistols were loud, dangerous, and when Jordan jumped onstage and partially disrobed, the cameras clicked.

BLONDIE the group, have a line up that has now grown to quintet with the addition of Jimi Destri (ex-Knickers) on keyboards. He joined Chris Stein on guitar, Gary Valentine on bass and drummer Clem Burke in October. The new line-up with five members makes their stage debut tonight at CBGB's. They've been in hiding since December working on their material and changing their image. Blondie are now ready to be taken seriously. In the *NY Rocker*, Debbie confesses, "I'm sick of bleaching my hair, but I have this feeling of obligation to the band. How could we call ourselves Blondie if I didn't have blonde hair."

SEX PISTOLS...........................private show   BLONDIE/MIAMIS.....................New York City, CBGB's

19th - Thursday..

SQUEEZE are disillusioned. The band's contract with RCA has been terminated. They had been so hopeful and had even recorded five demos at Rockfield Studios for RCA. Last month they were about to get rolling when the label was planning to issue their recording of "Take Me I'm Yours" as the group's debut single. Now they are back at square one. Glenn Tilbrook summed it up in the *NME* with, "They just weren't interested. It was almost like we were (used as) a tax loss."

KILBURN & THE HIGH ROADS ......London, Dingwalls   SEX PISTOLS ....St. Albans, Hertfordshire College

20th - Friday..

THE SEX PISTOLS' gig tonight in High Wycombe is the sight of more audience violence. The Pistols weren't actually booked in to the Buck's College of Higher Education's Valentine dance, they just showed up and said they were the opening act for Screaming Lord Sutch. Midway thru their set, in the middle of "No Fun," Johnny's mic goes dead. Nothing. Someone runs up onstage and picks up Johnny and sends him to the floor. The fight begins. The Sex Pistols friends are scrapping with the audience. It was the end of the show. The DJ even comes on afterward and taunts them about their post-Hot Rods comment about being into chaos.

    A few weeks ago Howard Devoto (aka Howard Trafford) and Pete Shelley (aka Pete McNeish) read a review about the Sex Pistols and how they do outrageous songs and covers of the Stooges' material. They're intrigued and have borrowed a car for the weekend to check out the Pistols. They've driven down from Manchester to see them in High Wycombe tonight and tomorrow in Welwyn. They're both very impressed and they meet Malcolm McLaren and try to set up two shows with the Sex Pistols in Manchester. Pete and Howard are thinking about the small hall that is above the Free Trade Hall that they could rent out inexpensively. Also in the crowd is Ron Watts who promoted tonight's gig. He also works for the 100 Club on Oxford Street in London. He likes the band and eventually offers the band a residency beginning at the end of next month. On the trip Pete and Howard go through a "Time Out" gig listing and spot a review of "Rock Follies" that says, "...it's getting a buzz, cocks!" It's the genesis of the name of the band they're about to begin, calling it the Buzzcocks.

PATTI SMITH clearly stated one of her goals in the *NME* this week, "You know, I'd rather be remembered as a great rock and roll star than a great poet. To reach the highest point of something our generation created."

SCREAMING LORD SUTCH/   STRANGLERS ....London, The Red Cow
SEX PISTOLS ....High Wycombe, College Of Arts   D.P. COSTELLO ....Putney, The Half Moon

22nd - Sunday..

ROUGH TRADE RECORDS has just opened up its first retail shop for special interests in London. They seek out and sell unusual singles, out of print discs and second hand vinyl. It's the project of Geoff Travis and his friend Ken. They can be found at 202 Kensington Park Road in Notting Hill.

STRANGLERS ....London, Hope & Anchor
DIVERSIONS ....London, The Red Cow

March 4th - Thursday..................

101'ERS enter Pathway Studios to set down some of their own songs, "Sweet Revenge" and a cover of Van Morrison's "Gloria." Mole on bass has been replaced with 'Desperate' Dan Kelleher, who also adds keyboards to the band.

MALCOLM McLAREN's philosophy of rock is quoted in this week's *NME*, "Rock is fundamentally a young people's music and a lot of kids feel cheated. They feel that the music's been taken away from them by that whole over 25 audience... there's this incredible antagonism coming from those older bands too, against the Sex Pistols. Bands like Wings, Queen...we've had rows with them and they're full of these miserable excuses for themselves."

DOCTORS OF MADNESS ....Coventry, Warwick Univ.   EDDIE & THE HOT RODS.............Penzance, Winter Garden

18th - Thursday..

EDDIE & THE HOT RODS are finally immortalized on vinyl. Their debut waxing for Island is the single "Writing On The Wall" b/w "Cruising (In The Lincoln)." Both are original compositions and had the benefit of producer Ed Hollis for the sessions.

MARCH 1976

PERE UBU have another single out on their own Hearthan Records label. It's titled "Final Solution" and is flipped with "Cloud 149." This track features a new member to the Pere Ubu line up. Dave Taylor is the synthesizer player who replaces Alen Ravenstine.

THE 101 ER'S ....High Wycombe, Nags Head   D.P. COSTELLO ....Houndslow, The Grail Folk Club

30th - Tuesday...

SEX PISTOLS get an important London booking as a result of their High Wycombe gig. The Sex Pistols are invited to play the 100 Club in the heart of London, a club that normally features jazz fare. This is their first "booking" there. Chrissie Hynde has brought musician/producer Chris Spedding to the 100 Club to see the band. He's interested and thinks there is definitely something there worth hearing, no matter what the press is saying. During the show, Johnny was caught up in the act and wasn't exactly singing with the music, more like singing around the music. Glen shouts "sing in time!" Johnny gets furious and starts to pick a fight. He flings one of Paul's cymbals across the stage and wanders out front to talk to the audience. Malcolm confronts him and tells him to get back onstage or he's finished. He won't even get taxi fare home! He makes his way back to the stage as the set dissolves into chaos. Then Johnny disappears with his friends. Johnny's found a new friend in American Chrissie Hynde, who he met around Malcolm's clothing shop Sex. She teaches John a thing or two on the guitar, even though Malcolm doesn't like the interference with HIS band.

THE STRANGLERS raise eyebrows across London with their new promo posters showing a Boston strangler victim in a pool of blood.

LIVE TONIGHT!

PLUMMET AIRLINES/   DOCTORS OF MADNESS ....London, The Marquee
SEX PISTOLS/SALT ....London, The 100 Club   STRANGLERS/SNAKES...............London, The Nashville

April 1st - Thursday...

THE BUZZCOCKS are in their infancy as a four piece band of Pete Shelley, Howard Devoto, Garth Smith and a fourth mystery drummer and entertain students at the Bolton Institute of Technology. Pete and Howard met three years ago when they were both students. The band play for the Overseas Students Association. Pete Shelley is involved in student politics with this group. When the annual get-together comes around, Pete books his own band in. They play a few numbers, including a tedius version of Bowie's "Diamond Dogs." The band must have been less than entertaining, as they were switched off after only three numbers.

THE REZILLOS are a new band of students at Edinburgh Art College. They're a large group, eight pieces, who play a mixture of new wave, music hall comedy and sixties a-go-go, twisted through the influences of Roxy Music and Dr. Feelgood. The band nicked their name from a comic book cafe called the Revilo Cafe. The band is Eugene Reynolds (aka Alan Forbes), Candy Floss (nee Fay Fifi, or Shelia Hyde), Hi-Fi Harris, Luke Warm (real name- Jo Callis), D.K. Smith, Angel Patterson, Gale Warning and William Mysterious. Eugene and Luke were previously in a pop group called The Knutsford Dominators.

4th - Sunday...

THE SEX PISTOLS are due to open a new Sunday venue in Soho at the site of the old El Paradise Club. It's a decaying strip joint, thirty feet long with black walls, a postage stamp of a stage backed with mirrors and sticky floor. Actually Malcolm has rented the space for £100 and says it will feature "much ruder things" than it does now. For starters, the Sex Pistols will be the resident band there, since nobody else will have them. It will also serve as a starting-off point for other new off-the-wall groups that can't get gigs at more traditional venues. Advertising for the gig is done with handbills passed around at the 100 Club, Nashville, the Marquee and other London rock clubs. The Sex Pistols gig tonight has strippers on before and after the band. During the show, Johnny trips on some of the stage lights, burns himself and trashes the bulbs. He gets very angry stares from the dangerous looking people who normally run the place. In a pre-show interview with *Sounds* magazines' John Ingham, Johnny Rotten flatly states, "I hate shit. I hate hippies and what they stand for. I hate long hair. I hate pub bands. I want to change it so there are rock bands like us. I'm against people who just complain about *Top Of The Pops* and don't do anything. I want people to go out and start something, to see us and start something, or else I'm just wasting my time."

      Their show last night with the 101'ers was reviewed in the rather staid *Melody Maker* by Alan Jones who did not have a good time. Jones tore into the band with unconcealed glee, writing, "...the predictably moronic vocalist was cheerfully idiotic and the lead guitarist, another surrogate punk suffering from a surfeit of Sterling Morrison, played with a determined disregard for taste or intelligence. The novelty of this retarded spectacle was, however, soon erased by their tiresome repetition of punk cliches. They do as much for music as World War Two did for the cause of peace. I hope we shall hear no more of them."

SEX PISTOLS....................London, El Paradise

13th - Tuesday...

PATTI SMITH's "Gloria" bears little resemblance to any previous version of the song. The first part is "Gloria-In Excelsis Deo," the second being Van Morrison's crusty chestnut "Gloria." Mix the two together and you have something wholly new. That's what Arista has out today as the new single from Patti Smith. It's flipped with the live version of the Who's "My Generation" as performed by Patti Smith with John Cale live in Cleveland some months back.

SLAUGHTER & THE DOGS are a new band around Manchester that have been stirring up punks in Northern pubs. They're said to have a stage act based on Ziggy, Diamond Dogs and Mick Ronson, as well as a singer with green hair. The sound is described as something between the MC5 and the early Stones. The group actually got together at Wythenshawe's Sharston High School, in South Manchester.

KILBURN & THE HIGH ROADS ......London, Dingwalls   CAFE SOCIETY/BRAG.................London, The Nashville
STRANGLERS ....London, The Speakeasy

APRIL 1976

17th - Saturday.....................................

THE SEX PISTOLS get a very favorable review in the *NME* of their concert at the Nashville on the 3rd. Reporter Geoff Hutt describes the punk band as "too good for anyone to really hate them…They try nothing flash, but play hard and sharp within limitations, which act as a discipline." Geoff also wonders if this is the first band to use "plants" in the audience that are paid to heckle the group. Commenting on the headliner of the evening, The 101'ers, Geoff Hutt mentions that "they are much better than last time I saw them and are no longer struggling against an inadequate sound system…The focus of their act is the self-styled Joe Strummer, lead singer and one of the few genuine guitarists around. He's everywhere at once, chopping out chords like there's no tomorrow." They finally graduate from being a Elgin Pub band to being a real R&B/rock band.

STRANGLERS ....London, The Raven Hotel

18th - Sunday.....................................

THE 101'ERS get the opening slot on a bill with Van Der Graaf Generator and The Spiders From Mars at tonight and tomorrow night's London Roundhouse concert. This is the largest audience they have ever played to. Acknowledging the historic moment, the band's sound engineer, Mickey Foote, captured the bands' brief set on cassette. Preserved on tape are their versions of Chuck Berry's "Too Much Monkey Business," "Shake Your Hips," the Bo Diddley song "Don't Let Go" and the traditional cajun song "Junco Partner" that the Clash would later cover on their LP "Sandinista."

MALICE have had a much needed shake up. They've been freed of their singer, who only got the job because he had a mic and an amp. Since the singer was the drummer's brother, he's left too, but that's alright, as they've found a new drummer named Lawrence Tolhurst, Lol for short. Now the pieces are in place for the Cure (Smith, Dempsey and Tolhurst) to evolve.

VAN DER GRAAF GENERATOR/   SPIDERS FROM MARS/BLITZ.......London, The Brecknock
THE 101 ER'S ....London, The Roundhouse

23rd - Friday.....................................

THE SEX PISTOLS are playing again at the Nashville and they've finally gotten the attention of the press, although it wasn't as spontaneous as it appeared. *NME* Reader and future Pet Shop Boy singer Neil Tennant wrote into the music paper with his thoughts on the concert: "As you know the Pistols are composed of three nice, clean, middle-class art students and a real live dementoid, Johnny Rotten. Now on Friday night, El Dementoid wasn't really on top form, although the rest of the band were doing their best to compensate. Johnny's heart wasn't in the music. His lack of interest was naturally reflected by the audience who, disappointed, weren't reacting sufficiently to the band. So how do the Pistols create their atmosphere when their music has failed? By beating up a member of the audience, how else?" Actually, insiders say that during the course of the concert, which was a little dull, Vivian Westwood (Malcolm's accomplice) began slapping another girl in the front row. The girl's boyfriend came barreling over to stop her and instantly the front row erupted in aggro. Not wanting to miss out, Johnny leaps in. Steve and Glen try to pull him out, but the fight continues. Cameras snap and journalists take notes. Finally the band gets back onstage and finishes their set. The mold has been cast. Violence at a Sex Pistols gig is not only accepted, it's expected.

Sons of Scuzz Hit Home Run in World Punk Series

THE RAMONES' debut LP, "The Ramones," is released. The quick session began on Feb. 2nd and concluded on the 19th. It was recorded at the illustrious Plaza Sound Studios in NYC's Radio City Music Hall on a budget of only $6,400. The album is non-stop frenetic energy with fourteen songs clocking in under twenty-eight minutes. The songs meld into each other in a frenzy of buzzing guitars, sounding a bit like the Beach Boys on amphetamines. They grind through originals like "Blitzkrieg Bop," "Beat On The Brat" and "Havana Affair." After two years, the Ramones are finally on vinyl. Commenting on this momentous day Joey admitted to the *NME*, "I've only heard it once. I don't even have a copy. I can't believe it, you know…if I turn on the radio and ever hear it, I think I'll go berserk."

THE 101ER'S/SEX PISTOLS..........London, The Nashville
HEARTBREAKERS/
Movie "The Blank Generation" .....New York City, CBGB'S

May 7th - Friday.....................................

THE STOOGES were recorded live by an audience member on their last tour. This bootleg cassette has now been released under the title "Metallic K.O." One side is probably from the American Theatre in St. Louis show on Sept. 18, '73, the other from the Michigan Palace show in February of '74. Songs include the never before available "Cock In My Pocket" and a rambling, obscene version of "Louie Louie."

TELEVISION are reeling from the attention they've been getting these days. They now have three (count 'em) offers to sign with various major labels and are currently weighing the possibilities of each.

STRANGLERS ....Bristol, Newlands Park College   IAN DURY & THE KILBURNS ....London, Dingwalls
THE 101er's/   EDDIE & THE HOT RODS............London, The Hunt Hotel
GENO WASHINGTON..................London, City Univ.

MAY 1976

8th - Saturday...

THE HEARTDROPS is the latest name for the London SS. Their members keep leaving to start other groups. Brian James and Rat Scabies had left to put together the Damned and even Chrissie Hynde has left. They never could find just the right drummer and gigs were impossible with a vacillating lineup. Paul Simonon, Keith Levine, Terry Chimes and Mick Jones have renamed the group again, calling themselves the Heartdrops. Other names that were considered briefly include The Mirrors, The Outsiders, Psychotic Negatives and the Phones. They began their rehearsals in a small squat near Shepherds Bush Green in London.

THE JAM ....London, Hope & Anchor

11th - Tuesday.......................................

THE SEX PISTOLS begin a Tuesday night residency at the 100 club. Their gigs at the tiny club are beginning to shake things up and change the shape of the music world around them. Tom Robinson, a member of Cafe Society is at the gig. He hates the band. Joe "Woody" Strummer of the 101er's is there as well. Two times last month the Sex Pistols opened for his band. Strummer and Robinson both see a different future in rock and roll in the Pistols energy and drive and Joe is considering his own future. Within the band itself, Johnny is beginning to have serious problems with Glen. Johnny's out to get up peoples noses, to be troublesome. Glen is just the opposite. He wants the band to succeed, but not necessarily offend to the point of killing the group's chances of playing in public.

LIVE TONIGHT! KRAKATOA/SEX PISTOLS/
THE LONDON BOOGIE BAND ....London, The 100 Club

16th - Sunday...

PATTI SMITH finally makes her UK debut at the London Roundhouse. Tonight's show is VERY New York. The only thing remotely familiar to the London audience is the opening act, The Stranglers, who some might have caught at some of the local clubs. She dedicated several songs in the set to the late Keith Relf (ex-Yardbirds) who died on Wednesday. With the notoriety comes the skeletons rattling out of the closet. An underground Greenwich Village newspaper called *The Planet* has hit the street with a few pages of full nude photos of Patti taken three years ago. To add insult to injury, they've also published Patti's home address. Lawyers are in hot pursuit.

PATTI SMITH/THE STRANGLERS ...London, The Roundhouse   D.P. COSTELLO ....Hillingdon, Unit 3

20th - Thursday.....................................

THE SEX PISTOLS begin "secretly" cutting tracks at Majestic Studios this week with Chris Spedding producing. He sets the band in the studio and asks them to run through their set. He doesn't tell them that tape decks are recording. The band is tight and electrifying. Three songs are the focus of the sessions. They're intent on capturing the ultimate versions of "No Feelings," "Pretty Vacant" and "Problems." Malcolm believes he can get his band signed with a good demo to play.

JOHN DOWIE &
BIG GIRLS BLOUSE ....London, Square One   CAFE SOCIETY.........................London, The Nashville
                                                            SEX PISTOLS ....Scarborough, The Penthouse

27th - Thursday.....................................

CAFE SOCIETY is about to split up. Tom Robinson is becoming disenchanted. The group has been together for three years and only had one album out in all that time. They had just started on recordings for a second, but Tom is tired of waiting for things to happen. Too little promotion, too few gigs and not enough action. After seeing the Sex Pistols at the 100 Club a few weeks earlier he's thinking about beginning a new band that will be a vehicle for his political and social statements, though not the in-your-face taunt style of the Pistols.

JOHN DOWIE &
BIG GIRL'S BLOUSE ....London, Rochester Arms   CAFE SOCIETY.........................London, The Nashville
                                                                STRANGE DAYS ....London, The Kings Arms

31st - Monday...

THE 101'ERS enter the singles world with the release of their debut 45 "Keys To Your Heart" and "Five Star Rock 'n' Roll Patrol." The single is on London-based indie Chiswick Records and comes in a picture sleeve with the band's name spray painted on a wall. The 101'ers have been playing almost nightly and are at the threshold of turning their career into something big with the release of this single. Since seeing the Sex Pistols, Joe has confirmed his thoughts about starting a new type of band beyond the 101'ers' limits.

STRANGLERS ....London, The Nashville

June 1st - Tuesday................

THE RUNAWAYS started as a bit of a lark. Back in the summer of 1974, California-based *Bomp Magazine* ran a competition, sponsored by Kim Fowley, open to, "Girls who can bring hysteria, magic, beauty and teen authority to a stage. Girls with youth, energy,

JUNE 1976

dedication, wildness and style." In the end, the Runaways were formed, first as a trio, then a quartet now a quintet. At the time they were all around fourteen or fifteen but now the most are sixteen, the oldest is Lita Ford at seventeen. The rest of the group are Joan Jett, Cherie Currie, Sandy West and Jackie Fox. Their debut LP "The Runaways" is out now on Mercury in the US. Critics claimed the album was dated from the moment it was released, perhaps dooming it to never going above number 194 on the U.S. album charts.

4th - Friday......................

THE SEX PISTOLS make their first trip to play in Manchester. This concert was arranged by Pete Shelley and Howard Devoto. Howard is currently writing the pub-rock listings for the *New Manchester Review*, a local listings magazine. The pair had kept in touch with Sex Pistols manager Malcolm McLaren since they saw the Pistols a few months ago as Malcolm was very interested in booking the band outside of London. Pete and Howard hired the Lesser Free Trade Hall for the event. They sell the tickets for 50p, but less than a hundred curious people show up. The hall would hold about 300-400 people. Howard and Pete's band the Buzzcocks had intended to play tonight, but they had trouble finding a drummer that they could teach the songs in time.

While Malcolm McLaren is outside trying to get customers into the hall, he sees someone waiting for a guitar player. Malcolm had heard earlier that Howard and Pete were looking for a bass player. Malcolm asks him if he's a bass player, he replies, "Yes, I am," and then directs him inside saying "the guys you're looking for are upstairs." The bass player, Steve Diggle, goes inside and meets with Howard and Pete, comes to a rehearsal or two, and ends up joining the Buzzcocks. The happy accident is that he was waiting for someone else and got steered upstairs by mistake. The Buzzcocks advert was in a different paper than the one he was replying to.

CBGB'S had tape decks rolling all weekend long as the "Live At CBGB'S" album is being taped. Bands that will appear for the recordings were selected as representative of the best bands that have appeared at CBGB'S in '75 and '76. Club owner Hilly Krystal said, "I have wanted to do this for a long time, I also wanted to pick the groups that were important from the beginning. I think a lot of writers started the idea of Punk Rock, meaning there's just one specific kind of music and one attitude and what they don't realize is that they're just labeling something which isn't so. Television, The Shirts and the Talking Heads are not Punk Rock. This is a whole new scene. I feel it's going to be very important." Bands participating in the live sessions this weekend will include Blondie, The Laughing Dogs, Manster, Mink DeVille, The Poppees, The Shirts, Stuart's Hammer, The Talking Heads and Tuff Darts. In the final LP, some of the top bands won't allow their tapes on the LP, leaving only the second tier bands.

JOHN DOWIE & BIG GIRL'S BLOUSE ....London, Dingwalls	SEX PISTOLS/MANDALA BAND.....Manchester, Lesser Free Trade Hall EDDIE & THE HOT RODS.............Plymouth, The Top Rank

6th - Sunday..........................

THE 101'ERS' lead singer Joe Strummer (real name John Mellor) splits his band after tonight's gig in Hayward's Heath. He's cut his hair short and tries on some new ideas. Paul Simonon, Mick Jones, Keith Levine and Terry Chimes have invited him to join the Heartdrops as their new vocalist and guitar player. Paul Simonon suggests a name change to the Clash. They begin rehearsals in a small squat near Shepherds Bush Green. The 101'ers were scheduled to play at the Midsummer Music Festival Benefit in Walthamstow tomorrow night, but will obviously not be there. Ironically, in their place are the Sex Pistols, the band responsible for their demise.

JAM ....London, Windsor Castle

15th - Tuesday...........................

THE HEARTBREAKERS have a new bass player. He's Billy Wrath and he joins the band as a veteran of the Boston music scene. He replaces Richard Hell, who has left the group to start his own. Since Richard is leaving, they won't be doing any of his songs any more. Thunders and his bandmates have to start writing new songs.

THE 101er's/SEX PISTOLS...........London, The 100 Club	STRANGLERS ....London, The Red Cow

17th - Thursday............................

IAN DURY & THE KILBURNS play their last date together in London's West End at the Walthamstow Assembly Hall. Ian's been told that if he continues, the pressures of touring would endanger his health. The triple bill also features the Stranglers and last minute fill-in Sex Pistols. Besides Ian himself, one of the most permanent members of the group, guitarist Keith Lucas, will resurface in 1977 under the name Nick Cash and fronting 999.

BLONDIE's debut single is released. "X Offender" and "In The Sun" is on Private Stock Records in the US. It was recorded by Marty Thau (ex-New York Dolls manager) and Craig Leon for a label they were planning called Instant Records. They thought it was such a smash that they leased it to a newer, bigger label called Private Stock. There was concern that the band would be lessened by their bass player departing for Television, but the record bears out that Blondie is more than any of it's members. Jim Green of *Trouser Press* describes it as, "...the Sufaris meeting the Sangri-Las down at CBGB'S. Pumping bass and Dick Dale guitar enhanced by a neat organ hook, with plenty of echo. The flip opens with a 'Wipe Out' drum roll, a casual 'surf's up' and off we ride into a nice outtake from the soundtrack to 'Beach Blanket Orgy.'" Blondie is in concert tonight (as well as Friday and Saturday) at C.B.G.B.'s. They're being eyed from the audience by Frankie Valli, the lead singer of the Four Seasons. Why Frankie? He's checking the band out so he can give final approval to record a full album for the Private Stock Records label he's financially involved with. The band themselves have been playing whenever they can, usually for about $60 a night and have recently filmed a bit to be included in Amos Poe's film *The Blank Generation*.

JUNE 1976

THE JAM ....London, Fulham Greyhound

IAN DURY & THE KILBURNS/
SEX PISTOLS/STRANGLERS ....London, Walthamstow Assembly Hall

18th - Friday..

MORRISSEY tosses in his 2p worth in the press, a reaction to the Sex Pistols concert in Manchester two weeks ago. Seventeen-year-old Steven Morrissey writes to both the *Melody Maker* and *NME*. He wants everyone to see that the Sex Pistols, who are supposedly so original, take much of what they do from his heroes, The New York Dolls. "The Pistols boast having no inspiration from the New York/Manhattan rock scene, yet their set includes, "I'm Not Your Stepping Stone," a number believed to be done almost to perfection by the Heartbreakers on any sleazy New York night and the Pistols' vocalist/exhibitionist Johnny Rotten's attitude and self-asserted 'love us or leave us' approach can be compared to both Iggy Pop and David JoHansen in their heyday." Morrissey concluded with, "I'd love to see the Pistols make it. Maybe they will be able to afford some clothes which don't look as though they've been slept in."

July 3rd - Saturday...

THE SEX PISTOLS play at the Pier Pavilion in Hastings and leave another convert in their wake. It's Mari Elliott's nineteenth birthday and she's watching the Pistols in awe. Two months ago she had cut a pop single of "Silly Billy" for GTO Records. The music the Sex Pistols are playing is something totally new to her. It's only a short jump from being Mari Elliott to becoming Poly Styrene.

ADAM ANT placed an advert in *Melody Maker* two days ago that read "Beat On A Bass with the B-Sides." Andy Warren called up and today they meet outside the Marquee. The B-Sides form and begin rehearsing in South Clapham. Members of the band include Adam Ant, Andy Warren, Lester Square and others.

BUDGIE/SEX PISTOLS ....Hastings, Pier Pavilion

Mari Elliott, aka Poly Styrene

4th - Sunday..

THE RAMONES make their UK debut in a triple bill with the Stranglers and the Flaming Groovies at the London Roundhouse. They're in the second slot, behind the Groovies. They had originally been booked for a European tour but their label on the continent backed out at the last minute, almost cancelling even the UK dates. The Flaming Groovies are now on the road to support their latest album "Shake Some Action." The Ramones will have their first UK single out later this week, with tracks from their debut album. Tomorrow night the band headline their own concert at Dingwalls. The two concerts were vastly different. The first, in front of 2,000 people was their largest concert ever, the other is a crammed, tiny club, just like back home. Their concert tonight at the Roundhouse is reviewed for the *NME* by Max Bell. "Closer to a comedy routine than a band...the guys on the mixer hated them and they hated the guys on the mixer back. I laughed solidly for half an hour...The appeal is purely negative, based on their not being able to play a shit or give a shit...imbecilic adolescent ditties but still oodles more exciting than the majority of bands.."

THE CLASH play their very first public gig tonight opening for the Sex Pistols way up in Sheffield. They've only been together for about three weeks.

RAMONES/STRANGLERS/
FLAMING GROOVIES ....London, The Roundhouse

SEX PISTOLS/THE CLASH ....Sheffield, Black Swan

6th - Tuesday...

THE SEX PISTOLS & THE DAMNED make a great double bill at the 100 Club in London. It's the Damned's first "real" gig. Their line-up is Dave Vanian, Brian James, Rat Scabies and Ray Burns. They had played a few times prior to this in Lisson Grove. Members of the group had been in previous bands like the London SS and Bastard. Rat Scabies, drummer for the Damned, told Tony Parsons of the *NME* how he got that most unusual moniker. "(I got the name) at rehearsal. I had the scabies and I was on me kit playing and scratching away when somebody asks me what's the matter with me and I say I got the scabies. And just as I said it a big hairy rat runs across the floor!...so that's how I got the name Rat Scabies." Some things are perhaps better left unsaid.

SEX PISTOLS/DAMNED...............London, The 100 Club

7th - Wednesday...

ULTRAVOX! is a new name, but not a new band. They began as Tiger Lily in the spring of '73. In the last six months though they've been alternately called The Zips, London Soundtrack and Fire Of London. They are now settled on Ultravox! The band members have also changed their names. Singer Dennis Leigh is now John Foxx and bassist Chris St. John is Chris Cross.

THE POLECATS ....London, Rochester Castle

9th - Friday..

THE RAMONES have their first single in the UK released today on Vertigo Records. It's "Blitzkrieg Bop" b/w "Havana Affair." Both tracks are from the band's debut LP.

JULY 1976

PRETTY THINGS/SUPERCHARGE/	STRANGLERS ....London, Forest School
SEX PISTOLS...........................London, The Lyceum	EDDIE & THE HOT RODS............London, The Marquee

12th - Monday.............................

KILBURN & THE HIGH ROADS have been forced to disband due to lead singer Ian Dury's health problems, or at least that's the story. Dury is a former polio victim and was found to be endangering his health every time he went on stage. This doesn't mean that he'll not be musically active though. He intends to continue writing and recording with Chas Jankel of the Kilburns, with a solo LP in the future a real possibility. Another more plausible story is that the Kilburns latest adventure with Pye Records sister label Dawn, has left Dury with a very great amount of debt over his head. This could be a great way to disappear and start over.

13th - Tuesday.............................

SNIFFIN' GLUE is a new fanzine inspired by a review of the first Ramones' LP by *NME's* Nick Kent. Mark Perry of Deptford leaves his job as a bank clerk to start the UK's first punk fanzine, *"Sniffin' Glue and Other Rock & Roll Habits."* It's a xeroxed multi-page handout that features articles about the Ramones, Blue Oyster Cult, The Stranglers and the Runaways. It's put together by Perry who has "high hopes" for his magazine, stating on the cover that, "…this thing is not meant to be read…it's for soaking in glue and sniffin'." Perry also put together a band. A dream for some time, the assembled group of friends is Mark Perry on vocals, Alex Ferguson on guitar, Mickey Smith on bass and John Towe on drums.

     STRANGLERS ....London, Hope & Anchor

EVERY NIGHT AT
THE HOPE & ANCHOR
THE
Fabulous, Original, Sensational
STRANGLERS
July 13th-July 17th
Upper Street, Islington, N.1

15th - Thursday.............................

THE JAM are looking for someone to complete their group. They're into the whole mod scene and it's clear that the Who, Yardbirds and early Stones are definite influences. The trio has been playing around for quite some time and only recently have started getting bookings in London, miles away from their home base in Woking. It's probably a good thing that the Jam don't find a keyboard player as they wanted. It would have changed the sound of the band away from the power trio feel that will make them superstars in the late '70s in England.

THE JAM require
KEYBOARD/VOCALS
Age 18-20
Early Tamla Motown, R&B
Good prospects of Recording contract
clean image
Phone: Woking 72460 or Byfleet 46521
(after 6 p.m.)

PERE UBU submit a track for Volume Two of "Max's Kansas City" LP. Their last single "Final Solution" was included on Volume One, so you would think that the band would be on the next one as well. Unfortunately their new track, "The Modern Dance" has been rejected because of the inaccessibility of the lyrics. The ever-changing lineup of Pere Ubu catches them as a sextet on this demo. Present are David Thomas, Tom Herman, Tim Wright, R. Scott Kraus, and synthesizer player Allen Ravenstine who has returned to the fold once again. Also, a new addition to the group is Allen Greenblatt on guitar. They can be found regularly at the Pirate's Cove in Cleveland almost every Thursday night.

EDDIE & THE HOT RODS ....High Wycombe, The Nags Head	STRANGLERS ....London, Hope & Anchor
DIVERSIONS ....London, The Speakeasy	

18th - Sunday.............................

SEX PISTOLS' soundman Dave Goodman demos the Pistols in their rehearsal space on Denmark Street. When the band play live, they use his sound system, so he's got a bit of interest in making the band sound as good as possible in a studio setting. The power of the Steve Jones' guitar was seriously undermixed on the previous session with Chris Spedding and they wanted a new take on things. The four track deck captures early versions of "Anarchy In The UK," "Satellite," "Pretty Vacant," "Submission," "Problems," "Seventeen" and "I Wanna Be Me." The finished songs are taken to the larger Riverside Studios for Jones to complete some guitar overdubs.

     THE POODLES ....London, The Marquee

20th - Tuesday.............................

BUZZCOCKS' members Pete Shelley and Howard Devoto book the Sex Pistols into the Lesser Free Trade Hall in Manchester for a second time. They had booked the band for their debut in Manchester six weeks ago. The Buzzcocks make their public debut at this sold out gig at the bottom of the bill below Slaughter & The Dogs. Although The Buzzcocks organized and promoted the gig, they were third on the bill when Slaughter & The Dogs convinced Malcolm that they had a huge following (numbering in the dozens!) and deserved better treatment. The Dogs' stage act is an unsettling cross between Alice Cooper and The New York Dolls. For their efforts the Buzzcocks made £10. Subtract that from a sell out take of four hundred tickets at one pound each. The crowd is totally into the show and have a chance to hear a new song the Pistols have been working on called "Anarchy In The UK."

SEX PISTOLS/SLAUGHTER & DOGS/	STRANGLERS ....London, The Nashville
THE BUZZCOCKS ....Manchester, Lesser Free Trade Hall	

JULY 1976

21st - Wednesday...........

MORRISSEY vs. THE RAMONES Under the headline "Ramones Are Rubbish," Steve Morrissey of Manchester sets pen to paper in a fevered missive slamming the Ramones. "The Ramones are the latest bumptious band of degenerate no-talents whose most notable achievement to date is their ability to advance beyond the boundaries of New York City and purely on the strength of a spate of convincing literature projecting the Ramones as God's gift to rock music." He's obviously upset with the "instant adulation" that the Ramones have gotten from the underground press since their triumphant Roundhouse concert. The frustrated "music reviewer" calls them "notoriously discordant" and hopes that they remain in New York in a life of obscurity. "The New York Dolls and Patti Smith have proved that there is some life pumping away in the swamps and gutters of New York and they are the only acts which originated from the N.Y. club scene worthy of any praise. The Ramones have absolutely nothing to add that is of relevance or importance and should be rightly filed and forgotten. Steve Morrissey, Kings Road, Stretford, Manchester."

Ramones are rubbish

THE RAMONES are the latest bumptious band of degenerate no-talents whose most notable achievement to date is their ability to advance beyond the boundaries of New York City, and purely on the strength of a spate of convincing literature projecting the Ramones as God's gift to rock music.

They have been greeted with instant adulation by an army of duped fans. Musically, they do not deal in subtlety or variation of any kind, their rule is to be as incompetent as possible.

For a band believed to project the youth of America, New York suburban life, anti-conformism, sex and struggle, or whatever, they fail miserably. And in the sober light of day their imperfections have a field day.

THE HEARTBREAKERS are back in action with a whole new set of material. Richard Hell took his songs with him, so the remaining Heartbreakers wrote new songs. Their set tonight included "It's Not Enough," "Pirate Love," "I Wanna Be Loved," "Get Off The Phone," and a song co-written with the Dee Dee Ramone called "Chinese Rocks." They'll be trying the songs out on the Max's Kansas City audience in New York on Friday night.

STRANGLERS ....London, Fulham Greyhound   VIBRATORS ....London, Windsor Castle

August 3rd - Tuesday.......................

WAYNE COUNTY, the DJ and occasional singer, has rerecorded his song "Max's Kansas City," updating the listing of bands in the song to include all the current bands on the NY scene and dedicating the new single to Lou Reed. The 45 is out on the Max's label and is available in the Village record shops. Mentioned in the new single are the Ramones, Heartbreakers, Harry Toledo, Fuse, Mong, The Fast, Richard Hell, Mink DeVille, Psychotic Frogs, Pere Ubu, Cherry Vanilla, Blondie and Patti Smith as well as the established stars like The New York Dolls, Lou Reed, Iggy Pop. On the flip side of the single is "Flip Your Wig." Present in Wayne's band, the Back Street Boys, are Greg Van Cook, Elliot Michaels and Jett "Bingo" Harris.

STRANGLERS/SUGAR DADDY.......London, The Nashville

10th - Tuesday.......................

CHELSEA A new band is coming together in London. It all started with Acme Attractions boss John Cravene's (Krivine) desire to have a band to manage. He already had a singer, a young, dark haired chap called Gene October. The only thing he needed was a group to back him. Cravene put an ad in *Melody Maker* for a band, and two friends, Billy Idol and Tony James (ex-member of the front room London SS) answered. With the addition of drummer John Towe the band is underway and is called Chelsea.

THE B-SIDES with Adam Ant, their leader, continue to rehearse, but fail to get any gigs. They did however record what they claim is the "definitive version" of the Nancy Sinatra '60s classic "These Boots Are Made For Walking."

SEX PISTOLS/VIBRATORS ....London, The 100 Club   FABULOUS POODLES ....London, The Nashville

11th - Wednesday.......................

TELEVISION Elektra Records has just announced that Tom Verlaine, Fred Smith, Richard Lloyd and Billy Ficca, collectively known as Television, have been signed to a contract. They'll begin recording their debut album in the next few months. It's been almost exactly a year since the band had their debut single "Little Johnny Jewel" out on ORK Records and they haven't had any vinyl out since.

VIBRATORS ....London, The White Hart

12th - Thursday.......................

TOM ROBINSON of Cafe Society has taken the event of Gay Pride Week to step out of his role as part of a group to perform an hour-long revue of gay songs from the last three decades. It was titled "Robinson Cruisin'" and is starting tonight for a four-night run at the Little Theatre Club in St. Martins Lane. In the revue, Robinson weaves through songs like Noel Coward's "Mad About The Boy," and David Bowie's "Lady Stardust." Interspersed with the songs are jokes, observations and dialogue about being gay in today's society. He even managed to work in a few of his own songs that, due to their nature, were never included in Cafe Society's sets. Song's like "Cruisin," "Long Hot Summer," and the end-of-the-evening singalong "Glad To Be Gay." Robinson has been supporting the gay cause in London since early '74 when he began answering calls at the controversial Gay Switchboard.

"ROBINSON CRUISIN'" ....London, Little Theatre Club

13th - Friday.......................

THE CLASH have played before an audience only once, in Sheffield a few weeks ago with the Sex Pistols. They're playing "a private

AUGUST 1976

performance" tonight for friends at their new rehearsal studio, Rehearsals Rehearsals, near the Roundhouse in Camden Town. It's an old British Rail warehouse that their manager Bernard Rhodes has rented. They've been busy painting a mural on the back wall of their studio space and their clothes are spattered with paint drops. The addition of a few painted slogans to the spatters on their shirts and trousers have given the Clash a look of their own, which sets the band apart from the Sex shop look of the Sex Pistols. The five piece band includes Mick Jones, Terry Chimes, Joe Strummer, Paul Simonon and Keith Levine.

STIFF RECORDS is launched by former Dr. Feelgood manager Andrew (Jake) Jakeman and Graham Parker/Brinzley Schwartz manager Dave Robinson on a £400 loan from the Feelgoods. The roots of the Stiff idea extend back to Jake's involvement with Chilli Willi and the Red Hot Peppers, plus the fact that he's had aspirations of being an A&R man. The real beginning can be tracked back to an unfulfilled side project for Dr. Feelgood that was to be called Spick Ace and the Blue Sharks. It was a low key goof-off with members of the Feelgoods, Nick Lowe and Pink Fairie Martin Stone. There was supposed to be an EP recorded for Skydog in Holland, but contractual entanglements halted it dead. In the meantime, Nick Lowe had his own demo that he brought forward. It was recorded on the microscopic budget of £45 and sounded great. Off to the pressing plant, a label is born. The single "So It Goes" b/w "Heart Of The City" is Stiff BUY-1. Looking at the matrix of the record (that narrow bit between groove and label) you can find the message "Earthlings Awake" and "Three Chord Trick, Yeh." Nick plays all the instruments on the record with the exception of Steve Goldings (borrowed from the Rumour) on drums. Nick Lowe told *Melody Maker's* Caroline Coon, "It's a sound that's happening now. Clever words over a simple rhythm. Basically, I'll do anything. I can write in any style, but all my friends have turned into punks overnight and I'm a great bandwagon climber."

Stiff has set up shop in Notting Hill section of London and are offering one-off deals with bands unable to get offers from the majors, the orphans of the music scene. They will be using the EMI pressing plant and hope to have any of their bands recorded, pressed, and out in the shops within two weeks of the initial deal being signed. As Riveria says, "for far too long there has been a gap between the million quid advance and scuffling about in a cellar. There has to be a middle ground and I believe Stiff is it."

SUBURBAN STUDS ....Hayward, The Seven Stars   "ROBINSON CRUISIN'" ....London, Little Theatre Club

15th - Sunday...

D.P. COSTELLO has his demos played on Charlie Gillett's BBC Sunday night program "Honky Tonk." The six tracks are "Cheap Reward" (later re-recorded with different lyrics as "Lip Service"), "Mystery Dance," "Jump Up," "Wave A White Flag," "Blame It On Cain" and "Poison Moon." The show is an overview of rock and roll, its roots and its branches. Charlie would play new re-issues of '50s rock traditions as well as new material that carried on that same tradition. The tracks would never be issued and circulate only in collectors circles until a box set compilation digs them out in late '93.

FABULOUS POODLES.................London, The Marquee   THE DAMNED..........................London, The Nashville
"ROBINSON CRUISIN'" ....London, Little Theatre Club

19th - Thursday.......................................

THE RAMONES get the attention of *The Glasgow Evening Times* who print the headline "Ramones In Teenage Glue Death Outrage." Labor Party MP James Dempsey of Scotland, makes a move to have the first Ramones LP banned from the country's record racks, citing the track "Now I Wanna Sniff Some Glue" as encouragement to young buyers to do just that. Dempsey is preparing to put a bill before Parliament that will put glue and similar solvents on a par with cigarettes and fireworks, to make them available to those only over the legal age of sixteen. In the last few years about two dozen youths have died in Scotland with deaths directly linked to sniffing these substances. A bemused Ramone contacted in Los Angeles tells *NME* that, "…we don't want the kids to sniff glue and we don't think the record will make them do it. We could write songs about people jumping off bridges, but we don't want people to jump off them. I hope that everyone understands that the song is a joke, we know the stuff is dangerous…you always feel sick afterwards." Ramones manager Danny Fields chimed in with, "Why should the song be banned? War films aren't banned on the grounds that they advocate violence."

SUBURBAN STUDS ....Birmingham, Barbarella's   SEX PISTOLS ....West Runton, Village Inn

21st - Saturday......................................

THE MONT DE MARSAN FESTIVAL is the idea of Skydog record executive Marc Zermati. He organized and sponsored what was to be the first European Punk Rock Festival at the Mont de Marsan bullring about an hour's drive south of Bordeaux. The line up is mostly bands that were labeled as "pub bands" a few months ago and view the tag of "punk" with varying degrees of amusement. Along on the show are Nick Lowe, the Pink Fairies, Eddie & The Hot Rods, the Hammersmith Gorillas, Tyla Gang, Count Bishops and the Damned. French bands at the event include Shakin' Street, Little Bob Story, Bijoux, Il Baritz and Kalfont Rockchaud. About 2,000 people turn up for this low key event. On the way to the Mont de Marsan Punk Rock festival the Damned stopped to buy some cheap new clothes. Ray bought a shirt with some epaulettes which he wore and pretended to be an airplane pilot guiding a doomed aircraft shouting, "It's alright, everything's under control!" Then someone in the group said, "Oh great, it's fucking Captain Sensible!" Ray now has a nickname that looks like it could stick. He's always been anything BUT sensible and it's a move up from his previous nickname "Eats."

EDDIE & THE HOT RODS have their liveliest single yet issued by Island Records. It's the "Live At The Marquee" EP and is an accurate document to the excitement of their stage show as recorded at their July 9th performance. All of the songs on the EP are cover versions,

AUGUST 1976

"96 Tears," "Get Out Of Denver," and the medley of "Gloria" and "Satisfaction." Not bad for the band's third vinyl outing.

LIVE TONIGHT! DEAF SCHOOL/ SUBURBAN STUDS ....Birmingham, Barbarella's

SEX PISTOLS ....Nottingham, The Boat Club

24th - Tuesday..

WIRE is a new front room band coming together. It's a quintet of Colin Newman on vocals and guitar, George Gill on guitar, Rob Gotobed on drums, Bruce Gilbert on guitar and Graham Lewis on bass. They are against the idea of using normal song structure, (verse, chorus, middle eight, verse, end) and are coming up with some very unusual and rather short songs. Although Wire would never have any Top 40 success, they would remain as a lasting influence over many bands through the '80s and into the '90s.

STRANGLERS ....London, The Nashville

27th - Friday...

XTC have recently completed more demos, this time recording at Sun Studios in Reading. Their former lead singer Steve Hutchins has left the band and the guitarist/ songwriter Andy Partridge is stepping up to the mic in these sessions. Songs include "Science Friction," "Quicksilver," "Spinning Top," "Hang On To The Night," "She's So Square" and "Refrigerator Blues."

29th - Sunday...

THE SEX PISTOLS & THE CLASH stage a concert together at the successor to the El Paradise, the Screen on the Green in Islington. This is the first public gig for the Clash in London. Third on the bill is a band from Manchester, the Buzzcocks on their first gig outside of their hometown. The "event" begins at midnight and the bands play until dawn and are punctuated with Kenneth Anger films which, in this setting, are more comic than erotic. Brushing past the Pistols and hardly noticing the Buzzcocks, *NME* reporter Charles Shaar Murray was annoyed at the Clash and wrote, "The Clash are the sort of garage band that should be speedily returned to the garage, preferably with the motor still running, which would undoubtedly be more of a loss to their friends and families than to rock and roll…their guitarist on the extreme left, allegedly known as Joe Strummer, has good moves but he and the band are a little shaky on ground that involves starting, stopping and changing chords at approximately the same times." Photos of the cinema concert almost always include at least one of the striking clothes (or lack of them) that Suzie was wearing. Fishnet stockings, a black cupless bra, swastika armband and mismatched leather shoes caught everyone's eyes. While there, Suzie and Steve Severin approach Pistols manager Malcolm McLaren about the possibility of their new band playing with the Sex Pistols at the upcoming 100 Club Punk Rock Festival in September. Malcolm agrees and asks them what they're called. They haven't a name yet but they plan to call him with one in the next few days.

SEX PISTOLS/THE CLASH/ THE BUZZCOCKS ....London, Screen On The Green

September 2nd - Thursday...

SIOUXSIE & THE BANSHEES is the name that Suzie and Steve Havoc have decided on for their new group. The inspiration was the Vincent Price horror movie *Cry Of The Banshee* which was on TV a few nights ago. With the Suzie changed to Siouxsie, Malcolm McLaren is called with the information about the name of the band. The only problem they face now is that none of the proposed group, with the exception of Billy Idol, had any real musical background. Billy was tagged to play guitar, he in turn would teach Steve bass and Siouxsie would sing for the group. They select a number of songs that they hated for their set. They planned to do the most outrageous and anarchistic versions possible of them. Among those discussed were "Money Money" by the Bay City Rollers, the Kingsmen's "Louie Louie" and "Goldfinger."

SEX PISTOLS/ SUBURBAN STUDS ....High Wycomb, Nags Head

3rd - Friday..

THE SEX PISTOLS trek to Paris for their first concert abroad. A new generation of rockers spring up in France as a result. They play the grand opening of a new 2,000 seat disco in the middle of the Bois du Boulogne called the Chalet du Lac. The stage has an unusual stripped floor that's lit from below. The club is packed with even more outside wanting to get in. The crowd isn't there to see the Sex Pistols, they've come because it's opening night and the admission is free. It's a strange cross section of Paris with "Mr. & Mrs. First Nighter" standing shoulder-to-shoulder with punks. Among the French bands there to check out "the real thing" were members of the Stinky Toys, Who's Art and European Sons.

SEPTEMBER 1976

On the road with the group are the collection of fans the press has already dubbed as the "Bromley Contingent." They've followed the Pistols to France in Billy Idol's beat up van that serves as transport and hotel. The group includes Billy Idol, Little Deb, Siouxsie, Steve Severin, Simon Barker and Michael. That evening in Paris, Siouxsie is punched by an Arab man who was outraged at her attire. She was dressed in a topless black mesh bra, fishnet tights with black vinyl stockings, a see through plastic mac with polka dots (checked at the door) and studded stiletto heels. Her normally jet black hair was cropped close and flecked with red flame highlights and to top off the ensemble, she had a black armband with a swastika pinned to it.

SEX PISTOLS............................Paris, Chalet du Lac

4th - Saturday...........................

SEX PISTOLS are one of the groups suggested as feature material for Granada TV's third series of *So It Goes* TV programs. Presenter Tony Wilson received two letters that caught his attention, both from Manchester. One from Howard Trafford suggesting they get the Sex Pistols. Howard was part of the Buzzcocks and had booked the Pistols to play in Manchester. The other is from Steven Morrissey suggested that they feature the New York Dolls, a band that turned to dust over a year ago. For their first TV appearance, a film of the Sex Pistols playing the song "Anarchy In The UK" is shown beside features on two other unsigned bands, the Gentlemen and The Bowles Brothers. Meanwhile in Paris, the Sex Pistols and their Bromley friends meet at Sartre's old hangout, Deux Magots and occupy a pair of tables displaying their outrageous punk attire. Johnny even looked vaguely Parisian in his beret. Before the tea and Heinekins arrived, the photographers were there clicking their cameras incessantly.

6th - Monday..............................

RICHARD HELL is busy assembling a new band after his departure from the Heartbreakers. He's recruited Marc Bell from Wayne County's band and had recently met a guitarist, Robert Quine, in the packing department of a bookstore where he is working. Their last guitarist appeared in answer to a newspaper ad and he's Ivan Julian. They're working on a batch of Hell's newest songs and finding their band's identity as the Voidoids.

STRANGLERS.........................London, The Rochester

8th - Wednesday...........................

THE SEX PISTOLS' most recent review in the *NME* brings up the following point, "You wanted the Sex Pistols and now you've got them. Trouble is, they look like they aren't going to go away, so what are you going to do with them? Alteratively- ha ha- what are they going to do with you? In a way it's the classic horror movie situation.... don't rub the lamp unless you can handle the genie."

IAN DURY and former Kilburn Chaz Jankel, are working together with Pete Van Hook and Kuma Harada, recording several tracks and looking for a record label. The projected title for the LP they're trying to sell is "Live At Lourdes."

VIBRATORS ....London, The White Hart   THE JAM ....London, Upstairs At Ronnie Scotts

13th - Monday..............................

DAMNED lead singer Dave Vanian must see some future with his new group. He's giving up his daytime job as a grave digger to devote all his energies to the Damned. He'll bear the looks of the graveyard throughout his career.

EATER gets fourteen-year-old Roger Bullen (aka Dee Generate), as their new drummer. He's a protégé of Rat Scabies of the Damned and replaces the band's first drummer, Social Demise, who had trouble taking time off from school. Singer Andy Blade got his name from his "hobby" of playing with his cutlery.

PUNK ROCK? To satiate the growing curiosity about the new punk movement for its befuddled readers, Michael Watts spends a full page trying to nail down what exactly punk is. He starts off in the *Oxford English Dictionary* where he notes it says "of poor quality, worthless." He describes punks as a working class. "Many of them left home and live in squats. Certainly they believe in aggro; they like to project an air of violence, real or not. Fun equals violence and love equals screwing, so therefore punk rock equals insensitivity and monotony both musically and lyrically. Punks are often drawn from the ranks of soccer hooligans." A stretch back to James Dean and Ed "Kookie" Byrnes gives punk some historic borders in the past and New York's punks are described as being no different than, "...old time greasers without the patchouli oil. Leather jackets, tight Levis and tee shirts sawn off almost at the collarbone."

SEX PISTOLS...........................Chester, Quaintways

17th - Friday..............................

THE SEX PISTOLS play at Chelmsford Top Security Prison for a crowd of about 500 inmates. They are allowed three hours inside the walls, to set up, play and tear down their gear. Their set of a dozen or more songs is greeted with cheers and catcalls. McLaren associate John Tiberi captures the concert on a portable deck. The concert will be issued as one of the many pseudo-legal bootlegs in the '90s.

SIOUXSIE & THE BANSHEES' guitarist Billy Idol informs Steve and Siouxsie that he is unable to participate in their 100 Club debut as he is committed to working with a new group called Chelsea and they don't like the idea of sharing a guitar player. The Banshees now have to find another guitarist and they still haven't found a drummer. Their debut is only days away.

SUBWAY SECT, a new London group, are preparing for their public debut at the 100 Club festival this next week. This group of conformist friends includes Vic Goddard on vocals, Paul Myers on guitar, Robert Simmons on bass and Paul Smith on drums. The group

SEPTEMBER 1976

aren't into chart bound sounds, quite the reverse. They enjoy incorporating elements and sounds not normally associated with rock music.

LIVE TONIGHT!

SEX PISTOLS...........................Chelmsford Prison

THE JAM.................................London, Fulham Greyhound

EDDIE & THE HOT RODS.............London, The Marquee

19th - Sunday...

SIOUXSIE & THE BANSHEES get Marco Pirroni (who has just left Chelsea as Billy Idol joins them) as the new Banshees' guitarist. Still missing a vital piece of the band, the Banshees meet with Malcolm McLaren again, bemoaning their lack of a drummer. He suggests they try Sid Vicious who is currently with a casual group called Flowers Of Romance. Sid refuses to play cymbals or sing, but nevertheless accepts the temporary position. Siouxsie and The Banshees, now a full band for the first time, organize a trial rehearsal at the Clash's practice space in Camden Town. It's decided that the previous song selection for the Festival is to be dropped in favor of a twenty-minute wall of noise over which Siouxsie would recite the Lord's Prayer while Marco interspersed guitar cliches from Deep Purple and the Rolling Stones. They're ready for their one time performance tomorrow night. Even though the group doesn't plan to be together beyond that, Siouxsie & The Banshees will persist into the '90s.

20-21st - Monday-Tuesday.........................

THE 100 CLUB PUNK FESTIVAL, in retrospect, is one of the most important two club nights in London in the late '70s. A line almost 600 kids long stretched from the entrance of the tiny 100 Club. Tonight's the first night of the first "Punk Festival" and the tribes have gathered. Onstage first to start off the two night festival is the Subway Sect playing their first ever gig. They're fronted by nineteen-year-old Vic Goddard, Paul Myers is on bass, Robert Miller on guitar and the late addition of Paul Packham helping out on drums for the evening. Next up is Siouxie and the Banshees. Caroline Coon reports on the band for *Melody Maker* as being part of the ever-present Bromley contingent at Sex Pistols' gigs. Tonight they're not only in the audience, they're sharing a stage with the Pistols as well. "This inseparable unit is Steve (21), Bill (22) and Simon (19)- he sells hot dogs off a mobile stand during the day- raspberry haired Debbie (15) and Suzi herself. She is nothing if not magnificent. Her short hair, which she sweeps in great waves over her head, is streaked with red, like flames. She'll wear black plastic, nonexistent bras, one mesh and one rubber stocking and suspender belts all covered by a polka-dotted transparent plastic mac." Without much pre-planning or rehearsal the hastily assembled band played a twenty-minute medley of "Twist & Shout," "The Lords Prayer" and "Knocking On Heaven's Door." The band included Sid Vicious on drums, Siouxsie on vocals, Steve Havoc on bass and Marco Pirroni on guitar. Their set was described as "unbearable" and "pure noise, unfit for anyone's ears." The band had intended to play much more than their allotted time. Siouxsie commented, "It was a mistake, we were going to keep playing till we were thrown off, but we got bored before the audience did!" Geoff Hill of the *NME* reviewed the debut writing, "With only one continuous but deeply-felt chord from the red-streaked hair guitarist...and the hypnotically compelling drumbeat like that of a bored five- year-old...the minimal art vocalizing of the thin dark young chanteuse with the Charity jacket and the striking Swastika armband...this band is finally received with politeness...and occasional spasms of pogo dancing."

The Clash played as a four piece. Guitarist Keith Levine is off starting another new band. They kick through a set of "White Riot," "London's Burning, I'm So Bored With The USA," "Protex Blues," Deadly Serious," "Janie Jones" and "1977." Geoff Hill of the *NME* described them with, "Their numbers are short and to the point...they preform as if they actually dig rock music."

Finishing up the evening were the Sex Pistols. It's easy to see that the Pistols are no longer a secret band. The bar is filled with record types checking out the buzz band and they're not impressed. The days of the Sex Pistols having an audience of twenty of their friends are over. They tear into their set with "Anarchy In The UK," and rip through "I Wanna Be Me," "Seventeen," "Pretty Vacant (Lazy Sod)," "New York," "Pushing And Shoving," "Submission," the Monkees' oldie "Stepping Stone," "Liar," and the Stooges' "No Fun."

The second night started out with France's contribution to the punk scene, The Stinky Toys. They are coolly received and are perhaps the only band at the festival that the crowd doesn't embrace. The Damned are up next. They've come an amazingly long way in the three months they've been gigging and their stage show and costumes are impeccable, even when their playing isn't. They played their soon-to-be-released single "New Rose" and a 300 mph version of the Beatles' song "Help." Somewhere in the middle of the set a disturbance at the back of the room halted the show. The club's manager jumps onstage and admonishes people for throwing beer glasses. One has just shattered and cut some people. This is the aspect of the event that is grabbed by the press. Some said that it was Sid Vicious that threw it. An ambulance was called in and the police were right behind. Police arrested both Sid Vicious and reporter Caroline Coon.

After the Damned, the Vibrators came on. They are the veterans of the show and aren't sure whether they're part of the movement or not. Even older guitarist Chris Spedding is onstage with them and they do a few covers of the Beatles' "I Saw Her Standing There" and the Stones' "Jumping Jack Flash." One original is tossed in the middle, Spedding's "Motorbike," and it's into more covers like "Great Balls Of Fire" and "Let's Twist Again." The audience is not amused. The Buzzcocks follow with a few blessed originals including

SEPTEMBER 1976

"Breakdown," "Orgasm Addict," "Boredom" and "Oh Shit," with vocalist Howard Devoto singing frantically. They've only been together two months and are already developing an underground following back in their hometown of Manchester.

Although this was by no means the first gig of the new punk rock boom, for many it is considered the moment that was the catalyst for the years to come. This was the gig that brought the underground punks together from all over England for a rally of the clans. In retrospect, the festival would make its mark in the press with the tragic wounding, painting a black specter of violence and disregard for law and order over the punk movement. Though it happened on the second day of the festival while the Sex Pistols were in Cardiff, Wales, the press blamed the Pistols. As a result of the incident, all punk bands are banned from the 100 Club.

Monday Night at the 100 Club	Tuesday Night at the 100 Club
SEX PISTOLS/THE CLASH/SUBWAY SECT/	THE DAMNED/CHRIS SPEDDING & THE VIBRATORS/
SIOUXSIE & BANSHEES	THE STINKY TOYS/THE BUZZCOCKS

22nd - Wednesday...............................

FLOWERS OF ROMANCE get their most enduring quality, their name, from Johnny Rotten. The Flowers of Romance are best described as a group with a rather fluid membership. Their sometimes singer/sax player, Sid Vicious, was onstage with Siouxsie & The Banshees last night at the 100 club as a drummer. Other members include, from time to time, Viv Albertine on guitar and Palmolive on drums, Steve Walsh on guitar and Sarah Hall on bass. They rehearse at various flats and spaces, including Rehearsal Rehearsals where their guitarist Keith Levine (ex-Clash) can get them in. The group fools around with Ramones' songs and a few originals of Sid's like "Piece Of Garbage," "Brains on Vacation" and "Belsen Was A Gas."

DR. FEELGOOD vocalist Lee Brilleaux, must be feeling a little jealousy having the focus on the new "pub rock" scene being shifted to the "punk rock" crowd just as things were warming up for the Feelgoods. He told the *NME*, "I think this whole punk thing, at the moment, has got too stylized. There's no such thing as punks anymore. This lot are consciously making themselves out to be something they're not. They're trying to come on like little yoboes. And they're not little fucking yoboes."

SEX PISTOLS...........................Dundee, Technical College

24th - Friday.................................

CHRISSIE HYNDE has been introduced to a most unusual group of musicians by Capt. Sensible of the Damned. The pair from South London are Fred Mills on bass and Dave Batchelor on drums. They've played in the past with Johnny Moped as Genetic Breakdown, Assault And Buggery and several other names. Now the duo have Chrissie out front as guitarist and singer. She refers to them as Fred and Dave Berk and calls the band The Unusuals. They rehearse in Fred's front room, working up about a dozen songs including one of Chrissie's "The Phonecall," that would later be recorded by the Pretenders. Unfortunally, Chrissie still lacks confidence on guitar to go onstage with the group. After a few months, the Berks get together again with Johnny Moped. Chrissie picks up a copy of Sniffin' Glue and reads that the "Johnny Moped Band" are looking for a guitarist. Nobody has told her she had gotten the bump. Again, Chrissie is out in the cold while a band is getting together without her.

ERIC'S is the newest club in Liverpool for live music. It's a basement at #9 on Matthew Street. Ironically enough, the historic '60s club "The Cavern" was just across the street at #10 Matthew Street, Liverpool. Eric's will be the breeding ground that gives first gigs to Echo & The Bunnymen, Teardrop Explodes, Orchestral Manoeuvres and dozens of others.

SEX PISTOLS...........................Burton on Trent, The 76 Club   RUNAWAYS...........................Liverpool, Eric's

28th - Tuesday.................................

THE SEX PISTOLS are the subject of discussion between EMI representative Dick Mobbs and Malcolm McLaren. Mobbs has been up all night listening to the Pistols' Goodman demos unconvinced that the group would translate to record. McLaren does his best sales spiel and with the help of EMI's Mike Thorne, Mobbs is brought over to the band's side. Now he has to take the offer upstairs to Bob Mercer. In this weeks *NME*, Geoff Hill is unconvinced as well about the music of the Pistols. "The fans pogo, singly and in twos and threes, breaking up and reforming here and there around the floor, amoebas on methedrine. After the fifth or sixth 'Born To Be Wild' soundalike, I am ready to split- right down the middle. Perhaps I can maintain my sanity by concentrating on just one instrument, since I can't find two that are playing together."

SEX PISTOLS...........................Guildford, Bunter's Club   STRANGLERS...........................London, Rock Garden
SQUEEZE...........................London, Golden Lion

October 9th - Saturday.........................

THE SEX PISTOLS were signed to EMI Records in a four hour rush meeting last night. Commented Nick Mobbs, A&R Manager of EMI, "For me the Sex Pistols are a backlash against the 'nice little band' syndrome and the general stagnation of the music industry. They've got to happen for all our sakes....here at last is a group with a bit of guts for the younger people to identify with." After being thrown out of the CBS offices, Malcolm must feel that he's accomplished something now. Johnny Rotten told *Sounds* magazine "The great ignorant public don't know why we're in a band, it's because we're bored with all that old crap. Like every decent human being should be."

Polydor Record's Chris Parry is left standing, thinking all the time that Polydor was going to get the Pistols and McLaren did nothing to dispel this belief. Parry had even scheduled a session with the Pistols and Dave Goodman for last night, to record "Anarchy In The U.K." The band's EMI deal is for £40,000, a lot of money for an unsigned, unknown band.

STRANGLERS...........................London, Digby Stuart College   KRAFTWERK...........................Sheffield, Univ.

OCTOBER 1976

10th - Sunday...

THE SEX PISTOLS, the leading British "punk rock" group, waste no time starting to record their EMI debut single "Anarchy In The U.K.," at the Lansdowne studios. The band runs through their whole set of songs, "Did You No Wrong," "Stepping Stone," "No Fun," "Substitute," "Whatcha Gonna Do About It" and "Anarchy In The UK." To inspire the band, Malcolm sprays "Anarchy" and "EMI Is Here" on the control room window in shaving cream. It's pandemonium and Dave Goodman is trying to produce the sessions. Other problems are appearing with the single. EMI wants the debut to be "Pretty Vacant" and the band wants "Anarchy."

ROCKSLIDE adds a new member (Gangrene Gus) and change their name and style from R&B to something more up-to-date. Their new name is The Drones, the new style is this exciting new punk rock that is sweeping the nation. Rockslide had been playing around Manchester for the last year and a half.

LIVE TONIGHT! KRAFTWERK/ PENGUIN CAFE ORCH. ....London, The Roundhouse

STRANGLERS ....London, The Nashville

11th - Monday..

WRECKLESS ERIC (aka twenty-two-year-old Eric Goulden) walks into the Stiff Records office with a sample cassette of his songs for Dave Robinson. He had recorded some of his original songs on a home cassette deck as a demo. After delivering the tape to the Stiff offices, he goes home to wait for an answer and to find a proper job. He's just gotten out of the Hull College Of Art.

12th - Tuesday...

PERE UBU have their third single out on their own Hearthan Records label this week. Tracks are "Street Waves" and "My Dark Ages." The record is more of the odd stuff we've come to expect from this odd Cleveland group. Their numbers have changed again for this single. The ever-vacillating lineup this time includes the ever present David Thomas on vocals, Tom Herman on guitar (formerly on bass), Alen Ravenstine returns to play synthesizer, R. Scott Kraus is on drums and a new addition is Tony Maimone on bass and piano. If this isn't carried in your local record store, it is possible to mail order the disc through some of the more off-beat music magazines.

SEX PISTOLS...........................Dundee, Technical College

FABULOUS POODLES ....London, Rock Garden

13th - Wednesday..

WRECKLESS ERIC is called back to Stiff Records and offered a recording deal rumored to be in the two figure range. He's not new to music. The lad from Hull had previously been in Addis and the Fliptops as well as Rudy and the Takeaways, groups that covered hit songs as well as most of the Chuck Berry songbook.

ROBYN HITCHCOCK finds himself fronting a band called Dennis & The Experts. Robyn himself is cast in the lead role as "Dennis," while the "Experts" are Rob Lamb, Andy Metcalf and Maurice Windsor. They play a few original's of Robyn's and some covers by artists like Little Feat, Steely Dan and select bits of David Bowie. While punk is screaming on in London, Robyn is stuck in Cambridge playing what he later described as "sedate hippy gibberish." The group would be only a brief stopping place on the way to becoming the Soft Boys, with quite a different style.

SEX PISTOLS...........................Wolverhampton, Layfayette Club

14th - Thursday...

THE SEX PISTOLS, unhappy with the results of Dave Goodman's sessions, record another half dozen tracks with Mike Thorne from EMI in an eight track demo studio.

THE DAMNED/JACK THE LAD........High Wycombe, The Nag's Head

STEVE GIBBONS/COCKSPARRER...London, The Marquee

17th - Sunday...

THE SEX PISTOLS still aren't satisfied with their studio recordings. After a pair of chaotic sessions, the whole affair is moved to Wessex with Chris Thomas behind the board. Chris had worked with Roxy Music and had mixed Pink Floyd's "Dark Side Of The Moon." Differing from Goodman's approach, Thomas layers the guitars over and over, creating a searing wall of sound. In all, Johnny claims that Steve was given twenty-one tracks for his guitar, leaving him only one for his vocal. Pressure is on to get the single out before Christmas and EMI is rush-releasing it. In the late hours while working on the sessions, the Sex Pistols also knock around a few non-Pistols songs, one of which is Chuck Berry's "Johnny B. Goode." The impromptu session is captured on tape, but considered too rough for use, since Johnny blew the lyrics during the song.

18th - Monday...

THROBBING GRISTLE are a new "industrial" combo making their first public appearance at the London Institute of Contemporary Art before an audience of 800. The show started with Throbbing Gristle, who is currently made up of Chris Carter, Cosi Fanni Tutti, Peter Christopherson and Genesis P. Orrige. Lead member Genesis actually had his name legally changed to Genesis P. Orrige from Neil Megson

OCTOBER 1976

about six or seven years ago. The set consisted of some very bizarre tape loops and improvised twitterings and doom-style lyrics delivered in a morose tone. Some of the members of Throbbing Gristle have long pasts in music. Since he was living in Hull in the late '60s, Genesis was part of a project called COUM. They were unpracticed, untalented musicians that promoted their rare appearances truthfully, yet people still kept coming to see them. Genesis' lady friend, Cosi, has been the frequent subject of porno pics and bondage sessions. All in the name of art, of course. After the opener came the strippers, then the closing act billed as L.S.D. They're actually Chelsea, the Gene October - Billy Idol combo under a psychedelic moniker. Billy Idol, bass player for Chelsea told Tony Parsons of the *NME* that "We've known the Pistols for years, we could be that big if they gave us the chance. We've been turning up at venues asking them if we can get up on stage and play but most of them tell us to piss off." Besides the bands, there is some very odd art nailed to the walls, a few pornographic photos and loads of artists and/or musicians in attendance. Reaction to this "event" is very mixed.

Tory MP Nicholas Fairbairn was maddened that the £80,000 a year grant for the Council should waste it's money on this described the event as, "…it's a sickening outrage, sadistic, obscene, evil. The Art's Council must be scrapped after this." The Daily Mirror described it as, "Porn Pop Art Show- distasteful and unartistic…hairbrained schemes of a few trendy elitists."

THROBBING GRISTLE/CHELSEA ....London, I.C.A. Theatre

22nd - Friday.....................

THE DAMNED have their debut single out only five months after their live debut at the Nashville. It was recorded at Pathway Studios on an eight track set up for a budget of less than £50. Stiff Records' artist Nick Lowe produced the effort. The Damned original "New Rose" is flipped with a frantic cover of the Beatles' song "Help." It's Stiff Records sixth release and sells 4,000 copies through mail order before U.A. distributes it. With distribution arranged through United Artists, this should be available at "every Damned record store in the UK." Reading the matrix of the record reveals the scratched in messages "Is This A Record" and "Damned Beatles." Among the originals that the band preforms live are such new numbers like "Feel The Pain," "See Her Tonight" and the delightful Rat Scabies' original, "Pickin' Spots." Nick Kent, in the *NME* writes, "They'll be very very big." Pub Rocker Graham Parker had this to say in the *NME* about them, "I saw the Damned and I thought they were like a figment of the Woodstock Generation's acid trip. They were like a bad flash, but they've got energy and youth and believe in what they're doing. But I don't think they're doing anything musically at all."

PATTI SMITH has her second album released. It's "Radio Ethiopia," and is described by Patti as, "…a field of exploration." The album contains tracks such as "Ask The Angels," "Poppies," "Distant Fingers" and "Pissing In A River." The title track, "Radio Ethiopia," as well as "Abyssinia" were recorded live on August 9th and are dedicated to Arthur Rimbaud and Constantin Brancusi. Patti can also be found on the cover of the new *New Musical Express* under the caption of "Two Lips From Amsterdam." She's preparing for a European tour with her new re-arranged band. Richard Sohl, who had been playing with Patti for two years now, leaves and is replaced, albeit temporarily, by Ivan Kral who switches from bass to piano. Leigh Foxx steps in on bass and Andy Paley has joined for the tour. Lenny Kaye is on guitar and J.D. Daugherty is on drums. Julie Burchill, writing for the *NME*, describes her impressions of the Patti Smith persona, "…Patti Smith may be chicken-faced and pigdeon-chested, but she comes over like a chance encounter in a dark alley…she makes the Runaways look like the Sisters Of Mercy (a charity organization)."

SEX PISTOLS	Liverpool, Eric's	FABULOUS POODLES	London, The Nashville
PATTI SMITH/STRANGLERS	London, Hammersmith Odeon	JACK THE LAD/SPLIT ENZ	Manchester, Palace Theatre

23rd - Saturday.....................

THE CLASH are the focus for another decadent night at the London ICA, the crowds of punks, poseurs and the curious have arrived for an evening with the Clash and their guests, the Subway Sect and Snatch Sounds. After the first two bands have come and gone, the Clash arrive onstage. They rip through the growing collection of original songs like "Garageland," "1977," "I'm So Bored With The USA" and "Career Opportunities." In the meantime, local punk Shane McGowan (future lead singer of the Pogues) and his girlfriend are having a bit of "fun" in front of stage right. This "fun" started off as fondling each others earlobes, when she suddenly leaps in and bites Shane's right earlobe off! She then wanted to add to the blood by taking a Guiness bottle, smashing it and trying to slash herself up a bit, but not before some alert security men helped her outside. What about the earlobe? Was it "Cannibalism at the ICA?"

THE JAM have come up with a noisy way to attract press attention. They've taken their gear down to the Soho Market, set up on the sidewalk, borrowed power from Ted Carrol's Rock On Records stall and fired up. It's about noon and they manage to attract a small crown of curious onlookers, including members of the Clash who are having breakfast nearby. The Jam are dressed in their matching black suits, skinny ties and white shoes. They are successful in their quest and get mentions in both *Melody Maker* and *Sounds*.

CLASH/SUBWAY SECT/		PATTI SMITH/STRANGLERS	London, Hammersmith Odeon
SNATCH SOUNDS	London, I.C.A.	THE JAM	London, Soho Market (afternoon)

28th - Thursday.....................

EDDIE & THE HOT RODS have their latest single out on Island today. It's the Rods' original song "Teenage Depression" b/w their version of the Sam Cook song "Shake." The "A" side is from their upcoming LP under the same title. In order to get some possible radio play on the song, the Rods have altered the lyrics from the live version of the song. The references to spending money on cocaine are changed to "things I shouldn't use," and instead of "none of your shit" is the innocuous "button your lip." Safe fare, even for the BBC, as the song climbs to #35, their biggest hit yet.

OCTOBER 1976

STRANGLERS ....Bristol, The Granary   PATTI SMITH/STRANGLERS ....Manchester, Free Trade Hall

November 5th - Friday..

THE REZILLOS are a new Scottish band making their stage debut tonight in their home town of Edinburgh. They're a combination of punk and '60s Thunderbirds-Are-Go chic, odd, quirky cover tunes and hilarious stage costumes. In their set are a few originals as well as covers of songs like "Land of 1,000 Dances," "Ballroom Blitz" and "Route 66."

CLASH/ROCKETS/SUBWAY SECT...London, Royal College Of Art   EDDIE & THE HOT RODS.............London, Thames Poly.

10th - Wednesday...

THE VIBRATORS have their first single released under the name Chris Spedding and the Vibrators. Chris is helping out the band, but not a "real" member. "Real" members include Ian "Knox" Carnochran, Pat Collier, John Ellis and John Edwards. The single is "Pogo Dancing" b/w "Pose." The pogo is the dance being made evident in the punk clubs that involves a simple leaping into the air in rough equivalent to the tempo of the music.

BUZZCOCKS/CHELSEA................Manchester, Electric Circus

12th - Friday...

SHAM 69 is another new band, spotted playing furious rock and roll around front rooms in London. They are Billy Bostik (drums), Johnny Goodfornothing on rhythm guitar, Albie Slider on bass, Neil Harris on lead guitar and Jimmy Pursey on vocals. In today's issue of *NME*, Julie Burchill calls then "potentially great." There is a rumor running around that before they decided to be a "punk" band they were calling themselves Jimmy And The Ferrets while playing Bay City Rollers' cover songs. What cruel friends they must have to spread talk like that, but then the friends also say they have photos! It's said that the band got the name "Sham 69" from a bit of graffiti in their neighborhood, Hersham. It used to say "Hersham '69." but a bit of it was worn away.

DERELICTS ....London, Fulham Town Hall   MANIACS...............................London, The Speakeasy

15th - Monday...................................

THE VIBRATORS finally have a record under their own name, without sharing billing with Chris Spedding. The 45 is "We Vibrate" b/w "Whips and Furs." It's a Mickey Most production and as such, is on his RAK record label. The Vibrators started out as a R&B outfit but changed recently to high energy, no nonsense, flailing rock and roll. They are Knox on lead vocals, John Ellis on guitar, Gary Tibbs on bass and John Edwards on drums. The Vibrators are not your normal "youth club" types. They're all almost at the advanced age of thirty!

SEX PISTOLS............................London, Notre Dame Hall   DEAD FINGERS TALK................London, The Rock Garden

18th - Thursday................

RICHARD HELL & THE VOIDOIDS make their public debut tonight at CBGB's. Hell had left the Heartbreakers back in June and had assembled and rehearsed this band since that time. Strangely enough, Hell had come to the attention of Jake Riveria (of UK Stiff Records) when he played with the Heartbreakers and that interest got Hell a single out in England just days before Richard Hell & the Voidoids had even played publicly. The single has been issued in a limited edition of 5,000 with a picture sleeve. Each single is numbered, the object of course, is to show how utterly cool you are by having the lowest number possible. Unfortunately, more than a few people have copies that bear the #0001. Could it be a pressing error? If it's on Stiff, think twice. Lead track on the 45 is a song that Hell was doing back in his days with Television called "Blank Generation." The intention isn't a put down, but rather for the listener to "fill in the blank" with whatever generation fits. The other tracks are "Another World" and "You Gotta Lose." The group is Richard Hell on bass and vocals, Robert Quine on guitar, Marc Bell on drums (the future Marky Ramone) and Ivan Julian on bass.

STRANGLERS ....Leeds, Fforde Green Hotel   WASPS ....London, The Bridgehouse
NATIONAL HEALTH/   DERELICTS/VIBRATORS ....London, The Nashville
LIVE TONIGHT! CRASS STUPIDITY ....London, Collegiate Theatre   BICYCLE THIEVES.....................Manchester, The White Lion

19th - Friday...

THE SEX PISTOLS make a bold vinyl debut with "Anarchy In The UK." The initial 1,000 are shipped with a solid black picture sleeve with no info on it whatsoever. One mistake has surfaced on the initial pressing of the single. The first copies off the press list the producer as Chris Thomas. It should in fact read Chris Thomas on "Anarchy," and Dave Goodman on the flip "I Wanna Be Me." In a glowing review of the single in *Melody Maker*, Caroline Coon exclaims that "They've done it!" They've captured the excitement of their stage show on vinyl in "Anarchy In The UK." *Sounds* lists it as Single Of The Week. The Sex Pistols are still planning a major tour of the UK with several other groups. Opening date for the tour is only a little over two weeks away, but plans still are not certain. Meanwhile the Sex Pistols play tonight at Hendon Poly., including in their set a new song that Johnny has been working on titled "No Future (God Save The Queen)." The song

NOVEMBER 1976

was so new to the set, that Johnny was reading the words off a cheat sheet onstage.

DAMNED/   SEX PISTOLS ....London, Hendon Poly.
SLAUGHTER & THE DOGS ....London, Manor Hill School

21st - Sunday...

CHELSEA open up for the Stranglers at the Nashville in London. It is their last gig with the original line-up of the band. The disagreement that caused the split was that the band played lots of Idol-James originals. The Idol-James team didn't like October's arrangements and wanted to do it themselves. Instead of kicking October out, they all quit the band. Billy Idol, Tony James and John Towe start a new band called Generation X. The name is from a paperback novel about '60s mod culture that was found at Billy Idol's mum's house. Generation X will have a few minor hits in the late '70s before Billy Idol goes solo for his most successful years in the '80s.

VIBRATORS ....High Wycombe, The Nag's Head   STRANGLERS/CHELSEA ....London, The Nashville

22nd - Monday...

EDDIE & THE HOT RODS stretch out and give the public a full 12 inches of music. Their debut LP is "Teenage Depression" and features some of the band's originals like "Get Across To You," "On The Run" and "Double Checkin' Woman." The album also has the three tracks that were on their "Live At The Marquee" single. Two additional covers are also included bringing the live content to five tracks.

SQUEEZE ....London, Rochester Castle   VIBRATORS ....London, The Rock Garden

27th - Saturday...

ROBYN HITCHCOCK announced to the crowd onstage tonight in Cambridge "We're the Soft Boys." It's a new direction for the group that was only hours ago calling itself Dennis & The Experts. The new name comes from the title of a song that Robyn recently made up in rehearsal called "Give It To The Soft Boys." Rob Lamb left the group when he felt the band was getting to be too scrappy. The Soft Boys are Robyn Hitchcock on lead vocals & guitar, Maurice Windsor on drums, Andy Metcalf on bass and new guitarist Alan "Wangbo" Davies, who takes departing Rob's place. Why the name the Soft Boys? Robyn explains "I'd had this concept of this thing called the Soft Boys, like a William Burroughs amalgam. Soft Machine and the Wild Boys. The implications were kind of homo-erotic and seedy, kind of crawling, bloodless, colorless things that crawled around like filleted human jellyfish around the corridors of power. Soft Boys controlled things but they had no spine. Basically insidious people and basically that's what we were."

VIBRATORS ....London, North East Polytechnic   CHARLIE/DENNIS & EXPERTS ......Cambridge, Polytechnic

28th - Sunday...

TOM ROBINSON debuts his new band at the Hope & Anchor in Islington only six months after leaving Cafe Society. His reputation as part of that band has helped him get his new group off the ground quickly. The band is a collection of friends, including Nick Trevisick on drums, Anton Mauve (aka Roy Butterfield) on guitar, Mark Griffiths on bass and Bret Sinclair on guitar.

THE SEX PISTOLS are featured on an ITV special about the punk rock phenomenon sweeping the UK, called the *London Weekend Show* this afternoon at 1:15. The program is hosted by Janet Street-Porter and is a very well done documentary on the punk rock scene. Filmed in the Notre Dame Roman Catholic Church near Leicester Square in London, the Sex Pistols segment catches the band in a most unusual setting. There are also interviews with the Clash and members of the Banshees.

EDDIE & THE HOT RODS ....Croydon, The Greyhound   SQUEEZE ....London, The Brecknock
KIK BUDI/   DAMNED/
TOM ROBINSON BAND ....London, Hope & Anchor   SLAUGHTER & THE DOGS ....Manchester, Electric Circus

29th - Monday...

IGGY POP's new LP that he's been working on with David Bowie is reportedly finished. It's tentatively titled "Nightclubbing" and allegedly contains a great deal of material that some would consider stark heavy metal. At this time there is still no release date since no label as yet has offered to meet the demand that Iggy has set for advance money. Iggy also says that he's finished a book simply titled "Fun."

THE SEX PISTOLS planned gig with the Clash, Damned and The Heartbreakers at Lancaster Polytechnic has been banned. The University heads as well as the town council didn't feel that the town needed "that sort of filth in the town limits." The gig, originally planned to take place on December 10th, will be moved to the Charter Theatre in Preston.

EDDIE & THE HOT RODS ....Guildford, Civic Hall   LEE KOSMIN BAND/
DERELICTS/SQUEEZE.................London, The Rock Garden   THE STRANGLERS....................London, The 100 Club

YOU CANNOT OFFEND ME

December 1st - Wednesday....................

THE SEX PISTOLS are invited as last-minute guests to appear on the Bill Grundy TV program *Today*. Today's guest band was supposed to be Queen (the group, not the regent) and they cancelled. Someone thought it would be a good idea to get the Pistols on. They're whisked from the midst of their rehearsals for their "Anarchy" tour to the ITV studios in a courtesy

DECEMBER 1976

limo. In the car complimentary drinks. In the waiting room at the TV station, more complementary drinks. By the time they're ready to go on, the wheels are well greased. Too bad the band weren't told this show was being broadcast live! The Sex Pistols are about to become a household word and a naughty one at that! Presenter Bill Grundy planned to expose them as unschooled ruffians with little wits about them. The interview lasted just under two minutes. The reverberations would last a long time.

Exploring the new punk rock craze sweeping England, Grundy set about asking the band questions that were designed to entice the band into upsetting the audience. Grundy asked Johnny about Beethoven, Mozart, Bach and Brahms and he replied, "They're all heroes of ours, ain't they?…they're wonderful people…they really turn us on." Grundy moved in with, "Suppose they turn other people on?" Then Johnny Rotten replied under his breath, "That's their tough shit." Grundy leapt on it. "It's what?" Johnny, moved on with, "Nothing. A rude word. Next question…" Grundy, "No, no, what was the rude word?" Prompted, he said, "Shit." "Good heavens, you frightened me to death!" Grundy joked. Then turning to Siouxsie (of the Banshees, standing behind the seated Pistols) they spoke briefly of meeting after the show. "You dirty sod, you dirty old man…" Steve cackled. "Go on chief, go on, you've got another five seconds. Say something outrageous," countered Grundy. "You dirty bastard." "Go on again," Grundy provoked. "You dirty fucker!" "What a clever boy," he chuckled. "What a fucking rotter." Grundy wasn't disappointed. The band said something outrageous, they said a lot outrageous and 6:25 on a peaceful Wednesday evening is not the time to be outrageous, unless you want to be noticed. Malcolm is worried and furious, he grabs the band, throws them into the limo and makes a quick escape. The phone are already beginning to melt with irate calls back at the station.

TOM ROBINSON BAND ....London, The Golden Lion   VIBRATORS.............................Swindon, The Affair

2nd - Thursday.................................

THE SEX PISTOLS' career is at a major turning point. Because of yesterdays encounter with Bill Grundy, the *Today* show with Bill Grundy is without Bill Grundy for the next two weeks. He's been suspended. The decision to put the Sex Pistols on was an ill-fated one, reached only ninety minutes before airtime. Because of the trouble from it, even the producer and director for the *Today* show were fired. The headlines are piling up as they roll out of Fleet Street. *The Daily Express* titled their story "The Filth And The Fury, uproar as viewers jam phones." The article included the story of "lorry driver James Holmes, forty-seven, who was outraged that his eight-year-old son had heard the swearing…and kicked in the screen of his TV. It blew up and I was knocked backwards," he said. "But I was so angry and disgusted with this filth that I took a swing with my boot." EMI held its own press conference with Leslie Hill stating that "we feel that in many cases the media deliberately provoked this act; in no way does this affect the group's relationship with EMI." As a result of the incident, cancellations are beginning to pour into McLaren's office. Glasgow, Southend, Norwich, Cardiff, they're all responding instantly to the Pistols.

LIVE TONIGHT!
DERELICTS/WIRE ....London, The Nashville
THE BOYS ....London, Rochester Castle
STRANGLERS ....London, The Red Cow

3rd - Friday.................................

THE SEX PISTOLS have even more fallout from the Grundy episode on the Beeb. Record packers at the EMI factory refuse to handle their 45. At least seven future engagements for the Pistols have been cancelled by the clubs and the BBC have banned the record from all future airplay, an amusing development since they never played it to begin with. *The Daily Mail* published an editorial titled "Never Mind The Morals Or Standards, the Only Notes That Matter Come In Wads." Frank Thislewaite, Vice Chancellor of East Anglia University has cancelled tonight's opening show of the tour, because after Wednesday's affair on the BBC he can't feel secure that the concert would proceed peacefully. Angry students protest the ban with a sit-in.

THE STRANGLERS, a veteran pub band cum punk band, have signed a deal with United Artists Records. Plans are for their debut album and a live one at that, to be recorded next Friday as they play at the Nashville.

STORMTROOPER.....................Bristol, The Naval Volunteer   MANIACS ....London, Rochester Castle

4th - Saturday.................................

LENE LOVICH of the Diversions has a single out just in time for the Christmas rush of singles, a version of "I Saw Mommy Kissing Santa Claus" issued on Polydor UK. A weird mixture of Shirley Temple style vocals and Hawaiian guitars.

THE SEX PISTOLS are in Derby today. The winsome foursome have been asked by the local council of Derby for a private matinee show to see if the band would be "approved" to play that night. Local Councillor Leslie Shipley said that the other bands could play, but the Derby Council will have to approve the Sex Pistols personally before the show. When the designated preview time of 4PM rolled around, the Sex Pistols refused to show up. The Derby Council made it's statement at 5, saying that the Pistols had their chance and had not taken part in the audition. Meanwhile back at the hotel, *News Of The World* reporters were vying for quotes, the other bands on the tour were giving their views on freedom of speech and the National Front were threatening to align themselves with the Pistols. The other bands showed solidarity with the Pistols ban and pulled out of the show as well, all except the Damned, who said they would go on anyway. This has infuriated Malcolm and the others. *NME* reporter Julie Burchill was noticeably irritated when she wrote, "…the Pistols are coming to change your town soon. Are you going to make sure they're allowed to partake in the fable of free speech of this democratic country or are

DECEMBER 1976

you going to sink back into stupor for another decade? The Fascists are in the council chambers, not on the stage."
MANIACS ....London, The Speakeasy

6th - Monday...................................

THE SEX PISTOLS' "Anarchy In The UK" tour, their first major tour, had been whittled down to three dates from an original nineteen. Support acts included the Damned, The Clash and Johnny Thunders with his new band the Heartbreakers. The first gig of the tour, originally planned as the fourth, was tonight at Leeds Polytechnic. Johnny scolded the audience at one point that, "You're not wrecking the place. The *News Of The World* will REALLY be disappointed." Back at EMI Headquarters in London, Leslie Hill has sent a note to EMI Chairman Sir John Read concerning the Sex Pistols' problems with the press. He laid out his plans for the group's next single in February of '77 and a future album. He also expressed his belief that the press had exaggerated the problem with the group.
SEX PISTOLS/DAMNED/CLASH/
HEARTBREAKERS ....Leeds, Poly.

7th - Tuesday.............................

THE SEX PISTOLS were the subject of the following statements about "Content of Records" at the EMI Annual General Meeting today by Sir John Read, Chairman of EMI Records, "The Sex Pistols incident, which started with a disgraceful interview given by this young pop group on Thames TV last week…the Sex Pistols have acquired a reputation for aggressive behavior which they certainly demonstrated in public. There is no excuse for this…I need hardly add that we shall do everything we can to restrain their public behavior…Our view within EMI is that we should seek to discourage records that are likely to give offense to the majority of the people…(yet) EMI should not set itself up as a public censor, (it does however) seek to encourage restraint." When the *Daily Mirror* asked Johnny Rotten what he thought of the statement he replied, "Tell him to go fuck himself!" The Sex Pistols tour was supposed to play in Bournemouth tonight, but with the concert cancelled like so many others, the band has quickly pushed on to Sheffield to play a hastily re-scheduled gig. As a result of their lack of solidarity with the ban in Derby, The Damned have been kicked off the tour.
ULTRAVOX!. ....London, The Nashville   SEX PISTOLS/CLASH
EDDIE & THE HOT RODS ....Manchester, Free Trade Hall   HEARTBREAKERS.....................Sheffield

8th - Wednesday.................................

THE VIBRATORS are suffering from the after-effects of the Sex Pistols on the BBC. Promoters, suddenly leery of any "punk" style bands, have cancelled their entire UK tour as well as an already booked tour of Holland, Germany and Belgium. They were originally booked to play on the package tour with the Sex Pistols, but backed out when the package was revamped not to include the Ramones and Talking Heads. Bassist Pat Collier told the *NME*, "We're suffering the worst, but we're not going to give in. There's nothing that the establishment can do to stop punk from coming through."

EATER are touched by the backlash against punk after the Bill Grundy thing. Under-age kid-punk band Eater had their recent gig at the London Hope & Anchor interrupted when police wanted to investigate the band members for being underage in a licensed premises. Parents of the band members prevented the interruption while police followed up on an anonymous complaint that drummer Dee Generate was under fourteen and should not be allowed on the premises. After speaking to Dee's parents the officers were satisfied he was fourteen and left the band playing. The average age of the Finchley youth punk band is fifteen.
SLAUGHTER & THE DOGS ....London, Hope & Anchor   XTC.....................................Swindon, The Affair

9th - Thursday.................................

THE SEX PISTOLS play the legendary Electric Circus in Manchester. Also on the bill are The Clash and Johnny Thunders and the Heartbreakers. Since the Damned were just kicked off the tour, there's room for one more and Manchester band, The Buzzcocks, have been asked to continue with the traveling circus. They're acquaintances of the Sex Pistols and were responsible for booking the band into Manchester for the first time. Tony Parsons, observes for the *NME,* "Johnny Rotten just hangs from the mike stand…burns the crowd with his glassy, taunting, cynical eyes…(and shouts) 'I hope you 'ate it!'" In *Sounds* magazine they have the comments of Manchester youth who are all in the process of starting their own punk bands. "Sentiments were echoed by almost every kid…all in the process of forming bands, Stiff Kittens (Hooky, Terry, Wroey and Bernard) being the most grotesque offering." Stiff Kittens were one of the many Manchester bands at the gig. They'll go through a succession of names, becoming Joy Division before the decade ends and eventually become New Order. Also at the gig is Steven Morrissey, one of the New York Doll's greatest Manchester fans, who has come out this evening to see ex-Doll Johnny Thunders band the Heartbreakers. This is the second time he's seen the Pistols and is moved to take out an ad in *Sounds* magazine calling for: "Dolls / Patti (Smith) fans wanted for Manchester-based punk band."

NINA HAGEN leaves East Germany with her uncle for the West. Her uncle is a political dissident and is being expelled and Nina leaps on the chance to get out of East Germany as well, even though she leaves behind a promising musical career. She had already been in two East German bands. The first was Automobil, with which she would play eight hour concerts; five hours of song and three hours of dance. This group left her exhausted and forced her seclusion (for a short while) to recuperate. Upon coming out again, she formed a second band called Dampferband. Now with the promise of a fresh start in a new, free country, she leaves her homeland.
DERELICTS ....London, The Nashville
SEX PISTOLS/DAMNED/CLASH/
THE HEARTBREAKERS/
THE BUZZCOCKS ....Manchester, The Electric Circus

DECEMBER 1976

10th - Friday...........................

GENERATION X is Billy Idol, John Towe and Tony James. They play their first gig as Generation X less than three weeks after leaving Chelsea. Lead singer Billy Idol has already made a picture of fashion by dying his hair various colors from green to red, to white, to blue, to orange, to…whatever suits him. They've also added an additional guitarist, Bob "Derwood" Andrews. Andrews was discovered at a Saturday Night Bash at the Fulham Arts Center playing in a band called Paradox. Idol was at the side of the hall giving Andrews motions to "come over here a minute." Andrews thought that this was some punk that wanted to beat him up. He finally walked over and was informed that he might have a future in another band, a band that didn't play cover songs. With this line-up the band makes its public debut playing tonight at the Central College of Art & Design.

THE STRANGLERS' gig tonight at the Nashville is being recorded for their LP debut with United Artists. The Island Mobile Recording Unit is being used and tickets for the event were only one pound each. The next recording session for the Stranglers will be right after Christmas when they go into the studio to record their debut single for release in January. Most likely titles are "Go Buddy Go," or the live favorite, "Grip."

THE SAINTS are an Australian punk band, who have their debut single re-released on the Power Exchange label down under. The band previously had a private pressing of the single on their own "Fatal Records" label after being turned down by every major label on the continent. Now Power Exchange has worked out world-wide rights and "I'm Stranded," as well as the flip "No Time," are available on a much wider basis than before. The private pressing had been a very rare item and commanding high prices in underground record shops. The Saints are: Chris Bailey on vocals, Ed Keupper on guitar, Kym Bradshaw on bass and Ivor Hay on drums.

LIVE TONIGHT!
SEX PISTOLS/DAMNED/ CLASH/ JOHNNY THUNDERS & THE HEARTBREAKERS/ THE BUZZCOCKS ....Preston, Charter Theatre

GENERATION X........................London, Central College Of Art STRANGLERS/ TOM ROBINSON BAND..............London, The Nashville

11th - Saturday....................

THE SEX PISTOLS' impact on the stagnant music scene is summed up in this week's *Record Mirror*. "The Sex Pistols are about as subtle as a sawn off shot gun. Like hit men, they have come out of the night to shoot the legs off a tired music industry that has relied on crutches too long." Music fan Shane McGowan (and future Pogues lead singer) wrote in his fanzine *Bondage* that "There isn't any public decency. People only know what's decent by being told by ITV and the rest of the media and EMI too."

DEAF SCHOOL/STRANGLERS ....Aylesbury, Friar's

DERELICTS ....London, Hope & Anchor

13th - Monday..........................

TOM ROBINSON is busy putting together a band. He had just been playing with pick-up groups of friends. His first true member was an old school friend of his guitarist Danny Kustow. Then they stumbled onto Brian "The Dolphin" Taylor. He was giving a bass-playing friend a ride to the audition and ended up as the band's drummer. During auditions for bassists, they found sixteen-year-old Mark Ambler, who can play anything by ear. The Tom Robinson Band was complete.

CLASH singer Joe Strummer makes it clear what they're rebeling against in the *NME*. "I think people ought to know that (The Clash is) anti-fascist, anti-violence, we're anti-racist and we're procreative. We're against ignorance."

EDDIE & THE HOT RODS ....Birmingham, Town Hall

NOBODADDY/STRANGLERS ....Edinburgh, Tiffany's

16th - Thursday..................

THE RESIDENTS are the dictionary definition of "odd." Their twisting of music into shapes different from anyone before are legendary. Their offering for the Christmas season is a most peculiar version of the Rolling Stones' song "Satisfaction." Jim Green of *Trouser Press* described hearing it for the first time. "I put on 'Satisfaction' and was at that point bombarded with the most determinedly repellant music I've ever heard, guaranteed to empty a room inside of ten or fifteen second electronically processed guitars forming painfully unsettling mutations of the original chords and riff and an electronically distorted voice resembling a downer freak from the ass-end of Uranus. Remember those cartoons of bug-eyed monsters riding drag race cars? If they could sing they'd be in the Residents." The single is flipped with "Loser (is congruent to) Weed" and comes in a limited edition silkscreened sleeve. It's on Ralph Records out of San Francisco.

STRANGLERS ....High Wycombe, The Nag's Head

18th - Saturday........................

MALICE are masquerading under another name to fool a booking agent into thinking they were a folk band and get a gig in Sussex at Worth Abbey. They turn in an acoustic set on the floor with bongos. They're also scheduled to play with Amulet at St. Wilfrid's Comprehensive School on the Monday the 20th. The newest line-up of Malice boasts Porl Thompson on guitar, who is the brother of the

DECEMBER 1976

Lol's current girlfriend, as well as Robert Smith on guitar and vocals, Lol on drums and Michael Dempsey on bass. The wait to becoming the Cure and making their first single is two years long.

> EDDIE & THE HOT RODS ....Liverpool, The Stadium

19th - Sunday.................................

THE SEX PISTOLS, The Clash, Johnny Thunders and the Heartbreakers all return to the Electric Circus in Manchester just ten days after their first booking there. They've had so many cancellations on their abortive Anarchy In The UK tour that some places can afford to book the band twice. Paul Cook's mother tells the *Daily Mail* that her son is no longer welcome at home. She's planning to make a nice little dinning room out of Paul's old bedroom. Twenty-year-old Cook is now a castaway.

> EDDIE & THE HOT RODS ....Glasgow, Apollo Centre
>
> SEX PISTOLS/THE CLASH
> JOHNNY THUNDERS &
> THE HEARTBREAKERS/
> THE BUZZCOCKS......................Manchester, Electric Circus

20th - Monday.................................

THE SEX PISTOLS' gig originally scheduled for the Town Hall in Birmingham has been cancelled due to "adverse press and potentially adverse conditions surrounding the band." The good news is that the show has been rescheduled for Cleethorpes tonight. To make matters even worse, Terry Collins, licensee of the new Roxy Theatre in London, stated that the Sex Pistol tour would not be playing the venue as planned near the end of the month. He had seen the Pistols when they used the Roxy as a rehearsal space some weeks back and found them "thoroughly disgusting." He will take more time to finish out his new club which is projected to open in mid-January. Bernard Rhodes, manager for the Clash commented to the *NME*, "Kids should have the chance to see the entertainment they want. The government tells them to work hard for their money and get the nation back on its feet and then they won't give them the chance to see the entertainment they want!"

21st - Tuesday.................................

THE SEX PISTOLS play the last of the three dates left after the backlash of the Bill Grundy incident. Sixteen cancelled and one to go. The Sex Pistols, The Clash, Johnny Thunders and the Heartbreakers and the Buzzcocks play at the Woods Centre in Plymouth tonight. Johnny Rotten is indignant, "Every time we get a gig, you get your local councils banning it and you get no complaints. So there's your local council officials thinking 'righteous- look at us. Look at what we're doing for society.' Nothing's gonna change. Even rehearsing and writing new songs is a problem 'cause you ain't given a chance to do 'em anywhere. It's my job and I'm being denied my job. But at the same time I'm being taxed 80% of everything I earn by people who are stopping me. The councils, they ban my concerts and they take my money. 'Cause we're the first, we're the only ones that mean what we say and mean a lot more than any of the rest…we make people think and that's frightening for those who'll like to make us morons."

GENERATION X play at the grand opening of a new punk club in London. It's the Roxy Club at Neal Street in Covent Garden. Opening the show for Gen X is Siouxsie & The Banshees. Billy Idol, before his stint in Chelsea, was once a Banshee himself, for a few days anyway. It's not so surprising that they were asked to open the club, as its manager is Andy Czezowski, who has been connected with Generation X members in their previous incarnation as Chelsea. The club itself enjoyed a bit of notoriety in 1974-75, when under the name Chaguarama's, it was a gay nightclub of some note. Club owner Rene Albert has accepted the offer of a three month contract to let Andy Czezowski and his two partners, Ralph Jedaschek and Barry Jones, run his club, renamed The Roxy. The tile and canopy that mark the small doorway on Neal Street W2 have instantly become 'THE' place to hang out and heckle passersby.

> GENERATION X/
> SIOUXSIE & THE BANSHEES ....London, Roxy Club
>
> SEX PISTOLS/THE CLASH
> JOHNNY THUNDERS &
> THE HEARTBREAKERS/
> THE BUZZCOCKS......................Plymouth, Woods Leisure Centre

22nd - Wednesday.................................

THE VIBRATORS have most of their gigs in Europe and England cancelled because of the punk rock backlash. Through careful negotiation. they have been able to talk themselves into a few gigs. One tonight at the London Holloway Lord Nelson and at the Middlesborough Rock Garden on Thursday and Friday. They are now still trying to re-book their cancelled European tour.

THE SEX PISTOLS' tour date set tonight for Torquay was banned by the local council. It shifted last week to Penelope's in Paignton which has also been cancelled. So now, the band has been held over in Plymouth. Unfortunately, the promoter hadn't had a chance to promote it on a day's notice, so only six Hell's Angels turn up for the show. Making history in a different way, the Sex Pistols are the first "punk" band to have a single enter the *NME* charts. It makes its historic debut this week at number #27. Speculation is that it would go even higher if the band were able to play concerts to promote it. At present it's selling approximately 1,500 copies per week.

THE ADVERTS are a new band from Devon County that have been playing a few nights at the Roxy as an opening act. Jake Riveria of Stiff saw them and even though the band is just starting out, he sees promise and offers them a one-off single contract.

> MANIACS ....London, Upstairs At R. Scott's
> VIBRATORS ....London, Lord Nelson
>
> SEX PISTOLS/THE CLASH
> JOHNNY THUNDERS &
> THE HEARTBREAKERS/
> THE BUZZCOCKS......................Plymouth, Woods Center

DECEMBER 1976

25th - Saturday.......

THE SEX PISTOLS are featured in the Christmas issue of *NME*, under the headline "Sex Pistols, This week's episode." More of the band's dates being cancelled are detailed and rocker Pat Travers issuing a challenge to the band. Travers has challenged the Pistols to a battle of the bands anytime, anywhere. They will even go so far as to feature their bassist playing with just two bass strings and drummer playing on a three piece kit. They bragged even with that handicap they could still out-play the Sex Pistols.

Bernard Brooke Partridge of the Greater London Council said of the Sex Pistols, "My personal view on punk rock is that it's nauseating, disgusting, degrading, ghastly, sleazy, purient, voyeuristic and nauseating. I think that just about covers it as far as I'm concerned. I think most of these groups would be vastly improved by sudden death. The worst of the punk rock groups currently are the Sex Pistols. They're unbelievably nauseating, they are the antithesis of humankind. I would like to see somebody dig a very, very large, exceedingly deep hole and drop the whole bloody lot down in it. The whole world would be vastly improved by their total and utter non existence."

SEX PISTOLS
This week's episode

TWO MORE cancellations hit the Sex Pistols' package tour, when scheduled gigs at Birmingham Bingley Hall (Monday) and Paignton Penelope's (Wednesday) were called off. But the show received a late boost in the shape of three last-minute bookings — gigs in Manchester and Cleethorpes earlier this week and a date at Ipswich Manor Ballroom tonight (Thursday). A further boost is the arrival of the Pistols ● **Pat Travers Band have issued a challenge to the Sex Pistols, to be performed any time and anywhere for charity. They say they would feature Peter Cowling playing with just two bass strings, Travers using three guitar strings, and drummer Nico McBrain playing high hat, snare drum and one cymbal — and they reckon they would still out-play the Pistols.**

27th - Monday.....................

THE SEX PISTOLS were the subject of a statement by EMI Group Chairman Sir John Read at their Annual General Meeting. Despite the rantings of Malcolm and the band, Read's comments were even-handed and more supportive than you'd have imagined. He said; "Throughout its history as a recording company, EMI has always sought to behave within contemporary limits of decency and good taste...Today, there is in EMI's experience...a good deal of questioning by various sections of society, both the young and old...What is decent or in good taste compared to the attitudes of, say twenty or even ten years ago?" It is against this present day social background that EMI has to make value judgments about the content of records in particular. The Sex Pistols are a pop group devoted to a new form of music known as "punk rock." It was contracted for recording purposes by EMI Records Limited in October 1976- an unknown group offering some promise,...like many other pop groups of different kinds that have signed...The Sex Pistols have acquired a reputation for aggressive behavior which they have certainly demonstrated in public. There is no excuse for this. Our recording company's experience of working with the group, however, is satisfactory. I need hardly add that we shall do everything we can to restrain their public behavior, although this is a matter over which we have no real control...Our view within EMI is that we should seek to discourage records that are likely to give offense to the majority of people. In this context, changing public attitudes have to be taken into account. EMI should not set itself up as a public censor, but it does seek to encourage restraint. The board of EMI certainly takes seriously the need to do everything possible to encourage the raising of standards in music and entertainment."

28th - Tuesday.....................

THE BUZZCOCKS become the first punk band in this do-it-yourself movement to start their own record label. It's called New Hormones and its first release will be their own debut EP. It required a loan of £250 from Pete Shelley's dad to get off the ground. The Manchester band has purchased five hours of studio time at Indigo Sound Studios in Manchester to record this "document". Four tracks were recorded today including "Breakdown," "Time's Up," "Boredom" and "Friends of Mine." The Buzzcocks are Pete Shelley on guitar, Steve Diggle on bass, John Maher on drums and Howard Devoto on vocals. It's off to the pressing plant now.

30th - Thursday.....................

FRIAR'S CLUB in Aylesbury, is the site of an unusual twist in the Sex Pistols banning in England. Generaly speaking, the result of this "filth & fury" frenzy is that promoters and town councils are barring the Sex Pistols and any band that might even vaguely resemble them. Here's a new twist. The punters that frequent Friar's have submitted a 1,000 name petition to the owners of the club asking them to never let bands like the Pistols play their venue.

THE DAMNED have been invited to record a session for the BBC and are in the studio tonight. They're recording a new version of their single "New Rose," as well as three new songs, "Neat Neat Neat," "Stab Your Back" and "I Fall."

31st - Friday.....................

"1976 YEAR END REPORT" in the *NME* is a summary of events, concerts, records and quotes. Among its list of the staff's "Singles of the Year 1976" are Nick Lowe's "So It Goes," The Sex Pistols "Anarchy In The UK," Eddie & The Hot Rods "Live At The Marquee" EP, and Television singing "Little Johnny Jewel." Also on the top twenty list are artists like Thin Lizzy, Steve Miller, Bob Dylan, Boz Scaggs and Joan Armatrading.

JANUARY 1977

January 3rd - Monday...............

THE VIBRATORS are slowly recovering from the national backlash against punk rock that began with the Sex Pistols. They have managed to salvage a few of the dozens of dates that were cancelled last month, beginning tomorrow night at the Covent Garden Rock Garden.

WIRE guitarist George Gill has left the band to start a new group called The Bears. This leaves Colin Newman, Bruce Gilbert, Graham Lewis and ex-Art Attack member Robert Gotobed to carry on.

JOHNNY THUNDER & THE HEARTBREAKERS	London, Dingwalls
EATER	London, Rochester Castle

4th - Tuesday......................

THE SEX PISTOLS make headlines again as they leave Heathrow Airport for a five day tour of Holland. They reportedly "Spat, vomited and swore" all of their way through the airport to the KLM departure lounge, where they hastily boarded on the plane. Stories vary greatly over this incident, but the truth wasn't important to the press hungry public. It was headlines that counted. In fact, the Sex Pistols were accompanied on the trip by an EMI representative, bypassing the KLM check-out desk because they were running so late when they got to the airport. The band never even went through the terminal. The exaggerations in the press for the sake of headlines is getting out of hand. A spokesman for the Pistols commented on the potential quitting of EMI by the band for lack of support by saying, "…for the present we are still with EMI. But I stress, that's for the present." The whole incident smacks of a recreation of a similar and real incident when Johnny Thunders got sick in an airport lounge back in the New York Dolls days. That incident got a great deal of press about the outrageous New York Dolls and there's little doubt that Malcolm McLaren was familiar with it, because he was on the trip with the Dolls at the time. He's was a keen observer and has taken every chance to re-create them in the guise of the Sex Pistols since the very beginning. Did the press get their stories firsthand, or could they have been planted for the sake of gaining more press?

VIBRATORS ....London, The Rock Garden

5th - Wednesday........................

THE VIBRATORS have let it slip that their follow up to "We Vibrate," will be a cover of the Rolling Stones' "Jumping Jack Flash." They'll be recording it when they return from their upcoming dates in Europe for release in February.

THE STRANGLERS' proposed live album debut has been scrapped in favor of a group of studio recordings, so they've taken themselves off the road to record with Martin Rushent at the backroad T. W. Studios in Fulham. They're recording some of their favorite live selections, as well as songs that are being written as they go along. They've got enough material saved up after three years to go a long way. The finished tracks will appear as their debut album for U.A. sometime this spring.

XTC are auditioning for CBS Records. It's the latest in a long string of tryouts, with the band having previously tested for Pye Records and Decca. They've selected for the session "Statue Of Liberty," "Monkey Woman" and "Star Park." For the sessions, they're joined by their newest member, Barry Andrews, who began playing keyboards with XTC only a few days ago.

6th - Thursday........................

THE SEX PISTOLS finally pushed just a bit too far. Claiming that the Heathrow incident was the last straw, EMI Chairman Sir John Read throws the Sex Pistols off EMI. In a statement issued to the press Reed stated that, "The Sex Pistols have acquired a reputation for aggressive behavior which they have certainly demonstrated in public." This parting of the ways comes as an unexpected surprise to manager Malcolm McLaren who had a meeting with EMI executives planned for January 12th after the band returned from their brief Dutch tour. This untimely parting of the ways comes only three months into a two year contract. EMI have directed their UK pressing plant, as well as the foreign ones to stop production the "Anarchy In The UK" single and delete it from the current catalogue immediately. Malcolm and the Sex Pistols, who should be pleased at this release from what they felt was a cool relationship, are threatening to sue, since EMI is breaking the contract prematurely. Malcolm told the *NME,* "It's been very nice. We've come away to Holland and someone's decided behind our back to 'mutually terminate' the contract. Legally we're still on EMI Records."

VIBRATORS ....London, The Red Cow

9th - Sunday........................

SEX PISTOLS' manager Malcolm McLaren meets with Derek Green of A&M Records concerning the Sex Pistols future possibilities with the label. A demo tape brought along for the meeting includes "Submission," "No Feelings," Pretty Vacant," "No Future" and three versions of "Anarchy in The UK." In the fanzine *Sniffin' Glue* Mark Perry writes, "The Pistols reflect life as it is in the council flats, not some fantasy world that most rock artists create. Yes, they will destroy, but it won't be mindless destruction. The likes of Led Zeppelin, Queen and Pink Floyd, need to be checked in the 'classical' music section. They've got to make way for the real people and the Sex Pistols are the first of them."

MANIACS ....London, Windsor Castle

JANUARY 1977

13th - Thursday..

THE TALKING HEADS are now one of the biggest draws that NYC's CBGB's has. Along with the Ramones, they are among that new music elite that will have a major label record out in the very near future. The Talking Heads are currently being courted by both Sire Records and Private Stock. Their first single will undoubtedly be "Psycho Killer." They are so prepared that they have already begun planning what tracks to set aside for their debut album. On the short list are "For Artists Only," "I Wish You Wouldn't Say That," "The Book I Read," "I'm Not In Love," and some covers like "1-2-3 Red Light," "Love Is All Around" and "96 Tears."

PATTI SMITH "I'm not going to sell my art. It never was for sale…Listen, I'm over 30, nobody tells me if I can spit on stage or not…," - Patti Smith in the *NME*.

LIVE TONIGHT!

JOHNNY THUNDERS &
THE HEARTBREAKERS ....London, The Red Cow

WASPS ....London, Rochester Castle

17th - Monday..

THE DAMNED & EATER play a double bill at the Roxy Club. The Damned are onstage first but make it clearly understood that they are NOT opening for underage punk band Eater. The Damned's Captain Sensible looks striking in his short blue nurse's dress and starched apron and Vanian is ghoulishly made up (as usual). Vanian dedicated the first number saying, "This is for Johnny Thunders, who's been busted." They then rip through a set including their single (both sides) as well as "Neat Neat Neat," "Born To Kill," "Fan Club" and a London SS song "Fish."

Eater take the stage later that night playing some originals as well as some mutant covers like an amusing version of Alice Cooper's "Eighteen" with the lyrics changed to be "Fifteen." This, to capitalize on fifteen-year-old vocalist Andy Blade. Other covers included David Bowie's "Queen Bitch" and the essential Lou Reed tune "Sweet Jane." These bands must be getting to be a bit of a curiosity among the more established musicians. Somebody has spotted both Jimmy Page and Robert Plant here tonight. Robert Plant gives the *NME* his thumbnail review of the show. "I came down (to the London Roxy Club) with Jimmy Page to check out the Damned. I was impressed by them, thought they were good, especially Rat Scabies, the drummer. He's really got it…All the talk about Old Farts and Young Farts is nonsense, age doesn't matter."

DAMNED/EATER ....London, The Roxy

MANIACS................................London, The Brecknock

19th - Wednesday..

SLAUGHTER & THE DOGS have about fifty curious punks turn up downstairs at the Roxy to see their gig. This Manchester band are having difficulty getting accepted in the South because of the prevalent attitude of "there can't be real punks up North. Not like us." In any event, Slaughter & The Dogs have been playing for over a year and already have a shtick and songs to go with it. Instead of a dry ice machine, the Dogs simply use talc powder to make a billowy mess. They are tight and have many originals to toss into the set. Titles include "Where Have All The Boot Boys Gone," "Cranked Up Really High" and "Bitch." They also do a tasty version of the Velvets' "White Light, White Heat." Opening up for the Dogs were a new group from Devon called the Adverts. This is their second ever gig and it's apparent that they're still learning their instruments.

ULTRAVOX have their new single released by Island in the UK. The songs "Dangerous Rhythm" and "My Sex" were recorded with the help of BOTH Brian Eno and Steve Lillywhite. The tracks are John Foxx/Chris Cross originals.

THE NASHVILLE ROOM

Thursday January 20th Free
THE GORILLAS
Friday January 21st Free
KITES
(Ex Starry Eyed & Groundhogs)
+ Last Exit
Saturday January 22nd 61p
MOON
Sunday January 23rd 75p
Continuing their successful residence
ROOGALATOR
Monday January 24th Free
BEES MAKE HONEY
Tuesday January 25th 75p
CLOVER

CORNER CROMWELL ROAD/NORTH END ROAD, W14
(Adjacent West Kensington Tube   Tel 01 603 6071)

- Sting plays live in London as a member of Last Exit.

SLAUGHTER & THE DOGS/
SUBURBAN STUDS ....Swindon, The Affair
ADVERTS ....London, The Roxy

22nd - Saturday..............

THE JAM's recent performance at the 100 Club gets a favorable review from John Tobler. He described them as having, "…the outward trappings of a punk band, with guitarist/vocalist Paul Weller wearing a stiff standup collar of the Eton variety and drummer Rick Buckler wearing what appeared to be masochistic goggles as used by those under sunray lamps…their musical ability was considerably in advance of that displayed by most young bands that I've seen." He noted that their material revolved around several sources including the Who songbook "So Sad About Us," "Heatwave" and "Much Too Much." Another source was soul/mod favorites like "Sweet Soul Music," "Mustang Sally" and "Slow Down," but their real talent was writing their own songs. Originals like "In The City" and "Sounds Of The Street" were well received and characterized them as, "Exceedingly promising."

JOHNNY THUNDERS &
THE HEARTBREAKERS/
GENERATION X ....Middlesbrough, Rock Garden

BEARDED LADY/THE JAM ....London, The Marquee

JANUARY 1977

25th - Tuesday.....................................

THE RAMONES's newest album is out today following in that well-honed machine gun groove they tread so well. The album is called "The Ramones Leave Home" and titles include "Gimme Gimme Shock Treatment," "Suzy Is A Headbanger," "Pinhead," "Commando" and "You're Gonna Kill That Girl." The inclusion of "Carbona Not Glue" must relate to the glue sniffing incident in Scotland last August. These guys are crying to be animated; they're turning into a comic-cartoon-type band that just keeps getting funnier and funnier.

THE CLASH have just signed a worldwide deal with CBS Records. It's to be expected that there are rumblings in the underground that the Clash, the perceived last bastion of the political left have sold out to a major corporation. This despite the Pistols being on EMI and then A&M and the Stranglers being snapped up by U.A. They plan to have their debut single out inside of eight weeks.

TOM ROBINSON BAND ....London, The Stapelton   MANIACS................................London, Windsor Castle

27th - Thursday.....................................

PATTI SMITH was struck by tragedy in concert last Sunday night in Tampa Florida. In the middle of the band's seventh song ("Ain't It Strange"), she fell fifteen feet off the edge of the stage and broke the seventh vertebrae in her neck. As she was taken away by the ambulance, her musical future was uncertain. Now, she is recovering in her hospital room and told *NME's* Tony Parsons about her dramatic fall that left her in twenty-two stitches and a broken neck as well, "I went for a space that wasn't there…it was one of those things, I feel like a discus thrower when they spin out of the circle." Strange enough she's already talking about going out on the road. Her neck brace should be off in six to eight weeks and she's looking forward to getting out on the road again! "As you know we had to cut our last (UK) tour short…so this time, as soon as I'm better, we're gonna come back and play all the places we didn't get a chance to last time." She says that will be sometime in the spring, probably March. What about that third album, when will we see that? "In the spring. I'm writing now, writing all the time, songs and poems. It's all one thing with me…working on the book and the new album….It's gonna be a celebration of the whole new scene, the whole new wave…it's rock and roll." Patti also expressed her support for bands like the Sex Pistols and the Clash, but cautioned them to keep working so they grow and progress. "They've gotta always maintain that original energy if it's all gonna last...and it mustn't be a fad." She concluded with "I want to tell all the kids over there not to worry about my broken neck, not to think about me. Zero in on themselves, keep working on their playing and writing…and keep growing."

THE SNAKES finally have out a record, even though they're long defunct. They knocked around London pubs for literally years and now are nostalgically remembered on vinyl. The songs selected by Dynamite Records are two of the band's best covers. Side one is the Flaming Groovies' song, "Teenage Head," and the flip is a '57 style rocker by Jerry Byrne called "Lights Out." Nick Garvey handled the vocals and can now be heard as a member of the Motors. Snakes also featured Robert Gotobed, now a drummer with Wire.

VIBRATORS/OUTSIDERS/   TOM ROBINSON BAND...............London, The Brecknock
THE DRONES..........................London, The Roxy

28th - Friday.....................................

THE SEX PISTOLS' organization have come to a mutual agreement that they will leave EMI, with a buy-out of £50,000. The group was originally signed for £40,000, half of which was paid in advance and has since been used to fund their ill-fated "Anarchy Tour." The other half, plus an additional £10,000 brings the total £50,000. Ten thousand over their company guarantee at signing. Not bad for less than four month's work. Meanwhile, Malcolm is at the Midem Festival in Cannes trying to find a new home for the Pistols.

THE STRANGLERS make their vinyl debut with the United Artists single "Grip" b/w "London Lady." The tracks are both Stranglers' originals recorded at T. W. Studios in Fulham under the production of Martin Rushent. The band was formed around the core of Hugh Cornwell, Jet Black and Jean Jacques Burnell, who met in 1974 at college and formed the Guildford Stranglers after Cornwell had split his band Johnny Sox. In 1975 they were joined by Dave Greenfield on keyboards who gave the Stranglers their unique "dark carnival" sound. The band was signed to UA last month and are currently about to embark on an extensive six-week tour of the UK.

GENERATION X ....Liverpool, Eric's   LAST EXIT..............................Middlesbrough, The Rock Garden
CLASH ....London, Central Poly.

29th - Saturday.....................

THE BUZZCOCKS have their self-financed debut EP out today. It's titled "Spiral Scratch" and features the four songs the band recorded four weeks ago at Manchester's Indigo Studios. This is one of the first self-made records of this underground movement. They've had an initial pressing of 1,000 on their own New Hormones record label and they hope to be able to sell them all and repay the borrowed money from Pete's Dad, manager Richard Boone and Howard Devoto's friends. On the sleeve is a Polaroid photo taken by Richard Boone, of the four members crowding into frame on the steps of a statue in Manchester Picadilly. The initial pressing with its textured label and four tracks is a brave step for an independent band.

PENETRATION get a fantastic lucky break. After playing only four gigs, they've been selected to come to London to open for Generation X at the Roxy Club. The Newcastle-based group has been playing together for scant weeks, getting the idea to put together a band after seeing the Sex Pistols play in Manchester. Their "big break" was playing at the Middlesbrough Rock Garden last week. Recently Penetration lost their drummer and

buzzcocks

spiral scratch

JANUARY 1977

bassist but they've been replaced for tonight's gig. Among the band's set are songs like "VIP," "Duty Free Technology" and "Never." Penetration is now Gary Chaplin (19) on guitar, Pauline Murray (19) on vocals, Gary Smallman (17) on drums and Robert Blamire on bass. The group is hoping for the success that will allow them to leave behind their new 50 watt PA and Ferryhill rehearsal flat to enter the big time.

LIVE TONIGHT!

GENERATION X/
PENETRATION ....London, The Roxy

FABULOUS POODLES ....Manchester, Electric Ballroom

30th - Sunday...

GENERATION X earn a half page article in this weeks *New Musical Express*. Tony Parsons writes, "Generation X may well be the "punk rock" group that many people have been waiting for; songs with lyrics about change and revolution, but with melodies cute enough for "boy meets girl." His interview catches the band's dislike of drug culture. All except John Perfect were once members of Chelsea, but insist that Chelsea and Generation X are completely different bands. Titles likely to be heard if you catch Gen X are "New Orders," ""70s Problems," "Ready Steady Go," "London Life," "Youth Youth Youth" and "Your Generation."

THE STRANGLERS are having troubles with the Greater London Council over everything from stage dress (and undress), to language. They have gained such a reputation for this mischief that the GLC put certain protective measures in place to control any future events. Some members of the GLC Public Committee saw the Stranglers at the Croydon Red Deer and had restrictions written into their contract with the Rainbow, assuring that certain words "would not appear on their apparel or over the amplification." While opening up for Climax Blues Band, The Stranglers went over the edge with obscenity and the sound and stage lights were shut off two-thirds into their set. That incorrigible Hugh Cornwell refused to replace his naughty t-shirt. It showed the Ford logo but was misspelled to read Fuck. He came onstage with the logo on the back, was asked to remove it, he did and fifteen minutes later replaced it with the logo in the front. Then he was promptly shut down. The Rainbow is under the scrutinizing eye of the GLC since they are the first major venue to book "punk" bands.

CLIMAX BLUES BAND/
STRANGLERS ....London, The Rainbow Theatre

February 2nd - Wednesday.........................

PATTI SMITH is signed to Arista Records, but competitor Sire Records has managed to get the rights to release a Patti Smith rarity that predated Arista's contract. The lost classic is Smith's 1974 recording of "Piss Factory" and "Hey Joe." They've done it up in a special limited edition picture sleeve. The single features current Smith sidemen Richard Sohl and Lenny Kaye, as well as the added attraction of Television guitarist/vocalist Tom Verlaine.

THE SEX PISTOLS came up in an *NME* interview this week with Mick Jagger. He guardedly said, "I saw the Sex Pistols at the 100 Club and I thought they were pretty good. Well…not good, really, but…they could be." Word has it, that the Sex Pistols manager, Malcolm McLaren was within a whisper of signing the band with Warner Brothers Records when he upped the deal to a six figure sum and the bottom fell out.

THE JAM ....London, The Nashville

CLASH ....Swindon, The Affair

9th - Wednesday...

BLONDIE's label Private Stock Records is busy filling orders for the new debut LP. Cuts include "X-Offender," "In The Flesh," "Rip Her To Shreds" and "Attack Of The Giant Ants." There is even the slightest hint of West Side Story in "A Shark In Jets Clothing." As the LP jacket says, "Blondie hates fun, but they have so much of it that they decided it's time to unload the real meaning of fun on this LP." It was recorded at Radio City Music Hall in the same studio that was set up for Stravinski. Several in the music scene in New York still find it very funny that this most unlikely band are beginning to succeed where so many others have failed. Blondie, the band, are Debbie Harry, James Destri, Clement Burke, Gary Valentine and Chris Stein.

ONLY ONES ....London, The Speakeasy

11th - Friday...

STIFF RECORDS expands to becomes much more than just a mail-order, one-off record company. Stiff and Island Records have signed a pact giving Island a licensing deal for the independent label for all markets in the world, except the USA. This agreement runs for two years and will give Stiff the worldwide promotion and distribution they couldn't do on their own. Stiff will retain it's mail order business but under the new deal the eight singles previous to signing, Stiff BUY #1 - BUY #8, are all now deleted and will no longer be available after present stock is depleted. The first new released under this arrangement will be a new single and album by the Damned to be released in the next two weeks.

REZILLOS..............................Glasgow, Jordanhill College	VIBRATORS............................London, The Nashville	
THROBBING GRISTLE ....High Wycombe, The Nag's Head	MANIACS................................London, The Speakeasy	
GENERATION X ....London, Hope & Anchor		

12th - Saturday...

THE POLICE rent Pathway Studios in Islington to record their debut single, before they've ever played a single gig. The group is made up of former Curved Air drummer Stewart Copeland, guitarist Henry Padovani and Last Exit vocalist and bassist, Sting. They've been

FEBRUARY 1977

rehearsing in Copeland's Mayfair apartment studio for the last three weeks. Things are coming together very fast for this new band. Although Sting still has some commitments with The Last Exit, he plans to quit the group in the next week or so. His changing musical direction, combined with Last Exit's unwillingness to move to London is causing the rift. Today at the Pathway sessions the group records two of Stewart's songs, the first "Fall Out," strangely enough features Stewart, the drummer for the band, playing the guitar solo! The other song "Nothing Achieving" is credited to both Stewart and his brother Ian Copeland. The Police borrowed £150 from Paul Mulligan to pay for the time at this tiny eight track studio.

STRANGLERS ....Glasgow, Queen Margaret Union   SLAUGHTER & THE DOGS...........London, The Roxy

13th - Sunday...

FANZINES are multiplying like rabbits. This week's *NME* has Tony Parsons writing about the growing scene with fanzines in the UK. He concentrates on Deptford scribe Mark Perry, creator of *Sniffin' Glue*, a combination of gossip, reviews of gigs and records, photos and news. Other fanzines mentioned are *Ripped & Torn* (from Glasgow), *London's Burning* (predominantly Clash oriented), *Bondage* (written by Shane McGowan) and *I Wanna Be Your Dog* from Paris. Others are *Sideburns, 48 Thrills, Fishnet Stockings* and *Malheureusement* (printed entirely in French).

THE SEX PISTOLS must be considering getting rid of bassist Glen Matlock. Sid Vicious is not even an official Sex Pistol yet, but he still does a trans-Atlantic phone interview with Los Angeles disc jockey Rodney Bingenheimer, where he describes meeting a girl who "licked out toilet bowls." Sid was referring to Nancy Spungen, who had recently arrived in the UK on the heels of the Heartbreakers. It's unclear whether Sid is in the group or not. He was "auditioning" for the band last Friday, but Glen hasn't been let go. Sid thinks he's in, but is he? Malcolm is unavailable for comment because he's in Los Angeles to meet with Jerry Moss of A&M Records as well as some other US labels based in LA. There's also some talk about a Sex Pistols film. Sid is also sporting a new piece of jewelry that would become a trademark of sorts. It's a little lock with the letter "R" on it. It's chained to his neck and will remain there the rest of his life. It was a present to him from his friend Chrissie Hynde. It used to be the padlock that she used in her London squat.

14th - Monday...

B-52's have a most memorable Valentine's Day. At a crowded house party in Athens, Georgia, at the corner of Prince and Milledge, just across from the Taco Stand, there is an odd collection of musicians having a party. The five members are dressed in shaggy wigs, dreadful '60s fashions and loud colors. Prior to tonight's party, Ricky Wilson and Keith Strickland made a tape recording of guitar and drums to use as a backing to sing over. At the party, Ricky's sister, Cindy Wilson, sang while hiding behind the curtains during the haphazard set. Kate held things together and Fred brought along some of his toys and fronts the aggregation in a "B-52's" t-shirt. There are only six songs in their set, among them are originals like "Strobe Light," "Planet Claire," "Rock Lobster" and "Killer B's." It's still a two-year wait until the B-52's will have an album you can buy with these party classics.

DAMNED................................London, The Roxy

15th - Tuesday...

CHELSEA begin making a few appearances around town. Lead singer Gene October was shocked last November when the other three members of his band left to start Generation X. He's now pulled together a new group containing Bob Jessie on bass, Marty Stacy on guitar and Carey Fortune on drums. Some great new originals include "High Rise," "Curfew" and "Got To Go."

VIBRATORS ....London, Putney Railway Hotel   GOGMAGOG ....Swindon, Brunel Rooms

17th - Thursday...

THE SAINTS follow up the roaring success of their single "I'm Stranded" with an album under that very title. It was recorded in their native Australia and features "No Time," "Demolition Girl," "Nights In Venice," "Messin' With The Kid" as well as "I'm Stranded." The Saints are one of the forerunners of the buzzsaw sound from down under and at present are Chris Bailey on vocals, Ed Kuepper on lead guitar, Kym Bradshaw on bass and Ivor Hay on drums.

VIBRATORS ....London, Hope & Anchor

18th - Friday...

THE DAMNED release their debut LP for Stiff Records. They claim that this is the first "punk" album to be released. Most of the songs were written by Brian James, with the notable exception of "Fan Club," which is a re-written version of "1970" by the Stooges. The LP was recorded at Pathway studios in ten days. A great rumor circulating now is that the musical backing was recorded at 15 ips, speeded up to 20 ips and then the vocals were added on top. Could it be!? Initial copies were supposedly erroneously pressed with a picture of Eddie & The Hot Rods on the back, however this smacks of another marketing scheme from Stiff to drive early sales.

THE BUZZCOCKS are busy stocking copies of their record "Spiral Scratch" in area shops. Meanwhile, lead singer Howard Devoto is spending his time at college studies and has decided to quit the group. He told the *NME* that, "...the break is to do with the fact that I'm tired of noise and short of breath. I'm sick of having to address people out of breath and under my breath." He's given some thought to

FEBRUARY 1977

starting on his own projects. To fill the hole left by his departure, Steve Diggle switches to guitar as Garth Smith is brought in on bass.

VIBRATORS ....London, Southbank Poly.   DAMNED ....Scarborough, The Penthouse

21st - Monday.......................................

THE ADVERTS get some encouragement in the *NME*. A review read, "...there's a touch of West Cost in their sound, both on guitar and on Lorry Driver's jerky drum rock style. The Adverts are new and inexperienced, but like the Clash, are an original new voice on the scene." Some of the band's own material they're playing is "Bored Teenagers," "One Chord Wonders" and "Great British Mistake."

SNATCH are the front room duo of Patti Palladin and Judy Nylon. Their debut single on Bomp Records is just out. Although pressed in the US, it's available in the UK only. The tracks themselves were cut in 1976 in Patti's Maida Vale living room. The result of the demo session was a lengthy tape that Greg Shaw of Bomp offered to press anything from. The two songs "I.R.T." and "Stanley" are only part of this longer tape.

STRANGLERS ....Canterbury, Kent Univ.   DAMNED/ADVERTS ....London, The Roxy

22nd - Tuesday.......................................

THE HEARTBREAKERS are going into Essex Studios this week to work on four tracks they hope to turn into a single this spring. Tracks in the mix include "Let Go," "Chinese Rocks," "Born To Lose" and "All By Myself." They still haven't got a record company and will put out the EP themselves if necessary.

LIVE TONIGHT!

STRANGLERS/DAMNED/
COUNT BISHOPS ....Colchester, Essex Univ.   SLAUGHTER & THE DOGS ....Manchester, Charlton Oaks

23rd - Wednesday.......................................

THE DAMNED have been asked to open up for glam rocker Marc Bolan and T-Rex on his upcoming UK tour. This will be a tremendous break for the band throwing them in front of thousands of people this Spring. The tour starts on March 10th. Marc Bolan of T-Rex told the *NME*, "The Damned I like a lot. I was introduced to them because one of them had the good taste to wear a Marc Bolan t-shirt. Of those new bands who don't seem to be breaking out of their environment, I thought it'd be nice to have them on tour." Tragically this is Marc Bolan's last tour and will conclude on March 20th. He'll die in a car crash on September 16th.

SLAUGHTER & THE DOGS ....London, The Roxy

24th - Thursday.......................................

SIOUXSIE & THE BANSHEES open up for the Heartbreakers at the Red Deer in Croydon and barely have enough material to fill their twenty minute set. Songs they play include originals like "Captain Scarlet," "Love in A Void," "Psychic," "Scrapheap," and the T-Rex tune "20th Century Boy." This line-up of Siouxsie & The Banshees is not the same as the group that played the 100 Club gig in September. The membership since November '76 has been Siouxsie Sioux on vocals, Steven DeVille (a.k.a. Steve Severin, Steve Havoc) on bass, P.T. Fenton on guitar and Kenny Morris on drums.

WIRE are playing in public for the first time tonight as the opening band for the Jam. The setting is the tragically hip Roxy Club. They're rather frantic, pseudo-electronic madness.

THE LAST EXIT have their last-ever gig with Gordon "Sting" Sumner. While living in Newcastle, he's been in and out of groups such as Earthrise, The Phoenix Jazz Men (trad jazz band) and the Newcastle Big Band as far back as 1971. He had been with The Last Exit since 1974. Also in the group were keyboardist Gerry Richardson, guitarist Terry Ellis and drummer Ronnie Pearson. The group had released one single, "Whispering Voices" and "Evensong," on Wudwink Records and there was also a cassette-only album of nine songs. If you could find it, you'd hear Sting originals like "We Got Something," "Carrion Prince," "On This Train," "Oh My God," "Truth Kills" and "Savage Beast." Although the Last Exit had begun as a jazz band, their material had grown to more than seventy numbers and had been drifting into much more of a pop vein. Sting had been yearning to move to London and with the encouragement of his new bride, actress Frances Tomelty, they did. He encouraged the group to relocate to London, but half of them weren't prepared to move. Around the end of December, Sting had met Curved Air drummer Stewart Copeland in Newcastle. They've decided to start a new group. Tonight is the end of the old Sting, the beginning of the new.

JOHNNY THUNDERS &
THE HEARTBREAKERS/
SIOUXSIE & The BANSHEES.........Croydon, The Red Deer

JAM/REJECTS/WIRE.................London, The Roxy
LAST EXIT.............................London, The Red Cow
TOM ROBINSON BAND..............London, Rochester Castle

25th - Friday.......................................

THE JAM are the leading band in a small but energetic and growing mod clique. *NME's* Tony Parsons caught a live show at the Roxy last night and was very impressed. He's let down, though, that the crowd thinks it's uncool to like The Jam. He writes, "Three months ago it wasn't cool to say you liked the Damned. Now the black sheep of the new wave are The Jam. It makes me puke, that kind of bullshit is just as vacuous as peace signs and half hour guitar solos." Hip or not, Polydor Records announces that they've signed the group. They're the discovery of A&R man and sharp talent scout Chris Parry who have given the band £6,000 for their contract with Polydor. The contract covers four years with as many albums and their debut single will be "In The City," to be released in a few weeks. Before the group splits in October of '82, they will have placed twenty songs in the UK top forty, with half of those in the top ten and four songs going to #1.

FEBRUARY 1977

THE DAMNED have their second single released by Stiff Records in the UK. It's a three track EP with "Neat Neat Neat," "Stab Your Back" and "Singalong Scabies." This is the first of the Stiff releases to be packaged and printed by Island Records. If you look to the matrix of the record, you'll see the message "This is your Captain Squeaking" scratched in the vinyl. The "bonus" track "Singalong Scabies" is actually "Stab Your Back" played backwards. Whoopie.

ULTRAVOX! ....London, The Marquee

28th - Monday.................

SEX PISTOLS' manager Malcolm McLaren sends telegrams to the music papers in London to report bassist Glen Matlock has been ousted from the Sex Pistols. One of the more intriguing reasons was, "…he went on too long about Paul McCartney." His replacement is Sid Vicious, a one-time member of Siouxsie & the Banshees and a long time friend of Johnny's. Matlock disagrees with McLaren's telegram reasons. He told the *NME's* Tony Parsons, "It was mutual agreement. I wanted to leave and they wanted me out. In the beginning it was just mates playing rock and roll and then later all the business side came in and spoiled it." Matlock outlined his plans for the future, "I just wanna make my music, get a band together. Maybe we'll call it the Rich Kids - with my mate Jimmy Norton, who plays guitar and sings…and I want it to be good! There's too much dross coming through, ain't there?"

JOHNNY MOPED and his band open for the Damned at the Roxy. Johnny Moped and the Damned have a common past, sharing members back in 1975 in front room band called Rot. Tonight Johnny is joined onstage by Captain Sensible for some very funny numbers. The band's four piece line up of Fred Berk on drums, Dave Berk on bass and Johnny Moped on vocals is augmented by Xerexes on Saxophone and a guitarist called Sissy Bar that the *NME* describes, "…who looks like Jane Fonda meets Joan Jett." The guitarist is Chrissie Hynde, who has joined the group as a second guitarist for just a while. Then she's shuffled out of the group, out on her own again. She'll make it onto record doing backing vocals on Chris Spedding's new LP "Hurt," but even that is a really pretty anonymous affair. Listen for her on the tracks "Hurt," "Lone Rider" and "Wild In The Street."

DAMNED/JOHNNY MOPED ....London, The Roxy

March 1st - Tuesday.............................

CHERRY VANILLA & THE POLICE are starting their UK tour tonight at the Stowaway Club in Newport, Wales. She's been playing the New York circuit for some time. A hanger-on in the Warhol crowd, she writes and sings erotic songs and was once David Bowie's press agent. Cherry Vanilla (aka Kathy Dorritie) is on tour without record company support and was only able to bring along her guitarist on tour. Working with his brother's talent agency, Stewart Copeland managed to strike a deal to "loan" Cherry a drummer and a bassist to round out her band. This also means that the Police would open the show. By the way, this is the band's first gig ever and they have to play both sets! For their appearance they have £15 to split between the three of them. That's their normal salary for opening the show on this tour and playing backup to Cherry. What a beginning. Copeland's outfit will have their debut single on his brother's Illegal Record label later this month.

ULTRAVOX! has come a long way since they were playing the pubs as Tiger Lily two years ago. Island has just issued their LP "Ultravox!" The songs were produced by veterans Brian Eno and Steve Lillywhite in the autumn of last year. The all-original album shows the band to have developed into a modern equivalent of David Bowie, breaking new ground with synthesizers not normally heard in clubs like The Nashville or the Roxy. Featured on the disc is their last single as well as studio versions of live favorites like "Saturday Night In The City Of The Dead," "I Want To Be A Machine," "Wide Boys" and "My Sex." Ultravox! is Stevie Shears, Warren Cann, Billy Currie, Chris Cross and Dennis Leigh (aka John Foxx).

IGGY POP ....Aylesbury, Friar's
TOM ROBINSON BAND ....London, Kensington Hotel

JAM ....London, Putney Rail Hotel
CHERRY VANILLA/POLICE...........Newport, Stowaway Club

2nd - Wednesday..................................

THE RAMONES are in the middle of a record company battle over lyrics on their latest LP "Ramones Leave Home." The track "Carbona Not Glue," is about sniffing Carbona, a solvent that was a cheap teen high in the Ramones youth. The complaint from Tony Morris, Managing Director of Phonogram UK is, "…we cannot promote any product which extols the virtue of dope. As you know, we had correspondence with the Home Office about glue sniffing and Carbona is apparently available and even more dangerous than glue." On the other side, Ramones manager Danny Fields replied that, "You're entitled to your feelings about the use of drugs of any sort. But what you're attempting to do is set yourself up as judge and jury. This is censorship, a far greater evil than either Carbona or glue and something that in good conscience, I cannot be a party to." The record company's idea is to replace the track on the LP with another song, possibly an already available, non-LP flipside called "Babysitter." If not this, they'll simply leave the album stand at thirteen tracks. There are currently about 5,000 copies of the LP in the shops on both side of the Atlantic with the "offensive" track. Whatever anyone thinks of the controversy, they do have to deal with the fact that "Carbona" is a trademark name that was used without permission. Whether the song

MARCH 1977

encourages deviant behavior or not may not be the deciding issue.

LIVE TONIGHT!

JOHNNY THUNDERS & THE HEARTBREAKERS ....London, The Roxy	JAM ....London, The Red Cow
	DAMNED ....London, Tufnell Park Res. Hall

4th - Friday...

TELEVISION have probably waited longer than other band around today to get their shot at an album. The wait is over. The LP is called "Marquee Moon" and is new on Elektra. Television have been together in one form or another since 1971 and this is the first time (besides their self-financed single in 1975) that their fans can actually take their songs home with them. Unlike other bands in the underground scene, Television aren't afraid of a long song and they find ample excuse to stretch a melody over more than 2:10. On "Marquee Moon" there are only eight tracks. The majority are over five minutes and the title track runs on for nearly ten. The songs are all Verlaine originals and include "Elevation," "Prove It," "Torn Curtain" and "Venus." There is no remake of the single "Little Johnny Jewel."

BUZZCOCKS' lead vocalist Howard Devoto left the band and now they're being overrun with offers from prospective Buzzcocks singers. Among them are overtures from aspiring musician Rob Prefect, Pete Nichols (of the Distractions) and some strange calls from the Clash's manager Bernard Rhodes who wants to steal Pete Shelley away from the Buzzcocks, move him to London and start a new group with Keith Levine. All offers are being politely refused, Pete Shelley says "the position's already been filled." Pete will be the new vocalist.

IGGY POP................................Birmingham, Barbarella's	WAYNE COUNTY ....London, The Roxy
CHERRY VANILLA/THE POLICE .....High Wycombe, The Nag's Head	DAMNED ....London, City Poly.
VIBRATORS ....Liverpool, Eric's	TOM ROBINSON BAND...............London, N. London Poly.

6th - Sunday...

SQUEEZE receive a very favorable write up of their live performance on the 16th of last month opening up for the Pirates. The *NME's* Geoff Hill, described them as, "...five guys all around twenty-twenty one years with a New Wave look but without the amateurishness of a lot of other such outfits. They're tight and professional with a good thick furry, R&Bish sound." The line-up was listed as Glenn Tilbrook on "pretty nifty lead vocals," Chris Difford on "heavy rhythm," Julian Holland on "ching-ching piano," Harry Kakoulli on bass and the jovial Gilson Lavis on drums. Geoff Hill ended his piece with, "...go and see them and buzz jelly-babies at 'em, because they're starving right now, although I expect to see things looking up for them pretty soon."

CHERRY VANILLA/THE POLICE .....London, The Nashville	ULTRAVOX!............................London, The Red Cow

7th - Monday...

THE TALKING HEADS, that quirky New York trio that's been turning heads at CBGB's, has finally got a record out. It's a 45 of two David Byrne originals, "Love → A Building On Fire" and "New Feeling." The single was produced by Tony Bongiovi and Tommy Erdeyli (aka Tommy Ramone). The three Talking Heads are David Byrne on vocals and guitar, Chris Frantz on drums and Martina Weymouth on bass.

THE RAMONES' new single is safe, has nothing to do with sniffing glue and is guaranteed not to upset anyone. "I Remember You" doesn't tear along at 100 mph. It's actually a melodic, medium tempo, pop song that can be found on the band's troublesome second album, "Ramones Leave Home." It's backed with two live songs, "I Don't Wanna Walk Around With You" and a surfin' cover of the Riverias' "California Sun."

IGGY POP................................London, The Rainbow Theatre	

10th - Thursday...

THE SEX PISTOLS publicly sign their recording contract with A&M Records and are greeted with overwhelming indifference by the press. The ceremonies, designed to cause outrage, are held today just outside of Buckingham Palace, although the actual signing took place yesterday at Rondor Music. Today is the show for the press with a table set up just across the street from Buckingham Palace. The group arrived in a special limousine at 9am. They burst from the car, signed the papers, clowned around for the cameras and jumped back into the limo, whisked away just as the police caught on. Their next appearance was moments later at Regent Palace Hotel for a press conference. The press was itching for some more of "the foul mouthed yobs" but didn't get it. The band refused to play along with their game. Exercising his usual discretion, Malcolm was quick to tell the press that the band had been signed for a sum of £150,000. A&M boss Derek Green refused to confirm or deny this figure.

Their first single will be "No Future (God Save The Queen)" b/w "No Feeling." Manager Malcolm McLaren told the *NME*, "It's not a punk rock version of the National Anthem, but the boys own genuine tribute to the Queen." The single is to be rush-released by A&M and is planned for release on March 25th, in ample time for the Queen's Jubilee celebration. Jamie Reid is already at work on the picture sleeve which is supposed to feature the group in front of Buckingham Palace with the guards asking them for autographs. Other designs include defacing the Queen's official portrait with a safety pin and swastikas over her eyes. Whether the Sex Pistols will tour to support the new single is still uncertain. The Pistols are banned by local councils in almost every major city in the UK, Malcolm claims. Some European dates are being planned for late April and then in May they plan to record their first LP for A&M. If they are still unable to play in the UK by that time, they might leave the country and set up residence somewhere else where they can play.

EATER is one of England's youngest active punk bands and their debut single of "Outside View" b/w "You" is out today. The group is on Dave Goodman's label, "The Label." The band is Andy Blade, Brian Chevette, Ian Woodcock and Dee Generate.

CHERRY VANILLA/THE POLICE .....Liverpool, Eric's	COCKSPARRER ....London, The Brecknock

MARCH 1977

11th - Friday...

THE CLASH and their friends play at the Harlesden Coliseum tonight and tomorrow. The Coliseum is actually an established bingo parlor that has been "rescued for occasional gigs by upcoming bands." The concert is really a trial for the upcoming "White Riot" tour for the Clash. The Buzzcocks and Subway Sect are there, as are the Clash's proteges, the Slits, who are making their live debut. In name, the Slits are the obvious opposite to the Sex Pistols, although not opposite in sound. The "new" line-up of the Buzzcocks debuting has Pete Shelley cast as the new lead singer and recent addition Garth making his stage debut with the band. The Clash have some internal friction that comes to a head tonight and this is the last date that original Clash drummer Terry Chimes will play with the band. He's been sitting in with them as a favor until they found a replacement.

GENERATION X lead guitarist Bob Andrews, had to be taken to the hospital to have his head stitched up after being hit with a beer glass at tonights gig at Leicester University. Troublemakers, described as "Led Zeppelin heavies" were held responsible. Throughout the evening, the bands played through a hail of plastic cups, beer cans and spit. About halfway through Gen X's set, a full can hit Andrews in the head, covering him in blood and requiring immediate attention. Unfortunately, this violent behavior is becoming more frequent as rival music groups fight at gigs. Recent incidents of violence have included bands like the Stranglers, The Damned and the Sex Pistols.

CHERRY VANILLA/	FABULOUS POODLES	...............London, Middlesex Poly.
JOHNNY THUNDERS &	CLASH/THE BUZZCOCKS/	
THE HEARTBREAKERS ....Birmingham, Univ.	THE SLITS/ SUBWAY SECT..........London, Harlesden Coliseum	
JAM......................................Canterbury, Kent Univ.	DIVERSIONS ....London, The Rock Garden	
GENERATION X/THE BOYS ....Leichester, Univ.	T. REX/THE DAMNED................Manchester, The Apollo	

12th - Saturday..

THE HEARTBREAKERS sign a one-off record contract with Track Records. Thunders has played around the club scene in a number of underground bands since his days as a New York Doll.

THE SEX PISTOLS seem to have gotten in trouble again. It happened at the Speakeasy Club in London. *Old Grey Whistle Test* presenter Bob Harris was at the club with a band called Bandit. Sex Pistols friend John Wardle (aka Jah Wobble), approached Harris and asked why he doesn't play the Pistols on the TV show. He supposedly replied, "We don't want the Sex Pistols on the program. Does that answer your question?" The band Bandit got in a few comments and the insults were flying. Sid was pushed, he grabbed his glass and went after Harris, with the rest of the Pistols behind him. By the end, a beer glass was broken over the head of recording engineer George Nicholson, who was with Harris. Nicholson required fourteen stitches.

BUZZCOCKS............................Brighton, The Vault	GENERATION X/SLITS...............London, Harlesden Coliseum
STRANGLERS ....Liverpool, C.F. Mont College	DIVERSIONS ....London, The Rock Garden

14th - Monday..

THE TABLE has been signed by Virgin Records. They're a quartet from Cardiff founded by Russell Young and Tony Barnes. These two originally had a band in the early '70s called "John Stabber." This name was dropped in favor of "Do You Want A Table." This duo played and sent out demo tapes. In 1974, Do You Want A Table played its first ever gig at the Windsor Festival with equipment borrowed from Burlesque. Late last year, Virgin Records signed the duo, they shorted the name to The Table and Len Lewis and Micky O'Connor were recruited to fill out the band. The group don't see themselves as a "real" band. They have no gear, no intent to tour, no long term future in music. They just want to go into the studio and record great records whenever, wherever and however long it takes them. Virgin Records has offered the band no financial support but they have given them free studio time.

WAYNE COUNTY ....London, Dingwalls	WASPS ....London, The Lord Nelson
TOM ROBINSON BAND ....London, Fulham Greyhound	MANIACS..............................London, Upstairs At Ronnie Scott's

16th - Wednesday..

THE SEX PISTOLS' recent barfight, results in A&M Records receiving a letter from Bob Harris' attorneys. Harris' management also handles Peter Frampton, one of A&M's top acts. Derek Green, who had signed the Pistols with some reservations, saw that this was a potentially dangerous situation. He felt that the violence that surrounded the group was far more than just posturing, it was real and could hurt A&M's reputation. After a phone call to Jerry Moss (the "M" in A&M Records) Derek Green decided that having the Sex Pistols on the label was not a good thing. It was confirmed by a follow up call from Herb Alpert (the "A" in A&M), who stood by Green's decision. This brief statement was drawn up. "A&M Records wishes to announce that its recording agreement with the Sex Pistols has been cancelled with immediate effect. The company therefore will not be releasing any product from the group and has no further association with them. Production of their single "God Save The Queen," which had been tentatively scheduled for release later this month, has been cancelled." Less than a week after signing their second recording contract, the Sex Pistols are without a label. The reasons were never fully stated as to why this happened at all. There were some unconfirmed reports, however, of the band returning to the A&M offices after last week's Buckingham Palace signing and destroying property as well as assaulting members of the A&M staff. Also the incident with Bob Harris. A&M managing directors have also reportedly received numerous complaints from artists on their label

GOD SAVE THE QUEEN
(Cook/Matlock/Rotten/Jones)

Original sound recording made by A & M Records Ltd.

Time 3.20

AMS 7284

SIDE 1
45 RPM

AMS 7284A*
P 1977 A & M Records Ltd.

Copyright Control

SEX PISTOLS
Produced by Chris Thomas

MARCH 1977

including harsh letters from Rick Wakeman, Karen Carpenter and Peter Frampton. Malcolm McLaren again negotiated a settlement to soothe their wounds. This time it was for half of their advance payment, a cool £75,000 for producing nothing with less than a week's work. Looking back, the Sex Pistols have amassed £125,000 in a few months, only playing a handful of gigs and just being themselves around their label and the press. There's little hope that another record company will take on the Pistols until their behavior can come under check. In the few days since the signing of the band last week, 25,000 copies of their next single "God Save The Queen (No Future)" were pressed up and boxed for shipment. These singles have now been sent to the scrap heap to be re-melted into a safer product. Some, however have leaked out.

LIVE TONIGHT!

BOYS	London, The Roxy	STRANGLERS	Swindon, The Affair
JAM	London, The Red Cow		

18th - Friday...........................

THE RAMONES' album "Leave Home" has been re-released with the song "Carbona Not Glue" dropped from the LP because it was a violation of the copyrighted name "Carbona." It's being replaced with another new Ramones track "Sheena Is A Punk Rocker." The Ramones were not pleased with what they felt was "censorship" and "over reaction."

THE CLASH release their debut single "White Riot." It was inspired by the Notting Hill Carnival riots (Sep. 1, 1976) and photos from those riots are used as backdrops for their live dates. The flip side is "1977." Despite the first impression created by the title and feel of the record the band rebels against the notion they're part of a new movement. Mick Jones of the Clash told the *NME*, "It ain't punk, it ain't new wave, it's the next logical progression for groups to move in. Call it what you want - all the terms stink. Just call it rock and roll."

REZILLOS	Glasgow, Queen's College	JAM	London, Southbank Poly.
TOM ROBINSON BAND	London, College of Art & Design	T. REX/THE DAMNED	London, Rainbow Theatre

23rd - Wednesday...........................

THE MODELS are a group put together by former Siouxsie & The Banshee guitarist Marco Pirroni, Cliff Fox, Mick Allen and Terry Day (aka Terry Lee Miall). They got together in October of last year after Marco left Siouxsie & The Banshees. After only two gigs at the Roxy under the name The Beastly Cads, they've changed their name to The Models. Marco will become an important part of Adam & The Ants early in 1980 and help create the new sound that takes Adam's career out of the pubs and into the large arenas. He'll stay a part of Adam's group for over a decade.

JOHN DOWIE	Birmingham, Repertory Theatre	JAM	London, The Roxy

25th - Friday...........................

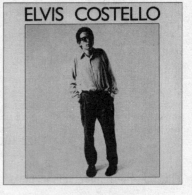

ELVIS COSTELLO makes his debut on Stiff Records with a single of "Less Than Zero" and "Radio Sweetheart." The sessions were produced by Nick Lowe and are recorded in "reasonable stereo." Reading the matrix on the records you'll find "Elvis Is King" and "Elvis Is King on this side too." *NME's* Charles Shaar Murray comments that it's a "great record. Doesn't have a snowball's chance in hell. What a bleedin' shame." Elvis is no newcomer to the music business. He is the son of former Joe Loss band singer Ross McManus. His grandfather was also in music going back to the turn of the century.

FANZINES are becoming more and more plentiful in market stalls, underground shops and clothiers. Among the latest crop are Paul Morley's *Out There, Au Contraire, Panache* and *Penetration*. There's also the *Aylesbury Roxette, New Wave Magazine, Cells, Buzz, Situation 3, Ripped and Torn, Out Now, Flicks, Ad Libs* and the Irish *Scene*. Prices range from the rare free fanzine to the average 10p-30p variety. One time bank clerk Mark Perry, who many credit with starting the fanzine revival, has decided to stop printing his long standing sheet *Sniffin' Glue*. The circulation for the fanzine has grown to more than 10,000 and it requires more of his time than is available. Perry wants give his group Alternative Television his full energies.

JOHN DOWIE	Birmingham, Repertory Theatre	ULTRAVOX!	London, The Marquee
THE JAM	London, Royal College Of Art		

28th - Monday...........................

THE SEX PISTOLS' first live concert of 1977, is a hastily set up event by Malcolm McLaren, who is organizing it so that NBC News can get some live footage for a documentary they're filming. After the firings from both EMI and A&M and the scandalous headlines, he was having a very difficult time getting a space for them to play. Nobody would have them. In a very strange turn of events, Malcolm has gotten permission from area Roman Catholic priests for the band to play at Leicester Square's Notre Dame Hall in London with only a few hours notice. Word of mouth spread the news and by 5:30 there were hundreds of people waiting outside, only 150 of which were let in. This is the first time that Sid has played publicly with the band and he's not shy at all. Johnny told the *NME*, "We're against bureaucracy, hypocrisy and anything else that ends in 'Y.'"

THE TALKING HEADS, originally a three-piece from the Rochester College of Design in New York, have added a fourth member to their ranks. The newest head is Jerry Harrison from Boston, formerly with the Modern Lovers. This brings the head count to four and Harrison is being quickly worked into the group, giving lead singer David Byrne more time to concentrate on singing. David told the *NME*, "At first

MARCH 1977

people said we were real intellectual and only smarties would like us - but then all these kids came along and liked us and that proves they were wrong!"

JOHNNY THUNDERS &
THE HEARTBREAKERS ....London, The Marquee

30th - Wednesday.....................................

STIFF RECORDS has its second album out this week in the UK. It's a compilation album titled "A Bunch Of Stiffs." It is also subtitled with true stiff humor, "Undertakers to the industry, if they're dead - we'll sign 'em." The LP features tracks by Stiff artists as well as a few guest appearances. Side one starts off with a song penned by the mysterious Lowe/Profile. Inside info has it that Mr. Profile and Mr. Riveria are one in the same. The track is performed convincingly by Nick Lowe and bears the heartfelt title "I Love My Label." A fitting beginning and touching tribute. Track two is a new Stiff signing (October of last year) named Wreckless Eric (aka Eric Goulden). He debuts on the label with "Whole Wide World." Elvis Costello is here with a different mix of his new single "Less Than Zero." Other tracks are by Motorhead, Magic Michael and an uncredited, unlabeled bonus track of "Back To Schooldays" by Graham Parker & The Rumour. The track is part of the band's first demo sessions recorded at the Hope & Anchor. It was first aired on Charlie Gillett's Honky Tonk program and is a different, earlier version than that on Parker's "Howling Wind" LP Phonogram released in April of 76. Since Stiff headmaster is Dave Robinson, who also manages Parker, perhaps its inclusion isn't much of a surprise. Side two features Stones Masonry, Jill Read, Dave Edmunds and The Tyla Gang. This album is admittedly a rather jumbled collection of demos, finished tracks and outtakes, but it's still a great collection of songs from some rather creative people. The ads say that "the first million are to be pressed with an attractive black vinyl finish, the second million will be pressed in gold."

XTC ....Aylesbury, Friar's	GENERATION X.......................Plymouth, Woods Leisure Ctr
THE JAM ....London, The Red Cow	ULTRAVOX!.............................Swindon, The Affair
DAMNED/JOHNNY MOPED...........London, Royal College Of Art	

31st - Thursday.....................................

EDDIE & THE HOT RODS have their fifth single released, the first of their new records for1977. It's two brand new tracks; "I Might Be Lying" b/w "Ignore Them (Always Crashing The Same Bar)." The first 10,000 are in a special picture sleeve. (Aren't they all?)

THE SEX PISTOLS are off on "holiday" in Berlin. They had tried to go to the Jersey Island, but were hassled so much while there that Malcolm has sent them on to Berlin. They're based at the Hotel Kapinsky and have hired a VW bus to tour around town in, specifically buzzing around the Berlin wall. The experience would be written into the song "Holiday In The Sun."

HOWARD DEVOTO begins working with John McGeoch on a few songs on the side. They begin discussing the possibility of a band quite different from Howard's frantic past life in the Buzzcocks. It's the begining of a new band that will blossom under the name Magazine.

GENERATION X ....London, The Marquee	THE JAM ....London, Rochester Castle
JOHNNY THUNDERS &	DAMNED/JOHNNY MOPED ....London, The Roxy
THE HEARTBREAKERS ....London, Dingwalls	

LIVE TONIGHT!

April 3rd - Sunday.....................................

THE SEX PISTOLS are back in town and showcasing in front of about 350 people at the Screen On The Green. Opening the show are the Slits and a pre-Pistols short film called *Number 1*. The twenty-five minute film is a pastiche of live footage and TV press reports and interviews. It's all cut together in chronological order and is a wonderful propaganda piece. The lights dim and after a false start, on come Rotten & Co., Johnny bedecked in his best velvet bowtie. Some of the older cover tunes are trashed and in their place are new originals. There's the should-have-been A&M single "God Save The Queen," a new rant titled "EMI," as well as "Submission," "No Feelings" and "Out Of View."

SEX PISTOLS/SLITS ....London, Screen on the Green	ULTRAVOX!............................Sheffield, Top Rank
CHERRY VANILLA/THE POLICE .....London, The Nashville	

5th - Tuesday.....................................

THE SEX PISTOLS' manager Malcolm McLaren gets a call from CBS Records to tell him they're no longer interested in the Sex Pistols. There is still lingering interest however, in France from Barclay Records and Richard Branson at Virgin is calling asking for a meeting. Just as the Sex Pistols are getting on their feet and playing, Sid gets himself in trouble that will curtail any live appearances for the next few weeks. After the last live show, Sid scored some heroin and a good case of hepatitis, sending him to the hospital.

48 HOURS are a Northampton group that are playing the first London gig. They're onstage tonight at the Nashville, opening up for The Jam. The group got together in December of last year, yet are already looking to put out a single to attract the attention of the major labels. The group is fronted by twenty-seven year old Nick Cash who was a former member of Ian Dury's group Kilburn & The High Roads. He left the Kilburns in the summer of '75. That wasn't his only band experience though. Prior to the Kilburns he began in the Pentagon Beat Group, was part of Graduate and just prior to joining the Kilburns in '71, was in the tantalizingly named Frosty Jodhpur. Nick lead the group on guitar and vocals, along with Pablo LaBritian on drums, John Watson on bass and Guy Days on guitar. The group won't find any success coming their way until they change their name to 999.

CHERRY VANILLA/THE POLICE .....Birmingham, Barbarella's	ADVERTS...............................London, Dingwalls
THE JAM/48 HOURS ....London, The Nashville	

APRIL 1977

7th - Thursday...

THE CLASH take an important step in their career with the release of their debut album "The Clash." Although they signed a worldwide deal, the American counterpart to CBS has refused to issue the album in the states. Feeling that it was to crudely produced and wouldn't sell. In retrospect, the import will eventually sell almost 100,000 copies before its US release. Titles include "White Riot," "I'm So Bored With The U.S.A.," "Hate & War," "London's Burning," "Cheat" and "Police & Thieves." The album's fourteen tracks capture most of the band's best songs from the live shows and is generally well praised in the music press. The photo on the front cover shows only three members of the group. That's because their drummer Terry Chimes (listed as Tory Crimes on the jacket) quit the group last year, and is only sitting in for the album sessions. They're still looking for a suitable replacement.

KRAFTWERK have their follow-up to "Radio-Activity" released this day. It's called "Trans-Europe Express" which the band describes as the electronic interpretation of the "metal and rhythms of the railway." Among the new tracks on the LP are "Showroom Dummies," "Franz Schubert," "Hall Of Mirrors," "Europe Endless," and the title track "Trans-Europe Express."

THE TABLE are awarded "Single of the week" status in the *NME* for their frantically up tempo "Do The Standing Still." A nifty photo sleeve pictures the band leering about in the ladies undergarments section of Marks & Spencer. This trio was signed to a one-off deal with Virgin but with a start like this they might go far. The single is flipped with "Magical Melon Of The Tropics."

WAYNE COUNTY ....Croydon, The Red Deer	ADVERTS ....London, Adam & Eve

9th - Saturday...............

THE CLASH offer up a unique freebie for readers of the *NME*. If there is a red sticker attached to the inner sleeve of your Clash LP, (and there's only 10,000 of those!), take out the sticker and clip out the *NME* coupon and send it in for a free record from the Clash. The interview on the 45 was conducted by Tony Parson on the tube with a tape deck on Joe's lap so the sound is a little muddy. On it you'll hear Joe Strummer and Mick Jones talk about various things. Here's what Joe had to say about seeing the Sex Pistols for the first time. "When I saw the Pistols, I suddenly realized that I wasn't alone in the fact that I couldn't play too well. I was in a group where all the people could play quite well and I felt inferior, and when I saw the Pistols I thought it was great. It just suddenly stuck me that it didn't have to matter that much." Over the top of the spoken bit is an instrumental they call "Listen" that makes the conversation even more unlistenable. Also on the 45 is a new song called "Capitol Radio." It won't be out in any form for two years, and this version won't officially be released until 1980's "Black Market Clash."

CLASH OFFER -FREE E.P.

THE DAMNED become the first of the British New Wave acts to tackle the American public. They're in the midst of a series of four headline nights at NY's CBGB's club. From there they will continue to Philadelphia, Long Island and Cleveland. Upon arriving at their New York hotel, they found that a package of "goodies" had been left for them by the Rolling Stones. The care package included seven meringue pies, a birthday cake and other funmakers, plus a trio of prostitutes to give any needed other comforts.

CHERRY VANILLA/	THE JAM ....London, Rochester Castle
THE POLICE ....London, The Nashville	VIBRATORS ....Manchester, Electric Circus

11th - Monday...

EASY CURE guitarist Robert Smith has torn out an advert he saw in the music paper he thinks is their possible ticket to riches. The ad features two rock bimbettes and the headline "Wanna Be A Recording Star?" It continued "Get Your Ass Up - Take Your Chance! Germany's leading pop label brought you Boney M and Donna Summer. Top recording studios, only experienced groups, singer/songwriters age fifteen-thirty should apply." They were hooked. Somebody out there would listen to their music. A tape was recorded in the dining room of Robert's parent's house and a photo was taken. The package to Hansa was on its way! Easy Cure is Robert Smith and Porl Thompson on guitar, Lol Tolhurst on drums, Michael Dempsey on bass and vocalist Peter O'Toole.

STRANGLERS ....Brighton, The Buccaneer	JOHN CALE/THE CLASH/
	SUBWAY SECT/THE BOYS ....London, The Roundhouse

12th - Tuesday...

THE BOYS are the latest signing to NEMS Records and are experts in up tempo power pop. Their debut single is "I Don't Care" b/w "Soda Pressing." It comes in a simple, cheaply produced one sided picture sleeve. The Boys were formed around members Casino Steel (ex-Hollywood Brats) and "Honest" John Plain (ex-London SS drummer, now a guitarist). The song writing team has been together since last June and since then they found members Matt Dangerfield on guitar and lead vocals, Duncan "Kid" Reid on bass and Jack Black on drums. The sound of the band is a variety of revved-up power pop.

THE VIBRATORS have switched labels, from RAK to CBS. Their situation with RAK was on a one-at-a-time basis and the new contract includes plans for singles and several albums. They've already begun recording in preparation for their first single. Among the already recorded tracks are "Bad Time," "Sweet, Sweet Heart," "Wrecked On You," "Petrol" and "No Heart."

APRIL 1977

LIVE TONIGHT!

ULTRAVOX! ....Brighton, The Top Rank	THE JAM ....London, The Nashville
WAYNE COUNTY ....London, Putney Railway Hotel	

14th - Thursday.......................................

XTC's gig at the Rochester Castle tonight is reviewed in *Sounds* by writer Chas De Whalley. "It's only the bands third trip to London (as XTC) and they're already beginning to draw a crowd. 'XTC R NRG' is the slogan they're using and it fits." The gig is marred by their keyboards breaking down, forcing the quartet to play the evening as a trio. "We had to play all the dumb stuff" claimed Andy Partridge. Among the "dumb stuff" was "1967 (She's So Square)," "Star Park," "Refrigeration Blues," "Science Friction" and "Neon Shuffle." De Whalley described them as being, "…like Television without the improvisation, or Be Bop Deluxe without the flatulence. Sinewy guitar from Partridge and throw-away cool corner vocals, a pounding, pummeling bass and a drummer who didn't make too many mistakes I noticed.. XTC have been kicked out of their West Country lethargy by the power of punk rock. Once they get that organ working properly they could be going places."

SAD CAFE/BUZZCOCKS...............Blackburn, The Golden Palms	XTC.......................................London, Rochester Castle

15th - Friday.......................................

THE STRANGLERS have their first album "Ratus Norvegicus" released by United Artists in the UK. It was originally titled "Dead On Arrival" but was changed to the proper Latin name of the Norwegian Rat, a huge bit of vermin. Tracks on the album are all originals with alluring titles like "Goodbye Toulouse," "London Lady," "Princess Of The Street," "Peaches," "Ugly" and the four part, eight minute mini-epic "Down In The Sewer." The album cover photograph features all four members of the band, with a fifth "man in black" in the background looking away from the camera. The Stranglers are touring extensively to support the LP and will play at the London Roundhouse, their only major London gig on Sunday. The first 15,000 will also include a free single of "Peasant In The Big Shitty" and "Choosey Susie."

ONLY ONES ....High Wycombe, The Nags Head	ULTRAVOX!.............................London, The Marquee

22nd - Friday.......................................

THE ADVERTS have their debut single released by Stiff Records. It's "One Chord Wonders" b/w "Quick Step." The band is T.V. Smith, Gaye Advert, Lorry Driver and Howard Pick-Up. Most of the band hails from Devon.

THE SAINTS are Australia's answer to the new wave. They follow their single "I'm Stranded" with "Erotic Neurotic" and "One Way Street." Both songs are from the band's debut album from two months ago.

THE RADIATORS FROM SPACE & SKREWDRIVER are two of the new bands that were discovered by Ted Carroll for Chiswick Records. He told *Music Week*, "There are more major record company A&R men than punters in the Roxy Club these days and the general vibe is if it moves and has a guitar 'round its neck - sign it!" His latest acquisitions are gathered from far outside London. From Dublin he's gotten the Radiators From Space (formerly called Greta Garbage & The Trash Cans) and a Blackpool group called Skrewdriver. Both will have singles out shortly.

EASY CURE.............................Crawley, St. Edward's Hall	THE JAM ....London, Poly.
SQUEEZE ....Dudley, JB's	JOHN CALE/COUNT BISHOPS/
SLAUGHTER & THE DOGS ....London, The Roxy	BOYS...................................Manchester, Free Trade Hall
S.A.L.T./WASPS ....London, The Marquee	

23rd - Saturday.......................................

DESPERATE BICYCLES are strictly D.I.Y. (Do It Yourself). The band was formed in March of this year "specifically for the purpose of recording and releasing a single on their own label. They booked a studio in Dalson for three hours and with a lot of courage and a little rehearsal they recorded "Smokescreen" and "Handlebars." Total cost of the studio, single and printing was £153. They cut the tracks back in April and the wait's finally over. It's released on their own Refill Records label. It is such a budget operation that the sleeve is a monochrome of a Bicycle Wheel printed on one side only; the single has only one printed label on one side only and the two tracks on the "A" side are repeated on the flip. "Smokescreen…leaps at the throat," as the band put it. There is a limited edition of 500 copies, with the potential of being re-pressed if it sells. At this recording, the Desperate Bicycles are Danny Wigley on vocals, Nicky Stephens on keyboards, Roger on bass, plus an unnamed guitarist and drummer. They call themselves the "Desperate" Bicycles because they're desperate for equipment. Besides the keyboards and bass, they have to depend on what the studio has lying about.

SIOUXSIE & BANSHEES are onstage at the The Roxy Club, oblivious to the fact that the Roxy is in trouble. In setting up the Roxy, manager Andy Czezowski agreed to the appallingly large sum of £25,000 a year to lease the club. He's not been paying the piper and the music's about to stop. The owner of the club has him physically thrown out the front door. Andy's involvement with the club is at an end. Meanwhile, a group of Hornsey Art College students are in the audience to see Siouxsie & The Banshees. The show inspires them to start a new band they call The Ants. They're led by Stuart Goddard and have been already been playing as the B-Sides.

JOHN CALE/COUNT BISHOPS/	SIOUXSIE & THE BANSHEES/
BOYS ....Birmingham, Barbarella's	THE VIOLATORS ....London, The Roxy
JAM/STUKAS...........................London, The Marquee	

APRIL 1977

25th - Monday..

RADIATORS FROM SPACE have their debut single out this week on Ted Carrol's Chiswick Record label. It's a 100mph thrash called "Television Screen," b/w "Love Detective." The group was discovered in Dublin by entrepreneur Carrol on one of his record excursions. The Radiators From Space are Steven Rapid on vocals, Philip Chevron and Peter Holidai on guitar, Mark Megaray on bass and James Crash on drums. This single marks Chiswick's tenth release as a new independent label and it's first of the new "punk" bands.

THE JAM & THE ADVERTS have both been invited to record a BBC session and are in the studio tonight. The Jam are recording versions of songs that will be on their debut album to be released next month. The four tracks are "In The City," "Art School," "I've Changed My Address," and a new song that's not on their forthcoming LP, "This Is The Modern World." It's rough mod sounds, driven by the attitude that Paul Weller displayed when he told the *NME*, "You can't play rock and roll with a beer gut."

The Adverts are recording new BBC versions of their Stiff single "One Chord Wonders" and "Quickstep," as well as new songs they've never recorded before called "Gary Gilmore's Eyes," "Bored Teenagers" and "New Boys."

27th - Wednesday...

THE CLASH are on the bill in Paris for what is called "Nuites de Punk." They've brought along their favorite opening act, The Subway Sect, who have improved over their earlier performances, but still can't approach their mentor's skills. The Clash's loss of drummer and charter member of the band, Terry Chimes, last month has forced them to find a drummer. After auditioning over 200 drummers, Nicky "Topper" Headon is filling in until a decision about a permanent replacement is reached. Tonight in Paris the Clash put on a furious show beginning with "London's Burning," proceeding through "1977," Toots' and the Maytals' song "Pressure Drop" and Junior Murvin's "Police & Thieves." They play almost everything from the new LP, ending with "Janie Jones," "Garageland" and a reprise of "White Riot."

EATER	London, Dingwalls	ONLY ONES	London, The Speakeasy
LOU REED	London, New Victoria Theatre		

29th - Friday..

THE JAM have their first single released by Polydor Records. They're a trio consisting of Paul Weller, Richard Buckler and Bruce Foxton from the town of Woking. The band is a dream come true for Weller. As a student back in 1973 he was awarded a prize for having the best local group. The single is two Jam originals "In The City" and "Taking My Love." The single will do moderately well in the charts, climbing up to #40, beginning a long lasting relatinship between the Jam and chart positions in the UK, where they will turn into one of England's biggest acts of the early '80s. Almost as significant, they spearhead the "mod scene," a revival or sorts of the revved up '60s UK soul inspired scene represented by the early Who. Unlike the punks they share bills with, the mod bands dress in neat suits, skinny black ties and short, neat haircuts.

BLONDIE have their single of "In The Flesh" b/w "Man Overboard" released on Private Stock Records. It's Blondie's second single and both tracks are from their debut album issued just three months ago.

WAYNE COUNTY is the former Max's Kansas City DJ who has turned flamboyant performer. He's decided to tone down his ribald act and drop what his press office calls "camp theatrical excesses." That means he won't be coming out in drag and making it with a microphone. His backing band is Greg Van Cook on guitar, Val Haller on bass and John J. Johnson on drums. They will now be performing under the collective banner "Wayne County and The Electric Chairs." Their debut as the "new" Wayne County is tonight at the London Hope & Anchor. This renouncement of style will in no way be reflected in the music however. Wayne County must be himself after all.

JAM/TYLA GANG/		FABULOUS POODLES/XTC	London, The Marquee
CIMMARONS	London, Royal College Of Art	CHELSEA/	
VIBRATORS	London, The Nashville	WAYNE COUNTY &	
PREFECTS	London, The Roxy	THE ELECTRIC CHAIRS	London, Hope & Anchor

30th - Saturday..

JUNGLELAND is a new fanzine that has sprung from the typewriters and xerox machines of Ayr, Scotland. The writer is eighteen year-old Mike Scott, a frequently frustrated musician who has fronted his own band Karma with friend John Caldwell for the last three years. Groups covered in the sheet include The Sex Pistols, The Clash, as well as Patti Smith, The Beach Boys, John Lennon and Bruce Springsteen. Mike Scott will tramp through a succession of bands before putting together the Waterboys in the early '80s.

GANG OF FOUR is a new group coming together in Kent. The name came from the group of people who ruled China after Mao's death. The name was suggested to them by Andy Corigan of the Mekons. They all met at Leeds University and are basing themselves there. Vocalist Jon King and guitarist Andy Gill had been in bands previously while still living in Seven Oaks. When moving to Leeds University they started the Gang Of Four with Hugo Burnam on drums and a "hippy bassist."

BUZZCOCKS/XTC	London, The Roxy	VIBRATORS	Southampton, Univ.

May 5th - Thursday...

ADAM ANT debuts his new band The Ants in a Muswell Hill front room. The Ants are Adam Ant, vocals and guitar, Andy Warren on bass, Paul Flanagan on drums and Lester Square on guitar as well. Ant Music for Sex People is still far in the future at this point. Instead of a pirate look, you're more likely to see Adam in leather bondage wear and eyeliner.

MAY 1977

THE CLASH play at Eric's in Liverpool. In the crowd, Pete Wylie meets a lad named Julian Cope dancing in front of him. They find that they have common interests in music and Pete introduces Julian to another friend of his, Ian McCulloch. The three decide to start their own band. This is the very moment that becomes the genesis for the bands Echo & The Bunnymen and the Teardrop Explodes, but even those two bands are still two years down the road.

EASY CURE guitarist Robert Smith receives a brief telegram from Hansa Records in London. It's from Kathy Prichard and simply states "Please Call Hansa Records Urgently." It's the stuff dreams are made of. Robert calls the number given and sets up an audition for the band on the 13th.

LIVE TONIGHT!

BUZZCOCKS	Birmingham, Rebecca's	JAM	Manchester, Chorlton Oaks
CLASH	Liverpool, Eric's		

6th - Friday.....................

THE STRANGLERS are grinning ear to ear. Their debut album has been selling faster than they ever could have imagined and is now the fourth best selling album in the United Kingdom. That puts the band in the company of Abba with "Arrival," "The Shadows 20 Golden Greats" and "Hotel California" by the Eagles. A position like that reflects over 30,000 albums have been sold in about three weeks. That's the level of success that Led Zeppelin and Elton John aspire to. The album's impetus will be aided by issuing a new single today, "Peaches" b/w "Go Buddy Go." The flipside was one of the many songs left over from the prolific sessions in January and not included on the LP.

THE JAM's debut album "In The City" is released on Polydor in the UK today. It's an even dozen tracks, ten of which are compositions by lead singer/guitarist Paul Weller. The only two covers are Larry Williams 1950s classic "Slow Down," and the theme from "Batman." Other tracks reflect the band's respect for being British, yet desire that people react to disagreeable situations. They're very much against apathy. The album was recorded in only eleven days at Polydor's Stratford Place studios. Tracks include "Art School," "Away From The Numbers," "Sounds From The Street," "Taking My Love," and the title track "In The City." Next month the band plan to start their first UK tour as the headlining act.

THE BOOMTOWN RATS play their first English concert at Studio 51, for a select crowd of Phonogram Records employees. They've just signed the band after a battle with five other labels. The band was very particular about their deal, taking greater care in selecting a record company than most other bands. Tonight is the first night they begin their assault on England. What are the band's greater goals? Bob Geldof said, "We are in this to get rich, to get famous and to get laid."

BIG IN JAPAN are a direct result of last night's concert in Liverpool by the Clash. Loads of kids in the audience are talking about putting together bands and doing it themselves. One trio of Merseyside lads start a band they call Big In Japan. The three are Kevin Ward on bass, Phil Allen on drums and Bill Drummond on guitar.

EASY CURE	Crawley, The Rocket	TOM ROBINSON BAND	London, Central London Poly.
WAYNE COUNTY &		SLAUGHTER & THE DOGS/	
THE ELECTRIC CHAIRS	Liverpool, Eric's	ED BANGER/THE DRONES	London, Royal College Of Art
48 HOURS	London, The Roxy		

8th - Sunday.....................

THE SEX PISTOLS are mentioned in London Weekend Television's *The London Programme* when an interviewer suggests there is a connection between the National Front movement and the Sex Pistols. Band manager Malcolm McLaren made a public reply to the statement public in the *NME* stating, "The Sex Pistols are not into ANY political party, least of all the loathsome National Front. I think it is extraordinarily irresponsible and dumb to give that scummy organization a load of free publicity by connecting them with us (The Sex Pistols)...Anarchy is not fascism but self rule and a belief in following one's own way of life without recourse to any form of dictatorship of nationalism. We hate this kind of army nonsense."

THE CRUCIAL THREE are Julian Cope, Ian McCulloch and Pete Wylie. The new trio is at Pete's house to begin practicing. They endlessly run through a nearly all-instrumental version of Lou Reed's "Waiting For The Man" with Ian singing under his breath because he was so embarrassed with his voice. The trio is soon turned into a quartet with the addition of Stephen Spence on drums.

XTC looks like they're on the fast track to getting signed. They've just been called back for a second demo session with CBS Records. This session will hear "Traffic Light Rock," "Neon Shuffle," "Saturn Boy" and "She's So Square" recorded.

CLASH/THE JAM/THE SLITS
BUZZCOCKS/SUBWAY SECT.........Manchester, Electric Circus

9th - Monday.....................

THE CLASH push the "new wave movement" to a new level tonight. The Clash have arrived at the point that the Sex Pistols aspired to and failed. They play a prestigious gig at the Rainbow Theatre with full label support, records in the charts and they are the headline act of their own package tour. The five band "White Riot Tour" date in London turned into a real riot which cost the Rainbow over 200 seats. The

MAY 1977

capacity crowd remained in their seats (with encouragement from the security staff) through sets by the Prefects, Subway Sect, The Buzzcocks and the Jam. Each band receiving a more excited response than the last. Energies mounted through the last of the Jam's set and by the time they left the stage the crowd did not want to be confined to their seats. When the Clash started their show by ripping into "London's Burning," the mayhem had already begun.

LIVE TONIGHT!

CLASH/THE JAM/THE SLITS	TOM ROBINSON BAND..............London, Dingwalls
BUZZCOCKS/SUBWAY SECT.........London, The Rainbow	48 HOURS............................London, Hope & Anchor

10th - Tuesday......................................

THE ANTS lose their replacement guitarist Lester Square, and after less than forty-eight hours, finds another. Adam had approached the ICA and told them that he had a country & western band and asked if they could play. Thus, the Ants make their official debut at the Institute Of Contemporary Arts restaurant at lunchtime. Adam appeared onstage in his leather gear with a hood and chains then began singing "Beat My Guest." Immediately following the number, the woman who had booked them, paid them their £8 and asked them to leave quietly. They were being enjoyed by at least one student. John Dowie asked them to come and finish their set during the break in his show later that night at the ICA Theatre.

THE HEARTBREAKERS have been asked to be extras in the Who's current movie project called *My Generation*. They know Townsend and crew through their Track Records deal. The Heartbreakers are to play the parts of 1965 beach-fighting mods in the Chris Stamp-directed film, tentatively titled *My Generation*. The film will eventually come out under the title *Quadrophenia*.

THE DAMNED are riding high on the wave of success. They've just returned from their first American tour, headlined at the Roundhouse and passed their first anniversary as a group. Now they've been invited back again to the BBC studios to record some songs for the John Peel Radio program. Tracks recorded tonight are new songs like "Sick Of Being Sick," "Stretcher Case Baby" and "Feel The Pain." They've also cut a new version of "Fan Club." The session is scheduled to be aired on the evening of the 16th.

THE ANTS................London, Instit. Of Contemporary Art	VIBRATORS............................Manchester, Chorlton Oaks Hotel

12th - Thursday......................................

THE SEX PISTOLS have been the subject of rampant speculation about where they will be working next. Now, Virgin Records announces that they've signed the Sex Pistols. It is the Pistols third recording contract in eight months. Perhaps they'll last a little longer with this company, a company that intends to let the band do what they do, not try to mold them into something they're not. Sid, who has been in the hospital battling hepatitis for the last few weeks is scheduled to be released tomorrow. During his stay his only regular visitor has been his girlfriend Nancy Spungen.

THE JAM's lead singer Paul Weller spoke out about politics and music in two different London magazines this week. In *Sniffin' Glue* he said, "I don't dig hippies but they achieved something in the '60s. They brought about a little more liberal thinking. We're all standing and saying how bored we are, but why don't we go and start an action group? In the *NME* he continued with, "I don't see any point in going against your own country...All this change the world thing is becoming a bit too trendy. I realize that we're not going to change anything unless it's on a nationwide scale. We'll be voting conservative at the next election."

JOHNNY THUNDERS &	ULTRAVOX!............................London, The Marquee
THE HEARTBREAKERS ....Birmingham, Rebecca's	EATER ....Manchester, Chorlton Oaks
CAFE JACQUES/REZILLOS ....Edinburgh, Art College	

13th - Friday......................................

THE EASY CURE have their Hansa Records audition today at Morgan Studios in London. It was low key with the band set up in a studio with a video camera and the Easy Cure told to run through a couple of numbers. Of all the bands that entered the contest, only sixty were selected for this audition.

NICK LOWE lets loose another burst of pop music loose. The EP (Extended Play) 45 crowds four songs together on one disc. The effort is practically solo Nick, only Steve Golding helping out on drums. The EP is titled "Bowi." This mysterious title makes more sense when Lowe explains his disappointment when Bowie misnamed his last LP "Low," omitting the "e." So he repaid the compliment with "Bowi," "e" excerpted. Nick's sound is billed as "Pure Pop For Now People" and the variety on the EP bears that out. Side one has Nick's cover of the 1966 Sandy Posy song "Born A Woman," and a rousing, original instrumental titled "Shake That Rat." Side two couples acoustic "Endless Sleep" with the "Hollywood Babylon" tale of "Marie Provost." The later bearing the touching couplet, "She was a winner, but became the doggie's dinner."

IT'S O.K. TO LIKE NICK LOWE

VIBRATORS............................London, Royal College Of Art	TOM ROBINSON BAND..............London, N. London Poly.
TALKING HEADS........................London, The Rock Garden	CHELSEA/MODELS ....London, The Winning Post
KICKS/THE POLICE ....London, Dingwalls	

16th - Monday......................................

SLAUGHTER & THE DOGS are Manchester's masters of talc powder punk. Their debut single is out this week in Manchester, some copies available through the more adventurous London indie shops on the Rabid Record label. The "A" side is "Cranked Up Really High," a jumpin' track which deals with being pumped up on amphetimines. The rest of the band is Mike Rossi on guitar, Zip Bates on bass and "The Mad Muffett" (a.k.a. Eric Grantham) on drums. This debut is made with the highest hopes of success as there is already a contact for

MAY 1977

the Slaughter & The Dogs fan club on the sleeve. One wonders which member's mother drew the short straw to have their home address listed.

48 HOURS, a London-based rock band, play one more gig before changing their name again. This time they'll begin to call themselves 999, after the emergency telephone code. They have been through a few names before this. They had previously been known as The Dials and The Frantics. They can be found playing a Monday night residency at the Hope & Anchor. No cover.

XTC ....High Wycombe, Nags Head		48 HOURS..............................London, Hope & Anchor	

18th - Wednesday......................................

THE SEX PISTOLS have two more roadblocks thrown into their race to get "God Save The Queen" out in time for the Jubilee celebrations. Yesterday, the workers making the pressing plates are upset with the content of the record and refuse to work on it. There's a hurried exchange of phone calls and production was resumed. Then today, the platemakers working on the sleeve have refused to work on it as well. Another round of phone calls and the record is moving again through the pressing plant. Perhaps they should have gone ahead with Malcolm's original idea of pressing up the single as a double thick flexi thus bypassing the usual strict pressing facilities.

RAMONES' guitarist Johnny Ramone confided to the *NME*, "We usually wear out our audiences before we wear out ourselves…Our normal set consists of seventeen songs and takes thirty minutes to perform. Last month the same set lasted thirty-seven minutes…and we're getting faster every day!"

THE EASY CURE are offered, and accept, a recording contract with Hansa Records. This was all started when they answered a music paper ad with 1,400 other bands. The group was one of eight London bands chosen from the contest. They've signed a five-year deal and are given a £1,000 to buy new equipment. Robert Smith told the local paper, "It's all happened so fast, but now we are really looking forward to making our first record."

CORTINAS ....Newport, The Roundabout	WAYNE COUNTY &
COUNT BISHOPS/SQUEEZE ....London, The Marquee	THE ELECTRIC CHAIRS ....London, Dingwalls
X-RAY SPEX/THE ANTS...............London, The Man In The Moon	TOM ROBINSON BAND...............London, The Red Cow

19th - Thursday.......................................

THE SEX PISTOLS were thwarted in their attempt to advertise their new single today on the Bill Grundy Show. Thames TV rejected a ten second advertisement just thirty minutes before it was to air. The ad had Johnny Rotten glaring at the camera saying, "You thought you'd got rid of us but you were wrong, old bean. We're back, with a vengeance." Then Steve shoves Johnny aside and toasts the camera with a beer and says, "God save the Queen." The Grundy show was the battleground for the band's first major exposure to television-watching England. Their previous visit on December 1st of last years, led to the temporary suspension of the host, Bill Grundy, the Sex Pisto's firing from EMI Records, the banning of them playing any live dates in the UK and much negative press headlines. Meanwhile, the Sex Pistols have a film shoot scheduled for Monday at the Marquee. The film will be of "God Save The Queen" for potential use on *Top Of The Pops*.

THE RICH KIDS have found their last member. *Sounds* magazine reports that former Pistol bass player Glen Matlock has concluded auditions for the guitar slot in the band, giving the position to ex-Slik vocalist, guitar player, Midge Ure. Glen has known Midge since before Johnny joined the Sex Pistols as their singer. In fact, Midge was asked to join the Pistols but turned it down to be with his new group Slik. One interesting musician that was turned down for the Rich Kids, was a young player from Wythenshawe named Billy Duffy. He'll find his own fame in the mid '80s as the guitarist for the Cult.

THE RAMONES have their first UK single "Sheena Is A Punk Rocker" released to coincide with their UK tour. There is a limited number of 12" singles pressed (12,000) and the offer of a free t-shirt to those first 1,000 who send in their proof of purchase. The Ramones begin their tour tonight at Eric's in Liverpool.

WAYNE COUNTY (DJ)/	JOLT/THE EXILE ....Glasgow, Strathclyde Univ.
THE HEARTBREAKERS	RAMONES/TALKING HEADS ....Liverpool, Eric's
SIOUXSIE & BANSHEES/	THE ADVERTS ....Manchester, Chorlton Oaks
THE RINGS ....London, Music Machine	

20th - Friday..

THE HEARTBREAKERS finally make their debut in the recording world after playing together for two years. The single is "Chinese Rocks." It was written last year, with the combined talents of Johnny Thunders, Dee Dee Ramone, Jerry Nolan and Richard Hell. Flipside "Born To Lose" is a Thunders song. Both were produced by Speedy Keen (ex-vocalist for Thunderclap Newman) and Chris Stamp.

STRANGLERS are getting some airplay on the BBC with their latest single release "Peaches," but it's not the same recording that you can buy at the shops. The lyrics have been altered to get the Stranglers on the nation's airwaves and it worked. "Oh Shit!" has become "Oh No!," …"What A Bummer!" becomes "What A Summer," and the immortal "…is she trying to get out of that clitoris?!" is changed to "…is she trying to get out of that bikini?!" The airplay helps the song sell and the single climbs to #8 in the UK, becoming the band's first real hit.

BLONDIE arrives in London for the first time last Tuesday. It's kind of weird. A little bit of New York confronts them in London as soon as they arrive. They go down to Dingwalls and see Wayne County ranting about in his wild dresses. It's like back home, only with warm beer. Now they're in Bournemouth doing the warm up show for their first UK tour. They're on in between Squeeze and their old friends The Talking Heads, who are headlining the show. The bands on the bill are all pop bands, even though the press lumps them in with the "punk" scene. In *Sounds* magazine, Talking Heads vocalist David Byrne said, "I'd just like it to be thought of as pop music. One thing we don't want is to be thought of as punk rock."

MAY 1977

LIVE TONIGHT!

EATER.....................................Birmingham, The Pose	WAYNE COUNTY &
TELEVISION/BLONDIE/SQUEEZE....Bornemouth, The Village	THE ELECTRIC CHAIRS..............Sheffield, City Hall
XTC/RAY PHILLIPS WOMAN.........London, The Rock Garden	WASPS.................................London, Roxy

23rd - Monday...

STIFF LITTLE FINGERS are the latest new band in Belfast. They take their name from a song they heard live by The Vibrators. Unlike the political posturing of the Southern bands like the Clash and the Sex Pistols, Stiff Little Fingers come from Belfast and intend to write and sing about their native trouble-torn town, with first hand knowledge. The group is comprised of Jake Burns lead guitarist and vocalist, Brian Faloon on drums, Ali McMordie on bass and Henry Cluney on rhythm guitar.

JAPAN are offered a recording contract with Hansa Records. This all started when they answered a music paper ad with 1,400 other bands. Japan was one of eight London bands chosen from the contest. Just like the Easy Cure, they've signed a five year deal with Hansa and are given a £1,000 to buy new equipment. The group is David Sylvian (aka David Batt) and his brother Steve Jansen (Steve Batt). There's also Richard Barbieri and Mick Karn (aka Anthony Michaelides). Japan will have a long career, scoring hits with "Ghosts" and an eerie cover of "I Second That Emotion" in mid '82. Lead singer David Sylvian will start working with other musicians on more ambient projects, eventually splitting Japan in the Summer of '83, embarking on a long solo career.

ADVERTS/LURKERS..................London, Music Machine	SKREWDRIVER......................London, Rochester Castle
DIVERSIONS............................London, The Nashville	THE BOYS/X-RAY SPEX..............London, The Marquee
NINE NINE NINE.......................London, Hope & Anchor	

27th - Friday.........................

THE SEX PISTOLS' new single "God Save The Queen" is released with a special pic bag and the largest advertising campaign Virgin has ever used. The ill-fated single was originally to be the band's debut with A&M, but the entire pressing was recycled after the band's run-in with A&M company officials at an after-signing party. There was some doubt as to whether the single would be struck by the same worker protests that accompanied EMI's 45. In fact, while the initial pressing of 50,000 singles was being processed by the CBS record plant, workers did indeed momentarily stop work and file their protests. It's doubtful the track will receive any daytime radio play, but John Peel has aired the song on his last few programs and intends to continue playing it on Radio One. More money into the Glitterbest coffers was provided by Barclay Records who have recently purchased the Sex Pistols Swiss and French rights for two years. The price? A cool £26,000. Their first priority is releasing a French 45 of "Anarchy In The UK" to import into the UK. Original EMI copies are already getting to be collectable.

ELVIS COSTELLO makes a rare appearance as an opening act for the Rumour. Since he has no band to back him, he plays a solo electric guitar with only his amplifier to keep him company on stage. He had previously been playing solo on the folk circuit under the name D.P. Costello. Also today, Stiff releases Costello's second single, a ballad titled "Alison" b/w "Welcome To The Working Week." The "A" side is an addictive ballad, the flip an up tempo rocker. Nick Lowe acted as producer again and in true Stiff humor the sides are listed as being in "Would-Have-Been-Stereo" and "Forty-Year-Old-Stereo." There's also more sloganeering on the record run-out groove that reads "Elvis Is King" and "Elvis Joins The FBI." The back of the picture sleeve for the single states Stiff's back catalogue policy- "pre planned deletions."

THE VIBRATORS have a new single out today. It's their first for CBS Records and the tracks "Baby Baby" and "Into The Future" have been selected as the sides. They were signed to CBS last month after a short stint with RAK Records.

THE CLASH have another single out called "Remote Control" flipped with a live version of "London's Burning." The Clash are not pleased with the choice of the single.

EATER have their second single released today. It's "Thinking Of The USA" b/w "Space Dreamin'/ Michaels Monetary System." The "A" side is typical 100mph Vortex style punk while the flip has a psychedelic dreamscape talk over.

TELEVISION/BLONDIE.,...............Birmingham, The Odeon	VIBRATORS...........................London, Southbank Poly.
SKREWDRIVER.......................London, Dingwalls	LURKERS/ZEROS....................London, The White Lion
THE RUMOUR/	NINE NINE NINE.....................London, Stockwell College
ELVIS COSTELLO.....................London, The Nashville	AGGRAVATORS/MENACE............London, Roxy

28th - Saturday..

THE POLICE are playing a one-time-only gig today under the banner of "Strontium 90." The event is a Gong reunion show in Paris, at the Circus Hippodrome. All of the ex-members of Gong are playing with the new groups they've assembled, then there is a Gong reunion show. This ten-hour affair features Pierre Moerlen, Steve Hillage, Didier Malherbe, Daevid Allen and Mike Howlett's temporary group Strontium 90. Howlett had asked Sting (who he had met through their mutual ties with Virgin Publishing), to join him for the one-off gig in Paris. He also invited Stewart to play drums, but felt that the services of guitarist Henry Padovani weren't necessary since he was already using former Zoot Money member Andy Summers. The four-piece, two bass band rehearsed last week and today make their appearance in front of 5,000 Gong fans. Within the band's set were two Police originals, "Dead End Job" and "Be My Girl." At Mike Howlett's insistence, the

MAY 1977

group plans for one more gig in London in the near future. Not wanting to confuse people with the new "Police" and Howlett's band, they decide to appear as the Elevators. It's basically the Police, plus Mike Howlett who sang. Two basses and one short career.

SEX PISTOLS vocalist Johnny Lydon is horrified to see *The Islington Gazette* print an exclusive interview with his mother, Eileen Lydon, who they referred to as Mrs. Rotten. When asked about the use of foul language Mrs Lydon replied that, "It's true I've brought up my children to be plain speaking, so Johnny will sometimes say things straight from the shoulder, but he's not the violent type at all." Throughout the article she supported her son's career "I'd even allow my sons to be roadsweepers if that's what made them happy." She also reported that punk rockers don't really stick safety pins through themselves "it just looks that way." She continued "my boy is doing his own thing. He's not going around murdering people. In fact, groups like Johnny's help society by bringing kids in off the street."

THE DAMNED/ADVERTS	Liverpool, Eric's	KICKS	London, Rochester Castle
NINE NINE NINE/LURKERS	London, The Red Cow	SKREWDRIVER	London, The Red Cow
XTC/SAHARA FARM	London, Roxy	TELEVISION/BLONDIE	London, Hammersmith Odeon

29th - Sunday.............................

THE STIFF KITTENS are chosen to open tonight's Electric Circus concert with the Buzzcocks, Penetration and John Cooper Clarke. This is the first public performance of the group and, although they've already advertised themselves as Stiff Kittens, they've suddenly changed their name to "Warsaw." The group is Ian Curtis on vocals, Bernard Dicken on guitar, Peter Hook on bass and newcomer Tony Tabac on drums (he's been in the group less than forty-eight hours). Warsaw will go through two names before finding fame. First as Joy Division, then when their lead singer dies in '80, they change their name and style and eventually find world-wide success as New Order in the '80s. The multi-band concert is reviewed by Paul Morley for the *NME* who describes Warsaw as having, "...a quirky cockiness that made me think of the Faces...Twinkling evil charm....there's an elusive spark of dissimilarity that suggests they've plenty to play around with. The bass player had a mustache. I liked them and will like them even more in six months time."

TELEVISION/BLONDIE	London, Hammersmith Odeon	BUZZCOCKS/WARSAW/
TOM ROBINSON BAND	London, Inst. Of Contemporary Arts	JOHN COOPER CLARKE/
		PENETRATION/
		JOHN THE POSTMAN ....Manchester, Electric Circus

30th - Monday.............................

THE POLICE are a mixed group of American drummer Stewart Copeland, Englishman bassist Gordon "Sting" Sumner and Corsican guitarist Henry Padovani. They have their debut single out this week. It's on the new indie "Illegal Records" label, funded and started by Stuart's brother, Miles Copeland. Practically everything about the recording had its genesis with Stewart Copeland. He wrote both songs, he started the band, arranged the recording session, set up the label with his brother and did the artwork for the sleeve. The tracks are "Fall Out," an up tempo screecher and "Nothing Achieving". The band has a varied background. Copeland only recently left progressive art-rockers Curved Air and Sting is a former member of Newcastle jazz band The Last Exit. The Police have just finished a short tour with Cherry Vanilla and hit the road on their own soon. As another milestone in the Police's career, their first headline gig is tomorrow night at the Putney Rail Hotel.

DIVERSIONS	London, The Nashville
MENACE	London, Rochester Castle
NINE NINE NINE	London, Hope & Anchor
SQUEEZE	London, Brecknock

31st - Tuesday.............................

ULTRAVOX! has their second single for Island released this week. It's "Young Savage" b/w "Slipaway." Both sides are original songs and were produced by Steve Lillywhite. The "B" side was recorded at the band's Rainbow concert. As an incentive to buy, the first 10,000 are in a special sleeve designed by John Foxx.

COCKSPARRER has their new single "Sister Suzie" and "Running Riot" released on Decca Records. The *NME* describes the single as, "New wave for the Woolworth's crowd. Punk by numbers."

THE POLICE/SKREWDRIVER	London, The Putney Rail Hotel	FAST BREEDER/WARSAW ....Manchester, Rafters

June 1st - Wednesday.............................

THE CORTINAS & CHELSEA are two new bands that Miles Copeland is using to launch another independent record company called Step Forward Records. Actually, Step Forward is the collective brainstorm of Miles, as well as Mark Perry and Harry Murlowski (of *Sniffin' Glue* magazine fame). Two new bands have been signed and have simultaneous debut releases. The Cortinas are from Bristol and have a pair of originals gracing the respective flips of their debut 45. One side is "Fascist Dictator," the other is "Television Families." The group is made up of Dexter Dalwood on bass, Daniel Swann on drums, Nick Sheppard on rhythm guitar, Jeremy Valentine on vocals and Mike Fewings on lead guitar. The Cortinas have been together about a year, originally starting out as an R&B outfit but switching to new wave with great sympathy. Average age in the band is sixteen. Drummer Dan Swann told the *NME*, "...we chose the name (the Cortinas) because it represents something cheap 'n' nasty."

The other band is Chelsea. This band should have had a record out months ago, but they had a major change since then.

JUNE 1977

Although Chelsea got together late in '76, the entire band left lead singer Gene October to start another band, Generation X. October, determined to overcome this loss, set his jaw and built a new band. The current line-up is James Stevenson on guitar, Henry Daze on bass and Carey Fortune (ex-Stranglers' roadie) on drums. The songs on their Step Forward outing are October songs, "Right To Work" and "The Loner." Both singles come in special picture sleeves and are scheduled to hit the shops this Friday.

THE DAMNED's gig planned for this Saturday at St. Alban's City Hall has been cancelled when the local police refused to attend the gig. No police, hence no security, so the hall cancels the gig. This eliminates the local council effecting a ban on the group. Clean, safe, notorious. The Damned's concert with the Adverts is now moved to Dunstable. The cancellations on this tour are becoming more and more commonplace. In Stafford, on the 19th, the concert was called off with only four hours notice. On the 23rd, Southampton porters and bar staff refused to show up for work in protest to the booking and on the 26th the Mecca Organization had their booking at Newcastle cancelled. It continues...The gig scheduled for this Friday in Cromer, at the West Runton Pavilion has been cancelled as well as the scheduled concert for the 16th at Cheltenham and Southend Kursaall on the 18th.

LIVE TONIGHT!

STRANGLERS	Birmingham, Barbarella's	CHELSEA	London, The Winning Post
THE BOYS	London, Hope & Anchor		

2nd - Thursday..

SHAM 69 have a new line-up. The new members are Mark Cain on drums and Dave Parsons on guitar. Three of the old members; Bostik, Goodfornothing and Harris have all been sacked. Only Jimmy Pursey and Albie Slider remain from the original band.

THE ANTS support Desolation Angels at Hornsey Art College (where Adam attended school). Their drummer, Dave Barbe, left the Angels to join the Ants. Adam's previous drummer, Paul Flanagan, left to get a day job. Kenny Morris of the Banshees was filling in.

STRANGLERS	Birmingham, Barbarella's	MODELS/THE FRAMED	London, Roxy
EDDIE & HOT RODS/		ONLY ONES	London, Rochester Castle
RADIO STARS	Birmingham, Town Hall	SQUEEZE/WIRE	London, The Nashville
MENACE	London, The Lord Nelson	SKREWDRIVER	Manchester, Chorlton Oaks

3rd - Friday..

THE SEX PISTOLS find themselves well on the way to a number one hit only a week after the release of "God Save The Queen." Obstacles thrown in their path include a ban by several major chain stores that sell top singles. Woolworths, Booths and Smiths have all refused to stock the single, although it entered the charts this week at #11 and will surely reach #1 next week. The stores are not alone in their ban on the record. The BBC took the decision to ban play on the single last Tuesday (31st) as they felt it was "in gross bad taste." The Independent Broadcasting Authority has issued a statements to all UK radio stations saying that in their opinion the record was in breach of Section 4:1:A of the IBA Act. This covers material that "offends good taste or decency, or is likely to encourage or incite to crime, or lead to disorder, or to be offensive to public feeling." The BBC, as well as BRMB, Picadilly, Clyde and Capitol Radio, all refuse even to play a paid advertisement for the single. Robin Nash, producer for *Top Of The Pops* declared "It is quite unsuitable for an entertainment show like *Top Of The Pops*." It will be interesting to see what happens when the Sex Pistols release their debut album at the end of the month.
    The Sex Pistols spoke their mind to the *Melody Maker* with the usual bravado from Johnny Rotten, "There's no one who can follow us. The rest of those fucking bands like The Clash, The Damned and The Stranglers are just doing what every other band has done. It's the same big fat hippy trip." He told the *NME*, "We're the only honest band that's hit this planet in about two thousand million years." It was guitarist Steve Jones who let the public peek behind the curtain at the Pistols when he told the *Melody Maker* "I don't see how anyone could describe us as a political band. I don't even know the name of the Prime Minister."

THE VIBRATORS' debut album is rush-released by CBS in the UK today. They've only been with the label for two months and have been very busy recording and planning their next assault on the UK to support the LP titled "Pure Mania." Tracks include versions of songs from their previous singles "Baby Baby," "Whips & Furs," "Bad Time" and "No Heart." Also included are "Petrol," "London Girls," "Stiff Little Fingers" and "Into The Future." All but two of the songs were written by Ian Carnochan (aka Knox), vocalist and guitarist for the band.

EASY CURE	Crawley, Queen's Square	WAYNE COUNTY &	
BOOMTOWN RATS/		THE ELECTRIC CHAIRS	London, Royal College Of Art
SIOUXSIE & THE BANSHEES	London, The Marquee	EDDIE & HOT RODS/	
NINE NINE NINE/BETHNAL	London, Roxy	RADIO STARS	Manchester, Apollo

6th - Monday..

THE JAM are hinting that the group will be dropping the use of the Union Jack emblem from their equipment, stage gear and promo materials. He says it's nothing against the Queen, it's just that there is some confusion whether they are involved with the fascist clique the National Front. This is an association that they don't want.

EATER are on the road to promote their new single "Thinking Of The USA." Their original drummer, fifteen year-old Dee Generate has left the band with the age old excuse of "musical differences." He is replaced by another youngster, sixteen year-old Phil Rowland.

THE OUTSIDERS are three ruddy faced, nineteen year-old Wimbledon lads named Adrian Borland, Adrian Janes and Bob Lawrence. Their self-financed debut album is out this week on their own Raw Edge record label. It's entitled "Calling On Youth" and features the same tracks that they've been using while opening up for the Vibrators and The Jam down at the Roxy. They run through nine compositions of their lead singer/guitarist. Titles include "Break Through," "On The Edge," "I'm Screwed Up," "Terminal Case" and "Weird." Sensing some teenage angst? The entire project is D.I.Y., from the cover art and songs, right down to the mixing, borrowing just enough money (from their parents) to cover the costs of 1,000 albums.

JUNE 1977

VIBRATORS ....Edinburgh, Tiffany's	SQUEEZE ....London, The Bell
RAMONES/TALKING HEADS/	DAMNED/ADVERTS...................London, Dingwalls
SAINTS................................London, The Roundhouse	NINE NINE NINE ....London, Hope & Anchor
BOOMTOWN RATS ....London, The Nashville	

7th - Tuesday...........................

THE SEX PISTOLS and Virgin Records invite some close and rambunctious friends out for an evening cruising down the Thames to celebrate the Queen's Jubilee. Invited guests are to assemble at the Charring Cross Pier to board the Queen Elizabeth at 6:15 this evening. The question remains, did Malcolm intend for this evening out to wind up splashed across the headlines of the UK's papers? The Sex Pistols and Virgin plotted together to stage a boat ride for 175 people and the Sex Pistols up and down the Thames the evening of the Jubilee celebration. The boat left, the banners proclaiming the new single unfurled and the party was underway. Meanwhile, back at the ranch, the boat's owner, feeling that he's gotten his boat into something more than he bargained for called the local authorities to report the goings on. Up the Thames the boat traveled, all the time gathering behind them police boats as they passed each bridge. Three hours after leaving the dock the guests of honor were just starting their seven song set. The atmosphere was quickly broken with the blaring strains of "Anarchy In The UK." Next up on the list was "God Save The Queen," "I Wanna Be Me," "Pretty Vacant," "No Feelings" and "Problems." By this time, the Queen Elizabeth had been joined by six police boats which were pulling up next to the party boat and demanding it pull over to the nearest pier. The band then asked for requests and launched into a venomous version of Iggy Pop's "No Fun." The band played on while the boat was boarded and finally the power to the amplification was pulled. At the pier the River Police were joined by the Metropolitan Police who then, in a very rough and surly manner, cleared the boat. Cameras were smashed, party-goers pummeled, punched and dragged away to the waiting police vans. All in all, only eleven people were arrested, including some members of the band, management, and organizers, as well as some of the guests and taken to the Bow Street Station.

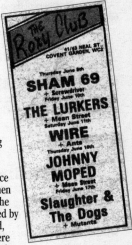

JAM..Birmingham, Barbarella's	EATER ....Manchester, Chorlton Oaks
SHANGHAI/MENACE ....London, Music Machine	

9th - Thursday...........................

THE CLASH are in trouble with London police. They arrested a troublemaker this evening caught spray painting some graffiti on a brick wall next to Dingwalls at Camden Lock in London. The culprit was identified as John Mellor (aka Joe Strummer) and the spray painted word as "Clash." He could get a publicist to do this, couldn't he? Joe/John is due to appear before magistrates tomorrow to answer charges at 4 PM. Joe's also due in Newcastle that same day at six PM to answer charges of theft of property (pillowcases) from a hotel there. The property was found on the group's coach after it was searched in St. Albans.

THE REZILLOS have been discovered and signed. The spotter was Lenny Love, the Scottish rep for Island Records. He's decided to start his own label called Sensible Records. He's sent the Rezillos into the Barclay Towers recording studios to lay down the tracks. Live favorites such as "Flying Saucer Attack" and "I Can't Stand My Baby" are favored titles. The band was put together back in April of last year. Typically, the Rezillos attack a variety of oldies with express train enthusiasm, as well as some originals, more often than not in a similar vein. Their comic book approach to music is also carried onstage with the band as lead singer Faye Fifi (aka Shelia Hyde) leaps around in her green PVC suit and silver painted mini boots. while sharing vocals with Eugene Reynolds (aka Alan Forbes). Guitar duties are shared by Hi-Fi Harris and Luke Warm. The rhythm section is Angel Patterson on drums and Willie Mysterious on bass.

BOYS/CHELSEA/	ELECTRODES ....London, Man In The Moon
THE TABLE ....London, Music Machine	ONLY ONES ....Manchester, Chorlton Oaks
SKREWDRIVER/SHAM 69.............London, Roxy	

10th - Friday...........................

"LIVE AT THE ROXY" is the new LP from Harvest Records that captures the dawn of the punk boom from the vantage point of the London Roxy. The tape decks were rolling as some of the best new groups in the country trekked through the club between January and April of this year. Among those on the LP are new wave veterans Slaughter & The Dogs, The Adverts, Eater and the Buzzcocks. Those bands making a vinyl debut are Wire, The Unwanted, X-Ray Spex and Johnny Moped.

DAMNED/ADVERTS ....Birmingham, Barbarella's	LURKERS/MEAN STREET/
JOLT.......................................Glasgow, The Amphora	SAINTS/STUKAS ....London, The Marquee
VIBRATORS ....Liverpool, Eric's	JOHNNY THUNDER &
	HEARTBREAKERS/THE MODELS ...London, Royal College Of Art

11th - Saturday...........................

CLASH members Joe Strummer and Nicky "Topper" Headon were arrested this morning in London on charges of failing to appear in Newcastle yesterday, to answer to petty theft charges. The reason they were unable to report to Newcastle court, was Strummer was answering charges in Kentish Town at the time. The two charges were filed in different towns but for the same day. After Strummer paid the five pound fine in Kentish town for spray painting "Clash" on a wall, they were taken into custody and spent the weekend in the Newcastle jail, after paying their fines there, of course.

JUNE 1977

LENE LOVICH is reviewed in *Sounds* magazine by Martha Zenfell while still a member of a funk-rock group called the Diversions at Dingwalls in London. "Image wise they are as shiny as a Jubilee penny, several members project caricatures hooking even the weariest of eyes... The Diversions have the musical resources to transcend disco obscurity." The photo and story picture a young lady named Lene Lovich who is likened to Dorothy Lamour.

Members of the group include Lene on sax and vocals, Steve Saxon and Glen Cartlidge on lead guitar and sax and Les Chapple on guitar. They reveal that they have recorded a full album with producer Mike Vernon but are currently looking for a worldwide deal.

DAMNED/ADVERTS ....Birmingham, Barbarella's　　　WIRE/THE ANTS......................London, Roxy

12th - Sunday..................................

SIOUXSIE & THE BANSHEES get time in the studio through an arrangement with their manager Nils. He's been working with Track Records, who are footing the bills. It's their first time in a recording studio. The six songs cut were "Love In A Void," "Captain Scarlett," "Bad Shape," "20th Century Boy," "Carcass" and "Make Up To Break Up."

SAINTS....................London, Dingwalls	IAN HUNTER/VIBRATORS ....London, Hammersmith Odeon
JOHNNY MOPED ....London, The Roxy	JAM/CHELSEA.........................London, Chelsea Football Ground
ULTRAVOX! ....London, Marquee	STRANGLERS ....Sheffield, Top Tank

LIVE TONIGHT!

15th - Wednesday..................................

SKREWDRIVER, a punk band from Blackpool, have their debut single out this week on Chiswick Records. It's the lively thrash "You're So Dumb," b/w "Better Off Crazy." Skrewdriver is Ian Stuart on vocals, Phil Walmsley on guitar, Grinny on drums and Kev on bass.

MORE FANZINES keep appearing and the *NME* runs yet another article about them. Among those that are mentioned are a whole new lot like *Sounds Of The Westway, New Wave, I Wanna Be Yur Dog, Stranded, Sideburns, These Things* and *Spittin' Blood*. Devoted entirely to the Stranglers is a new one called *Strangled* and from Scandinavia comes *Rock Filla*, which spends a lot of time on the Runaways and Patti Smith.

NINE NINE NINE ....London, The Red Cow

18th - Saturday..................................

THE SEX PISTOLS' new single "God Save The Queen," hits the #1 spot in the UK in its second week of release despite it's suppression on British radio, the ban on sales at many shops, and the many outlets who refused to advertise it. There is a great deal of worry about the single since it's listed as #2 behind Rod Stewart's "I Don't Want To Talk About It." Distributor's, marketer's and sale's figures show that the Sex Pistols single is far ahead of Rod's, but the British Market Research Bureau have other ideas about what should be number one. In a strange ruling that was effective the week that this chart was compiled, all the Virgin Records stores reports of sales were struck from the figures and Virgin was selling thousands of records for the Sex Pistols. It was all a very thin-veiled conspiracy to keep the Pistols from holding the number one spot on Jubilee week. Lambeth MP Marcus Lipton said this week, "If pop music is going to be used to destroy our established institutions, then it ought to be destroyed first." In an unrelated story, Johnny Rotten, producer Chris Thomas and studio manager Bill Price are attacked by a gang of five with knives in the car park of the Pegasus pub where they were taking a break between sessions at a Highbury North London recording studio. Johnny's arm was severely cut, severing two tendons and Chris Thomas was injured as well.

THE MODELS have their debut single released today. It's "Freeze" and "Man Of The Year." The band is made up of former Siouxsie & The Banshees member Marco Pirroni on guitar, Cliff Fox on guitar and vocals, Mick Allen on bass and Terry Day on drums. They use to appear around London as "The Beastly Cads". One of the songs they've dropped from their set is their "beastly" "I Wanna Form A Nazi Party."

REZILLOS...........................Glasgow, Jordanhill College
NAUGHTY LUMPS ....Liverpool Univ.
THE BOYS/MEAN STREET.............London, The Roxy
CORTINAS/JOHNNY MOPED.........London, The Marquee
THE JAM ....London, Poplar Civic Theatre
KICKS/WIRE............................London, Rochester Castle
THE ONLY ONES.....................London, The Speakeasy
WAYNE COUNTY &
THE ELECTRIC CHAIRS ....Manchester, Cholrton Oaks

20th - Monday..................................

XTC take up John Peel's invitation to record a session for his radio show. He had seen them at Ronnie Scott's back in April. The songs recorded are "Radios In Motion," "Crosswires," "She's So Square" and "Science Friction." The band is playing London as much as possible and is beginning to stir up some attention.

THE CRUCIAL THREE have split up without ever playing a single gig. Singer Ian McCulloch as well as drummer Stephen Spence quit the group. Remaining members Julian Cope and Pete Wylie are thinking over their next move. Among the original songs written during their short

JUNE 1977

life together are "Salomine Shuffle," Space Hopper" and "Bloody Sure You're On Dope." Julian and Pete consider starting a new band. Julian will be on the scene in a major way as the singer for the Teardrop Explodes in '79, while Ian McCulloch will front Echo & The Bunnymen.

GENERATION X	London, Cooks Ferry Inn	THE MODELS	London, The Marquee
THE SAINTS/999	London, The Nashville		

21st - Tuesday.............................

THE FUTURE is the new name for a Sheffield front-room band up until recently known as The Dead Daughters. The protagonists in the band are Martin Ware and Ian Craig Marsh. They're both computer operator shift leaders working at Spear & Jackson Intl. and Lucas Service, respectively. Their music is technically-based with synthesizer and tape loops. Their style of music is something unlike the current punk scene. Ian and Martyn find Phil Oakey to sing for the band, providing the final missing link to a group that will one day be called the Human League. Phil is currently working as a porter in a plastic surgery operating theatre. None are trained musicians but share an interest in electronics and the desire to do something different. They have been calling themselves The Dead Daughters but with the addition of Addy Newton and Philip Oakey, they change their name to The Future. They're still about four years away from a chart hit.

SKREWDRIVER	London, The Putney Rail Hotel	GENERATION X	London, Dingwalls
JOHNNY MOPED	London, Upstairs at Ronnie Scott's	THE SAINTS/999	London, The Nashville

23rd - Thursday.............................

THE SEX PISTOLS have a unique distinction among the record world now. Their single "God Save The Queen" has now surpassed the 250,000 mark, giving the disc the status of "going silver." This in light of almost no radio play, no TV promotion and many shops refusing to stock the single at all. There will probably be some preposterous event staged to celebrate the award. In yet another Sex Pistols bashing, Johnny Rotten is set upon while at a Pirate's gig in Dingwalls. Tables are overturned, bottles shattered and his previous wounds reopened.

GENERATION X have found a new drummer since the departure of John Towe last month. He's eighteen year-old Mark Laff (AKA Mark Laffoley) a former member of the Subway Sect, who left his previous band in the midst of their lengthy tour with the Clash. He was the choice of the band after going through some fifty-four other candidates. Spokesman for the band told the *NME* that he was chosen because of, "…his ability to batter his kit into submission without the obligatory showmanship."

EXILE	Glasgow, The Amphora	ED BANGER & NOSEBLEEDS	London, The Roxy
THE SAINTS	London, Hope & Anchor		

24th - Friday.............................

WAYNE COUNTY & THE ELECTRIC CHAIRS release their debut EP today on Miles Copeland's Illegal Records. That's the same company that released the single by the Police last month. The Electric Chairs got together two months ago when Wayne radically changed his rock image. The "A" side is a seven and a half minute version of the Rolling Stones song "The Last Time" coupled with "Paranoia Paradise" and "Stuck On You." It's quite tame stuff, compared to Wayne's normally bawdy stage act.

999	Birmingham, The Pose	THE SAINTS/NEO	London, The Roxy
THE POLICE/LURKERS	London, The Marquee		

25th - Saturday.............................

THE POLICE are about to get a new guitar player and don't even know it. Guitarist Andy Summers, who played with the group on the one-off gig with Gong in Paris, came down to the Marquee to see them again last night. Today he's tracking down both Stewart and Sting and proposing that he join the group and they sack Henry. He's certainly more qualified for the position. He's played with Kevin Coyne, The Animals, Zoot Money and numerous other groups. The real crux of the situation is the firing of Henry. Henry was just not up to the capabilities that Sting wanted in the group, but he was the "token punk." It's as if the Police were trying to be a punk band, but were far too good for the ruse. To have Andy join the group and abandon Henry, is to change the aims of the band.

ELVIS COSTELLO's recordings for the John Peel show are aired. They include "Red Shoes," "Mystery Dance," "Blame It On Cain" and "Less Than Zero." This is Elvis' first recording with his new backing group The Attractions. He put the band together in May and they've been rehearsing for the last seven weeks. The group consists of Steve Naive (Steve Mason) on keyboards, a graduate of the Royal College Of Music; Pete Thomas on drums, ex-member of Chilli Willi, and Bruce Thomas on bass, an ex-member of The Sutherland Brothers. In an interview with *Melody Maker*, Elvis revealed one of his guiding axioms in songwriting, "I hate anything with extended solos or bands that are concerned with any kind of musical virtuosity. I get bored. That's why I write short songs. You can't cover up songs like that by dragging in banks of synthesizers and choirs of angels. I've written hundreds of songs. They're not all classics."

SUBURBAN STUDS	Birmingham, Digbeth Civic Hall	BUZZCOCKS/THE FALL/	
RADIATORS FROM SPACE/		VERBAL	London, NE Poly.
UNDERTONES/REVOLVER/		SQUEEZE	London, The Marquee
GAMBLERS/VIPERS	Dublin, Univ.	999	London, The Nashville
TOM ROBINSON BAND	London, Wandsworth Town Hall	THE SAINTS/MEAN STREET	London, The Roxy

69

JUNE 1977

30th - Thursday................................

WARSAW drummer Tony Tabac has left the group "for health reasons," and has been replaced by Steve Brotherdale. The Manchester group found him using the "musicians needed" adverts in local fanzine "Shy Talk." Tonight is his live debut with Warsaw, opening for Johnny Thunder's Heartbreakers in Manchester.

THE INVADERS are a goofy band that mostly play covers of '50s R&B songs, ska and bluebeat. They got together last year around the nucleus of keyboard player Mike Barson, guitarist Chris Foreman and sax player and vocalist Lee Thompson. They are all eighteen years old. Since that time, they've added drummer John Hassler and Carl Smyth on bass. Their debut performance tonight is at Simon Birdsall's house party, a skinhead friend of theirs. The quirky group will shift members and styles until they ultimately become known as Madness in 1979 and start having hit after hit after hit.

THE SUBURBAN STUDS have their single "Questions" b/w "No Faith" out today on the aptly named Pogo label. Distribution for the record is handled by Warner Brothers, so somebody in high places must be interested.

LIVE TONIGHT!

JAM	Birmingham, Rebecca's	WAYNE COUNTY &	
ULTRAVOX!/STUKAS	London, The Marquee	THE ELECTRIC CHAIRS/	
XTC	London, Hope & Anchor	ALTERNATIVE T.V.	London, Roxy
BOOMTOWN RATS/999/		GENERATION X	Manchester, Chorlton Oaks
SKREWDRIVER	London, Music Machine	HEARTBREAKERS/WARSAW	Manchester, Rafters

July 1st - Friday................................

THE SEX PISTOLS release their new single today, "Pretty Vacant" b/w "No Fun." It's the band's third 45 and comes only five weeks since Virgin released "God Save The Queen." This new waxing flips a Pistols' original with an Iggy Pop & Stooges' standard. Lyrically, it's not as controversial as "God Save The Queen," and is expected to be able to receive airplay not accorded their previous singles. There is still no word as to whether this single will get the same boycott that shops levied against their last two records. Chain stores like Boots, Woolworth's and W.H. Smith are reserving comment until hearing the disc.

THE SAINTS, Australia's best known punk export, have their third single released today by Harvest Records. The "A" side, "This Perfect Day," is culled from their debut LP, the flip side, "L-I-E-S," can only be found on the single. In an interesting marketing ploy, the first 12,000 copies of the 12" have an extra track with an apologetic warning sticker attached. It says that "Due to an administrative error…this 12" pressing contains a third, additional title not available on the normal 7" pressing. The additional title, 'Do The Robot,' has consequently been withdrawn from future release consideration and will now be available only on this 12" pressing."

CELIA & THE MUTATIONS is the name that Stranglers' fans will be surprised to see their favorite band masquerading under. The new "group" is on UA (the same label as the Stranglers) and features Celia Collin, a new singer discovered by the Stranglers' manager Dai Davies, singing the old Tommy James & the Shondells' hit "Mony Mony". It's coupled with "Mean To Me," which was written by J. Black, J. Burnel, H. Cornwell and one D. Greenfield. That should be a giveaway to any doubter.

CHELSEA	Birmingham, Barbarellas	EATER	London, Fulham Greyhound
WAYNE COUNTY &		X-RAY SPEX	London, Hope & Anchor
THE ELECTRIC CHAIRS/		MODELS	London, The Red Cow
ALTERNATIVE TELEVISION/		HEART ATTACK/999/	
TONES/SKREWDRIVER	London, The Roxy	PENETRATION	London, Royal College Of Art
LURKERS/ZERO	London, White Lion		

3rd - Sunday................................

THE DAMNED made their debut one year ago onstage at the Marquee, opening up for the Sex Pistols. In celebration of this note worthy anniversary, The Damned give each fan in the audience a special Stiff commemorative 45 with picture sleeve. There are 5,000 singles to be passed out over the next four nights that they play at the Marquee. The songs are two new tracks, "Stretcher Case Baby" and "Sick Of Being Sick." It comes in a special pic sleeve with a drawing of a Victorian woman at a bureau looking in a mirror. At a distance the image isn't a woman at all, it's a huge skull! Stiff Records makes sure the single will have no future value by imprinting on the label "Special snob collectors artifact of no historical/cultural value. Throw it away. Why sell 'em away when you can give 'em away?"

SIOUXSIE & THE BANSHEES undergo another personnel change. This time guitarist Peter Fenton (aka P.P. Barnum) is replaced by John McKay, a great fan of the band and a Roxy club regular. He himself had noticed that the band "…seemed really uncomfortable onstage - even to the point of looking awkwardly at each other all the time they were playing." McKay is a self-taught musician from Hemel Hempstead.

Damned

DAMNED/THE RINGS	London, The Marquee
THE SAINTS	Manchester, Electric Circus

4th - Monday................................

THE VORTEX opens its doors tonight with what seems to be "Manchester Night," as The Buzzcocks, The Fall and Manchester punk poet

JULY 1977

John Cooper Clark all play. It's located at Wardor Street where Crackers Disco used to be. The club has a capacity of 600 more than the Roxy with a higher stage and a better view. The management found that the new wave was drawing crowds on early week nights and decided to give it a try. The "Crackers" sign outside doesn't change, only the atmosphere, clientele and music inside. "Vortex" is a most appropriate name since it refers to a swirling mixture that draws into the center. So far, it's only on Mondays but if all goes well it will move to Tuesdays as well. Opening act The Fall are greeted with great indifference. Their music is aggressive but not as banal as some openers can be. It's only the Fall's sixth-ever gig. They got together in Manchester late last year and have a harsh, unschooled approach to music. As a surprise to everyone in attendance, Johnny Thunders and the Heartbreakers make a "farewell to Britain" appearance after the Buzzcocks. They're due to be deported soon and it could be a while before they return. During their set, Garth from the Buzzcocks is thrown out of the club for throwing things at the Heartbreakers. Other acts already booked to play in the near future include Siouxsie & Banshees, Wayne County & the Electric Chairs, The Models and Generation X.

BLONDIE July 4th, Independence Day. It's independence for Gary Valentine of Blondie. The bassist for the group has been told he's out of the band. It's no surprise though. He'd been thinking of heading for California the past few months. Blondie is using a friend of Clem Burke's, Frank Infante, to fill in on bass, as they're scheduled to start recording their second album very soon.

DAMNED/JOHNNY MOPED	London, The Marquee	BUZZCOCKS/THE FALL	
NEW HEARTS	London, Hope & Anchor	JOHN COOPER CLARKE/	
999	London, Nashville	JOHNNY THUNDERS &	
		THE HEARTBREAKERS	London, The Vortex

5th - Tuesday.....................................

THE ANTS are involved in the filming of another punk movie that's just started shooting. Derek Jarman is directing the movie *Jubilee*. It stars Jenny Runacre and Richard O'Brien as well as bit parts for Little Nell from *Rocky Horror Picture Show* and Kings Road Sex Shop waitress Jordan. It's set in the year 2,000 and in a punk rocker's dream comes true London. For the most part filming will take place in a warehouse near Tower Bridge in London as well as on location in Northamptonshire and Dorset. There will undoubtedly be lots of music in the film, with performances by many current underground acts. A new Hornsey Art College band called The Ants film their bit for the movie with Siouxie & The Banshees drummer Kenny Morris borrowed, just for the video.

THE SEX PISTOLS' video for "Pretty Vacant" has the band playing on a simple set in front of Jamie Reid's posters for "God Save The Queen." Steve is in a rough weave sweater with a knotted hankie on his head, Johnny in his "Destroy" t-shirt and red Ben Franklin glasses and leather jacketed Sid flails away like a punk Pete Townsend on his bass. Bill Cotton, Head of Light Entertainment BBC doesn't really care what the video looks like. "I wouldn't have the Sex Pistols on anything. I don't think anybody wants to see those types of people."

WAYNE COUNTY &		THE BOYS/XTC/	
THE ELECTRIC CHAIRS	Birmingham, Barbarella's	DAMNED/SKREWDRIVER	London, The Marquee
ONLY ONES	London, Rochester Castle	999/BETHNAL	London, Putney Rail Hotel

6th - Wednesday.................................

THE SEX PISTOLS score a victory of sorts today when a representative of Boot's stores agreed to stock the new release "Pretty Vacant." W.H. Smith and Woolworth's are soon to follow. The records, which has received advance orders of 20,000 will be shipped in a plain white sleeve since there was no time to prepare a proper picture jacket. A Virgin spokesman told *Sounds* magazine "This record does not contain anything remotely offensive. It will be interesting to observe whether it was the Sex Pistols or their song that got banned last time." Malcolm is currently in Los Angeles trying to set up a deal for the Sex Pistols in America. He's also contacting various film industry people about a movie idea he has.

X-RAY SPEX	London, Man In The Moon	VIBRATORS	London, Winning Post
DAMNED/ADVERTS	London, The Marquee	THE RINGS	London, The Red Cow
MODEL MANIA/ZERO	London, Roxy Club (audition night)		

7th - Thursday.................................

ELVIS COSTELLO has his third single released by Stiff Records. It's "(Angels Wanna Wear My) Red Shoes" b/w "Mystery Dance." These songs are from the sessions for Elvis' first album, still unreleased although it was finished over six months ago. Matrix readers find the message "Help Us Hype Elvis" and "Larger Than Life and More Fun Than People - Elvis."

THE SAINTS	Birmingham, Rebecca's	999	London, Hope & Anchor
YACHTS	Liverpool, Eric's		

8th - Friday.................................

THE JAM have a two new songs out today on Polydor Records. It's "All Around The World" b/w "Carnaby Street." Both cuts are originals and neither song is on their LP "In The City." The Jam will headline a major concert in London at the Hammersmith Odeon on the 24th, their first major concert in London and a remarkable milestone in the growing acceptance of the new wave amongst audiences.

JOHNNY MOPED finally has a record after years of playing in underground bands and it's through the good graces of Ted Carrol's Chiswick Records. The single couples two Slimy Toad (the band's guitarist) originals, "No One" and "Incendiary Device." The band's line-up is now a four-piece, since the departure of guitarist Sissy Bar (aka Chrissie Hynde).

JULY 1977

XTC, who have been the subject of auditions of Pye, Decca and Columbia Records are now being checked out again. Tonight's performance at the Red Cow had representatives from both Island and Virgin Records in the audience.

LIVE TONIGHT!

SAINTS....................................Liverpool, Eric's   POLICE ....London, Hope & Anchor
XTC ....London, The Red Cow

9th - Saturday..

THE ONLY ONES release their debut single on their own Vengeance label. It's the haunting "Lovers Of Today" and "Peter And The Pets." Unlike other bands on the scene, the Only Ones members have musical pasts. Their leader, Peter Perret, had been in a previous band called England's Glory that use to play around London until about two years ago. They even cut a self-financed album in hopes of getting a recording deal. The band's bass player, Alan Mair, use to be in a Scottish band called The Beatstalkers, that existed sometime back in the mid-sixties. Drummer Mike Kellie had played with the V.I.P.'s in the mid-sixties and more recently with Peter Frampton on his first solo project as well as some time with Spooky Tooth. Guitarist John Perry played some licks on an unreleased album with the Grateful Dead. Peter put the band together after he saw a group called Rat Bites From Hell. They were a not-so-serious party group and Peter was impressed enough with John Perry to start another band. They recorded some tapes and were joined by Mike Kellie and Alan Mair. They aren't new kids, they aren't new wave. It's uncertain what they, are but it's for sure that their debut single is one of the best of the month, possibly the year.

ELVIS COSTELLO quits his day job at the Elizabeth Arden cosmetics factory to pursue his new musical career with all his energies. He had been taking "sick days" to work on his recordings for Stiff Records.

SAINTS....................................Liverpool, Eric's   X-RAY SPEX/EATER/
                                                                         JOHNNY MOPED
                                                                         SLAUGHTER & THE DOGS ....Manchester, Elizabeth Suite

10th - Sunday...

WARSAW's concert last week at a central Manchester dive called "The Squat" is reviewed in *Sounds* magazine by Tony Moon. It's Warsaw's sixth-ever gig, but word is out that it's a show worth seeing. The double bill pairs two of Manchester's newest bands, The Worst and Warsaw. The Worst open the show since it's their second gig, Warsaw, veterans of five other live shows are the main act. Moon writes, "They have slightly better gear than the Worst and since they have done a couple more gigs, are a bit tighter. Tony Tabac is on drums…he only joined a few weeks agao, Pete hook is on bass/plastic cap, Barney Rubble is on guitar and Ian Curtis is the voice. Lotsa Action and jumping in the air to "Tension" and "Kill." Since the show, Warsaw have a new drummer, Steve Brotherdale. In local magazine *Kids Stuff*, future Smiths lead singer Steven Morrissey writes, "Of the new bands, Warsaw, The Worst, The Drones and the Fall look the most likely to make any headway. Warsaw were formed some time ago by vocalist Ian Curtis and have performed alongside more prominent bands like The Heartbreakers. Although they offer little originality with Ian's offstage antics resembling one Iggy Pop."

VIBRATORS ....Manchester, Electric Circus   THE JAM ....Sheffield, Top Rank

11th - Monday.....................

THE SALE are a rather off-beat Edinburgh band. They have been playing around Edinburgh a while and have landed the chance to open for the Saints at their first Edinburgh concert. The lucky thing for them, is that on a customer's insistence, Bruce Findlay attends their show. Findlay runs Bruce's Records, a collectors shop that specialized in hard to find records. Findlay is suitably impressed and offers to press up a single of the band's material. A deal is struck and the band's future is clear. The one thing they do change is the name. The new moniker located after much discussion is The Valves. The group is Dee Robot (a.k.a David Robertson) on vocals, Ronnie Mackinnon on guitar, Gordon Scott on bass and Gordon "Teddy" Dair on drums.

SAINTS/SALE ....Edinburgh, Tiffany's   SIOUXSIE & BANSHEES/
999 ....London, The Nashville   SLITS/THE ANTS....................London, The Vortex

13th - Wednesday.............................

SEX PISTOLS Sid and his American girlfriend Nancy Spungen, had found themselves a cozy little dive in the Maida Vale section of London. They were found by some friends of Johnny, who were terrorizing Nancy and trashing the apartment, forcing the landlord to put them out on the street. This problem, as well as others, could be the cause of Sid missing the plane as his bandmates left today for a short tour of Scandinavia. Malcolm is keeping all the dates and venues a secret until the last minute to avoid being cancelled out of shows.

HEARTBREAKERS Johnny Thunders and the Heartbreakers are deported from the UK but will only be gone temporarily (we're told).

JAM......................................Glasgow, Shuffle's   WAYNE COUNTY &
XTC ....London, Fulham Greyhound   THE ELECTRIC CHAIRS ....London, Wining Post

14th - Thursday...............................

THE SEX PISTOLS on *Top Of The Pops!* Since the ban has been lifted on the Sex Pistols the most amazing things have happened. You can buy their new record at Boot's. You can see adverts for them in local press and now you can see them right in you own home on *Top*

JULY 1977

of The Pops. Eight million viewers tuned in to find that the Sex Pistols video of "Pretty Vacant" was indeed a part of ITV's evening program. Letters and editorials in the *Sun* are certain to follow. Stay tuned.

THE ANTS record their songs "Plastic Surgery" and "Beat My Guest" at Chapple Lane Studios. It is the first Antmusic destined for vinyl.

EATER ....Birmingham, Erdington Roebuck   ULTRAVOX! ....London, The Marquee

16th - Saturday...

SEX PISTOLS' singer Johnny Rotten gets his own radio show. It's only a one-time, pre-recorded affair on London's Capitol Radio, but what a start. The hour and a half show was called "A Punk And His Music" and featured Johnny playing bits of some of his favorite discs. Among the tracks he selected were Bowie's "Rebel Rebel," Tim Buckley's "Sweet Surrender," Gary Glitter's chart topper "Doing Alright With The Boys," Neil Young's "Revolution Blues," Aswad's "Jah Wonderful," "Don't Determine My Right" by Dr. Alimantado, the Chieftains' "Jig A Jig," Kevin Coyne's "Eastbourne Ladies" and Captain Beefheart's "It's The Blimp." Conversation between songs wandered over topics such as his Catholic school upbringing, Johnny's early memories of music and the expected forays into musical oblivion with recordings by Nico, Lou Reed, Can, The Gladiators and others. At one point Johnny lashed out at the participants of the very scene he fostered. He said "A lot of (punk) is real rubbish. I mean real rubbish, pathetic and just giving it a terrible name. They're either getting too much into the star trip, or they're going the exact opposite way. Neither way is really honest. If you know what you're really doing you can completely ignore the whole damn thing which is what we've always done." It was likely that Capitol Radio DJ Tommy Vance was taken aback when Johnny concluded the chat with: "Let's wrap up a really tedious interview...Just play the records and they speak for themselves. There's nothing I can say that'll make people change their minds if they hate me, so why bother?" Vance countered with "So what would you like to say to people who like you?" Johnny replied- "Big deal."

17th - Sunday...

THE CLASH showed up at the Birmingham site for their aborted indoor punk festival. The festival was announced three weeks ago and it took only a matter of days before the local council found a way to prevent it. Nevertheless the Clash showed up to talk to several hundred fans who turned out anyway. Only minutes after they arrived so did the local constabulary who threatened arrest for inciting an unlawful gathering and for obstruction. The Clash moved on to local club Barbarellas, where they persuaded local heavy metal band Warhead to loan them their gear. With a reluctantly borrowed kit, the Clash played a forty-five minute set for the 500 punks that came to see them. Strummer told the *NME*, "I feel like a pimple that's about to burst." Other bands that were to have played the festival included The Heartbreakers, The Saints, Motorhead, The Buzzcocks, The Stinky Toys, Subway Sect and The Rich Kids (ex-Pistol Glen Matlock's new band).

18th - Monday...

RAMONES There's a new single this week from the Ramones of the comic "Pinhead" b/w a heartfelt ballad, "Swallow My Pride."

THE ANTS film their song "Plastic Surgery" for the film *Jubilee*. It's shot at the Drury Lane Theatre in London and during the actual take Adam dislocates his knee.

WARSAW pool their funds and to record some demos at Pennine Studios in Manchester. They begin just after noon and ten hours later leave with proper studio tapes of their live favorites. They hope to use the recordings to get more gigs around Manchester and perhaps farther afield. Songs recorded in this first session are "Gutz," "At A Later Date," "The Kill" and "Inside The Line." The recordings go unissued until interest in Joy Division encourages bootleggers to put out a black market 45 of all four songs.

STINKY TOYS ....London, The Vortex

19th - Tuesday...

GENERATION X have signed a long term, world-wide recording contract with Chrysalis Records. The band will immediately go into the recording studio to record their debut single which a Chrysalis spokesperson described as being, "...a special unlimited edition on 7-inch black vinyl with a green Chrysalis logo and a hole in the middle." The band's managers John Ingham and Stuart Joseph said: "Having been associated with so many fine English bands in the '60s, it was time that Chrysalis were dragged into the new decade. We look forward to them exploiting us as much as we intend to exploit them."

DESPERATE BICYCLES, that D.I.Y. band from Dalston have done it again, all by themselves. Their second single is "The Medium Was Tedium" b/w "Don't Back The Front." They've had 1,000 pressed up on their own Refill Records label today and it is said to be recorded in "slightly stereo." As with their last single, the label is on one side only, the two tracks repeating back to front. The Desperate Bicycles are discouraged that more people haven't followed their lead and made their own records. The Desperate Bicycles on this recording are founder members Danny Wigley and Nicky Stephens, joined by fourteen year-old Dave Papworth on drums and Roger Stephens on bass. Their last single was so successful that they've sold 1,500 copies, the income from which has made this second effort possible.

20th - Wednesday...

EDDIE & THE HOT RODS have their sixth single out on Island in the UK. It's "Do Anything You Wanna Do" b/w "Schoolgirl Love." Both tracks are new, originals that could be part of their upcoming LP for the fall. The single comes in a picture sleeve with the somewhat sinister Aleister Crowley in a mousketeer hat. It's destined to be the 'Rods biggest hit, climbing unrelentingly to #9 in England.

GENERATION X have their coming-out party in celebration of being signed by Chrysalis Records. Their new guardians have filled the

JULY 1977

stage sides with heavy lighting to make a video of the event. The Marquee is packed inside with a queue stretching for blocks outside. The set consisted of originals and some surprising covers. They start their set with Gary Glitter's classic "Rock On," then follow with "From The Heart," "London Life," "Above Love," "New Orders," "Listen" and "Wild Youth." The crowd gets even more worked up as they continue with "Ready Steady Go," "Day By Day," and several others.

Opening the show were Fulham's own Ramones styled band The Lurkers. They've been gigging around in pubs for the last few months and have been handed quite a break to open this event. This band is Pete Stride on guitar, Howard Wall on vocals, Manic Esso (Pete Haynes) on drums and Arturo Bassick (Arthur Billingsley) on bass. They say they'll have out an independent single of their song "Shadow" out soon but aren't sure on what label.

XTC	London, Fulham Greyhound	STINKY TOYS/KILLJOYS	London, The Roxy
GENERATION X/LURKERS	London, The Marquee		

21st - Thursday.....................................

THE SEX PISTOLS are on *Top Of The Pops* again, despite letters of protest, phone calls and editorials. Their single "Pretty Vacant" has now climbed to the #7 slot. The video was recorded under the production wizardry of Mike Mansfield. Presenter Dave Lee Travis couldn't escape this time; the Pistols are still Top 20 material.

JOHNNY MOPED and band play their farewell gig at the Red Deer in Croydon tonight. The band have also been busy recording an album for Chiswick Records which will certainly be out sometime before everyone forgets who Johnny Moped was.

THE POLICE appeared as Strontium 90 at a Gong reunion with Gong bassist Mike Howletton May 28th . Now they're back in England playing another gig today under a different name. For today only, the group is called "The Elevators," and are Mike Howlett, Stewart Copeland on drums, Andy Summers on guitar and Sting on vocals and bass. The tentative group politely splits, leaving Howlett to find other collaborators.

BOYS	High Wycombe, Nags Head	THE ELEVATORS	London, Nashville
MUTANTS	Liverpool, Havana Club	SIOUXSIE & BANSHEES/	
999	London, Hope & Anchor	UNWANTED	London, The Roxy
ONLY ONES	London, Rochester Castle	STINKY TOYS	London, Rock Garden
CHELSEA/CORTINAS/		ELVIS COSTELLO/ LURKERS	Manchester, The Rafters
LURKERS/SHAM 69	London, The Acklam Hall		

LIVE TONIGHT!

22nd - Friday.....................................

SQUEEZE make their vinyl debut today with "A Packet of Three." The band has been shopping their tapes around to every label in London but with little luck, so it's D.I.Y. time. They have the new Deptford Fun City label all to themselves. It's another new company launched by Miles Copeland. His other indie label is Step Forward Records. The single is available in 7" and 12" formats. The three tracks are "Cat On The Wall," "Night Ride" and "Back Track." The sessions were recorded at Pathway studios and produced by veteran musician John Cale. Squeeze are Glenn Tilbrook, Chris Difford, Julian Holland, Harry Kakoulli and Gilson Lavis. The single is available in a special picture cover version, with a photo from the band's day-long free concert outside The Bell pub on Jubilee Day (June 6th). Songs in the band's live set included Difford/Tilbrook love songs like "Out Of My Head" and "Heaven In Your Kiss," as well as "Makes Me Mad" and "Deep Cuts."

squeeze

PACKET OF THREE

THE ADVERTS have just been signed to Anchor Records. Their first 45 will be "Gary Gilmore's Eyes" slated for early August. The Adverts have been bouncing around the Isle with the Damned lately and their following has increased greatly in the last few weeks.

ELVIS COSTELLO finished the sessions for "My Aim Is True" six months ago. Unfortunately, Stiff Records was having contractual problems with Island UK, so it sat on the shelf until now. This album was actually recorded long before Costello's backing band, the Attractions was put together, however there is no mention of these studio musicians anywhere on the disc. Sources have revealed that they were a group of US West Coast musicians that record as Clover. They are John McFee, Sean Hopper, Mickey Shine and Johnny Ciambotti. Vocalist Huey Louis is not present for these recordings. "My Aim Is True" is the title of the album. It's a line taken from his single "Alison." The sometimes venomous album features songs like "Watching The Detectives," "Miracle Man," "Blame It On Cane" and "Sneaky Feelings." There's also some of his tracks gathered from his first three singles like "Less Than Zero," "Alison," "Welcome To The Working Week," "Red Shoes" and "Mystery Dance." The bespectacled singer has the whole of manager Jake Riveria's attention focused as they try a promotional stunt never before done. The first pressing of the LP contained a "Help Us Hype Elvis" flyer that encouraged buyers to send in postage as well as a twenty-five word description of why you like the "English" Elvis. If you're among the first 1,000, they send a friend of yours a free copy of the album you just bought. Clever, eh?

TUBEWAY ARMY is the new name for the Lasers. They used to play mostly covers, but now their new lead guitar player, Gary Webb, is writing originals for them. Gary, a huge sci-fi fan, is now calling himself "Valeriun." Paul Gardiner is the bassist "Scarlet," and Gary's uncle Gerald Lidyard is on drums as "Rael." Gary was briefly in another band from late '75 to early '76 that kept changing it's name. They were Riot, then Heroin, and also Stiletto. He was thrown out just before they renamed themselves Mean Streets. Now he's found the group that will bring him fame and fortune.

STRANGLERS have given the record public a glimpse of their next LP in the form of their new single "Something Better Change." It's the result of their recently completed LP sessions at T.W. Studios in Fulham. Martin Rushent produced the sides which includes the non-LP flipside "Straighten Out." Following the example set by "Peaches," the new single climbs into the top ten also, peaking at #9.

JULY 1977

THE DRONES are one of the new wave of Manchester bands. Their debut is on their own O.H.M.S label. It's a 7" mini album (4 songs) called "Temptations Of A White Collar Worker" and was recorded in on April the 7th at Countdown Studios. Songs include"Lookalikes," "Corgi Crap," "Hard On Me", "You'll Lose." The Drones are M.J. Drone on vocals, Gus Gangrene on guitar, Whisper on bass and Peter Purrfect on drums.

SAINTS.....................................Birmingham, Barbarella's	X-RAY SPEX/TUBEWAY ARMY......London, The Roxy
STINKY TOYS ....London, The Rock Garden	BUZZCOCKS/THE FALL ....Manchester, Hulme Labour Club

25th - Monday...

THE POLICE make their debut as a four-piece. The regular line-up of Sting, Stewart and Henry have now been joined by guitarist Andy Summers. Tension in the group is growing and it's unlikely that they'll remain a quartet much longer.

THE NOSEBLEEDS are another Manchester punk band making it to record. It's the second release from independent Rabid Records and is aptly titled "Ain't Bin To No Music School," flipped with the similarly humble "Fascist Pigs." The Nosebleeds have actually been together for several years, starting out some time ago under the name Wild Ram. They recently adopted the new "punky" name and under it have been playing around the Birmingham, Manchester and Liverpool area for the last six months. These musically unschooled lads are Ed Banger (aka Eddie Garrity) on vocals, Vincent (Vini) Reilly on guitar, Pete Crookes on bass and Toby (Phillip Tolman) on drums.

POLICE/WASPS/FLICKS ....London, The Music Machine	NEW HEARTS...........................London, Putney Rail Hotel
999 ....London, The Nashville	ADVERTS/JOHNNY MOPED/
RADIATORS ....London, The Rock Garden	REZILLOS/NEO ....London, The Vortex

26th - Tuesday...

ELVIS COSTELLO is busking on the sidewalk in front of the London Hilton where the Columbia Records world-wide convention is being held. Elvis, who has just had his debut LP "My Aim Is True" released on independent Stiff Records in the UK, has a Voxx practice amp strapped over one shoulder and sets about like a strolling musician entertaining arrivals hotel. The curious onlookers heard Elvis in a once-in-a-lifetime performance. He started with "Welcome To The Working Week" "Waiting For The End Of The World," then into the subtle "Less Than Zero." CBS conventioneers gape at the spectacle. By now the Hilton Security staff are already sniffing around for the leader to this circus. A confrontation with manager Jake Riveria sends the concierge off for reinforcements. By now the sidewalk is crowded with clapping and shouting CBS representatives with Elvis singing "Mystery Dance" in the center of it all. Then the law arrives and accuses Costello of busking, a punishable offense. "He's not busking, he's just singing in the street" Jake yells at the officer, "you can't stop people from singing!" The officer asks Elvis to move along. Elvis takes a step aside and continues singing. He is arrested and taken to the Vine Street station where he is charged with obstruction and fined £5. He is released and departs to prepare for a set that evening at Dingwalls in Camden Town. Needless to say, the gig at Dingwalls was packed with regulars and CBS conventioneers as well. It was a stunt to capture the attention of a record giant that was nothing short of brilliant and it worked!.

NEW HEARTS/VIBRATORS...........London, The Vortex (CBS Party)	REZILLOS ....London, Fulham Greyhound
ELVIS COSTELLO &	SQUEEZE ....London, Hope & Anchor
ATTRACTIONS ....London, Dingwalls	RADIATORS...........................London, The Rock Garden

27th - Wednesday...

THE BOYS release their second record despite the title "First Time." It's paired with "Whatcha Gonna Do" and "Turning Grey".

THE KILLJOYS are a new group built around ex-Lucy And The Lovers guitarist Kevin Rowland. Based out of Birmingham, they are thrilled to have their debut single "Johnny Won't Get To Heaven" released under the new Raw Records logo. The Killjoys are Kevin Rowland on vocals, Gem on bass, Mark Phillips on guitar, Heather Tonge on vocals and Joe 45 (aka Trevor) on drums. The single was recorded at Spaceward Studios in Cambridge and both screaming sides are Rowland originals. The Killjoys are light years distant from the sound that will eventually give Kevin Rowland his first hit. He'll make it to the big time in in 1980 with the song "Geno" and again in '82 with "C'mon Eileen" under the name Dexy's Midnight Runners.

ONLY ONES ....Birmingham, Rebecca's	REZILLOS ....London, Man in The Moon
ELVIS COSTELLO &	XTC ....London, Fulham Greyhound
ATTRACTIONS ....London, Hope & Anchor	RADIATORS...........................London, Rock Garden
BOOMTOWN RATS ....London, The Marquee	

28th - Thursday...

BLITZKREIG BOP are a Teeside band that debut with a three track single on the Mortonsound label. We'll guess right off that this band took their name from the Ramones tune. The songs are "Let's Go," "9 till 5" and "Bugger Off." Blitzkrieg Bop are Blank Frank on vocals and keyboards, Gloria on guitar, Mick Sick on bass and Nicky Knoxx on drums. The best track is "Let's Go," a vague re-working of Scott McKenzie's "San Francisco" from back in the summer of love in '67. They sing,"If you're going to San Francisco, you can wear some flowers in your hair. If you go to San Francisco, you will meet a lot of weirdos there.."

BOOMTOWN RATS ....Birmingham, Rebecca's	TOM ROBINSON BAND...............London, Brecknock
999 ....London, Hope & Anchor	ULTRAVOX!............................London, The Marquee
RINGS/REZILLOS/	SQUEEZE/DIRE STRAITS.............London, The Albany Empire
MENACE ....London, The Roxy	

JULY 1977

30th - Saturday......................................

THE MANCHESTER SCENE is exposed in a two page article in the *New Musical Express* by Paul Morley. The Buzzcocks are addressed and a lengthy interview with former lead singer Howard Devoto reveals that he is putting together another, as yet unnamed, band that will play fast AND slow songs that he'll write up in his own style. He'll be showing the world his command of the language and college band. Another new band mentioned is Warsaw, characterized as "one of the many recent new wave functional bands: easily digestible, doomed maybe to eternal support spots. Whether they will find a style of their own is questionable but probably not important. Their instinctive energy often compensates for the occasional lameness of their songs, but they seem unaware of the audience while performing." Other bands mentioned include Slaughter & the Dogs, The Drones, Ed Banger and the Nosebleeds, the Fall, John Cooper Clarke and the Worst.

LIVE TONIGHT!

XTC ....Birmingham, Hopwood Waterside Club	
NEW HEARTS/NEO ....London, Roxy	THE MODELS ....London, The Red Cow
REZILLOS/GONZALES ....London, Dingwalls	VIBRATORS/PENETRATION ....London, The Marquee

August 1st - Monday......................................

CHRISSIE HYNDE is about to involve Johnny Rotten in a scheme to stay in England. He's a friend and had offered to help her out. Now, as the days are dwindling, she has trouble getting back into England on a trip back from Paris. She's turned away at customs in Dover. "So I had to go back to Paris, pretend I lost my passport, get a new one, the whole thing and then go in through another port of entry. And at this point I was really desperate because my time was really running out. And so Rotten said 'Yeah, I'll marry you if that helps you stay in the country.' Then they did that Bill Grundy thing and I couldn't get hold of Rotten and I was really nervous, my time was running out. Finally find him in a pub somewhere and say, 'what's happening with our thing (the marriage of convenience)?' He went 'Ow gawd!' cause he's so bummed out he's super famous all of the sudden and Sid asked 'What's going on, what's going on?' I explained what about my problem and he volunteered 'I'll do it, but there has to be something in it for me.' I said, 'I'll give you two quid' and he said, 'OK.' So we picked up Sid, got his birth certificate at his mothers house cause he was under age, come back home to my house, where we could keep him and he wouldn't escape. He was with this girl and the three of us slept in my bed and they were having a squelching session all night. And I was like 'God you guys, I'm trying to sleep.' I just kept getting knees and elbows in my back all night. And then in the morning, we still had Sid by the scruff of the neck, took him to the registry office and it was closed for an extended holiday. And he couldn't go the next day cause he was in court himself. That's how close I came. I eventually worked something else out in order to stay."

THE SEX PISTOLS' first bootleg LP is on the street this week. It's titled "No Fun" and features the Matlock era Pistols romping through several songs they've already recorded and released as well as some most unusual cover songs. The album is described as "grade z mono, that makes the Beatles At The Star Club look like a Yes album." The LP includes Sex Pistols originals like "Did You No Wrong," "Pushin' & Shovin'," "Seventeen," "New York," "Pretty Vacant" and "No Fun." They also are featured doing covers of the Small Faces' tune "Whatcha Gonna Do About It?," the Monkees "Stepping Stone," and the Who's "Substitute." Most of the songs are from the Dave Goodman sessions that preceded the EMI single.

THE BOYS release their debut album "The Boys". It had been delayed a week to correct some artwork that was found objectionable. It contains their first and second single as well as several other beaty tracks guaranteed to set young toes a-tappin'. A highlight is the rave-up version of the Beatles classic "I Call Your Name." Originals on the LP are "Kiss Like A Nun," "Living In The City," "Cop Cars," "Tumble With Me" and "No Money."

2.3 CHILDREN are another new group from Sheffield. They take their name from the average number of children in the nuclear family. The group is formed around the talents of guitarist Paul Bower (editor of the *Gunrubber* fanzine), Paul Shaft on bass and Haydn Boyes-Weston on drums. They are taking a try to incorporate good hooks in music while still presenting something different.

GENERATION X/LURKERS/	REZILLOS ....London, The Rock Garden
ART ATTACKS/STEEL PULSE ....London, The Vortex	THE VIBRATORS/
999/SWORDS ....London, The Nashville	PENETRATION ....London, The Marquee

2nd - Tuesday......................................

THE SNIVELING SHITS prove there can be a truly comic side to punk rock. The Sniveling Shits' single is reportedly called "Terminal Stupid." In 1:32, the band speed bops thru a ditty that "sets the cause of militant feminism back ten years, maybe fifteen." It's flipped with "I Can't Come" and is on their own Ghetto Rockers label. The band only got together in late June and have kept their identities a secret, which the band claim, "...mostly because we need cheap publicity." Since nobody except certain reviewers in the elite music press have ever seen a copy, some doubt that it exists at all and is just a joke. Who is the band? It's said that they also gig under the name Arthur Comics and there's thought that at least one shit is Vibrator John Ellis.

SEX PISTOLS bassist Sid Vicious dons a suit and tie to appear at his hearing at the Wells Street Magistrates Court. He'd been charged with carrying a knife when searched at the 100 Club Punk Festival last September. Appearing as character witness for Sid are Mick Jones and Paul Simonon of the Clash, *NME* writer Caroline Coon and Generation X manager John Ingham. Even though his case appeared trumped up, a stiff minded judge charged Sid to pay a £125 fine. He paid and left to rejoin his bandmates as they toured Scandinavia. Interviewed in this week's *NME*, Sid confided, "I hate the name Sid, it's a right poxy name, it's really vile. I stayed in for about two weeks because everyone kept calling me Sid, but they just wouldn't stop. Rotten started. He's 'orrible like that, he's always picking on me..."

AUGUST 1977

ELVIS COSTELLO/THE YACHTS .....Liverpool, Eric's
GENERATION X/SKREWDRIVER/
PENETRATION ....London, The Vortex
STUKAS ....London, Rochester Castle

X-RAY SPEX ....London, Hope & Anchor
BOOMTOWN RATS/TONIGHT ....London, The Nashville
REZILLOS ....London, The Golden Lion

3rd - Wednesday...

THE REZILLOS, one of the first of the new breed from Scotland, had already taken in 2,000 advance orders for their debut single before it was even recorded! It's out this week as the first release on Sensible Records. Quite a statement when the band is anything BUT sensible. The song "I Can't Stand My Baby" is flipped with the Lennon-McCartney song "I Wanna Be Your Man." It's delivered at breakneck speed with doubled up vocals that drive the point home. The Rezillos have been bouncing about London lately dressed like refugees from Thunderbirds Are Go! and should soon be at a pub near you.

THE RAMONES wonder what people expect from them. They're just trying to be themselves. In the *NME* this week Tommy Ramone said, "Dey say we're STOOPID. Whadda dey want?? Fer us to use flugel horn 'n' strings, or sumting?"

Roxy audition night with
CRUTCH PLATES/BEARS/NOTHING ...London, Roxy

BOOMTOWN RATS ....London, The Marquee
NO DICE/REZILLOS ....London, Music Machine

9th - Tuesday...

THE DAMNED have returned from France and are now working on some new recordings with their current five piece line-up. They say that the membership of the band could would be even more improved if they could find a sax player! Recording sessions are being held at Pink Floyd's Islington studios with Nick Mason producing. This isn't their first departure from working with Stiff's own Nick Lowe. They had tried a few trial recordings with '60s veteran Shel Talmy but didn't like the studios that he was able to work in.

THE PORK DUKES turn in the most absurd records of this month and possibly the worst in taste. It's titled "Bend & Flush." The sleeve supplies a note describing the effort as being from the "meat productions stable,...sexist punk at its throbbing orgasmic best." Sheeeze! The Pork Dukes are probably a group of studio musicians that love to share a dirty joke or two in off hours. Their debut single is flipped with "Throbbing Gristle." It's on Wood Records and comes in a special crudely drawn sleeve. Who are they ? The sleeve credits Vilos Styles on vocals, Ron Dodge on guitar, Scabs on bass and Bonk on drums. It is strange that singles like this go unnoticed while the Sex Pistols get the focus of the GLC's attention.

SQUEEZE ....London, Dingwalls
XTC/WASPS ....London, Music Machine
BOOMTOWN RATS ....London, The Nashville
JOHNNY MOPED ....London, The Village Inn

SLAUGHTER & DOGS/
MEAN STREET/THE FLICKS/
FRUIT EATING BEARS ....London, The Vortex

10th - Wednesday...

THE CLASH have a bootleg LP appearing at record stalls around London. It is a recording of their performance at the Electric Circus in Manchester on May 8th. Look for it under the title "Take It Or Leave It." CBS Records are doing everything in their power to stop it from being distributed. Tracks from the show include "London's Burning," "1977," "I'm So Bored With The USA," "Pressure Drop," "Hate & War," "48 Hours," "Protex Blue" (mis-titled "Danny"), "Capitol Radio," "Police and Thieves," "Cheat," "Remote Control," "Career Opportunities," "Janie Jones," "White Riot," "Garageland," and still another version of "1977."

XTC have been signed by Virgin. The deal involves a quarter of a £1,000,000 for six albums. XTC will now be able to quit their day jobs (those that still have them) and begin playing full-time. They'll be working on their debut single soon after completing a series of dates around London this week. They signed their contracts in their manager's club, The Affair, in Swindon.

THOSE NAUGHTY LUMPS are a new Liverpool band that can't seem to get booked to play at Eric's, so they turn to the heretofore unknown Havana Club for help. They have convinced its manager to begin booking in new wave acts in the middle of the week. Bands which are for some reason not being booked at Eric's. Among the groups this will affect immediately will include Those Naughty Lumps, The Mutants, The Accelerators, 051, Radio Blank and the Storm Troopers.

THE NAUGHTY LUMPS ....Liverpool, The Havana Club
CHELSEA ....London, The Marquee

999 ....London, The Winning Post

12th - Friday...

THE ADVERTS release the haunting single "Gary Gilmore's Eyes." It's the story of an eye transplant patient who is on the receiving end of the executed murderers eyes. It's flipped with a studio version of "Bored Teenagers," which was featured on the "Live At The Roxy" album two months ago.

TOM ROBINSON has been signed by EMI Records. The outspoken gay activist has caused some concern among the EMI board who want to block his desired first release for the label, the homosexual anthem "Glad To Be Gay." Their selection for a debut single is the safe and popular live number "2-4-6-8 Motorway." (EMI doesn't seem to catch the repeated reference to cocaine in the song.). The Robinson Band, or T.R.B. (which they prefer) is made up of Tom on vocals, Danny Kustow on guitar, Mark Amber on keyboards and Brian Taylor on drums. Robinson has only had his new band going for nine months, previously being in a folk style band, Cafe Society. He is, in a minor way still connected to his former band in that he is under agreement to pay out a 10% royalty and advance bonus to Ray Davies' Konk

AUGUST 1977

publishing for the next two years, a result of a prior arrangement that he had some trouble shaking.

THE MEMBERS are a new group from the London suburbs of Camberly and West Drayton fronted by Nicky Tesco. They have their live debut tonight at the Roxy Club. They'll almost make it to the top ten in the UK in '79 and then have another minor hit in the US with a song called "Working Girl" in America in late 1982.

LIVE TONIGHT!

NOSEBLEEDS/MEMBERS		ROKOTO/JAPAN	London, Music Machine
SHAM 69/THE VICTIMS	London, Roxy	LURKERS/	
GENERATION X	London, The Marquee	AMYL NITRATE/TAKE OFFS	London, The White Lion
SQUEEZE	London, Brecknock	BOOMTOWN RATS/WASPS	Sheffield, The Top Rank

14th - Sunday.....................................

GLASGOW, SCOTLAND has levied a ban on all "punk" shows in the city. The city councilors were shocked by the "atrocities" they witnessed on a punk special that was screened on TV in Scotland on the 3rd. Although there has been no violence at any punk gigs in Glasgow yet, this is seen as a preventative measure, not a punitive one. It's unfortunate that Glasgow based bands such as The Exile, The Jolt and the Cuban Heels cannot play their hometown any longer.

THE RUTS are a new band coming together in the London suburb of Southall. Bassist Dave Ruffy and guitar player Paul Fox had just left a cover band called Hit And Run. Paul's friend Malcolm Owen is going to sing for the group. They still need a drummer and for the time being, they're having ex-Hit And Run drummer Paul Mattock sitting in. They're rehearsing at a small studio in Rotherhithe, in the docklands. The group is totally into the new punk scene and are regulars in the crowd at the Vortex. Songs that are being kicked around in this primal stage are "Rich Bitch," "Out Of Order," "I Ain't Sophisticated" and "Lobotomy." A lot of things are still up in the air with this group. They've not settled on a name yet, and have been considering Malcolm and the Sulking Loafers.

SQUEEZE	London, Roundhouse	FRUIT EATING BEARS	London, The Roundhouse
ELVIS COSTELLO	London, The Nashville	DOCTORS OF MADNESS/	
MEAN STREET	London, Roxy	PENETRATION	Manchester, Electric Circus

16th - Tuesday.....................................

THE SEX PISTOLS are tracked down by *Melody Maker* magazine to get their reaction to the shocking news of the untimely death of rock & roll legend Elvis Presley. Reacting in the expected caustic manner, Johnny Rotten said "Elvis was dead before he died and his gut was so big it cast a shadow over rock and roll in the last few years. Our music is what's important now."

THE BUZZCOCKS, Manchester's most famous punk band, have been signed by United Artists Records, the contract itself being signed over the bar of the Electric Circus in Manchester. They'll go into the studios immediately to record their next single. It'll probably be one of their most successful stage numbers, "Orgasm Addict." They'll also be planning their debut album. Pete Shelley says "…we signed to make records, not to be in debt to a record company." The Buzzcocks are Pete Shelley on vocals and guitar, Steve Diggle on rhythm guitar, John Maher on drums and Garth Smith on bass.

CHELSEA/CORTINAS	Birmingham, Barbarella's	THE JAM	London, 100 Club
ADVERTS/STEEL PULSE/		XTC	London, Rochester Castle
LURKERS/MASTERSWITCH/		BOOMTOWN RATS	London, The Nashville
OUTSIDERS	London, The Vortex	PENETRATION	London, The Marquee

18th - Thursday.....................................

SHAM 69's August 12th gig at the Roxy is reviewed by *NME's* Tony Parsons who parks his report under the headline "Next Week's Big Thing." Parsons likens the band to the Sex Pistols and enjoys their fresh, genuine appeal. "Jimmy Pursey of Sham 69 is a star. Hardly anyone has heard of him or his band, he doesn't get interviewed by *Vogue* or *Sunday Times* magazine and he probably don't pull any more birds than you do. Nevertheless, Jimmy Pursey of Sham 69 is a star…Sham 69 are ex-skinheads who don't have the cash or the inclination to dazzle you with the mandatory sartorial elegance of corporate sponsored urban guerillas. They're content to use their performance to provoke REACTION! God, I wish you could have been there. Sham 69 are a band who do everything except lie." Songs played include "I Wanna Have A Fight," "Hey Little Rich Boy," "I Don't Wanna," "Red London," and a track that screams from the crossfire, "Ulster."

THE POLICE have booted guitarist Henry Padovani from their line-up, trimming the group from a quartet back to a trio. This follows unsuccessful recording sessions with John Cale for their follow up to this summers debut 45 "Fall Out." The band tried to carry on as a four-piece for a while but this proved difficult and with Padovani out, the new player is Andy Summers. He's a guitarist of substance, with backgrounds playing in the Animals in the late '60s, as well as backing Kevin Ayers and Kevin Coyne. The band plan to go to Paris with Wayne County in the coming weeks, after which they plan to record again. Tonight they make their live debut as the "new" three-piece.

POLICE	Birmingham, Barbarella's	SQUEEZE	London, Hope & Anchor
DAMNED/ADVERTS/		BOOMTOWN RATS	London, The Marquee
FRUIT EATING BEARS	London, The Sundown	WASPS	London, Rochester Castle

19th - Friday.....................................

THE VIBRATORS are bored with London. The new, exciting town for music, to them, is Berlin. So they've packed up and moved to Berlin on a semi-permanent basis. Today also sees the release of their latest single "London Girls" which was recorded at a recent gig at the Marquee. It's their fifth single and is flipped with another original song called "Stiff Little Fingers," the very song that the likewise named Irish band took their name from.

AUGUST 1977

SEX PISTOLS have found it increasingly difficult for them to play in their own country. To get around this the band is making occasional appearances as the S.P.O.T.S. That's short for "Sex Pistols On Tour Secretly." Tonight's secret affair was at the Lafayette in Wolverhampton with a one pound fifty admission. The band started the set with "Anarchy In The UK," then right into "I Wanna Be Me." Following that, "Pretty Vacant," "New York," "EMI," "Holidays In The Sun," "No Feelings," "Problems" and "God Save The Queen." The band return for a one song encore of the Stooge's "No Fun." It was the Sex Pistols first gig in England since December. A Virgin spokesman said that these concerts have to be held clandestinely and if word were to leak out about one it would be cancelled immediately.

THE BOOMTOWN RATS, Ireland's newest rock band on the club scene lately, release their debut single on Ensign Records. It's the stage favorite "Looking After Number One" flipped with "Born To Burn" and Robert Parker's '60s hit "Barefootin'" recorded live in Amsterdam. A limited edition of (only) 20,000 of the 12" version, includes a BTR armband.

GENERATION X/		ADVERTS	London, The Nashville
JOHNNY & SELF ABUSERS	Edinburgh, The Clouds	EATER	London, The Roxy
STUKAS	London, Hope & Anchor	S.P.O.T.S./PREFECTS	Wolverhampton, The Lafayette

20th - Saturday...

GENERATION X gig scheduled for Clouds at Edinburgh got off to a rather rocky start. About 6:30 PM police arrived and said that the band couldn't play since the club had no music license. This excuse held up, even though the Jam played there three weeks ago. Generation X wanted to play and see that the 400 mile trip up to Scotland was not wasted. They offered to play for nothing in order to get around the law. The police agreed but but didn't have an officer to stand watch. Stalemate. So Generation X moved the concert to a place that did have a license, the Pantiles Hotel in West Lindon, just outside of Edinburgh. Moving the band was easy, but then they had to organize transport for the 300 punks that had already arrived for the gig. Once the show was underway, kids were pogoing in the halls and the hotel manager wondering what he had gotten himself into. The opener for the evening is a local band called Johnny & the Self Abusers who went on after Generation X in case the local police busted the gig.

NINE NINE NINE have just released an optimistic 10,000 copies of their debut single on their own LaBritain label. The songs are "I'm Alive" and "Quite Disappointing." They've been playing around London for almost a year under several different names, beginning as The Dials, then The Frantics and also as 48 Hours. Four months ago, they became Nine Nine Nine. Preparing for the big move to stardom, the members of Nine Nine Nine quit their jobs after seeing some hope of making a name for themselves. Employment offices around London are searching for a replacement postal clerk, painter, hall porter and GLC groundsman.

THE LURKERS make their grand debut with the single "Shadow" and "Love Story." It's the first release for the new Beggars Banquet Records label. The band is Pete Stride on guitar, Manic Esso on drums, Arturo Bassick on bass and Howard Wall on vocals.

REZILLOS	Glasgow, Shuffle's	ADVERTS	London, The Nashville
EATER	Liverpool, Eric's		

21st - Sunday...

ELVIS COSTELLO makes his third Sunday night appearance at the Nashville Rooms. This time word has gotten out about the bespectacled wunderkin and a crowd of 1,000 arrive to listen. The problem is that the Nashville only has a capacity of 300. The mob outside wouldn't go home and transport workers at the West Kensington Station (next door) called in the police. Twelve officers arrive and begin thinning the mob. There were eight arrested this evening that did refuse to leave though. Five of the eight were journalists there to cover the story. The charges were "willful obstruction." There is no doubt that the journalists will have something to write about while fighting the charges. By the way, Elvis was great.

CHRISSIE HYNDE is cutting demos for a new record company called Real Records. It's being run by Dave Hill, who worked A&R for Anchor Records. He's interested in Chrissie's songs and has her cut a demo of "The Phone Call." She still has to get a band together to realize her dreams, but that's been a three-year struggle.

BOOMTOWN RATS	Dublin, Dalymount Festival	SQUEEZE	London, Other Cinema
999/SWORDS/NEW HEARTS	London, The Sundown	EDDIE & HOT RODS	London, The Marquee
ELVIS COSTELLO	London, The Nashville	FRUIT EATING BEARS	London, Hammersmith Swan

24th - Wednesday...

THE SEX PISTOLS are preparing to enter the movie world. A film is being planned and the script is supposedly finished, however details are a highly guarded secret. It is known that Russ Meyer (of Super Vixen film fame) is being brought in to shoot the piece. Also keeping the Sex Pistols busy, is planning their first album. The recording is hoped to be available for release in late September or early August. The Sex Pistols continue their "secret tour" tonight in Doncaster at the Outlook Club under the name "The Tax Exiles."

GENERATION X and their record company get beaten to the punch by bootlegers who have issued an EP with versions of "Your Generation," "Save My Life" and "Ready Steady Go." The recordings are taken from the band's demo sessions in February and are very rough versions. The folks at Chrysalis will have to get after it quick if they intend to capture any of the market with their single.

WARSAW have another personnel change. Their drummer Steve Brotherdale, who only joined Warsaw eight weeks ago, has quit to join The Panik. Warsaw have posted notices again and have found Steve Morris of Maccelssfield. Unlike Warsaw's last two drummers who only lasted a few weeks with the band, Steve (later Stephen) will remain with Warsaw as they change their name to Joy Division and then again

AUGUST 1977

to New Order. He's still with New Order sixteen years after joining.

LIVE TONIGHT!

PIGS/SOCIAL SECURITY	Bristol, Bamboo Club	TYLA GANG/SOFT BOYS	London, The Rock Garden
CHELSEA	Glasgow, Disco Harry	XTC	London, Hope & Anchor
NAUGHTY LUMPS	Liverpool, Havana Club	EDDIE & HOT RODS	London, The Marquee

25th - Thursday.................................

PERE UBU has "The Modern Dance" and "Heaven" out in the US on their own Hearthan Records label. They had previously recorded the "A" side for the US compilation LP "Max's Kansas City Vol. Two," but it was rejected because of the organizers inability to understand, much less make out the lyrics. Now the group has re-recorded the song and released it as a limited edition 45 with a pressing of only 1,000 copies. This might be the last indie record for Pere Ubu. Recently, Phonogram-Mercury A&R man Cliff Burnstein signed the band up to his new Blank Records subsidiary. They are already planning their debut album for the label, which is tentatively titled "The Modern Dance" as well. As always, the band has shifted personnel again. This time out the group maintains the Thomas - Ravenstine - Kraus core, but includes the latest member Tony Maimone, who joined Pere Ubu for "Street Waves" in October of last year. Now playing elsewhere is guitarist Tom Herman.

THE SEX PISTOLS play another in the series of "secret" gigs. They've appeared as S.P.O.T.S. and the Tax Exiles. Watching carefully for odd names that aren't recognized usually pays off, but tonight in Scarborough the band is simply billed as "Special Guest." One could easily overlook it. Tomorrow though they're booked into the Middlesborough Rock Garden as "Acne Rabble."

WRECKLESS ERIC makes his world debut whining on about how he'll search the "Whole Wide World" for his true love. Not exactly your social comment stuff but honest enough to be attractive. The flip is "Semaphore Signals" and is very similar. The single is on Stiff Records, that inflexible label that shows what it's like to be different.

SQUEEZE/THE DRONES	London, The Nashville	SLAUGHTER & DOGS/DRONES	London, Roxy
EDDIE & HOT RODS	London, The Marquee	ED BANGER & NOSEBLEEDS	Manchester, The Rafters
XTC	London, The Red Cow		

28th - Sunday..................................

MAGAZINE is the new band that Howard Devoto has finally assembled since he left the Buzzcocks. He had said he felt tired of shouting vocals and wanted something more intelligent to sing. After posting adverts for musicians at the Manchester Virgin Record center, a band is built. There are rumors about that he's setting Kafka to music. The band will make its debut soon. Members of the group include Howard Devoto on vocals and guitar, John McGeoch on guitar and sax, Barry Adamson on bass, Martin Jackson on drums and Bob Dickinson on keyboards.

ELVIS COSTELLO's music has a common thread running through it that he's not shy about pointing out to readers of the *NME* this week. "The only two things that matter to me, the only motivation points for me writing all these songs, are revenge and guilt. Those are the only emotions that I know about, that I know I can feel. Love? I dunno what it means, really and it doesn't exist in my songs."

WAYNE COUNTY & THE ELECTRIC CHAIRS are VERY out of place in the mudpen that is this year's Reading Rock Festival. They're not what the long haired, gritty audience are used to. When they launch into their third number, "If You Don't Wanna Fuck Me, Fuck Off," they are taken quite literally and retreat the stage under a hail of beer cans, rocks and mud. They attempt to re-take the stage minutes later to finish their set but are again driven off. Wayne County vows to never play at a festival again.

ELVIS COSTELLO & ATTRACTIONS	London, The Nashville	999/ADVERTS/LONDON	Manchester, Electric Circus
TOM ROBINSON BAND	London, The Other Cinema	WAYNE COUNTY & THE ELECTRIC CHAIRS +	Reading, the Festival

29th - Monday.................................

SHAM 69 are the latest signings to Step Forward Records, home to The Cortinas, The Models and Chelsea. They recorded their debut single at Pathway Studios with John Cale producing. The tracks include "Ulster," "I Don't Wanna" and "Red London." Sham 69 are Jimmy Sham (aka Jimmy Pursey) on vocals, Albie Slider (aka Albie Maskell) on "Tea Boy" bass, Mark Doidie (Mark Cain) on drums and dustbins and Dave Vicar (aka Dave Parsons) on lead guitar.

MENACE are a London band that are making their debut with the 45 "Insane Society" b/w "Screwed Up." It's released today on Illegal Records, the company started by Miles Copeland to release his brothers record (The Police- "Fall Out"). Menace are Morgan Webster, Steve Tannett, Charley Casey and Noel Martin.

SQUEEZE	London, Russell Gardens	TOM ROBINSON BAND	London, The Golden Lion
XTC	London, The Nashville	CHELSEA/NEO/SWANK	London, The Vortex
LURKERS/JAPAN	London, The Rock Garden	SLAUGHTER & DOGS/DRONES	Sheffield, Top Rank

30th - Tuesday.................................

THE RICH KIDS play two unannounced dates. One last night at the Vortex and another tonight opening for Tom Robinson. These are the first concerts for ex-Pistol Matlock since being fired/leaving seven months back. The band was still one member short of their ideal line-up so they asked Mick Jones of the Clash to join them for the night. Matlock sat in for the missing bassist for the Clash when they were putting it together so consider it a debt repaid. If you were there either night you would have heard "Burning Sounds," "Rich Kids," "No Lip," "I Ain't Hung Up On You," "I Think We're Alone Now" (a Tommy James '60s tune), "Empty Words," "Strange One" and finally their own

AUGUST 1977

version of "Pretty Vacant." The Rich Kids are Glen Matlock on bass & vocals, Steve New on guitar and Rusty Egan on drums. They're still looking for that magic fourth member. They call him "Jimmy Norman" for lack of anything else. Glen had done some other secret gigs with ex-Slik popster Midge Ure, but claimed that it didn't work out. Midge didn't want to move down to London from Scotland.

MIDGE URE has been living and playing within the confines of successful pop group Slik since '75 and is beginning to feel compressed, unable to do he wants to do. After two chart toppers in late '75 and early '76, Slik failed to recapture the success they once enjoyed. They certainly aren't rolling in the royalties they dreamed they would have either. Times have changed. It's 1977 and this punk movement is where the excitement is, but they don't want to be seen as bandwagon jumpers. So, the members of Slik are hiding themselves under the name PVC 2. Midge Ure and Kenny Hyslop have written some songs and recorded three songs live on a two track tape deck. The finished 45 was released disguised under the name PVC 2 on local label Zoom Records. The three tracks on vinyl are "Pain," "Put You In The Picture" and "Deranged, Demented and Free."

THE VALVES have their debut single released by Zoom Records in Edinburgh. Their 45 is "For Adolfs Only" and "Robot Love." They're very much like a Scottish version of the Ramones and don't take things too serious. The Valves are Dee Robot (aka Dave Robertson) on vocals, Teddy Dair on drums, Ronnie MacKinnon on lead guitar and Gordon Scott on bass. Label owner Bruce Findlay is also acting as the distributor for the Dundee based label NRG who have out a new record called "Jerkin'" and "Push n' Shove" by the Drive.

LIVE TONIGHT!

ADVERTS	Edinburgh, Tiffany's	999/ART ATTAX/	
TOM ROBINSON BAND	London, Brecknock	NOW/THE FLIES	London, The Vortex
BONE IDOL	London, Duke Of Lancaster	THE LURKERS	London, Putney Rail Hotel
XTC/THE MODELS	London, The Nashville	THE MODELS/SWORDS	London, The Rock Garden

31st - Wednesday......................................

THE SEX PISTOLS play another one of their secret concerts tonight in Plymouth as "The Hamsters." Other names they've used go from the mundane "Special Guest" to "Acne Rabble" and "S.P.O.T.S." The Hamsters moniker must certainly be a nod to Johnny's childhood pet hamster Sid. Rumors about these secret concerts is spreading so far afield that people are traveling great distances to see the Sex Pistols and then being disappointed when they can't play, or don't show up at all. There also is the growing feeling that the hype about the Sex Pistols being banned in London is just that, hype. In reality, there have been no applications with the Greater London Council for a Sex Pistols gig in London this year. Is the ban for real or is it just hype?

DAMNED	Birmingham, Barbarella's	NAUGHTY LUMPS	Liverpool, Havana Club
ELVIS COSTELLO &		XTC	London, Hope & Anchor
ATTRACTIONS	Edinburgh, FESTIVAL	S.P.O.T.S.	Plymouth, Castaway's

September 1st - Thursday....................

THE BOOMTOWN RATS are riding high these days. Their debut single "Looking After Number One" is selling quickly and has been included on their LP on Ensign released this week. It was recorded in Koln Germany with Robert "Mutt" Lange producing. The LP features all of the band's stage favorites, like "Mary Of The 4th Form," "Never Bite The Hand That Feeds," "Joey's On The Street Again" and "Neon Heart." On the cover of the album, the Rats themselves appear to be dead in individual plastic bags. This gives the American Mercury Records Artist Development manager Mike Bone a brainstorm about the ideal way to start radio programmers talking about the 'Rats. Following the lead of the photo on the cover, he decides to send US radio stations the new single "Looking After Number One" along with a freeze dried dead rat in a plastic bag! The result is that not only the label managers at Mercury US come down on Bone, but so does the band, their management and the US Post Office (for sending hazardous material through the mail.) It does little to convert anyone to being a 'Rats fan but it's a story still talked about.

There is still a little confusion about what the Boomtown Rats are. In *Melody Maker* they question "what will we label them? Rock and roll, rhythm and blues, pop and new wave? All tags apply but no one alone totally fits the bill." In the band's own press kit, lead singer Bob Geldof states clearly, "We are not punks. The Boomtown Rats are 1977 pop." Contrary to these opinions, their misled American label reclassifies the band. From the minutes of a corporate meeting of Mercury Records, "Though the band does not think of itself as a "punk rock" band, we are promoting them as such...Mike Gormley will type the bio so it will have a high number of typographical errors which will be left in." Ultimately, this lack of understanding in the US is the band's undoing. Their album and attendant singles are huge successes in the UK and disappear without a trace in America, until the band changes labels and has a world-wide smash hit in 1979 with "I Don't Like Mondays."

THE SEX PISTOLS pop up again at the Winter Garden in Penzance for a secret gig. The club billed them as "A mystery band of international repute." Only about 400 people witness the event. Strangely enough this is one of the few gigs on this secret tour where the secret was too well kept.

GENERATION X , who signed with Chrysalis four weeks ago, have their debut 45 "Your Generation" released today. The single is destined to be a theme song for the new wave movement in it's stance of, "Trying to forget your generation...your generation don't mean a thing to me." *Sounds* magazine described it as sounding like, "Cliff Richards and the Shadows on sulfate." In *Record Mirror*, pop star Elton John reviews the single saying..."This is really dreadful garbage. It doesn't do anything for me and the Ramones do this sort of thing so much better...Hear it first thing in the morning and you'll want to go straight back to bed. It's hideously recorded." The track is flipped with the powerful "Day By Day."

SEPTEMBER 1977

XTC ....London, The Red Cow	BUZZCOCKS ....Manchester, The Rafters
ONLY ONES ....London, The Nashville	"A mystery band…." ....Penzance, Winter Gardens

4th - Sunday...

THE HEARTBREAKERS return to the UK with "renewed work visas." Quite a turn around, since they were deported two months ago. They were initially thinking they'd be out of England for about eighteen months, but somehow found a shortcut back. There are some musicians claiming the Heartbreakers were self-exiled and used this as an excuse for headlines. Thunders & Co. are planning to record their new single in the next few days. Their debut album, recorded with producer Chris Stamp last spring, will be issued next month.

THE CLASH get grouped with The Sex Pistols and Tom Robinson Band as a "political" group, but there's disagreement on the matter from within. Paul Simonon of the Clash told the *NME*, "I don't understand what people are talking about when they say The Clash is a political band. I didn't know who the Prime Minister was until a few weeks ago!" Sounds a little familiar doesn't it? Isn't that almost exactly what Steve Jones of the Sex Pistols said back on June 4th?

ELVIS COSTELLO ....London, The Nashville	BUZZCOCKS/THE WORST ....London, The Sundown

6th - Tuesday...

THE SKIDS emerge from Scotland, inspired by the punk movement that's swarming down in London. The root of the new band rose out of a Bowie cover band called Tattoo. Its two principle members, Stuart Adamson and Willie Simpson have gotten together with Alistair Moore and Richard Jobson, to form a new group called the Skids. They found their drummer Thomas Kellichan using a newspaper advert. They're all from the mining towns surrounding Dunfermline. The Skids are rehearsing and rehearsing, hoping to get that break that'll take them South to be discovered. Although the Skids will have some small impact on the music scene, Stuart Adamson's group Big Country will eleven top forty hits in the UK in the '80s.

THE PUNK ROCK MOVIE is an amature film by Don Letts, the black DJ at the Roxy Club. He used his position and good sense to capture what was going on all around him on film. He shot 8mm sound film of some of the most important moments in this new music movement, edited them together and has presented it as *The Punk Rock Movie*. Among the clips in the final edit are the Sex Pistols gig at the Screen on the Green in Islington, the Clash White Riot Tour, Shane McGowan trashing the Jams' drum kit, backstage candids of Generation X, The Slits, Wayne County, Siouxsie & The Banshees and some live footage of fans that captures the feeling of 1977 perfectly. The film, like the movement itself, is rough cut and homemade. You can be guaranteed that it will never win awards, but that's not the point is it? Don Letts became a musician himself, becoming one of the vocalists for the group Big Audio Dynamite in the early '80s.

GENERATION X/THE JOLT............London, The Marquee	ELECTRIC CHAIRS/KILLJOYS/
BUZZCOCKS...........................Birmingham, Barbarella's	LOCAL OPERATOR/
THE SLITS ....London, Dingwalls	IGNERANTS ....London, The Vortex

7th - Wednesday...

FANZINES are featured in a double page spread this week in *Sounds*. Notable in the zerox paper-storm are *No Future, Tacky, Jolt, Skum, Shews, Black Sun, Live Wire* and *Negative Reaction*. There is also mention of Sheffield-based *Gunrubber*, Tumbridge Wells-based *Septic Ears, Manchester's Ghast Up,* and Glasgow's *Trash-77*. Old favorites like *Sniffin Glue, 48 Thrills, Flicks* and *Ripped & Torn* are also covered. Most are available from 10-40p each, on a very irregular basis from your local indie record shop.

THE BUZZCOCKS have been invited to record some songs for the John Peel BBC Radio program. They've just been signed to United Artists and these will be their first recordings since Howard Devoto left the group. Songs laid down include "Fast Cars," "(Moving Away From The) Pulsebeat" and "What Do I Get?" They're scheduled to begin work on their debut single for UA on Friday.

BOOMTOWN RATS ....Edinburgh, FESTIVAL	THE MEAT/CYCLES/TICKET..........London, Roxy Club
STUKAS/THE JOLT ....London, Hope & Anchor	LURKERS ....London, The Red Cow
ELECTRIC CHAIRS ....London, Dingwalls	

9th - Friday...

ALBERTO Y LOS TRIOS PARANOIAS are sailing high these days on the success of their macabre, albeit humorous musical *Sleak!* so why not have a vinyl artifact to go along with it? Well now you have one. It's the "Snuff Rock" EP and features four songs from *Sleak!* In the grooves are "Kill," "Gobbin On Life," "Snuffin' Like That," and the reggae track "Snuffin' In Babylon." It was produced under the watchful eye of Nick Lowe. Besides being a document of the highlights of a successful stage show, it's one of the funniest and most on-the-mark parodies of punk rock that's been done.

PATTI SMITH's original April '76 version of "Gloria" is reissued as a 12" single, with her live version of "My Generation" on the flip. It's the same single they issued last year with the exception that the lyrics are complete and unedited. The over-cautious managers at EMI had it edited when they distributed Arista. New distributor, new version. It's available now in a 12" format only.

GENERATION X ....Birmingham, Barbarella's	ONLY ONES ....London, The Speak Easy
SQUEEZE/REALISTS ....London, Albany Empire	LITTLE ACRE/RIFF RAFF.............London, The Nashville
999/TOOLS ....London, The Marquee	WASPS/SKREWDRIVER.............London, The Roxy

SEPTEMBER 1977

10th - Saturday.....................

IAN DURY, the former Kilburn and the High Roads singer, makes his Stiff debut today. It's the oft-quoted, indisputable theme song for the rock and roll lifestyle, "Sex & Drugs & Rock & Roll." The 45 is flipped with "Razzle In My Pocket." Those looking for secret messages scratched in the inner groove will read "Watch For Hand Signals" and "Crime Does Pay."

THE RADIATORS FROM SPACE squeezes out another single from Chiswick Records. It's "Enemies," flipped with a cover of the '60s Count Five classic "Psychotic Reaction." Both tracks were recorded in Dublin and are the precursor to a full LP from the quintet. Its release is planned to coincide with the first "mainland" tour by this Irish punk band.

GENERATION X	Birmingham, Barbarella's	TOM ROBINSON BAND/	
RIOT SQUAD/TUBEWAY ARMY	London, The Roxy Theatre	SORE THROAT	London, Dingwalls
THE JAM/THE JOLT	London, The Nashville	NEW HEARTS/BAZOOMIES	London, The Roxy
SANTANA/ ELVIS COSTELLO		RIFF RAFF	London, The Red Cow
+ others	London, Crystal Palace Garden	SUBURBAN STUDS/SNATCH	Manchester, Electric Circus

14th - Wednesday.....................

ALTERNATIVE T.V. make their first appearance with their new, permanent line-up tonight at the Rat Club in London. The band is now locked in as Mark Perry on vocals, guitars, tapes, Alex Fergussen on guitar, Tyrone Thomas on bass and Chris Bennett on drums. Tyrone joined the group when original drummer Mickey Smith quit after playing only one gig with the group.

EASY CURE find out about instability in a begining band. It's something you learn to live with. Just as things were going great for the Easy Cure, their lead vocalist Peter O'Toole quits the band. Why? He wants to go to Israel and live on a kibbutz. Guitarist Robert Smith steps up as the band's new singer. Ahhhh. That's better.

X-RAY SPEX have just been signed by Virgin Records. The group is fronted by a mulatto Brixton youth calling herself Poly Styrene. She's no stranger to the recording world and had a single out under her real name Marion Elliot last year. Since seeing the Pistols play, she's become a regular around the Roxy Club, resplendent in her dayglo vinyl, psychedelic kilt and full set of dental braces. They'll be releasing X-Ray Spex's debut single on the 30th. This is not X-Ray Spex's first appearance on vinyl though. You remember they were included on the "Roxy" album singing "Oh Bondage Up Yours," the same song they will re-record for Virgin in the next few weeks. Other members of the group include Jak Airport on guitar, Paul Dean on bass, B.P. Hurding on drums and Laura Logic on saxophone. They've been playing together since January and now are prepared to hit the big time, invading the male dominated punk world.

LURKERS	London, The Red Cow	BOOMTOWN RATS/	
PEKOE ORANGE/		BERNI TORME	London, The Marquee
ALTERNATIVE T.V.	London, The Rat Club	999	London, Hope & Anchor

16th - Friday.....................

SLAUGHTER & THE DOGS have something new to bang their talc bags about. It's their first single for their new bosses, the ladies and gents at Decca Records. The tracks are "Where Have All The Boot Boys Gone," b/w "You're A Bore."

THE ID are a new band that have sprung up in Northern England, put together by friends Andy McCluskey and Paul Humphries. They have played together and separately in several short lived Liverpool school bands. The rest of the large group includes Julia Kneale (vocals), Neil Shenton on guitar, John Floyd on vocals, Malcolm Holmes on drums, Steve Hollis on bass and Gary Hodgson on guitar. They are all from Wirrall. The Id will stick with their electronic style, refine it and eventually find their fortunes as Orchestral Manoeuvres in the Dark. They'll have a string of four top ten hits begining late in 1980 and continue having hits through today.

BOOMTOWN RATS	Swindon, The Brunel Rooms	EATER/DOLE Q	London, The Roxy Club
ADVERTS	Liverpool, Eric's	X-RAY SPEX	London, Red Cow
FABULOUS POODLES	London, Marquee	PLUMMET AIRLINES/	
		TERRY CHIMES BAND	London, Nashville

19th - Monday.....................

ALTERNATIVE T.V. are giving away a free flexi-disc of "Love Lies Limp" in this week's issue of *Sniffin' Glue*. The fanzine is Mark Perry of ATV. They'll be available until the 10,000 copies printed run out. The song was originally recorded for EMI, but were rejected for being too political. The band on this recording is made up of writer Mark Perry on vocals, Alex Fergusson on guitar, Tyrone Thomas on bass and John Towe on drums. Since the recording was made, drummer John Towe (former Chelsea & Generation X) left and was replaced by Dennis Bennet, ATV's third drummer.

THE SLITS are one of the most talked about new groups around London. They're seen as the female version of the Sex Pistols that more people that have heard of, than have actually heard. That's about to change. The Slits are in the BBC studios recording four songs for the John Peel program. Songs recorded are "Love And Romance," "Vindictive," "New Town" and "Shoplifting."

THE FLIES	Birmingham, Rebecca's	ONLY ONES	London, Southside City
ANTS/BLACK SLATE/		JOLT	London, Rock Garden
RAGE/SLUGS	London, The Vortex		

SEPTEMBER 1977

20th - Tuesday...

THE NEW HEARTS are an Essex four-piece "pop punk" band. They have just signed with CBS Records in the UK and will be recording their debut single immediately. Titles considered have been narrowed down to two originals, "Just Another Teenage Anthem" and "Blood On The Knife." Producer Kenny Laguna will oversee the sessions. The band is made up of eighteen year-old David Cairns lead guitar, John Harty on bass, Ian Paine on lead vocals and drummer Matt MacIntyre. The New Hearts' style of pop will shift full gear to a mod style when Ian and Dave split off to start Secret Affair and start having UK chart hits in '79.

LIVE TONIGHT!

ADVERTS	Birmingham, Barbarella's	XTC/DOLE Q	London, 100 Club
GENERATION X/		NEW HEARTS	London, Dingwalls
JOHNNY CURIOUS	London, The Marquee	X-RAY SPEX/THE TOOLS/	
SPITFIRE BOYS	London, Roxy	THE CRABS/THE LOSERS	London, The Vortex

21st - Wednesday...

ADAM & THE ANTS have their Sept. 8th gig at the Nashville reviewed in *Sounds* by Jane Suck. Among the evening's songs were his latest songs for the film *Jubilee*; "Plastic Surgery" and "Deutcher Girls" as well as "Puerto Rican" and "B-Side Baby." Adam was even joined onstage by his "manager" Jordan, who sang lead on "Lou." Suck concluded her review with, "The Ants, their barbed sound- guitar, bass drums (now a second guitar of keyboards would really be nice)- and jugular attack are not an immediate band, but the best bands never are. Unplug the jukebox, kids and learn about addiction..."

THE HUMAN LEAGUE is the new name being used by the Sheffield electronic band that used to call itself The Future. They've changed their personnel when Addy Newton left to join Clock DVA. Adrian Wright has been brought in to handle a slide and light show for the band. The name "The Human League" is culled from a science fiction war game that band member Ian Marsh was given as a birthday present.

THE STRANGLERS were forced to pull out of their three Swedish dates after mass fighting at the first venue. A group of about 300 Swedish thugs (a cross between National Front skins and '50s style Teds) allegedly broke into the club and destroyed some £2,000 worth of equipment as well as injuring members of the road crew and battering all of the band. A group known as the Raggare were held accountable. Other bands are concerned about the trouble, most immediately the Jam, who are planning to tour in Sweden soon.

THE LURKERS	London, The Red Cow

23rd - Friday...

THE VORTEX has been expanded to become London's first twenty-four hour punk venue. The club will feature recorded music during the day, live bands at night and a record shop as well. Scheduled to play today at the grand re-opening are The Models, Nue, Sham 69, Mean Street and the Outsiders. Pre-opening press billed this as "Carnaby Street was to the Mods...Hanway is to the Punks." This is an offshoot of the Crackers Disco "Vortex" that found they had many of their audience unable to get home after the gigs because of transport shut downs and such. Opening up the club proved more of an adventure than imagined. By 1 PM, two hours after the opening, the press and a lot of punks had gathered at the new Vortex. The intention was for one band to play inside and another on the sidewalk outside. When Sham 69 arrived a little while later, they proceed to the rooftop of the building next door to play instead of risking arrest on the sidewalk, a real possibility. With camera crew in tow, they set up on the rooftop and began to run through their songs. (A little bit like the Beatles rooftop serenade isn't it?). After playing "I Don't Wanna," "George Davis Is Innocent" and "Ulster" the boys in blue arrived. It only took a moment for them to find the power source, cut it and remove the band from the rooftop. The band's perch didn't belong to the Vortex after all and they were off to jail. It couldn't have worked out better though. Jimmy Pursey (the lead singer) was out on bail and their debut EP is out today on the new Step Forward label. Sham 69's EP couples "I Don't Wanna" with "Ulster" and "Red London." All are original songs and reflect the band's pent up frustrations at day-to-day life in the UK. The single comes with a picture sleeve of nine policemen carrying off a protester from the site of the Lewisham Riots. It's ironic that today reality imitates art.

IAN DURY's debut solo LP is released by Stiff Records today. It's called "New Boots and Panties" and includes tracks such as "Billericay Dickie," "I'm Partial To Your Abracadabra," "Clever Trevor" and "Plaistow Patricia." Ian was the vocalist for London pub band Kilburn & the High Roads for most of the '70s and has finally found an understanding home at Stiff Records as a solo artist. From what the press are saying, after all the disappointing records from Kilburn & The High Roads, they're glad to see the true Ian Dury caught in an album up to his abilities.

THE STRANGLERS release their second album "No More Heroes" today and already have advance orders for 62,000 copies. The LP features the title track (their last single), as well as such dainties as "I Feel Like A Wog," "Bitchin," "Bring On The Nubiles" and the toe tapper "Peasant In The Big Shitty." A single of "No More Heroes" is on its way to #8 in the UK. The 45 is available in shops with "In The Shadows." It's a non-LP track that features their unique "Barracuda Bass." It's guaranteed to shake the plaster from your walls.

THE CLASH release their third single, "Complete Control" coupled with "City Of The Dead." The lead track deals with the band's feeling about being signed to such a major record company as CBS. Small problems like trying to get your friends into the show for free and large problems like a feeling of a lack of control over your career.

ULTRAVOX!	Liverpool, Eric's	GENERATION X/CRABS	Manchester, The Rafters
DRONES	London, The Red Cow		

26th - Monday...

THE JAM received a less than gracious welcome in Scandinavia this weekend. Onstage at Ronneby they were pelted with chair legs and

SEPTEMBER 1977

eggs after their first number. The stage was then assaulted and much of the band's gear was laid to waste. The Jam beat a well timed retreat and left the hall. They have announced that their date this Wednesday in Holland will be cancelled since they don't have proper gear to play now.

X-RAY SPEX have just been announced that their sax player, Laura Logic, has left the band so that she could continue her schooling. She's only sixteen and would have trouble making gigs and grades at the same time. She'll be replaced with Glyn John for the time being. Laura has expressed interest in starting her own band at the end of the school year. Stepping into line in her place is Steve Rudi.

Chainstore ChainSmoke
I consume you all
Chainstore Chainstore
I don't think at all

OUT NOW ON VIRGIN
12" LIMITED EDITION SINGLE VS18912
7" SINGLE IN A PICTURE BAG VS189

BOOMTOWN RATS/ X-RAY SPEX	London, Marquee...................999	London, Southside Club
STEEL PULSE/WASPS	XTC/ SCREENS/ VIOLATORS ......London, The Rock Garden	
CYANIDE/THE JETS ......London, The Vortex	MEMBERS ....London, Speakeasy	

28th - Wednesday......................

THE SEX PISTOLS begin advertising the next Sex Pistols single "Holidays In The Sun." It's a series of cartoon scenes of people on holiday with suitable "Sex Pistols" captions, which upon closer examination turn out to be the lyrics to the song. "Holidays" is scheduled for release in about three weeks.

In this week's *NME*, Randy Newman shows his dislike for the Pistols. "I hate the way the Sex Pistols remove all musical standards. That 'No future in England's dreaming' is not bad, but it's kind of demagogue. If you look at it hard, what do they mean? What's England got to do with fascism? Why get worked up about the God-damned Queen anyway?" Randy's currently getting "worked up" (the charts) about "Short People" on his new album "Little Criminals."

STIFF'S GREATEST STIFFS is an album designed to capture the collectors market. When Stiff Records signed with Island Records for distribution, their first ten singles were deleted. Since February the stocks have been dwindling until now; there is a demand for the songs and no product. Record dealers have been charging unusually high prices for early works. To solve this problem, Stiff Records has gathered up one side of each of these lost singles (two songs from the Tyla Gang) for a compilation LP. There's Nick Lowe's "Heart Of The City," The Damned's debut "Help," Richard Hell's "You Gotta Lose," and Elvis Costello's "Radio Sweetheart." Among these flip sides were padding with tracks by Roogalator, The Pink Fairies, Lew Lewis, Motorhead and Plummet Airlines. Early copies also included a free copy of Max Wall's single "England's Glory" (Stiff #12). This was a move to deplete swollen stocks of the monumentally slow selling single.

JOLT......................................Edinburgh, Clouds (RAR)	RADIATORS FROM SPACE/	
LURKERS ....London, Red Cow	NEW HEARTS/THE CRABS...........London, Music Machine	

30th - Friday......................

TOM ROBINSON BAND have their debut 45 rush-released by EMI. It's called "2-4-6-8 Motorway" and is predicted to be a chart-topper. The fact is, the single will climb the charts to #5 and become Tom's signature song and a hit unequalled for the rest of his career. Robinson hopes to have his song "Glad To Be Gay" pressed and released as soon as possible. Still no word from press conscious EMI on its imminent release.

X-RAY SPEX make their single debut with "Oh Bondage Up Yours" b/w "I Am A Cliche" on Virgin today. The vocals are discordant, the sax drifts in and out of tune. It could have what it takes to become a classic.

ULTRAVOX! ....Birmingham, Barbarella's	XTC...London, Rochester Castle	
X-RAY SPEX..........................Liverpool, Eric's	BUZZCOCKS/CIMMARONS ....London, North Poly.	
IGGY POP/ADVERTS ....London, Rainbow Theatre	999/ART ATTAX ....London, Nashville	
SHAM 69/	DRONES................................London, Red Cow	
RADIATORS FROM SPACE...........London, Roxy		

October 1st - Saturday......................

THE ELECTRIC CIRCUS is about to close. This is the weekend that Manchester dreaded. It's the final two nights of the legendary club. The Circus was the first of the Manchester new wave venues and an important catalyst in the brewing underground music scene. All of the local talent has gathered for the two day blow-out. Tonight's show starts off with sets from The Panik, The Negatives and John The Postman. Then Manicured Noise and their associated electronic noodlings, followed by The Swords and Liverpool's latest combo, Big In Japan. Next up are Steel Pulse with the best in reggae this side of Birmingham, followed by a closing set from The Drones. Being charitable to the very end, the receipts from the club's closing nights is being directed to benefit cancer research. To capture the excitement of this two day event, the Virgin Sound Mobile recording studio is on hand to catch every moment on tape, for a recording that will come out next year under the title "Short Circuit."

THE DRONES have publicly signed to Manchester's Valer Records. The signing took place a few weeks ago live on Picadilly Radio's "Reflextions" program. Their first single for the label is out today and is "Bone Idle" b/w " Just Want To Be Myself." The band had previously released a single on their own back in July.

THE HEARTBREAKERS have started a promotional tour to hype their forthcoming LP "L.A.M.F." (Like A Mutha Fuckah). Yesterday afternoon at four o'clock without warning, drummer Jerry Nolan announced that he was quitting the band. Johnny Thunders hurriedly gathered up some phone numbers and called Sex Pistol drummer Paul Cook down to the gig at Bristol Poly Technic to help out for the evening. Paul was more than happy to come and brought along bandmate Steve Jones. This isn't a permanent replacement, just friends helping friends out. At the gig, a group of about forty football rowdies broke into the club and started a fight that left the promoter unconscious and tables and patrons overturned. The gig continued and was a great success, and they were called back for five encores.

OCTOBER 1977

THE YACHTS are another Stiff success story. After only six months together these Liverpool art school students have their debut single released. It's a catchy little ditty called "Suffice To Say" b/w "Freedom (Is A Heady Wine)." The band evolved out of Albert Dock and the Codfish Warriors and are vocalist John Campbell, keyboard player Henry Preistman, guitarist Martin Watson, bassist Martin Dempsey and drummer Bob Bellis. The name The Yachts was chosen out of a list of answers to a crossword puzzle. They liked its bright, clean overtones.

ULTRAVOX!	Birmingham, Barbarella's	XTC	London, Rochester Castle
THE MODELS	Liverpool, Eric's	DRONES/PREFECTS/	
IGGY POP/ADVERTS	London, Rainbow Theatre	BIG IN JAPAN/RIP OFF/	
PIRATES/ GENERATION X/		SWORDS/ MANICURED NOISE/	
SOFT BOYS	London, North-East Poly.	NEGATIVES/	
RADIATORS FROM SPACE	London, Red Cow	JOHN THE POSTMAN/	
ONLY ONES/BAZOOMIES	London, Marquee	STEEL PULSE	Manchester, Electric Circus
999/ART ATTAX	London, Nashville		

2nd - Sunday.....................................

THE ELECTRIC CIRCUS is having its final night. Manchester says farewell as the newest and the best come out and play. The show starts with doom-rockers Warsaw. Then come The Prefects and The Worst. There's also some in between band interruptions by the hilarious punk-poet John Cooper Clarke. Then another new group, The Fall, who are followed by the long awaited debut of Magazine. This is the new group fronted by ex-Buzzcock Howard Devoto. With equipment they borrow from the Buzzcocks, Magazine play three songs; "Shot By Both Sides," "I Love You You Big Dummy" and "The Light Pours Out Of Me." After Magazine, the Buzzcocks come on to bring a rousing end to the evening. As a final closing, John The Postman (aka John Ormerod, a real-life singing postman) comes onstage and lurches into "Louie Louie" as the stage fills with a sing-along audience.

THE DAMNED drummer, Rat Scabies, quit last night in the midst of the band's European tour and flew home to London. The Damned are having a damned bad time. Their recent tour of the US, which failed to find them a record deal, left them exhausted. Their lack of press attention on the subsequent UK tour and now the riots and cancellations are greeting them in France and Switzerland. In a fit of depression Rat left the Damned. For the time being, Dave Berk, borrowed from Johnny Moped's band, sits in to complete the dates already committed to. Rat has been unhappy with his lot in the Damned for some time and is now considering the current opening in the Heartbreakers. His disenchantment with the whole scene came out in an interview in *Sounds* magazine where Rat said, "The punk thing has become the quickest sell-out I've ever seen. Now it's completely run by businessmen. It's just a trend to make money out of. That was one of the main things getting me down. Instead of Boring Old Farts, we had Boring Young Farts. We were all getting fat, especially me and the Captain. Suddenly we were on £50 a week when we were used to a tenner on the dole. We had it easier than we'd ever had it in our life and with that the desperation went."

DEPRESSIONS	London, Fulham Greyhound	BUZZCOCKS/	
NEW HEARTS	London, The Nashville	JOHN COOPER CLARKE/FALL/	
BOOMTOWN RATS/YACHTS/		WORST/PREFECTS/WARSAW	Manchester, Electric Circus
LEW LEWIS	London, The Roundhouse		

3rd - Monday....................................

THE TALKING HEADS critically acclaimed debut album is called "Talking Heads '77". Its stark red cover is in blinding contrast to the busy and airbrushed album jackets of the rest of the rock world. The LP features "New Feeling," "Don't Worry About The Government," "Pulled Up" and the throbbing "Psycho Killer." There's a single out as well of album track "Uh Oh, Love Comes To Town," and the non-LP flipside "I Wish You Wouldn't Say That."

RICHARD HELL is no stranger to making records. He had his vinyl debut with "Blank Generation" almost exactly a year ago on Stiff Records. Since then his band has grown tighter and tighter and his voice more psychotic. On his Sire debut LP you find "Love Comes In Spurts," "New Pleasures," "Walking On The Water," and among others, still another version of "Blank Generation." This is the thing that led *Newsweek* magazine to label him, "The Mick Jagger of punk."

THE HEARTBREAKERS have their debut LP "L.A.M.F." released by Track Records today. The band has been playing around town for quite some time and public demand for something other than a single has been great. The album features live favorites like "Get Off The Phone," "All By Myself," "Born Too Lose" and a remixed version of "Chinese Rocks". The album was produced by Speedy Keen (of Thunderclap Newman fame) and features ex-NY Dolls Thunders as well as Walter Lure and Billy Rath. It's leaked that the fingerprints on the back of the Heartbreakers LP "L.A.M.F" are not those of Johnny Thunders as represented. They are, in fact, those of Francis Cookson, a friend of the Buzzcocks. As a sidelight to Jerry Nolan's walk-out last Friday, the auditions for a replacement find ex-Damned drummer Rat Scabies trying out today.

STIFF'S GREATEST STIFFS LIVE TOUR is the cumbersome title of the package of shows that include Elvis Costello, Nick Lowe and Wreckless Eric, Larry Wallis and former Kilburn High-Roader Ian Dury. The package tour, reminiscent of '50s style roadshows with many acts playing short sets, opens an extensive UK tour tonight in High Wycombe. Ian Dury will be making his first live appearance on the road since leaving Kilburn & the High Roads for health reasons well over a year ago. He is backed by his new band, (The Blockheads) consisting of Chaz Jankel on guitar, Davey Payne on sax, Norman Watt-Roy on bass and Charley Charles on drums. Also on the bill is Elvis Costello, appearing onstage with his new band, the Attractions, and Nick Lowe with his new backing group. Wreckless Eric will also be drawing from the pool of talent on the road by using Davey Payne and Ian Dury himself, both borrowed from the Blockheads.

ULTRAVOX! have their third single for Island out this week. It's "Rockwrok" b/w "Hiroshima Mon Amour." Both are original compositions that will be featured on their upcoming LP "Ha Ha Ha."

OCTOBER 1977

SPITFIRE BOYS ....Birmingham, Rebecca's	ONLY ONES/DEPRESSIONS
YACHTS..................................London, Dingwalls	SPEEDOMETERS/SKUNKS...........London, The Vortex
WIRE ....London, Hope & Anchor	COCK SPARER.........................London, Rochester Castle
MANIACS/WARSAW PAKT ....London, The Nashville	

4th - Tuesday...

STIFF RECORDS has a shakeup back at the main office. A disagreement between co-founders Dave Robinson and Jake Riveria has resulted in Jake leaving Stiff and taking two of their best potential assets with him; Elvis Costello and producer/performer Nick Lowe.

SHAM 69 is getting a big break in a most unusual way. Just when you thought that the establishment in London was against the very idea of punk rock, Sham 69 are asked to appear in a TV documentary about "new wave music" for the Inner London Education Authority. They performed two songs for the series "Confessions Of A Music Lover." It was shown to various colleges on cable TV. In the TV program there will also be a brief interview with Alternative TV leader Mark Perry.

RADIATORS FROM SPACE...........London, Hope & Anchor	BUZZCOCKS/ANTS....................London, The Marquee
TOM ROBINSON BAND/	SHAM 69/WIRE/
RICH KIDS ....London, 100 Club	SOLID WASTE/BAZOOKA JOE.......London, The Vortex

7th - Friday...

XTC have their debut EP out after numberous delays. Swindon's scientific pop band makes the splash with a 12" called the "3-D EP," with three tracks, "Science Friction," "Dance Band" and "She's So Square." There is also a limited number of a 7" pressing available, without "She's So Square." To promote the release Virgin is already lining up appearances on TV programs like *Magpie* and *Tis/Was*. XTC are Andy Partridge on guitar and vocals, Colin Moulding on bass, Barry Andrews on keyboards and Terry Chambers on drums.

EATER release their new single "Jeepster" today with Dave Goodman's record company "The Label." It's a cover of the Marc Bolan track, possibly a tribute, since Marc's unfortunate passing in a car crash two weeks ago. Their debut LP will be issued this Tuesday and will be just the beginning of Eater's three-year contract with The Label.

THE SAINTS have out a four track single titled "One, Two, Three, Four." Two are originals, "One Way Street" and "Demolition Girl" and two are covers "Lipstick On Your Collar" (Connie Francis) and "River Deep Mountain High" (Animals, Tina Turner et al.).

JOHN COOPER CLARKE is the Manchester "punk poet" who is seen occasionally at Northern clubs opening shows with rapid fire poetry and bad jokes. The Rabid Records EP features a trio of songs; "Suspended Sentence," "Innocents" and "Psycle Sluts." His rapid fire delivery of offbeat images of back street scenes has been entertaining crowds before concerts in Manchester for the past several months. The backing band, not listed on the single, is referred to as The Narks. They're hardly noticeable once you tune into the record though. Early pressings are available in a special gate-fold sleeve.

SAINTS......................Birmingham, Barbarella's	TOM ROBINSON BAND ....Liverpool, Eric's
ULTRAVOX! ....Edinburgh, Heriot Watt Univ.	ADVERTS/
BUZZCOCKS/	BLUNT INSTRUMENT.............London, Imperial Col.
JOHN COOPER CLARKE/	RADIATORS FROM SPACE.......London, N Poly.
NEW HEARTS ....Liverpool, Poly.	

8th - Saturday...

THE BUZZCOCKS make their debut on United Artists with the provocative "Orgasm Addict." They can't reeeeealy think that the BBC is going to play this, can they? It's paired with "What Ever Happened To?" Although the single will never even touch the charts, it'll remain one of the Buzzcocks more memorable songs with its breathy chorus. Among the celebrations with the release, bassist Garth has been fired just before they start their UK tour. He had been antagonizing Pete Shelley all day yesterday and the two had to dragged apart at times. Garth had reportedly been drinking heavily all day and when time came to play, he dropped his bass onstage and left, leaving the others to carry on without and that's just what they intend to do. The Buzzcocks have also just found out that their date for Wigan on November 17th has been cancelled by local police. The Wigan Council had enforced a new ban including any punk shows, especially at the Wigan Casino.

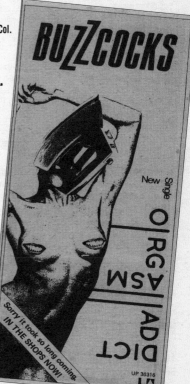

THE CRAMPS are in Memphis for sessions at Ardent Studios. They cut the an original song called "Human Fly" as well as covers of Jack Scott's "The Way I Walk," Sam Phillips' (the founder and owner of Sun Records) "Domino" and the Trashmen's 1964 surf classic "Surfin' Bird." The psychobilly quartet is Bryan Gregory, Lux Interior, Nick Knox and Ivy Rorschach. They are a strange mixture of rockabilly and jungle voodoo music. Very odd.

SKREWDRIVER have another in-your-face single out on Chiswick Records today. It's "Anti-Social" b/w a version of The Rolling Stones classic "19th Nervous Breakdown." The band have also acquired a new guitarist named Ron Hartley.

STRANGLERS/RADIO STARS ....Belfast, Ulster Hall	WIRE...................London, Red Cow	
SAINTS/X-RAY SPEX ....Birmingham, Barbarella's	SHAM 69 ....London, Roxy	

OCTOBER 1977

9th - Sunday...

THE CLASH are currently touring in Scandinavia and last night played in Ronneby, Sweden, at the same hall where The Jam, Stranglers and Sex Pistols had problems. Local promoters feared that the ted-car-club-cum-hooligan group called the Raggare would turn up to cause problems. To their surprise no gangs, no problems. Before tonight's gig in Orebro, Club 700 received a bomb threat that delayed the opening of the venue. Then, once the Clash did come on, in came the Raggare. They immediately began shouting and throwing things, specifically at the band. In a surprise move, The Clash turned on the mob and threw and shouted right back. This shocked them to the point where they backed down and let the show proceed unimpeded.

LIVE TONIGHT!

RUNAWAYS/999	Birmingham, The Odeon	RADIATORS FROM SPACE	London, Rochester Castle
TOM ROBINSON BAND	High Wycombe, Nags Head	ULTRAVOX!/ RADIO STARS/	
X-RAY SPEX	London, Nashville	XTC	London, The Roundhouse

10th - Monday...

THE SPITFIRE BOYS formed only five months ago in Liverpool and already have their debut single out on ROK Records. The single is "Mein Kampf" b/w "British Refugee." The songs are both originals. The group is Zero on bass (Pete Griffiths), Maggot (Paul Rutherford) on vocals, Jones (Dave Littler) on guitar and a drummer named Blister (Budgie). They enjoy playing uptempo punk. Two of their "punk" names make sense in a sideways manner. "Blister" has blisters from incessant drumming and "Jones" wanted to be another David Bowie (Davie Jones). From the group, Blister (aka Budgie, ne' Peter Clark) will join a variety of bands eventually finding lasting employment as the drummer for Siouxsie & The Banshees. Maggot (aka Paul Rutherford) will find the spotlight in '83 as one of the vocalists for Frankie Goes To Hollywood.

SOFT BOYS Cambridge-based band, The Soft Boys, have their debut EP released on Raw Records. The Soft Boys were formed out of the convergence of Andy Metcalfe and Robyn Hitchcock when Andy auditioned Robyn for a position as vocalist in a white soul combo that became Dennis & The Experts back in 1976. The band then reformed with Kimberly Rew brought in on guitar and Morris Windsor on drums. A song that Robyn wrote called "Give It To The Soft Boys" gave the band their name. Their EP has the tracks "Wading Through A Ventilator," "The Face Of Death" and "Hear My Brane." All of the songs are Soft Boys originals. The other tracks from the sessions, "The Yodelling Hoover," "Vyra Knowl Is A Headbanger" and "Give It To The Soft Boys" are all left unissued until 1984.

SIOUXSIE & THE BANSHEES are trying to get the attention of the record companies that are gobbling up punk groups left and right. They're feeling left out and don't understand why. They draw large crowds when they play and and even have a handful of demos to play for people. Someone connected with the band, and no one's saying who, has spray-painted slogans like "Sign Siouxsie Now" on no less than a dozen record company office buildings. The phone's not ringing, yet.

LURKERS	Birmingham, Rebecca's	WASPS/BERNI TORME/	
TOM ROBINSON BAND	London, Marquee	MANIACS/NEO/	
RADIATORS FROM SPACE/		MEAN STREET	London, The Vortex
WIRE	London, Rochester Castle	NEW HEARTS	London, Southside Club

11th - Tuesday...

EATER's debut album is finally here. It's entitled "Eater" and has a giant ant on the front. Geddit? Ant-Eater! The band has been recording for Dave Goodman's Label "The Label" since March and have also been through three drummers. Their new album finds them pulling out something old ("No Brains" from the first sessions with Dee Generate), something new (nine originals) and something borrowed "Sweet Jane" and "Waiting For My Man" from Lou Reed, "Queen Bitch" from Bowie and the song "Eighteen" (sung as "Fifteen") by Alice Cooper.

THE EASY CURE are finally in the studio doing their first recordings for Hansa Records. The sessions at SAV Studios in London give the band the chance to record "See The Children," "I Just Need Myself," "I Want To Be Old," "Pillbox Tales" and "Meathook." None of the songs would ever be released, with the exception of "Pillbox Tales" which is issued as a bonus track on the "Boys Don't Cry (remix)" dance 12" in 1986.

ALTERNATIVE T.V. have a personnel change that some see as a major setback for the group. Founder member, guitar player Alex Ferguson has quit. He's interested in pursuing a more accessible, pop direction than ATV. Many consider that Ferguson was the main writer for the group. With his departure, a change in direction for the band is certain.

SHAM 69 have another personnel change. Founder member Albie Slider leaves the band and is replaced by Dave Treganna on bass. Pursey remains the only "original" in the band.

Stiff's Greatest Stiffs	Liverpool, The Empire	JOHNNY THUNDERS &	
NEW HEARTS	London, Rock Garden	THE HEARTBREAKERS/	
JOHNNY CURIOUS/		SIOUXSIE & BANSHEES/	
ART ATTAX/SUSPECTS	London, The Vortex	MODELS	Sheffield, Top Rank

12th - Wednesday...

BLONDIE emerge from negotiations with several major labels, announcing that the band has now signed to Chrysalis Records worldwide. They had previously been with Private Stock Records.

THE RADIATORS FROM SPACE finally have an LP to their name. As their previous two singles, the LP "T.V. Tube Heart" is on Chiswick Records. The thirteen track LP is all originals, with only one exception. Songs include their previous two singles "Enemies" and

OCTOBER 1977

"Television Screen," although the latter has been totally re-recorded with 50% less fury and speed. Other titles are "Sunday World," "Press Gang," "Blitzin At The Ritz," "Ripped and Torn" and "Roxy Girl." For the most part the album will sound different from the other two Radiators records you own. Shortly before recording the LP, lead vocalist Steven Rapid quit the band and vocals were taken over by Phil Chevron. Rapid is present only on the recording of "Enemies," and will begin a new group with an electronic base at times called The Modern Heirs, Zed, Various Artists and Tell Tale Heart.

ONLY ONES ....London, Dingwalls	DEPRESSIONS ....London, The Speakeasy

13th - Thursday...

PUNCTURE are the band selected to start another indie label in London. The Small Wonder Record shop, an East London (Walthamstow) specialty shop now have their own, "Small Wonder" record company. Puncture have the first single with their original songs "Mucky Pup" and "You Can't Rock And Roll." The quartet is Paul McCallum on guitar and vocals, Steve Counsel on bass, Anthony Keen on synthesizer and "The Fabulous" Marty Truss on drums.

RADIATORS FROM SPACE ....Birmingham, Rebecca's	STRANGLERS/DRONES ....Manchester, The Apollo
Stiff's Greatest Stiffs ....Glasgow, The Apollo	YACHTS ....Manchester, Rafters
COCKSPARRER ....London, John Bull	

14th - Friday...

THE CATCH is that this is the begining of Annie Lennox's career. It's almost five years before anyone will notice the Eurythmics. The creative axis of Annie Lennox and Dave Stewart in a group called the Catch. They didn't intend to be a recording group, they just wanted to write hits for other people. The trio was put together by ex-Longdancer member Dave Stewart, who spent some time busking around Europe with Pete Coombes, a friend who had just come from a band called Peculiar Star. Pete knew of a girl with an amazing voice that worked in a vegetarian restaurant in Hampstead. According to the story that they tell, Dave Stewart's first words to her was "Will you marry me?" They decided to start with writing songs together to sell to other bands. There was no intention to actually release anything themselves. They found a contact with a publishing company who though that their demos were good enough that they ought to be released. The band balked at the idea, but went along anyway. Now the trio, dubbed "The Catch" have a single out. It's on Logo Records and is "Borderline" b/w "Black Blood." Publicity photos of the group show Annie with remarkably short cropped blonde hair. With a single out, the band might actually have to work on playing a live set from time to time.

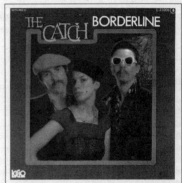

ULTRAVOX! release their second album "Ha! Ha! Ha!" today on Island Records and will support it with a string of thirteen dates across the UK. Both sides of their single "Rockwrok" and "Hiroshima Mon Amour," are on the album, as well as new songs "Man Who Dies Every Day," "Artifical Life," "Frozen Ones" and "Distant Smile."

THE DAMNED have their new single "Problem Child" and "You Take My Money" released by Stiff Records in the UK. "Problem Child" in no way reflects the recent departure of Rat Scabies.

ELVIS COSTELLO has his fourth Stiff single released today. It's "Watching The Detectives" b/w "Blame It On Cain" and "Mystery Dance." The "A" side was recorded back in May, before the Attractions even existed with Steve recording the keyboards this fall. Otherwise, the backing musicians were Graham Parker's sidemen Steve Goulding on drums and Andrew Bodnar on bass. The two songs on the flip side are live recordings from their Nashville Club appearance on August 7th. The matrix is a cryptic "little triggers but big tears" and "I think you know what I mean." By the way, Elvis' keyboard player Steve Mason is now referring to himself as Steve A'dore.

JOHNNY THUNDERS &	999/YACHTS ....London, N Central Poly.
THE HEARTBREAKERS/	BABYLON/WASPS ....London, Dingwalls
SIOUXSIE & BANSHEES/	"Blank Generation" film/
MODELS ....Edinburgh, Clouds	ALTERNATIVE T.V. ....London, The Other Cinema
REZILLOS...............................Glasgow, Jordan Hill College	TOM ROBINSON BAND ....Manchester, Rafters
STRANGLERS/DRONES ....Liverpool, Univ.	Stiff's Greatest Stiffs ....Sheffield, Poly.

15th - Saturday..

THE JAM have a new single out this weekend. "This Is The Modern World" is flipped with a portion of a live gig at the 100 club from September 9th. "B" side tracks include two soul classics "Sweet Soul Music" and "Back In My Arms Again," with a little portion of their own "Bricks and Mortar" thrown in to boot. The "A" side is the title track from their next LP, due out in November.

THE SEX PISTOLS' latest single hits stores today. Original plans were to have it be "Bodies," but Virgin felt shied away from the song because of the censorship problems EMI had. The safer choice was "Holidays In The Sun" and "Satellite." It is being released in a special picture bag with lyrics superimposed over cartoons of a happy family on holiday. Virgin still has no set date for the awaited debut album. Another controversial song has surfaced in the Pistols' rehearsals. It's a song that new Pistol Sid Vicious brought from his previous band called "Belsen Was A Gas." When asked if "Belsen" has been submitted as part of the album, Virgin said they knew of no such song.

THE UNWANTED are the latest band to be picked up by Raw Records. Their 45 debut is "Withdrawal/1984" b/w "Bleak Outlook." The band was a regular feature down at the Roxy Club and these tracks debut their new postman turned guitarist, twenty year-old Dave Lynch who replaces Paul Gardner.

OCTOBER 1977

THE BLANK GENERATION is a documentary film on the New York punk scene now being screened in London. It features Television, Patti Smith, Tom Petty & The Heartbreakers, Wayne County, Blondie and many others. The movie begins its thirteen-day run at the "Other Cinema" on Tottenham Street. As a special bonus, *Sniffin' Glue* fanzine editor Mark Perry's band, Alternative T.V. will be playing onstage for the opening tonight. Tomorrow and for the rest of the run, the Dr. Feelgood film *Going Back Home* will be the first feature.

LIVE TONIGHT!

REZILLOS	Edinburgh, Heriot Watt Univ.	SQUEEZE/MENACE	London, Deptford Broadway Queen
STRANGLERS/DRONES/		RADIATORS FROM SPACE	London, Marquee
LURKERS/THE ANTS	Liverpool, Eric's	999	London, Univ. Union
WIRE	London, Red Cow	JOHNNY THUNDERS &	
ALTERNATIVE T.V./NEO/		THE HEARTBREAKERS/	
SPITFIRE BOYS	London, The Bell	KILLJOYS/MODELS	Manchester, Univ.

19th - Wednesday.....................................

SQUEEZE have been picked up by A&M Records in a worldwide deal. They will shortly begin work on their debut LP using John Cale as producer, just as they did on their single. The group had been trying to get a record deal for two years and in desperation, released their own indie single this summer. This isn't the band's first trip to the altar. Back in the fall of '75, Squeeze were signed to RCA Records and even got so far as cutting five demos. Back then, Squeeze intended for the song "Take Me I'm Yours" as the group's debut single. John Cale described the new sessions under way to *Sounds* as, "...weirder than you'd ever believe."

THOSE NAUGHTY LUMPS	Liverpool, Havana Club	DISTRACTIONS/SNYDE/	
ONLY ONES	London, Rock Garden	WARSAW/	
MISTAKES/OM	London, Roxy	NERVOUS BREAKDOWN	Manchester, Pipers Disco
DEPRESSIONS	London, Speakeasy	STRANGLERS/DRONES	Sheffield, Top Rank

20th - Thursday...................

THE CLASH were scheduled to play at Belfast's Ulster Hall tonight in the city's first major punk concert. Fans began gathering around tea time, then word came around that the gig was cancelled because insurance coverage hadn't arrived in time. The crowd got ugly. The 200 strong punk mob then went to the Belfast Europe Hotel where the group were rumored to be staying. This is one of the most bombed out hotels in Belfast and a security guard, seeing the mob on its way toward him, called out for help. The crowd surrounded the cyclone fence outside of the hotel and began shouting for the band. Hotel guests were horrified. The Clash came out front about the same time that rovers full of police arrived behind the crowd. The Clash explained and told the mob that they were trying to set up the show down the road at Queens University. Meanwhile at the University, plans to stage the show were squashed when the motion to hold it was defeated by superiors in the college administration felt it would be economically and physically damaging. Belfast has been a town that was critical of never having any major punk acts play. Now that the first one comes through the show is cancelled. It is still uncertain whether the Stranglers will meet a similar fate with their dates here on the 8th and 9th.

THE SEX PISTOLS are named in a suit filed against Virgin Records from further distribution and sale of the picture cover for their latest release "Holidays In The Sun." The cover was not altogether original artwork. It was a doctored version of a summer holiday brochure published by the Belgian Travel Service. 60,000 records sleeves are taken from warehouses and Virgin shops and replaced with plain white sleeves. It is estimated that some 5,000 single have been sold already and are beyond Virgin's reach. By the way, the back of the single was a photo-parody as well. The "happy family" scene was cribbed from a late '60s pamphlet that was distributed by a French revolutionary group called the "International Situationists."

For those into something on the more dangerous side, a bootleg is making the rounds called "Spunk," that beats Virgin Records to their album release. It's the second time the Pistols have been booted on LP. It features the demo sessions that McLaren was taking from label to label last summer. The dozen song titles are identical to the new album with the exception of the inclusion of "Satellite", "I Wanna Be Me," and the missing titles "Holidays In The Sun" and "Bodies." There's even a little bit of Beatles parody when Jones says "On behalf of the band, I hoped we passed the audition" into the intro of "Lots Of Fun" (otherwise known as "Pretty Vacant.") If you ask around, you can find a copy, but it will cost you £4.50, a pound more than the legit album that's out in a matter of days.

THE STIFF/CHISWICK CHALLENGE Here's a new idea in promotions. A record company sorting out potential signings at a live gig. Both Stiff and Chiswick have contributed three bands each to tonight's gig at London's Acklam Hall. The bands were selected from the hundreds of applicants for contracts they receive every week. Groups for the concert include The Clutch Plates, The Outsiders, Molesters, Strangeways, Wild Thing and The Alligators. The best part is that the gig is absolutely free to punters, but there is a stiff charge for A&R men. To insure that none slip through unnoticed, there are veteran A&R men spotters at the door. Here's the opportunity to see next weeks big thing, today.

CLASH/RICHARD HELL	Belfast, N Ireland Poly.	JOHNNY THUNDER &	
WIRE	Birmingham, Rebecca's	THE HEARTBREAKERS/	
STRANGLERS	Birmingham, The Mayfair	SIOUXSIE & BANSHEES/	
SQUEEZE/SWORDS	London, Deptford Albany Empire	MODELS	London, Rainbow Theatre
SPITFIRE BOYS/SUSPECTS	London, Roxy	X-RAY SPEX	Manchester, Rafters
Stiff-Chiswick Challenge	London, Acklam Hall		

21st - Friday.................................

THE HEARTBREAKERS' concert last night at the Rainbow was the site of more violence as the band's fans were roughed up by members of the security force there to control the "unruly mob." For some reason after the gig, Siouxsie and Kenny Morris (from the

OCTOBER 1977

Banshees) and Pablo LaBritian (of 999) were detained by local police on charges of obstruction. The three got to spend the night at the Holloway Road Station and paid their £20 fines in the morning. Siouxsie's shoes are confiscated as potential "offensive weapons."

CELIA & THE MUTATIONS are the not-so-mysterious Stranglers acting as backing to Celia Collin singing "You Better Believe Me" and "Round and Round." There's a Mr. Burnel collecting publishing on this one, could that be a clue? A behind the facade check located not only J.J. on bass but ex-Feelgood Wilko Johnson on guitar.

SOME CHICKEN are a Cambridge band that has just had their debut single released by Raw Records. This debut 45 is "New Religion" b/w "Blood On The Wall." The group is made up of Ivor Badcock on vocals, Jess Chicken on guitar, Galway Kinnell on drums and Terry Bull on bass.

CLASH/		SUSPECTS/THE MEAT/	
RICHARD HELL & VOIDOIDS	Dublin, Trinity College	OUTSIDERS	London, Rainbow (upstairs)
FABULOUS POODLES	London, Goldsmith's College	MANIACS	London, Red Cow
SHAM 69/KILLJOYS	London, Marquee	MENACE/SOME CHICKEN	London, Roxy
		REZILLOS/CRABS	Manchester, Rafters

24th - Monday...

THE SEX PISTOLS' debut LP release is close at hand. The LP is to be titled "Never Mind The Bollocks...Here's The Sex Pistols." It's scheduled to be available from November 4th. By the end of today, advance orders topped 125,000. This gives the LP, Gold Disc status even before it's left the Virgin warehouses. The album will be pressed up by Warner Brothers in the US, however advance orders for the album were not nearly as frantic there as in the UK. The album will be a collection of the band's past single sides and new material. Since Sid is still learning his way around a bass, Steve Jones had to play bass on most of the sessions. There is a smattering of Matlock though. He plays bass on "Anarchy In The UK." The newest songs on the LP are "Bodies" and "Holidays In The Sun" which were written since Sid joined the band. Otherwise, the LP catches fans up on studio versions of the Sex Pistols' best known songs.

SPIZZ 77 are a new band that only made their (his) debut a few days ago in Birmingham. It's basically Spizz, his real name a mystery, and his guitar. At the Birmingham festival he was given ten minutes to screech away onstage before the management cut the power. Now he's come down to London to try his wares out at the Vortex.

SHAM 69 have been signed to Polydor Records and will start shortly to record their debut single for the label. There will also be some tapes rolling when they play the Vortex tonight, for possible inclusion on one of their upcoming Polydor Records. Some of the attention that stirred up the record companies was that "educational" TV documentary that they were in. Sometimes breaks come from the oddest places, even for Hersham lads.

UNWANTED	Birmingham, Barbarella's	MANIACS	London, Hope & Anchor
KILLJOYS/MODEL MANIA/		TOM ROBINSON BAND	London, Marquee
SPIZZ 77/SPITFIRE BOYS/RIVVETS London, The Vortex			

25th - Tuesday...

METAL URBAIN is a new punk band in France. The group have been around about a six months now have their debut single "Panik" b/w "Lady Coca Cola" in France on the Cobra Records label. Members include Claude Panik on vocals, Eric Debris on synths, Nancy Luger and Herman Schwartz on guitar.

THE POLICE are in Munich, Germany recording with experimental electronic composer Eberhard Schoener. This is because of a prior commitment that Andy Summers had made before joining the Police. He's managed to get his bandmates worked into the sessions as well, even to the point of using Sting for some of the vocals. These sessions come at a great time, since their recent planned European tour with the Electric Chairs had fallen through and they could use the cash. The trio play alongside an avant garde orchestra featuring Eberhard himself on various keyboards and Olaf Kubler on sax. Among the tracks laid down are "Frame Of Mind" and "Signs Of Emotion." While in Germany, the Police are also refining a new song that Sting has been working on as a result of the band's recent trip to Paris. While there he wandered into the red-light district and wondered at the beautiful prostitutes, thinking that they probably had boyfriends that wished they had different jobs. The resulting song in progress is called "Roxanne."

Stiff's Greatest Stiffs	Birmingham, Town Hall	CLASH/	
JOHNNY THUNDERS &		RICHARD HELL & VOIDOIDS	Glasgow, Apollo
THE HEARTBREAKERS/		SHAM 69/MENACE	London, 100 Club
SIOUXSIE & BANSHEES/		X-RAY SPEX/JOLT	London, Marquee
MODEL	Birmingham, Barbarella's	JAH WOOSH/TERMINALS/	
RADIATORS FROM SPACE	Edinburgh, Clouds	CRABS/THE PRIMATES	London, The Vortex

26th - Wednesday...

RICH KIDS get a new guitarist and vocalist. Midge Ure has joined Glen Matlock's Rich Kids. He was a chart topper with his teen-pop band Slik, but has since turned to other tastes. He had played a few dates with the Rich Kids but rejected the idea of joining the band because of a reluctance to relocate to London. That reluctance is gone now and Midge Ure, Slik popster, is now a Rich Kids guitarist.

NINE NINE NINE have just issued their second single for United Artists. It's "Nasty Nasty." For some reason there has been a special

OCTOBER 1977

promotional issue of the single on a 78 rpm record. It's flipped with the track "No Pity."

LIVE TONIGHT!

RUNAWAYS/RADIO STARS ....Dublin, Stadium	THOSE NAUGHTY LUMPS ....Liverpool, Havana Club
CLASH/	SKUNKS ....London, Man In The Moon
RICHARD HELL & VOIDOIDS ....Edinburgh, Leith Town Hall	DEAD FINGERS TALK.................London, Rochester Castle
JOHNNY THUNDERS &	X-RAY SPEX/THE JOLT............London, The Marquee
HEARTBREAKERS/MODELS ....Liverpool, Eric's	DEPRESSIONS ....London, The Speakeasy

27th - Thursday..

THE SEX PISTOLS' debut album is being rush shipped-tomorrow, a week earlier than originally planned. The LP has been the subject of change after change after change from McLaren, with Jamie Reid's sleeve artwork being re-worked repeatedly up until the last minute. Even the disc itself was originally planned to have eleven tracks, but now it will feature the additional song "Submission" at the band's request. Since the presses were already busy when this decision was made, the extra track will have to be included on a one sided single in a small quantity of the initial 200,000 albums. The LP has the provocative title "Never Mind The Bollocks, Here's The Sex Pistols."

THE RICH KIDS have just been signed to a recording deal with EMI Records. This is the same company that had lead singer Glen Matlock under contract last year as a member of the Sex Pistols. The group have already cut some demos and now prepare for their first single. The group has had some recent changes and is now made up of Glen Matlock on vocals and bass, ex-Slik vocalist and guitarist Midge Ure, Steve new on guitar and Rusty Egan on drums.

THE ADVERTS follow up the success of "Gary Gilmore's Eyes" with their latest offering "Safety In Numbers" and "We Who Wait."

REZILLOS/THE MOTELS..............Glasgow, Saints & Sinners	JOHNNY CURIOUS &
MUTANTS ....Liverpool, The Havana Club	THE STRANGERS ....London, The Red Cow
SHAM 69................................London, Middlesex Poly.	BLUNT INSTRUMENT/
SAINTS..................................Manchester, The Rafters	THE VOID..............................London, Wimbledon Art Col.

28th - Friday...

THE SEX PISTOLS' album "Never Mind The Bollocks" is on the streets less than an hour and has already been blocked from sale at Boots, Woolworth's and W.H. Smith. It contains the "A" sides of the band's previous four singles, as well seven new recordings. Side one starts with their current 45 "Holidays In The Sun." Then comes "Liar," "No Feelings," and their biggest hit, "God Save The Queen." The side closes out with "Problems." Side two has "Seventeen" just prior to the EMI recorded track "Anarchy In The UK." Then there's "Bodies," "Pretty Vacant," "New York," and the biting, autobiographical "EMI." Besides the single sided 45 of "Submission," which is in some of the first copies, there is also a full color poster montage. There were plans to re-issue the album, deleting some tracks to allow it to be stocked by the major chain stores, but these plans have now been dropped.

MAGAZINE and the *NME* spend some time verbally sparing while Paul Morley tries to find out what Howard Devoto and Magazine are all about. Devoto plays three recording for him; "Shot By Both Sides," "The Light Pours Out Of Me," and a whimsical tune called "Suddenly Eating Sandwiches." There a negotiations underway at the moment with Virgin Records but the details are kept secret. Trying to pin him down is very difficult. Devoto told Morley, "I'm not stupid and I refuse to pretend to be smart. Somebody said I'm smart; well read and well groomed. What e.e. cummings called an intelligentleman...I deal in ideals and the effects of ideas. That's a real distinction. I'm not going to tell you what the ideas are right now, but I'll give you a clue. The last place to look for them is in the songs." Magazine, played their first full length gig tonight as a benefit for another magazine, the *Manchester Review*. This is a magazine that features articles and public comment about Manchester. The periodical had been raising money by sponsoring new wave nights at the Rafters Club. Lead singer Howard Devoto started the show with "Hello we're Magazine and my name is Adam Faith.." Then they launched into "Shot By Both Sides." Very original stuff. A great start for a band that came together only about two months ago. Opening up the show is another hometown band, The Fall. Hopefully Devoto remembered the words to this new set of material. He confessed to *Sounds* this week that "When I forget the words I make noises that sound like words."

THE HEARTBREAKERS have a three track maxi single issued today by Track Records. The "A" side is "One Track Mind," a track from their LP "L.A.M.F." The "B" side features two previously unreleased recordings of "Can't Keep My Eyes Off You" and "Do You Love Me."

ADVERTS/SAINTS/RAGE.....Edinburgh, The Clouds	OUTSIDERS/
X-RAY SPEX ....Liverpool, Eric's	NIPPLE ERECTORS ....London, The Roxy
ONLY ONES....................London, Bedford College	MAGAZINE/THE FALL........Manchester, Rafters
GENERATION X ....London, Kings College	

November 1st - Tuesday..............

THE SNIVELING SHITS' record that was shipped to the music papers at the end of September is now available in shops around London. It's an import though, being pressed up in France. It's titled "Terminal Stupid" and "I Can't Come." The original copies were on A C Disc Records and left people to speculate about who was in the band. Now some French imports of the 45 are in the UK with listing of the artists in the band. It's enough to make the writers at the *NME* who gave it "Single Of The Week" status blush. At the time they wrote that the 45 was, "...another kick up the arse for Rock & Roll from a bunch of geezers as yet relatively unknown, but once Stiff Records gets their hands on them, The Sniveling Shits will change the face of blather, blather, etc." Now the secret is out. The Sniveling Shits are actually a secret

NOVEMBER 1977

band put together by Giovanni Dadomo, Pete Makowski, Dave Fudger and Steve Nicol from *Sounds* magazine. I wonder what rating the *NME* will give it now?

THE SEX PISTOLS' proposed movie, *Who Killed Bambi*, under the direction of American Russ Meyer, has been cancelled in pre-production when one of the financial backers quit as costs began to skyrocket. Intended to be a low budget affair, expenses climbed to one million dollars. There have already been several weeks of preparation to begin shooting the project at Bray Studios, but now Meyer has returned to Los Angeles and the sets are being dismantled. The proposed film was to have a reported love scene pairing Marianne Faithful and Johnny Rotten.

THE VALVES have already followed up their single eight weeks ago with another. It's called "Tarzan Of The King's Road" and deals with the Tarzan persona having to live in a tree in a plastic bondage suit while hangin' with Cheetah. Hearty stuff. It's coupled with "Ain't No Surf In Portobello," one of the few Scottish bands to use the word "Surf" in a song. It's about surfing in part of Edinburgh called Portobello where a sewage plant is nearby. The Valves sing about riding on the crest of an oil slick with city sewage in their hair. A great sense of humor and a funny record.

SAINTS	London, Marquee	MODELS/HEADACHE/TONES	
MANIACS	London, Hope & Anchor	PEROXIDE ROMANCE	London, The Vortex
LURKERS	London, Dingwalls	CLASH/	
XTC/WIRE	London, Music Machine	RICHARD HELL & VOIDOIDS	Sheffield, The Top Rank
ALTERNATIVE T.V.	London, 100 Club		

4th - Friday.....................................

THE JAM's second album is on release today in the UK. It's "This Is The Modern World." The record finds the band perilously close to the mid-sixties riffs that they use as influences. The LP contains their current top forty single "The Modern World" as well as tracks such as "Standards," "In The Street Today," "London Traffic," "Here Comes The Weekend" and "Tonight At Noon." The band wrote the LP after returning from their last American tour. They spend quite some time at rehearsal space outside of London trying to find the right songs. Here's the result. By the way, Paul Weller has now moved to London, the others are still living in the trio's hometown of Woking with their parents. Some distancing between Paul and the others is beginning to show.

THE MYSTERY GIRLS are a new Liverpool band that's onstage tonight at Eric's opening up for Sham 69. The band rose out of the ashes of the Crucial Three. Tonight is their first (and last) appearance before an audience. They play a powerful set consisting mostly of cover versions of songs like "I Wanna Be Your Dog," "Diddy Wah Diddy," "The Night Time" and "I Can See For Miles." The group is made up of Pete Burns on vocals, Phil Hurst on drums, Julian Cope on bass and Pete Wylie on guitar. Pete Burns will go on to start a group called Nightmares In Wax that would turn into Dead Or Alive. Pete Wylie would go off and start Wah! Heat and Julian Cope would be involved with a group of friends calling themselves Teardrop Explodes.

SKREWDRIVER's debut album "All Skrewed Up" is released by Chiswick Records in two different pressings. The initial 3,000 have the disc spinning at 45 rpm with a total of thirteen songs. The rest of the pressing reverts to 33 rpm with fifteen songs. The faster version will retail at less than the fuller, slower version. Skinhead titles include the single "Anti-Social" as well as "Government Action," "Gotta Be Young," "I Don't Like You," "I Don't Need Your Love," "Jailbait," "We Don't Pose" and a cover of the Who's "Won't Get Fooled Again."

EDDIE & THE HOT RODS' new LP is "Life On The Line." It features their previous top ten single "Do Anything You Wanna Do" as well as a longer version of "Ignore Them," the flipside to "I Might Be Lying," plus many new songs. There are problems with the album overseas, specifically with new Hot Rod Graeme Douglas. Six months ago he was member of The Kursaal Flyers and his former bosses feel they still have his talents on a string. Talents that have been reflected by Graeme's name turning up in the credits to six of the nine songs on the album. Entanglements ensue and the LP has Graeme's picture deleted from the cover art and a "courtesy of CBS Records" next to his name. Further complications await if this is a hit record.

COCKSPARRER have their new Decca single released today, a reworking of the Rolling Stones song "We Love You," flipped with the appropriate "Chip On My Shoulder." The group got together early in '76 with what they make clear is "Skinhead Rock" not "punk rock." They are Mick Beaufey on guitar, Colin McFaull on vocals, Charlie Bruce on drums, Steve Burgess on bass and Garrie Lammin on guitar.

BUZZCOCKS/		THOSE NAUGHTY LUMPS	Liverpool, Red Star Club
JOHNNY & SELF ABUSERS	Edinburgh, Clouds	VOID/ MONOTONES/MANIACS	London, The Roxy Club
REZILLOS	Edinburgh, Art College	STRANGLERS/ DICTATORS/	
SHAM 69 /MYSTERY GIRLS	Liverpool, Eric's	THE POP GROUP	London, The Roundhouse

5th - Saturday.....................................

PENETRATION cut a rough demo some five months ago in Newcastle and the manager of the Virgin shop there liked it enough that he forwarded it to headquarters in London. Since then, Virgin has signed the Penetration and issue their debut single today as part of a one-off deal. The new 45 is the high energy rocker "Don't Dictate" b/w "Money Talks."

MORRISSEY is still in love with the New York Dolls. Over the past three years he's been writing to whoever would print his letters about his favorite group. Now that the Dolls split, he has to concentrate on the various parts. Lead singer David Johansen is working on a solo LP and Morrissey has gotten a tape. He wrote to *Sounds,* "I have just received some tapes from a friend in California of the David JoHansen Group and all I have to say is LOOK OUT, because when David gets over here, new wave will age rapidly. Something happening over Manhattan and British Punk is eight blocks behind (sad!). Jerry Nolan- explain yourself...Steven Morrissey, Stretford, Manchester."

THE LURKERS release their second single "Freak Show" on the indie Beggars Banquet label. Artwork for the picture cover is provided by *Sounds* artist "Savage Pencil" (Edwin Pouncey). The band sum up the true story of all blind dates and the fears that go with them.

NOVEMBER 1977

DEPRESSIONS/MEAN STREET ......London, The Marquee	WIRE.....................................London, Rochester Castle
COCKSPARRER ....London, N.E.Poly.	STRANGLERS/DICTATORS/
MENACE ....London, Red Cow	THE POP GROUP ....London, The Roundhouse
SKUNKS/BLITZ/NIGHTS ....London, Roxy	

7th - Monday...

SEX PISTOLS have shocked the nation again. Their new album "Never Mind The Bollocks" has been stricken from many shop windows as being indecent. It's an under-the-counter item if sold at all. All of this stems from the police enforcing an 1889 Indecent Advertisements Act as well as an equally antique Vagrancy Act. The record shop that set this in motion was the Virgin Records in Kings Road in Nottingham. Last Saturday a police sergeant was shocked to see a 6 x 9 foot poster of the cover in the window. It was removed and replaced when she left. The sergeant returned with reinforcements and arrested the shop manager, Chris Seale. Records have been impounded, shop keepers (even independents) harassed and fines levied. All over a record jacket. Virgin Records boss Richard Branson has said that Virgin will continue to display it in their shop windows. "We would be hypocritical if we took them down" he said. Trial date is set for November 24th. Not only is the album unable to be displayed, £40,000 worth of advertising has been rejected (even though it was earlier approved) by the Association of Independent Radio Contractors. No ads will be seen on TV or heard on the radio. So far Woolworth's, W.H. Smiths and Boots have all forbade sale of the album. Others are covering up the offensive word. On the other hand, the Virgin retail store in Notting Hill Gate has stocked that store with nothing BUT "Never Mind The Bollocks."

THE DAMNED are holding auditions today and tomorrow for a new drummer. The are already planning to see twenty-five today, twenty-five tomorrow. The first four dates on their UK tour (Middlesbrough, Leeds, Dublin & Belfast) have been cancelled so the band can regroup.

CLASH/	MANIACS/MONOTONES	
RICHARD HELL & VOIDOIDS ....Birmingham, Top Rank	BAZOOKA JOE/JETZ ....London, The Vortex	
YACHTS.................................London, Marquee	RUNAWAYS/999 ....Sheffield, City Hall	
NEW HEARTS ....London, Hope & Anchor		

9th - Wednesday.......................................

IAN DURY's recording of "Sex & Drugs & Rock & Roll" has been deleted by Stiff Records only two months after it was issued. They claim two reasons: one, they don't have warehouse space to keep storing backstock; two, they are interested in the business of new records, not becoming a museum. Yeah, but only two months afterwards?

BOOMTOWN RATS have once again been immortalized on polystyrene. This time it's "Mary Of The Fourth Form" (an alternate version of the LP track), flipped with "Do The Rat," a popular audience participation number.

SHAM 69 lead singer Jimmy Pursey knows what he is and does. He doesn't see his place in music as anything more than an entertainer. This week in the *NME* he said, "I know I'm not gonna change the world- if I ever believed I was gonna change the world I'd be a complete nutcase. All I can do is get out on that stage, sing about it and make people enjoy it at the same time. I'm not a politician, I'm not a leader, all I am is a bloke who gets on stage and sings rock and roll."

RAPED/DISTURBED ....London, Man In The Moon

10th - Thursday......................................

WAYNE COUNTY & THE ELECTRIC CHAIRS are no doubt controversial. It's this latest song that Illegal refused to issue. Perhaps because they thought it really was illegal. The song is "(If You Don't Want To Fuck Me Baby) Fuck Off!" This tender love ballad is on the band's own Sweet F.A. label, flipped with "On The Crest." The band remains Greg Van Cook, Val Haller and J.J. Johnson, but there is the addition of Jools Holland on piano. He's not joining the band, just adding that rolling Chicago blues undercarriage that he knows so well.

THE LURKERS have been joined by ex-Saints bassist Kym Bradshaw. He's turned up as the replacement for Arturo Bassick. Bradshaw takes over just in time to hit the road with the Lurkers on their latest tour. Meanwhile, Bassick is starting his own group, "Pinpoint."

THE TUBES/WIRE ....Birmingham, The Odeon	RIFF RAFF ....London, The Red Cow	
PENETRATION ....London, Ealing College Of Tech.	SHAM 69 ....Manchester, Rafters	
REZILLOS/IGNATZ....................London, The Nashville		

11th - Friday.......................................

LOCKJAW are a new group from Crawley, Sussex. They've leave behind one of the most ridiculous versions of Cliff Richards 1961 hit "The Young Ones" ever on vinyl. It's out today on the Raw Records label. One of their members is Simon Gallup, who will join the Cure in January of '80. Lockjaw will encounter the Cure several times in the late '70s, after all, they're both from the same neighborhood.

THE WASPS have their debut single out today on 4-Play Records. These teenagers are regulars down at the Vortex and Rochester Castle. They're a quartet from Walthamstow made up of Steve Wollaston on bass, John Rich on drums, Gary Wellman on guitar and Jesse Lynd-Dean on vocals. The single pairs "She Made Magic" with "Teenage Treats."

BLONDIE ....Birmingham, Barbarella's	DEPRESSIONS/MISTAKES/	
STRANGLERS ....Dublin, Trinity College	ACME SEWAGE COMPANY ....London, Roxy	
RUNAWAYS/999......................Glasgow, Apollo	THE TUBES/WIRE ....London, Hammersmith Odeon	
THOSE NAUGHTY LUMPS...........Liverpool, Red Star Club	X-RAY SPEX/BLACK SLATE.........London, Lambeth Town Hall	

NOVEMBER 1977

12th - Saturday.....................................

WIRE has been a band about one year now. They started out as a five piece and after the departure of guitarist George Gill in January '77, they remained as a quartet. Their minimalist rapid fire approach and their subsequent tracks on the "Live At The Roxy" LP, brought them to the attention of Harvest Records. Their debut single is out today. It's a three track EP coupling "Mannequin," "Feeling Called Love" and "12XU." It is considered very, very weird and brilliant.

BIG IN JAPAN & THE CHUDDY NUDDIES are two Liverpool bands sharing a record put out by a local club called Eric's. The single is billed on the sleeve as "Brutality - Religion and a Dance Beat." One side has Big In Japan singing their theme song "Big In Japan." Listening to the shrill record you can't make out any of the lyrics, but you do catch the phrase "Big In Japan" at least eighty times. Big In Japan are Kevin Ward on bass and vocals, Jayne Casey on lead vocals, Phil Allen on drums, Ian Broudie on guitar, Bill Drummond on guitar and vocals and Clive Langer on guitar. The Chuddy Nuddies are actually the Yachts. They appear here in disguise since they are under contract to Stiff Records who have just issued their debut single "Suffice To Say." Their song contribution is "Do The Chud."

BLONDIE	Aylesbury, Friar's	MENACE/BLITZ/RED LIGHT	London, Roxy
STRANGLERS/RADIO STARS	Dublin, Trinity College	TUBES/WIRE	London, Hammersmith Odeon
THIN LIZZY/		LONDON/ONLY ONES/	
RADIATORS FROM SPACE	Glasgow, The Apollo	TANYA HYDE & TORMENTERS	London, N.E. London Poly.
WASPS	London, Red Cow	BUZZCOCKS	Manchester, Poly.
ADAM & THE ANTS	London, Marquee	RUNAWAYS/999	Manchester, Free Trade Hall

14th - Monday...........................

Wouldn't you like to rip her to shreds?

Blondie's new single out now.

BLONDIE's latest single is "Rip Her To Shreds," "X-Offender" and "In The Flesh." All three songs are from the Private Stock LP, now being picked up by Chrysalis Records. Blondie have found their new bass player. He's Nigel Harrison (ex-Silverhead) and has a long past in bands, most recently playing with ex-Doors keyboardist Ray Manzarek. He's been flown in from New York and told to learn the twenty-five song set quickly. Frank Infante moves over to rhythm guitar. Tonight is the debut of the new band with the Harry- Stein- Burke- Destri- Infante- Harrison lineup.

"STREETS" is the new compilation put together by Beggars Banquet, a chain of record shops in London that have been paying close attention to underground and indie records. The flegling label now issues a collection of punk bands titled "Streets." Some of these recordings have never been released before and many bands appear for the first time anywhere. Among those we've heard from before are the Lurkers with a new one "Be My Prisoner," John Cooper Clarke's "Innocents," "Hungry" by the Zeros, The Drones' "Lookalikes," the Pork Dukes' disgusting "Bend & Flush" and the Drive's "Jerkin'." New bands to surface on this LP include The Doll, Arthur Comics?, The Members, Art Attacks, Cane and Tractor. The majority of the tracks for the album were produced by Steve Lillywhite and Ed Hollis and represent bands from France, Dundee, Glasgow, Manchester and London.

Most notable on the album is a group called The Reaction. Do you remember the song "Talk Talk" by Talk Talk in 1982? The beginning of that hit, is farther back than you'd expect. Producer Ed Hollis (ever heard of Eddie & The Hot Rods?) has a little brother, Mark Hollis and this is his band's debut. The Reaction is more or less a studio group working out Mark Hollis' demo of "Talk Talk Talk Talk," the prototype of the 1982 Talk Talk hit single. This version is twice the tempo and a completely different feel.

THIN LIZZY/		SLAUGHTER & DOGS/	
RADIATORS FROM SPACE	Edinburgh, Odeon	SPIZZ 77/	
RICHARD HELL & VOIDOIDS/		RAPED/METAL URBAIN	London, The Vortex
SIOUXSIE & BANSHEES/		NEW HEARTS/DRONES	London, Marquee
LOUS/NEO	London, The Music Machine		

15th - Tuesday........................

EASY CURE are in SAV Studios in London again recording their second round of songs for Hansa Records. Today's session included originals like "I'm Cold," "Little Girl" and "Killing An Arab," as well as covers of Bowie's "Rebel Rebel," and the Beatles' "I Saw Her Standing There." Having to record other people's material grates on the new band. They pride themselves on their originals and are just going along with the test recordings like good little soldiers.

BUZZCOCKS	Birmingham, Barbarella's	LURKERS/ART ATTAX/	
VIPERS	Dublin, Trinity College	DOLL/BIZARROS	London, The Vortex
COUNT BISHOPS/OUTSIDERS	London, The 100 Club	WHY NOT?/BERLIN	London, Roxy Club
BLONDIE/XTC	London, Rainbow Theatre	THE CLASH	Manchester, Elizabethan Ballroom

16th - Wednesday............................

THE SEX PISTOLS' aborted Sex Pistols' movie *Who Killed Bambi?* has been given new life as another backer for the venture has been found. The script for the film has been drastically re-written and Russ Meyer has not been retained to direct the picture. Shooting is slated to start at the first of next month with Marianne Faithful still cast as the leading lady. It is still unclear whether the title *Who Killed Bambi?*

NOVEMBER 1977

will remain. There are also rumblings around that the Sex Pistols will be planning a major UK tour for the spring. So far no dates, no venues. Interviewed in the London Times, manager Malcolm McLaren is upfront about what marketing the Pistols is about. "If people bought the records for the music, this thing would have died a death long ago."

LIVE TONIGHT!

THIN LIZZY/		ADVERTISING/MANIACS	London, Rochester Castle
RADIATORS FROM SPACE	Liverpool, The Empire	SUBURBAN STUDS	London, Spooky Lady
OPEN SAW	London, Roxy	LURKERS	Manchester, Electric Circus (opens)

17th - Thursday.....................

THE RAMONES' new LP is their "Rocket To Russia." The LP contains their previous hit single "Sheena Is A Punk Rocker," as well as other up tempo romps like "Teenage Lobotomy," "I Wanna Be Well," "Rockaway Beach" and "Cretin Hop." There are two covers of '60s hits; "Surfin Bird," (by the Trashmen) and "Do You Wanna Dance? " (by Bobby Freeman). The production of the album was supervised by Tony Bongovi as well as Tommy Erdelyi (aka Tommy Ramone). There's going to be no complaints against the band on this album. They even have a song about American home life, "We're A Happy Family."

THE REZILLOS have signed to Sire Records. They were among the first of the Scottish punk bands and have previously had one single on their own Sensible Records label which sold about 15,000 copies around the UK. They are currently planning their first 45 for Sire which will be "(My Baby Does) Good Sculptures." The bad news is that the Rezillos intended single for Sire is already at the pressing plant with the Sensible label. The band placed the order before the deal came down. The Sensible single will have to be disposed of immediately, potentially making them an instant collectible. Since the band came to London a week ago, they've cut the line-up from an unwieldy seven members down to five. Bassist Dr. D.K. Smyth and backup singer Gale Warning have returned to Scotland.

XTC	Birmingham, Rebecca's	OUTSIDERS/AUTOMATICS/	
THIN LIZZY/		GOATS	London, Roxy
RADIATORS FROM SPACE	Liverpool, The Empire	WIRE/RIFF RAFF	London, The Red Cow
ADVERTS/JOHNNY MOPED		DEPRESSIONS	London, Rochester Castle
ELECTRIC CHAIRS/ATV	London, The Roundhouse	ONLY ONES	Manchester, The Rafters

18th - Friday.............................

THE DAMNED have a new album on the shelves today. It's "Music For Pleasure." Surprise of the week is that Pink Floyd drummer Nick Mason produced the LP. Being from a generation where time spent in the studio is an asset and not a liability, it was probably a shock having to work on a budget. The album is also packaged in a cheerful Barney Bubble cover. Not the normal package for punk records these days. Where's the safety pins? The LP has the current singles "Problem Child," "You Take My Money," "Don't Cry Wolf" and "One Way Love." For the first time the Damned appear as a five piece on vinyl. The mystery man is Robert Edmunds, who everyone calls Lu. Rat Scabies, who left the band back at the first of October, will not be present to play these tracks live at the band's upcoming dates. As far as the songwriting goes, we get to hear what sort of songs Scabies, Sensible and Vanian can turn out. That's something missed in the past because of the prolific Brian James and one of the alleged reasons that Rat walked, not enough credit(s).

ADVERTS	Birmingham, Barbarella's	WASPS/TICKETS/	
BUZZCOCKS	Liverpool, Eric's	SHOPLIFTERS	London, Roxy
YACHTS	Liverpool, Poly.	DICTATORS/999/STUKAS	London, The Roundhouse
WAYNE COUNTY &		X-RAY SPEX	London, The Marquee
THE ELECTRIC CHAIRS	London, Central Poly.	USERS/SOFT BOYS	London, School of Economics
FABULOUS POODLES	London, Kings College		

19th - Saturday.............................

THE CLASH have their debut album "The Clash" released by CBS Records, just in time for 1978. Songs on the album include their singles "Remote Control," "London's Burning" and "White Riot," as well as many live favorites. The reverse of the jacket features a back photo of the Notting Hill Carnival Riots of last year that inspired the song "White Riot" as well as provided the band a photo backdrop for their tours. The band has found it increasingly difficult to play live as their insurance coverage has been rescinded by their agents as well as the fear that venues have of booking the band.

GENERATION X have their second single released by Chrysalis here today. Although fans had been wanting several stage favorites of the group, they have chosen a brand new song called "Wild Youth." It's backed with "Wild Dub," a drastically remixed version of the song. There was a bit of a cock-up at the pressing plant and some singles have slipped out with a new song called "No No No" on the flip instead. The labels all say "Wild Dub," the only way to tell is to listen to it. Generation X are currently in the studio with producer Phil Wainman recording their debut LP.

ADVERTS	Birmingham, Barbarella's	XTC/RUMBLE STRIPS	London, Imperial College
TOM ROBINSON BAND	Glasgow, Univ.	METAL URBAIN/	
THE REZILLOS	Liverpool, Eric's	BLUNT INSTRUMENT/	
SLITS/TICKETS	London, Chiselhurst Caves	THE TARTS	London, Roxy

NOVEMBER 1977

21st - Monday.............................

STROMTROOPER doesn't even exist anymore- it hasn't since the winter of '75. Now, two years after it was recorded, Stormtrooper roar to life on vinyl. Some of the former members felt their music is now "in style" and have gotten together the money to put the demo on a single. It's out on Solent Records, the tracks being "I'm A Mess" and "It's Not Me." A two-inch badge saying "I'm A Mess" will become part of Sid Vicious' wardrobe of badges on his leather jacket in the middle of the Pistols' U.S. tour.

THE HEARTBREAKERS play two nights at the Vortex to break in their new drummer. Original drummer and ex-NY Doll, Jerry Nolan, left the band at the first of October, is to be replaced by Terry Chimes (a.k.a. Tory Crimes), ex-member of the Clash.

THE NEW HEARTS have just had their debut single released by CBS in the UK. It's their crowd pleaser "Just Another Teenage Anthem." The band will be out on tour soon with the Jam, possibly influencing them to go mod in '79 when Dave and Ian from the band split off to become Secret Affair.

DAMNED/DEAD BOYS	Birmingham, Top Rank	BUZZCOCKS/THE FLIES	London, Marquee
TOM ROBINSON BAND	Edinburgh, Univ.	HEARTBREAKERS/	
THE ELECTRIC CHAIRS/		DEPRESSIONS/MEAN STREET/	
ALTERNATIVE T.V.	High Wycombe, Nags Head	SPIZZ 77	London, The Vortex

23rd - Wednesday.............................

THE CORTINAS had been planning to spend a week playing dates at the Gibus Club in Paris soon but have cancelled their trip because of red tape. There is a 1933 law on the books in Paris that prevents a young person from playing in a foreign country without a special license. The band went to the local authorities to work out matters but found that the application could not be finished before the dates. They have just released their second single for Step Forward Records "Defiant Pose" b/w "Independence."

THE HEARTBREAKERS implode after two nights at the Vortex. The band are splitting up. It's not the club, it's the personal tensions that have been running high all year long.

THOSE NAUGHTY LUMPS	Liverpool, The Havana Club	RIFF RAFF	London, The Kensington
THE ELECTRIC CHAIRS/		BOOMTOWN RATS	Sheffield, Poly.
ALTERNATIVE T.V.	Liverpool, Eric's	THIN LIZZY/	
XTC	London, The Marquee	RADIATORS FROM SPACE	Sheffield, City Hall
PENETRATION	London, Rochester Castle	DAMNED/DEAD BOYS	Sheffield, The Top Rank

24th - Thursday.............................

THE SEX PISTOLS finally have their day in court. The issue at hand is the word "Bollocks" on their new LP sleeve. The prosecution feels that the word is offensive and violates the 1889 Indecent Advertising Act and intends to use the case in Nottingham as a test case. Prosecuting the case for the Crown was David Ritchie. He described the circumstances surrounding the arrest of Christopher Seale, the shop keeper who displayed a 9 x 6 foot display of the album jacket. Seals' attorney, John Mortimer raised the question of why Seale was prosecuted for displaying the sleeve while the newspapers that used the same image as an illustration were not. Mortimer continued to outline the history of the term "Bollocks" tracing it back to roots in the Middle Ages. Mortimer continued by bringing in a Professor Kingsley, head of English Studies at local Nottingham University. Kingsley told the court that the term had been used from the year 1,000 to describe a small ball (or things of a similar shape) and that it has appeared in Medieval Bibles, veterinary books and literature through the ages. He also revealed (not surprisingly) that it also served as part of place names throughout the UK. Eyebrows were raised when Kingsley said that the term had been used to describe the clergy of the previous century. In that connotation it was used in a similar fashion as the word rubbish and used to describe a clergyman that spoke nonsense. The defense continued to intimate that perhaps the prosecution was not interested in decency of the word in question but instead were waging war against the band themselves. After making the case clear, the judiciary deliberated for twenty minutes and felt compelled to dismiss all charges against Seale. The Sex Pistols' cover was ruled as "decent" and set a precedent that would protect other shop owners who displayed the cover.

THE DRONES have their first album released by independent Valer Records today. It's called "Further Temptations," the follow up to their EP "Temptations Of A White Collar Worker." It has two tracks re-recorded from the EP, as well as both sides of the band's last single. Besides the twelve original songs, there is an odd remake of the Ronette's "Be My Baby."

THE OUTSIDERS are a "new wave" trio from Wembley. They have a new EP out this week in the UK of all new material not included in their debut album in September. Tracks include "One To Infinity," "New Uniform," "Consequences" and "Freeway." As their last record was, this one's also on Raw Edge Records.

DEPRESSIONS	London, Rochester Castle	Stiff-Chiswick Challenge	London, Royal College Of Art
RIFF RAFF	London, The Red Cow	WAYNE COUNTY &	
LONDON/RABIES/TARTS	London, The Roxy Club	THE ELECTRIC CHAIRS/	
		ALTERNATIVE T.V.	Manchester, The Poly.

25th - Friday.............................

THE DAMNED release their fifth single today. It's "One Way Love" b/w "Don't Cry Wolf." If your lucky enough to be in the first 20,000 purchasers (and who couldn't be?) you'll get this vinyl goodie pressed on purple vinyl. Dave Berk, who had been replacing Rat Scabies has been replaced as well by John Moss.

NOVEMBER 1977

CHRISTMAS PUNK? The first of a genre. A punk Christmas record. The mystery band is called The Yobs, (that's The boY's backwards innit?). The effort had the Chuck Berry Christmas classic "Run Rudolph Run" flipped with "The Worm Song." The "Rudolph" on the picture sleeve is Rudolph Hess.

2.3 are the Sheffield based trio that started off back in July as 2.3 Children (the average number of children in the nuclear family). They've shortened their name and got their big break after only five months of work. Their recent gig in Doncaster opening for the Rezillos didn't go unnoticed by Bob Last. He was so impressed he quickly got a tape deck and recorded the last portion of their set. Afterwards, he offered the lads a record deal with a new label he's starting up in the coming year. Although the exact amount is unknown, it's said the band received a two figure advance. 2.3 have nothing but good luck come their way. Their debut gig in August at the Penthouse Club in Sheffield was a rousing success, now only months after getting together they're on their way to their first record.

LIVE TONIGHT!

EATER/MONOTONES..................Edinburgh, Clouds	ONLY ONES/NEWS ....London, Dingwalls
DAMNED/DEAD BOYS/	BURLESQUE/
DRONES ....London, The Roundhouse	JOHN COOPER CLARKE..............London, The Nashville
THIS HEAT.............................London, School Of Economics	THIN LIZZY/
SUBURBAN STUDS/	RADIATORS FROM SPACE ....Manchester, Free Trade Hall
BLITZ/UK SUBS ....London, The Roxy Club	

28th - Monday...

SEX PISTOLS' manager Malcolm McLaren revealed intentions to tour the Sex Pistols abroad in an interview with Tony Parsons for the *NME*. Thoughts of going to Spain, Italy and Yugoslavia all were made clear. There were also plans for the bands to play in the US. Malcolm said, "What I'd like to do is pick some place on the map that no-one has ever heard of before. Somewhere in Alabama or near the Mexican border and do a gig there. Even if they hate it, at least it's helping to decentralize and get away from playing New York and Los Angeles because everyone plays those shitholes."

WIRE release their groundbreaking debut album "Pink Flag." The twenty-one songs flash by quickly. There's "Reuters," "Field Day For The Sundays," "Surgeon's Girl," "Mannequin," "Didderent To Me" and "12XU." The LP is a distillation of the band's remarkably left field sense of music. Songs with unheard of chord structures, built more like aural sculptures than pop melodies. It's unusual stuff and the music papers are talking about it as the "album of the year." The photo on the cover was taken by a friend of theirs in Plymouth last July. They had a notion about a flag and pole, just the stark image. Walking along the road they saw it. Just like that, a gift. Wire is Colin Newman on vocals, Robert Gotobed on drums, B.C. Gilbert on guitar and Craig Lewis on bass.

BIG IN JAPAN don't want to be taken seriously! They've come down from Liverpool to play their first London gig at the Music Machine, even though they only have a handful of songs to play. New addition to the group is future Frankie Goes To Hollywood singer Holly Johnson on bass. Tonight he's delightfully decked out in crew-cut, bowtie, leather jacket and tartan trousers. Gear! The band also has a few copies of their single "Big In Japan" to sell after the gig, if you're interested.

JAM/NEW HEARTS ....Birmingham, The Top Rank	THE UNWANTED/TICKETS
BIG IN JAPAN/SUBURBAN STUDS/.	BLITZ/MISTAKES ....London, The Vortex
PEROXIDE ROMANCE ....London, Music Machine	ART ATTACKS ....London, Rochester Castle

29th - Tuesday...

ALTERNATIVE T.V. have released their first proper record on Deptford Fun City Records. That's the label that Miles Copeland (manager of Climax Blues Band) set up to record some of his own interests. Titles are "How Much Longer" and "You Bastard." ATV's previous release was a flexi disc in lead singer Mark Perry's fanzine *Sniffin' Glue*.

SIOUXSIE & THE BANSHEES are the subject of tonight's John Peel session aired during his show on Radio One. Songs recorded for this radio debut are "Love In A Void," "Metal Postcard," "Suburban Relapse" and "Make Up To Break Up." This is the first chance for anyone who has not been to the band's few appearances to hear what the buzz is about.

999/PLEASERS ....London, Hope & Anchor	KILLJOYS/MIRRORS
YACHTS/ADVERTISING ....London, Nashville	PATRIK FITZGERALD/
THE WASPS ....London, Rochester Castle	THE CANE ....London, The Vortex
LARRY ZOOM/PLASTICS ....London, Roxy	THE JAM/NEW HEARTS ....Manchester, The Apollo

30th - Wednesday...

SEX PISTOLS' bassist Sid Vicious turns up for prearranged rehearsals for the Sex Pistols' secret three month world tour, only to find that none of the other members are there. He's very put-off and wonders why they are letting time run out when their departure for the tour is quickly coming. Morose and disappointed, Sid got very depressed and drank himself even deeper. At one point he tried to throw himself out of the window of his Ambassador Hotel room in Bayswater. The only thing that stopped Sid's suicidal plunge was girlfriend Nancy Spungen who wouldn't turn loose of his belt and dragged him back into the room. Once inside, Sid turned even more violent and knocked Nancy's head against a wall repeatedly, leaving her almost unconscious and very bloody. After more hysterics (this all taking place in the pre-dawn morning hours) they calmed down and went to bed. The hotel's receptionist entered the room, saw the blood and general disarray of the room, assumed the worst and called the authorities. The police entered on grounds of searching for "a stolen ring," and while there confiscated some "suspicious substance." The two were taken to the station, questioned and charges were dropped. Because of this morning's incident, the rest of the band are supposedly adamant about having Sid booted from the group. If he doesn't leave they want him to be separated from Nancy, who they consider the reason for all his troubles and constant excesses.

NOVEMBER 1977

SLAUGHTER & THE DOGS' third single is "Dame To Blame" and "Johnny T." It's their second Decca release, gearing the band up for an album in the new year.

JAM/NEW HEARTS	Glasgow, The Apollo	WIRE/NEO/TRASH	London, Music Machine
THOSE NAUGHTY LUMPS	Liverpool, Havana Club	SHAM 69/SLUGS	Manchester, Electric Circus
RIFF RAFF	London, Kensington Hotel	EATER	Manchester, Roundtree's Corn Ex.
CRABS/MONOTONES	London, Marquee	ADVERTS	Sheffield, Poly.
EXORCIST/SUFFOCATION	London, Roxy		

December 1st - Thursday............

PLASTIC BERTRAND is a new act that's surfaced through the import record bins in the UK and America. He's Plastic Bertrand and is the comic Belgian/French answer to punk rock. His real name is Roger Jouret and he had previously been in a punk trio called Hubble Bubble, who had recorded an entire album of odd songs. There were unusual covers of Scott McKenzie's "San Francisco" and the Kinks' song "I'm Not Like Everybody Else." The "Plastic Bertrand" persona was created as a comedy act called "Two Man Sound" with Roger teaming up with producer Lou Deprijck. His solo debut single is out this week on the continental Vogue Records label. The tracks are "Pogo Pogo" and "Ca Plan Pour Moi."

THE CATCH is onstage tonight at the Red Cow. Annie Lennox must be feeling some thrill that their single "Borderline" is beginning to get a little attention in Holland, even though it still hasn't set London on fire yet. The Red Cow is a tiny, tiny way to start on a big, big career.

SPLIT ENZ	Edinburgh, College Of Art	DIRTY DOGS/RAPED/	
ALTERNATIVE T.V./		TICKETS	London, Roxy
MYSTERIONS	London, Deptford Albany Empire	THE CATCH	London, The Red Cow

2nd - Friday.................

THE RAMONES' latest single is "Rockaway Beach," a tribute of sorts to a beach on Long Island, New York. It's taken from their latest LP "Rocket To Russia." It's flipped with two old stage favorites, "Beat On The Brat" and "Teenage Lobotomy." If you're among the first 10,000 buyers of the UK single, you will also receive a limited edition poster of the Ramones.

IAN DURY & THE BLOCKHEADS have their tribute to rocker Gene Vincent released on Stiff Records today. It's "Sweet Gene Vincent" b/w "You're More Than Fair." The "A" side a wonderful tribute, the flip, an old Kilburn's song reworked.

THE REZILLOS have their first single release since signing with Sire Records. It's the live favorite "(My Baby Does) Good Sculptures" b/w "Flying Saucer Attack."

ADVERTS	Edinburgh, Univ.	999/ MERGER/ART ATTACKS	London, Royal College Of Art
LEYTON BUZZARDS	London, Art College	DEAD FINGERS TALK	London, Pegasus
THIS HEAT/ACME QUARTET	London, Arts Centre	PIRATES/ONLY ONES	London, Central London Poly.
DEPRESSIONS/YOUTHENASIA/		BONE IDOL	London, Brecknock
CHARGE	London, Roxy	WARSAW	Manchester, Electric Circus

5th - Monday..................

"LIVE AT THE VORTEX!" In keeping with the live compilations connected with clubs like The Roxy and CBGB's, The Vortex have their own vinyl document now. It contains tracks from regulars of the club, but not the absolute best of their live bands. Side one starts off with The Wasps' "Can't Wait Till '78," and then proceeds with songs by Mean Street, Neo, Bernie Torme and The Art Attacks. Side two begins with Bernie Torme again, then The Art Attacks, Neo, The Suspects and two songs by The Maniacs. All of the bands are unsigned, with the exception of The Wasps, who have a one off single on 4 Play Records and the Maniacs who are now with United Artists.

THE SEX PISTOLS are off to Holland for ten days. Sid's troubles are seeping into the rest of the band, and the distraction of a tour would be a good way to get their minds off of the internal problems. Holland just might be the start of the "Never Mind The Bans" tour. There are plans when the band returns from ten days in Holland to send them on to Finland, Sweden, Yugoslavia, Spain and France. Even the Sex Pistols' film project, that has been the subject to financial troubles as well as rewrites, seems an insurmountable task.

WASPS/MANIACS/NEO/		WIRE/BETHNAL	London, Nashville
MEAN STREET/ART ATTAX	London, The Vortex		

6th - Tuesday..................

"GOBBING: *(verb)* - to spurt spit at you favorite rock star IN APPRECIATION of their talents." This is the sport of gobbing. It started in London earlier this year with the tide (appropriate!) growing in outlying communities. At concerts now, it appears that there is an everpresent horizontal rainstorm aimed at the stage from the front rows. Punks claim to actually spit INTO a performers mouth is second only to french kissing! Bands are beginning to dislike the practice. Some are speaking out against it because it's a very easy way for a musician to contract hepatitis and it's already happened several times. Bands are actually playing more reserved, shorter sets to escape it. Encores are becoming rare. This custom must be replaced by something else and quickly!

DECEMBER 1977

LIVE TONIGHT!

BOOMTOWN RATS ....Edinburgh, The Odeon	ASSAULT/BLOOD DONOR ....London, Roxy
TOM ROBINSON BAND ....London, Lyceum	MERGER/RAGE/
RADIATORS FROM SPACE ....London, Nashville	BAZOOMIES/TUBEWAY ARMY......London, The Vortex
LURKERS/ADVERTISING ....London, Rock Garden	IAN DURY ....Sheffield, The Top Rank

8th - Thursday...................

TALKING HEADS' latest 45 is a single of "Psycho Killer." It's taken from their debut album and is flipped with a non-LP acoustic version of the same song, with different lyrics. Jon Savage reviewed the single for *Sounds* writing, "Perhaps the perfect Talking Heads song, in which David Byrne's electrocuted Anthony Perkins' persona meets the subject matter." The 12" version of the single includes another non-LP track, "I Wish You Wouldn't Say That." The song is one of the first songs that the Talking Heads wrote back in early '74 when they were called the Artistics.

XTC are at the Manor recording their debut album for Virgin Records. So far this week they've already laid down sixteen tracks, twelve of which will be used for the record. Already on tape is a fractured version of Dylan's "All Along The Watchtower," originals like "Spinning Top," "New Town Animal" and their own version of the '60s TV theme song to "Fireball XL5." The oldest song in the sessions is "Neon Shuffle" that dates back over two years. Colin has a new song submitted for the LP called "Set Myself On Fire."

LURKERS/THE DOLL/	UK SUBS/ACME SEWAGE CO./
REACTION ....Birmingham, Rebecca's	OPEN SORE ....London, Roxy
SKIDS ....Burntisland, Hall Circle	PENETRATION ....Manchester, Rafters
IAN DURY &	
THE BLOCKHEADS ....Edinburgh, Univ.	

9th -Friday.....................

SEX PISTOLS' bassist Sid Vicious and his live-in American girlfriend Nancy are separated, following their violent scene at the Ambassador Hotel in Bayswater several days ago. The authorities were called in by the manager and police investigating took away "suspicious substances," substances that were claimed to be prescribed medication for Nancy. No charges have been filed in this incident, which took place last week, but it is reflective of the many troubles surrounding Sid, his girlfriend and his place in the Sex Pistols. Before the band's quick trip through Scandinavia at the end of July, Sid and Nancy, as well as Johnny and some friends were living in a house in Maida Vale. Upon returning from the Scandinavian dates (from which Nancy was purposely, some say forcefully, excluded), they found that they had to find another place to live. Johnny was set up in a Chelsea residence and Sid & Nancy were left to their own devices. After failing to find suitable digs, they moved in with Sid's mother. From the beginning of Sid's membership in The Pistols, he always paired off against Paul and Steve, with Johnny on his side. Now, the growing tension is apparently pulling even Sid and Johnny apart. The band want Sid to straighten out, or get out.

DEAD BOYS ....Edinburgh, The Cloud Ballroom	LURKERS/THE DOLL ....London, Rochester Castle
WIRE/TRASH ....High Wycombe, Nags Head	STREETS/YOUTHENASIA/
SQUEEZE/THE MOVIES/	DEFECTS ....London, Roxy
TONIGHT................................London, Middlesex Poly.	LURKERS ....London, Rochester Castle

11th - Sunday.....................

JOHNNY & THE SELF ABUSERS are more than just another punk band from Glasgow. They're veterans of Scotland's underground going on six months now and they're the latest Chiswick signing. Their debut single is "Saints And Sinners" b/w "Dead Vandals." *NME*, in an advance review of the record were not impressed. Bob Edmands wrote, "Sadly, Johnny and The Self Abusers live entirely up to their name. The song is a drab parade of New Wave cliches that jerks off aimlessly into the void. While they're keeping their hands to themselves, perhaps they should do the same to their records." The group is frequently splits on issues on two sides and today's release of their single finds the two sides breaking apart irreparably. One part of the split has Jim Kerr on vocals, Charlie Burchill on guitar, Brian McGee on drums. They'll regroup under the new name "Simple Minds." The other half of the Abusers is Michael McNeil, Ali Mackenzie, Donald and John Milarky who will put together a new band called the "Cuban Heels." On the day that Johnny & The Self Abusers should be celebrating their record release, they're breaking up.

THE CARPETTES are another group that owe their existence on vinyl today to London's Small Wonder Records. Their vinyl debut is a four track, 7" extended play single. Among the tracks (all originals) are "How About Me And You," "Help, I'm Trapped," "Radio Wunderbar" and "Cream Of The Youth." The Carpettes are a trio of George Maddison on bass and vocals, Neil Thompson on guitar and vocals and Kevin Heard on drums and vocals.

CLASH ....Glasgow, The Apollo	ADAM & THE ANTS ....London, Marquee
IAN DURY & BLOCKHEADS /	THE JAM/NEW HEARTS ....London, Croydon Grayhound
DEKE LEONARDS ICEBERG ....Liverpool, Eric's	

DECEMBER 1977

THIN LIZZY/	BUZZCOCKS/
RADIATORS FROM SPACE...........London, Hammersmith Odeon	SIOUXSIE & THE BANSHEES/
SUBWAY SECT.......................London, The Roundhouse	SUBWAY SECT ....London, The Roundhouse

14th - Wednesday...

THE PORK DUKES are actually more disgusting than the Sex Pistols, yet get none of the press. Their second single "Making Bacon" b/w "Tight Pussy" is in less discerning shops today. It's on their own Wood Records label. As on their last record, there are no pictures of the group, no "real" names, no taste in lyrics. On the first Pork Dukes record the band was listed as being Vilos Styles, Ron Dodge, Scabs and Bonk. This one lists Vilo's sidemen as Harrendus Styles, Mack E Valley and Germum Le Pig. We'll probably never know just who is in this band and it's probably best that way.

ELVIS COSTELLO & NICK LOWE have a recording contract again. You might remember, the pair of artists, along with Jake Riveria walked out of Stiff Records two months ago. Now all three are at home at Radar Records. It's a totally new label started by former United Artist managing director Martin Davis and A&R man Andrew Lauder. The deal covers WEA territories worldwide with the exception of the US, Canada and parts of Scandinavia, where their deals with Columbia Records remain intact. Elvis even has a new album on the way called "The King Of Belgium."

BOOMTOWN RATS/YACHTS ....Birmingham, Top Rank	DEPRESSIONS ....London, Pegasus
THOSE NAUGHTY LUMPS...........Liverpool, Havana Club	BOYFRIENDS ....London, Red Cow
RIFF RAFF...............................London, Kensington Hotel	CLASH/DEAF SCHOOL
THIN LIZZY/	DRUNK & DISORDERLY ....London, Rainbow Theatre
RADIATORS FROM SPACE...........London, Lewisham Odeon	PITFUL/FURS ....London, Roxy
CORTINAS ....London, Marquee	FABULOUS POODLES ....London, Royal College Of Art
XTC/MEMBERS ....London, The Music Machine	PENETRATION ....London, Spooky Lady

16th - Friday...

CHELSEA have been the focus of recent rumors that they had split up, but it couldn't be farther from the truth. Chelsea have re-emerged from a break with a new second guitarist (Dave Martin) and a new single on Step Forward Records. The single is "High Rise Livin'" b/w "No Admission." They'll be undertaking a UK tour in the new year.

1977 READERS POLL This years *NME* "Readers Poll" finds the Sex Pistols gathering top honors as Best Group (finishing ahead of Led Zeppelin and Genesis), Best Album and Best Single honors ("God Save The Queen"), Best Dressed Sleeve, Best Drummer and Johnny Rotten was voted as "Most Wonderful Human Being." Best New Group went to the Tom Robinson Band, with The Stranglers and Boomtown Rats coming in second and third. The number one event of the year was Elvis' demise, with the Sex Pistols' December 1, 1976 appearance on the Bill Grundy BBC TV show *Today* a close second. The Sex Pistols virtually dominate the chart. They have three of the top ten singles of the year, figured in as the third best songwriters and were responsible for three of the top ten events of the year. Other bands that figured in the poll respectfully were the Clash and Tom Robinson Band. Eddie & The Hot Rods, who were voted on heavily in 1976, were virtually absent.

RICH KIDS ....Birmingham, Barbarella's	PENETRATION ....London, Rochester Castle
SLAUGHTER & THE DOGS/	ADAM & ANTS/RED LIGHTS/
URBAN DISTURBANCE ....High Wycombe, Nags Head	THE TAX EXILES ....London, Roxy
MAGAZINE/	PUNCTURE ....London, The Basement
JOHN COOPER CLARKE ....Liverpool, Eric's	FALL/MANICURED NOISE/
LURKERS/SNIVELING SHITS ....London, Hope & Anchor	ELITE.................................Manchester, St. Johns College
MOLESTERS ....London, Red Cow	SEX PISTOLS ....Uxbridge, Brunel Univ.

17th - Saturday...

ELVIS COSTELLO and the Attractions appear live on the NBC program *Saturday Night Live*. The Sex Pistols were originally booked but are currently in Holland on tour, so Elvis was brought in from his first US tour to play instead. Early in the show he played "Watching The Detectives." Then they came back for a second song later in the show. It started innocently with an introduction and Elvis starting into "Less Than Zero" Halfway into the first verse Elvis stopped. "I'm sorry ladies and gentlemen...there's no reason for me to do this song here." He then launched into "Radio Radio." This was a totally new song for the US. He has been playing it live but it had not yet been recorded. At the side of the stage, the show's producer was furious with the sudden change. This transferred to Elvis who became more and more angry in his singing of the song. At the end of "Radio Radio," Elvis did a quick bow and jerked his guitar lead out, storming off stage with the Attractions.

THE RICH KIDS are finally making their official stage debut. They had only previously been seen in public as surprise guests of the Tom Robinson band in August and have since then been the object of speculation and conjecture. The debut gig is staged in Nottingham as the beginning of a UK tour this winter.

SEX PISTOLS..........................Coventry, Mr. George's	SQUEEZE ....London, Rochester Castle
FALL/PENETRATION ....Liverpool, Eric's	DEPRESSIONS/ACME SEWAGE CO.
THROBBING GRISTLE ....London, Bedford Corner Hotel	OPEN SORE ....London, Roxy
BOOMTOWN RATS/YACHTS ....London, Rainbow	

DECEMBER 1977

20th - Tuesday.....................................

THE DAMNED are hitting on hard times and times just got harder. They have recently weathered a tour with marginal attendance, rumors about their breaking up and the loss of drummer Rat Scabies. Now they're faced with the loss of their recording contract with Stiff Records, as well as management by Dave Robinson. You can understand why the band is so despondent. The Damned felt that Robinson wasn't spending enough time with them, but rather with Graham Parker. Robinson stated that he split his time equally between Stiff, The Damned and Parker but had lately found the band rather unmanageable. He continued by stating The Damned could record again for Stiff or any other label if they could only find the right manager. He wasn't the "right" manager any longer.

WARSAW return to Pennine Recording Studios again to record after extensive rehearsals. The result is a four-song tape that they're hoping to turn into a record. Tracks include "No Love Lost," "Failures," "Warsaw" and "Leaders Of Men."

THOSE NAUGHTY LUMPS.............Liverpool, Havana Club	CAFE JACQUES/KILLJOYS...........London, Music Machine
Stiff Xmas Party ....London, Hope & Anchor	PENETRATION.......................Manchester, Electric Circus

24th - Saturday.....................................

PARTY! The infamous *NME* Christmas party is underway at Dingwalls. It's a star studded event with entertainment provided by Dave Edmunds and later by the Flaming Groovies. The event is attended by members of The Clash, Generation X, Snatch, The Lous, Ramones, Heartbreakers, Thin Lizzy, Motorhead, Fabulous Poodles, Squeeze, The Kursaals, The Damned, Adverts, Tom Robinson, Steel Pulse and many others. As a gift to the partygoers this evening, Stiff Records and *NME* pressed up a limited edition single by Ian Dury. The instant collectors item had "Sex & Drugs & Rock & Roll" on the "A" side, on the flip were two unreleased live Kilburn & The High Roads tracks, "Two Steep Hills" and "England's Glory."

LIVE TONIGHT!

SEX PISTOLS...........................Cromer, Links Pavilion	EDDIE & THE HOT RODS/STUKAS
THE SKIDS..............................Edinburgh, Nicky Tams Tavern	ONLY ONES ....London, Roundhouse
SAUSAGES FROM MARS/	ELVIS COSTELLO/POP GROUP .....London, The Nashville
RADIO DOOM/FAST BREEDER ......Liverpool, Eric's	THE SOFT BOYS.......................London, Rochester Castle

25th - Sunday..............

THE SEX PISTOLS have been booked to play a children's Christmas party today. The party is to benefit the children of Huddersfield firemen, laid-off workers from the nearby Brown's Park Works and one-parent families. Over 500 invitations were sent out and Virgin has arranged for busses to bring in the children to the Ivanhoes. There's also 1,000 bottles of soda pop and a huge cake brought in. The party lasts between 3pm and 6pm for disco, tea and the Pistols. There's also an evening show that's not so reserved.

PEROXIDE ROMANCE/PLASTIX/
RAPED/OPEN SORES/BLITZ/
TICKETS/THE GOATS/
WRIST ACTION/UK SUBS/
THE JETS/STREETS ....London, Roxy
SEX PISTOLS.........................Huddersfield, Ivanhoes Club

---

BANKHOUSE ENTERTAINMENT

£1.75   presents —   £1.75

SEX PISTOLS

on CHRISTMAS DAY

at IVANHOES, Manchester Road, Huddersfield

Doors open at 7.00 p.m.

Please note: to prevent forgers, this ticket can only be purchased from Pickwicks, Dewsbury or Ivanhoes, Huddersfield and will have required signing for. In the event of any cancellation your money will be returned less 25p administration fees.

29th - Thursday.....................................

THE SEX PISTOLS were to begin their assault on the American public today, but were stopped dead in their tracks by the US immigration officials. The group is refused entry visas until the band's criminal record are explained. All four members have records of offenses ranging from drug possession, burglary, theft, to assault. They'll be scrutinized and receive the necessary papers tomorrow.

THE NOVA MOB is the new Liverpool band that sprang to life only three days since the split up of the Spitfire Boys. This one has ex-Spitfire veteran Pete Griffiths, spliced to Julian Cope and Pete Wylie of the Mystery Girls. Griffiths claim to the "professional" status, as he had a single with his previous band out on ROK Records two months ago. Budgie, now with Big In Japan, describes them as, "...a merchandising set-up based on a William Burroughs thing, which is basically t-shirts with Jane Casey from Big In Japan with a bullet hole through her head." The Nova Mob seems to have spent the majority of their energies heckling Big In Japan instead of playing live.

BOYFRIENDS/EL SEVEN.............High Wycombe, Nags Head	THE ADVERTS ....London, Dingwalls
FABULOUS POODLES ....London, The Marquee	PUNCTURE...........................London, The Roxy

31st - Saturday.....................................

THE RAMONES concert tonight at the Rainbow is being recorded for a live LP. The crowd is going nuts and the band is in top form. Joey's even been writing some new songs. One is called "I Wanna Be Sedated."

SCARE BLEU ....Dublin, The Tivoli	EASY CURE............................Orpington, General Hospital
WARSAW ....Liverpool, The Swinging Apple	RAMONES/REZILLOS/
ULTRAVOX! ....London, The Marquee	GENERATION X.......................London, The Rainbow

JANUARY 1978

January 3rd - Tuesday.......................................

2.3 have been playing in Sheffield front rooms for about five months and at their occasional club appearances some original titles are turning up. So far there are "New Clear Waves," "I Don't Care About London," "Nowhere" and "All Time Low." They are having some regional success but are adamant about staying in the North instead of moving south to London. Their debut single on Fast Records should hit the shops in the next month or so.

METAL URBAIN/
CHEAP STARS ....London, 100 Club

SHAM 69/CRABS
MIRRORS/THE JERKS................London, The Vortex

5th - Thursday................

THE SEX PISTOLS make their American debut at the Great SouthEast Music Hall. There are about five hundred curious American punks there to worship their heroes and an equal number of journalists and law enforcement officers from all across the US. After a less-than-stellar show, Sid disappears to pursue his heroin habit in unfamiliar territory. There's a great deal of concern over Sid, so much that their US label (Warner Brothers) has hired what amounts to a "baby-sitter" for Sid to take care of him and see that he doesn't get into trouble. Sid had easily ducked him this first day on the road.

YACHTS ....London, Dingwalls
ADAM & THE ANTS...................London, The Marquee
SEX PISTOLS/CRUISE-O-MATIC....Atlanta, Great S.E. Music Hall & Emporium

Melody Maker

PISTOLS SHOCK USA!

McCartney's 'Mull' — it's a record!

JANUARY 14, 1978   15p weekly   USA 75 cents

The complete music weekly
— and still only 15p

And the MM is with them. Report from Memphis: page 3▶▶

6th - Friday................

THE SEX PISTOLS make headlines across the US with articles decrying the "punk rock horror" that they have loosed on America. Even the UK papers get involved. The *London Evening News* headline today read "I Hate Britain, Says Screaming Johnny." Vice squads from Memphis, Baton Rouge, San Antonio and Tulsa flew in to preview the notorious troublemakers soon coming to their towns. Memphis Vice Officer, Lieutenant Ronald Howell told the press what the band would be allowed under their guidelines. He said "We've heard a lot about these boys and if they behave themselves we'll give them a right friendly welcome. Memphis is a clean city. We aim to keep it that way. We will not tolerate any real or simulated sex onstage. No sir. They can be nude if they like. They can spit. They can even vomit. No laws against that, but there must be no lewd or indecent behavior." Generally, the Sex Pistols are coming across to US audiences as a lot more tame than the crowd had been led to believe. There was some violence at their Memphis concert tonight though. About 300 fans were unable to get into the sold out show and there was a scuffle with the local police. Sid was beginning to show off his toughness with the first US incident of self-inflicted wounds. To start things off, he's used a knife to make a two-inch gash on his left arm.

XTC have their "Statue Of Liberty" and "Hang On To The Night" single issued by Virgin. Their debut LP is expected later in the month. The BBC has already banned this innocuous little pop song because of the lyric about wanting to sail beneath the statue's skirt.

SHAM 69 could be seen as Polydor's answer to the Sex Pistols, only a little more controlled. They've started down that trail with Sham 69's Polydor debut, the rave up "There's Gonna Be A Borstal Breakout" b/w "Hey Little Rich Boy." To support the single they'll be undertaking a series of dates starting tonight at Braintree College.

SLAUGHTER & THE DOGS ....Liverpool, Eric's
SEX PISTOLS...........................Memphis, Taliesyn Ballroom

SIOUXSIE & THE BANSHEES/
THE UNWANTED ....London, The Nashville

7th - Saturday................

ADAM & THE ANTS are featured in a half-page article in the *NME* this week. Every time they receive some press, it's a comic look at their s&m bondage stage show. Granted, there is a comic side to the music, but the press seems to delight in poking fun at Adam's image and very young following. In the course of a lengthy interview Adam confesses that the rumors about the way he runs the band are all true. He makes pre-recorded tapes of the various band members parts for them to learn, beatings when they don't get it correct, total devotion to the band. Adam claims only that he expects the band to work as hard as he himself works. The article points out that "the Ants play fast, negative pop to corrupt the innocent. They've got this following, a fanatical crew of 14-year-old head bangers who have ANTS written all over their clothes and chuck themselves about with the same total disregard for personal safety that Adam himself displays." Among his current song list are tracks such as "Zerox," "Cleopatra," "Whip In My Valise," "Hampstead," "Juanito the Bandito," "Dirk Wears White Socks," (Adam's tribute to Dirk Bogarde) and "Light A Beacon On A Puerto Rican." Currently the line up in the ever-changing Ants is Adam on guitar, "Handsome" Johnny Bivouac on guitar, Dave Barbe on drums and Andy Warren on bass. Of course, Jordan (their manager) helps on vocals from time to time, as well as contributing her own song to the set, "Lou" (a tune about Lou Reed).

THE SEX PISTOLS' traveling circus arrives in Austin, Texas for a day off on their way to San Antonio. The routing on the tour is

JANUARY 1978

torturous, zig-zagging the band across the country with no thought given to the distances between concerts. They've gone from Atlanta to Memphis, down to San Antonio in three days. It's got to be wearing on the band. Johnny Ramone wasn't real impressed with the Sex Pistols when he saw them, telling Lester Bangs of *Trouser Press* "They were terrible live. Sloppy…maybe they got better during the American tour, I dunno, but they were very unprofessional and I'd expected to see a somewhat professional group. I guess I shouldn't have thought that because they hadn't played for a year. The records sound very good if you take one song out of it here and there; a little monotonous. Y'know, they had their backdrop with all this stuff spray painted on, I guess that's their thing, but no drum platform, no lights at all, the PA sounded awful, little tiny amplifiers- it was just a rinky-dink show. Maybe they're supposed to be unprofessional but there's a certain standard kids in America expect."

Stiff Chiswick Challenge ....Liverpool, Erics   JAPAN ....London, The Red Cow

8th - Sunday...

THE SEX PISTOLS arrive in San Antonio to play at Randy's Rodeo, their largest American date so far, holding about two thousand people. The band is beginning to fray at the edges. Paul and Steve hang together, Sid is off with groupies and drugs, and Johnny is disgusted with everyone. Johnny has been working on some new songs, one of which is called "Religion." It's intense, perhaps too intense for Steve and Paul who aren't sure about taking on that heavy of a problem. Onstage the band has to play in a hail of spit, popcorn, beer cups and bottles. Sid erupts onstage and hits an audience member with his bass, he himself is hit in the face and bloodies his nose. *The San Antonio Express* sets their headline for tomorrow's paper as, "Sex Pistols Win S.A. Shootout."

STIFF/CHISWICK CHALLENGE It's the third in a series of Stiff/Chiswick Challenges and it's happening at Eric's in Liverpool. These "challenges" are the specially arranged, free concerts with regional bands selected from the demo stacks of Stiff and Chiswick Records. These are not only a chance to see groups ahead of their time, it's also a chance for interested A&R men to see the best of a towns unsigned bands in one setting. Tonights show was a sixteen-hour carnival. First up was Bryan Farrell who performed songs in the "Graham Parker mould." Then came the UK Subs, Hard Up Heroes and Coincidence. Lester Parrot played a short acoustic set and two members of Big In Japan also took the stage as "The Sausages From Space." The Smirks, a relatively new band (barely six weeks old) were thought to be the high point of the evening. They seemed to outshine The Look, who were thought to be the favorites for the event. Also up were Strangeways and the final band for the evening, Willi And The Visitors. The evening was considered a great success and everyone is looking forward to the first Stiff-Chiswick Challenge in Glasgow next month. It'll be an all-Scottish competition.

SEX PISTOLS............................San Antonio, Randy's Rodeo

9th - Monday...

MAGAZINE have just signed to Virgin. In the past few months they have become one of the most talked about bands in the UK, mostly because of their tight-lipped vocalist Howard Devoto. Second only to Siouxsie & The Banshees, they were considered one of the most "eligible" unsigned bands. Virgin Records were impressed with Magazine's reputation and the three-song demo they recorded last October. Since their appearance on *So It Goes* keyboardist Bob Dickinson has left the band as a quartet looking for a replacement. They will begin work on their debut single immediately for release next month.

MONOTONES............................London, Fulham Greyhound   SLAUGHTER & THE DOGS...........London, The Marquee
SEX PISTOLS............................Baton Rouge, Kingfish Ballroom

10th - Tuesday...

THE ONLY ONES have signed on with CBS Records in the UK. Their previous single and constant gigging has helped them build a solid audience. They'll be starting on the sessions for their first single for CBS, which should be released in next month.

CABARET VOLTAIRE who rarely play live, have turned up again onstage in Sheffield. They've been together for about three years now but have only played live a half dozen times. The group is a self-described "experimental pop band." It is clear that they are drawing ideas from abstract and minimalist German bands like Can, Kraftwerk and Neu. They fracture music and piece it back together in a very intriguing way. Some of their titles include "Talkover," "Do The Mussolini" and "Control Addicts." They don't restrict themselves to music alone at their rare performances. They incorporate slide shows and film loops as well. It will be interesting to see when the rest of the world catches up to them. Their current line up is Stephen Mallinder on bass and vocals, Chris Watson on keyboards, electronics and tapes and Richard Kirk on guitar and clarinet.

THE SEX PISTOLS come back to Texas to play the Longhorn Ballroom in Dallas. The Ballroom was the stomping ground for Country & Western legend Bob Wills & The Playboys and had been owned for decades by local C&W legend Dewey Groom. Even the stage spoke of the Ballroom's country status. Around its border is a wooden split rail fence to separate the band from the audience and on the golden curtain that hangs over the edge of the stage were the portraits of legends like Johnny Cash, Hank Williams, Tex Ritter and Bob Wills. That night, there are about 500 Sex Pistols fans and 500 C&W fans

came out on an icy night to defend their territory. Anticipating trouble that never arrived were about a hundred police and several TV camera crews. Sid came onstage with the words "Gimmie A Fix" scratched into his bare chest. During the course of the evening he would again be hit in the face by a member of the audience. In an article in the *Dallas Morning News* Sid told reporter Pete Oppel, "She is only the second girl who ever hit me. One time at a Ramones gig this girl came up to me and said, 'are you Sid Vicious?' and when I said I was, she hit me. Only I didn't

JANUARY 1978

know it was a girl. She looked just like a guy so I stomped her." Sid wasn't the only one getting angry with the crowd. Steve has someone climbing the fence to taunt him and struck him with the short end of his guitar.

SHAM 69.....................Birmingham, Barbarella's	SEX PISTOLS/
BOYFRIENDS.....................London, Hope & Anchor	NEREVEBREAKERS ....Dallas, The Longhorn Ballroom
MONOTONES.....................London, The Vortex	

11th - Wednesday...

ELECTRIC CHAIRS have taken in ex-Police guitarist Henry Padovani. He was an original member of The Police but was booted from the band last September shortly after Andy Summers joined. Henry's now a member of The Electric Chairs. He plays his first gig with the band this Saturday at the Rochester Castle in London. He's joined just in time for the band's signing to Safari Records. They had previously been cutting one-off records with companies, but this is a lengthy contract that calls for multiple singles and albums.

THOSE NAUGHTY LUMPS.............Liverpool, Havana Club	ADVERTISING/ART ATTACKS ....London, Music Machine
THE JOLT ....London, Rochester Castle	SEX PISTOLS ....Tulsa, Oklahoma, Cain's Ballroom

12th - Thursday...

NINE NINE NINE tease their fans with their upcoming album by releasing their new single "Emergency." It's their second 45 since signing with United Artists. The single is flipped with the non-LP track "My Street Stinks."

THE MARBLE INDEX are a front-room band that is made up of sixteen year-old Matt Johnson, Charlie Blackburn and Martin Brand. Martin and Matt both work at DeWolfe's eight track studio learning about recording business and making tea for everyone else. He's taken the stuff he's learned and has recorded himself with his tape machine, effects and microphones. The result being a cassette tape called "See Without Being Seen" that he gives away at gigs. Back last summer Matt had taken out an advert looking for people into Syd Barrett and these musicians responded. Matt is still years away from finding his reward with a group called The The. They'll begin having minor hits in '82 and will continue making records for the next decade.

LIVE TONIGHT!

X-RAY SPEX ....Birmingham,, Rebecca's	SQUEEZE ....London, Dingwalls
RADIATORS FROM SPACE...........Dublin, Trinity College	ADAM & ANTS.....................London, The Marquee
SHAM 69 ....Leeds' Ace Of Clubs	RICH KIDS/ACCELERATORS.........Manchester, Rafters
SHOPLIFTERS ....London, The Roxy	

13th - Friday...

THE RICH KIDS Ex-Pistol Glen Matlock's band, The Rich Kids, have just released their debut single for EMI. They began gigging around London in August of last year and have become the critic's favorite. Tracks out are their theme song "Rich Kids" as well as "Empty Words." Both are originals and, if you buy them early enough, both are presented on red vinyl, red label and in a solid red sleeve. The Rich Kids are Glen Matlock on bass and vocals, Steve New on guitar, Rusty Egan behind the drums and the latest addition, Midge Ure on guitar.

RICH KIDS ....Birmingham, Barbarella's	SQUEEZE ....London, The Marquee

14th - Saturday...

THE SEX PISTOLS close their first US tour with a show at the Winterland in San Francisco. It's their second biggest show ever, in front of over four thousand fans. Before the concert, Johnny and Sid stop in at KSAN in San Francisco and Paul and Steve go to KSJO in San Jose and take phone calls on the air. Sid on KSAN says, "Rules were meant to be broken right? When there are no more rules or categorizations, when there are no more niggers or whites or, when there's just people, when there's no more punks and there's no more dirt, that is when things are going to be OK. We'll probably be dead in like two years." Local punk acts the Nuns and The Avengers opened the show. Just before the band came on, the twenty-five-minute film *Number 1* was shown. It's the pastiche of news clips and interviews that serves as a propaganda piece to stirs the audience up. When the band finally hits the stage, the crowd goes wild. Six songs into the set, the Sex Pistols play the only new song they've yet to premier before an audience. "Belsen Was A Gas," it's an old Sid Vicious song from his days with the Flowers Of Romance. The concert continues with "Anarchy In The USA," and falls apart at the end of "No Fun." KSAN records the gig with their remote truck. In the end, after all the band's expenses were subtracted from their money, they were left with only $67.

THE RAPED have their debut single out on Parole Records. The "Pretty Paedophiles" EP includes "Moving Target," "Raped," "Escalator Hater" and "Normal." Raped reportedly got an impromptu commentary on their EP when they dropped it off at the Rough Trade Record Shop. Harry Lime, the manager of the group, claims that the proprietor of the shop threw the record to the floor, stomped vigorously on it, then set it aflame. We'll have to see what the public has to say about "Pretty Paedophiles."

RICH KIDS ....Birmingham, Barbarella's	WAYNE COUNTY &
BLACK SLATE/	THE ELECTRIC CHAIRS ....London, Rochester Castle
KRYPTON TUNES.....................London, The Nashville	SLAUGHTER & THE DOGS/
SHAM 69.....................Sheffield, Poly.	SEX PISTOLS ....San Francisco, The Winterland

15th - Sunday...

SIOUXSIE & THE BANSHEES are making headlines, drawing enormous crowds and getting great reviews. The only problem is that, for some reason, no major record company is interested in signing them. Their manager Nils Stevenson was contemplating releasing their

JANUARY 1978

John Peel session from November as a four track EP on the BBC Records label. However the red tape and bureaucracy involved has so far kept the sessions out of reach.

THE BUZZCOCKS' new 45 is being delayed by the sensitive workers at EMI Records. Their forthcoming single is "What Do I Get?" It's on United Artists Records and you'd think they would have the final say, but UA singles are pressed by EMI, who find the "B" side, "Oh Shit," offensive. The Buzzcocks insist that it's only a love song and should not bother anyone who's been in a make-up and break-up relationship. United Artists representatives are currently meeting with EMI to work out the difficulties so the single can come out close to its scheduled release date.

SEX PISTOLS Sid and Johnny are staying at a hotel in nearby San Jose with the road crew from the tour. Johnny tries to reach McLaren at his hotel and talks with a writer named Joe Stevens. He says that Malcolm has arranged for the band to all fly off to Rio tomorrow morning. Johnny's gotten increasingly ill on the road and doesn't want to go, especially when it's to pal around and film with Ronnie Biggs, the convicted participant in the UK's 1963 "Great Train Robbery." Besides, the Sex Pistols are due to play in Stockholm on the 20th. How can they get to Rio and still make it to the gig on time?

LIVE TONIGHT!

X-RAY SPEX/BLACK SLATE			
DEAD FINGERS TALK	London, The Roundhouse	WAYNE COUNTY &	
THE DAMNED/JOHNNY MOPED	London, Foxe's Greyhound	THE ELECTRIC CHAIRS	London, The Pegasus
		YACHTS/BRAKES	London, The Nashville

16th - Monday........................

THE SEX PISTOLS are in chaos. Malcolm, Steve and Paul leave their hotel in the early morning hours. On the way they get Johnny in San Jose and they pick up Sid, who supposedly complains about Johnny being apart from the band and acting the part of a rock star. They turn back the cars and return to their hotel San Francisco, content to wait until the problems with Sid and Johnny are worked out. Sid calls John's hotel room at five in the morning and tells him that Malcolm was complaining about both he and Johnny being in the band. Sid was with some fans who took him in after the gig and have quenched his thirst for heroin. Meanwhile, Johnny calls Cook and Jones and find out he's possibly being ousted from the group. He goes to the hotel where they're staying to confront them and Malcolm face to face. Johnny first meets with his bandmates and learns that the two were supposed to already be on their way to Rio and that they didn't want to work with him or Sid anymore. Johnny looks for Malcolm but he's nowhere to be found. It turns out that Malcolm had gotten a call from Sid's new friends and he had to rush off to help Sid who was unconscious and OD'd on a mattress in Haight Ashbury turning blue. He was rescued in the nick of time.. Johnny ends up leaving before McLaren returns to the hotel.

MAGAZINE have their first single issued by Virgin in the UK. It's "Shot By Both Sides" and "My Mind Ain't So Open." Magazine began in August of last year when Howard Devoto left the Buzzcocks. The current line up is, Howard Devoto on vocals, Barry Adamson on bass, Martin Jackson on drums and John McGeoch on guitar and sax. They begin their promotional tour of the UK on the 24th at London's 100 Club.

MAGAZINE
SHOT BY BOTH SIDES
OUT NOW ON VIRGIN RECORDS VS200

THE ART ATTACKS have announced that they're quitting after tonight's gig at the Vortex. Vocalist Edwin Pouncy, who doubled as the erstwhile cartoonist "Savage Pencil," left the band shortly before Christmas. Since then they've been limping along. Now they've decided to go their separate ways, each departing member starting their own new group also called The Art Attacks. They'll be numbered Art Attacks #2 through Art Attacks #5.

LURKERS/THE DOLL/		ART ATTACKS/MEAN STREET /	
JOHNNY G	London, Dingwalls	ACCELERATORS/	
WAYNE COUNTY &		PERVERSE VELVET	London, The Vortex
THE ELECTRIC CHAIRS	London, Hope & Anchor		

17th - Tuesday........................

SEX PISTOLS' vocalist Johnny Rotten returned to the Miyako Hotel to confront Malcolm this morning. McLaren confirms what Cook and Jones had said. The Pistols were finished with Johnny and Sid. They would be going to Rio without them. Jones, Cook and McLaren fly down to Los Angeles to meet with Warner Brothers Records before leaving for Rio. Sid is also on his way to LA under the watchful eye of Glitterbest associate Sophie Richmond. With only a few dollars in his pocket, Rotten borrows enough to get on a plane to New York. The Sex Pistols were due to start their next Scandinavian tour on Friday, but Malcolm's plans have been abruptly changed. The question of "is this the end of the Sex Pistols" hangs with an enormous question mark.

STEEL PULSE/BACK STABBERS		ADAM & THE ANTS/	
SIMPLE MINDS/NU SONICS	Glasgow, Tiffany's	WAYNE COUNTY &	
DEPRESSIONS/		THE ELECTRIC CHAIRS	London, Dingwalls
SUBURBAN STUDS		LURKERS/MAKERS	London, The Rock Garden
MUVVER'S PRIDE	London, The Vortex		

18th - Wednesday........................

SEX PISTOLS' singer Johnny Rotten announces to the *New York Post* that the Sex Pistols are no more. "I am sick of working with the Sex

JANUARY 1978

Pistols," he said. He stays with various New York bands, attends gigs at some of the more seedy clubs and disappears into the city.

MOORS MURDERERS are a "mystery" group that has gathered a lot of press attention in the last two weeks. Word came through the offices of the *NME* that it was in fact ex-*NME* writer Chrissie Hynde behind the group. It's not true and she's furious! Chrissie has contacted the paper to disavow any permanent involvement in the group. After all, she's trying to start her own band and doesn't need the bad press. She claimed that the group was the idea of a guy from Wales named Steve Strange (aka Steve Brady). Chrissie was looking for musicians to play with and met Steve at the Vortex. Chrissie remembers, "I saw him in the Vortex club and he came up to me and said 'I have these three songs' and he sang three songs to me just acapella there at the bar. And they were all about different criminals. There was one about Myra Hindley called 'Free Hindley,' it went 'In nineteen hundred and sixty four, Myra Hindley was nothing more than a woman who fell for a man. So why can't she be free? Free Hindley! Brady was her lover, he told her what to do. A psychopathic killer, nothing new. So why can't she be free? Free Hindley!' And it was absurd. Then he had another song about the Capones and another about the Kray twins. That was his theme, these criminals." Steve Strange asked Chrissie to come down an play guitar and help give a record company guy the impression he has a band together. Pretty soon, there's someone from *Sounds* magazine to do a piece on the band! She didn't want to be in the photo with the article so they all wore plastic bin liners over their heads. In *Sounds* her name was listed as "Christine Hindley," and the other papers take the next step saying it was HER BAND!" Suddenly she's being called by everybody outraged over the idea of the song when she was only helping out on demos. The press make it seem that there is a record of "Free Myra Hindley" and "The 10 Commandments" on the semi-bootleg Popcorn label, but no one seems to have seen it, even the band. The "real" Moors Murderers are the reason for the scandal around this group. They were Myra Hindley and Ian Brady. In the '60s they tortured and murdered several children and the story of their heinous crime still lives in the minds of Britains. To name a band after such people, is…well…unthinkable!

WIRE are in the BBC studios recording a session for John Peel's Radio 1 program. The songs are a new version of "106 Beats That," and three totally new songs, "Practice Makes Perfect," "I Am The Fly" and "Culture Vultures." The session is scheduled to be aired on the 31st.

KRYPTON TUNES/	THOSE NAUGHTY LUMPS ....Liverpool, Havana Club
THE BRAKES ....London, Hope & Anchor	CHELSEA ....London, The Marquee

19th - Thursday...

THE MONOCHROME SET have existed as a loose front-room group since June and are the latest testament to Liverpool's swelling ranks of new bands. In some ways they might be seen as an Ants spin-off. Canadian born vocalist Bid sang with Adam Ant in the Hornsey Art College band the B-Sides and Lester Square played guitar in the first version of Adam's Ants. But Drummer J.D. Haney came from Art Attaxx and Charley X is a mystery on bass. The Monochrome Set will never have chart hits, but will be an enduring part of the underground scene, turning out suave and sophisticated new albums through the next twelve years.

SEX PISTOLS' bassist Sid Vicious seems to have trouble follow wherever he goes. Prior to boarding his flight to New York from Los Angeles, Sid takes 80mgs of methadone, falls asleep in first class and slips into a drug induced coma. Besides the methadone, he had also taken some valiums. He's been rushed to Jamaica Hospital to be kept under observation. A blizzard rages into New York and Sid is utterly alone. In London, Malcolm McLaren makes a stunning announcement at 4pm. The statement reads; "The management is bored with managing a successful rock and roll band. The group is bored with being a successful rock and roll band. Burning venues and destroying record companies is more creative than making it." He has second thoughts afterwards and withdraws the statement two hours later.

YACHTS.................................High Wycombe, The Nag's Head	THIS HEAT ....London, Inst. of Contemporary Arts
VOICE SQUAD...........................London, Dingwalls	ADAM & THE ANTS ....London, The Marquee
SOFT BOYS.............................London, Hope & Anchor	

20th - Friday...

THE BUZZCOCKS have triumphed over the troubles with EMI's pressing plant over the title of their new "B" side and have their fourth single released. It's "What Do I Get?" and the controversial (to EMI that is) "Oh Shit." The entire effort was recorded in two days with Martin Rushent at the Olympic Studios helm.

ADVERTS have their latest "No Time To Be 21" b/w "New Day Dawning" released today on Bright Records.

BRIAN ENO has a new single out in the UK. "Kings Lead Hat" has been remixed and is flipped with a non-LP track called "R.A.F." The flipside is a collaboration with Patti Paladin and Judy Nylon, otherwise known as Snatch. "R.A.F." is a rhythmic Eno backing track with voice bits strewn over the top. The samples were gotten by Judy when she was in Germany. They're recordings of the telephone announcements broadcast to help identify members of the Baader-Meinhof gang. It's said the Snatch/Eno collaboration only took four and a half hours to record. It's available on Polydor Records in the UK.

XTC are finally an album band. When planning the LP, the band wanted to call it "Black Music" but Virgin thought the title would be misunderstood. It's been re-titled an released instead as "White Music" and contains the "A" side of their current single "Statue Of Liberty." The song "Neon Shuffle" is a golden oldie with the band, going back to their days as the glitter rock band "The Helium Kidz" two years ago. Perhaps the most unusual song on the record is their unlikely cover of the Hendrix (Dylan) song "All Along The Watchtower." The effort was produced by John Leckie.

THE MEKONS have their debut single released today on the indie Fast Records label. They are from Leeds and only came together in the autumn of last year. The Mekons are a large band with Kevin Lycette & Tom Greenhalgh on guitar, Jon Langford on drums, Mary on bass and Mark White and Andrew Corrigan sharing vocals. They were the first group on the new Fast label, who has ambitiously pressed up 4,000 copies. Tony Parsons, in a *NME* single review, describes the Mekons single "Never Been In A Riot" as "…making the Sex Pistols look like Paper Lace."

RADIATORS FROM SPACE...........Birmingham, Barbarella's	ELVIS COSTELLO/
THE POP GROUP ....London, College Of Printing	WHIRLWIND/SOFT BOYS............London, The Roundhouse (free gig)

JANUARY 1978

XTC ....London, Middlesex Poly.
WAYNE COUNTY &
THE ELECTRIC CHAIRS/SWORDS...London, The Nashville

THE PLAGUE...........................London, The Roxy
DEPRESSIONS ....London, Royal College Of Art
TALKING HEADS/DIRE STRAITS....Sheffield, Univ.

21st - Saturday.....................................

SEX PISTOLS' singer Johnny Rotten arrived in London with a comment for the *London Evening News* about the rumored demise of the Sex Pistols. Confirming the rumors, he said he, "…was bored chronic of singing the same set that we'd played for two years and (he was) bored stiff with Sid's juvenile behavior." He continued, "I won't work again with any of them and that's no great pity. Steve can go off and be Peter Frampton, Sid can go off and kill himself and nobody will care, Paul can go back to being an electrician and Malcolm will always be a Wally." Virgin Records still denies the allegations that the Sex Pistols have split. In New York City, Sid has been discharged from Jamaica Hospital with the strong recommendation of Dr. Gussoff that he get follow up care in London. He's got a touch of bronchitis, a little cough and looks like hell.

RADIATORS FROM SPACE ....Birmingham, Barbarella's
SPLIT ENZ................Edinburgh, Queen Margaret Union
CORTINAS ....London, Rochester Castle

SQUEEZE ....London, Thames Poly.
ADAM & THE ANTS ....London, The Roxy
TALKING HEADS/DIRE STRAITS ....Manchester, Poly.

22nd - Sunday.....................................

THE POLICE are in the midst of recording sessions at sixteen track Surrey Sound Studios in Leatherhead. They're laying down the songs that will comprise their debut album. Sessions include "Dead End Job," "Landlord," "Can't Stand Losing You," "Roxanne" and "Be My Girl." Sting is anxiously looking ahead with the Police as he's just gone through a "reunion" with his previous band Last Exit. The packed University Theatre in Newcastle was witness to the absolute last gig for Last Exit and Sting. No looking back, full steam ahead.

ULTRAVOX!/THE DOLL...............Glasgow, The Apollo
TALKING HEADS/DIRE STRAITS....Liverpool, Eric's
POLICE ....London, The Marquee

RADIO STARS/THE DYAKS ....London, The Nashville
YACHTS/METABOLIST......................London, Pegasus
MANIACS ....London, Rochester Castle

23rd - Monday.....................................

THE SEX PISTOLS' break up is finally addressed by Virgin Records. Their version of the facts about the current situation is that the band, as they were, no longer exist and that Johnny Rotten was kicked out of the band and had not quit on his own accord. Sid is currently in London where he is recovering from a drug overdose while in New York. Meanwhile, Paul Cook and Steve Jones are in Rio recording with Ronald Biggs, infamous in the UK for his part in the "Great Train Robbery" and now living outside the law in Brazil. Malcolm McLaren has joined them and is overseeing all of the recording for the Swindle movie. Reasons for the split are still unclear, although most likely is Johnny's refusal to make a proposed appearance with the band in Rio and disillusionment over the American tour. Virgin Records made it clear that they still have the Sex Pistols under contract, both as a group and as individual performers. Meanwhile, Johnny Rotten arrived in London tonight and told reporters "The Sex Pistols haven't broken up. It's all a publicity gimmick. I'm totally amused by the whole business." The story continues.

ADAM & THE ANTS are invited to record a session for John Peel's BBC 1 Radio show. They record four songs, "Deutcher Girls," "Puerto Rican," "It Doesn't Matter" and "Lou" which features Jordan on vocals. This will be the first time that people who haven't seen the live show will have a chance to hear the band. Their debut on vinyl will be on the Jubilee soundtrack but that's still two months away.

ULTRAVOX!/THE DOLL...............Edinburgh, Clouds
SPLIT ENZ................Edinburgh, Tiffany's
YACHTS ....London, Hope & Anchor
NEW HEARTS...........................London, The Marquee

RADIATORS FROM SPACE ....London, Music Machine
CORTINAS/AUTOMATICS/
THE CHEAP STARS ....London, The Vortex

25th - Wednesday.....................................

THE TARTAN HORDE single is a rather unusual record to be re-issued. Back in 1975, when Brinsley Schwartz split, United Artists were quite keen on keeping Nick Lowe under contract. He had written the songs, he was the "valuable one." He desperately wanted out of the contract so he could pursue his own things and puzzled about how to do it he decided to submit some really bad records to UA. Lowe recalled "I couldn't be obvious about it by turning in Country & Western songs with sitars…so I decided to make one of those fan type records like in the 60s….at the time there was no escaping the Bay City Rollers, they were everywhere! So I wrote this stupid little song called 'Bay City Rollers We Love You.' I recorded it and, it was actually the very first thing I'd done all by myself." United Artists released the single and it almost disappeared except in Japan where it went to #1. He submitted another song called "Let's Go To The Disco" under the name The Disco Brothers and UA let him out of his contract. On the sleeve of the re-issue is a 1977 photo of the fictional "Tartan Horde." Going left to right are Nick Lowe (as Terry Modern), Rat Scabies (as Mouse Modern), a girl who shared a flat with Jake and Nick (as Suzie Marmalade), a roadie (as Ray Marmalade) and the secretary at Stiff Records (as Mary McKeon). The reverse of the sleeve carries a fictional history of the band.

JANUARY 1978

WARSAW have decided to change their name to "Joy Division." The name is from the seamy novel *The House Of Dolls* and describes the portion of some German concentration camp where certain female captives were kept for the officers pleasure. When Warsaw started playing down South, there was some confusion because of London-based band Warsaw Pakt. They have their first gig as Joy Division tonight at Pip's in Manchester.

THOSE NAUGHTY LUMPS ....Liverpool, Havana Club   JOY DIVISION/CONNECTION ....Manchester, Pip's

27th - Friday.......................................

THE STRANGLERS' fifth single is out on United Artists today. It's two of their popular live numbers, "5 Minutes" and "Rok It To The Moon." The band is currently recording their third LP, yet neither of these tracks will be included on the LP. As is the norm, a limited number of the singles will have special picture covers.

PATRIK FITZGERALD prompts the question, "Is there room in the underground for two punk poets?" Fast on the heels of John Cooper Clark comes Patrik Fitzgerald. He's been the opening act on several shows and now is a recording artist in his own right. His debut single is a five track EP on Small Wonder Records. Titles include "Banging And Shouting," "Safety Pin Stuck In My Heart," "Work, Rest & Play Reggae," "Set Me Free" and "Optimism / Reject."

YACHTS.................................Birmingham, Edgehill College	SAINTS/THE JOLT....................London, The Marquee
BUZZCOCKS.............................Dublin, Trinity College	CORTINAS/DEENO ....London, The Nashville
MAGAZINE..............................Liverpool, Eric's	SUBURBAN STUDS ....London, Rochester Castle
WIRE/	STEEL PULSE.........................London, South Bank Polytechnic
SIOUXSIE & THE BANSHEES ....London, College Of Fashion	ULTRAVOX!/THE DOLL...............Manchester, Middletown Civic Hall

28th - Saturday.................................

SEX PISTOLS' manager Malcolm McLaren receives a letter from an out-of-touch advertising agency who wants to use Sid and Johnny in a shampoo advertisement for print. The brief letter assured Malcolm that "the advertisements are in no way derogatory to your clients." The proposal went unanswered. In the *NME* Malcolm admitted, "Rock and Roll is dead."

PROTEX BLUE are a new band in Belfast and are the result of two members of the Incredibly Boring Band splitting off and starting a new group. Those members, guitarist Aidan Murtagh and drummer Owen MacFadden, teamed up with bassist Paul Maxwell and guitarist David MacMaster. Aidan is the lead singer. At the present they're rehearsing in MacFadden's bedroom. They take their name from a brand of condoms frequently found in pub bathroom dispensers.

FRANK SINATRA in this week's *NME*, "Punk rock is a bad scene and I don't understand why it has to exist when there's so much in life."

XTC/THE SECRET.....................Glasgow, Queen Margaret Union	LURKERS ....London, Rochester Castle
RADIATORS FROM SPACE...........Liverpool, Eric's	ADAM & THE ANTS ....London, The Roxy
DEPRESSIONS/PIRANHAS ....London, The Marquee	SHAM 69/SPEEDOMETERS...........London, School Of Economics
PENETRATION/AUTOMATICS........London, The Nashville	

30th - Monday..................................

THE SWELL MAPS first offering is a three track single on their own Rather record label. The band is Nikki Sudden, Phones Sportsmen, Epic Soundtracks and Jowe Head. The tracks "Read About Seymour," "Ripped & Torn" and "Black Velvet" were actually recorded in 1976. This is an unsettling record today, perhaps it's still out of its time. The group has 2,000 copies pressed up and hope for the best.

YACHTS...............................Edinburgh, Tiffany's	KILLJOYS ....London, The Marquee
UNDERHAND JONES/	MAGAZINE/SKEETS BOLIVAR ....London, The Nashville
CUBAN HEELS ....Glasgow, Strathclyde Univ.	POLICE/MENACE/
ADAM & THE ANTS/	MUVVERS PRIDE ....London, The Vortex
PINK PARTS ....London, 100 Club	PASSAGE/THE ELITE ....Manchester, Band On The Wall

February 3rd - Friday.......................

JOHN COOPER CLARKE, the Manchester poet/comic, has been signed to CBS Records in Britain. His rapid fire images have sputtered across many stages around the isle preceding the best of the new wave crop. His humor is obvious although it takes some listening to get through the combination of Mancunian accent and 100 MPH delivery. It is unknown whether he will record just his poems or will "sing" with a group. He considers his poetry and stories as glimpses of life viewed in somebody else's windows as you fly by on an express train.

GUILLOTINE is the title of the Virgin Records 10" sampler of some of their more unusual product. It contains songs from Virgin's current singles as well as a surprise or two. Side one starts off with the Motors' "You Beat The Hell Outta Me." It's the flipside of last fall's single "Be What You Gotta Be." Next up is the "A" side of Newcastle band Penetration's debut for Virgin, "Don't Dictate." This is followed by The Table and "Do The Standing Still" and Russell Murch's group Avant Gardener and "Strange Gurl In Clothes." Side two starts off with XTC and the non LP track "Traffic Light Rock." The song was included on a free EP given away with the Christmas edition of the *Record Mirror*. The recording on Guillotine however, is a studio version, not live as on the RM single. This is followed by former 13th Floor Elevator lead singer, Roky Erickson's latest single "Bermuda." Next up is reggae group Poet And The Roots with "All Wi Doin' Is Defendin." The very capable group is headed up by Linton Kweski Johnson. Side two finishes with X-Ray Spex' debut song for Virgin, "Oh Bondage Up Yours."

FEBRUARY 1978

THE SEX PISTOLS' former singer, Johnny Rotten, is off on a trip to Jamaica to sign up bands for the new Front Line label with the head of Virgin Records. Richard Branson has invited Johnny Rotten to go along since he's a great fan of reggae music. Branson wants his opinions on what's worthwhile and it's no secret he's also a little concerned about saving a real Virgin moneymaker band from itself. Along on the junket are Don Letts, Dennis Morris and journalist Vivienne Goldman. They're planning on spending the next three weeks on the island. Meanwhile, the Sex Pistols' favorite self destructor Sid Vicious is talking to the press, telling the *NME*, "When I get so annoyed over something, I need an enemy, somebody who's done something to me so that I can take it out on them and beat them to a pulp. And I always find I'm sitting in a room with a load of friends and I can't do anything to them, so I just go upstairs and smash a glass and cut myself. Then I feel better."

LIVE TONIGHT!

ROBERT GORDON & LINK WRAY ...Birmingham, Barbarella's		WIRE	Liverpool, Eric's
ADVERTS	Dublin, Trinity College	KILLJOYS	London, The Nashville
XTC/THE SECRET	Edinburgh, Univ.		

4th - Saturday.....................................

THROBBING GRISTLE have released their debut album "Second Annual Report" as a very limited edition. Only 785 copies have been pressed up of the ground-breaking industrial album. That's all the band could afford. They have found that the cost of re-pressing is about the same as cutting a new disc, so instead of a reissue of old works they'll move ahead to another release. "Second Annual Report" is composed of recordings made during last year up to September 3, 1977. Throbbing Gristle is Chris Carter, Genesis P Orridge, Cosey Fanni Tutti and Peter Christopherson. The "music" isn't punk rock, it isn't pop, it's something entirely nameless.

BLONDIE's second LP is rush-released by Chrysalis this weekend. It's titled "Plastic Letters." Blondie's backing group has now slimmed to a trio. Bassist Gary Valentine, now pursuing a solo career in California, has not been replaced. His duties have been assumed by guitarist Chris Stein. Among the tracks on the Richard Gottehrer produced album are "Contact In Red Square," "(I'm Always Touched By Your) Presence Dear," "Denis," "Bermuda Triangle Blues" and "Fan Mail."

ULTRAVOX!/THE DOLL	Birmingham, Barbarella's	KILLJOYS	London, Music Machine
EDDIE & THE HOT RODS	Glasgow, The Apollo	ADAM & THE ANTS	London, Rochester Castle
RICH KIDS	Liverpool, Eric's	ROBERT GORDON & LINK WRAY ..Sheffield, Poly.	

6th - Monday.....................................

DEVO are unusual exports from Akron Ohio to the UK and have just signed a deal with Stiff Records for three singles. The first of the three Stiff singles will be a reissue of 5,000 copies of their US single "Mongoloid" b/w "Jocko Homo" with a removable sticker on the fold out sleeve. That will be followed by the riotous Rolling Stones cover "Satisfaction" and a third not yet named. They'll be signing with Warner Brothers in the States soon as well.

SIOUXSIE & THE BANSHEES, London's hottest unsigned band, are invited back tonight for another Radio 1 session at the invitation of John Peel. Songs are "Honk Kong Garden," "Overground," "Carcass," and a version of the Beatles song "Helter Skelter." The group is still looking for a deal or a way to get an indie single out.

SOFT BOYS	London, Hope & Anchor	SLAUGHTER & THE DOGS	London, The Nashville
KILLJOYS/RESISTANCE	London, The Moonlight Club		

8th - Wednesday.....................................

NICK LOWE has his latest single "I Love The Sound Of Breaking Glass" released on the new Radar Record label. It's Radar Records #1. The "A" side is "I Love The Sound Of Breaking Glass." Nick Lowe said that when recording the track: "I did the song and Elvis (Costello) came into the studio one night and I said what do you think of this and he said blimey, you've just lifted a Bowie title. And it's not like lifting 'I Love You' or something ordinary like that, I mean it was an odd title, but I'd never heard of the Bowie song. Totally unknown…it's got a great bass line and the piano is really weird. The piano bits are played by Bob Andrews. He asked me what sort of piano do you want on it, cause I can't quite fit in. I said just go out and play like breaking glass, don't worry about the chords or any of that, I said try and play just like breaking glass and he just went out and that is the very first take on the record there." The flipside is "They Called It Rock." It was the first recording by Rockpile. Both songs are to be featured on Nick's upcoming debut album.

TOM ROBINSON has his wish granted. When the TRB signed to EMI he wanted to release the song "Glad To Be Gay." Instead, they released the more commercial "2-4-6-8 Motorway," which, though it did reach #5 on the UK charts, was not really representative of TRB. As if in reward for the success of the last single, EMI has released an EP of "Glad To Be Gay" as well as "Martin," "Right On Sister" and "Don't Take No For An Answer," a song about Tom's failed business relationship with Ray Davies of the Kinks and a publishing deal that went sour two years ago. The sixteen-minute "Rising Free" EP was recorded live at the TRB dates at the end of November and start of December, in High Wycombe and London. Although EMI General Manager Peter Buckleigh said "we're treating it like any other release."

THOSE NAUGHTY LUMPS	Liverpool, Havana Club	METHOD/MEAN STREET	London, The Rock Garden
SPLIT ENZ	Liverpool, The Mountford	UK SUBS	London, Upstairs at Ronnie Scott's
SLAUGHTER & THE DOGS	London, Dingwalls	CRABS/PLASTIX	London, The Marquee
YACHTS	London, Hope & Anchor	RIFF RAFF	London, The Pegasus

9th - Thursday.....................................

MAGAZINE show off their musical integrity. They were invited to play a slot on *Top Of The Pops* tonight but refused to mime to a tape as all bands do on the program. Magazine insisted on playing live. BBC 1 wouldn't have it and Magazine declined the television appearance.

FEBRUARY 1978

THE POP GROUP are gathering momentum. They've been together about eight months now and that's the width and depth of their musical expertise, but it doesn't slow them down a bit. The quintet is made up of Mark Stewart on vocals, Simon Underwood on bass, Gareth Sager and John Waddington on guitar and Bruce Smith on drums. Although they've named themselves the "Pop Group," they're anything but "Pop" as most people think of it. In an interview with *NME's* Steve Walsh lead singer Mark Stewart outlined what the group was about, "We want to create something that is capable of being good and evil at the same time. We want to be the beatniks of tomorrow." They cite influences from John Cage and Kirlian photographs to anti-note/psycho-acoustic philosophies. Among their set are originals such as "Color-Blind," "A Sense Of Purpose," and the disturbing "Life Is A Chair/Death Why Don't You Come Out And Play." The Pop Group are unsettling and very determined. As time goes by, the Pop Group will split up with Simon starting a group called Pigbag, Mark Stewart going solo and making a name for himself with Tackhead and Gareth beginning Rip Rig & Panic.

SQUEEZE ....Birmingham, Rebecca's	UK SUBS/DICK ENVY ....London, The Plough
THE VIBRATORS/	POLICE ....London, Hope & Anchor
FAST BREEDER/	YACHTS/MEMBERS ....London, Kings College
TORCHY & THE MOONBEAMS.......Liverpool, Eric's	NEW HEARTS...........................London, The Marquee
ONLY ONES/	ULTRAVOX!/THE DOLL..............Manchester, The Rafters
PUMPHOUSE GANG..................London, The Nashville	EDDIE & THE HOT RODS............Sheffield, City Hall
CHARGE/SCHMO ....London, Roxy	

10th - Friday........................

"TAKE ME I'M YOURS"
The Squeeze Single

BLONDIE has a new EP out this week. New York's favorite platinum blonde has cut a cover version of an unlikely do-wop classic called "Denis." It was originally recorded by Randy & The Rainbows in the summer of '63 going to #10 on the US charts. The new version of the song won't touch the US Top 40, but it will become Blondie's first UK hit, going all the way to #2. Also on the single is LP track "Contact in Red Square" and "Kung Fu Girls" from her first LP

GENERATION X has another carefully calculated single out. It's "Ready Steady Go." In it Billy professes his love for *Ready Steady Go's* presenter Cathy McGowan. It's flipped with "No No No."

SQUEEZE have their first major record released on A&M. Their previous EP (Packet Of Three) was on a indie, but this is the big time. The tracks are "Take Me I'm Yours" and "Night Nurse." It's clear that there was far more money and time put into production on this record than the last and the band has grown tighter than ever before.

THE ELECTRIC CHAIRS make it to album with their self-titled debut. Gaining the reputation as one of the most outspoken (read: offensive) of the new bands, they had some difficulty finding a record company to handle their recordings, but new UK indie Safari Records has taken the responsibility. The album features the band's "safe" current single "Eddie & Sheena," a re-recorded version of Wayne's "Max's Kansas City." and new tracks like "On The Crest," "Bad In Bed," "Out Of Control," "Rock & Roll Resurrection" and "Worry Wart." Squeeze pianist Jools Holland guests on "Hot Blood."

WRECKLESS ERIC has his second single for Stiff Records out today, sporting a new red label design that reads "Stiff Wreckords." The tracks are "Reconnez Cherie" and "Rags and Tatters." Order yours as Stiff BUY-25 in a spiffy pic sleeve.

SHAM 69.......................Edinburgh, The Univ.	SUBURBAN STUDS ....London, South Bank Poly.
ULTRAVOX!/THE DOLL ......Liverpool, Eric's	NEW HEARTS.....................London, The Marquee
MENACE........................London, Rochester Castle	

13th - Monday........................

TUBEWAY ARMY have their debut single released by Beggars Banquet in London. The band was put together some months back after their lead singer joined cover band The Lasers. Since that time, Gary's written loads of original material for the band and now they've got their first opportunity to present it on a record. Valeriun (aka Gary Webb) is so convinced of his future success, that he's flaunted the old adage and quit his day job at W.H. Smith. They're a trio with Valeriun on guitar/vocals, Scarlet (aka Paul Gardiner) on bass and Rael (Gary's uncle- Gerald Lidyard) on drums. The single is "That's Too Bad" b/w "Oh! Didn't I Say." *NME's* Bob Edmands reviews the single as, "..a feeble Johnny Rotten imitator gabbles indistinctly over 'Day Tripper' riff."

SQUEEZE follow up the release of "Take Me I'm Yours" with a full album on A&M. On the cover is bodybuilder Arnold Schwartzenegger of "Pumping Iron" fame. Behind what is possibly one of the ugliest dayglow covers in rock history lurk a dozen original songs from the Difford-Tilbrook writing machine. The LP contains the band's current single "Take Me I'm Yours" as well as "Bang Bang," "First Thing Wrong" and "Hesitation (Rool Britannia)." John Cale produced most of the album. Of the songs that were recorded, but didn't make the LP, the most intriguing is a track called "Deep Cuts." It's about obscene phone calls and was deemed "not suitable" by A&M record execs.

MIKE SCOTT is upset with the profiteering going on in the punk record shops. The future Waterboy Mike Scott writes to *Sounds* magazine, "Isn't it about time someone told those jokers who advertise "Holidays In The Sun" in a picture sleeve for daft sums like £10, that you can still get it (with sleeve) in many shops at 65p?...Looks like money-grubbing in the UK reigns in the small ads! Mike Scott (editor of *Jungleland* rock magazine) Dalkeith Road, Edinburgh.

THE INVADERS ....Birmingham, Rebecca's's	ADAM ANT/STRAIGHT 8 ....London, The Cavern
MENACE ....London, Moonlight Club	THE SOFT BOYS.......................London, Hope & Anchor
ULTRAVOX!/THE DOLL ....London, The Marquee	

FEBRUARY 1978

14th - Tuesday...

THE STRANGLERS are trying out new material at a secret live gig under the name Johnny Sox; the name is the one Hugh Cornwell's band used back in 1974, prior to the Stranglers. Some of the new material has titles such as "All Quiet On The Eastern Front" and "Tank."

METAL URBAIN is a French band that Kensington Park indie shop, Rough Trade Records has selected as the first band on their new label. They're by no means the first to venture into the indie record waters. Labels such as Raw, Chiswick, Lightning, Small Wonder and Zoom, were all set up by indie record shops. Unlike the other labels that picked up neighborhood bands and recorded them, Rough Trade has selected a French group for their first single. The band is Metal Urbain. Membership includes Claude Panik on vocals, Eric Debris on synths, Nancy Luger on guitar and Herman Schwartz, also on guitar. The group have been around about a year and have previously had a single "Panik" released last October in France on the Cobra Records label. Their UK debut is "Paris Maquis" b/w "Cle De Contact."

V2 are a new Manchester band that are making their debut in the punk marketplace this week with a three track EP of "Speed Freak," "Nothing To Do" and "That's It." It's on Bent Records. The quintet is comprised of Johnathan E. on vocals, Rev. P.P. Smythe on guitar and vocals, Stan The Man on bass and Steve Brotherdale on drums. Steve was briefly drummer with Warsaw and The Panik.

LIVE TONIGHT!

VALVES/ZONES/		SOFT BOYS/BRAKES	London, The Nashville
CUBAN HEELS	Glasgow, The Apollo Center	LEVI & THE ROCKATS	London, The Speakeasy
SIOUXSIE & THE BANSHEES	London, The 100 Club	ADAM & THE ANTS	London, Hope & Anchor
ULTRAVOX !/THE DOLL	London, The Marquee	JOHNNY SOX	London, Duke Of Lancaster

17th - Friday...

THE ADVERTS have made it to those slim ranks of punks with albums to their credit with the release of "Crossing The Red Sea With The Adverts." It features their last several singles "One Chord Wonders," "Safety in Numbers" and "No Time To Be 21," as well as other disturbing gems. For some reason the classic "Gary Gilmore's Eyes" has been left off. All of the titles were written by T.V. Smith. John Leckie produced the LP for Bright Records and it's now gracing shops around the UK.

THE CLASH have their latest slice of vinyl available today. It's "Clash City Rockers" and a reworking of the old 101'ers tune "Jail Guitar Doors." The two songs are new tracks and are not planned to be included in their next LP.

SHAM 69 are now album artists. Their debut album for Sire Records has today been released in the US and in the UK. It's called "Tell Us The Truth" and pictures the band in a confronting pose (presumably against authority) backed into a corner. The unusual thing about the album is that it has one side of studio recordings and another that was recorded live. It contains three of their previous 45s including "Ulster (live)," "Borstal Breakout (live)" and "Hey Little Rich Boy." The LP was produced by lead singer Jimmy Pursey.

THE DAMNED	Birmingham, Barbarella's	BLACK SLATE/PENETRATION	London, The Univ.
THE PREFECTS	Colwyn, The Bay Pier	BONE IDOL	London, The Brecknock
IGNATZ/THE VALVES	Edinburgh, The Univ.	THE SLITS	London, The Cryptic One Club
THE PLAGUE	London, The Roxy	ADAM & THE ANTS	London, Rochester Castle
EDDIE & THE HOT RODS	London, The Lyceum	RADIATORS FROM SPACE	London, Bedford College

18th - Saturday.........................

THE RADIATORS FROM SPACE are now just "The Radiators" (it took up too much room on the marquee) and release their new single "Million Dollar Hero (In A 5 & 10 Cent Store)" on Chiswick today. The flip of the single is "Blitzin' At The Ritz" recorded live at their Roundhouse gig on February 18th. It was produced by the legendary Tony Visconti. The band are still considering legal action over their recent banning from The Nashville. The Radiator's concert at the Roundhouse tomorrow night with The Count Bishops and Johnny Moped is going to be recorded for a budget line live album for Chiswick.

JOHNNY THUNDERS is helping to blur the question of whether the Heartbreakers have split up or not. In November of last year the Heartbreakers played two nights at the Vortex while "breaking in" their new drummer Terry Chimes (ex-Clash). Since that time they still have no record deal, no publicist and bassist Billy Rath and guitarist Water Lure have both returned to New York. Thunder's present state in unclear. He's either taking a break until the band returns, or he's plotting a solo career. Thunders has already reportedly recorded three demos at Island Studios. Of the numbers recorded, one new one is "Dead Or Alive" while another, "Leave Me Alone" is the New York Dolls' song "Chatterbox" slightly rewritten. Tonight he makes a rare appearance with a temporary combo called The Living Dead. It's comprised of Hot Rods' rhythm section members Paul Gray and Steve Nichol, as well as Only Ones' lead singer Peter Perrett, plus Patti Palladin on backing vocals and Sid Vicious on drums.

SHAM 69	Birmingham, Aston Univ.	RAPED	London, Middlesex Poly.
XTC/THE SECRET	Birmingham, Barbarella's	THE LURKERS	London, Rochester Castle
ADAM & THE ANTS	London, The Nashville	DEPRESSIONS	Manchester, UMIST
THE LIVING DEAD	London, The Speakeasy	ADVERTS	Manchester, The Univ.

19th - Sunday...

STIFF LIVE! The October '77 Stiff Records live tour has been preserved on film and on vinyl. Here's your first opportunity to own a piece

FEBRUARY 1978

of it. The LP of the tour captures high points of the first UK Stiff "caravan of stars." Side one starts with two unique Nick Lowe performances. The first is "I Knew The Bride (When She Use To Rock And Roll) and then "Let's Eat." Both are unavailable in any form in the Stiff catalogue. That's followed by Wreckless Eric and live versions of his singles, "Semaphore Signals" and "Reconnez Cherie." Finishing up side one is Larry Wallis and "Police Car." Side two is launched with Elvis Costello's performance of the Bacharach - David song "I Just Don't Know What To Do With Myself." If the songs sounds familiar, Dusty Springfield had a top ten hit with it in 1964. Elvis follows that with "Miracle Man." Next up is Ian Dury with live versions of three tracks from his current LP. They're "Billericay Dickie," "Wake Up," and the rousing finale with everyone joining in for "Sex and Drugs and Rock and Roll." "For the sake of trivia buffs, the autographed leather jacket on the reverse of the album belongs to Kosmo Vinyl, roadie extraordinare.

LOCKJAW & THE EASY CURE are playing a double bill at the Crawley Rocket tonight. They're both local bands. Lockjaw are in some ways similar to the Buzzcocks and the Lurkers and they get the headlining spot since they had a single out four months ago on an indie label. Lockjaw's bassist Simon Gallup through friends knows members of the Easy Cure, but this is the first time they've ever played together. When Lockjaw break up next year, Simon will join the Cure and be part of the band (on and off) through the '90s.

LOCKJAW/EASY CURE	...............Crawley, The Rocket		WIRE/STUKAS	.........................London, Foxe's Greyhound
DEAF SCHOOL/RADIATORS/			VIBRATORS/SMIRKS	.................London, The Nashville (free gig)
DOCTORS OF MADNESS /			LURKERS/TUBEWAY ARMY	.........London, The Marquee
JOHNNY MOPED	.......................London, The Roundhouse		BE BOP DELUXE/	
			JOHN COOPER CLARKE	...............Manchester, The Apollo

22nd - Wednesday...

JUBILEE (the film) assaults the big screen tonight at the Bloomsbury Square Odeon in London. The Derek Jarman film stars Jenny Runacre as "Bod," Adam Ant as "the kid" propelled to stardom by "Crabs" played by Little Nell. Wayne County plays the part of "Lounge Lizard," an aging transvestite punk star who bears a remarkable resemblance to Phyllis Diller and even Chelsea's Gene October wanders in as Crab's paramour only to be suffocated before his time. The leader of a punk band called "The Maneaters" is given to a new unknown singer Toyah Wilcox. Even Adam's manager, and face of '77, Jordan gets a part as "Amyl Nitrate," the singing, dancing historian. Most of the bands in the film are half glimpsed in passing. Siouxsie & The Banshees appear briefly on television behind the action. Rampant violence, gratuitous non-erotic sex and little plot. The production itself is set in an anarchy-ridden London in the far-flung future of 1984, when all forms of government are obsolete and violence reigns supreme. It is a generally irresponsible and sensational view of the punk movement. Music for the movie is provided by Wayne County & the Electric Chairs, Chelsea, Adam Ant (making his first appearance on vinyl) and Brian Eno. The film opens tomorrow night at the Notting Hill Gate Cinema in London.

THE POLICE are still having to do whatever they can to make ends meet. They don't have a record out, they aren't packing them in at live shows, but they are making ends meet however they can. These aren't kids all living together in a squat, these are adults with families to support! Sting has already, from time to time, helped provide rent money by appearing in adverts for everything from Brutus Jeans, to Triumph Bras. Now he's won an audition for himself and the band to appear in a Wrigley's Chewing Gum commercial as a punk band. The one stipulation was that the band would have to be all blonde. No problem, Stewart wasn't far off, Sting was right on and Andy was the only non-blonde in the group. They take the job, which is to dye for (sorry!).

PRAG VEC is a new group coming together in London. The nucleus of the band is vocalist Sue Grogan and guitarist John Studholme. Back in 1976 they had a rather leftist R&B group called the Derelicts. When the group split the duo kept in touch and now are starting a new group. They've just secured a drummer in the person of Nick Cash (as in "Steal Money," not THE Nick Cash that sings for 999).

EDDIE & THE HOT RODS	.............Birmingham, Town Hall		YACHTS/SMIRKS	.....................London, Music Machine
THE DEPRESSIONS	...................Birmingham, St. Peter's College		XTC/WIRE	...............................London, The Lyceum
SPLIT ENZ	.............................Glasgow, Queen Margaret Union		THE MANIACS	........................London, Hope & Anchor
THOSE NAUGHTY LUMPS	............Liverpool, The Havana Club		ONLY ONES	............................London, The Rock Garden
IAN DURY & BLOCKHEADS /			RIFF RAFF	.............................London, Pegasus
WARSAW PAKT	........................London, Dingwalls			

23rd - Thursday...

WIRE have their second single in shops today, it's a new song called "I Am The Fly" flipped with "Ex Lion Tamer" from their debut album. Kids who watch the *Tiswas* TV program are doing a dance these days called the "dead fly." Will Wire's label turn this into the soundtrack for a new dance craze?

ALTERNATIVE T.V. have their third single out this week on the Deptford Fun City label. The tracks are "Life After Life" and "Life After Dub." On the recordings, A.T.V. is augmented by guitarist Kim Turner and Squeeze keyboardist Jools Holland.

SIMPLE MINDS	........................Glasgow, Doune Castle		DRONES/	
RIFF RAFF	............................London, The Pegasus		JOHN COOPER CLARKE/	
ONLY ONES/NEW HEARTS	..........London, The Rock Garden		THE SLUGS	...........................London, Rainbow (Upstairs)
THE POLICE	...........................London, Hope & Anchor		THE BOYS	..............................Manchester, The Rafters

24th - Friday...

SHAM 69 are worried about their image. At their last several concerts the crowd has become very unruly and police called in to quell the violence. They are beginning to get a reputation of being a violent band. This concerns lead singer Jimmy Pursey to the point where he said, "...this concert is the last chance for people who say they are Sham 69 fans...I am worried sick about the violence that faces the kids who come to our shows...if they really are Sham 69 fans, there must be NO violence." Pursey has claimed that if this show lives up to

FEBRUARY 1978

the violence of the last several London gigs they will play there never more! There is also the threat that supporters of the National Front will arrive to cause trouble. They had their Ilford March banned and are hungry for action. To help keep a lid on things, the London Police will be on hand with more than the usual amount of security men inside. Tonight's event is a "Rock Against Racism" event with four bands. Opening up the show is Charge, The Desperate Bicycles and reggae band Misty. They will play tonight at Central London Polytechnic.

NINE NINE NINE have their debut LP in shops this week. The group had a bit of difficulty settling on an album title. They started off with "Emergency," then tried "100% 999," switched to "Strike A Light" and "Songs Of Praise," before settling on the imaginative "999." It has only two of their previous singles "I'm Alive" and "Emergency." The album is all original material and quite colorfully packaged. The actual recording was finished last winter at Olympic Studios. To promote the release in a different way, the band held their reception for the press at a local art gallery and displayed the works of a number of arty rock & rollers. Among the collected works was a soiled t-shirt displayed by Billy Idol, a large jailer's key from Steel Pulse, a painting of a junkyard by Paul Simonon of the Clash, some rather oblique canvases by Glen Matlock and Nick Cash, some nice work by Andy Partridge of XTC and Dave Vanian of the Damned and a mutilated Picasso print by Brian James, also of the Damned.

THE VIBRATORS have a new single "Automatic Lover" b/w "Destroy" released on Epic today. Both are advance tracks from their forthcoming album.

DEVO brings de-volution comes to the UK. Devo have their single "Jocko Homo" released in England on the Booji-Boy/Stiff label. They have had it out in the US on their own label since last year.

STIFF/CHISWICK CHALLENGE The fourth Stiff/Chiswick challenge is underway in Edinburgh tonight. The battleground is the Clouds Disco. Among the bands that participated were the Skids who *NME* writer Kim Davis described as, "...local heros...providing awful, droning heavy metal punk with interminable feedback wails from the super macho guitarist." Nevertheless, they do have quite a large following north of the border. Also on the bill were the Glasgow-based Subs, who already have a Stiff one-off single. The Monos, not the London-based mob, but a Northern version. The Cuban Heels got the notice of being "the ones to watch for" and there was honorable mention for The Freeze as well. Other participants included The Scars and Groper. The next stop on the tour for talent are the fertile musical fields of Manchester.

LIVE TONIGHT!

CUBAN HEELS/SCARS/ GROPER/THE SUBS/ THE SKIDS/FREEZE	Edinburgh, Clouds	BONE IDOL	London, The Brecknock
THE VALVES	Glasgow, The Art College	THE JAM/LATE SHOW	London, The Marquee
SIMPLE MINDS	Glasgow, Third Eye Centre	RADIATORS	London, Middlesex Poly.
MUTANTS	Liverpool, Mountford Hall	SATELLITES/PRISONERS	London, Park Royal Hotel
MENACE	London, The Roxy Club	SHAM 69/MISTY/ DESPERATE BICYCLES	London, Central London Poly.
LURKERS	London, Lincoln College	BLONDIE/ADVERTISING	Sheffield, The Univ.
		VIBRATORS	Sheffield, Poly.

25th - Saturday..........................

NICK LOWE has his solo LP "The Jesus Of Cool" released this weekend. That's an endearment that Nick read in a review of his work in the U.S. He's on the cover in six different poses, six different faces. His indeed is a man of many talents and backgrounds. From his days in the mid-sixties pop band Kippington Lodge, through pub rock Brinsley Schwartz and now to power pop, Stiff-style. Songs include Nick's current single "Breaking Glass" as well as a different version of the flipside "They Called It Rock." The LP version has the lyric changed to "Shake And Pop." Also included on the LP are Nick's past Stiff 45's "So It Goes," "Heart Of The City" and "Marie Provost." New tracks include "Music For Money," "Little Hitler," "Tonight," "No Reason," "36 Inches High" and "Nutted By Reality."

ADVERTS' drummer Lorry Driver has quit the band. He says it's because of remarks singer Gay Advert made about his using up twenty-seven takes to get a part right in their recent recording sessions and also felt the band wasn't progressing as fast as he was. He's planning to start a new band to be called the Drivers, but not a punk band, "...cos that's all finished!" Lorry's replacement is John Towe, a founder member of Chelsea who has since been in Generation X, then started his own band The Rage. He's starting with the Adverts immediately and will play drums behind the group tonight at Dundee University.

BLONDIE/ADVERTISING	Glasgow, Strathclyde Univ.	THE JAM /THE JOLT	London, The Marquee
THE BOYS	Liverpool, Eric's	DRONES/ JOHN COOPER CLARKE/ SLUGS	London, Wilmot Youth Club
THOSE NAUGHTY LUMPS	Liverpool, C.F. Mont College		
ADVERTS	London, N.E.Poly.		
YACHTS	London, The Rock Garden	DEAD FINGERS TALK	London, Red Cow

27th - Monday..........................

JOHNNY ROTTEN has returned to the UK after spending a few weeks in Jamaica. He says he visited some recording studios and visited with some local musicians. Virgin Records is anxious to claim that he has a record in the works but nothing has been announced. Meanwhile in Los Angeles, Malcolm McLaren is playing people two new "Sex Pistols" songs recorded in Rio by Cook and Jones. They're teamed up in the studio and before the cameras with Ronnie Biggs for a re-worked version of "Belsen Was A Gas" and a new one called "A Punk Prayer." Films of these performances in the studio and on board a ship going up the Amazon are dressed up with American actor Jim Jetter playing the part of Nazi Martin Borman in full Nazi dress uniform. While in Los Angeles McLaren and Warner Brothers have a confrontation with Johnny Rotten, who has been flown in especially for the meeting. Johnny is adamant about his new band and Malcolm is adamant about his film. Neither side budges.

Sid's also on the scene, although it's not as you're use to seeing him. He was the drummer for a "superstar" one-off combo called The Living Dead at a Speakeasy gig in London last week. The rest of the group was Johnny Thunders, Peter Perrett of the Only Ones, Patti Palladin of Snatch and two members of the Hot Rods.

FEBRUARY 1978

SLAUGHTER & THE DOGS have a new single out this week, which is a very unusual cover song. They've selected the 1968 Kasenetz-Katz Singing Orchestral Circus song "Quick Joey Small." The record goes to great strides to make obvious that Mick Ronson is also featured on the disc. It's a very unusual selection for a cover in that Slaughter have recently tried to establish themselves as "the last bastion of punk." The effort is flipped with "Come On Back."

DEPRESSIONS/		CRABS/THE HARDS/	
SPEEDOMETERS ....London, The Vortex		STAMPS ....London, Dingwalls	
SLAUGHTER & THE DOGS ....London, The Cavern		STATISTICS/THE HEAT/	
THE JAM/THE STUKAS ....London, The 100 Club		DOSE ....London, Moonlight Club	
THE BOYS/ BERLIN/ JERKS ....London, The Marquee		SOFT BOYS ....London, Hope & Anchor	

March 1st - Wednesday........

THE DAMNED are page three news in both *Sounds* and *NME*. It is announced that The Damned are splitting up. Founding member and guitarist Brian James is off on a solo career. James felt that the band had outlived its usefulness and had acquired a "clown image" with the stage antics of Sensible and Scabies and the horror makeup of Vanian. Most speculation is being made about Dave Vanian and Captain Sensible. The Captain had been approached about four months ago about replacing Sid Vicious in the Sex Pistols and is currently seeking Johnny Rotten, recently returned from Jamaica. Dave could go on the road with his friend's band "Doctors Of Madness" since the departure of Urban Blitz. Newest member Lu and drummer Jon Moss may continue together.

THE JAM have just had their fourth single released by Polydor. It's "News of The World" flipped with "Aunties & Uncles (Impulsive Youths)" and "Innocent Man." All are fair, up-tempo examples of what club-goers have come to expect from this trio from Woking.

ULTRAVOX Steve Shears, one of the original member of Ultravox!, has left the band. His replacement is former Neo guitarist, Robin Simon. A new Ultravox! EP of live material is just out. It's titled "Live Retro" and will feature concert versions of "The Wild, The Beautiful, & The Damned," "My Sex," "Young Savage" and "The Man Who Dies Everyday."

SUBWAY SECT/THE LOUS ....Birmingham, Barbarella's			
THE EXILE ....Glasgow, The Third Eye Centre			
WAYNE COUNTY &		YACHTS ....London, The Hope & Anchor	
THE ELECTRIC CHAIRS/		XTC...Manchester, The Rafters	
LEVI & THE ROCKATS ....London, Dingwalls		RICH KIDS ....Manchester, Middletown Civic Hall	

3rd - Friday.....................................

PATTI SMITH has her third LP for Arista released today. It's simply called "Easter," and comes after a long recovery from her neck injury last year. Patti sees the LP as her "resurrection" back into the music scene since she was absent almost the entirety of 1977. The LP is mostly originals with the exception of "Because The Night" which she co-wrote with Bruce Springsteen and the song "Privilege" from the Paul Jones movie of the same name. The album was produced by Jimmy Iovine.

THROBBING GRISTLE make another one of their unusual appearances at the Architectural Association in London's West End tonight. They'll be playing while suspended in a cage above a yard between five buildings. They'll be viewable from rooftops, the ground, windows or television monitors inside. Earthbound support bands will include punk poet Patrik Fitzgerald, Exzibitor, Incidence and various strippers and dancers. It's all part of a twelve-hour outdoor festival.

ELVIS COSTELLO has his first Radar single out today with the release of "I Don't Want To Go To Chelsea" and "You Belong To Me."

WRECKLESS ERIC's new Stiff LP comes in two different varieties. One is the regular, twelve inch, ten track LP; the other is a ten inch version with only eight songs. The tracks left off include "Whole Wide World" and "Telephoning Home." The unfortunate situation for the ten inch version is that both album sizes retail at the same price. You can choose novelty and brevity, or value for money. On the album with Wreckless is David Lutton on drums (ex-member of T-Rex), Davey Payne on sax (temporarily borrowed from Ian Dury), Charlie Hart on organ and Barry Payne (Davey's brother) on bass. Eric's new road band, The New Rockets, are Lutton on drums, John Glyn on sax (ex-member of X-Ray Spex), "Hello" Henry on keyboards (an ex-member of Chelsea) and Barry Payne on bass.

THE BOYS have their third single for NEMS record released today. It's "Brickfield Nights" b/w "Teachers Pet."

VIBRATORS ....Edinburgh, Clouds		EDDIE & THE HOT RODS/	
EXILE/MOTELS.......................Glasgow, Third Eye Centre		RADIO STARS/SQUEEZE ....Manchester, The Belle Vue	
THOSE NAUGHTY LUMPS...........Liverpool, The Univ.		THE ELECTRIC CHAIRS/	
DYAKS ....London, Duke Of Sussex		FALL ....Manchester, The Rafters	
THROBBING GRISTLE/		DEPRESSIONS ....Manchester, Pips	
PATRIK FITZGERALD/		Live Stiffs On Tour.....................Sheffield, Poly.	
INCIDENCE/EXZIBITOR ....London, Architect Association			

4th - Saturday...................................

THE HUMAN LEAGUE have turned into a quartet, but not to add another instrument or vocalist to the band. The addition is Adrian

115

MARCH 1978

Wright, who will provide "visual energy" to the music the rest of the band generates. He'll be responsible for a growing array of lights, projectors and slide backdrops that have made the Sheffield-based electronic band as interesting to watch as they are to listen to. Unlike his bandmates, who moonlight as computer operators and medical assistants, Adrian drives an ice cream van in Wakefield. The Human League have been playing around their native Sheffield in front rooms since last June, but have made a few public appearances locally in the last few weeks. They've also hooked up with Bob Fast, the entrepreneur who runs Fast Records. He'll be their manager and is looking to put out a record of the band very soon.

LIVE TONIGHT!

EDDIE & THE HOT RODS/	
RADIO STARS/SQUEEZE ....Glasgow, The Apollo Center	
ADVERTS ....Glasgow, Queen Margaret Union	
WAYNE COUNTY &	
THE ELECTRIC CHAIRS ....Liverpool, Eric's	
THOSE NAUGHTY LUMPS/	
DESTROYERS ....Liverpool, The Swinging Apple	
JAPAN/THE STICKERS ....London, The Music Machine	
COCKSPARRER ....Manchester, The Rafters	

MONOCHROME SET ....London, N.E.Poly.
THE POLICE.............................London, Rochester Castle
BUZZCOCKS/SLITS/
PENETRATION ....London, Thames Poly.
SUBWAY SECT/THE LOUS ....London, The Nashville
YACHTS ....London, The Pegasus
DEPRESSIONS/
PATRIK FITZGERALD ....London, The Roxy Club

6th - Monday...........................

ELVIS COSTELLO closes his second North American tour with two nights at the El Mocambo in Toronto Canada. All the stops are pulled and the band tears through a set of old Costello favorites and new material from his forthcoming album "This Year's Model." The concert is also being broadcast by CHUM FM in Toronto. All throughout the US tour he's been singing a different version of "Less Than Zero." Most Americans had never heard of Sir Oswald Mosely (the head of the UK version of the Nazi party in pre-war Britain) and misunderstood the "Oswald" to be assassin Lee Harvey Oswald. Instead of explaining the reference, Elvis just changed the lyrics to suit the misconception.

SNATCH The mysterious and alluring duo, have their second single out this week in the UK. It's been almost a year since their last record and that one was a limited edition. The songs presented are "All I Want" and "When I'm Bored." The tracks were recorded almost a year ago! What's taken so long? Snatch is the combined talents of Patti Palladin and Judy Nylon. Along on the record are Keeth Paul on guitar, Bruce Douglas on bass, Nick Plytas on piano and Jerry Nolan on drums. This issue has a very unusual, limited sleeve.

DESPERATE BICYCLES have spent a year saving their money to print up another Do It Yourself single, but the wait is over. Their third outing is on their self-financed Refill Records and is the 45 "New Cross, New Cross" EP. Six new songs for the bargain price of 70p! Titles are "Holidays," "The Housewife Song," "Cars," "(I Make The) Product," "Paradise Lost" and "Advice On Arrest."

SNATCH
'ALL I WANT'
the new single from
SNATCH
Special limited edition in a
Multi-coloured shimmer sleeve!

THE SUBS ....London, Hope & Anchor		SUBURBAN STUDS/UK SUBS/
ADAM & THE ANTS/		FRENCH LESSON ....London, The Vortex
HOT POINTS...........................London, The 100 Club		SUBWAY SECT/THE LOUS ....London, The Music Machine

8th - Wednesday........................

2.3 is more than a number, it's a Sheffield band that has their vinyl debut with "Where To Now" and "All Time Low" on Fast Records. Tony Parsons reviews the single in *NME*, describing the single as sounding like "an out-take from the annals of the 'Nuggets' album. Quintessential listening during a nervous breakdown." 2.3 are based around Paul Bower, one-time editor of one of Sheffield's first fanzines *Gunrubber*. They also have Paul Shaft on Bass and Haydn Boyes-Weston on drums. Their first live appearance was at Sheffield's Penthouse Club.

MENACE have their second single out this week on Small Wonder Records. It's the well aimed "G.L.C." and "I'm Civilized." Initial copies have the mandatory black, white and red picture cover.

LURKERS ....London, Deptford Albany Empire		THE SUBS ....London, Rochester Castle
RADIO BIRDMAN ....London, The Rock Garden		

9th - Thursday...........................

DEVO have finished their album sessions in Germany with Brian Eno. On their way back to Akron Ohio, the De-volutionists stop off in England for a short tour. They make their UK debut at Eric's in Liverpool tonight.

PERE UBU have released several indie singls on their own, but now they take the next step, with their debut album on the new Mercury subsidiary "Blank Records." It's called "The Modern Dance" and features some of the strangest songs to emerge from America of late. Tracks are "Nonalignment Pact," "The Modern Dance," "Laughing," "Street Waves," "Chinese Radiation," "Life Stinks," "Real World," "Over My Head," "Sentimental Journey" and "Humor Me."

DEVO ....Liverpool, Eric's		RIFF RAFF ....London, The Pegasus
THOSE NAUGHTY LUMPS...........Liverpool, The Havana Club		THE LURKERS ....London, The 100 Club
MENACE ....London, South Bank Poly.		999 ....Manchester, The Rafters

MARCH 1978

10th - Friday...

THE BUZZCOCKS have their first album, "Another Music From A Different Kitchen," released today in the UK. The LP starts off with a few seconds of the intro to "Boredom" then slides into "Fast Cars." After a full set of delightful Buzzcock melodies it then concludes with a few more seconds of "Boredom" after the last track, "Moving Away From The Pulsebeat." The Buzzcocks plan to record a follow-up to "What Do I Get." Top of the list of consideration is "Noise Annoys" and "Love You More." To help promote the new Buzzcocks LP, Virgin record shops in London, Leeds, Liverpool, Manchester and Newcastle each released 500 helium filled balloons, each containing a ticket good for a free copy of the LP. Catch a balloon- win a record.

SOME CHICKEN follow-up last October's single with a new one called "Number Seven" and "Arabian Daze." It's being released on Raw Records with two different numbers at the same time. One as Raw #13 and for the sake of the superstitious, Raw #17.

999	Birmingham, Barbarella's	COCKSPARRER	London, Croydon Greyhound
BETHNAL/THE SKIDS	Edinburgh, The Univ.	NEW HEARTS	London, Middlesex Poly.
GENERATION X	Liverpool, Eric's	YACHTS/RADIO BIRDMAN	London, Hope & Anchor
GRAND HOTEL/ TUBEWAY ARMY	London, Dingwalls	TRAPEZE/MONOCHROME SET	London, The Nashville
BUZZCOCKS/		THE SUBS	London, The Red Cow
JOHN COOPER CLARKE/		SUBWAY SECT/THE LOUS	Manchester, The Mayflower
THE SLITS	London, The Lyceum	ANY TROUBLE	Manchester, The Commercial
WAYNE COUNTY &		XTRAS/TEST TUBE BABIES	Sheffield, Dance Centre
THE ELECTRIC CHAIRS	London, Rochester Castle		

11th - Saturday...

IAN DURY gave away 500 copies of a specially pressed single at the *NME* party at Dingwalls last Christmas. Since none of these went to the public at large, the *NME* and Stiff have started a "Blockheads" competition to distribute the remaining 500. The grand prize is a night out with Ian Dury himself, an autographed copy of the album, the special single and a new pair of boots and panties. Entry is made by filling in a form in today's *NME* and submitting a photo of your blockhead self. Contest closes on the 23rd.

THE DRONES are arrested today for rehearsing their set. Perhaps the reason for the law to step in was they the rehearsal took place at about 5pm, atop their practice hall on Oxford Street in Manchester. The rehearsal didn't go unnoticed since they had their 3,000 watt sound system turned up full.

Live Stiffs On Tour	Glasgow, Queen Margaret Union	SPIRIT/ATV/THE POLICE	London, The Rainbow
NEW HEARTS	Birmingham, Barbarella's	LURKERS	London, Rochester Castle
999	Liverpool, Eric's	SHAM 69	Sheffield, Poly.
EDDIE & THE HOT RODS/		WRECKLESS ERIC	Manchester, Queen Margaret Union
RADIO STARS/SQUEEZE	Liverpool, Univ.	SUBWAY SECT/THE LOUS	Manchester, The Mayflower
JOHNNY THUNDERS	London, Speakeasy	ALBERTO Y LOS TRIOS/DEVO	Manchester, Free Trade Hall

13th - Monday...

THE SAINTS Australia's best known new wave combo, have their second LP out this week, titled "Eternally Yours" Side one starts with "Know Your Product," and ends with the complimentary "No, Your Product." In between is "Lost & Found," "Memories Are Made Of This," "Private Affair" and "A Minor Aversion." Side two begins with their single "This Perfect Day," and proceeds through "Run Down," Orstralia," New Center Of The Universe," "Untitled," "I'm Misunderstood" and "International Robots." The album was recorded late last year at the Roundhouse and Wessex Studios and was produced by vocalist Chris Bailey and lead guitarist Ed Kuepper.

Live Stiffs on Tour	Edinburgh, Tiffany's	DEPRESSIONS/WARM JETS	London, The Cavern
REZILLOS	Glasgow, Tiffany's	NEW HEARTS/SPEEDOMETERS	London, The Vortex
VIRUS/ZIPPS	London, Rochester Castle	ONLY ONES	London, The Marquee

14th - Tuesday...

THE SKIDS getting the attention of Virgin Records, who liked it enough to distribute it and are considering signing the group. The EP has three songs, "Charles," "Reasons" and "Test Tube Babies," and the first 5,000 are available in a picture sleeve. Somewhere along the way, lead singer Joey Jolson has evolved into Richard Jobson.

SQUEEZE singer Glenn Tilbrook thinks of Squeeze totally apart from the movement that has produced the Sex Pistols, the Clash and Sham 69. In this week's *NME* he said, "Although punk has been an influence, I don't think we ever want to be associated with it...When I first heard (the Sex Pistol's) 'Anarchy In The UK,' I thought it was a load of crap. I thought the chord sequence was dumb."

THE ELECTRIC CHAIRS/		THE BOYS/LITTLE ACRE	London, Music Machine
LEVI & ROCKATS	Birmingham, Barbarella's	THE DEPRESSIONS	Manchester, Poly.
EATER/MENACE/		BUZZCOCKS/SLITS	Sheffield, Top Rank
BLITZKRIEG BOP	London, The Vortex		

15th - Wednesday...

STIFF LITTLE FINGERS got together almost a year ago in Belfast and now have a searing debut single. It's "Suspect Device," and reeks

MARCH 1978

of the life that the band must find a day-to-day basis in wartorn Belfast. The group's vocalist Jake Burns told the *NME*, "Punks in England complain about hassles in the street…but they've never seen hooded men at a barricade. Their cops don't carry sub machine guns." Stiff Little Fingers financed the first 500 copies of the single at a cost of about one pound each. They're repressing another 500 copies of the disc for shops in Liverpool and all points South. The single is flipped with "Wasted Life" and you'll find it on their own Rigid Digits label. With enough material for an album, the group is anxious to find a label that will take a chance on such a controversial band. They already think that having a song of this sort will make it difficult for them to get gigs in Ireland. They might have to play under an assumed name as the Sex Pistols did.

THE SAINTS	Birmingham, Barbarella's	YACHTS	London, Hope & Anchor
REZILLOS	Edinburgh, Leigh Town Hall	DEPRESSIONS	Manchester, Poly.

16th - Thursday.............................

THE DAMNED are finding out what that old song "Breaking Up Is Hard To Do" was all about. They officially announced that they were parting ways and have plans for a final, farewell concert. Plans but no venue. The Roundhouse is fully booked, so is the Lyceum. They are now considering the Hammersmith Odeon or the Rainbow. Perhaps they'll just have to wait to break up until next year.

LIVE TONIGHT!

ELVIS COSTELLO	Dublin, Stella Cinema	MEAN STREET/THE RUTS	London, The Phoenix
DESTROYERS/		RADIATORS	London, Dingwalls
THOSE NAUGHTY LUMPS	Liverpool, Eric's	RADIO BIRDMAN/	
EDDIE & THE HOT RODS		THE BUSINESS	London, The Nashville
RADIO STARS/SQUEEZE	London, The Lyceum	SIOUXSIE & THE BANSHEES	
THE BANNED	London, Hope & Anchor	REGGAE REGULARS/ UNWANTED	London, Alexandra Palace
ADAM & THE ANTS/		RIFF RAFF	London, Rochester Castle
GENERATION X/			
BLITZKRIEG BOP	Manchester, The Rafters		

17th - Friday.......................

GENERATION X finally have their first LP released by Chrysalis. The album features the best of their current single "Ready Steady Go." The songs are all Idol-James originals and bear the titles "Day By Day," "Kiss Me Deadly," "Kleenex," One Hundred Punks," "Promises, Promises" and several others. The band are supporting the release with a major UK tour that began last week in Norwich. The LP is also out in America with a marked difference. The US album doesn't include "Listen," "The Invisible Man" and "Too Personal." It does however include four tracks not on the UK version; "Wild Youth" and Wild Dub," "Your Generation" and a cover of John Lennon's "Gimmie Some Truth." While the other three sides are available in the UK as single sides, the Lennon cover is unique to the US LP and had not been released in the UK at all!

ELVIS COSTELLO's second album is "This Year Model." The LP contains eleven originals including the band's latest single "I Don't Want To Go To Chelsea" and "You Belong To Me." Other tracks are "No Action," "Little Triggers," "Pump It Up" and "Night Rally." On the album is a "new" song that is actually quite old. "Pay It Back" was originally written back when Elvis led a group called Flip City in 1975. The inside groove of the record has this message written in it; "Special pressing number 003, ring Moira on 434-3232 for your special prize." The prize that goes out to the first 5,000 callers is a bonus Costello single of "Stranger In The House" and "Neat Neat Neat" (previously released by the Damned). Elvis Costello and the Attractions massive UK tour started last night in Dublin and will arrive in London on April 15th for two nights at the Roundhouse.

THE BOYS' second album "Alternative Chartbusters" is out today. It included their current single "Brickfield Nights" as well as "Do The Contract," "Not Ready," "Cast Of Thousands" and "Backstage Pass." There are also two covers, a version of the Hollies' hit "Stop, Stop, Stop," and the Dean Martin '54 chart topper "Sway."

Be the first on your block.

THE DEBUT ALBUM

Generation X

ELVIS COSTELLO	Belfast, Ulster Hall	BARON CULTURE &	
SUBURBAN STUDS	Birmingham, Barbarella's	RAINCOATS IN SEX	London, Cryptic One Club
U2/REVOLVER	Dublin, Project Arts Center	RADIATORS	London, The Univ.
999	Edinburgh, The Clouds	WRECKLESS ERIC	London, Kings College
BUZZCOCKS/SLITS	Liverpool, Eric's	LANDSCAPE/BERLIN/	
EDDIE & THE HOT RODS		UK SUBS	London, The Roxy Club
RADIO STARS/SQUEEZE	London, The Lyceum	RADIO BIRDMAN	London, Rochester Castle
SKIDS	London, The Red Cow		

18th - Saturday...............................

JOOLS HOLLAND, Squeeze's flamboyant keyboard player, has out a solo EP today. It's pressed on the Deptford Fun City label, the same label that pressed their debut single. The songs are, for the most part, Holland originals. They include a naughty version of "Buick 48," "Mess Around," "Should Have Known Better" and two others. The backing group should sound familiar. It's Glenn Tilbrook and Gilson Lavis, both from Squeeze as well. There's also the addition of Brent Cross on bass. These are the type of songs that Squeeze could never

MARCH 1978

commit to one of their own albums. Obvious in the tracks is Jool's love for rock-boogie musicians like Big Joe Turner and Louie Jordan. It's a real romper-stomper.

SIOUXSIE & BANSHEES are the subject of a half page article in *Sounds* where Pete Silverton asks the record companies of the world "…have you got cloth ears or something?!" He runs down the A&R history of Siouxsie & the Banshees; being turned down by Anchor, EMI, RCA, Chrysalis, Arista, CBS and Decca. All this when the band is drawing enormous crowds and many lesser bands are being gobbled up. Maybe the Banshees should find the funds to put out a do-it-theirselves album. They'd sell thousands.

THE HYPE's drummer Larry Mullen Jr. read in the *Evening Press* a notice that the Harp Lager Talent Contest for new groups is to be held in Limerick as part of the city's Civic Week. The first prize in the contest is £500 and a chance to audition for CBS Records. Larry passed word onto the band and they've decided to enter the contest. Adam gets the band together and they go to Limerick. Only a few days ago, they change their name to something shorter, to the point, snappier. U2 is suggested by Radiators lead singer Steve Averill and it sounds just right. There's almost thirty bands that are going to be playing, most of them dreary beginners. U2 manage to stand out because of their energy and attitude. The Hype, now calling themselves U2, end up winning the contest and the audition with CBS A&R man Jackie Hayden at Keystone Studios. It's a positive, far reaching career move and sets the band on the road to becoming 80s superstars.

SHAM 69.................................Liverpool, Eric's   JOHNNY THUNDERS' LIVING DEAD..London, Speakeasy

19th - Sunday...

THE FALL have been playing around Manchester since June of '77. They're fiercely independent and intend to stay that way. This week, Mark E. Smith discussed the problems and advantages of being in a minor band with *NME's* Malcolm Heyhoe, "We've never been signed up. It's a big help. We're independent and that's how we want it…We use a public phone box for gettin' gigs. It's great, works right to our advantage. People can't get in touch with you unless they want to." The bands supposedly take their name from a Camus novel (La Chute) and project a beatnik existentialist image. There's far more going on than 1-2-3 punk.

SKREWDRIVER's Ian Stuart, in an open letter to this week's *NME*, lays down a few facts about his band. "Skrewdriver is no longer a skinhead band, due to the violence at our gigs…I do not mind who attends our gigs, whoever they are so long as they're there to enjoy the music and not to beat the hell out of each other. We are making a conscious effort to stop any violence at our gigs and I only wish the audience would do the same." Stuart went on to reply to Sham 69's Jimmy Pursey, who has reportedly encouraged violence prone members of the audience to leave his gigs and go see Skrewdriver. Stuart wished that, "Pursey would keep the problems in his audiences to himself. We've got enough of our own."

SACRE BLEU ....Dublin, Baggot Inn   COCKSPARRER ....London, The Bridge House
999/BLACK SLATE/STUKAS..........London, The Roundhouse   ADVERTS...............................Sheffield, Top Rank

20th - Monday...

THE DAMNED are waiting to make their farewell and already the members are finding new jobs. Lead singer Dave Vanian has been invited to sing with The Doctors Of Madness. Kid (Richard) Strange has been acquainted with Vanian for quite a long while and was one of the Damned's biggest fans. He felt that Vanian was misused in the group. Now Strange has the opportunity to do something different in his group, as well as capitalize on what he considers one of the best talents around. Vanian will be making his stage debut as a member of the Doctors Of Madness on Easter Sunday.

GENERATION X/THE JOLT............Birmingham, The Mayfair   RADIO BIRDMAN/ALLIGATOR ......London, The Vortex
SUBWAY SECT/THE LOUS ....Edinburgh, The Clouds   BUZZCOCKS/SLITS ....Swindon, The Affair
PENETRATION/DICK ENVY..........London, The 100 Club

23rd - Thursday...

THE SUBWAY SECT make their debut with a single on the Braik label. It's the company that Bernard Rhodes (manager for The Clash) set up for them to record on. Rhodes told the *NME* that the new label, "…will only deal in extremes. The scene is getting predictable. There's not enough spice getting into things." The Clash and Sect go back together to when they were seen at the 100 Club punk festival. Since then they have opened up for the Clash on their '77 tour and have been appearing around the UK with French band, The Lous. Their single, "Nobody's Scared" b/w "DontSplitIt," was recorded six months ago.

THE CUBAN HEELS are half of the Glaswegian punk band Johnny & The Self Abusers who split up last December. Ali MacKenzie and John Milarky from the group immediately began this new group. They've been playing the clubs and pubs around Scotland and now are about to make the big move. For their first foray into the recording world they've chosen "Downtown" (the same song that Pet Clark had a hit with in the '60s) and their original composition, "Do The Smok Walk." The Cuban Heels are John Milarky on vocals, Paul Armour on bass, Laurie Cuffe on guitar and Davie Duncan on drums. The single is out now on Housewives Choice Records.

CRABS/SPITFIRE BOYS ....London, Deptford Albany Empire   REZILLOS ....London, The Nashville
BANNED ....London, Hope & Anchor   NEW HEARTS.........................Manchester, The Rafters

24th - Friday...

JOHNNY MOPED's first album "Cycledelic" has a trick groove on the first song. A special pressing has been worked out so that track one is actually two different songs, one inside the other, done by using a double, parallel groove. One is a rave-up titled "V.D. Boiler," the other is simple called "the Mystery Track." The mystery is why the mystery track was ever included. It's little more than false starts, belches and muttering with echo effects. How you set your needle on the disc determines your fate.

MARCH 1978

THE RAMONES release another 100 mph pop song. This time it's the 1958 Bobby Freeman classic "Do You Wanna Dance" b/w "Cretin Hop" and "It's A Long Way Back To Germany." The latter track being exclusive to the single and unavailable on any album. The Ramones are planning to tour Europe in May and then return to England.

LIVE TONIGHT!

BUZZCOCKS/SLITS/	ELVIS COSTELLO ....Liverpool, Eric's
PATRIK FITZGERALD ....Birmingham, Top Rank	BOOMTOWN RATS/
TANGERINE DREAM ....Glasgow, Apollo Centre	BLAST FURNACE ....London, The Lyceum

26th - Sunday.......................

JUBILEE is the soundtrack hot on the heels of the release of Derek Jarman's film *Jubilee*. The LP has two distinctly different sides. The "rock" side starts and ends with Adam And The Ant's debut tracks on vinyl, the songs are "Deutscher Girls" and "Plastic Surgery." In between are Wayne County and the Electric Chairs with "Paranoia Paradise," Chelsea with their semi-hit "Right To Work" and an heretofore unknown band called the Maneaters with "Nine To Five." Side two on the LP is the "mood" side. The first two tracks are credited to Suzi Pinns, the singing, dancing historian in the film, played by Jordan. The first of these tracks is "Rule Britannia," as preformed by Jordan, the second is somebody else but still bearing Suzi Pinn's name. This is followed by another unknown group called Amilcar preforming thematic music. The side closes with two from Brian Eno. Tracks are "Slow Water" and "Dover Beach." Siouxsie & The Banshees appear briefly in the movie and had the opportunity to be on the soundtrack. They've been yearning for a major label record. They've turned it down because they didn't want to be associated with what they saw as a camp, exploitative movie. Siouxsie & the Banshees remain, again, unsigned though not uninvited.

THE AUTOMATICS are the unique Coventry-based punk-meets-reggae group making their London debut tonight as the opening act for the Saints at the Marquee. Saints manager Chris Gilber was quite taken with the group and he's put up the funds for the band to cut some demos while in town. The Automatics are Jerry Dammers on keyboards, Horace Panter on bass (ex-Breaker), Silverton Hutchinson on drums (ex-Chapter 5), Neol Davies (ex-Chapter 5), Roddy "Radiation" Byers (ex-Wild Boys), Lynval Golding and vocalist Terry Hall (ex singer for punk band The Squad). Because of another group called the Automatics, they'll have to change their name to the Specials. Under that name, they'll help shape music in 1979 and be responsible for the nationwide "two tone" movement that brings a modern version of "ska" music to the masses. Along the way, they'll have eight top ten singles in the early '80s.

VIBRATORS/CHELSEA/	NEW HEARTS/BUSINESS ....London, Nashville
CORTINAS/	LEYTON BUZZARDS ....London, The Red Lion
SNIVELING SHITS ....London, The Roundhouse	BUZZCOCKS/THE SLITS/
SAINTS/AUTOMATICS ....London, Marquee	PATRIK FITZGERALD ....Manchester, Mayflower

29th - Wednesday......................

EASY CURE are faced with a hard decision. After entering a band contest, going thru an audition and finally earning a major label recording contract, the Easy Cure are chucking it all and cancelling their deal with Hansa Records. At the end of their second recording session they were given some "oldies" to try as covers. Then when they were in session again in January, they were again encouraged to record cover versions of other people's old songs. The band were aghast. This was 1978! They weren't about to help revive the '60s! To make matters worse when a single was being talked about in these sessions, Hansa refused to release "Killing An Arab." So the Easy Cure are back where they started, if not a little wiser about how the business sometimes works.

EDDIE & HOT RODS/	WIRE.....................................London, Marquee
RADIO STARS/SQUEEZE ....Dublin, Stadium	DEPRESSIONS ....London, Speakeasy
SOFT BOYS ....London, Hope & Anchor	BUZZCOCKS/THE SLITS.............Manchester, Middletown Civic Hall

30th - Thursday......................

CLASH members Paul Simonon and Nicky Headon were arrested this evening at 7 PM for shooting pigeons from the rooftop of their Chalk Farm studio, "Rehearsal, Rehearsals." A helicopter, three detectives and several boys in blue were called in to deal with the "rooftop gun gang" by employees of British Rail, who have property behind the studio. They were taken to Kentish Town station, charged with criminal damage to three racing pigeons and held in cells overnight. They're to be released tomorrow on £1,500 bail each and the case is to come before the magistrate on May 10th.

BOOMTOWN RATS ....Birmingham, Barbarella's	SLAUGHTER & THE DOGS...........London, The Marquee
THE VIPERS ....London, The Bridge House	X-RAY SPEX ....Manchester, The Rafters
NEW HEARTS/FAVORITE/	SIOUXSIE & THE BANSHEES ....Sheffield, The Limits
STRANGEWAYS ....London, Music Machine	

31st - Friday......................

PATTI SMITH makes a single comeback with her first 45 in ages. It's "Because The Night," the track she co-wrote with Bruce

MARCH 1978

Springsteen and will become her biggest hit ever, climbing to #5 in the UK and to #13 in America. It's also included on her current album "Easter." It's paired with the non-LP ballad "God Speed." As a blast from the past, Patti's debut single "Hey Joe" and "Piss Factory" is being reissued on Sire. It's in a special pic sleeve and is a limited edition at only 80p. Owning the original '74 version of this single was a true sign of being a hip insider, now everyone else will have a chance to hear it.

DEVO have signed a worldwide contract (excluding the US) with Virgin Records boss Richard Branson. The papers were signed in Los Angeles earlier this week as the band returned from Cologne with finished tapes of the debut album. The cost of recording the LP was paid for by producer Brian Eno, giving a strong bargaining position to the band. There is gossip that US Warners is upset about the deal since they claim to have signed a contract with Devo's management on March 23rd. Unfortunately, those who represented themselves as Devo's management were not on Devo's payroll. With the US licensing still up in the air, Warners is consulting their lawyers.

BOOMTOWN RATS A new single today for Dublin's Boomtown Rats. This time it's "She's So Modern," a real jumper that's one of the band's live favorites. It's flipped with the non-LP track "Lying Again."

PENETRATION	Edinburgh, The Clouds	VIC RUBB & the VAPORS ....London, The Duke Of Lancaster
WRECKLESS ERIC	Liverpool, Eric's	

April 4th - Tuesday.....................................

SEX PISTOLS' bassist Sid Vicious is in Paris shooting bits for the upcoming Sex Pistols movie. The filming takes place at the Olympia Theatre on a set built for Serge Gainsbourg and the song is the Frank Sinatra hit "My Way." Sid descends a long, lit flight of stairs and saunters to the microphone. During the course of the song, Sid in a solo performance writhes like a lounge singer and concludes by shooting the audience.

THE CRAMPS have made a historic first record. It's the first of a new genre of music being called "psychobilly." That's Rockabilly music (a cross between country and rock) with psychotic or psychedelic overtones. It's southern-fried weirdness that is uniquely American. Although there's people like Robert Gordon and the Polecats singing in this style, nobody can even approach the totally over-the-top, gibbering psychosis of the Cramps. Their first single is a pair of cover tunes, "Surfin' Bird" and "The Way I Walk." It's out on the band's own Vengeance Records label #666.

ELVIS COSTELLO	Glasgow, Satellite City	PATTI SMITH ....London, The Rainbow
ADAM & The ANTS	London, The 100 Club	

5th - Wednesday.....................................

"FAREWELL TO THE ROXY" is another live "club" album released today. Today's subject is the Covent Garden Roxy Club. The album is a collection of live tracks by some of the more representative, unsigned bands that played the club late in 1977. The LP was recorded by the RAK mobile studio over the three-day New Year weekend. Side one starts with Blitz and "Strange Boy." Then follow Acme Sewage Co with "Smile and Wave Goodbye," "Billy Karloff and the Goats with "Relics From The Past," and the UK Subs with "Live In A Car" and "Telephone Numbers." Closing out the first side are The Tickets with "Get Yourself Killed" and "Never Wanna Leave" by The Red Lights. Side two features XL5 with "Here Comes The Knife," The Jets with "TV Drink," and The Streets with "Sniper." There's also "Tough On You" by Plastix," The Bears with "Fun Fun Fun," "Vertigo" by Open Sore, and lastly, The Crabs' "Lullabies Lie."

COCKSPARRER	Birmingham, Barbarellas	THOSE NAUGHTY LUMPS ....Manchester, Pips
SKIDS	London, Rochester Castle	ELVIS COSTELLO ....Sheffield, The Top Rank

6th - Thursday.....................................

THE VIBRATORS' guitarist John Ellis has announced that he's leaving the band, just as the Vibrators second LP "V2" is hitting the shops. When asked what he was going to do next he told the press he intends to, "...devote more time to watching TV and playing bridge." He also plans to, "...work on his valuable collection of rare wax cylinder recordings of speeches made by Neville Chamberlain." The Vibrators' second LP is simply titled "V2." It contains their current single "Automatic Lover" as well as "Pure Mania," "Nazi Baby," "Feel Alright," "Wake Up" and "Public Enemy Number One." With Ellis' departure, it's uncertain whether the band can find a replacement that can live up to their new LP, live. Is this the end of the Vibrators?

THE NORMAL is the subject of speculation as test pressings of "T.V.O.D." begin to leak out of indie Mute Records. It's described as a cross between Kraftwerk electronics and Lou Reed drug lyrics. In truth it's one of the first completely electronic new wave records. It's Daniel Miller, who runs Mute, on the record. There is no band, no chance of a live show or tour. The single is flipped with "Warm Leatherette."

THE MUTANTS	Liverpool, The Sportsmen	THE ELECTRIC CHAIRS/
VIC RUBB & The VAPORS	London, Western Counties	LEVI & THE ROCKATS ....London, Music Machine
SKIDS	London, The Red Cow	ELVIS COSTELLO ....Manchester, The Rafters
THE SAINTS/THE FRONT	London, The Nashville	EATER ....Manchester, Pips

7th - Friday.....................................

DEVO have another Stiff 45 out today. It's the Akron spuds bizarre version of the classic Rolling Stone's song "Satisfaction" b/w the original "(I Saw My Baby Getting) Sloppy" If they disappear tomorrow without ever making another record, it would have all been worth it just to hear this version of Satisfaction. It's the weirdest cover version in eons, or at least since the Residents' version in December '76.

APRIL 1978

THE POLICE release their single "Roxanne" on A&M Records in the UK. It's their follow up to "Fall Out" and is the first to feature their new guitarist Andy Summers. They had tried once before to record "Roxanne" but the sessions were a disaster. That was back several months ago when Henry Padovani was still in the group and Andy Summers has just joined. Since that time, Padovani left to join the Electric Chairs and the Police became a trio again. At the moment, the Police are back in Munich, Germany with Eberhard Schoener's Laser Theatre. They had recorded with Eberhard last October. The money's good and the job's an easy one.

TELEVISION New York band Television release their second album "Adventure" today. It features seven tracks written by Verlaine and was produced by Verlaine and Jon Jansen.

LIVE TONIGHT!

SACRE BLEU ....Dublin, Baggot Inn	THE FALL ....Liverpool, Eric's
UK SUBS/THE PLAGUE/	SKIDS ....London, Hope & Anchor
DICK ENVY ....London, Battersea Arts Centre	ELVIS COSTELLO ....Manchester, The Rafters

8th - Saturday.....................................

THE DAMNED have their official "Farewell Concert" tonight. After weeks of trying to find a suitable available venue, the Rainbow became available. Opening up the show is a rather comic, somewhat Alberto-esque group called Prof. and The Proffets followed by Cambridge combo The Soft Boys. The Damned for this final concert were NOT the original 1976 line-up. Onstage at the beginning of the show was Brian James, Captain Sensible, Dave Vanian and latecomers Lu Edmunds and John Moss. Halfway through the set, the band was joined by original member Chris Millar (aka Rat Scabies) bringing the crowd onstage to their original 1976 membership, plus two. The show continued with the energy usually associated with ending a tour and there was one encore of "I Feel Alright." That's it.

JAPAN release their debut album and coincidentally have photos of their collective crotches posted around London. It's a promotion campaign for their new LP "Adolescent Sex." Each poster features the front of a member's trousers, a hand inserted halfway into the open fly with the banner "Get Into Japan" above it. The LP is a mix somewhere between Roxy Music with The Velvets. The group have been playing around London since 1976 and now they have something to give the public. The songs are all originals with titles like "Wish You Were Black," "Lovers On Main Street," the one exception being the song "Don't Rain On My Parade," lifted from the soundtrack to *Funny Girl*. Japan is David Sylvian on vocals & rhythm guitar, Mick Karn on bass, Steve Jansen on drums, Rob Dean on lead guitar and Richard Barbieri on keyboards.

SID VICIOUS is the subject of a three-page *Record Mirror* interview. The cover of the magazine headlines the question "Why does Sid Vicious think he'll be dead in two years." Sid was half right, he would be dead in 300 days. Sid and his girlfriend, American dancer Nancy Spungen, tell how they met, how the Pistols disintegrated and how they both don't expect to reach the old folks home. Sid said, "I'll die before I'm very old...I don't know why. I just have this feeling. There have been plenty of other times that I've nearly died." Sid talks at great length about the number of fights he's been in, how he got his boot in or got slashed himself. He seems really proud of being a scrapper.

SAINTS.....................Liverpool, Eric's	DAMNED/SOFT BOYS/
RADIO STARS/SKIDS ....London, The Nashville	JOHNNY MOPED/
WRECKLESS ERIC/TOURISTS ....London, Oxford College	PROF. & PROFFETS ....London, The Rainbow

9th - Sunday.....................................

GENERATION X lead singer Billy Idol pinpoints one of the elements that sets Generation X apart from other "punk" bands. In an interview this week in the *NME* he said, "The one thing I've got against punk is this concept of no emotion. Surely the music should be ringing with emotion. No wonder people in straight jobs can't take rock and roll. It must be so painful to see people enjoying themselves...and then they've gotta get up and go to work in the morning. I realized when I saw the Sex Pistols that if I didn't do it then, I'd be just like all those people I hated."

THE TELEVISON PERSONALITIES are responsible for giving us another oddball record. Their debut single is "14th Floor" and "Oxford Street, W1." It's a limited edition on GLC Records. The group is alleged to be Nicholas Parsons on guitar, John Peel on vocals and drums, Russell Harty on guitar and Bruce Forsyth on bass. The tracks were recorded in November of last year, but the band has only now been able to afford to have the disc pressed. There is an initial edition of 1,500 singles.

GENERATION X/THE JOLT	SKIDS...................................London, The Nashville
REGGAE REGULARS ....London, The Roundhouse	THE MEMBERS ....London, The Red Cow

14th - Friday.....................................

X-RAY SPEX have their first record for EMI released today. EMI must have some pride in signing the group, as they've allowed them to use their own "X-Ray Spex" logo as the major image on the label. Tracks selected for the 45 are "The Day The World Turned Dayglo" b/w "I'm a Poseur," and the first 15,000 are pressed in dayglo orange vinyl with a special picture bag. The "A" side is a love song to a plastic world, a plastic society, sung (of course) by Poly Styrene.

THE BUZZCOCKS have their latest hitting the shops this day. It's "I Don't Mind" b/w "Autonomy." Both tracks are from their debut LP.

APRIL 1978

IAN DURY & The Blockheads have another classic in the making. This time it's their new single of "What A Waste" filled with could-have-beens and what-ifs. It's flipped with another soon to be classic "Wake Up (And Make Love To Me)."

STIFF/CHISWICK CHALLENGE is staged at the Rafters tonight in Manchester. Eleven bands participated beginning with Fly, then came Ed Banger, The Prime Time Suckers, Jilted John and 2.3. As the evening wore on out trooped V2, The Yo Yo's, Time Out, Mike King and the Tunes. Joy Division were the last band on and it was now 2:30 AM. Mick Wall reviewed the challenge for *Sounds* and was not overly impressed with any of the bands, including Joy Division. He described them as "Mock-heroics all around from Iggy imitators acting out their Sons-Of-World-War-Two histrionics I can do without."

ELVIS COSTELLO.....................Birmingham, Barbarella's	ADAM & THE ANTS...................London, The Marquee
GENERATION X/THE JOLT............High Wycombe, Town Hall	Stiff-Chiswick Challenge ....Manchester, The Rafters

15th - Saturday...

MAGAZINE's new single is "Touch And Go" coupled with the James Bond theme "Goldfinger." This precedes a short, eight date promotional tour in England. Barry Formula, who had been with Magazine on their last tour, as now joined the group full time.

NINE NINE NINE release their new single "Me And My Desire" b/w "Crazy." As usual, the first run of the United Artists single will be shipped with a special picture cover. It's the group's fourth single.

THE NOSEBLEEDS are playing at Manchester Polytechnic as part of a Manchester mini-festival. Way down at the bottom of the bill are the new version of the Nosebleeds. Ed Banger (aka Eddie Garrity) had left the band recently to pursue a solo career and they had to find a replacement. The new singer is Steven Morrissey, a nineteen year old local writer - lyricist who was brought into the band by fellow New York Dolls enthusiast Billy Duffy. The Nosebleeds new version still features the old rhythm section of Pete Crookes and Toby, with the addition of guitarist Billy Duffy and his friend Steven. They do well tonight and are warmly received although they're bottom of the bill.

VIPERS..................................Cork, Downtown Kampus	SLAUGHTER & THE DOGS/
ELVIS COSTELL/WHIRLWIND ....London, The Roundhouse	GYRO/JOHN COOPER CLARKE/
SOFT BOYS............................London, Hope & Anchor	JILTED JOHN/THE NOSEBLEEDS ...Manchester, Poly.

19th - Wednesday...

KRAFTWERK releases another future-soaked LP called "The Man Machine," that takes the group closer to the dance beat than ever before. Tracks include "The Man Machine," "The Model," "Neon Lights," "The Robots," "Spacelab" and "Metropolis." The album is available in their native Germany in an all-German version, except you have to ask for "Die Mensch Maschine."

SIOUXSIE & THE BANSHEES almost set a house record at the Music Machine in London tonight. Their advance ticket sales were second only to the latest Tom Robinson gig and he's signed, successful and on the radio. For an unsigned band, Siouxsie & The Banshees are a very successful, unrecorded, unsigned band. Frequently Siouxsie aims quips at the A&R men she supposes are lurking in the back recesses of the club. Perhaps these barbs are what has kept them unsigned. Siouxsie & The Banshees have an expanding playlist of new songs such as "Love In A Void," "Nicotine," "Captain Scarlet," "Metal," "Hong Kong Garden," "Overground" and "Suburban Relapse." Of the imaginative covers, there's a striking version of "Helter Skelter."

SIOUXSIE & BANSHEES	BANNED/THE MONOS ....London, Nashville
THE TABLE/SPIZZOIL ....London, The Music Machine	

21st - Friday...

BLONDIE's first UK hit is their version of the 1963 Randy & The Rainbows' song "Denis." It went all the way to #2 on the British charts and is still selling. Now a new single is in the shops. It's "(Always Touched By) Your Presence Dear," b/w "Poet's Problem" and "Detroit 442." Two of the tracks are from the current LP "Plastic Letters," while "Poets Problem" is unique to the single.

THE ONLY ONES release their first single since signing to CBS Records. It has been a wait of almost a year since their well-received indie "Lovers Of Today." The song selected for this fresh start is the haunting "Another Girl, Another Planet" b/w "Special View." They are currently touring as support band for Television.

XTC releases their latest single. It's a simple statement about the "type" of music they play. It's not punk, it's not the new wave."This Is Pop!" It's coupled with "Heatwave."

THE FRESHIES are strictly do-it-yourself. their debut single is a limited edition of "Baiser (Taste Of A Boy, Taste Of A Girl)" on their own Razz Records label. Other tracks on the EP are "Moonmidsummer," "Two Of The Same Girl" and " Washed Up." The group's lead vocalist, songwriter and protagonist is the energetic Chris Sievey.

MEKONS ....Birmingham, Bournebrook Hotel	JOHNNY MOPED ....London, South Bank Poly.
THE BANNED ....Liverpool, Rock Garden	RADIO BIRDMAN.....................London, The Red Cow
SIOUXSIE & THE BANSHEES ....Liverpool, Eric's	RICH KIDS/WHITE CATS ....Cambridge, The Corn Exchange
SOFT BOYS.............................London, Hope & Anchor	

22nd - Saturday...

JOHNNY THUNDERS stages a surprise gig at the Speakeasy with Paul Cook and Steve Jones of the Sex Pistols. Aided by french teenager Henri Paul on bass, they trudge through a collection of rock classics and some originals. Songs included "Pipeline," "These Boots Are

APRIL 1978

Made For Walking," "Daddy Rolling Stone" and Thunders' originals like "So Alone," "London" and "Dead Or Alive." One new song written by Steve Jones was played. It's called "Black Leather" but seems to be still be in the process of being written. There is still talk whether tonight's line-up of Thunders' band will exist as a preforming unit, a one-off or a studio group. Nothing is sure so far, although at the moment it looks good for being a real band. Johnny Thunders has his first solo single out this weekend on the new Real Records label. Songs include "Dead Or Alive" and "Downtown." Helping Johnny out on the disc is the Hot Rods rhythm section, Steve Nichol and Paul Gray. The pair have appeared with Thunders numerous times in the recent past. The songs were produced by Thunders and Steve Lillywhite and is the guitarist's first recording since the Heartbreakers fell out with Track Records.

THE PRETENDERS are coming together. Chrissie was originally teamed up with a drummer named Gas Wilde. He brought along a friend of his, a bass player named Pete Farndon. He has previously been in a Hereford group Cold River Lady and only just returned from Australia where he was in a group called the Bushwackers. After a few rehearsals, Gas drops out and they have to find another drummer. Chrissie was trying to get the attention of Motorhead's drummer Phil Taylor, because there were rumors that Motorhead was about to split. She figured is she could just let Phil hear her band, then he'll join when they split. They get Phil's attention by telling him they have an audition. He can't make it but suggests two other guitar players. One is a older guy with kids, the other is a young kid, Jimmy Scott. Jimmy is the total opposite of Chrissie. She's into punk and he loves Abba and the Beach Boys. He's from Hereford and has been playing since he was only a lad of twelve, most recently with The Cheeks. They played together and it was magic. So now Chrissie has a bass, a lead guitarist and still has to find a suitable drummer. For the sake of the demo session, they hired a session player. He's the Irish drummer named Gerry Mackleduff who plays part time with Juice On The Loose. After the session, Jimmy Scott returns to Hereford to lead his life of near-musical retirement. Chrissie tries again to find her perfect band.

| THE MEMBERS | London, The Red Cow | RICH KIDS | Sheffield, Poly. |

25th - Tuesday................................

ALTERNATIVE T.V. will be the last punk band to play the 100 Club tonight. It was decided by the club owners that graffiti, theft and property damage were cutting too far into their profits to continue booking punk bands. The club will stay open but will continue in its earlier, longer tradition as a jazz and reggae showcase. The 100 Club has been the site of many significant and landmark concerts in the past two years. Most notably, it was the site of the September '76 "Punk Festival" that brought England's scattered punk tribes together into one movement.

THE PORK DUKES supply more juve humor with their new single "Telephone Masturbator" b/w "Melody Makers." The single's production is credited to Willie Dunnit.

SIOUXSIE & THE BANSHEES/		THE ELECTRIC CHAIRS/	
EATER/ THE FRONT	Birmingham, Barbarella's	LEVI & ROCKATS	London, The Marquee
MAGAZINE	Liverpool, Eric's	A.T.V./EL SEVEN	London, The 100 Club
UK SUBS/CRACK/CRASS	London, The White Lion		

26th - Wednesday................................

THE STRANGLERS have a new single out today. It's "Nice & Sleazy" and is said to be part of their forthcoming LP "Black & White." It's flipped with the non-LP "Shut Up," which clocks in at one minute and six seconds, one of the shortest punk songs.

THE ART ATTACKS release their debut single, months after they've split up. The posthumous recording of "I Am A Dalek" and "Neutron Bomb" is on Albatross Records. By now, lead singer Edwin Pouncey is quite well known under the cartooning guise of Savage Pencil. The song is almost "What Do I Get" a lá Buzzcocks but no real copyright threat considering how few copies it will ever sell.

THROBBING GRISTLE have released a throbbing, churning, post punk single of "United" and "Zyklon B Zombie" on Industrial Records. It's music of its own definition. *Sounds* magazine described it as "Syd Barrett meets Kraftwerk;" very appropriate.

| MAGAZINE | Birmingham, Barbarella's | RICH KIDS/WHITE CATS/ | |
| THOSE NAUGHTY LUMPS | Liverpool, Christ's College | SNEAKERS | London, The Lyceum |

28th - Friday................................

SHAM 69's new single, their second for Polydor Records, is "Angels With Dirty Faces" b/w "The Cockney Kids Are Innocent."

ELVIS COSTELLO has a new 45 out only two months since the release of "I Don't Want To Go To Chelsea." It's "Pump It Up" b/w "Big Tears." The "A" side is from the album "This Years Model." The flipside is an outtake from those same sessions, with Clash member Mick Jones guesting on lead guitar.

PERE UBU make their UK live debut tonight in Manchester. Pere Ubu's debut LP "The Modern Dance" had been rush released earlier this month in the UK and expectations are running high for their avant guarde live show. To coincide with the tour, Radar Records is issuing a five track EP called "Datapanik In The Year Zero" that features the band's rare, early singles, that were difficult to find, even if you lived in Cleveland where they came out. On the 12" is Pere Ubu's first single from 1975, "Heart Of Darkness" and "30 Seconds Over Tokyo." There's also one side of their second single "Cloud 149," and the rare flipside of their limited single "The Modern Dance"; a track called "Heaven." The song listed as "Untitled" is apparently a previously unreleased song from the same sessions as "Street Waves."

WIRE	Birmingham, Barbarella's	SOFT BOYS	London, The Red Cow
SIOUXSIE & THE BANSHEES/		PENETRATION	London, The Nashville
EL SEVEN/SPIZZ OIL	High Wycombe, Town Hall	LEVI & the ROCKATS	London, The Speakeasy
RADIO BIRDMAN	London, Hope & Anchor	PERE UBU/THE POP GROUP	Manchester, Rafters

MAY 1978

May 3rd - Wednesday...

THE GANG OF FOUR will be having more than the usual number of rehearsals in their front-rooms in Leeds. They've gotten rid of their "hippy bassist" and replaced him with Dave Allen who they found by posting a notice on the university bulletin board. They've also been contacted by Bob Last of Fast Records and plan to be recording their debut single when Dave is up to speed with the rest of the group.

EASY CURE guitarist Porl Thompson, one of the founder members of the group, has quit. Robert said, "The songs were getting more stark, more minimal and I was beginning to loathe Porl's lead guitar. I tried to get him to play chords but he didn't like that...we decided not to have any more rehearsals for a couple of weeks and when we started again, we just didn't tell him." They've also changed the name of the band. The new trio will be known by the shorter and "less hippyish" name The Cure. Porl will once again be a member of the Cure, when he re-joins the band in 1986.

EATER/	THE MONOS/UK SUBS ....London, The Pegasus
SLAUGHTER & THE DOGS ....Birmingham, Town Hall	THE LURKERS ....London, The Rock Garden

4th - Thursday.....................

B-52's have just released their debut single on their own B-52's Records label. The band got together last Valentine's Day and have built a body of songs that are best described as a goofy cross between surf music, new wave and total camp. The sides on the debut 45 are "Rock Lobster" and "52 Girls." Both songs are primitive versions far different from the versions that would be heard on the band's debut album. The inital pressing of the single comes in a green and white sleeve with the band's contact address on the back as the El Dorado Restaurant. That's where Fred works. The band are begining to get some record company attention yet have only a handful of songs in their live set. Other songs you're likely to hear are "Strobe Light," "The Killer B's" and "Planet Claire." The B-52's are Kate Pierson, Fred Schneider, Ricky and Cindy Wilson and Keith Strickland.

SHAM 69, are beginning to be isolated by some of their biggest fans. National Front supporters (modern Nazi skinheads) have taken on Sham 69 as THEIR BAND. They pack the gigs, crowd the stage and abuse those not in their clique. Jimmy Pursey spends time with these misled youths trying to diffuse the problem but generally just winds up even more frustrated. Some have split from the NF to start in with another, more radical group called the British Movement. Although Sham 69 has a solid audience in this crowd, they could be on the way to alienating their average fans. Pursey makes it continually clear that he's not aligned politically with the NF, they've just attached themselves to his music for some reason. The controversy that comes with this audience is not something he wants.

NICK LOWE has a new single out on the new Radar Records label, "Little Hitler," b/w "Cruel To Be Kind." The first track is from his new album, while the flipside is non-LP.

LIVE TONIGHT!

U2/VIPERS ....Dublin, McGonagles (residency)	ELECTRIC CHAIRS/FISHER Z........London, The Nashville
BIG IN JAPAN ....Liverpool, Eric's	THE BANNED/
	THOSE NAUGHTY LUMPS ....Manchester, The Rafters

5th - Friday...

ALTERNATIVE T.V. have a new single (their fourth) and their debut album released this week on Deptford Fun City Records. The album is "The Image Has Cracked." Of the nine tracks on the LP are some studio material, plus some live tracks recorded at the 100 Club in London. The simultaneous single is "A.T.V.," that's A= Action, T= Time and V= Vision; Action Time Vision. It's the bands clearest and most concise release to date. The flip side, "Another Coke" was recorded at the 100 Club on February the 7th of this year.

JOY DIVISION have been in Arrow Recording Studios in Manchester since Monday. The session was arranged by promoter Richard Sterling and John Anderson, head of northern soul label Grapevine Records. Joy Division have recorded eleven tracks so far: " The Drawback," "Leaders Of Men," "Walked In Line," "Failures," "Novelty," "No Love Lost," "Transmission," "Ice Age," "Interzone," "Warsaw" and "Shadowplay." During today's mixdown of the album with John Anderson, he insisted that some synthesizer be mixed into it to soften the sound. The band are all against it. Their tape is to offered to RCA Records but now Joy Division are considering getting out of the contracts. They think that the terms are most unfavorable (although standard for contracts with major labels) and the trials with the addition of synthesizers might be the last straw.

TOM ROBINSON's first album has begun to leak out of EMI Records. On the LP are studio versions of the group's most popular live tracks such as "Grey Cortina," "Ain't Gonna Take It," "The Winter of '79," "You Gotta Survive" and their current single "Up Against The Wall." Nowhere on the album is their pop chart hit, "2-4-6-8 Motorway." The powerful LP is titled "Power In The Darkness."

VIBRATORS ....Edinburgh, Univ.	MISTY/PLEASURE ZONE/
BUZZCOCKS/PENETRATION ....Liverpool, Univ.	PASSIONS ....London, Acklam Hall
THE ELECTRIC CHAIRS ....London, Rochester Castle	COCKSPARRER ....London, Hollies

6th - Saturday.....................................

TANZ DER YOUTH is the new group led by Brian James since he left the Damned. James says the idea for the name came when The Damned were on tour in Berlin. He saw a German poster for a Roman Polanski film titled *Dance Of The Vampires*. In German it was

MAY 1978

"Tanz Der Vampires." He said he liked the "Tanz Der" but felt that "Youth" fit better at the end. Tanz Der Youth includes Alan Powell on drums (ex-Hawkwind), Andy Colquhoun on bass (ex-Warsaw Pakt) and Tony Moor on keyboards. The quartet got together about four weeks ago, have been busy rehearsing and have reportedly already cut some demos. They plan to make their live debut at Brighton on the 20th of May, although their first London date may be put off until mid-summer.

THE SKIDS have signed with Virgin Records. They already have one single to their credit, the "Charles" EP on the No Bad record label, which was distributed by Virgin. The Dunfermline Scotland group has a growing following in the North. Since their Southern debut in March, they're developing a following as well in London. The Skids are guitarist Stuart Adamson, vocalist Richard Jobson, drummer Tom Kellichan and bassist Willie Simpson.

LIVE TONIGHT!

WIRE ....Liverpool, Eric's	SOFT BOYS ....London, Hope & Anchor
JOHNNY MOPED/DRUG ADDIX......London, The Marquee	WAYNE COUNTY &
CHELSEA ....London, The Speakeasy	THE ELECTRIC CHAIRS ....London, Rochester Castle

8th - Monday..........................

THE NOSEBLEEDS with Steven Morrissey as lead vocalist, play their second (and final) live date before splitting up. Morrissey has written several songs for the band, among them "I Get Nervous," "(I Think) I'm Ready For The Electric Chair," "The Living Jukebox" and "Peppermint Heaven." The surprise of the evening was the Nosebleeds version of the '60s Shangri-La's cover "Give Him A Great Big Kiss." Morrissey didn't change the gender of the song (scandal!) and handed out candies to the audience while singing it. The *NME's* Paul Morley wrote this about the new version of the band, "The Nosebleeds re-surface boasting A Front Man With Charisma, always an advantage. Lead singer is now minor local legend Steve Morrison (sic) who, in his own way, is at least aware that rock'n'roll is about magic and inspiration. So the Nosebleeds are now a more obvious rock'n'roll group than they've ever been. Only their name can prevent them being this year's surprise."

THE PARIS VALENTINOS are responsible for a bedroom full of youthful sounds coming from Manchester. The roots of this group of kids are in guitar heros like the Allman Brothers, Thin Lizzy and Rory Gallagher. Their line-up now is Kevin Williams on bass and vocals, Bobby Durkin on drums, Andy Rourke on rhythm guitar and Johnny Maher on lead guitar. They are all about fifteen so they can't play in pubs yet, but they get to play at the regular 5:30 Sunday "folk" Mass at Sacred Heart Catholic. In 1982, Johnny Maher, as "Johnny Marr," along with Andy Rourke will start a new Manchester group called the Smiths.

WILD BILL CHILDISH &	PERE UBU/NICO/
THE POP RIVITS...................Chatham, Tam 'O Shanter	PATRIK FITZGERALD ....London, The Marquee
SLAUGHTER & THE DOGS/	THE TOURISTS/
JOHNNY MOPED ....Liverpool, Eric's	BETTER LOOKING ....London, The Nashville
	MAGAZINE/NOSEBLEEDS ....Manchester, The Ritz

10th - Wednesday.........................

THE STRANGLERS continue to wage war with the Greater London Council over their concerts. It seems unlikely now they'll be granted permission to play at their open air rock concert at Queens Park on June 10th. The Stranglers have been thwarted twice by the GLC in their attempts to stage two consecutive concert dates at the Alexandra Palace in North London. The GLC, long in their dislike of anything vaguely threatening to the status quo, have also given the Roundhouse trouble over soundproofing and a weekday live music permit. This forced cancellation of many concerts planned for this summer including dates by the Buzzcocks. The mountains of red tape thrown in the path of promoters is forcing many to stage their events just outside of the London area.

RUDI give pause to all those who thought that Stiff Little Fingers were all that Belfast had to offer. They're a four-piece Belfast combo that have just released their debut single, "Big Time" flipped with "Number One." The group is built around guitar and vocalists Ronnie Matthews and Brian Young. Gordon Blair on bass and Graham Marshall on drums provide the backbeat. The single is out on a new indie Belfast label called Good Vibrations Records. They hope to put out singles by the more promising Belfast bands such as Victim, The Outcasts, Idiots and The Flying Squad.

CHELSEA/BRIMSTONE/	VIBRATORS...........................Birmingham, Barbarella's
PATRIK FITZGERALD ....London, The Music Machine	THOSE NAUGHTY LUMPS ....Manchester, Pip's

11th - Thursday..........................

FAST BREEDER & NUCLEAR REACTORS are described as a "secret enclave of past & future stars." Their Anti-Nuke song "Nuclear Waste" is released today on Charley Records. Minor investigation reveal that the Radio Actors have Sting of the Police on vocals, Steve Broughton (ex-Roy Harper, Mike Oldfield) on drums, Nik Turner (of Hawkwind) on sax, Mike Howlett (of Gong) on drums, as well as Gilli Smyth, Harry Williamson and the enigmatic "Steve." According to Sting, the group tried to get Johnny Rotten in to sing the song, but he wouldn't have anything to do with old hippies, so Sting stepped in.

THE RESIDENTS re-release their single "Satisfaction" and "Loser (is congruent to) Weed." It originally came out in 1976 and is one of

MAY 1978

Ralph Records rarest pressings. This pressing is on yellow vinyl and has a printed sleeve, unlike the black vinyl-silk screened sleeve on the 1976 limited issue. Considering that Devo are currently making noise with an unusual remake of this same track, it's interesting that another band can have available an even stranger version of this Rolling Stone's classic.

SHAM 69	Birmingham, The Mayfair		WAYNE COUNTY &	
IAN DURY/WHIRLWIND/RICO	Birmingham, The Odeon		THE ELECTRIC CHAIRS	High Wycombe, Nag's Head
U2/VIPERS	Dublin, McGonagles (residency)		BAD MANNERS	London, The Broom

12th - Friday...

THE STRANGLERS' new album, their third, is out in the UK. It's called "Black & White" and was produced by Martin Rushent. Several of the tracks on the album, such as "Tank," "Death And Night And Blood," "Hey" and "Nice & Sleazy," were tried out live at a series of secret gigs they played earlier in the year. The first 75,000 copies of the LP include a free single of the Bacharach-David tune "Walk On By" flipped with "Mean To Me" and a live recording of a band introduction cum solo-piece called "Tits." A terse message on the black label of this white vinyl effort reads in part, "This record has been given free. If it is offered for sale by a shop, write with details and they will be dealt with."

JOHN COOPER CLARKE/		SLAUGHTER & THE DOGS/	
JILTED JOHN/GYRO/		BLEACH BOYS	London, The Nashville
NOSEBLEEDS	Liverpool, Eric's	SHAM 69/PATRIK FITZGERALD/	
JOHNNY MOPED /THE VIOLINS	London, Dalston Cubies	GIRLSCHOOL	London, Harlesden Roxy Theatre
CHELSEA	London, Hollies	LEYTON BUZZARDS	London, The Red Lion
YACHTS	London, Hope & Anchor	VIBRATORS	Manchester, Rafters

13th - Saturday..

PLASTIC BERTRAND Belgian pop singer-comic Plastic Bertrand, has his single of "Ca Plane Pour Moi" enter the UK charts at #58. The single has been a great success on the continent and is catching on quick in England, too. It attracts the ear in that it is sung almost entirely in what appears to be French and is said to be a "punque smash internationale." The lyrics are generally (so the press has been told) made up of French slang, so literal translation comes out a bit odd. According to a Vogue Records press release the first verse runs something like this...."Allez Oop, my bird has thrown up, Is knocked out, in fact the whole place is a mess. The settee, the bar, leaving me here alone like a big nerd. Ohhhh Ohhhhh Ohhhhh Ohhhh. My foot on a plate." The actual title, unlike the BBC interpretation is not "That's alright by me" but rather "I'm high because of it all." Actually, Plastic Bertrand doesn't care what you make of the record, "If you are naive, the effect will be naive. If you are perverse the effect will be perverse and if you are clever the effect will be clever." (Deep stuff!)

JOHN COOPER CLARKE/		IAN DURY/	
PASSAGE/		WHIRLWIND/RICO	London, The Hammersmith Odeon
PATRIK FITZGERALD	London, Goldsmith's College	TOURISTS	London, Hope & Anchor

16th - Tuesday...

THE NIPPLE ERECTORS are the band fronted by Shane MacGowan. He has been a prominent face in the crowd at punk gigs since '76 and was apparently not content with staying in the audience. His group has been playing around the London circuit for some months and now they have a vinyl legacy. The debut single is "King Of The Bop" and "Nervous Wreck." It's available on the Soho Records label. Officially speaking, The Nipple Erectors are Shane O'Holligan (aka Shane McGowan) on vocals, Shanne Bradley on bass, Roger Towndrow on guitar and Jerry Arcane on drums.

THE ONLY ONES' debut album is released by CBS this week. It includes their latest single "Another Girl, Another Planet," as well as new songs such as "City Of Fun," "Creature Of Doom," "No Peace For The Wicked," "The Whole Of The Law" and "The Immortal Story." Curiously enough the LP declines to include their debut hit single, "Lovers Of Today." All of the songs were composed by vocalist Peter Perrett, with the band producing the LP themselves.

THE SIMPLE MINDS have emerged from the rubble after the split up of Johnny & The Self Abusers. The group is three ex-Abusers, Jim Kerr on vocals, Charlie Burchill on guitar and violin and Brian McGee on drums. The others are Mick MacNeil on keyboards, Duncan Barnwell on guitar and Derek Forbes on bass. They're working on demos now and a have six songs recorded, "Pleasantly Disturbed," "Act Of Love," "The Cocteau Twins," "Wasteland," "Chelsea Girl" and "Did You Ever." They're ready to start making the rounds of labels to look for a deal. They're working now with Bruces' Record Stores owner Bruce Findley, who is helping to arrange gigs, drive them around and will eventually help them put out a record.

ADVERTS	Birmingham, Barbarella's	SORE THROAT/DYAKS	London, Nashville
NEW HEARTS	London, Dingwalls	UK SUBS/RAPED	London, White Lion
CHERRY VANILLA/MEMBERS	London, The Marquee		

19th - Friday...

THE BUZZCOCKS' concert at St. George's Hall in Bradford tonight is marred by violence. Penetration opened the show and everything went normally. When the Buzzcocks went onstage, a lone National Front supporter started some incessant slogan chanting just in front of the stage that annoyed people down around him. Though asked to stop, he kept on shouting. Infuriated, a crowd set upon him in an attempt to shut him up, the NF supporter's friends materialized and a small battle ensued in which somebody was stabbed. The local

MAY 1978

constables arrived, shut the PA down and tried to find the culprit and the victim. Neither could be located. Meanwhile the interrupted gig continued even though the sound system had been shut off. Pete Shelley found a megaphone to sing through while the Buzzcocks played only through the power of their stage equipment. To help along, the audience sang along to near instrumental versions of the Buzzcocks better known songs.

THE LURKERS have their new single "Ain't Got A Clue" released today on Beggars Banquet Records. It's paired with "Ooh Ooh I Love You." If you buy it early, you get a free record included with the single. It's a gold flexi disc called "Fulham Fallout Forty Free." It's about five minutes of an unedited tape of the Lurkers in the recording studio rehearsing and finally recording a song that one can guess is called "The Chaos Brothers." Their first album should be out by the first week of June.

THE ANGELIC UPSTARTS have their debut single released on their own independent label. 1,000 copies of "The Murder Of Liddle Towers" hit the shops today. The subject matter is the "justifiable homicide" of gay Liddle Towers after he was arrested and "helped to the ground" by the local boys in blue. This searing record does in punk form what Tom Robinson has been doing in pop for ages. The Angelic Upstarts are Mensi on vocals, Mond on guitar, Sticks (predictably enough) on drums and Steve on bass. They all hail from Newcastle.

THE DURITTI COLUMN are a new Manchester band that are managed by Tony Wilson (of TV's *So It Goes*). Tonight they make their live debut at the Factory Club in Manchester. Several members of this new band come from the now defunct group Fast Breeder. The five-piece combo is made up of Tony Bowers on bass (formerly of the Albertos), Dave Rowbotham on rhythm and bass, Chris Joyce on drums, (ex-Nosebleed) Vini Reilly on guitar and keyboards and Phil Raynham on vocals. "The Factory" is a special Friday night affair that Tony Wilson has started at the Russell club. There are four "events" planned for the next four weeks.

THE PASSIONS	Birmingham, The Crown	IAN DURY/	
FLAMING GROOVIES/		WHIRLWIND/RICO	London, Lewisham Odeon
RADIO BIRDMAN	Edinburgh, Tiffany's	THIS HEAT	London, The Broom
SHAM 69	Edinburgh, The Clouds	MICH ABRAHAMS/LURKERS	Manchester, Pip's
LURKERS	Liverpool, Eric's	JILTED JOHN/	
PINK PARTS/RAINCOATS	London, Chelsea College	DURUTTI COLUMN	Manchester, The Factory

LIVE TONIGHT!

21st - Sunday...

JOHN LYDON helps the *NME* scoop the world on the secret identities of the Lydon's new bandmates. John Lydon (aka Johnny Rotten) is unable to use his stage name because Malcolm McLaren has claimed that he owns it. Until it's straightened out in court, Rotten returns to his given name, Lydon. The new quartet is built around Johnny, longtime friend and bassist Jah Wobble "the Ride Man" (aka John Wardle), guitarist Keith Levine and drummer Keith Walker. Still no name has been made public for the band although they did flirt with the name "The Carnivorous Butterflies." They have been working on some original material though, with titles like "Religion" (formerly titled "Sod In Heaven"), "Public Image" and toying with tracks like "My Generation" and "EMI." Jah Wobble has been active on the London scene for a few years and has known Lydon since their school days at the Kingsway College of Further Education some five years ago. Keith Levine was a member of the Clash in their earliest days and since leaving the group has been found mixing sound at Slits gigs. Drummer Keith Walker is a Canadian who only recently immigrated from Vancouver to the UK, leaving his previous band, The Furys, behind.

ESSENTIAL LOGIC is the group put together by former X-Ray Spex saxophonist Lora Logic (aka Susan Whitby). She had left the Spex because touring and school didn't mix, as well as a growing coolness between her and Poly when Lora started showing that she could write songs as well as play. Now that school's out, so is her single of "World Friction" and "Aerosol Burns." It's on Cells Records and distributed by Rough Trade. The backing band are Stuart on guitar, Tim on bass, Rich on drums and Lora on sax and vocals. It's not a proper group, just four friends and the result of a few rehearsals.

THOSE NAUGHTY LUMPS	Liverpool, The Havana Club	JOHNNY MOPED/	
SOFT BOYS	London, The Marquee	NIPPLE ERECTORS	London, The Music Machine
PATRIK FITZGERALD	London, Rochester Castle	MISTY/THE RUTS	London, The Albany Empire

23rd - Tuesday...

THE PURPLE HEARTS are young, impressionable and they're grizzled veterans of the mode scene for almost a year. They got together back in June of '77 and called themselves Robbie Hatchet and the Sockets. Their first big break was getting to open for the Buzzcocks. They played only a few other times and broke up last January. Now's they've updated their name and their image. They've taken the '60s slang term for a Mod drug, Purple Hearts, as their new name. The group is Bob Manton, Simon Stebbing, Jeff Shadbolt and Gary Sparks.

PENETRATION have their second single released today. It's a pair of originals titled "Firing Squad" and "Neverr." This is the band first recording since the addition of Neale Floyd on guitar. He's a long time fan and follower of Penetration. He replaces former lead guitarist Gary Chaplin. This is Neale's first band and even though he didn't enjoy being gobbed on the first time out he said, "It's something you just have to get used to." What a trooper.

FLAMING GROOVIES/		CHELSEA	London, Marquee
RADIO BIRDMAN	Birmingham, Barbarella's		

25th - Thursday...

SQUEEZE have their second A&M single out this week. It's "Bang Bang" coupled with "All Fed Up." The "A" side is from their debut LP, but the flip is unique to the single. There's more. A special limited number of the first pressing on clear green vinyl with a body builder photo sleeve.

MAY 1978

U2 are opening for The Gamblers tonight at the Project in Dublin and have an influential person eyeing them from the back. Paul McGuinness has been tipped-off to check out U2. He's impressed with the band, although they are less experienced than any band he would normally consider managing. McGuinness takes them next door to the Granary pub to talk tuff about the music business with them. He went with his guts and told the band that he'd manage them. He also wanted to get them into the studio as soon as possible to cut some demos. U2 are part of a social group that refer to

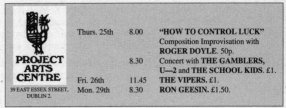

PROJECT ARTS CENTRE			
39 EAST ESSEX STREET, DUBLIN 2.			
Thurs. 25th	8.00		"HOW TO CONTROL LUCK" Composition Improvisation with ROGER DOYLE. 50p.
	8.30		Concert with THE GAMBLERS, U—2 and THE SCHOOL KIDS. £1.
Fri. 26th	11.45		THE VIPERS. £1.
Mon. 29th	8.30		RON GEESIN. £1.50.

themselves as "Lypton Village." It a collection of artistic students who see the systems around themselves as backward. They're inventing their own systems. They've even re-named themselves. There are two brothers Guggi and Strongman (Derek and Trevor Rowen), Bono Vox (Paul Hewson), Reggie Manuel, Gavin Friday (Fionan Hanvey), Pod (Anthony Murphy), Dave-id (David) and Niggles Watson.

GAMBLERS/U2/		JOHNNY MOPED/THE HITS/	
SCHOOL BOYS	Dublin, The Project Arts Centre	THE NIPPLE ERECTORS	London, Music Machine
THOSE NAUGHTY LUMPS	Liverpool, Havana Club	UK SUBS	London, Rochester Castle
SOFT BOYS	London, Marquee		

26th - Friday...

THE MEMBERS are a Camberly quintet who have just had their single of "Solitary Confinement" released on the One Off label by Stiff Records. It's a springboard device for upcoming bands Stiff doesn't want to sign right away. It's flipped with "Rat Up A Drainpipe." The "A" side deals with the boredom of a youth with no girl, nothing to do and no money to spend. The Members are Nicky Tesco on vocals, Jean-Marie Carroll on guitar, Chris Payne on bass, Adrian Lillywhite on drums an lead guitarist Nigel Bennett. Lasting fame will always elude the band, but they will have one brief shining moment in the sun when their song "Sounds Of The Suburbs" becomes a hit in 1979.

SOFT BOYS have their second 45 "(I Want To Be An) Anglepoise Lamp" released by Radar Records. It's backed with "Fat Man's Son," both Robyn Hitchcock compositions. The Cambridge based group is lead singer Robyn Hitchcock, along with Andy Metcalfe, Morris Windsor, Jim Melton and Kimberley Rew. Hitchcock has been in bands for many years.

THE YACHTS	Birmingham, Barbarella's	ATV/PATRIK FITZGERALD	Liverpool, Eric's
BUZZCOCKS/		CHELSEA	London, Rochester Castle
PENETRATION	Birmingham, The Mayfair	SOFT BOYS/SOLID WASTE	London, The Nashville
STRANGLERS	Glasgow, The Apollo	JACKIE LYNTON/MEMBERS	London, The Music Machine
SLAUGHTER & THE DOGS/		BIG IN JAPAN/	
BLITZKRIEG BOP	Glasgow, Queen Margaret Union	MANICURED NOISE	Manchester, The Factory

27th - Saturday...

KLARK KENT is supposed to be an enigma. The mystery record of the week is a 7" green vinyl, green sleeve, green label pressing of "Don't Care," "Office Girls" and "Thrills." Klark Kent's debut on Kryptonite. (Now wasn't Kent supposedly weakened by Kryptonite?) According to the press release, "Klark Kent first materialized in Llandyckkk, a Welsh fishing village where, despite only speaking in a New Orleans' patois, he became the church organist. It was the first in an increasingly bizarre sequence of events which was to culminate in New York at the height of his fame. His personal manners began to excite adverse attention following the unfortunate 'lasagna affair' when the beautiful eponymous triplets, stricken into sadness after he had rejected their sexual advances, threw themselves holding hands from the top floor of the Mobil Oil Building singing 'Ave Maria' before splashing themselves on to 42nd Street below." Kent, claiming he was the author of this traditional song, sued the grieving parents of the dead girls on the grounds that they had 'gained unwanted notoriety' for a song which he had written in some previous life and which, as he put it, 'belongs to posterity and not to me.' Some weeks later the *Daily News* ran a front page picture of Klark Kent urinating on the graves of the sisters, thus signaling an abrupt end to his short-lived popularity." End press release. Or this could all be a hoax.

THE CURE are in Chestnut, a small eight track studio in West Essex recording demos. They're being financed by Lockjaw bassist Simon Gallup's brother Rick. The total cost is less than £50 and they manage to knock out four songs. They are "Boys Don't Cry," "10:15 Saturday Night," "It's Not You" and "Fire In Cairo." These demos and the new photos of the band as a trio are to be sent out to all the major record companies immediately.

XTC	Birmingham, Barbarella's	HI FI/EATER	London, The Marquee
SOFT BOYS	High Wycombe, The Nag's Head	TOURISTS	London, Hope & Anchor
999/BIG IN JAPAN	Liverpool, Eric's	YACHTS/BLITZ	London, The Nashville

June 2nd - Friday...

JOHNNY ROTTEN or **JOHNNY RUBBISH?** The Virgin press office has announced that the Sex Pistols will continue without Johnny Rotten. Manager Malcolm McLaren said that the other three members, Cook, Jones and Vicious will continue and are auditioning for a new vocalist. McLaren hints that the new Pistols' single will feature Ronald Biggs with Cook and Jones, in his own version of "God Save The Queen." The flipside is supposedly Sid singing "My Way" with a full orchestra backing. Both songs are said to be from the soundtrack of the forthcoming Sex Pistols movie, recorded while Cook & Jones were in Rio. McLaren's objectives in keeping the Sex Pistols going is clear in his statement to the *NME*, "What most people don't realize is that the whole thing is about getting as much money as possible, in as short of time as possible and with as much style as possible."

JUNE 1978

On the Sex Pistols exploitation trail, Johnny Rubbish comes forward with a parody of "Anarchy In The UK" titled "Living In NW3 4JR." It's lots of fun, albeit eighteen months late. The single's backing track sounds identical to the Sex Pistols' record. The vocals are different though. Delivered in a surly Johnny Rotten style, this Johnny sings "I am a capitalist, I am a profiteer. I know what I want, Malcolm knows how to get it. I wanna be rich, make money. Cos I wanna live in NW3."

STIFF LITTLE FINGERS have been supposedly been signed to Island Records for a reported £30,000. Their first single is slated to be "1978" b/w "Alternative Ulster." The group are planning now to immediately move to London and start recording.

O LEVEL "East Sheen" is the name of the debut single from O Level. "East Sheen" is also a London suburb, presumably familiar territory to this combo. The single is on Psycho Records and is flipped with "Pseudo Punk." The members of this group also masquerade as the Television Personalities.

EATER have their new live EP released today. It's titled "Get Your Yo Yo's Out" (after the Rolling Stones live LP of a similar name). The songs were recorded at the band's performance on April 24 at Dingwalls in London. Tracks include "Debutantes Ball," "Holland," "No More Bedroom Fits" and "Thinking Of The USA." It's an unlimited pressing on white vinyl.

THE RICH KIDS' latest single is "Marching Men" flipped with a live recording of "Here Come The Nice." The first 20,000 copies will be in a special color sleeve. The flip is a cover of a Small Faces' song, a stage favorite of Matlock.

LIVE TONIGHT!

IAN DURY/		REACTION	London, Hollie's
WHIRLWIND/RICO	Glasgow, Apollo Centre	WHITE CATS	London, Hope & Anchor
PENETRATION/VICE CREAMS/		DURUTTI COLUMN/	
VENTICATORS/YONKERS	High Wycombe, Town Hall	CABARET VOLTAIRE	Manchester, The Factory
SHAM 69	Liverpool, Eric's	CORTINAS /BIG IN JAPAN/	
JOHN DOWIE	London, Battersea Arts Centre	DISTRACTIONS	Manchester, The Rafters
UK SUBS	London, Carshalton Park	XTC	Sheffield, The Top Rank

4th - Sunday...

JOY DIVISION release their debut EP on their own Enigma Records label, "An Ideal For Living." The debut EP has a special fold out, black & white cover. The disc contains four original Joy Division songs, "Warsaw," "No Love Lost," "Leaders Of Men" and "Failures." On the cover they state that, "…this is not a concept EP, it is an enigma. Joy Division is Bernard Albrecht on guitar, Ian Curtis on vocals, Stephen Morris on Drums and Peter Hook on bass. They have had numerous mentions in the press, most of them bleak reviews of their live dates going back to July 30th issue of last year's *New Musical Express*. In a review of last month's Stiff-Chiswick Challenge concert in Manchester, *NME's* Paul Morley described them as, "…a dry, doomy group who depend promisingly on the possibility of repetition, sudden stripping away, with deceptive dynamics, whilst they use sound in a more orthodox hard rock manner than either Fall or Magazine."

ROBERT & THE REMOULDS	Birmingham, Barbarella's
ONLY ONES/SOFT BOYS	Edinburgh, Tiffany's
BUZZCOCKS/PENETRATION	Glasgow, Apollo
THE MONOCHROME SET	London, The Rock Garden

7th - Wednesday..

SLAUGHTER & THE DOGS have split up. It's official. One of the first punk bands to emerge from Manchester, they have left several records and several pounds of talc powder in their wake. There is talk that the members of the two halves will start bands of their own.

CLOCK DVA are an electronic band from Sheffield that make the Human League seem positively tame. Clock DVA (pronounced "clock-de-vey") were recently interviewed by Chris Westwood of *Zig Zag* magazine. The band impress him as being, "…w-e-i-r-d, no two ways about it…they smacked of winkle pickers, dope, Clockwork Orange logos and waaay out theories about the mating of onstage punk aggression and precision electronics…there's distinct sex/perversion/gore fixations and Newton confesses to personal Iggy, Bowie, Warhol and Ballard fascinations…the actual sound brooding and rhythmic with (Adi) Newton's wavering, mournful vocals wiping every last trace of 'accessibility' clean off the board." Besides their music, it's revealed that they're working on a film called *Genitals and Genesis* which is constructed of (Throbbing Gristle's) Genesis P-Orrige and live footage from one of their gigs interspliced with taped of the Myra Hindley trial. "The film will include four sections, described simply as serial images, pornography, surrealism and esoteric." The line-up at this time is Adi Newton on vocals, violin and tapes, Jud (or Veet) on guitars and treatments, David Hammond on bass, treatments, tapes and Simon Mark Elliot-Kemp on synth and electronic percussion.

SHAM 69's Jimmy Pursey is adamant about what type of music they play. "We're not a New Wave band, we're not a Power Pop band - we're a PUNK BAND!"

LURKERS	Glasgow, Cinders	IAN DURY/	
		WHIRLWIND/RICO	Sheffield, City Hall

8th - Thursday...

THE TALKING HEADS' new single for the UK is "Pulled Up" and " Don't Worry About The Government." Unlike several of their previous singles, both sides of this release are also available on album, both tracks coming from "Talking Heads '77."

JUNE 1978

THROBBING GRISTLE are reportedly providing half the soundtrack to a new film, currently in production. "Millions Like Us" is written by Fred and Judy Vermorel, who have out a new Sex Pistols book. The unusual film is in two parts. The first half is "Concrete And Blood" and will be similar to a German documentary. It will detail the decline of the UK since 1945. Throbbing Gristle play the part of an "anti-rock" group called Millions. The second half is "Blue Skies Over England," and will be set off by a bland pop band called Susan And Her Feelings who will be played by a band being put together by Alex Fergusson of ATV.

BANNED	High Wycombe, Nag's Head	KILLJOYS	London, Hope & Anchor
TANZ DER YOUTH/		LEYTON BUZZARDS	London, Middletown Arms
COVENTRY AUTOMATICS	London, The Nashville	MONOS	London, Rochester Castle
SUBWAY SECT/		UK SUBS	London, N E Poly.
BLACK ARABS/REDS	London, Fulham Town Hall	THE ONLY ONES/JAB JAB	Manchester, Poly.

9th - Friday...

SIOUXSIE & THE BANSHEES can all breathe now. It took forever, but Siouxsie and the Banshees have finally been signed. Being one of the most popular bands live in the underground scene over the last year, it was unbelievable they hadn't been snapped up by one of the major labels when so many lesser bands had. In a few weeks they'll begin recording their debut 45 for Polydor at Pathway Studios in Highbury and then start work on a full LP. The contract is just about the best they could have wanted three albums over the next three years, with the band having full approval over artwork, production and marketing. The current line-up of the band has Siouxsie Sue on vocals, Steve Severin on bass, John McKay on guitar and Kenny Morris on drums.

PETE SHELLEY, lead singer of the Buzzcocks makes a one-off appearance at the Russell Club (The Factory) in Manchester with the backing of the Tiller Boys. This is part of a four week experimental series for Shelley using written and improvised songs, tape loops, electronic sounds and a drum machine. The Tiller Boys are Eric Random and Francis Cookson. The gig finds the band behind a pyramid shaped wall of chairs singing "Hey, Hey, We're The Tiller Boys." There's a sign posted on the wall of "Name That Tune."

THE BOOMTOWN RATS release their new single "Like Clockwork" today on Ensign Records. It's an advance track from the band's forthcoming album and is flipped with the non-LP "How Do You Do."

THE LURKERS have their first LP released today. First copies of "Fulham Fallout" include a free "gold record" flexi disc, the same flexi that accompanied their last single. The LP starts off with their latest single "Ain't Got A Clue," and strides through eleven Lurkers originals. Titles are "Total War," "Time Of Year," "I'm On Heat," "Be My Prisoner," and a re-recording of their debut song "Shadow." There's also a cover of the '50s rockabilly song "Go-Go-Go" and a humorously re-worked version of the Greenwich-Barry '60s song "Then I Kissed Her," which the Lurkers sing as "Then I Kicked Her." The quartet of Wall, Stride, Esso and Moore are joined by Pete Edwards on backing vocals and harmonica on the album.

MAGAZINE release the LP that's been speculated about for months. It's called "Real Life," and is their debut album for Virgin Records. The LP features a new version of "Shot By Both Sides" as well as live favorites like "Motorcade" and "The Light Pours Out of Me." Songs provoke thought with titles like "The Great Beautician In The Sky," "Recoil," "Definitive Gaze" and "My Tulpa." If you don't know what they're about, don't ask. Devoto won't tell you. If you can't figure it out, that's tough. The band is Howard Devoto on vocals, Barry Adamson on bass, Dave Formula on keyboards, Martin Jackson on percussion and John McGeoch on guitar and sax. The effort was recorded at EMI's Abbey Road studios with John Leckie producing.

THE VIBRATORS reach a rare pinnacle of success today with the release of their seventh single. Tracks are "Judy Says (Knock You In The Head)" and "Pure Mania."

VALVES/SKIDS/MONOS	Edinburgh, Art College	NEW HEARTS	London, Cubies
THE REZILLOS/MEKONS	London, The Marquee	SOFT BOYS	Manchester, Rafters
LEYTON BUZZARDS	London, N.E.Poly.	PETE SHELLEY & THE TILLER BOYS/	
POISON GIRLS	London, N. London Poly.	JOY DIVISION	Manchester, Russell Club (Factory)

11th - Sunday...

THE LINES are further proof that there is no end to new bands starting new labels and selling their wares through Rough Trade, Small Wonder or Bruce's record shops. The latest entry is London-based quartet, The Lines. They're fronted by Richard Conning on vocals and guitar, along with Joe Forty, Phillips and Harker. Their debut single is on their own Liner Records and pairs two original tracks, "White Night" and "Barbican."

U2 bassist Adam Clayton engages in a little bit of subterfuge. He trades his pair of tickets to see hometown heros The Boomtown Rats, for a secret phone number which leads him to Gerry Cott, the lead guitarist from the Rats. They're the newest Irish rock stars (a rare commodity) and Adam wants some advice how to further U2's career. He gets Cott on the phone and does get a little advice, but the call itself does wonders for the band's morale.

BOOMTOWN RATS/VIPERS	Dublin, Olympia Theatre	JAM/THE JOLT/JAB JAB	London, The Lyceum
IAN DURY/WHIRLWIND/RICO	Liverpool, The Empire	ONLY ONES	London, Foxe's Greyhound
FLAMING GROOVIES/		SUBWAY SECT	Manchester, The Rafters
RADIO BIRDMAN	London, Roundhouse	ANY TROUBLE	Manchester, Spread Eagle

13th - Tuesday...

SLAUGHTER & THE DOGS have 12" worth of material available this week, just after the news of their split. Titled "Do It Dog Style," it's

JUNE 1978

their first-ever album and it's out on Decca Records. The songs include their last three "A" sides and a lot of filler. What they lack in originality they make up for in energy. Last years thing, today. The LP features some of the band's previous singles tracks like "Where Have All The Boot Boys Gone," "You're A Bore," "Dame To Blame" and "Quick Joey Small." There's also new recordings like "Victims Of The Vampire," "I'm Mad," and a cover of the New York Dolls' classic "Who Are The Mystery Girls."

THE DRUG ADDIX are a Surrey combo that definitely have a sense of humor. Their debut EP is just out on Chiswick Records in the UK and it's titled "Close Encounters of an Unsavory Kind…" The songs are reminiscent of the Albertos in their tongue in cheek look at punk/underground culture. Titles include "Gay Boys In Bondage," "The Addington Shuffle," "Special Clinic" and "Glutton For Punishment." The group are listed as Art Nouveau on guitar and vocals, Sterling Silver, Alan Offa on bass, Ron Griffin on drums and Mandy Doubt (aka Kirsty MacColl) on backing vocals.

SUBWAY SECT...................Birmingham, Barbarella's	BANNED/THE PANTIES..............London, Nashville
BOOMTOWN RATS/BLUE STEAM ...Belfast, Ulster Hall	BLACK SABBATH/
IGGY POP/MEMBERS ....London, Music Machine	TANZ DER YOUTH ....Manchester, The Apollo

14th - Wednesday...

THE ELECTRIC CHAIRS have their "Blatantly Offensive" EP released by Safari Records. In the adverts for the record it is described as "…crammed with the depraved parlance of the gutter, rancid with nauseous fantasies,…(it) will certainly want to make you puke." The "offensive" songs are "Mean Motherfucking Man," "Fuck Off," and the '60s dance classic "Night Time." The first million copies of the disc are said to be pressed on gold vinyl. The Electric Chairs are American transvestite Wayne County, with Val Haller, Elliot Michaels and J.J. Johnson. There are also some older bits on the record with ex-member Greg Van Cook on them.

IDIOTS/RUEFREX/	ROBERT GORDON & LINK WRAY ..London, Music Machine
DETONATORS/OUTCASTS/	KILLJOYS ....London, The Marquee
UNDERTONES/RUDI ....Belfast, McMordie Hall	VIC RUBB & VAPORS ....London, Windsor Castle
THE GERMS ....Liverpool, Masonic Hall	BLACK SABBATH/
LURKERS/SATELLITES ....London, Last Bastion	TANZ DER YOUTH ....Manchester, The Apollo

16th - Friday...

THE BOOMTOWN RATS' second LP "Tonic For The Troops" is released today. It's their most pop record yet and contains the band's last two singles, "Like Clockwork" and "She's So Modern." It also sports several new tracks that are proven live favorites and finally available on record. Among those are "Rat Trap" (possibly the next single), "Living On An Island," "Me And Howard Hughes," "Eva Braun" and a re-recorded version of last years "Mary Of The Fourth Form."

THE CLASH have a new single out today. It's "White Man In Hammersmith Palais" and "The Prisoner." It comes in a special pink or green bag with the band's name on it; halfway between a plain cover and special picture sleeve.

THE ELECTRIC CIRCUS had tapes deck rolling during their last weekend. Those two days of Manchester's newest and brightest is brought back to mind with today's release of "Short Circuit: Live at the Electric Circus" by Virgin. It's a curious 10" recorded document and a bittersweet tribute to a lost club. Recorded on October 1st and 2nd, the album captures hometown punk stars The Buzzcocks, poet John Cooper Clarke, up-and-coming bands such as The Drones and The Fall, reggae stars Steel Pulse and a still-forming band called Warsaw (although they have changed their name to Joy Division since that recording was made.)

THE UNDERTONES are in Wizard Studios in Belfast working on their debut single for Good Vibrations Records on a meagre budget of only £180. They were beginning to get a little disappointed with their lack of progress. They'd sent demos around to various labels and had received back rejection slips from Radar Records, Stiff and Chiswick. They had decided a while back that if they didn't get a record out by late in '78, they'd split up the band. So here they are, forestalling their demise by recording four songs for local release. On the tape deck are versions of "True Confessions," "Emergency Cases," Smarter Than U" and "Teenage Kicks."

THE JAM/THE JOLT .... Birmingham, Barbarella's	KILLJOYS ....London, Hope & Anchor
BLITZ/UK SUBS/XL 5/	CHELSEA/RAPED....................London, The Marquee
PLAGUE/RED LIGHT/	HERE & NOW/
OPEN SORE/JETS/	ALTERNATIVE TELEVISION.........London, Queen Elizabeth's College
ACME SEWAGE CO./TICKETS........Edinburgh, Clouds	WHITE CATS.........................London, Rochester Castle
BOOMTOWN RATS ....Liverpool, The Empire	VIC RUBB & THE VAPORS..........London, Western Counties
PASSIONS ....London, Hammersmith Town Hall	

17th - Saturday...

SIOUXSIE & THE BANSHEES enter Pathway Studios in Highbury to begin recording some demos for Polydor Records. They need to record several songs so that their album can be planned and a single picked. The three songs recorded today in a brief two-hour session are "Metal Postcard," "Switch" and "Staircase." For some reason that the band can't quite figure out, American soul producer Bruce Albertine has been flown in for the sessions.

JUNE 1978

PENETRATION	Liverpool, Eric's	ADAM & ANTS/	
SUBWAY SECT	London, Alexandra Palace	THE ENCHANTERS/CRISIS	London, South Bank Poly.
PATRIK FITZGERALD	London, Virgin Record Store	AMSTERDAM/SEVENTEEN	Rhyl, The Morville Hotel

22nd - Thursday...

U2 manager Paul McGuinness takes Adam Clayton to London to see the Irish double header at Wembly Arena. Thin Lizzy is topping the bill but Paul wants to go backstage to talk to Barry Devlin, the bass player for opening act, Horselips. Although Barry has never produced, he knows his way around the studio and accepts Paul's offer to record the young Irish band in the near future to work on some demos.

THE TEARDROP EXPLODES are a new bedroom band emerging in Liverpool. It's headed up by Julian Cope, who has previously experimented with bands like the Crucial Three, Mystery Girls and, most recently, the Nova Mob. The Teardrop Explodes take their unusual name from a panel in a DC comic book. Cope's favorite bands have all gotten their names from books; The Fall, Pere Ubu, Steely Dan, Soft Machine. In the group are Julian Cope, Gary Dwyer, Michael Finkler and ex-Dalek I member Dave Balfe. They're very into Capt Beefheart, funk and Motown, early psychedelics and The Doors. Their sound uses keyboards and soaring guitar lines. Presently, they're rehearsing below the office of Big In Japan member Bill Drummond.

BOOMTOWN RATS	Edinburgh, The Odeon	DICKIES/LEYTON BUZZARDS	London, The Rock Garden
MEMBERS	London, John Bull	KRYPTON TUNES	Sheffield, The Limit
MINK DEVILLE/RICH KIDS	London, Hammersmith Odeon		

23rd - Friday...

RIFF RAFF have been playing together as a bedroom band since '75. The five-piece group have a coarse, devil-may-care attitude about music. Back in the spring they moved from their home in London, to Peterborough's "Wobbling Heights," where they have become local celebrities by constantly playing. They even opened for the Stranglers, which convinced the locals that Riff Raff were a force to be reckoned with. Now, their "manager" has gotten them a deal with Chiswick Records. Their debut single is a four track, 7" EP with "(I Wanna Be A) Cosmonaut," "Romford Girls," "What's The Latest" and "Sweet As Pie." The songs are all the sole composition of lead singer Billy Bragg with the exception of Romford Girls, who also includes drummer Ron Handley's ideas. The rest of the group is Ruan O'Lochlainn on bass, S.D.R. Gol'fish on keyboards and Wiggy on guitar.

BILLY BRAGG
2nd guitar / vocals

THE DICKIES sound as if they are California's comic answer to NY's Ramones. They've just released their debut single, a version of Black Sabbath's classic "Paranoid" b/w "I'm OK, You're OK." Both uptempo romps are sure to raise a smile. They'll be supporting the new release with a tour of the UK. Initial copies are pressed on clear vinyl with a custom A&M label.

PATRIK FITZGERALD has a new single out today on Small Wonder Records. It's a four track EP called "Backstreet Boys" and features the title track as well as "Buy Me, Sell Me," "Little Dippers" and "Trendy."

WIRE has out their third single today. The song "Dot Dash" was written by Graham about an experience driving on a winding road through fog with about ten-foot visibility near Nottingham. It's flipped with "Options R." Both of the songs are new and can't be found on the band's LP "Pink Flag." Wire are taking a short break from their longest tour ever and in a few weeks will break new ground by playing in America at CBGB's.

BOOMTOWN RATS	Glasgow, Apollo Centre	OXY & THE MORONS/SMACK/	
LURKERS	Liverpool, Eric's	ELIGIBLE BACHELORS	London, Chat's Place
ANGLETRAX/PRAG VEC/		MEMBERS	London, The Red Cow
REALITY/THE RAINCOATS	London, Acklam Hall	POLICE	London, Rochester Castle
DICKIES	London, Hope & Anchor	RICH KIDS	London, Dingwalls (5th Anniv.)
KILLJOYS	London, The Marquee	JOHNNY MOPED/TONTRIX	Manchester, The Rafters
THIS HEAT	London, College Of Printing	PENETRATION/SUBWAY SECT	Sheffield, The Limit

25th - Sunday...

THE VIBRATORS were making headlines in all the music newspapers last week. Now comes the news that the announcement of their demise was a bit premature. They are continuing with a different line-up. Founder members John "Eddie" Edwards and Ian "Knox" Carnochran are busy finding new members for the long running band. Bassist Gary Tibbs has left to play with Roxy Music and Birch and Snow are out of the lineup with their replacements still unnamed.

LEYTON BUZZARDS	London, Hollies	VIC RUBB & VAPORS	London, Western Counties
BANNED/STARJETS	London, The Marquee	FALL/SPHERICAL OBJECTS	Manchester, Band On The Wall

27th - Tuesday...

CABARET VOLTAIRE's gig last night at Sheffield University was reviewed for *NME* by Andy Gill. The group started out with "Photophobia," a new song that featured a forbidding monologue with Kirk's squeaking clarinet in the background. Then into "Talkover," and a pair of songs about drugs, "Heaven And Hell" and "Capsules." Next up was the old favorite "Do The Mussolini (Headkick)" and "Oh Roger." Closing the unusual show were "The Set Up," and a cover of the 1966 Seeds' psychedelic track "No Escape." Gill closes his review

JUNE 1978

with, "I firmly believe that Cabaret Voltaire could well turn out to be one of the most important new bands to achieve wider recognition this year. Wait and see." The opening group for the show was, "...another drummerless trio (that makes four in at the last count in Sheffield alone)." They're called They Must Be Russians and are halfway between garage rock and the Cabs themselves. They do very unusual things to covers of "Louie Louie," "Waiting For My Man," and the Buzzcocks' "Boredom."

THE CURE receive letters rejecting their demo of original music from Island and Phonogram Records.

LIVE TONIGHT!

PENETRATION	Birmingham, Barbarella's	MENACE	London, White Lion
BOOMTOWN RATS	Birmingham, The Odeon	NEW HEARTS	London, Marquee
SKIDS	High Wycombe, Nag's Head	LIGHTNING RAIDERS/	
ROBERT & THE REMOULDS	London, The City Arms	MONOCHROME SET	London, Moonlight Club
TOYAH	London, Duke Of Lancaster		

28th - Wednesday..............

THE SPECIALS play tonight at Friar's in Aylesbury and change their name just hours before the show. They started as The Coventry Automatics and had been playing since mid-1977. Lately there has been another pop group making the rounds called The Automatics. The confusion was just too much. Just hours before their opening for the Clash, they announce that from now on they're to be called "The Specials AKA." The group is a five member, multi-racial punk-reggae group. They are more true to form in their reggae than The Clash and perhaps fall into the Ska style more comfortably than any reggae tag. These guys are definitely not Steel Pulse. They were formed around the core of Jerry Dammers (Gerald Dankin) on keyboards, Sir Horace Gentleman on bass (Horace Panter), Lynval Golding on guitar and Neville Staples on vocals. Recent additions to the group are vocalist Terry Hall, drummer Silverton and guitarist Roddy Radiation (Rod Byers.) Titles played tonight include "It's Up To You," "Dawning Of A New Era," "Wake Up," "Concrete Jungle," and the old ska standard "Liquidator." The Clash delivered as expected and the 1,800 fans that came to churn to the searing sounds were not disappointed.

FRIARS AT THE MAXWELL HALL
AYLESBURY
THE LAST OUTPOST
Wednesday June 28th at 7.30 pm
OUT ON PAROLE
THE CLASH
+ THE AUTOMATICS
Unfortunately no tickets will be available at door on night. Completely sold out.
Uncomplicated Complete Control Blue Beat Country Punk Good Timers
(evening dress optional)

THE CLASH/THE SPECIALS	Aylesbury, The Friars	MEMBERS	London, Red Cow
TUBEWAY ARMY/SKIDS	London, The White Hart	KRYPTON TUNES	London, Rochester Castle
DOCTORS OF MADNESS/WIRE	London, Lyceum	VIC RUBB & VAPORS	London, Windsor Castle

30th - Friday.................................

THE SEX PISTOLS' latest single is "No One Is Innocent" (aka "The Biggest Blow (A Punk Prayer by Ronnie Biggs)") and the supper club classic "My Way" by Sid Vicious. The "A" side had the basic tracks recorded in a studio in Rio, then was overdubbed in London's Wessex studios. The single has gone through at least half a dozen name changes in the past few weeks, one which actually threatened its release. By way of explaining, Ronnie Biggs was involved in "the great train robbery". His part was to knock out the driver of the train, which he did a little too efficiently. The driver has subsequently died. Biggs escaped justice and is now a fugitive in Brazil. The single was at one time titled "Cosh The Driver." This title raised problems with workers at the CBS Record Plant who are pressing the effort. Since then it's been renamed several times. Sources in McLaren's company hint that on the song "My Way," the basic tracks were laid down by Paul and Steve (on both bass and guitar) with Sid cutting the vocal portion while filming in Paris. There reportedly has been no contact between Sid and the others for quite a while. In Roy Carr's review of the single in *NME* he notes, "Just a passing thought, but the last person to record 'My Way' died soon after."

THE BUZZCOCKS' new single is out today. It's "Love You More" b/w "Noise Annoys." Timing in at 1:45, it is stated to be the second shortest single ever to be released in the UK. In response to the Buzzcock's claim, the Swell Maps claim first place with their January '78 release of "Read About Seymor" that clocks in at 1:27, only one second shorter than the 1961 Maurice Williams hit "Stay" at 1:28.

WIRE	Liverpool, Erics	WHITE CATS	London, Pegasus
PENETRATION/		TOYAH	London, Chelsea Wheatsheaf
JOHN COOPER CLARKE		POP GROUP/THIS HEAT	London, Collegiate Theatre
REINFORCEMENT/		BOOMTOWN RATS	Manchester, The Apollo
MONOCHROME SET	London, Royal College Of Art	CLASH/CHELSEA/	
LEYTON BUZZARDS	London, Hollies	SPECIALS	Sheffield, The Top Rank

July 2nd - Sunday.............................

MAGAZINE were forced to cancel the opening date of their UK tour, not because of a split, not because of police problems, but because they were locked out of the club. The road crew arrived at Barbarella's at 2pm to set up their gear and were unable to get in until moments before the club actually opened. With a perfectionist like Devoto running things, he simply couldn't preform without a proper sound check. Apologies are being made to the fans and the band will attempt to reschedule the gig towards the end of the tour.

REACTION follow up their appearance on the "Streets" LP with a single of "I Can't Resist" b/w "I Am A Case." The songs are quite reminiscent of some earlier records by the Hollies and the Who. Retrogressive pop. The Reaction has been playing live in London at the Rock Garden, Hollies and even as far afield as the Band On The Wall in Manchester. The group are Mark Hollis on vocals and guitar, George Page on guitar, Gino P. Williams on drums and Bruce Douglas on bass. This will be the band's only single, with the group splitting up next year. In '82 Mark Hollis will get together Talk Talk and begin a long string of hit singles and albums that will extend over the next decade. Tracks like "Life's What You Make It" and "It's My Life" will redefine the softer side of alternative pop.

WIRE/DOCTORS OF MADNESS	London, Lyceum	SOFT BOYS	London, Nashville

JULY 1978

U2/THE VIPORS/SCHOOL KIDS/	SKIDS .... London, Rochester Castle
BPY SCOUTZ/VELVET VALUES/	THE CLASH/SUICIDE .... Manchester, The Apollo
ROCKY de la VERA .... Dublin, Blackrock Park	

6th - Thursday...

DEVO release their third and final single for Stiff Records in the UK. It's titled "Be Stiff" and was not written for Stiff Records. It was in the Devo set list long before they ever heard of Stiff. It was however, one of the things that brought Devo to the attention of the UK indie.

THE LEYTON BUZZARDS take their name from the London neighborhood Leyton Buzzard. They're now immortalized on styrene with their debut disc for Small Wonder Records. It's "19 And Mad," b/w "Villain" and "Youthanasia." The Leyton Buzzards are David Jaymes on bass, Kevin Steptoe on drums, Vernon Austin on lead guitar and Geoff Deane out front with vocals.

WHITE CATS/ROBINS .... High Wycombe, Nag's Head	THE HEATWAVES/SKIDS .... London, The Nashville
ZORKIES/DALEK I .... Liverpool, Eric's	DRONES .... London, The Red Cow
BLAST FURNACE &	THROBBING GRISTLE .... London, Film-Makers Co-Op
THE HEATWAVES/SKIDS .... London, The Nashville	PATRIK FITZGERALD .... Manchester, The Rafters

10th - Monday...

SHAM 69 were to fly to the USA for a few dates in New York City and a gig in Philadelphia, however, immigration authorities have refused an entry visa for lead singer Jimmy Pursey. He's had a criminal offense in the last twelve months and that's grounds for refusal. Remember? Pursey was charged with causing a disturbance and resisting arrest last September when they played on the rooftop of the Vortex.

ADAM & THE ANTS are invited back for another BBC Radio 1 John Peel session. Tonight's session features four new songs including "Zerox," "Friends," "You're So Physical" and "Cleopatra."

IGNATZ/DICKIES .... Edinburgh, Tiffany's	MENACE/NOBODYZ .... London, Moonlight Club
DEAD TROUT .... Liverpool, The Moonstone	UK SUBS/SIREN .... London, The Rock Garden

11th - Tuesday...

THE TOURISTS' gig at the Marquee is caught by *NME's* Mark Ellen. They are singer/keyboardist/flautist Annie Lennox at the fore on vocals, Jim "Do It" Toomey on drums, Dave Stewart on guitar, Eddie Chin on bass and Peet Coomes on guitar and backing vocals. The core of the group have been playing in bands with diverse pasts like The Catch and Longdancer and it's reflected in the various styles the band can take on with apparent ease. Reviewing the show for *NME*, Mark Ellen writes, "It doesn't take long to realize that The Tourists can handle just about any style with consummate ease. 'Ain't No Room' is straight reggae, with Annie Lennox on flute and 'Exclusive' eases into a full Caribbean - swing version of 'Islands In The Sun'...rarely have I seen an audience react so fast...they're one of the most refreshing and entertaining (bands) that I've seen in a long time. If I was an A&R man, I'd be camping on their doorstep and stuffing banknotes through the letterbox."

WHITE CATS .... London, Dingwalls	PATRIK FITZGERALD/
TOURISTS .... London, The Marquee	GLORIA MUNDI .... London, Music Machine

12th - Wednesday...

PLASTIC BERTRAND (is this guy for real?) has a full album out now in the UK. It contains his previous single of "Pogo Pogo" as well as his top ten UK hit "Ca Plan Pour Moi." The rest of the LP (all in French) covers Small Faces songs "Sha La La La La Le," to some childish songs, sillier than any Jonathan Richman tune. What is it? C'est punque? C'est rocque? C'est boogie-woogie? C'est Plastic!

THE CLASH/SUICIDE .... Birmingham, Top Rank The Apollo	DICKIES .... London, Hope & Anchor
GRAHAM PARKER/	TALKING HEADS/MERGER .... London, Lyceum
BIG IN JAPAN .... Birmingham, Barbarella's	REZILLOS .... London, Nashville
THOSE NAUGHTY LUMPS .... Liverpool, Masonic Hall	WHITE CATS .... London, Music Machine

13th - Thursday...

X-RAY SPEX are back on the road again. There had been some problems in the last few weeks with lead singer Poly Styrene collapsing in rehearsals from exhaustion. Dates were cancelled and schedules re-arranged. Now she's back with all of her strength and EMI is releasing their new single "Identity." The song is about people's confused idea of who they are as reflected by what they wear. It's paired with "Let's Submerge" and a limited quantity of the first pressing will include a picture sleeve and be pressed on pink vinyl. X-Ray Spex are also about to finish their debut album which should be out by this fall.

PEOPLE UNITE! In the past we've seen record companies spring from record studios and even from independent record stores. Here's a new twist. People Unite is a "musicians collective" that's intended as a safe haven for bands that want an alternative to the major labels. Acting as a true cooperative, all bands will be treated as equals with the more popular bands aiding the lesser known ones. Already signed up are roots band Misty, The Ruts, The Enchanters and Milk. Singles and albums for all of these groups are said to be imminent.

ADAM & THE ANTS .... London, Marquee	REZILLOS/INVADERS .... London, The Nashville

JULY 1978

RAMBOW/THE RUTS ....London, Rock Garden
THOMPSON TWINS ....London, South Bank Poly.

TOYAH /THE RAINCOATS ....London, Young Vic Festival
LURKERS/DICKIES ....Sheffield, The Limit

14th - Friday...

SHAM 69 have their fourth single out today. It's the rousing, audience participation chant "If The Kids Are United," which also includes Dave Parsons on organ. It's rather loosely based on a Socialist Worker Party/North Bank Highbury chant. The track is said to be an advance from their debut LP, soon to be released on Polydor. It's flipped with a new song called "Sunday Morning Nightmare."

THE LURKERS have yet another new single out. This time around it's "Pills" and "I Don't Need To Tell Her." Neither track is from the album "Fulham Fallout," and there is a choice of four different picture covers for the single. One with each member of the Lurkers on the face. Beggars has also reissued 3,000 copies of their debut single "Shadow," with 1,000 each on red, white and blue vinyl.

LIVE TONIGHT!

RUNAWAYS ....Birmingham, Barbarella's
LURKERS/WHITE CATS/
THE VENTS ....High Wycombe, Nag's Head
NEW HEARTS/SPARE PARTS.......London, Marquee
TOURISTS/INVADERS ....London, Music Machine
RAMBOW/THE RUTS.................London, Windsor Castle

ANGLE TRAX/PRAG VEC ....London, Young Vic
REGGAE REGULARS/BLITZ.........London, Fulham Town Hall
RICH KIDS/THE FALL................Manchester, UMIST
THOSE NAUGHTY LUMPS ....Manchester, Tyldesley R.C.
GANG OF FOUR ....Manchester, The Factory

21st - Friday...

THE TALKING HEADS have their second album released today. It's called "More Songs About Buildings And Food" and features an intriguing cover photo(s). The image of the band is made up of 529 close-up Polaroids of the band, arranged in a mosaic picture. The album was recorded in April at Compass Point Studios in the Bahamas with Brian Eno producing alongside the Heads. Songs include "Thank You For Sending Me An Angel," "I'm Not In Love" and the Al Green composition "Take Me To The River."

REZILLOS finally have their LP debut, "Can't Stand The Rezillos." The Edinburgh band have been playing together since April of '76 and it's been a long climb. The album was recorded at the Power Station in New York City back in February. The Rezillos are the first of the UK new wave bands to record an LP in the US. Although Bob Clearmountain is listed as producer, insiders say that engineer Tony Bongiovi should get most of the credit. The album contains their debut single track "I Can't Stand My Baby" as well as "Good Sculptures," "Top Of The Pops," "Flying Saucer Attack" and the Dave Clark Five hit "Glad All Over." Early copies of the LP will include a free set of postcards. The Rezillos are Fay Fifi, Eugene Reynolds, Jo Callis, William Mysterious and Angel Paterson.

ERIC'S/THE FACTORY Eric's in Liverpool was such a success that a similar club is begun in nearby Manchester. With the recent closure of Rafters in Manchester, there's a need for another place for music. On Friday nights from now on, the Russell Club will be transformed into "The Factory" for special gigs. Tonight's concert with reggae group Culture is the first in the series.

WAYNE COUNTY, singer for the Electric Chairs, was refused permission to enter the UK today. Wayne and the group are now living in Berlin, a community they feel is more sympathetic to their style of music. Wayne currently is undergoing the necessary medical procedures prior to having a sex change. He was on his way to see his doctor and was stopped at immigration. How this will affect his operation, much less the band's future touring possibilities is uncertain.

THE CURE's demo that was sent to Polydor Records is heard by Chris Parry. He's keen on signing a band that's involved in the exciting new music scene that's erupting all around him. He'd missed the Clash, Sex Pistols and Siouxsie & The Banshees but had managed to sign the Jam. He was determined to find the next big thing and this new trio caught his attention, specifically with the song "10:15 Saturday Night." He writes to The Cure and arranges to meet them.

RAW/JOHN COOPER CLARKE/
PHANTOM/
PATRIK FITZGERALD ....London, Club Row Club

DICKIES/THE EDGE ....London, Music Machine
WHITE CATS ....London, Rock Garden
RAMBOW/THE RUTS ....London, Windsor Castle

22nd - Saturday.......................................

FANZINES continue to flourish in the UK and this week's *NME* does another overview of the Fanzines available to the die-hard punk fan. Some are American like *Teenage Rampage* from Columbus Ohio, or Chicago's *La Mere Gabba Gabba Gazette*. There's also West Germany's *Honey, That Ain't No Romance* that's devoted entirely to Iggy Pop worship and the everpresent *Ripped & Torn* as distributed by Rough Trade Records. Even Ireland gets into the action with two of their own. From Dublin comes *Hot Press* and *Private World* issues from Belfast.

THE RAMONES' former drummer Tommy Ramone confessed to the *NME* that the band wasn't as organized in the beginning as they are now. "In the early days Dee Dee would shout '1-2-3-4' and all the band would start playing a different song. Then we'd throw the instruments around and walk off. And it wasn't a put-on either. But it became easy, it became drilled into us. What the hell, it's all the same song anyhow." Tommy left the band last month and plans to continue record production full time under his given name, Tommy Erdeyli. He's not new at producing and has produced the Ramones' past albums.

RICH KIDS/SLITS ....Birmingham, Barbarella's

MISTY/CHARGE/IDOLS...............London, White Horse

JULY 1978

WHITE CATS ....London, Golden Lion	REACTION ....Manchester, Merry-Go-Round
RAMBOW/THE RUTS ....London, Red Cow	

24th - Monday...

THE PRETENDERS finally have all the pieces together. Chrissie knows that she has to have Jimmy Scott on guitar, he can play anything. He agrees to come into Regents Park studios in London for the sessions. They cut versions of "Precious," "The Phonecall," a cover of the Kink's "Stop Your Sobbing," a country-flavoured song called "Tequila" and a cover of the Troggs' "I Can't Control Myself." She also finds out that Jimmy loves Nick Lowe, who is a friend of hers. Dave Hill from Real Records takes the demo to Nick Lowe and loves Chrissie's voice on "Stop Your Sobbing" and wants to write a new arrangement. Jimmy's been listening to the tape as well and tells Chrissie that he wants to join the band. She tops it by telling him that Nick's going to produce the single. He came down one night and they played with the three others and Chrissie says, "I had to turn my back to them 'cause I was laughing the whole time, 'cause I knew this is it. This is my band. I'd found them. It was a wonderful thing."

THE HUMAN LEAGUE & VICE VERSA shared a gig in Sheffield recently and were reviewed by *NME's* Andy Gill. The event was one of the many gigs staged by the "Now Society," a university-based organization that books events from time to time with the more experimental northern bands. Some of the songs in their current repertoire include "Dance Like A Star," "The Path Of Least Resistance," and a rather unusual electronic version of "You've Lost That Loving Feeling." Vice Versa opening the concert. They're a new electronic band fronted by Martin Fry who Gill describes, "…is going on about 'not wanting your fashion scene'- (yet) he used to run a fanzine called *Steve's Paper*, whose main subject matter was the availability of plastic sandals in the Sheffield area. As it is, it looks as though he spends more time combing his hair than playing the guitar." Otherwise he rates the band as, "…a bizarro trio who show occasional flashes of promise, but whose pretentiousness becomes ultimately quite tiresome."

The Human League are celebrating their "Electronically Yours" vinyl debut. It's a single on Last's "Fast Product" label. The "A" side is "Being Boiled," a song about the silk trade. According to the band, the flipside, "Circus Of Death," works in, "…the actual arrival of Steve McGarret (Hawaii Five-0) at Heathrow Airport, a circus, an article in the Guardian from '62 and a short wave message from the last man on earth." The Human League will ultimately have the fame they're striving for but it will take some time. The band's first few singles will sell moderately until "Sound Of The Crowd" nearly breaks the UK top ten. After that, the Human League will place seven songs into the upper chart over the next six years.

ADVERTISING/U2........................Dublin, McGonagles	MONOCHROME SET/SLANDER .....London, Rock Garden
THOSE NAUGHTY LUMPS............Liverpool, Phab Club	BLACK SLATE/
SHIRTS/REACTION ....London, Marquee	PATRIK FITZGERALD ....London, N E Poly.
CLASH/SUICIDE/SPECIALS ....London, Music Machine	UK SUBS ....London, Upstairs At Ronnie Scotts'

26th - Wednesday.................................

THE REZILLOS' new record is "Top Of The Pops" and "20,000 Rezillos Under The Sea." The "A" side is from their debut album, the flipside is on the single only. They initially wrote the song to poke fun at the show of the same name, however this single is good enough they might just have to appear on *Top Of The Pops* to sing "Top Of The Pops".

MAGAZINE "I'm not interested in poetry at all. Poetry is…I…dunno…it's smelly." Howard Devoto in this week's *NME*.

CLASH/ SUICIDE/ SPECIALS ....London, Music Machine	MENACE/RAPED ....London, Last Bastion
ADVERTS ....London, Marquee	RAMBOW/THE RUTS ....London, Rock Garden
SOME CHICKEN........................London, Angel City Arms	

27th - Thursday....................................

SNAKEFINGER (real name Philip Lithman) is a part of the growing enigma the "Residents legend," a press barrage that is quite obviously rooted in storytelling, exaggeration and misinformation. He's a cohort of Nick Lowe and was managed at one time by Jake Riveria, now manager of Nick Lowe and Elvis Costello. He'd been through the usual run of bands, even finding himself in the US in 1971 where he met up in San Francisco with "Mysterious En Senada." In '72 he migrated back to the UK where he put together Chilli Willi & The Red Hot Peppers. His connections to the Residents run deep but nobody is telling. His solo single is the off-beat 45 "The Spot" b/w "Smelly Tongues". It is on the Residents' own Ralph Records label and early pressings include both a picture cover AND blue vinyl! The single was produced by the Residents as well.

RICH KIDS/SLITS ....Glasgow, Shuffles'	WHITE CATS ....London, Rock Garden
THOSE NAUGHTY LUMPS............Liverpool, Eric's	CLASH/SUICIDE/SPECIALS ....London, Music Machine
SOME CHICKEN........................London, John Bull	ADVERTS...............................London, Marquee
NINE NINE NINE ....London, Nashville	

28th - Friday.......................................

FRESHIES Chris Sievey and The Freshies are the DIY band that have set up their own Razz Record Company. They had their debut single out last April, now their first LP is available. Called "All Sleep's Secrets," it contains twelve continuous songs, that run one-into-another to make a complete composition.

THE PROLES are the South London group making a debut on seven inches of vinyl under the title "The Proles Go To The Seaside." The

JULY 1978

five track EP is on Can't Play Records. The Proles wrote all of the material on the disc and might just collect the prize for having the new, shortest song on record. The last track runs just twenty seconds and is called "I Hate Modern Music." Good thing it's over quick.

LENE LOVICH makes her debut as a Stiff artist. She's covered the '60s Tommy James song "I Think We're Alone Now" and recorded an original titled "Lucky Number." Only 5,000 copies are pressed up and will be available through mail order only. Lene had previously been involved with a funk-rock group called the Diversions, that also included as a member Les Chapple on guitar (now in Lene's band). The Diversions released one single ("Fattie Bum Bum") and had recorded a full album with producer Mike Vernon that still remains unissued. As recently as six months ago Les and Lene were appearing in "Ovals Exiles," a revue of Bobby Henry songs put together by Radio DJ Charlie Gilette. There was a tie between Oval and Stiff's Jake Riveria, who heard a demo of this Shondells song, so the story goes.

RICH KIDS/SLITS	Edinburgh, Clouds	CHELSEA	London, Marquee
FALL	Liverpool, Eric's	NINE NINE NINE	London, Nashville
WHITE CATS	London, Hope & Anchor		

31th - Monday..

TELEVISION One of the first of the "new wave" bands has split in New York City. After completing a series of three successful nights (27th-29th) at the Bottom Line, Television is no more. Tom Verlaine intends to work with bassist Fred Smith, and Richard Lloyd will probably continue as a producer for NY-based ORK Records and possibly work with drummer Billy Ficca. Verlaine said that, "There was a full moon the night that Moby Grape broke up so we wanted to do that as well." The band had recently returned from a disappointing tour of Europe where they often played to half-full houses. Disharmony in the band was not unfamiliar in Television. Tom Verlaine and co-founder Richard Hell had a falling out years ago and in the last few years Richard Lloyd had quit twice!

MIKE SCOTT & D.N.V. Future lead singer of the Waterboys, is college student Mike Scott. He's a keen fan of poetry and writes to *Sounds* magazine about John Gill's piece about Burroughs, and presses the case of T.S. Eliot and his influence on rock lyrics, "Check out 'The Lovesong of J. Alfred Prufrock' and then read Dylan's 'Visions Of Johanna.' Thomas Stearn even gets a mention in the master's 'Desolation Row' epic, which itself, like Bowie's 'Cygnet Committee' owes more than a little to Eliot's 'The Wasteland.' There are other throwbacks too- Patti Smith's 'Elegie' and the juxtaposition of the 23rd psalm with the song 'Set Me Free' on the 'Easter' album and Tom Verlaine's 'Torn Curtain' all call up Visions Of Eliot. Perhaps if he'd been American by culture as well as by birth, Eliot would be more recognized as the influence on rock 'n' roll lyric he undoubtedly is. Everything has not been returned which was owed. Mike Scott, Bellevale Ave. Ayr, Scotland" Mike fronts a rock band called D.N.V. who have done a little recording but haven't gotten the money to actually release anything. He's very into lyrics, in case you couldn't tell.

DEMON PREACHER/CARPETTES Small Wonder Records has two more singles to add to its growing catalogue. They've already had records out by Puncture, The Zeros, Patrik Fitzgerald, Menace, Carpettes and the Leyton Buzzards. Quite a list! Now they have two more, #9 and #10. The ninth is the second single from The Carpettes, "Small Wonder?" flipped with "2 NE 1." Next up is a new signing, a group called Demon Preacher. Their debut is "Little Miss Perfect" flipped with a dub version, "Perfect Dub." The song is about Joyce McKinney, the sex-in-chains gal. Demon Preacher are Nick E. Wade on vocals, Tony Ward on guitar, Camilla Armstrong on bass and Gerry Healy on drums. Secret messages scratched in the vinyl read "She Can Rattle My Chains Anytime" on the vocal side and "Juicy Joycey Bed A Dread" on the Dub side.

U2/REVOLVER	Dublin, McGonagles	TOURISTS	London, Marquee
SUICIDE	Edinburgh, Tiffany's	ADAM & ANTS	London, Moonlight Club
LEYTON BUZZARDS	London, Bridge House	JAPAN/WHITE CATS	London, Music Machine

August 4th - Friday..

PATTI SMITH has a new EP that is a mixture of old, new and live material. The UK issue leads with "Privilege (Set Me Free)." The song was originally recorded by Paul Jones (former lead singer of Manfred Mann) in the movie "Privilege." It's paired with "Ask The Angels" from the "Radio Ethiopia" album and on the flip is a live version of "25th Floor" as well as a poetry reading of "Babelfield" from her book.

THE RUDE KIDS are a Swedish band that are just asking for trouble. They're from Stockholm, home of a teds-cum-nazi group of hooligans called the Raggare. Members of this clique have disrupted so many concerts in Sweden, that many bands refuse to play there. They've caused damage to clubs, terrorized their patrons and have managers walking on eggshells just to keep trouble to a minimum. Facing the problem, The Rude Kids have cut a single on Polydor (Scandinavia) called "Raggare Is A Bunch Of Motherf**kers." It takes no shortcuts in describing the antipathy they hold for the group. The group is Bona on vocals, Lasse on guitar and backing vocals, Spaceman on bass and Lasse (Throw It) on drums. It's flipped with "Charlie." There's also the note on the sleeve, "This is a pardonless record to be played at a pardonless volume. R.A.R. Rock Against Raggare."

TANZ DER YOUTH/		INJECTIONS	London, Hambro' Tavern
SORE THROAT/		RICH KIDS	London, Music Machine
PATRIK FITZGERALD/		DEAD FINGERS TALK	London, Red Cow
THE ACTORS	High Wycombe, Town Hall		

8th - Tuesday..

THE JAM release their fifth single, "A Bomb In Wardour Street." They select as the "B" side an obscure Kinks track called "David Watts."

AUGUST 1978

ULTRAVOX's new single "Slow Motion" b/w "Dislocation" is a sample of the sessions they're in at producer Conny Plank's studio near Cologne Germany. The LP "Systems of Romance" will be released this fall.

STEVE GIBBONS BAND/   PIRANHAS ....London, Angel City Arms
AUTOGRAPHS/
JOHN COOPER CLARKE/SLITS ......London, Music Machine

9th - Wednesday...

WAYNE COUNTY & ELECTRIC CHAIRS have their next single released by Safari Records, the oh-so-acceptable pop song "Trying To Get On The Radio." The track is saccharin sweet and even includes a piano introduction with the inclusion of a sweet violin for the chorus. After previous records like the "Blatantly Offensive EP" and "Fuck Off," it will be a wonder if any radio station will even touch this…although it's truly squeaky clean! A list of stations that have banned Wayne in the past is on the back of the pic sleeve.

TRANSMITTERS/BLITZ/   UK SUBS/TICKETS ....London, Forrester Arms
THE ROTTIN KLITZ ....London, Last Bastion

10th - Thursday...

BILL NELSON has just put to rest one of the '70s more interesting art rock bands, Be Bop Deluxe. Tired of "the limitations of a rigid group structure" he split the band on the eve of the release of the seventh album. Now rehearsing with his new band called "Red Noise," Bill plans to explore fully some of the musical ideas touched upon by Be Bop Deluxe.

TUBEWAY ARMY release their second single on Beggars Banquet Records and it's a curious attempt at mating punk and pop. The churning guitar is definitely from the punk D.I.Y. school, but the synth dubbed in over the song lends it an odd, eerie sound unlike many of its contemporaries. The lead track is "Bombers," while "Blue Eyes" and "O.D. Receiver" occupy the flip. All three songs are credited to the imagination of Valeriun (the future Gary Numan), a bleach blonde, sullen-eyed leader of this quartet.

GENERATION X ....Edinburgh, The Astoria   NO SWEAT/SKUNKS ....London, Eel Pie Rock Club
TANZ DER YOUTH/   CHAMPION/DRONES ....London, Nashville
PATRIK FITZGERALD   ADAM & ANTS........................London, Rock Garden
CABARET VOLTAIRE ....London, Music Machine

11th - Friday...

THE RICH KIDS have their latest single out today. It's called "Ghosts Of Princes In Towers" and is the lead track from their debut album that will be out next week. It's cut with "Only Arsenic," both Rich Kids originals.

THE FALL make their vinyl debut on indie Step Forward Records. This is the first step in a career spanning more than fifteen years. The "A" side is "Bingo - Master's Break - Out!," flipped with "Psycho Mafia," Bingo Master" and "Repetition." At the time of the recording the band consisted of Martin Bramah on guitar, Karl Burns on drums, Kark Smith on vocals, Una Baines on piano and Tony Friel on bass. Since that time Yvonne Paulette and Marc Bailey have replaced Una and Tony. Songs in the band's live set that have yet to be recorded include "Industrial Estate," "Hey Fascist," "Mother Sister," "(Envy Of The) Music Scene," "Two Steps Back," "Last Orders," "I Like To Blow," "Mess Of My," "Rebellious Jukebox" and "It's The New Thing."

THE STRANGLERS gave away 75,000 copies of a free EP with the initial pressing of the Stranglers "Black & White" album in mid-May. Those have all disappeared and the demand is such for the EP that United Artist have reissued it, separate from the album. The EP features the Bacharach-David tune "Walk On By" flipped with "Mean To Me" and a live recording of a band introduction cum solo-piece called "Tits." Unlike its free counterpart, this one will come with a black and white picture sleeve and cost money.

SONS OF JAH/MAT STAGGER/   REGGAE REGULAR/SPIZZ OIL ......London, Nashville
PRAG VEC ....London, Acklam Hall   MEMBERS ....London, Windsor Castle

12th - Saturday...

SEX PISTOLS It's been only seven days since Sid was on *Revolver* singing "My Way," now Steve and Paul (along with Ronnie Biggs) are scheduled to be on the same show with their new song "No One Is Innocent." The track, which has Biggs singing the lead vocals, was filmed on location in Rio, where Ronnie is currently hiding from the law. The record is selling moderately well but is getting no radio play. The BBC claims there's no ban on the group, it's just that, "…it's not that good of a record and none of our jocks like it." However, just hours before airtime it was decided that the film clip was "unsuitable." There were those who felt a film of an outlaw living the life of leisure with England's bad boys was not proper TV fare. On the program, Peter Cook introduced the track, it was censored and he continued into the next segment. Sharing the spotlight this evening with the Sex Pistols blocked video are The Jam, The Boomtown Rats, Fabulous Poodles, Jab Jab and Dire Straits.

QUADROPHENIA would seem to have little connection to the punk world, but not in the eyes and ears of the Who's Pete Townsend. They're both about rebellion. Pete has been searching for a band that will be central to the movie and he's looking for just the right person to play the lead role of "Jimmy" in the film. There are two current candidates in Townsends mind. One is Johnny Lydon, late of the Sex Pistols, the other is Sham 69's Jimmy Pursey. Talks are underway and others besides the duo are also being considered.

MODERNE MAN ....Glasgow, Curler's Tavern   RANDOM HOLD ....London, Battersea Park
REZILLOS...........................Liverpool, Eric's   REGGAE REGULAR/SPIZZ OIL ......London, Nashville
       MISTY/MENACE/TICKETS............London, E. Ham Town Hall RAR gig

AUGUST 1978

TOURISTS/
LEE FARDON'S LEGIONNAIRES .....London, Music Machine

GENERATION X........................Sheffield, The Limit

14th - Monday.............................

THE DICKIES' second single in the UK is out, following the formula that make them famous; 100 mph cover songs. This release is no different. The victim this time is the 1965 protest song "Eve Of Destruction." Instead of the original version of 3:28 length, they've run through it in only 1:55. It's flipped with a Dickies original, "Doggie Do." The Dickies are Leonard Graves Phillips on vocals, Karlos Kaballero on drums, Stan Lee on guitar, Chuck Wagon on keyboards and Billy Club on bass.

THE POLICE have their second single for A&M released, "Can't Stand Losing You" b/w "Dead End Job." The picture cover has some poor lad hung from the ceiling after the ice block he was standing on melted from the heater placed beside it. Surely a slow method of doing yourself in. Strangely enough, he seems to be holding a photo of the Police. Bob Edmans, reviewing the record for the *NME* said this, "The Police- a great name for an outrageous punk band. Lousy name for a feeble white reggae act. Last observed proceeding in the direction of the waste bin. Not worth apprehending." Meanwhile, in *NME's* Jaws section, Geoff Barton lambastes The Police under the heading "You Can't Hide An Old Hippie." He writes about their *Top Of The Pops* appearance under the guise of Klark Kent. He writes,"Who do they really think they're kidding? Even in they were shrouded in what looked like pigs masks…there was no way the Police could hide the distinctive form of guitarist Andy Summers. Mind you for an old hippie, he could pogo pretty well." Meanwhile, Sting has gotten himself in front of the camera again. He's tagged to play the role of "Ace" in the Who's new film *Quadrophenia* now being filmed.

TOM ROBINSON BAND "Too Good To Be True" is the new TRB single on Harvest in the UK. Hopes are it will follow the success of his previous singles "2-4-6-8 Motorway" (#5), "Don't Take No For An Answer" (#18) and "Up Against The Wall" (#33).

LIVE TONIGHT!

BEARS ....Glasgow, The Amphora
PATRIK FITZGERALD ....London, Hope & Anchor

VIBRATORS ....London, Marquee
JAPAN ....London, Music Machine

16th - Wednesday................

LUDUS is one of Manchester's newest bands. They feature local hero Linder (Linda Mulvey) as the vocalist. She's made a bit of a name for herself around Manchester by using her training from Manchester Poly designing distinctive posters for the Buzzcocks as well as the sleeves to "Orgasm Addict," and Magazine's "Real Life" album jacket. Supposedly the Buzzcocks song "What Do I Get" is about her. The group got their drummer Toby (aka Philip Tolman) from the Manchester band Nosebleeds and the rest is filled out by Willie Trotter on bass and Arthur Cadmon (aka Peter Sadler, ex-Manicured Noise) on guitar. They were originally thinking of calling the band Bloodsport, but have decided on Ludus instead.

RAPED/DICK ENVY/
INNOCENTS ....London, Forrester Arms

ADAM & ANTS........................London, Last Bastion
ADVERTISING/VAPORS ....London, Music Machine

17th - Thursday.........................

THE HUMAN LEAGUE make the long trip from Sheffield to debut in London at the Music Machine opening up for The Rezillos. They had at first thought that they should don motorcycle helmets onstage, fearing the London punks would pelt them with beer bottles. Instead they went out sans headgear but armed with a riot shield for their pricey equipment. No sense in seeing months worth of wages for electronic gadgets and knobs go down with a well aimed pint glass. The Human League are Ian Marsh, Martyn Ware, Adrian Wright and vocalist Phil Oakey.

JAPAN have a new single out today, coupling two songs from their debut album. It's "The Unconventional" b/w "Adolescent Sex." The group are currently working on a second LP for Ariola-Hansa.

BEARS ....Glasgow, Doune Castle
REZILLOS/HUMAN LEAGUE..........London, Music Machine

IDOLS....................................London, Windsor Castle

18th - Friday.........................

SIOUXSIE & THE BANSHEES have their debut single released by Polydor Records in the UK. It's "Hong Kong Garden" b/w "Voices," and the first 10,000 copies come out in a special gatefold sleeve with lyrics included. It's a great beginning for an equally great band and the song will climb up the UK charts to #7. It will stand as the band's top hit until they cover the Beatles' "Dear Prudence" in '83. They started recording the single the week they were signed. The tedious, expensive sessions yeilded up a version of the song the band thought was unbearable. A new producer, Steve Lillywhite, was brought in, re-recorded "Hong Kong Garden" and a hit was born. Only "Voices" on the flip remained from the first session.

THE RICH KIDS have their debut album out. The LP is "Ghosts Of Princes In Towers" and features their singles "Rich Kids," "Ghosts Of Princes" and "Marching Men." Side two of the LP starts with "Put You In The Picture." It's a Midge Ure song and isn't the first time it was recorded. Remember? That's right, it was on the punk single that Ure cut with the members of Slik, under the name PVC 2. The band's fascination and respect for the Small Faces extends to having Face Ian McLagan play piano on "Cheap Emotions." He's played onstage with the band as well in the past. The LP was produced by Lou Reed/David Bowie protege and glitterperson Mick Ronson. The Rich Kids remain Glen Matlock, Midge Ure, Steve New and Rusty Egan.

AUGUST 1978

NINE NINE NINE have two new songs in shops for their fans, "Feeling Alright With The Crew" and "You Can't Buy Me." A third track on the EP "Titanic" was on the band's last album.

BLONDIE have the sessions for their next album finished and there's a sneak peek at them in the release of their new single. It's two new tracks, "Picture This" and "Fade Away (and radiate)." There is a special limited edition 12" in "Blonde" vinyl!

SIOUXSIE & THE BANSHEES/		MENACE	London, Bowling Green Ln Youth Club
SPIZZOIL	Edinburgh, The Clouds	SKREWDRIVER/DOGWATCH	London, Tidal Basin Tavern
REZILLOS/		JOHN COOPER CLARKE/	
PATRIK FITZGERALD/		ED BANGER/GIRO/	
THE VENTS	High Wycombe, Town Hall	GORDON THE MORON	Manchester, Russel Club

19th - Saturday.....

SKREWDRIVER have been hit with a heavy backlash surrounding the band's drawing of skinheads to venues not welcoming violence. These crowds that have attached themselves to bands like Skrewdriver or Sham 69, have made it increasingly difficult for clubs to manage the necessary insurance coverage to pay for potential damages. Out of a thirty-two date tour, twenty-one have been canceled. Skrewdriver's manager claims that the band's reputation may break them financially.

REVOLVER When the taping session for tonight's ATV program *Revolver* was scheduled, Public Image was slated to make an appearance. Guitarist Keith Levine showed up, but none of the other members did. They all were supposedly in Camber, drinking and sunning themselves, without a care about the havoc in the ATV studios. As a last minute replacement, the Rich Kids were called into action. Public Image is indeed Limited and they are making sure that it's understood that they control the group, not a record company. It's also ironic that one part of the defunct Sex Pistols is called in to fill for another splinter of the split group.

JOHN COOPER CLARKE/		ULTRAVOX	London, The Marquee
GYRO/ED BANGER/			
GORDON THE MORON	Liverpool, Eric's		

20th - Sunday.....

DEXY'S MIDNIGHT RUNNERS are a new group being carefully put together in Birmingham by Kevin Rowland. He's planning a group that works in some of the great soul sound of Geno Washington with some of his own ideas about music, even finding his sax player, J.D., from among Geno Washington's Ram Jam Band. He's also recruited drummer Addy Gowcott in a nightclub and organist Pete Saunders. Also in for the ride are guitarist Al Archer, bassist Pete Williams, "Big" Jimmy Patterson on trombone and Steve "Babyface" Spooner on alto sax. The look of the band is something that is straight out of DeNiro's "Mean Streets," and the name is a shortened tribute to the pep pill dexidrine. Kevin had previously been in punk band The Killjoys and has one single to his credit and prior to that was a veteran of Lucy & The Lovers, another Birmingham-based band.

LURKERS	Dublin, McGonagles	PENETRATION/THE FALL/	
ULTRAVOX	London, The Marquee	ED BANGER/	
VAPORS	London, The John Bull Pub	PUNISHMENT OF LUXURY	London, The Lyceum

22nd - Tuesday.....

SID VICIOUS is the center of attention at The Electric Circus tonight in a super-session of sorts. This evening it's the appearance of The Vicious White Kids. It's Sid's farewell gig before he and his girlfriend move to New York. Among the friends onstage are Rat Scabies (drums), Glen Matlock (bass), Steve New (guitar) and Sid's girlfriend Nancy Spungen (backing vocals). Sid, of course, sings lead. Songs this evening covered old Pistols' standards like "Belsen Was A Gas" and "No Lip (Pushin' and Shovin')," sound check faves like "Stepping Stone," "Raw Power" and "I Wanna Be Your Dog," the latter apparently being a band favorite as it was played three times. Also included was the surprise addition of Sid's latest single "My Way." It's as much an event for musicians as it was for music fans. Whether they were waiting to be invited onstage for a supposed chorus of "I Shall Be Released" is unknown. In the audience that evening were the remainder of The Rich Kids, Elvis Costello and Pete Thomas, Paul Jones of the Pistols, all of the Slits, Captain Sensible, Martin Belmont, Blondie and Joan Jett. This was a more stellar night than the Greedies superjam here some months ago.

HERE & NOW/THE FALL	Liverpool, Pickwick Club	ULTRAVOX	London, The Marquee
VICIOUS WHITE KIDS/		AUTOGRAPH/PASSIONS	London, Moonlight Club
ADDIX	London, Electric Ballroom	DUST/MEKONS/CREATION	Manchester, Band On The Wall

23rd - Wednesday.....

STEVE TREATMENT is the second artist to have a disc out on Rather Records, the other being the enigmatic Swell Maps. Treatment wraps himself in mystery as well. Backing musicians on the disc are Edrun Kubelwagen, Chris n' Chris (the Emergency Set), Mr. Matilda Tank, RJ Half Track and Amphibious Landing Craft. Tracks on the debut disc include "Danger Zone," "Negative Nights," "Taste Your Own Medicine," "Hooked On A Trend" and "The Hippy Posed Engrossment." The songs themselves were recorded in June at Spaceward Studios in Cambridge.

THE CURE receive letters rejecting their demo of original music from both Virgin Records and EMI Records.

LURKERS	Belfast, The Pound	ULTRAVOX	London, The Marquee
BEARS	Glasgow, Doune Castle		

AUGUST 1978

CHELSEA ....London, Last Bastion	PATRIK FITZGERALD/
UK SUBS...............................London, Forester Arms	LEYTON BUZZARDS/
	PUNISHMENT OF LUXURY ....London, Music Machine

25th - Friday..

DEVO release their new single "Come Back Jonee" in a special sleeve with a girl looking longingly into the eyes of a plaster bust. Like Warhol's banana on the Velvet Underground's LP, there's a surprise underneath the face sticker. A little surprise, nothing big. A film has been made by the band with the group singing the song in a bowling alley dressed in pseudo western wear.

CHELSEA Gene October's ever-changing band Chelsea, have their third single on Step Forward out today. It's two more originals "Urban Kids" and "No Flowers," and Step Forward has actually gone to the expense of giving the band their first full color picture sleeve. Although the single was produced by veteran Who producer Kit Lambert, it sounds like anything but a mod band.

LIVE TONIGHT!

STIFF LITTLE FINGERS...............Dublin, Moran's	SQUARES/THE SYSTEM ....Manchester, Tyldesley Rugby Club
REZILLOS/MEKONS..................Edinburgh, The Clouds	SKREWDRIVER.......................Manchester, The Mayflower
MEMBERS/THE NUNS ....London, Walmer Castle	

26th - Saturday..

WAYNE COUNTY & THE ELECTRIC CHAIRS have out their second album this year. The prolific Mr./Ms. County's latest is "Storm The Gates Of Heaven." It features their current 45 "Trying To Get On The Radio," the autobiographical "Man Enough To Be A Woman," and a cover of the Electric Prunes' 1967 hit "I Had Too Much To Dream Last Night." With the personnel of the Electric Chairs changing so much recently, Safari Records hasn't listed who's in the group. Here's the membership on the LP. Wayne County, John Johnson on drums, Val Haller on bass and Greg Van Cook on guitar, Van Cook was replaced in March by Elliot Michaels, yet the album sessions predate this change. Wayne himself has now been granted permission to enter the UK and pursue the medical procedures for his sex change. He has been denied entry to the UK previously and had been living in Berlin.

SID VICIOUS Sid and Nancy are reportedly on their way to New York. After the "farewell concert," Sid hurriedly finished filming his remaining bits for the film *The Great Rock & Roll Swindle*. They are both videos for two Eddie Cochran (another dead rock star!) songs that he's covered. "Something Else," features nearly naked Sid in the most microscopic pair of underwear, his Honda motorcycle and a beer bottle. Use your imagination. "C'Mon Everybody" has Sid riding his motorcycle down an English road. Reports in the *NME* claim that he's working on his autobiography, "My Life, Or What I Can Remember Of It."

Other Pistols peoples are busy on the film as well. Manager Malcolm McLaren is featured in one scene tap dancing while singing "You Need Hands," while in another scene Steve Jones is singing "Silly Thing."

BIG IN JAPAN is Liverpool's odd, theatre cum rock band. Now they've decided to call it a day. The group had been together since May of last year and has alternately been the subject of both praise and ridicule because of their unusual stage show. They leave behind one single, last year's "Big In Japan" on Eric's Records. Tonight is Big In Japan's final show at Eric's. The band have simply "run out of steam." Watch for Holly Johnson to eventually turn up as the creative focus behind Frankie Goes To Hollywood in 1980.

THE PRETENDERS are playing in front of a live audience for the first time. They're way out in Wakefield, opening up for Strangeways. They're a local band out here, who've just been signed to Real Records, the same label as the Pretenders. They're going to be playing some low-key gigs while breaking in new material. In October the band are to play a series of gigs at the Gibus Club in Paris. The Pretenders are Chrissie Hynde, Pete Farndon, Jimmy Scott and Gerry Mackleduff.

STIFF LITTLE FINGERS...............Dublin, Dingo's Rock Palace	MEMBERS ....London, Windsor Castle
BIG IN JAPAN ....Liverpool, Eric's	

27th - Sunday..........................

THE CURE play on the floor in front of the stage at The Lakers Pub, in Redhill. Chris Parry is in front and likes what he sees. After the gig, the Cure and Parry go to another pub and talk about their future together. He's uncertain what he's going to call his label. His first thought was Night Nurse but the Cure balked at that. What about 18 age? "How about when we all turn 21?" (They were all nineteen at the time). How about Fiction then? Chris tells them that he'll arrange the papers and set up studio time.

28th - Monday..........................

DEVO After settling lawsuits with record companies and an advertising campaign that makes "Devo" one of the most hated/loved household words, their debut album is out. It's titled "Q:Are We Not Men? A:We Are Devo!," a line taken from their song "Jocko Homo." The album was recorded with Brian Eno, who has polished the rough edges off the group and taken their unusual ideas about music two steps further into space. Song include new versions of their indie records "Satisfaction," "Jocko Homo" and "Mongoloid," as well as "Too Much Paranoias," "Space Junk" and "Praying Hands." It's just the sort of sound to make you dress up in a yellow chemical suit and 3-D glasses. To make things difficult and to play up to the vinyl collectors out there, Virgin had the LP pressed up on black, grey, red,

Q:ARE WE NOT MEN?

OUT NOW ON VIRGIN V2106

A NEW ALBUM

A:WE ARE DEVO!

AUGUST 1978

blue and yellow vinyl as well as a picture disc. This gives you some freedom of choice when purchasing one or more "collector" editions.

JOHN COOPER CLARKE Under the heading "Reprieved for Eccentricity," *Melody Maker* reviews the latest disc from the man who launched a thousand haircuts, John Cooper Clarke. This is his first since signing to CBS and is a poem with MOR musical backing. "Post War Glamour Girl is the "A" side. The flip, "Kung Fu International," recorded live at Eric's, is much more akin to what you expect from this 100 mph Mancunian.

MERGER/THE MONOS ....Edinburgh, Tiffany's	CUBAN HEELS ....Glasgow, Burns Howff

September 1th - Friday.....................................

TUBEWAY ARMY Less than two weeks after the release of their second single for Beggars Banquet, Beggars Banquet has announced that Tubeway Army have gone their separate ways, but that's not actually true. They're just changing their names. Valeriun (aka Gary Webb) will continue as the band's lead singer and writer, under the new name Gary Numan. Scarlet, will go under his real name, Paul Gardiner and Rael will do likewise as Gerald Lidyard. Gary got his new name from the Yellow Pages entry for "Neumann Kitchen Appliances." Wanting to stay away from the Berlin bit that Bowie was doing, Gary drops the "e" and the "n" arriving at "Numan."

THE SKIDS have their single "Sweet Suburbia" released on Virgin Records, with the first 15,000 on white vinyl. Their debut EP, which was released on the band's own "No Bad" record label, is being reissued on No Bad, but distributed by Virgin Records.

TANZ DER YOUTH had promised to have their debut single out in August and have almost kept to their word. Today they release of "I'm Sorry, I'm Sorry" and the aptly titled "Delay." The "A" side is a Brian James original, the flip being penned by bassist Andy Colquhoun and drummer Alan Powell. The disc will be released by Jake Riveria's Radar Records as ADA #19.

THE PHYSICALS are the new band put together by Alan Shaw since he left the Maniacs. He's joined by Steve Schmidt on guitar, Crister Sol on bass and Steve Bye on drums. Their debut EP is a 7" with "Breakdown/On Stage" and "No Life/In The City" flipped with "You Do Me In" and "All Sexed Up." It's on their own Physical Records label.

SHAM 69/THE VALVES ....Edinburgh, The Clouds	RICH KIDS/HARLOW ....London, The Nashville
HUMAN LEAGUE......................Liverpool, Eric's	WHITE CATS ....London, Rochester Castle

3rd - Sunday.....................................

THE STRANGLERS have been having a difficult time finding a venue that they can play in London. Like other bands shut out of clubs because of their name, they play a secret gig at the Nashville in London. They'll be appearing under the name "The Old Codgers." Last night they played the Red Cow as "The Shakesperoes." It's a word culled from their song "No More Heroes."

SIMPLE MINDS are reviewed by *NME's* Ian Cranna as he visits Glasgow's Mars Bar. He starts his review with this, "You know the band that everybody's been waiting for, the one that will achieve that magic fusion of the Bowie\Harley\Verlaine twilight academy with the fertile firepower of the New Wave, that early Roxy Music with a rock n roll heart? Well here they are." He is struck by their unorthodox use of lighting and their charismatic vocalist Jim Kerr. Some of the songs that they played were their first single's "B" side, "Dead Vandals," (recorded back when they were called Johnny & The Self Abusers), also "Subway Sex," "Better Watch Out," "The Cocteau Twins," "Chelsea" and "Pleasantly Disturbed." Cranna ends his enthusiastic review with "...it's hard to recall the last time I witnessed such an exciting yet thoughtful new talent." In the years to come, The Cocteau Twins will take their name from the unrecorded Simple Minds song of the same name.

THE RAMONES ....Belfast, Ulster Hall	THE OLD CODGERS...................London, Nashville
PATTI SMITH (poetry)/POP GROUP.....Dublin, Project Arts Center	JOLT ....London, The Marquee
SIMPLE MINDS ....Glasgow, Mars Bar	PATRIK FITZGERALD ....London, Rochester Castle

5th - Tuesday.....................................

LES PUNKS is a reunion of sorts for three quarters of the Damned. Les Punks is a one-off band made up of Rat Scabies, Dave Vanian and Captain Sensible along with Lemmy from Motorhead. The gig is tonight at the Electric Ballroom in Camden Town.

JOY DIVISION Paul Morley reviews the Joy Division gig last night in Manchester for the *NME*. Morley was one of the first to ever write about the band, going back to July 30th edition of *NME* last year when they were called Warsaw. He characterized them then as, "...one doomed maybe to eternal support spots...a new wave functional band, easily digestible." Now the band has improved. Morley caught them at the Band On The Wall and was impressed enough to write, "They have matured considerably. They have learned to sculpt, not merely to emit...a group with eloquence and direction. Their music is mercilessly attacking, it rotates, persists, repeats, always well balanced... somewhere on a line between the conventional and the unconventional...That good." Clearly, Joy Division are well on their way to being a band to be reckoned with in the future.

SIOUXSIE & THE BANSHEES/	LES PUNKS ....London, The Electric Ballroom
THE CURE ....Belfast, Ulster Hall	TOYAH ....Sheffield, The Penthouse
ADAM & THE ANTS ....London, The Marquee	CABARET VOLTAIRE/
EDGE ....London, Dingwalls	DEAF AIDS/MOLODOY ....Sheffield, The Limits (Bandfest)
MONOCHROME SET ....London, Upstairs At Ronnie Scotts'	

6th - Wednesday.....................................

CLUBS CLOSINGS Things are getting more and more difficult for UK club owners. Newcastle clubs are having difficulty getting bands to

SEPTEMBER 1978

play because of increased violence at some punk gigs. Recently the Glasgow Apollo has decided to not allow any more live rock shows. In London, the Red Cow closed recently at the insistence of the local councilors, The Speakeasy closed because of problems with patrons and drugs and The 100 Club banned all punk bands back in April. Now some new problems are arising. The Musicians Union are demanding that all musicians receive an elevated hourly minimum. This is causing great problems for the Marquee. The Rochester Castle has lost its live music license and will no longer have bands playing, and in Leeds, The Fan Club is not allowed live bands under their new liquor license. The difficulties of finding a club, no matter how willing, to support local music, are increasing.

LIVE TONIGHT!

SKIDS	London, Hope & Anchor	TOYAH	London, Old Winchester Arms
ADAM & THE ANTS	London, The Marquee	IDOLS	London, Swan Hotel
JOHNNY MOPED/THE DOLE	London, The White Hart	LURKERS	Sheffield, The Limits

7th - Thursday...............................

STIFF RECORDS operates under the idea of being a "new" record company and "not a record museum." To keep the racks thinned and fresh they've planned more deletions from the Stiff catalogue, including the both of the Damned's LPs and compilations "Hit's Greatest Stiffs" and "A Bunch Of Stiffs." Singles getting the boot include Nick Lowe's "Halfway To Paradise," The Damned's "Problem Child," and Wreckless Eric's "Reconnez Cherie" to name but a few. Stiff will not be recalling the product and will not press any more. Conversely, Stiff are making their first ten singles available again. Collectors shops have been pushing the price up and up on the early releases, long deleted and Stiff is jumping in to the mess by re-issuing the whole lot of 10 in a limited edition box set. The individual singles will not be sold except as a set and as soon as the set reached the Stiff offices, IT was deleted. There will be no more 1-10 ever! Or so they say.

CASUALTIES The Music Industry Casualties show is onstage at Max's tonight. It features Cheetah Chrome and Jeff Magnum of the Dead Boys, as well as a new immigrant to the "Big Apple," Sid Vicious. Sid has recently moved to New York and he and his girlfriend Nancy Spungeon have moved into the Chelsea Hotel on West 23rd. Sid's band features the ex-New York Dolls rhythm section of Jerry Nolan and Killer Kane. Mick Jones of the Clash guests on guitar. There are loads of covers in the set, mixing '50s, '60s and recent tunes. Songs included "I Wanna Be Your Dog," "Stepping Stone," "My Way," "Belsen Was A Gas," "Something Else," "Search & Destroy," "Chatterbox," "Chinese Rocks," "Take A Chance On Me" and "Born To Lose."

STRANGLERS	Belfast, Ulster Hall	SKIDS/THE ZONES	London, Music Machine
MEMBERS	London, The City Arms	TANZ DER YOUTH	Sheffield, The Limits
VIBRATORS	London, Dingwalls		

8th - Friday.................................

WIRE One of the more unusual quartets playing around London is Wire, a four-piece band that has been cutting great swathes through modern music ever since their debut LP "Pink Flag." Today sees the release of their second album, "Chairs Missing." It's a fifteen track compilation of widely divergent styles. On the LP are "Practice Makes Perfect," "Outdoor Miner" and "Marooned." Also included is their second single "I Am The Fly" but not their current 45 "Dot Dash." It's a disturbing album that will surely upset some. The band are about to embark on a month long tour of the UK at the end of the month.

BUZZCOCKS release their first taste of their next album in single form. It's "Ever Fallen in Love" and "Just Lust." Although the song will reach #12 on the UK charts, in March of '87 Fine Young Cannibals will make it to #9 with their version of "Ever Fallen In Love."

BLONDIE's third album has arrived. It's "Parallel Lines" and contains "twelve pulsating tracks that'll make you go round in circles." The LP was produced by Mike Chapman (Suzie Quatro, Sweet...) and contains the band's current hit "Picture This." Other tracks include "Heart Of Glass," "Sunday Girl," "Hanging On The Telephone" and "One Way Or Another."

TANZ DER YOUTH/QUARTZ	Birmingham, Barbarella's	SKIDS/ZONES	London, The Nashville
BARRY FORD/MEMBERS	London, Acklam Hall	B 52's	London, Hope & Anchor
FALL/GARDEZ DARKX	London, The Marquee		

9th - Saturday..........................

STIFF LITTLE FINGERS Only two days ago, Irish band Stiff Little Fingers arrived in England for the first time. With only pocket change in their trousers, they're headed for London to make their fortunes. Their best selling single "Suspect Device" has brought them to the attention of Island Records five months ago, who have arranged demo time in the studio with Hot Rods producer Ed Hollis. They make their London debut tonight at The Electric Ballroom.

U2 open for the Stranglers tonight at the Top Hat Ballroom in Dun Laoghaire, just south of Dublin. The Stranglers had arrived early and taken both dressing rooms. Here is U2's first opportunity to play with a big-time band and they have to get into their stage clothes crouched behind the speakers. U2 go onstage and try to blow the Stranglers away but the crowd is with the visiting heros and not the hometown team.

BERLIN	Dublin, Moran's	MEMBERS	London, Windsor Castle
STRANGLERS/U2	Dublin, Top Hat Ballroom	BANNED	London, Hope & Anchor
EXILE	Glasgow, Mars Bar	SKIDS/VALVES	London, Rock Garden
TANZ DER YOUTH/		MENACE	London, Town Hall
JOY DIVISION	Liverpool, Eric's	POLICE/NEW HEARTS	London, The Marquee
STIFF LITTLE FINGERS/		BLONDIE/BOYFRIENDS	London, Hammersmith Odeon
PHYSICALS/RUDI	London, Electric Ballroom	RICH KIDS	London, Caroline Radio Road Show

SEPTEMBER 1978

12th - Tuesday....................................

ULTRAVOX have their third LP "Systems Of Romance" released today by Island Records. It was recorded near Cologne, Germany at Conny Plank's studio. The openness that the band felt being outside the crush of the throbbing city is reflected in the change in sound that the band exhibits on the album. This also pushes the band further from being just a rock band and includes many synth bits that add a new dimension to the group. Titles included are "Quiet Men," "Maximum Acceleration," "Dislocation" and their previous single "Slow Motion." Ultravox is Warren Cann on drums, Chris Cross on bass, John Foxx on vocals, Billie Currie on keyboards and violin and Robin Simon on guitar. All provide backing vocals and most double on synths as well. John Foxx exhibits his passion for photography on the subdued and high tech cover.

STIFF LITTLE FINGERS Only three days ago, Stiff Little Fingers arrived in London from Belfast. They're trying their best to tie down a record deal. They were supposedly going to sign with Island, but that has fallen through. A good way of getting exposure is on the radio and John Peel from BBC1 has invited the band to record a session at the BBC's expense. The songs recorded tonight are "Johnny Was," "Law & Order," "Barbed Wire Love" and a new version of their debut single "Suspect Device."

JOY DIVISION Remember the album session that Joy Division did for those two promoters who thought they could get the band a deal with RCA Records? Well, the sessions are still unissued because their new manager Rob Gretton and RCA haven't been able to come to an agreement yet. The contracts that Joy Division signed (based on an American contract), had some points that made them questionable under UK laws. The group was unhappy with the percentages to be granted them and RCA was offering them no advance monies. The album is dead. Joy Division's lawyer has put the promoters on notice that they will be sued if they try to release the sessions. The group has offered to buy back the tape and forget everything. It's a deal.

CHELSEA	Birmingham, Barbarellas	LATE SHOW/TOYAH	London, The Nashville
SINCEROS	London, Hope & Anchor	FRANTIC ELEVATORS/THE UNITS	
ZONES/THE VALVES	London, The Bridgehouse	NOT SENSIBLES	Manchester, Band On The Wall
JAPAN	London, Music Machine	XTC	Sheffield, The Top Rank

13th - Wednesday....................................

THE RAMONES give singles buyers a glimpse of their upcoming album. The single is the unusually slow ballad "Don't Come Close" backed up with "I Don't Want You." The tracks include the Ramones' new drummer Marky Ramone. He joined the band in at the end of May when Tommy left to go into producing full time. Marky (aka Mark Bell) was formerly part of Richard Hell's Voidoids.

THE CURE have now officially signed to a six month contract with newly formed Fiction Records. They begin recording in a week.

POLICE	Birmingham, The Odeon	MEMBERS	London, Hope & Anchor
BLONDIE/BOYFRIENDS	Edinburgh, Odeon	SKREWDRIVER/THE VALVES	London, The Last Bastion
RAMONES	Glasgow, The Apollo	TANZ DER YOUTH	London, The Marquee
THOSE NAUGHTY LUMPS	Liverpool, The Wispa		

14th - Thursday....................................

SCRITTI POLITTI find do-it-yourself inspiration in the trio of singles the Desperate Bicycles did last year. These transplanted Leeds lads have all moved in together in a bare flat in Camden Town. They first met at college and agreed that nothing waited for them in Leeds. South to the big city, to London. They had been listening to a load of Pere Ubu, the Abyssinians and the Fall. They wanted to do something different, perhaps involving jazz, reggae and modern rock ideas. Scritti Politti is Green on vocals and guitar, Tom on drums, Neil on bass and Simon who handles the tape loops. They're on their way to their peak in '84-'85, when they'll have a pair of top ten singles.

SACRE BLEU	Dublin, Project Arts Center	POLICE	London, Rock Garden
CONTROLLED ATTACK/		MENACE	London, Walmer Castle
PATRIK FITZGERALD	London, Half Moon Theatre	RAMONES	Manchester, The Apollo
SQUEEZE	London, The Marquee	BLONDIE/BOYFRIENDS	Manchester, Free Trade Hall
ZONES/VALVES	London, The Nashville	YACHTS	Manchester, Russell's Club

15th - Friday....................................

THE RAMONES have their fourth LP "Road To Ruin" released in the UK today. The first 30,000 are pressed on yellow vinyl. Although Tommy Erdelyi (Tommy Ramone) quit the band earlier this year, he remained involved enough to produce the new album. All of the songs are originals with the exception of their cover of the Searcher's 1964 hit of "Needles & Pins." Other titles include "Don't Come Close," "I Wanna Be Sedated" and "I Just Want To Have Something To Do." The Ramones return to the UK for the first time since last Christmas, on September 23rd in Belfast.

ROBERT RENTAL/THOMAS LEER A pair of odd singles hit the shops this weekend. Bits of speech, voice clips and electronic meanderings are woven together into a unique pastiche of sound called "Private Plane." Thomas Leer is the artist on this experimental recording on his own Company \ Oblique Records label. Also on the same label is another called "Paralysis" and "A.C.C.," and is under the solo name Robert Rental, although Thomas Leer plays on it as well. Rental and Leer are two Scottish friends that dabble in experimental music. The two singles were recorded in their respective apartments on the cheapest of equipment. Then the pair had their singles pressed up and did the xeroxing of the covers, folded and took them to the indie shops. They have only had 650 of each made up and it took them some time to fold the jackets and hand stamp the labels. The duo have been into electronic music for quite some time

SEPTEMBER 1978

and have considered putting together a proper band in the future.

BLONDIE/BOYFRIENDS	Birmingham, The Odeon
RAMONES	Liverpool, The Empire
UK SUBS (Peel Road Show)	London, Battersea Arts Center
EATER/SECURITY RISK	London, Middle Of The Road
TOURISTS/STRAIGHT EIGHT	London, Music Machine
MENACE	London, Walmer Castle
THOSE NAUGHTY LUMPS	London, Rock Garden
SOFT BOYS/GAFFA	London, Nashville
SKREWDRIVER	Manchester, The Mayflower

20th - Wednesday..

THE CURE Chris Parry arranges time for The Cure to record in studio 4 at Morgan Studios in London, the same studios that they had their Hansa audition in back in May of '77. Throughout the evening they work on songs, eventually finishing recordings of "Killing An Arab," "10:15 Saturday Night," "Fire In Cairo," "Plastic Passion" and "Three Imaginary Boys."

JOHNNY THUNDERS has a new single out. He's going solo now that the Heartbreakers have split and is recording an LP called "So Alone." The advanced 45 is the track "You Can't Out Your Arms Around A Memory" with the non-LP song "Hurtin'." Guests on the single include Only Ones vocalist Peter Perrett on guitar and vocals on the "A" side and Thin Lizzy vocalist Phil Lynott on guest bass on the "B."

XTC	Edinburgh, The Odeon	STRANGLERS	Sheffield, Top Rank Suite

21st - Thursday..

SLAUGHTER & THE DOGS re-appear. It was June when the band split. Not finding any other jobs and the lure of the stage being so strong, the group re-forms. Their first gig back is tonight in Manchester. Among the new line-up is ex-Nosebleeds guitarist Billy Duffy and he's gotten his friend Steven Morrissey in as the new vocalist. It's Morrissey's chance to step in front of a mic for the first time.

STRANGLERS When the Strangler went to Scandinavia last year, they didn't leave on the best of terms. Trouble at the gigs plagued the band. Now, they've done something special for the Swedish fans. They've taken "Sweden (All Quiet On The Eastern Front)" from their newest LP "Black & White" and re-recorded it in Swedish as "Sverige"! It's available in Sweden with a special picture sleeve. It's flipped with "In The Shadows," also from the LP.

THE YACHTS are the Liverpool combo that had a one-off single of "Suffice To Say" last year on Stiff. They've followed Jake to his new label, Radar Records. Their new single is "Look Back In Love (Not In Anger)" b/w "I Can't Stay Long." The first 5,000 copies have a picture sleeve and are pressed in blue vinyl.

THE RAMONES "What we do takes a lot of concentration." —Johnny Ramone in this week's *NME*.

RECORDS/THE VALVES	London, The Nashville	ULTRAVOX	Sheffield, The Limit
SLAUGHTER & THE DOGS	Manchester, Russell's Club		

22nd - Friday..

THE BUZZCOCKS release their second album, "Love Bites" today. It was recorded in less than two weeks at Olympic Studios with Martin Rushent. Titles include "Nostalgia," "Operators Manual," "Sixteen Again," and eight others including their last single "Ever Fallen In Love" and "Just Lust." The LP also contains the writing debut of bassist Steve Garvey with his song "Walking Distance." The band remains Pete Shelley, Steve Diggle, Steve Garvey and John Maher.

THE UK SUBS, a long time favorite of many punk pub goers, have their debut single out. It's "C.I.D" b/w "Live In A Car" and "B.I.C." The band had previously been featured on two tracks contained in the "Farewell To The Roxy" LP earlier this year. The band's chief songwriter, Charlie Harper, describes the song, "It's about going down Soho where you're always liable to get picked up and frisked by the law. You're always looking around to see if there's any police. You just have to keep you eyes open for them." The UK Subs are fronted by rock veteran Charlie Harper (real name Manuel Vader.) His musical past can be traced back to various London R&B/rock combos. He began by fronting Charlie Harpers Free Press and by 1977 was in a group called the Marauders, that slowly mutated into the United Kingdom Subversives, UK Subs for short. Also in the band are Peter Davies on drummers, Paul Slack on bass and Nick Garratt on the guitarist. The single is available on indie City Records.

XTC Swindon band XTC have their latest single out today. It's the Andy Partridge tune "Are You Receiving Me" b/w Colin Moulding's "Instant Tunes." John Leckie produced the sides, the first of which will be included in the band's new album "Go 2" to be released later in the month. Initial pressings come in a full white sleeve with a giant "?" on one side and a similar "!" on the other.

KRAFTWERK German synth-dance band Kraftwerk has laid claim to issuing the first luminous vinyl single. It's their new recording of "Neon Lights" b/w "The Model" and "Trans Europe Express." The 12" single is part of a Capitol series of singles and albums, all falling in line with the current colored vinyl craze. This one's on luminous vinyl and glows in the dark.

JOHNNY MOPED	Liverpool, Eric's	VALVES/THE EDGE	London, The Nashville
UK SUBS/THE TICKETS/		YACHTS	London, Hope & Anchor
SECURITY RISK	London, Battersea Arts Center	RAINCOATS/B-52's/	
MEMBERS/MONOCHROME SET	London, Middle Of The Road	PASSIONS	London, Cryptic Club

SEPTEMBER 1978

23rd - Saturday...

THE UNDERTONES are Derry's answer to The Ramones. They're fast, sharp and write singable pop songs. Their debut EP is "Teenage Kicks" and it's out this week on Belfast's Good Vibration Records. The 7" EP features "True Confessions," "Emergency Cases," "Teenage Kicks" and "Smarter Than U." The Undertones are Feargal Sharkey on vocals, Damien and John O'Neill on guitar, Mickey Bradley on bass and Billy Doherty on drums. This is Good Vibrations' fourth release and most ambitious, with 7,000 copies being pressed up with a fold-out poster sleeve.

RAMONES	Belfast, Ulster Hall	YACHTS/WARM JETS	London, The Nashville
ULTRAVOX	Liverpool, Eric's	VALVES	London, Hope & Anchor
TAN DER YOUTH	London, Electric Ballroom	LURKERS	Manchester, The Mayflower

25th - Monday...

ALTERNATIVE T.V. Remember when ATV and Here & Now were tramping around the UK, playing gigs for donations and appearing at all sorts of hippie events? The result of that tour is an album called "What You See...Is What You Are." There's one live side by each band. ATV have "Action Time Vision" (sung as "Action Time Lemon"), "Going Round In Circles," "Fellow Sufferer" and "Splitting In 2" captured. Here & Now contribute "What You See Is What You Are," "Dog In Hell" and "Addicted." The sound quality isn't the best but the spirit is just the same as the concert tour was; what you saw, is what you got. A note on the cover pleads that you should not pay more than £1.75 for the LP. It's probably the best advice one could give about the record .

THE SAINTS' third album is "Prehistoric Sounds." It features the Australian combos current single "Security" as well as "Church Of Indifference," "Crazy Googenheimer Blues," "Everything's Fine," "The Prisoner" and "The Chameleon." There's also two '60s soul covers, Otis Redding's "Security" and Aretha Franklin's "Save Me." The Saints are still Chris Bailey on vocals, Edmund Kuepper on guitar, Alastair Ward on bass and Ivor Hay on drums.

TOM ROBINSON BAND/		CHELSEA/THE FALL/	
STIFF LITTLE FINGERS	Birmingham, The Odeon	THE SNIVELLING SHITS	London, The Music Machine
PATRIK FITZGERALD	London, Hope & Anchor	DISTRACTIONS	Manchester, Band On The Wall

26th - Tuesday...

THE CORTINAS debut album for CBS is out this week in the UK. It's called "True Romances," a rather soft title for a group whose previous singles had been "Fascist Dictator" and "Defiant Pose." The group has been together a little over two years and started out as a R&B cover band in their native Bristol. This could explain their cover of Smokey Robinson's "First I Look At The Purse" on their album. Other titles are all new original material. Songs include "Heartache," "Youth Club Dance," "Tribe Of The City," "Broken Not Twisted" and "Further Education." The band retains their original 1976 line-up and seems to have stylistically slipped back to their pre-punk days.

JOHN COOPER CLARKE's debut album is titled "Disguise In Love." Clarke is primarily a poet, but on the album he "talk-sings" some of his best known poems over musical backing tracks. Featured is a new version of the single recorded "Psycle Sluts," as well as "Teenage Werewolf," "Health Fanatic," "(I Married A) Monster From Outer Space," "Valley Of The Lost Women" and "Tracksuit." On the album is a host of friends and guest helping out. Ex-Be Bop Deluxe Bill Nelson is on a few songs, as is Buzzcock Pete Shelley. Even producer Martin Hannett jumps to the other side of the console to play bass.

MEKONS (RAR gig)	London, Blue Coat Boy

27th - Wednesday...

SHAM 69 play a secret gig at the Bridge House tonight in the London suburb of Canning Town. Just as the Sex Pistols appeared as "S.P.O.T.S.," the Stranglers as "The Shakespereos" and "Old Codgers," and Generation X under the name "Wild Youth," Sham 69 appear as "The Harry All Stars." It's a play on the name of their next single, "Hurry Up Harry." The crowd of about 200 insiders caught the show.

BUZZCOCKS/SUBWAY SECT	Dublin, Dingo's Rock Palace	HARRY ALL STARS	London, Bridge House
THOSE NAUGHTY LUMPS	Liverpool, The Masonic	JONA LEWIE/LENE LOVICH	London, Wimbledon Football Club

28th - Thursday...

METAL URBAIN have their third single out on their third record label. This time the French band is the guest of Radar Records who issues their "Hysterie Connective" and "Pas Poubelle" through a licensing arrangement with Rough Trade Records.

SID VICIOUS is onstage again in New York in a series of three nights at Max's Kansas City with a band called The Idols. It's comprised of ex-NY Dolls Arthur Kane and Jerry Nolan, along with Steve Dior. Sid has abandoned the bass and confines himself to vocals. Songs in his sets at these shows are mostly cover songs he's comfortable with. The NY Doll's song "Chatterbox," Iggy's "Wanna Be Your Dog," the Monkees' song "Stepping Stone," "Eddie Cochran's "Something Else," and the Heartbreakers' "Chinese Rocks."

THE VIRGIN PRUNES are one of the new bands that's sprung from the clubs in Dublin, Ireland. They're members of the same social set that count U2 among their number and have been playing together since the end of 1977. The Virgin Prunes are Gavin Friday (Fionan Hanvey) and Guggi (Derek Rowen) on vocals, Strongman (Trevor Rowen) on bass, Pod (Anthony Murphy) on drums, Dik Evans on bass (U2's Dave "The Edge" Evans' brother) and Dave-id (David Watson) on vocals. They've already played at a party in Glasnevin and another at the Dublin Project Arts Center featuring an entire specially constructed stage set.

SEPTEMBER 1978

LIVE TONIGHT!

BUZZCOCKS/SUBWAY SECT	Belfast, Ulster Hall
TOM ROBINSON BAND/	
STIFF LITTLE FINGERS	Edinburgh, The Odeon
XTC	Glasgow, Queen Margaret Union
WAYNE COUNTY &	
THE ELECTRIC CHAIRS	High Wycombe, Nag's Head
SOFT BOYS	London, The Rock Garden

UK SUBS/THE TICKETS/	
SECURITY RISK	London, Streatham Park Tavern
MICKEY JUPP/	
RACHEL SWEET	London, The Nashville
STRANGLERS	Manchester, The Apollo
NEON HEARTS	Manchester, Pip's

29th - Friday.....................

THE BOOMTOWN RATS are rapidly climbing the road to success and will reach a new high with their latest single "Rat Trap" b/w "So Strange." The "A" side is culled from their LP "Tonic For The Troops" while the flip is previously unreleased. "Ratmania" is sweeping the UK and the Rats will finally get their chance to be on *Top Of The Pops* when "Rat Trap" hits number one.

NINE NINE NINE have their second album out today. It's called "Separates" and features their current single "Feeling All Right With The Crew" as well as "Homicide," "High Energy Plan," "Rael Rean" and "Tulse Hill Night." The LP was produced by Martin Rushent. The first pressings of the album include a leaflet telling the purchaser how they can get a free 12" single (if they act fast) of "Action" and "Waiting," on the band's own Labritian label.

TALKING HEADS' latest single, "Take Me To The River," is a cover of a soul number written by Al Green that was a major hit in '75 by Syl Johnson on the American soul charts. It's coupled with "Found A Job." Both are taken from their current LP "More Songs About Buildings And Food." This will be the Talking Head's first Top 40 US hit. If you buy a UK pressing and you're among the first 10,000 to do so, you get a bonus. The surprise is an extra single of "Psycho Killer" b/w "Love →Building On Fire" in a special double sleeve.

DOOMED/TANZ DER YOUTH Three members of the Damned have joined to play a series of "informal reunion" gigs. All have had difficulties with careers away from the Damned. Dave Vanian has left the Doctors Of Madness, Rat Scabies experiments with the White Cats were less than rewarding and Captain Sensible left the Softies, only to start a new group, King, which lasted for about six dates. The trio are joined by guitarist Henry Badowski and begin playing together again tonight at the Plymouth Metro. Interesting enough, Tanz Der Youth, the band that Brian James started after the Damned split, has also gone their separate ways. James has no plans for joining his past cohorts, but instead plans to undertake a solo career. The Trio will be playing these dates, not as the Damned, but as the Doomed, since Brian James has claimed ownership of the name "The Damned" and refuses to let his former bandmates use it.

THE NIPS (formerly known as the Nipple Erectors) have their second single out on Soho Records. The "A" side is "All The Time In The World" and is flipped with "Private Eye." On the reverse of the sleeve, Shane asks "Why hasn't John Peel given us a session yet?"

XTC	Belfast, The Pound
TOM ROBINSON BAND/	
STIFF LITTLE FINGERS	Glasgow, The Apollo
PEARLY SPENCER	
TERESA D'ABREU/CRASS	London, Acklam Hall
ROCKPILE	Sheffield, Poly.

SOFT BOYS/THE VYE	London, The Rock Garden
WRECKLESS ERIC/	
LENE LOVICH	London, The Nashville
RAMONES	Manchester, Free Trade Hall
CHELSEA/THE FALL	Manchester, Factory

October 3rd - Tuesday.....................

ULTRAVOX have a new single taken from their new LP "Systems Of Romance." The track "Quiet Men" is paired with the non-LP track "Crossfade." Early copies come in a special limited pic sleeve.

SPIZZ OIL is an odd two-piece combo with Spizz on vocals and kazoo and Pete Petrol on guitar. Get it? Spizz-Oil. Rough Trade Records release the debut 45 today called "6,000 Crazy" b/w "1989" and "Fibre."

ULTRAVOX	Birmingham, Barbarella's
DOOMED	Birmingham, The Gig
XTC	Dublin, McGonagles
SLITS/INNOCENTS	London, Acklam Hall
PUNISHMENT OF LUXURY	London, Marquee

JAGS	London, Pegasus
POLICE	London, The Nashville
JOE JACKSON	London, Hope & Anchor
JOHN COOPER CLARKE	
GIRO/ED BANGER	London, N London Poly.
NINE NINE NINE	Sheffield, The Limits

5th - Thursday.....................

SHAM 69 C'mon, c'mon, Hurry up Harry, c'mon. We're going down the pub…"Hurry Up Harry" is the latest waxing from Sham 69. Nothing deep or social here, only a pub singalong about going to get a pint with your mates. It's flipped with "No Entry." Sounds more like Ian Dury than Sham 69. The snatty piano track is provided by producer Peter Wilson.

JAH WOBBLE is not only a member of Public Image, he's a solo artist as well with a white reggae 12" called "Dreadlock Don't Deal In Wedlock." Virgin advertises this new release under the enthusiastic heading "Do Not Play This To Your Plants." They conclude the advertisement with the hopeful addendum "Snap it up before we reprocess the vinyl." The 12" is flipped with "Pthilius Pubis" Both tracks were written by Wobble along with help from co-producer Wayne Jobson.

XTC	Belfast, The Pound
ONLY ONES	Edinburgh, The Astoria

MEMBERS	London, Rock Garden
TROOPS/SKIDS	London, Nashville

OCTOBER 1978

THE ELECTRIC CHAIRS/	STIFF LITTLE FINGERS ....Manchester, Apollo Centre
SKUNKS....................London, Music Machine	SUBWAY SECT/
FALL/DISTRACTIONS	TOM ROBINSON BAND.............Manchester, Middletown Civic Hall
MILITANT FRANK....................Manchester, Kelly's	

6th - Friday...

XTC would surely get the award for most wordy album cover if there was such a thing. "Go 2" is a simple black jacket with small white typing filling up every square inch explaining the obvious facts of the record. They embark on a philosophical treatise about how LP jackets lure you into purchase and are controlling by their very nature. Among the songs are "Meccanik Dancing," "I Am The Audience," "Beattown" and "Jumping In Gommorah." 15,000 early purchasers will be rewarded by a limited edition "Moulding's Map Of Swindon," a large fold-out poster for "White Music" and a spare 12" disc titled "Go+" containing five additional tracks which are marked "Play It Loud Or Not At All." John Leckie produced the sessions.

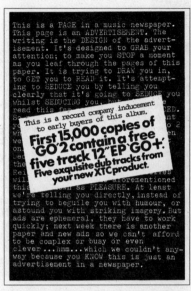

STIFF BARRAGE To celebrate the Stiff Tour '78, all five acts on the tour have a new album released today by Stiff Records. The new one from Wreckless Eric is "The Wonderful World Of Wreckless Eric." Its cover is a parody of the 50s UK Television program productions like Jack Good's *Oh Boy!* Songs are a mixed bag of originals like "Take The Cash," "Roll Over Rockola," "I Wish it Would Rain," and two covers, Buddy Holly's "Crying, Waiting, Hoping," and Tommy Roe's "Dizzy." Second of the five LP's is "Stateless" from Lene Lovich. She's no newcomer to the music scene and was prominent in the London pub scene in 1975-77 with a funk-rock-dance band called The Diversions. She's chosen Diversion bandmate Les Chappell to accompany her and co-write the majority of her new album. Tracks include her previously difficult-to-find single of "I Think We're Alone Now" as well as "Lucky Number," "Home," "Say When," "Too Tender To Touch" and Nick Lowe's ballad "Tonight." The three remaining Stiff album releases are Mickey Jupp's "Jupaneese," Jona Lewie's "On The Other Hand, There's A Fist," and Rachell Sweet's "Fool Around." Stiff chief Dave Robinson said, "It's time for the random finger of fate to select more victims for the cult hero machinery."

THE JAM have their new single out this weekend on Polydor. It's the haunting late night tale "Down In The Tube Station At Midnight." On the flipside is Pete Townsend's "So Sad About Us" and Bruce Foxton's "The Night." The Townsend song wasn't so much a tribute to Weller's inspirational hero, Pete Townsend, but as a tribute to the late Keith Moon. This is the Jam's sixth single and is a precursor to their new album to be released soon.

JOHNNY THUNDERS first solo album is "So Alone." He might feel alone since leaving the confines of the Heartbreakers, but the borrowed personnel on the album leaves him in the company of many of his drinking mates, gatecrashers and fellow musicians. On the album are Only Ones members Peter Perrett and Mike Kellie, Steve Jones and Paul Cook of the Sex Pistols, Phil Lynott from Thin Lizzy, Paul Gray from The Hot Rods, Patti Palladin from Snatch, Walter Lure and Billy Rath from the former Heartbreakers, Chrissie Hynde from a new band called the Pretenders, ex-Small Faces Steve Marriot and several others. The material spans oldies like the surf-classic "Pipeline" and "Daddy Rolling Stone," to new originals like "Leave Me Alone," "Untouchable" and "Ask Me No Questions."

NIPS...........................Belfast, The Harp Bar	SOFT BOYS ....London, Hope & Anchor
RAMONES ....Edinburgh, The University	WIRE/THE CURE ....London, Poly.
YACHTS ....Glasgow, Strathclyde University	ULTRAVOX...........................Manchester, The Factory
TOM ROBINSON BAND/	BUZZCOCKS/SUBWAY SECT ....Manchester, Middletown Civic Hall
STIFF LITTLE FINGERS.............Liverpool, Empire	LURKERS ....Sheffield, The Limits
MEMBERS ....London, A Little Bit Ritzy	

7th - Saturday...

PATRIK FITZGERALD is the poet-singer who is frequently confused with John Cooper Clarke. His new record is a "strictly limited edition of 5,000" EP called "Paranoid Ward." The tracks for the disc were recorded at two widely differing times and conditions. The "A" side of "Baby-sitter," "Irrelevant Battles," "Cruelest Crime," "Paranoid Ward" and "The Bingo Crowd," were recorded at the Covent Garden Redwood Studios three months ago. The "B" side of "Life At The Top," "Ragged Generation For Real," "Live Out My Stars" and "George," was recorded in Patrik's bedroom on a cassette last winter.

NIPS...........................Belfast, The Harp Bar	BUZZCOCKS/SUBWAY SECT/
FABULOUS POODLES.................Birmingham, University	ACCELERATORS ....Liverpool, The Empire
RAMONES ....Glasgow, Queen Margaret Union	EDGE/THE PACK ....London, The Nashville
SPLIT ENZ ....Liverpool, Eric's	

10th - Tuesday...

UNDERTONES Belfast band The Undertones have been signed to a long-term, world-wide record deal by Sire. Their indie EP on Belfast's Good Vibrations Records has done amazingly well, selling thousands even outside of Ireland and Sire wanted a piece of this hot new band.

OCTOBER 1978

Sire will re-issue the EP on their own label and put the band on the road to tour toward the end of October.

JOY DIVISION have had their EP "An Ideal For Living" re-released as a 12" disc. They were unhappy with the sound quality of the earlier 7" pressing, a problem solved with remastering the record. This time instead of being on Enigma Records (there already was another Enigma Records), it's issued on Anonymous Records. It comes in a limited edition of 1,200 in its own special photo sleeve. Joy Division will be in Cargo Studios in Rochdale tomorrow recording two songs for a sampler of Northern bands to be called "A Factory Sample."

LIVE TONIGHT!

WIRE	Birmingham, Barbarella's	JOE JACKSON	London, Hope & Anchor
ULTRAVOX	Edinburgh, The Astoria	DRONES	London, The Marquee

11th - Wednesday..................

PENETRATION The latest single from Penetration is "Life's A Gamble," from their new LP "Moving Targets." It's flipped with the non-LP "V.I.P." The songs include the band's newest addition, Fred Purser who joined on guitar in July.

PUBLIC IMAGE make their public debut with "Public Image." The single is flipped with "The Cowboy Song." Destined to be a collectable, early editions are wrapped in a special newspaper sleeve that folds out into a tabloid sized, two-page parody of *The Sun*. Public Image is the first opportunity for the disenchanted John Lydon to deal with fans, detractors, critics and the press. The flipside of the single has no discernible lyrics. It's a torrent of noise and feedback with a "clippity clop" on top. In the *NME* reviews, Julie Burchill writes, "It's a shame, but Rotten will probably end up around 1988 like Iggy Pop. Being touted around by some businessman on the strength of the outrageous band he used to be with, making offbeat records that impress a certain section of art-groupies and trying to play it straight to young audiences who were too young to be touched when he was good." Despite his attempts to distance himself from what the public wants, they want what Johnny's doing. The single "Public Image" sells rapidly enough to pop into the charts for two months, climbing to an unbelievable #9.

CLASH/OUTCASTS	Belfast, Ulster Hall	ULTRAVOX!	London, Marquee
DELINX/THE DELETED	Edinburgh, Stewart's	JAGS	London, The Pegasus
Stiffs On Tour	Liverpool, University	UK SUBS/MEMBERS	London, White Hart

12th - Thursday...................

SID VICIOUS (aka John Simon Ritchie) is arrested at his Chelsea Hotel apartment in New York and charged with the fatal stabbing of his girlfriend, Nancy Spungen. It's believed that the actual stabbing took place in the early morning hours. The story that Sid relates is basically this: he remembers being awakened late in the night and seeing Nancy with the knife they had bought earlier that day in Times Square when they were out shopping with another hotel resident, Neon Leon. Then, he woke again later (around 11:15 am) and found the bed covered in blood and Nancy under a sink in the bathroom, also covered in blood, with the knife sticking out of her side. He then called the front desk and asked for an ambulance to be sent. When the ambulance arrived it was accompanied by a police squad, who arrested Sid, detained and questioned him and charged him with the murder at the East 51st Street Station at approximately 5:30 pm. Back at the Chelsea, Nancy's body was removed from their first floor apartment, #100.

There are some conflicting stories about the events of last night and this morning. Here's the one uncovered by *Rolling Stone's* Michael Segell. Apparently Nancy (who handled the couple's finances) had just received a personal check from Malcolm on Wednesday, as well as $3,000 from Sid's Max's appearances. Nancy then called a friend of the pair named Rockets Redglare for some Dilaudid (synthetic morphine). He visited the couple this morning around 1:30 am, staying with them until about 5 am. When he left, he saw another drug supplier in the lobby heading for the elevator. More *Rolling Stone* investigation turned up Neon Leon, a punk musician who lived just down the hall from Sid and Nancy. Some of Sid's prize possessions were in his room. Items like a handful of Sex Pistols clippings, Sid's leather jacket and gold records. Unlikely things to be given away. Leon claims that the couple knocked on his door around 3 am and left the stuff. He continues with saying that Sid and Nancy called him around 4:30 that morning looking for a joint. Rockets, who claims to have been with Sid and Nancy between 1:30 and 5:00 am, recalls no phone calls or other visitors.

A third story making the rounds involves Sid and Nancy buying the entire drug stash from a dealer who was hanging around the Chelsea. The two went back to their room and hit. Sid was out cold when there's a knock on the door at about 3 am. It's the dealer, back to get a little bit of his stash back so he can hit in the morning. Nancy answers the door, refuses him the drugs and the dealer grabs the knife from a nearby table, stabs her and leaves with the drugs. There would be no prints if he's wearing gloves and Sid's fingerprints would be all over the knife since he's been playing with it all day since he bought it.

Most of the stories sound more credible than the one that the press is printing that Sid killed Nancy. All of his friends are coming forward saying that Sid was so terribly devoted to Nancy that he would never do anything to hurt her. Detectives found no money in the apartment, but have not linked the murder with a robbery. They think the money could have been taken by some of the scavenging junkies before the police arrived.

THE SUBWAY SECT have a new sound and a new single. The record is "Ambition" and "A Different Story." There has been a personal change in the band to lend it a different sound from the old Subway Sect. The new band is John on rhythm guitar, Colin on bass, Steve on piano, Bob Ward on drums and Vic Goddard providing vocals. Goddard describes his new group in the *NME* as, "A jazz funk bassist, a rock & roll guitarist, a cabaret pianist and a Bethnal Green docker on drums."

SPLIT ENZ	Birmingham, The Gig	UK SUBS/RAPED/RUDI	London, The Green Man
CLASH/ BERLIN	Dublin, The Top Hat	JOHNNY THUNDERS/	
TONTRIX	Liverpool, Everyman's Bistro	STRANGEWAYS	London, The Lyceum

OCTOBER 1978

LINTON KWESKI JOHNSON/NICO/	JOY DIVISION/THE RISK ....Manchester, Kelly's
CABARET VOLTAIRE/	THE ELECTRIC CHAIRS/
THE POP GROUP ....London, Electric Ballroom	EMERGENCY ....Manchester, Russell's Club

13th - Friday..

SID VICIOUS was brought before a judge and charged with second degree murder. Bail has been set at $50,000. The New York press has covered its pages with headlines that pronounce Sid guilty before he even has a trial.

PENETRATION'S debut album appears in UK record stores. It's called "Moving Targets" and early copies are pressed up in luminous vinyl which faintly glows in the dark. The album contains Penetration originals such as "Future Daze," "Life's A Gamble," "Too Many Friends," as well as two covers, Pete Shelley's "Nostalgia" and Patti Smith's "Free Money." Penetration is Pauline Murray on lead vocals, Fred Purser on lead guitar, Neal Floyd on rhythm guitar, Robert Blamire on bass and Gary Smallman on drums. The album was produced by Mike Howlett and Mick Glossop.

VALVES ....Belfast, The Pound	MISTY/MEMBERS/THE CRACK......London, Acklam Hall
WRECKLESS ERIC/	VIBRATORS ....London, Poly.
LENE LOVICH/JONA LEWIE/	YACHTS ....London, Bedford College
MICKEY JUPP/RACHEL SWEET .....Birmingham, Aston University	WIRE....................................Manchester, The Factory
ADVERTS ....Birmingham, Poly.	DAMNED/STRAITS/JOHNNY G ......Manchester, The Mayflower
THE ELECTRIC CHAIRS ....Liverpool, Eric's	SIMPLE MINDS.......................Paisley, Bungalow Bar

14th - Saturday..

SID VICIOUS Malcolm has arrived in New York and hired the firm of Prior, Cashman, Sherman and Flynn to defend Sid. He's also trying to arrange bail through Virgin or Warner Brothers Records. He been saying that he's got plans for an album from Sid, one that could pay for the estimated $100,000 in legal costs. In the meantime, Sid has been moved to the hospital wing of Riker's Prison to undergo heroin detoxification.

VALVES ....Belfast, The Pound	LURKERS ....London, Thames Poly.
TOM ROBINSON BAND/	PIRANHAS/IDOLS.....................London, Swan Hotel
THIRD WORLD.........................Dublin, The University	SOFT BOYS/GANG OF FOUR ....London, The Nashville

15th - Sunday..

SID VICIOUS' mother, Ann Beverly, has flown in to New York to see her son, but only after raising $10,000 from the sale of the rights to her inside story to the *New York Post*. Back in England, Malcolm McLaren's Kings Road clothing shop is already selling T-shirts with Sid surrounded by a bunch of dead roses and the slogan "I'm Alive, She's Dead, I'm Yours." Meanwhile, Nancy is buried in her parent's hometown of Philadelphia.

KLEENEX is evidence that even the Swiss alps can't keep punk influences from spreading. They're a group from Zurich and have just released a four track EP on the Sunrise Records label. Kleenex are Regula Sing on vocals, Klaudia Schiff on bass, Marlene Marder on guitar and Lisolt Ha on drums. Marlene's the only one any musical experience when the quartet got together back in March. Their debut EP includes "Beri-Beri," "Nice," "Ain't You" and "Hedi's Head." Only 1,000 copies were pressed up and they sold out immediately.

TOM ROBINSON BAND/	YACHTS/TONTRIX ....London, The Nashville
THIRD WORLD.........................Belfast, Queens University	BUZZCOCKS/SUBWAY SECT ....Sheffield, Top Rank Suite
D.C.NEIN ....Dublin, Baggot Inn	

16th - Monday..

SID VICIOUS Virgin Records has telegraphed Malcolm McLaren the $50,000 bail for Sid Vicious' release.

PRAG VEC Here's a new group with a new record as well. They're called Prag Vec. Their first outing is on their own Spec Records label and is called the "Existential EP." It's filled with "Wolf," "Cigarettes," "Bits," and the title track "Existential." The group have been together as Prag Vec since February and are Sue Grogan on vocals, Nick Cash on drums (not to be confused with 999's singer!), David Boyd on bass and John Studholme on guitar.

STIFF LITTLE FINGERS Belfast's Stiff Little Fingers have followed up their debut single with another rousing sound from the front lines. Titles are "Alternative Ulster" and "'78 Revolutions A Minute." Back in September, they were about to sign with Island, when the offer was withdrawn at the last minute. Since that time, their own Rigid Digits label has been picked up by indie Rough Trade Records. The collaboration makes the band's record available all across the UK instead of just a few cities as before.

THE UNDERTONES, a recent signing to Sire Records, have their debut "Teenage Kicks" EP reissued. It was originally released last month on Good Vibrations Records. The Sire reissue is hoping to capture some of the demand for the record generated by John Peel's constant airplay on his BBC Radio show.

FAY RAY ....Birmingham, Railway Hotel	WRECKLESS ERIC/
MEMBERS ....London, Hope & Anchor	LENE LOVICH/
ERIC BELL BAND/	JONA LEWIE/MICKEY JUPP
JOE JACKSON ....London, The Nashville	RACHEL SWEET ....Manchester, U.M.I.S.T.
ED BANGER ....Manchester, Band On The Wall	NEON HEARTS........................Sheffield, The Limits

OCTOBER 1978

17th - Tuesday...

SID VICIOUS Malcolm goes to Riker's Prison and gets Sid out on bail.

THE SAINTS One of Australia's premier new wave bands has called it quits. The Saints are going their separate ways. They're depressed over their situation with EMI that's left them high and dry in some crucial moments. Their first setback was when Kym Bradshaw, the original bass player for the group, left last year to join the Lurkers. In July of 1977, The Saints' single, "This Perfect Day," had a leap in the charts from #84 to #34 in one week. EMI hadn't planned on such brisk sales and shops in major cities had to do without any copies to sell for several weeks. No records- no chart action. The single dropped from the singles chart after only four weeks. Poor timing on EMI's part. Since this disaster the band,s manager and EMI were at odds, the result being that their manager (Chris Gilbey) left for Australia leaving the band behind with no management and a not so wonderful relationship with EMI. Add to that, the pressures of trying to set up a tour to promote their new LP "Prehistoric Sounds" and the band has reached their breaking point. Drummer Ivor Hay will be flying back to Brisbane on Thursday and guitarist Ed Kuepper will follow sometime next month. Meanwhile, lead singer Chris Bailey is hoping to work some songs over in his home studio and perhaps put another Saints together in the near future.

THE FLYING LIZARDS are the invention of Irish artist David Cunningham. He takes a completely different approach to music than anything around today. His "instruments," consist of an array of noisemakers, household appliances and studio tricks. Vocals are added by a college friends named Michael and Deborah Upton. In '76 David cut a shattered version of Eddie Cochran's "Summertime Blues" and took it to several labels who all refused it. Two years later Virgin has issued it as well as the flipside "All Guitars." David Cunningham is no newcomer to recording. He has been interested in the avant guarde music scene for several years. His first contribution to it was his self financed LP "Grey Scale," recorded back in 1976. It was at that time that the "Summertime Blues" recording released today was made. He also manages the experimental group This Heat. *NME's* Paul Morley relates this about a possible follow up, "A joke is a joke never worth repeating. There may be an album, whether Virgin put it out or now, which would put all his ideas into the pop idiom, serious and silly. He (Cunningham) would love to be popular, but realistically doubts that he ever will be."

LIVE TONIGHT!

NINE NINE NINE	Birmingham, Barbarella's	CHELSEA/PRAG VEC	London, The Marquee
TICKETS/UK SUBS/		CREATION/ALIEN TINT/	
CORVETTES	London, Bridge House	St. MATILDA'S BOYS	Manchester, Band On The Wall
JOE JACKSON	London, Hope & Anchor		

19th - Thursday..

THE GANG OF FOUR are a Leeds combo making their debut on Fast Records. The group came together in May of 1977 with John King on vocals and melodica, Hugo Burnham on drums and Andy Gill on guitar. After a year they brought in Dave Allen on bass and something magic happened. The groundbreaking group have selected "Damaged Goods" as the "A" side with "Love Like Anthrax" and "Armalite Rifle" on the reverse. Unlike other punkish bands in the movement, Gang Of Four rely more on sparse sounds, heavy bass and rhythm.

THE STRANGLERS' latest concert at Guilfords' Surrey University has left the band upset, the BBC furious and the college steaming. The Stranglers were contracted to perform a concert at Surrey which was to be taped by BBC TV for its *Rock Goes To College* series. The band was told that the free tickets would be distributed to students and public alike. When they arrived they found that all of the tickets were given to the university and none to the public at large. Furthermore, there were a great many students selling their tickets at greatly inflated prices outside the gig. The Stranglers took the stage and allegedly swore at the audience, sang obscene songs and smashed stage equipment. Then, after only fifteen minutes, they left. The entire production has been scrapped and the Stranglers' involvement with BBC TV in the future is in peril. The Beeb is still upset over recent problems with the group on *Top Of The Pops*, where (it's claimed) the band broke down the door to their dressing room.

JAPAN have their second Ariola single released. It's a new song titled "Sometimes I Feel So Low."

THE ELECTRIC CHAIRS	Birmingham, The Gig	RICH KIDS	London, Music Machine
WRECKLESS ERIC/		UK SUBS/MUVVERS PRIDE	London, The Green Man
LENE LOVICH/JONA LEWIE/		DOOMED/MEMBERS/	
MICKEY JUPP/		SOFTIES/THE CRACK	London, Royal College Of Art
RACHEL SWEET	Glasgow, Strathclyde University	YACHTS/SOFT BOYS	London, College Of Printing
PUNISHMENT OF LUXURY/		SLAUGHTER & THE DOGS/	
CYANIDE	London, Nashville	FRANTIC ELEVATORS	Manchester, Russell's Club

20th - Friday...

ELVIS COSTELLO has another biting single out in the UK. It's "Radio Radio" (remember the song he suddenly leapt into on *Saturday Night Live*?). It's a searing indictment of pap-pop radio. The song has been available to US consumers for a few months as it was included on the US version of "This Years Model." It came to life a few years ago as a demo called "Radio Soul" which was more of a song about what was great about late night radio than what is the dark underside. I guess rejection can change your opinion. It's coupled with "Tiny Steps," an outtake from the sessions for Elvis' forthcoming album, "Emotional Facism."

OCTOBER 1978

XTC is this week's *NME* feature story. Reporter Steve Clarke bundles into the transit van with the group and journeys to Cork, Dublin and beyond. They're on the road supporting their "Go 2" LP and are having mixed reactions in Ireland. Though the band are taking the experience with some grace, there is a noticeable dark cloud in the mind of keyboardist Barry Andrews. Ego clashes within the group have led Barry confide, "I don't see it lasting a hell of a lot longer. I think it'll explode pretty soon. Maybe one more album. I think we're soon going to exhaust the rock band format." He continued with, "At the moment I feel that there are a lot of things that are wrong and maybe getting up onstage and poking a few keyboards and bellowing words is a bit irresponsible." Clearly, Barry is not happy with his lot.

THE POLICE have just begun their first American tour. They've just come across from London (arriving at 11:00 PM, jumped in a cab at the airport and raced across town to get onstage at CBGB's.) They plan to play twenty-three dates in twenty-seven days, driving across the US in a station wagon packed to the windows with their gear.

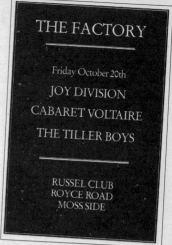

THE FACTORY

Friday October 20th

JOY DIVISION
CABARET VOLTAIRE
THE TILLER BOYS

RUSSEL CLUB
ROYCE ROAD
MOSS SIDE

THE DOOMED ....Brighton, Sussex University	SOFT BOYS................London, Hope & Anchor
NINE NINE NINE............Glasgow, Queen Margarets Union	CABARET VOLTAIRE/
PRAG VEC/SWELL MAPS/	THE TILLER BOYS ....Manchester, Factory
RAPED.......................London, Acklam Hall	

21st - Saturday..

THE SLITS have parted company with their drummer Palmolive (real name Paloma), who will continue to work with her other band, The Raincoats. That leaves Vivien Albertine, Tessa Pollit and Ariana "Ari" Up. Palmolive joined the group right at the beginning, late in 1976. Ex-Big In Japan drummer Budgie, is sitting in while they look for a suitable replacement.

IAN DURY is the subject of a rushed re-release by Warners. It's more than two years since Kilburn & The High Roads split up and now Warner Brothers UK reissues the album they deleted in '75. Retitled "Wotabunch," the LP is all previously released material taken from the Kilburn's various singles and 1975 LP "Handsome." Tracks include "Crippled With Nerves," "Upminster Kid," "The Roadette Song," "Rough Kids," "The Badger & The Rabbit" and "Billy Bentley." According to a story in the *NME*, Ian Dury heard about the impending release of this LP went to Warner Brothers Records with a proposal to have all of the tracks re-cut using his current band The Blockheads. The costs for these sessions was estimated to be only about £5,000. Warners reportedly told Dury that they only expected the album to sell about 25,000 copies and it wasn't worth the money to re-cut the tracks.

GENERATION X The news was wrong. Generation X haven't split up. They've been recording their second album with producer/musician Ian Hunter. It's set for release next month and is tentatively titled "Intercourse (Old Meets New)."

DR. FEELGOOD/SQUEEZE............Birmingham, Odeon	VIBRATORS...........................London, The Marquee
BUZZCOCKS/SUBWAY SECT.........Glasgow, The Apollo	MEMBERS/LOCAL OPERATOR......London, New Windsor Castle
WIRE/MANICURED NOISE ....Liverpool, Eric's (2 shows)	ADVERTS/IMPRINTS ....London, Thames Poly.
TOURISTS/PHYSICALS ....London, The Electric Ballroom	XTC....................................Manchester, The University
PRESSURE SHOCKS/	LURKERS ....Manchester, Middletown Civic Hall
ESSENTIAL LOGIC.....................London, Nashville	FALL ....Manchester, Poly.

22nd - Sunday..

THE VIBRATORS could be splitting up. Only two months after getting two new members into the Vibrators, founding member and lead vocalist Knox (aka Ian Carnochran), is quitting the group to go solo. Tonight could be the last night of the Vibrators. The rest of their current tour has been cancelled. Other members, Jon Edwards, Greg Van Cook and Ben Brierly are taking time off to consider the group's uncertain future.

SID VICIOUS is despondent over Nancy's death and perhaps confused about whether he had any part in it or not. He tries to commit suicide by taking all of his supply of methadone and slashing one of his arms. Sid's mother discovers him and quickly calls McLaren who races uptown to Sid, who weakly begs for someone to finish him off. This attempt further drives home the theory that it was a failed suicide pact between Nancy and Sid.

SLAUGHTER & THE DOGS, who were understandably dropped from Decca Records when the group split up earlier this year, find themselves in London for another record company audition. Their new lead singer Stevie Morrissey has incorporated some of his Motown influences in the band's set, working in the Velvettes' song "Needle In A Haystack." The band fails the audition and returns to Manchester very depressed about their future. Morrissey will eventually find more rewarding work with another band called The Smiths.

UNDERTONES Only a few months ago the Undertones were living in Northern Ireland and dreaming about being a successful band. Now they've not only got a major label contract, a chart single on their hands, they're also on television. Tonight's broadcast of *Top Of The Pops* features the band miming to their single "Teenage Kicks." They're also about to start out on a national tour opening up for the Rezillos.

D.C. NEIN...............................Dublin, Baggot Inn	WIRE....................................London, The Marquee
EXILES/FRICTION ....Glasgow, Doune Castle	CURE...................................Red Hill, Lakers Hotel

25th - Wednesday......................................

THE SKIDS' first record under their new contract with Virgin is called the "Wide Open EP." It's four songs on 12" of vinyl. Tracks

OCTOBER 1978

include "The Saints Are Coming," "Of One Skin," "Contusion" and "Night and Day." The initial pressing is on red vinyl. There is a two track version of this on 7" black vinyl as well.

CABARET VOLTAIRE are one of the most unusual bands to come out of Sheffield in years. They're an electronic dadist group that almost defy description. A cult following in the North brought them to the attention of Rough Trade Records who have just issued their debut EP. It is titled "Extended Play," and contains four of the band's originals. Side one has "Talkover" paired with "Here She Comes Now." Side two is "Do The Mussolini (Headkick!)" and "The Set Up." Cabaret Voltaire is Christopher R. Watson on electronics and tapes, Richard H. Kirk on guitar, vocalist and wind instruments and Stephen "Mal" Mallinder on lead vocals, bass and electronic percussive bits.

RICH KIDS	...........................Birmingham, Poly.	CLASH ....London, Harlesden Roxy Theatre
WRECKLESS ERIC/		METABOLIST/CRASS ....London, Moonlight Club
LENE LOVICH/JONA LEWIE/		YOUNG BUCKS/THE CURE ....London, Windsor Castle
MICKEY JUPP/		MENACE/ROTTING KLITZ/
RACHEL SWEET	......................Edinburgh, Clouds	THE CONDEMNED ....London, The Last Bastion

LIVE TONIGHT!

26th - Thursday.......................................

ADAM & THE ANTS were signed to Decca Records three months ago, recorded a month later and now have their debut single in the stores. They had previously had some cuts on the *Jubilee* movie soundtrack. Their new single is "Young Parisians," b/w "Lady." These days the ever-changing line-up of The Ants is Dave "family-man" Barbe on drums, Andy Warren on bass, Matthew Ashman on guitar and piano and Adam Ant on vocals and guitar. They've also used the services of Greg Mason on sax and Joseph Julian on piano for the sessions. It's still two years until Adam Ant will shift his sound to the double drum "Antmusic" sound that will change his life.

DOCTORS OF MADNESS/	
CABARET VOLTAIRE ....London, Music Machine	
SOFT BOYS ....London, The Rock Garden	
NOT SENSIBLES/	
FRANTIC ELEVATORS ....Manchester, Kelly's	
WIRE ....Sheffield, University	
MANICURED NOISE ....Sheffield, Limit	

27th - Friday.......................................

X-RAY SPEX Poly Styrene and X-Ray Spex have their new single released on EMI today. It's "Germ Free Adolescents" and "Age." The title track will be featured on the band's forthcoming album in November.

BLONDIE's second single from "Parallel Lines" is "Hanging On The Telephone" and "Will Anything Happen?" There is also a limited edition of 10,000 picture disc versions of "Parallel Lines" available today. The song is a big hit, reaching #5 in the UK without even breathing hard. "Hanging On The Telephone" was originally written and recorded by a California band called the Nerves that featured Paul Collins (future member of The Beat), Peter Case (future vocalist for The Plimsouls) and Jack Lee (future Rubber City Rebels).

JAPAN have their second LP within a year released. It was only six months ago that they made their debut and now they have a new LP called "Obscure Alternatives" in shops. It contains their single "Sometimes I Feel So Low," as well as "Automatic Gun," "Rhodesia," "Love Is Infectious," "Deviation," "Suburban Berlin," The Tenant" and the title track "Obscure Alternatives."

ADVERTS	.............................Birmingham, Aston University	RAPED/THE NIPS/RUDI ....London, The Cryptic Club
PLEASERS/SIMPLE MINDS	..........Edinburgh, University	X-RAY SPEX/INVADERS ....London, Hammersmith Odeon
SIOUXSIE & THE BANSHEES/		SOFT BOYS/
SPIZZOIL	.............................Glasgow, The Apollo	LUXOUND DE LUXE ....London, The Rock Garden
RICH KIDS	.............................Liverpool, Poly.	BUZZCOCKS/SUBWAY SECT ....Manchester, Apollo

28th - Saturday.......................................

THE JAM's third album (if you don't count the album they scrapped before its release earlier this year) is out on Polydor Records. It's titled "All Mod Cons," a name that is filled with puns, insight and even rendered in a 60s "Immediate" type face. It contains their previous singles "Down In The Tube Station," "David Watts" and "A" Bomb In Wardor Street." There's also one of the band's quietest ballads, "English Rose." Other songs include "To Be Someone," "Billy Hunt," "The Place I Love" and "Fly." The album was produced by Vic Coppersmith-Heaven with Polydor A&R man Chris Parry helping out as well.

THE SPECIALS have reached the breaking point. During their tour with the Clash five months back, Clash manager Bernie Rhodes started working with the group. He's kept them in rehearsals, rehearsals and more rehearsals and didn't allow them to play any gigs. The band is so frustrated that their drummer has quit the group. Jerry Dammers has now split with their "manager" and gone back to Coventry to start up again. After the tour and the great reviews they feel they've lost a lot of momentum.

PENETRATION (2 shows)	.............Liverpool, Eric's	DR. FEELGOOD/SQUEEZE ....London, Hammersmith Odeon
THE BISHOPS/		HUMAN LEAGUE/MEKONS/
HUMAN LEAGUE/MEKONS/		GANG OF FOUR ....London, The Electric Ballroom
GANG OF FOUR	........................London, The Electric Ballroom	THE LURKERS/SKREWDRIVER .....Manchester, The Mayflower
ONLY ONES/PATRIK FITZGERALD/		RICH KIDS ....Manchester, The U.M.I.S.T.
BLAST FURNACE & HEATWAVES	...London, University of London Union	THOMPSON TWINS ....Sheffield, Broadfield Hotel

OCTOBER 1978

29th - Sunday.......................................

PATRIK FITZGERALD Do-it-himself punk poet/singer Patrik Fitzgerald had moved on to something bigger than Small Wonder Records. He's just signed a contract with Polydor Records in the UK and will start recording his second album for release after the first of the year.

THE STRANGLERS are now being widely banned by other colleges as a result of the problems that Guilford University had with the Stranglers' concert there and the embarrassing scrapping of a BBC TV production of *Rock Goes To College*. The problems arose from a misunderstanding over the handling of free tickets passed out for the concert. Guilford University has circulated an open letter to other institutions encouraging them not to book the Stranglers either.

WRECKLESS ERIC/LENE LOVICH		DR. FEELGOOD/SQUEEZE	London, Hammersmith Odeon
JONA LEWIE/MICKEY JUPP		YACHTS	London, The Marquee
RACHEL SWEET	Belfast, Queens University	PENETRATION/	
SIMPLE MINDS	Glasgow, Doune Castle	BLACK SLATE/FUSION	London, The Roundhouse

30th - Monday.......................................

SHAM 69 have their second LP "That's Life" released. It features the single of "Hurry Up Harry" and their new one "Angels With Dirty Faces." There's also "Evil Way," "Is This Me Or Is This You," "Who Gives A Damn" and "Win Or Lose." The gatefold package not only holds the LP, but also a poster of "Sham 69 Fanx" for the fans.

PROTEX are one of the youngest of the bands that ever have played the Harp Pub in Belfast. All the members are under eighteen and pub manager Terry Hooley was well impressed with their approach to pop music in a punky vein. They don't wind songs around the sensitive political situation inherent in Belfast dismissing it as "not a very interesting topic." Hooley has added the band to the roster of his Good Vibrations label and has today released the band's single of "Don't Ring Me Up" b/w "(Just Want) Your Attention" and "Listening In." As with other Good Vibrations releases, the special sleeve to the disc folds out into a 11 x 15 inch poster. To stop any guessing about the group, they include a hand-written history of Protex inside the sleeve. It's taken from local fanzine *Alternative Ulster*. Gav writes, "Protex (Blue) came together in Jan 1978 when David McMaster and Paul Maxwell joined the remnants of the Incredibly Boring Band- namely Aidan Murtagh and Owen McFadden. The members of Protex are all seventeen years old. The only similarity between Protex and Led Zeppelin is that they're both four-piece, all male groups. I don't care coz their version of 'Jeepster' has all the right moves in the right places, somewhere Marc Bolan is smiling. Dion DiMucci likewise if he had have heard their version of 'Teenager In Love.'"

RAPED was such a harsh name. It made bookings difficult to get without anyone even hearing the band. Just last month they released their second single of "Cheap Night Out" but still had problems. They've given up on being Raped and have now decided to call themselves the much safer name "The Cuddly Toys." One of their first gigs under the new name is tonight at the Kirklands bar in Liverpool. This abrupt change shifts the focus of the band away from their previous punk image to a more early 70s glam stance.

WRECKLESS ERIC/LENE LOVICH		MARK GAUMONT/	
JONA LEWIE/MICKEY JUPP		ESSENTIAL LOGIC	London, Moonlight Club
RACHEL SWEET	Dublin, The Stardust	JOE JACKSON/C GAS 5	London, The Nashville
D.C. NEIN	Dublin, Baggot Inn	FALL/RODENT ENTERPRISES	Manchester, Band On The Wall
CUDDLY TOYS	Liverpool, Kirkland's Cafe Bar	THOMPSON TWINS	Sheffield, University

31st - Tuesday.......................................

JOE JACKSON's last time on record was as the piano player in Arms & Legs. Now he's a solo act and has been snapped up by A&M Records. His debut single is two originals "Is She Really Going Out With Him?" and "Do The Instant Mash." Jackson is a self-taught musician and was talented enough to win himself a place at the Royal Academy of Music. While still living in his native Portsmouth he was part of a working class cover group called Edward Bear. When a Canadian group using the same name put a record out, Jackson's combo was renamed Arms & Legs. Jackson sang backing vocals and played piano. Instead of covering other people's hits, they were now writing their own material, their own arrangements. After three singles on MAM Records with Arms & Legs, Jackson left to concentrate on his writing and singing. He got a £100 a week job playing as part of the backing trio at the Portsmouth Playboy Club as well as working as the Music Director with a local cabaret act "Coffee and Cream." In his spare time he put together some musicians and recorded a full album of his songs. Rejected by Virgin and Stiff, he submitted the tape to United Artists who turned him over to Albion Music. John Telfer of Albion snapped him up and became Joe's manager as well. The tapes then went to Dave Kershenbaum of A&M who signed Jackson last August. Now Joe has gotten this musician friends together, Graham Maby on bass, Dave Houghton on drums and lead guitarist Gary Sanford. They've re-recorded the album and the first track from it is out today.

RESIDENTS A three-fold press conference is called in London on behalf of The Residents. The occasion is another album release by the mysterious group on Ralph Records and the impending release of their next offering is announced as well. The new album is titled "Not Available" and the notes from Ralph Records claim the album was recorded back in 1974, although truth is stretched a bit thin with Ralph Records at times. The album features more weirdness, similar to their past efforts, with titles like "Never Known Questions" and "The Making Of A Soul." Supposedly Ralph were planning to release "Eskimo" (a sound epic telling the daily life of the Eskimo without words), but it was unfinished in time to go to the pressing plant, so they released this previously unavailable tape, "to maintain their credibility as a company." The next announced release on Ralph is to be "Buster And Glen," and will be ready "in the due course of time." There was also the ceremonious handing over of the master tapes of the future Residents' epic "Eskimo."

PENETRATION	Birmingham, Barbarella's	JOE JACKSON	London, Hope & Anchor
SOFT BOYS	London, Dingwalls	MEKONS/CREATION/	
UK SUBS/NECROMATS	London, Moonlight Club	ALIEN TINT	Manchester, Band On The Wall

OCTOBER 1978

LIVE TONIGHT!

RADIATORS/
STIFF LITTLE FINGERS ....London, Electric Ballroom

SIOUXSIE & BANSHEES/
SPIZZOIL ....Sheffield, The Top Rank

November 1st - Wednesday......................

U2 get their second chance in a studio working on demos. Unlike the last time when they worked with CBS's Jackie Hayden, who recorded them live to tape, Horselips' bassist Barry Devlin and their manager Paul McGuiness are making sure they take time to catch the band at their best. The sessions are at Keystone Studios and the band work on three original songs, "Street Mission," "Shadows And Tall Trees" and "The Fool." Of the three songs, only "Shadows And Tall Trees" would ever be reach a record and then in a re-recorded version.

SHAM 69 ....Edinburgh, The Odeon
JAM/DICKIES/........................
PATRIK FITZGERALD ....Liverpool, The Empire
XTC ....Liverpool, Mountford Hall
GERMS ....Liverpool, The Masonic

PASSIONS/PINK PARTS ....London, Moonlight Club
JOHN COOPER CLARKE..............London, Battersea Arts Center
EATER/IMPRINTS ....London, Last Bastion
SKIDS...................................London, Marquee
ADAM & ANTS/
MONOCHROME SET/UK SUBS ......London, Music Machine

3rd - Friday...........................

SQUEEZE and A&M Records team up to present a new record gimmick. There have been many issues lately with color vinyl, picture discs, shaped discs, gatefold sleeves, poster inserts but nothing like this. The new Squeeze single comes in a limited edition with a special sculptured sleeve. The sleeve itself is a frame out of a panel cartoon, with the actual figures in it raised and rounded. It's literally raised up almost half an inch in some places! The single getting this special treatment is the band's new effort "Goodbye Girl." It's backed with "Saints Alive." Both tracks are new and previously unreleased.

PERE UBU The second Pere Ubu album is out this week in the UK on Chrysalis Records. The album features "Navvy," "Caligari's Mirror," "I Will Wait," "Blow Daddy-o," and the title track "Dub Housing." Pere Ubu is now David Thomas, Tom Herman, Tony Maimone, Scott Kraus and Allen Ravenstine.

ADVERTS The result of the Adverts' switch from Bright Records to RCA is this week's single "Television's Over." It's flipped with "Back From The Dead," both new recordings. The Adverts have been through four labels in a little over a year: Stiff, Anchor, Bright and RCA.

YACHTS' latest single for Radar Records is out this weekend. It's stage favorite "Yachting Type," b/w "Hypnotizing Lies." Their gig last night at the Nashville was recorded by Radar and might be issued as a live album.

SPECIALS/DENIZENS (RAR) ....Birmingham, Poly.
CUBAN HEELS ....Glasgow, The Amphora
SHAM 69.................................Glasgow, The Apollo
THOSE NAUGHTY LUMPS............Liverpool, Christ's College
SIOUXSIE & THE BANSHEES/
SPIZZOIL ....Liverpool, Mountford Hall

BLACK SLATE/MEMBERS............London, City Poly.
VALVES/PLEASERS...................London, Nashville
CYGNUS/IDOLS/THE NIGHT ....London, Acklam Hall
PENETRATION ....Manchester, The Factory
ANY TROUBLE ....Manchester, Hattersley Com. Center
XTC ....Sheffield, The University

10th - Friday............................

THE CLASH have their second album and their new single released in the UK. "Give 'Em Enough Rope" comes almost a year to the day after their debut album. There had been a misunderstanding with CBS's US counterpart over the release of any Clash product in the US. The band settled the argument by refusing to record this album until it was agreed that the Clash would be available to the US market as well. The odd backlash to this is that this LP, their second, will be their American debut and their UK debut will become their follow-up album. The LP itself is entirely made up of all new material. The cover is a composite of an old American post card of a body in a desert with two buzzards and Chinese magazine art. The single is cut from their new LP "Give Em Enough Rope" and is titled "Tommy Gun." It's flipped with a Mick Jones vocal, (complete with wailing sax!) called "1-2, Crush On You." It is from the band's "Marquee" tapes recorded at the Marquee Studios in back in June.

THE REZILLOS' new single is "Destination Venus" b/w "Mystery Action." Both tracks are previously unreleased. The Rezillos are currently on a massive UK tour with new labelmates The Undertones as support.

DICKIES There's a fresh new Dickie for you today. It's "Give It Back" and "You Drive Me Ape (You Big Gorilla)."

JOHN LYDON, formerly Johnny Rotten, has started court proceedings to end the Sex Pistols relationship between the band, and most importantly to him, with Malcolm McLaren. A date is set for the hearing in the second week of February of next year and the notices to the various parties are sent out.

Thanks for giving us enough rope...

Joe, Topper, Paul +Mick.

NOVEMBER 1978

NINE NINE NINE There's a new single out by Nine Nine Nine this weekend. It's "Homicide" (from their "Separates" album) and it's coupled with the non-LP "Soldier." In another bout of vinyl gimmickry, the single is in a special picture bag with the first 20,000 pressed in green vinyl.

XTC	Birmingham, Town Hall	VALVES/INVADERS	London, Acklam Hall
SIMPLE MINDS	Edinburgh, Heriot Watt Univ.	PERIOD/RAINCOATS/	
EDDIE & THE HOT RODS/		DISTRIBUTORS	London, The Cryptic One Club
SQUEEZE	Glasgow, The Apollo	MEMBERS/ADDIX	London, Windsor Castle
UK SUBS/TICKETS/		SKREWDRIVER/BITCH	Manchester, The Mayflower
SECURITY RISK	London, Battersea Arts Center	JAM/THE DICKIES/	
		PATRIK FITZGERALD	Sheffield, Poly.

14th - Tuesday...........................

SIOUXSIE & THE BANSHEES' debut album "The Scream" is released by Polydor. It was recorded in August at the RAK Studios and features the some of the band's best known live material, as well as their current chart single "Hong Kong Garden." Titles include "Overground," "Carcass," "Metal Postcard," "Suburban Relapse," and their cataclysmic cover of the Beatles' "Helter Skelter." Production of the album is by Steve Lillywhite.

TUBEWAY ARMY make their long play debut. It's the last of the Tubeway Army, since they've renamed themselves. The LP comes in a special gate-fold sleeve with the first 5,000 in blue vinyl. Tracks are all new songs. There's "Listen To The Sirens," "My Shadow In Vain," "Everyday I Die," "My Love Is A Liquid," "The Dream Police" and a solo acoustic song called "Jo The Waiter (Mr. Smith)."

SQUEEZE	Birmingham, Barbarella's	CHELSEA/DECORATORS	London, Marquee
JAM/THE DICKIES/		PASSIONS/	
PATRIK FITZGERALD	Birmingham, Odeon	THE NIPPLE ERECTORS/	
JOY DIVISION	Canterbury, Odeon	CLAPPERCLAW	London, Acklam Hall
UK SUBS/TICKETS/SECURITY RISK	London, Bridge House	FRANTIC ELEVATORS/	
JOE JACKSON	London, Hope & Anchor	THE MEKONS/FAST CARS	Manchester, Band On The Wall

16th - Thursday...................

THE BUZZCOCKS release another single, although their current 45, "Ever Fallen In Love" is at #17 in the UK charts. The all new single is "Promises," b/w "Lipstick." Both are new songs, not included on the "Love Bites" album, though they were recorded at the same sessions. There is however an uncanny resemblance between the guitar line in "Lipstick" to that of the line in Magazine's "Shot By Both Sides." There's no Devoto credit on the Buzzcocks song, and one wonders if it was written before Devoto left the Buzzcocks over a year and a half ago.

THE POLICE have their debut album out today on A&M Records. It's titled "Outlands d'Armour," and features their single "Roxanne," "Can't Stand Losing You," and their new 45, "So Lonely." The new single is flipped with "No Time, This Time," a non-LP track.

X-RAY SPEX have their debut album released by EMI today. It's titled "Germ Free Adolescents" and contains a version of the title track as well as their single sides "Identity," "Let's Submerge" and "I Am A Poseur." Among new tracks featured are "Warrior In Woolworth's," "Art-i-fical," "Genetic Engineering," "I Live Off You," "I Can't Do Anything" and "Plastic Bag." On the record jacket, the tiny members of the band are trapped in test tubes.

CLASH/SLITS/			
PRESSURE SHOCKS			
(Sid Vicious Benefit)	Edinburgh, The Odeon		
JOLT/SIMPLE MINDS	Edinburgh, The Astoria		
PURE HELL/JOHNNY CURIOUS	London, Music Machine		
PERE UBU/RED CRAYOLA	London, 100 Club (Secret Gig)	SOFT BOYS/	
WIRE	London, The Venue	PLAIN CHARACTERS	London, The Nashville
		SKIDS	Manchester, Russell's Club

17th - Friday...............................

WRECKLESS ERIC has his cover version of Buddy Holly's song "Crying Waiting, Hoping" released by Stiff Records. It's flipped with "I Wish It Would Rain." Both songs are taken from his current LP "The Wonderful World Of Wreckless Eric."

THE LURKERS have out their fifth single today, "Just Thirteen" and "Countdown." Both songs are new and previously unreleased.

HEARTBREAKERS reunion! Just when it seemed that the Heartbreakers were finished, the principal members, Johnny Thunders, Walter Lure and Billy Rath, get together in New York for two nights at Max's Kansas City. It's nothing permanent, it's just a pair of friendly gigs for old time's sake. By the way, tape decks are rolling so this moment won't be lost.

THE FALL make another step forward with their latest single "It's The New Thing" backed with "Various Times." This is the first vinyl appearance with the Fall of new members Yvonne Pawlett and Marc Riley.

NOVEMBER 1978

LIVE TONIGHT!

SKIDS/THE NEX	Birmingham, Barbarella's	JOHNNY MOPED	London, N London Poly.
SIMPLE MINDS	Edinburgh, Art College	BOYS	London, Poly.
X-RAY SPEX/INVADERS	Liverpool, Eric's	HUMAN LEAGUE/MEKONS/	
PERE UBU	Liverpool, Rock Garden	GANG OF FOUR/SCARS	Manchester, The Factory
XTC	London, Electric Ballroom	PURE HELL	Manchester, The Mayflower
JOLT	London, Hope & Anchor	BLITZKRIEG BOP	Sheffield, The Limits

18th - Saturday....................................

SCRITTI POLITTI is a London combo who've taken their name from the political book "Scritto's Republic." The group are in the D.I.Y. vein, a cross between jazz, reggae, Robert Wyatt and Can. The single that marks their debut is entirely homespun, from the confessions about recording costs (recording- £98, mastering- £40, pressings- £369), to the xerox sleeve and rubber stamped labels. Beginning bands can get a handful of information on how to make their own record by just reading the wordy sleeve. The record is out on the band's own St. Pancras Records. Tracks on the single are "Skank Bloc Bologna," "28-8-78" and "Is And Ought The Western World." The one thing that the sleeve doesn't mention is who is in the group, who are Green, Neil and Tom and an additional "occasional" member.

RICH KIDS	Dublin, The University	RED CRAYOLA/TOURISTS	
U2	Dublin, Trinity College	CABARET VOLTAIRE/	
SIMPLE MINDS	Edinburgh, Univ. Pollock Hall	PRAG VEC/ SCRITTI POLITTI	London, Acklam Hall
X-RAY SPEX/INVADERS	Glasgow, Queen Margaret's Union	AUTOGRAPHS	London, Electric Ballroom
PURE HELL/SKIDS	Liverpool, Eric's	JAPAN	Manchester, The Mayflower
JOE JACKSON/THE PANTIES	London, Nashville	JOLT	Manchester, The Venue

21st - Tuesday....................................

BIG IN JAPAN were Liverpool originals. Even though the band has gone their separate ways, Zoo Records has issued the posthumous "From Y To Z And Never Again" EP. The four tracks were recorded throughout the band's career. Side one starts with "Nothing Special." It's from July '78 and is followed by "Cindy And The Barbie Dolls," from August '78. Side two has the Nov. '77 recording of "Suicide A Go Go" (their only London recording) and is followed up with "Taxi" from May of this year. The latter Big In Japan recordings generally had Ian Broudie on guitar, Bill Drummond on guitar, Dave Balfe on bass, Budgie on drums and Jayne on vocals. The exceptions being the substitution of bassist Holly for David Balfe on side two and Jayne's absence from "Cindy." Liner notes on the special fold out sleeve read, "Big In Japan began in the summer of 1977 along with a million other bands. We had no experience, we made a single, had a lot of fun and thought we were going to be stars, but we made mistakes, ran out of steam and broke up in the Summer of 1978."

FASHION are a new group from Birmingham. Earlier this year, video artist John Mulligan got involved with drummer Dik Davis while working on a one-off performance in Birmingham, necessating a group of live musicians to accompany a multi-screen performance. Thus were born Fashion. Since that time they've added the Luke on guitar and the trio started to play around Birmingham. They've put together their own label (Fashion Music Records) and have arranged distribution through Miles Copeland's Faulty Products. Their debut single is "Steady Eddie Steady," b/w "Killing Time."

FASHION	Birmingham, Barrel Organ	FALL/CERTAIN/RATIO/	
PHYSICALS	Dublin, McGonagles	GROW UP	Manchester, Band On The Wall
JOE JACKSON	London, Hope & Anchor	SHAM 69/CIMMARONS	Manchester, Apollo

23rd - Thursday....................................

ELVIS COSTELLO's new single is out today, but you won't find it under his name. It's hidden on the flipside of the new Nick Lowe single "American Squirm." Listing on the Costello track is "Nick Lowe And His Sound." It's a cover of a 1974 song originally recorded by Nick Lowe and Brinsley Schwarz called "What's So Funny About Peace, Love and Understanding." The song is said to be from Costello's new album tentatively titled "Emotional Fascism." There is a bit of a clue on the picture sleeve that Costello is on the record. The photo on the back has Nick standing in front of a window with a reflection of Elvis from his "This Years Model" photo session near the bottom.

ORCHESTRAL MANOEUVRES IN THE DARK An unusual electronic duo is playing tonight at Eric's in Liverpool. They have the lumbering name Orchestral Manoeuvres In The Dark and sound like a more accessible version of Kraftwerk. The two nineteen-year-olds in OMD are Andy McCluskey and Paul Humphries and were recently part of the Id, which split up only few months ago. Since then McCluskey joined up with Dalek I Love You and has since left that to get together with Paul again. The played around with the name VCL XI (which is supposedly a transistor part) and have now settled on Orchestral Manoeuvres In The Dark. The duo fill the stage with various keyboards, oscilloscopes, signal generators and pianos. Unusual stuff in the heady punky days.

IAN DURY and the Blockheads have an all new single out today. It's the humorous dance track "Hit Me With Your Rhythm Stick," coupled with "There Ain't Half Been Some Clever Bastards." This silly song will turn into Ian Dury's biggest hit, climbing to the top of the UK charts in five weeks.

EATER have their fifth single out this weekend. It's "What She Wants She Needs" and "Reach For The Sky." Both are Eater originals and feature the band's new guitarist Gary Steadman who replaces Brian Chevette.

LURKERS	Belfast, The Pound	REGGAE REGULAR/JAGS	London, Music Machine
VALVES/THE TOOLS	Edinburgh, The Astoria	HOMOSEXUALS	London, Chelsea Drug Store
ORCHESTRAL MANOEUVRES		MAGAZINE (2 shows)	London, The Venue
IN THE DARK/		CLASH/SLITS/	
TEARDROP EXPLODES	Liverpool, Eric's	PRESSURE SHOCKS	Manchester, Apollo

NOVEMBER 1978

WIRE ....London, The Marquee	FAST CARS/SISTER RAY.............Manchester, Kelly's

28th - Tuesday.............................

ADAM & THE ANTS' concert at the Marquee is caught and reviewed by *NME's* Deanne Pearson. The group is enthusiastically greeted by their fans and a Ants supporter told Deanne, "They're the only ones who've stuck to the small club circuit and their King's Road followers." Their set of songs were all originals including "Boil In The Bag Man," "Press Darlings," "The Day I Met God," "Lady," "Young Parisians," and an encore of one of the band's oldest songs, "Beat My Guest." Throughout the review, Deanne saw the band as repeating the ideas of 1977 and not contributing anything new to the music scene. Closing the *NME* review was, "…let's face it, they're just not going to make it. Punk's dying and Adam and the Ants are dying with it."

MAGAZINE have a "secret" record released today. The new Virgin 45 of "Give Me Everything" b/w a cover of the Capt. Beefheart song "I Love You You Big Dummy," is out without benefit of advertising or hype. According to Virgin Records, "…the people who want the record will find out about it anyway." Even singer Howard Devoto failed to mention the new single at his recent concerts when he sang these very songs. The tasteful image on the picture sleeve is "The Cactus Man" by French artist Odilon Redon.

THE OUTCASTS' goal is to be even bigger than the Undertones. Belfast's Good Vibrations Records releases a single by group of "Just Another Teenage Rebel" and "Love Is For Sops." It's full of teenage bluster and frequently strays from tune. The Outcasts are Greg on lead vocals and bass, Martin on backing vocals and guitar, Colin on drums and Getty on lead guitar. As with all Good Vibrations releases, it comes in a deluxe fold out sleeve that doubles as a group poster.

PERE UBU/RED CRAYOLA/ SOFT BOYS/ JOHNNY RUBBISH.....London, Electric Circus	PASSIONS/THE VEINS ....London, Moonlight Club
ADAM & ANTS ....London, The Marquee	DOGS/SKREWDRIVER................London, Music Machine
CHORDS ....London, Thomas A. Beckett	POLICE ....Sheffield, The Limits

29th - Wednesday.............................

MEKONS have their second single issued on Fast Records. It's "Where Were You?" and "I'll Have To Dance Then (On My Own.)"

THE MEMBERS have been signed by Virgin Records. They've previously had a one-off single with Stiff Records and have just been slotted in as openers for the Devo's UK tour. They replace Doll By Doll and there is some talk that Virgin (Devo's label as well) were responsible for the change, not Devo themselves. The group is fronted by former insurance salesman Nicky Tesco, who assembled the group from friends in his hometown of Camberly. The rest of the group is Adrian Lillywhite on Drums, Nigel Bennett on guitar, Jean-Marie Carroll on rhythm guitar and Chris Payne on bass

MAGAZINE/NEO......................Liverpool, Mountford Hall	MENACE/THE NIGHT ....London, The Last Bastion
ADAM & ANTS ....London, The Marquee	DOGS/SKREWDRIVER................London, Music Machine
JAM/SLADE/PIRATES/ PATRIK FITZGERALD/ GENERATION X/BERNIE TORME ....London, Wembley Arena	X-RAY SPEX/SORE THROAT ....Manchester, Apollo
	JAPAN ....Sheffield, Poly.

December 4th - Monday.................

THE CURE record a sound session for John Peel's radio show. Songs include "Killing An Arab," "10:15 Saturday Night," "Boy's Don't Cry" and "Fire In Cairo." This will give Peel something to play on the radio since the band have yet to release a record yet.

THE CRAMPS have their second single out. It's the original "Human Fly" and a cover of Sam Phillip's (the founder and owner of Sun Records) "Domino." Both songs are from the session they had with Alex Chilton in October of '77 and are out on the band's own Vengeance Records.

DEVO/THE MEMBERS..................Manchester, Free Trade Hall
MAGAZINE/NEO.......................Sheffield, Sheffield University

7th - Thursday.........................

THE DICKIES' new single is out just in time for Christmas. It's their 125 mph version of the holiday standard "Silent Night." Also in the festive mood is the flipside of Simon & Garfunkel's "Sounds Of Silence." The record is available today in a limited white vinyl pressing.

SID VICIOUS is in trouble again, this time at Hurrah's disco in New York. It's the early morning hours and Sid is out on the town with his new girlfriend Michelle Robinson. About 2:30 in the morning, Sid gets into a fight with Patti Smith's brother Todd. Todd throws a punch and Sid retaliates with a broken bottle, cutting Todd in the face. Police are called in and Sid, in clear violation of his parole, is hauled off to Riker's again.

THE XDREAMYSTS are another talented Irish band spotted by Terry Hooley playing at his pub. They're probably ten years older than any of the other groups on the label, but they still have the '78 spirit. He believes enough in the group to include them in his roster of talent and put out a single on his Good Vibrations Record label. Joining labelmates Rudi, The Outcasts, Protex and the Undertones, the

159

DECEMBER 1978

Xdreamysts become Good Vibrations #6 with "Right Way Home" and "Dance Away Love." The Xdreamysts are Brian (Moffy) Moffatt on drums, Roe Butcher on bass, Uel Walls on vocals and rhythm guitar and John (Wee Doc) Doherty on lead guitar. The release is in the usual Good Vibrations fold-out poster sleeve.

LIVE TONIGHT!

DOGS	Belfast, The Pound	PINK MILITARY STANDS ALONE	Liverpool, Eric's
HERE & NOW/THE FALL/		BOOMTOWN RATS/VIPERS	London, Hammersmith Odeon
PATRIK FITZGERALD	Glasgow, Strathclyde Univ.	ADVERTS	Manchester, Russell Club

8th - Friday...

PUBLIC IMAGE The long anticipated debut album "Public Image" arrives this weekend. It's ironic that Virgin signed the Sex Pistols when all other companies didn't want the risk, and now Virgin themselves are apprehensive about Johnny's new album. The disc contains several songs that can be seen as frontal attacks on the church. Side one starts with "Theme," then launches into the monotone drone of "Religion I" and "Religion II," ending with "Annalisa." Side two begins with their single "Public Image," then slides into "Low Life," "Attack," and ends with "Fodderstompf." The entire album is woven through with a disco-anti-disco feel. Strangely enough, Malcolm McLaren has wanted to begin an anti-disco band (and actually has tried with his group The Black Arabs.) The cover of the album and inner sleeve have the four members of the group posed into faked fronts of popular magazines. The sleeve bears the legend "Public Image Ltd. would like to thank absolutely nobody, thank you."

THE PRETENDERS have changed drummers. Chrissie and the rest of the group are not happy with the drummer they've been using. He was more or less hired on and paid a wage for gigs and sessions. He never really fit into the group. Guitarist Jimmy Scott has been telling Chrissie about a great drummer named Martin Chambers who had played with Scott in the Cheeks. He turned out to be living around the corner in Tufnell Park. On the way to the photo session for the single, they had to stop and break the news to Gerry Mackleduff he was out and Martin was in. Martin Chambers is onstage with the Pretenders for the first time Sunday night at the Nashville. The Pretenders were a group and on their way.

DOGS	Belfast, The Pound	SOFT BOYS	London, Hope & Anchor
JAPAN	Birmingham, The University	ROBERT & THE REMOULDS	London, Clapham Lark Hall
NINE NINE NINE	Birmingham, Barbarella's	ADVERTS	Sheffield, The Limit
PERE UBU/HUMAN LEAGUE	Edinburgh, The University	GENERATION X	Sheffield, Poly.
DOOMED	Liverpool, Eric's		

12th - Tuesday...

THE YOBS is the name that the Boys use to hide under each Christmas. Last year the Yobs graced record racks with a remake of the Chuck Berry song "Run Rudolph Run." This year their Christmas offering is their version of "Silent Night," The same song that the Dickies are singing in a 125 mph version! It's flipped with "Stille Nacht," - the same song sung in German. This record is on Yob Records and is limited to a pressing of 2,000 (so claim the Yobs).

THE RESIDENTS have a well timed, seasonal single out this week. It's "Santa Dog," b/w "Santa Dog '78." It's actually a harkening back to their beginnings. The cardboard sleeve of the single tells the story, "Following a large number of adventures, The Residents ventured to San Francisco and went straight to the studio and spent the entire night recording this new version of "Santa Dog," which was their first record (it is included on this disc for those unfamiliar with this 1972 classic). They decided to record this song again as a tribute to the innocence of their former days." It comes in a hard cardboard sleeve with a most odd photo of the Residents as four Santas.

FASHION	Birmingham, Barrel Organ	TICKETS/THE CORVETTES/	
WRECKLESS ERIC	Birmingham, Barbarella's	SECURITY RISK	London, Bridge House
VALVES	London, Hope & Anchor	PUNISHMENT OF LUXURY/	
ULTRAVOX	London, Lyceum	GARDEZ DARKX	London, Nashville

15th - Friday...

STRANGLERS In this week's *NME*, their elusive reporter M.A. Choman (geddit? Macho-man?) turns in a report about the supposedly new Stranglers' album that United Artists is suppressing. The article claims that the new LP is titled "Eastern Front." None of the titles can be remembered in any past Stranglers' live performance. Side one is, "Fuck My Old Boots," "Burt Bacharach's 'Alfie," "MiG," "Two Balls Are Better Than None (Any Day)" and "Only Faggots Hate The Sight Of Blood." Side two supposedly contains two Christmas songs, "No More Santa" and "Let My Reindeer Be My Weapon And My Statement." The exclusive *NME* article continues to claim that the real troubles about the album started concerning the cover. "The Stranglers had already submitted artwork depicting a giant phallus dressed as a Waffen SS Trooper (with the foreskin doing double duty as a coal-scuttle helmet), protruding from a snow covered battlefield." However the heads of UA rejected the cover, "in favor of a photograph of a dead girl with big tits." The Stranglers (as represented by this article) claim, "It's a really good album- far better than the boring, monotonous, simplistic load of half-baked sexist crap we released last time." Of course, knowing the *NME* and their natural ability to make things up for their entertainment value, there is every chance that this article by "Macho Man" is all bullshit.

TOYAH WILCOX and her band have been signed to a contract with Safari Records. The actress put together her group almost exactly a year ago. Her band is Pete Bush on keyboards, Mark Henry on bass, Joel Bogen on guitar, Steve Bray on drums and Toyah on vocals. Toyah can be seen in the role of "Mad" in the film *Jubilee*, as well as "Monkey" in the Who's *Quadrophenia* when it's completed.

THE DOOMED	Edinburgh, Clouds	UK SUBS	London, College Of Furniture
YOUNG ONES/THE CURE	London, Windsor Castle	BOOMTOWN RATS/VIPERS	London, The Rainbow

DECEMBER 1978

17th - Sunday......................................

RICHARD HELL is a new wave legend that has been actively involved in the underground scene since 1971. Legend or not, he's been dropped from the Sire Records roster. He's bounced back by joining up with the man who gave him his first big break in the record business, Jake Riveria, ex-Stiff mastermind and current head of Radar Records. Richard is now planning his next single, set for a January release. He's also filled out his band since his drummer Mark Bell left to join the Ramones in May. The new group is original members Robert Quine and Ivan Julian, plus Jerry Antonius on bass (which Hell originally played) and drummer Frank Mauro.

EDDIE & HOT RODS/		THE FALL/
MEMBERS/		MANICURED NOISE ....London, The Marquee
THE INNOCENTS....................London, Electric Ballroom		SKIDS/PINPOINT.....................London, The Nashville
IAN DURY & THE BLOCKHEADS ....London, Lewisham Odeon		ANTI-SOCIAL ....Manchester, Electric Circus
THIN LIZZY/UNDERTONES ....London, Hammersmith Odeon		

18th - Monday......................................

THE CURE get their first Nationwide press in the *NME* with an article titled "Ain't No Blues For The Summertime Cure." Adrian Thrills writes about the £20 Woolworth's Top Twenty guitar that lead singer Robert Smith plays onstage. "Hands up those who still reckon you need expensive instruments to play rock n' roll? I suggest you catch the Cure immediately. An abrasive light metal trio hailing from Crawley, a far-flung southern outpost of London's commuter hinterland. The Cure are like a breath of fresh suburban air on the capital's smog-ridden pub and club circuit."

AIN'T NO BLUES FOR THE SUMMERTIME CURE

ELVIS COSTELLO fans at the Dominion concerts this Christmas week get a free single of "Talking In The Dark" b/w "Wednesday Week." There is a total of 9,000 singles to be distributed over the seven nights. There will be a small quantity of the singles retained in the Radar bunker for poor sods who lose theirs, complain loudly enough or can pry one out of Jake's hands.

FASHION...............................Birmingham, The Barrel Organ		VALVES...................................London, Moonlight Club
DED BYRDS ....Liverpool, Kirklands Cafe Bar		ELVIS COSTELLO/
UNDERTONES/THE SQUARES ....London, The Nashville		RICHARD HELL
IAN DURY & THE BLOCKHEADS ....London, Lewisham Odeon		JOHN COOPER CLARKE ....London, The Dominion

21st - Thursday......................................

THE CURE have their debut single released by Small Wonder. The band was "discovered" by Polydor A&R man Chris Parry. He has recently started up his own label called Fiction Records. In order to get things rolling as fast as possible, Chris has licensed the tracks "Killing An Arab" and "10:15 Saturday Night" to Small Wonder Records. The initial pressing of 15,000 hits the shops today. Polydor, who will handle pressing and distributing the new label was unable to get things together before Christmas. The song "Killing An Arab" is based on the book "The Stranger" by Albert Camus, recommended reading for most O level English students. The "Arab" is not an Arab per se, just someone called Arab. The group has been together with various line-ups since 1976. They were signed to a five-year contract with Hansa Records last year after winning a talent competition, but got out of the contract by the end of last year. They're now under the guidance of Polydor A&R man Chris Parry.

U2 will be onstage tonight opening up for the Greedy Bastards at the Stardust Ballroom in Dublin. They're the "superstar" band that plays for fun occasionally. The group is Thin Lizzy's Phil Lynott and Gary More, Scott Gorman and ex-Pistols Steve Jones and Paul Cook. They're joined by Boomtown Rats members Bob Geldof and Johnny Fingers.

THE PHYSICALS know that banning a record can boost sales. That is, if the record is something worth banning, really something controversial. The Physicals' EP "All Sexed Up" was banned by the I.B.A. (Independent Broadcasting Authority) on the basis of its title and nothing's happened. In fact, sales have been slow enough that the band is giving away an undisclosed number of the singles free at tonight's Hope & Anchor gig. The four-track disc has the allegedly offensive songs "Breakdown/On Stage," "No Life/In The City," "You Do Me In," and the title track "All Sexed Up." The Physicals are Alan Lee Shaw on guitar and vocals, Steve Schmidt on guitar, Crister Sol on bass and Steve Bye on drums.

CUDDLY TOYS/RUDI..................Belfast, The Pound		ELVIS COSTELLO/
DEXY'S MIDNIGHT RUNNERS.......Birmingham, Barbarella's		RICHARD HELL
SIMPLE MINDS		JOHN COOPER CLARKE ....London, The Dominion
MOWGLI & THE DONUTS ....Edinburgh, The Astoria		JAM/JAB JAB/
CUBAN HEELS ....Glasgow, The Amphora		GANG OF FOUR/
IAN GOMM/		THE NIPS...............................London, Music Machine
JOE JACKSON BAND ....High Wycombe, Nag's Head		JERKS ....London, Tramshed
PHYSICALS...............................London, Hope & Anchor		UNDERTONES ....Manchester, Russell's Club

DECEMBER 1978

23rd - Saturday...

THE DOOMED are now reverting back to their original name, The Damned, which has been relinquished by former member Brian James. Their reunion is near complete with three of the original four members returning to the fold. Only Brian is still at large. Their first gig under their original name was scheduled for tomorrow at the Croydon Greyhound but has now been moved back to January 7th. Their last date as The Doomed is tonight's show at the Electric Ballroom. If you're among the first 250 fans you'll get a free 45 from the band as well. The disc is a demo advance of their new single "Love Song" and "Burglar(b)."

THE REZILLOS have decided to break up/start anew. Some members of the group have set tonight as the farewell appearance of The Rezillos. Lead singers Fay Fifi and Eugene Reynolds are quitting. The remainder of the group, Jo Callis, Angel Patterson and Simon Templar are all interested in continuing, in some form, with the Rezillos idea and sound.

IAN DURY fans had that sinking feeling at Dury's concert tonight at the Ilford Odeon. The over-excited fans were midway through the show when the floorboards gave way under excessive pogo dancing and caved in. The only thing that saved the punters from a quick trip to the basement was the sagging carpet.

LIVE TONIGHT!

REZILLOS/UNDERTONES ....Glasgow, The Apollo	DOOMED ....London, Electric Ballroom
THE ELECTRIC CHAIRS.............Liverpool, Erics	IAN DURY & THE BLOCKHEADS ....London, Illford Odeon
ELVIS COSTELLO/RICHARD HELL	THE JOLT ....London, Hope & Anchor
JOHN COOPER CLARKE ....London, The Dominion	IAN GOMM/JOE JACKSON ....London, The Nashville

24th - Sunday...

PUBLIC IMAGE's outspoken leader John Lydon does what he wants, but in an *NME* interview this week he seems dissappointed with the direction music is headed, "You know, people are bitching that the album doesn't sound like the Sex Pistols, bit if I'd had my way the Pistols would've sounded like Public Image. It was good when we started, the Pistols. Rubbish Rock it should've been called. I just loved the cluttering of it all. Complete breakdown of music, but you can't do it anymore. It's been washed out, watered down."

DEXY'S MIDNIGHT RUNNERS.......Birmingham, Winson Green Prison	PETER GABRIEL/
ELVIS COSTELLO /	TOM ROBINSON........................London, Hammersmith Odeon
RICHARD HELL/	THE IDOLS ....London, Windsor Castle
JOHN COOPER CLARKE ....London, The Dominion	

25th - Monday...

A FACTORY SAMPLE is the new offering from Manchester's indie Factory Records and is product from the fertile imagination of Tony Wilson, Peter Saville and Alan Erasmus. The notion was to put together a double pack 7" single with songs by four different groups that all played at the Russell Club in Manchester, known these days as The Factory. Featured on the EP is Joy Division with "Digital" and "Glass," and Durutti Column contribute "Thin Ice (detail)" and "No Communication." On disc two are John Dowie with "Acne," "Idiot" and "Hitler's Lover," while Cabaret Voltaire have "Baader-Meinhof" and "Sex in Secret." The special double single comes in a special silvery picture sleeve with sticker inserts for the price of £1.80p.

PUBLIC IMAGE LTD. ....London, The Rainbow	
BERLIN/NEW VERSIONS ....Dublin, Liberty Hall	

FAC 2

A FACTORY SAMPLE

27th - Wednesday...................

JOY DIVISION trek south to play London for the first time. Earlier they had avoided London because of Warsaw Pakt and the confusion that might arise with their names being similar (when they were called Warsaw). Now, they've simply been putting off London till they had more recorded product. They play tonight at the Hope & Anchor and admission is only 60p. *Sounds* spy Nick Tester was in the audience to check out this band that's been getting the buzz up north. Nick writes, "They stutter on stage wearing sulky, long looks. The vocalist, Ian Curtis, seems intensely irritated but he doesn't say anything between songs...the music is matt colored, often flat and usually undistinguished. I found Joy Division's 'tedium' a blunt, hollow medium, comical in its superfluous angst...Joy Division could be a good band if they placed more emphasis on poise than pose."

THE ZONES ....Edinburgh, The Abercorn	
SHAM 69/THE RECORDS/	
MERGER/THE INVADERS/	
JOHNNY RUBBISH..................London, Rainbow	
JOY DIVISION ....London, Hope & Anchor	
THE CURE............................London, Marquee	
STEEL PULSE ....Sheffield, The Limits	

JANUARY 1979

1st - Monday...

SIMPLE MINDS have signed with Edinburgh-based band's indie, " Zoom Records. In the past Zoom has championed Scottish music by issuing singles by The Valves, The Zones, The Questions and Nightshift. They even released a 1977 "mystery punk" single by Rich Kid member Midge Ure and Slik in their final days. Zoom is run by enthusiast Bruce Findlay and is now distributed by Arista Records. Simple Minds will start recording their debut album for the label this next week.

THE INVADERS, short for the North London Invaders, are playing their last gig under that name tonight at the London Film Makers Co-op. The trio of Graham "Suggs" McPherson on vocals and guitar, Mark Bedford on bass, and Dan "Woody" Woodgate on drums have decided that after tonight they'll be known as "Madness." It's an identity that will serve the band well through an enormous string of hit singles in the early '80s.

FASHION	.............................Birmingham, The Barrel Organ	WHIRLWIND	.........................London, Hope & Anchor
RADIATORS	.............................Dublin, McGonagles		

3rd - Wednesday...

THE MONOCHROME SET have their debut 45 of "He's Frank," and "Alphaville" released on Rough Trade Records. The songs were produced by ex-Red Krayola member Mayo Thompson. Organized almost exactly a year ago, The Monochrome Set is guitarist and vocalist Bid (ex B-Sides), Lester Square on guitar (ex-Adam & Ants), J.D. Haney on drums (ex-Art Attacks), and Jeremy Harrington on bass.

THE RUDE KIDS are the Swedish punk band that released the anti-Raggare single last August, and put themselves in danger of retaliation. The Raggare are a social clique of racist teds-cum-hooligans. Now, the Rude Kids are out again, stepping on toes. Their latest 45 is an answer to the Stranglers' "Sweden (All Quiet On The Eastern Front.)" Their reply in the form of a question is "Stranglers (If It's So Quiet, Why Don't You Play)?" The Stranglers were victims of the violence of the Raggare on their last tour and now refuse to play in Sweden. The single is flipped with the song "Punk Will Never Die." The 45 is available only on Polydor Records in Sweden.

U2	....Dublin, McGonagles	CUDDLY TOYS/RUDI	.................London, White Hart
EATER	.................................London, Music Machine	CLASH	.................................London, Lyceum

4th - Thursday...

BLONDIE'S new single is "Heart Of Glass." It's a cut from their album "Parallel Lines" but has been re-mixed for dance clubs. The five-minutes-plus version is on a limited edition 12" single with a dub version on the flipside. The single couples "Heart Of Glass" with "11:59," also included on the album. The song "Heart Of Glass" has been in the band's songlist since '75, and will be Blondie's first #1 hit in the UK and America. The song started off as "The Disco Song" a disco parody number that was part of Debbie Harry's sets with the Stilettos four years ago.

THE RAINCOATS are one of the thousands of new bands in London, most of which have a constantly changing membership. Their new drummer is ex-Slit Palmolive. She joins vocalist / guitarist Ann DaSilva, bassist Gina Birch, and Jeremie Frank on lead guitar. Strangely enough, Palmolive replaces her own brother-in-law, Richard (Snakes) Dudanski, who left to put together a new band called the Bank Of Dresden. If you go back to 1975-77, you'll find that "Snakes" played in the 101'ers with Joe Strummer. Both The Raincoats and the Bank Of Dresden will be appearing on the bill at London's Acklam Hall tonight.

RICHARD HELL doesn't really see himself involved in "real work." He admitted to the *NME* this week that, "Any kinda line o' work that I'm gonna be in is gonna be something that sorta depends on public response for it's success. So I figured at least I had a head start in this one, and I also had a whole lotta great songs…I mean, they wouldn't take me on the Apollo moonshots, so I decided to accept my fate and be venomous from the boards."

LIVE TONIGHT!

FASHION	.............................Birmingham, Barbarella's	JOE JACKSON	.........................London, Hope & Anchor
BANK OF DRESDEN/		GLORIA MUNDI/THE JERKS	.........London, Music Machine
RAINCOATS/			
SHOCKING STOCKINGS	.............London, Acklam Hall		

5th - Friday...

ELVIS COSTELLO'S new album was supposed to be called "Emotional Fascism," but the title was changed to "Armed Forces" instead. Nick Lowe produced the LP which includes Costello's secret single, "What's So Funny About Peace Love And Understanding," that appeared recently as a Lowe flipside. There's also new songs like "Accidents Will Happen," "Oliver's Army," "Party Girl," "Goon Squad," "Chemistry Class" and "Two Little Hitlers." Early copies of the album include a free EP with three songs recorded live at Hollywood High School in California last June. Tracks are the new song "Accidents Will Happen" as well as two oldies, "Watching The Detectives," and "Alison." The UK version has a limited edition that includes an unusual fold out sleeve and four color postcards.

GENERATION X The new 45 from Generation X is a thinly veiled tribute to Elvis Presley. It's titled "King Rocker," and is flipped with a real Generation X rarity, their version of John Lennon's "Gimmie Some Truth." Originally recorded as part of their John Peel session of June 12th, 1977, this 45 version is vastly different than the one included on the US album, last March. The single is available in the UK in four different picture sleeves, each one featuring a different member of the band, in a different color of vinyl. Still more fodder for collectors from Chrysalis.

RICHARD HELL/		RED NIGHT	.............................London, Three Rabbits
JOHN COOPER CLARKE	.............Birmingham, The Odeon	NINE NINE NINE	.......................Manchester, Russell Club
ELVIS COSTELLO/JERKS	.............London, Music Machine		

JANUARY 1979

7th - Sunday...

THE DAMNED show at the Croydon Greyhound comes with the added bonus of a freebie 45. Since before Christmas, the Damned have been giving away free singles to the first 250 people to arrive. They did it at their Electric Ballroom gig last night, and again tonight. The collector's single, "Dodgy Demo," featuring two new and unreleased tracks, "Love Song" and "Burglar(B)." The disc has plain white labels with a sticker on one side with the titles.

ELVIS COSTELLO/RICHARD HELL/
JOHN COOPER CLARKE..............Liverpool, The Empire

LEYTON BUZZARDS ....London, Hope & Anchor

9th - Tuesday...

WIRE have a new single out today. It's "Outdoor Miner" flipped with "Practice Makes Perfect." Both tracks are included on their current LP "Chairs Missing," but "Outdoor Miner" is a longer version than the album track. Where the album version fades after the second chorus, the 45 version continues through a guitar break and into a reprise of sorts. The initial pressing is on white vinyl.

THE FALL have a new drummer. He's Mike Leigh and formerly played with a rockabilly band called the Velvet Collars. Their old drummer Carl Burns left the Fall over "music differences" and because of "his desire to play with other top Manchester musical personalities." The Fall take to the road next month for a few weeks to generate interest in the band's next album "Live At The Witch Trials."

THE GANG OF FOUR are still looking for a record deal, and their appearance on the John Peel Show in a BBC1 session is coming at a great time. The group are recording four new songs, "I Found That Essence Rare," "5:45," "Return The Gift" and "At Home He's A Tourist." The session will air on the 18th. In this week's *Sounds* magazine Andy Gill explained the band's unusual sound, "The avant guarde way is to reject everything so that you can be seen as being totally different. Cutting out everything that sounds like anything else and losing all rhythm and beat along the way. "

LIGHTNING RAIDERS/................ Birmingham, Barrel Organ
FASHION ACCIDENTS ....London, Moonlight Club

THE VYE ....Sheffield, Limit Club

10th - Wednesday...

THE RAMONES' latest 45 is "She's The One" b/w "I Wanna Be Sedated." Both songs are from their current album "Road To Ruin."

GARY NUMAN & TUBEWAY ARMY have been invited to record a session for John Peel's Radio 1 show on the BBC. Gary Numan's selected three new songs for tonight, "Me, I Disconnect From You," "Down In The Park" and "I Nearly Married A Human."

LOCAL OPERATOR/
SOUL BOYS ....London, W Hampstead Rail. Hotel

THE DAMNED........................London, Hope & Anchor
JAGS ....London, Brecknock

12th - Friday...

THE ELECTRIC DREAD are bassist Jah Wobble, guitarist Keith Levine, and drummer Keith "Stratetime" Walker. They have out a mystery dub 12" single under the name "Steel Leg vs. The Electric Dread." It is unknown who the hooded figure of "Steel Leg" is but it's easy to hear it's not Johnny Rotten as they'd like you to believe. Tracks on the 12" include "Haile Unlikely By The Electric Dread," "Unlikely Pub," "Steel Leg" and "Stratetime And The Wide Man."

RICHARD HELL is back after a vinyl absence of over a year. "The Kid With The Replaceable Head," is his new Radar single and it's flipped with "I'm Your Man." Hell's also has two new members in his band. When drummer Mark Bell departed to join the Ramones last year he was replaced with a new drummer named Johnny, and a new bass/keyboard/sax player named Frankie. Richard is currently on tour with labelmate Elvis Costello.

KLEENEX are a Swiss new wave group that have just had their first UK single released by Rough Trade. The group got together in Zurich in March '78, and had their debut 45 out six months later. Kleenex are Lislot Ha on drums, Klaudia Schiff on bass, Regula Sing is on vocals and Marlene Marder on guitar. They're described in the press as being an unusual version of Siouxsie & The Banshees. Their debut EP featured four songs, two of which are coupled for their UK debut, "Ain't You" and "Hedi's Head."

LIVE TONIGHT!

SLITS ....Birmingham, Barbarella's
SIMPLE MINDS/VALVES/
THE MONOS ....Edinburgh, University
ELVIS COSTELLO/RICHARD HELL/
JOHN COOPER CLARKE..............Glasgow, The Apollo

SOFT BOYS ....London, Hope & Anchor
DRONES...............................London, Moonlight Club
JOE JACKSON ....London, Nashville
JOY DIVISION ....Manchester, Wythenshawe Col.
THOMPSON TWINS...................Sheffield, Limit Club

14th - Sunday...

RAMONES High School? A few weeks ago, the Ramones came to Hollywood and began filming their bits for the Roger Corman film *Rock And Roll High School*. It's an exploitation movie about a hard core Ramones' fan's reaction when her favorite band comes to town. The

JANUARY 1979

band will play about a half dozen numbers in the film and even have few lines of dialogue. New World Pictures plans for an April release. One scene calls for the Ramones to drive up to the front door of the Mayor Theatre in a big pink Cadillac with Leopard upholstery, performing "I Just Want To Have Something To Do." The New York license plate in the front says "Gabba-Gabba-Hey."

The film has it's beginnings a few years back when director Allen Arbush tried to get it going under the title *High School Spirit of '76*. It then changed to *Heavy Metal Kids*, and ultimately to *Rock & Roll High School*. Musicians considered early in the project included Todd Rundgren, Cheap Trick and Tom Petty. Roger Corman was sold on the idea of using the Ramones after seeing the comic-tabloid of *Mutant Monster Beach Party* that Joey Ramone and Debbie Harry did for *Punk Magazine*. Joey's a fan of Corman because of his past movies like *Attack Of The Crab Monsters*. The filming is being done at Mount Carmel High School in Watts, a long abandoned building that will be perfect for the finale when the school is demolished. Strangely enough, it's the same school where the '55 Glen Ford movie *Rock Around The Clock* was filmed. For this new movie it's rechristened Vince Lombardi High.

SCRITTI POLITTI "It wouldn't make a lot of sense for us to do what the Clash were doing then (1977)...'cos that wouldn't communicate the ideas and thoughts we're trying to convey, that's not dynamic!" — Green of Scritti Politti in this week's *Sounds*.

16th - Tuesday...

EATER has split. The group had played together since 1976 and were one of the youngest bands in the first generation of punks. There is talk of a final LP and some farewell gigs, but this is still in the planning stages.

DEVO have an album compilation of their Stiff singles released on Stiff Records this week. It's a six track, special priced EP that includes "Be Stiff," "Sloppy," "Satisfaction," "Social Fools," "Jocko Homo" and "Mongoloid." All of the material has previously been released. Early editions contain a bonus 45 of four primitive, previously unreleased Devo demos of "Mechanical Man," "Auto-Mowdown," "Blockhead" and "Blackout." The four track EP is on Elevator Records and is credited to the group "Mechanical Man."

THE UNDERTONES have their first "real" Sire release. Their previous EP had only been a re-issue of their Good Vibrations disc. This 45 features three new songs, "Get Over You," "Really Really" and "She Can Only Say No." They've also been invited to record some songs for John Peel's BBC Radio 1 show and studio time has already been booked for Sunday. They'll be recording four new songs, "Listening In," "Family Entertainment," "Billy's Third" and "Here Comes The Summer." The session will air on February 5th.

LIVE TONIGHT!

ELVIS COSTELLO/	FASHION ....Birmingham, Barrel Organ
RICHARD HELL/	UK SUBS/STOAT/
JOHN COOPER CLARKE ....Edinburgh, The Odeon	THE OTHERS.........................London, Music Machine

18th - Thursday..

CRASS are a radical seven piece group from Essex who are the victims of unlikely censorship. Their debut EP for Small Wonder "The Feeding Of The 5,000," was submitted to the Irish pressing plant that did all of the other pressings for Small Wonder Records. When one of the foreman at the plant heard the contents of the opening track of the disc, he demanded the track "Asylum" to be stricken from the disc or he would call a general strike and nothing would be pressed. Small Wonder got on the phone to try to find another plant that would handle it and all of the independent English pressing facilities turned down the job. Faced with the probability that it wouldn't come out at all if the track wasn't changed, Crass relented and struck the song from the record.

The EP now contains a two-minute silence at the beginning, entitled "Free Speech." The First 5,000 buyers of the record had the opportunity to write and get a cassette of "Asylum." The other sixteen tracks have provocative titles like "They've Got A Bomb," "Punk Is Dead," "Banned From The Roxy," "Fight Wars, Not War," "Sucks," "What A Shame," "Do They Owe us A Living," and eight other toe-tappers. Crass is Penny Rimbaud on drums, Pete Wright on bass, Andy Palmer and Phil Free on guitar, Steve Ignorant, Eve Libertine and Joy on vocals. They live in an open house near Epping. "The music is just the icing on the cake. We're not just talking about alternatives, we're trying them in the way we live. We try to live without the institutions and conditioning that's been applied to us - without normal structures like family, church and finance" says Pete Wright of Crass. They've been a band for two years. They're not into playing for money, just enough to cover their basic needs. The Crass are adamant that their message get out above all.

The *NME's* Tony Parsons reviewed the EP, characterizing it as, "...very trite, and very boring. The Clash and Tom Robinson's politics are facile but inoffensive, whereas Crass are facile and offensive, directing their self-righteous superiority, vehement cluck-clucking disapproval and anachronistic three chord thrashing at such rubber duckies as Securicor guards, factory workers, and of course... society." As for the deleted track "Asylum," Parsons referred to it as, "...contrived, sordid, ignorant piffle... At least PiL's "Religion" is a bit of fun."

ELVIS COSTELLO/RICHARD HELL/
JOHN COOPER CLARKE ....Sheffield, City Hall

21st - Sunday..

XTC Keyboardist Barry Andrews has left XTC. The reason was the standard "personal differences," yet it's more likely that he felt frustrated that his compositions for the band were passed up in favor of those of Andy Partridge and Colin Moulding. He told The *NME*, "...there was too much music to come out through the same outlet." Andrews had been feeling ill at ease in XTC for many months and took his chance at a change. He's planning to record a solo EP later this month for Virgin and then play around with several musicians to find a new direction. XTC are continuing without a keyboard player for the moment, and are auditioning guitarists. They say they're looking for somebody to bring new character to the band. One of Andy's first calls was to ex-Alehouse member Dave Gregory.

THE LURKERS play the first of two warm-up gigs before their major London appearance at the Electric Ballroom. The Lurkers offer a free picture disc to all attendants of this evenings concert at the Electric Ballroom. These are the discs that they were originally going to offer at their cancelled concert in London. The special picture disc is a flexi (the same flexi that came with their "Fulham Fallout" LP). The

JANUARY 1979

difference is instead of being pressed in gold, it's clear with the band's photo on it. Along with the free flexi, and probably to keep it from getting creased up, there is an accompanying free copy of their 45 "Ain't Got A Clue."

THROBBING GRISTLE have their new LP "D.o. A. (Third And Final Report)." It's a collection of live tapes from 1977, new tracks, solo performances of the members of the collective and even a recorded death threat from their phone answering machine. The impression from the liner notes is that this is to be the last Throbbing Gristle record. Perhaps in celebration of the release, they're staging another one of their occasional events tonight at the London's Centro Iberico in Harrow Road. Proceeds from tonight's show benefit Spanish anarchists. The performance will be an "instant soundtrack" to the screening of their latest film *After Cease To Exist,* which includes a castration sequence.

LIVE TONIGHT!

THE LURKERS/
ADAM & THE ANTS/THE EDGE......London, The Lyceum
YOUNG BUCKS/PORTRAITS.........London, Marquee

THROBBING GRISTLE ....London, Centro Iberico

22nd - Monday.....................................

THE PASSAGE Manchester group The Passage may be changing drummers. It's reported that ex-Fall drummer Karl Burns has joined the Passage, but there is no confirmed word that Passage drummer Dick Witts has left the group, a rumor the band finds amusing. Witts, a classically trained percussionist, and ex-Halle orchestra member, have been dabbling in experimental music for years and helped put The Passage together in December of 1977. The rest of the Passage are Tony Friel on bass and vocals, and Lorraine Hilton on keyboards. They have only one recording, the "New Love Songs" EP just out on Object Music Records. Tracks include "Love Song," Competition," "Slit Machine" and "New Kind Of Love." All four of the tracks are originals recorded in a scant three hours.

UK SUBS ....London, Marquee
JAGS/SNEAKERS.....................London, Rock Garden

ZZITZ/CARPETTES ....London, Moonlight Club
SINCEROS ....London, Hope & Anchor

23rd - Tuesday.....................................

THE MEMBERS have followed up their debut 45 on Stiff last year. The critically acclaimed "Solitary Confinement" is now joined by "Sound Of The Suburbs." Since their one-off deal with Stiff, the Members have been signed to Virgin Records in the UK and already have plans for an album and tour later in the season. Early editions of the single are pressed on clear vinyl and inserted in a package that features a TV screen sleeve with the picture clipped out. This allows you to look through the sleeve, through the record and onto a "suburban" picture printed inside the sleeve. The 45 is flipped with "Handling The Big Jets." The group distance themselves from the punk groups telling *Sounds* magazine "too much punk is based on heavy metal, or at least a very few permutations of power chords... what we want to do is get the feel, the rhythms of reggae into white music, build something new."

ART FAILURE ....Birmingham, Aston University
CUDDLY TOYS/THE LOUS/
STILETTO/GREY ....London, Acklam Hall

PORTRAITS ....London, Brecknock
THE STOPS/PRETENDERS ....London, W Hampstead Railway Hotel

24th - Wednesday...................................

THE RUTS avoid the perils of the major labels. The first two People Unite releases were by reggae band Misty. The Ruts debut features "In A Rut" and "H-Eyes." The Ruts describe themselves as "an aspiring comedy punk band." They organized back in the fall of '77 in the West London borough of Southall. Their earliest gigs were at RAR rallies, youth clubs and college gigs. The Ruts are Malcolm Owen on lead vocals, Paul Fox on guitars, John "Segs" Jennings on bass and Dave Ruffy on drums.

SHAM 69 have a new member in their ranks. He's Tot Taylor, a keyboard player who previously played in pop-rock band Advertising. He's to start with Sham at the Hendon gig this Friday night "just to see how he works out." He'll then follow the band and play with them for their next three gigs. If the addition of keyboards works he could become a permanent member.

25th - Thursday....................................

RED NOISE Bill Nelson and his new group Red Noise have out their first 45 today on Harvest Records. It's "Furniture Music" b/w "Acquitted By Mirrors," and "Wonder Toys That Last Forever." It's frenetic pop with synth stabs and swirls. Nelson's band was formed last August after the demise of Be Bop Deluxe and will have their debut album out in about two weeks.

KLARK KENT is back. Just when you thought that the Klark Kent joke had been told, here it is again. A new single from Police drummer Stewart Copeland's alter ego is on Krypton Records. It's "Too Kool To Kalypso" and "Kinetic Ritual." Still on green vinyl, still carrying on as if we can't see behind the disguise.

WRECKLESS ERIC/SOFTIES.........London, Strand Kings College
VALVES/NIGHTFLIGHT ....London, Nashville
MISTY BLUE/RUTS ....London, Albany Empire
WARM JETS/STAA MARX...........London, Ealing College Of Tech.
STRANGE DAYS ....Sheffield, Shiregreen Club

Too Kool To Kalypso

JANUARY 1979

26th - Friday...

GENERATION X take their fans to the "Valley Of The Dolls" with their new album out today. It's the result of the sessions last October with veteran musician/producer Ian Hunter. The LP includes their current single "King Rocker" as well as "Friday's Angels," "Night Of The Cadillacs," "Running With The Boss Sound," "English Dream" and "Paradise West." The band have also lowered the price of the album 40p below other new releases because they felt that the current prices was far too high and wanted to help their fans.

SHAM 69 are shaken tonight by more violence at a hometown gig in Hendon, North London. The group had been plagued with trouble at their shows since right wing factions have labeled the group as their chosen spokesmen. Pursey, who abhors aggro at gigs, has repeatedly tried to defuse the problem before it gets out of hand, and had refused to play London because of violence at a London concert in March of last year. The gig was preceded by the soundtrack to *A Clockwork Orange* and the nationalist "Land Of Hope & Glory." This couldn't help but stir up feelings in the waiting boot boys. Midway through the group's third number, "Cockney Kids Are Innocent," the fighting escalated and reached the stage. The problems were arising between the rough jackboot fans down front wanting to get onstage and join in with the group, and the band's own security team. Middlesex Poly, the site of the gig, had also brought in uniformed security guards with dogs as well. To compound matters, the BBC camera crews were on hand to film the gig for an upcoming viewing on *Arena*. The presence of TV cameras did nothing to inhibit the crowd.

Thirty minutes into Sham's set the band stopped and walked offstage amongst intense fighting in the audience. Pursey was visibly upset, in tears and was filled with disappointed with his hometown crowd. No matter what new direction Pursey sets for himself, he continually is shackled to his past by the violent and ill-mannered groups that have adopted him as their own. This is ultimately limiting his future.

LIVE TONIGHT!

FASHION ....Birmingham, Mr. Sam's	SHAM 69 ....London, Middlesex Poly.
U2 ....Dublin, Howth Community Centre	VALVES/PHIL RAM BAND ....London, Music Machine
BETTE BRIGHT &	GINO & THE SHARKS/REDS........London, Moonlight Club
THE ILLUMINATIONS.................Liverpool, Eric's	SINCEROS/THE MODS ....London, Dingwalls
THIS HEAT/WRECKLESS ERIC ......London, King's College	FATA MORGANA (film) ....London, Screen On The Green
OXY & THE MORONS.................London, Brecknock	ADAM & THE ANTS ....Manchester, The Mayflower
SOFT BOYS ....London, N.East London Poly.	PATHETIX/GROW UP ....Manchester, The Squat
MEMBERS ....London, Windsor Castle	

27th - Saturday...

XTC are in their rehearsal barn turning keyboard parts into guitar parts for their potential new member Dave Gregory. He's a little reluctant to take over Barry's parts and feels that XTC was going great and could potentially alienate a lot of fans changing their sound now. Andy persisted and the "new" XTC is being worked on in the snowy midlands.

THE CURE's gig tonight at the Marquee was a surprise for band and club alike. The surprise for the Marquee was that this band, still relatively unknown, had such a crowd turn out that there was a line down the block to get into an already packed club. The surprise for band was described by Dave Laing of the *NME* when they, "...came under attack from hard core punks, apparently because they were sporting blowwaves and baggy trousers, who gobbed copiously upon them all through their set, while the majority of the audience refused to let them off stage, the band having to play nearly their entire set all over again."

U2 ....Dublin Trinity College (The Buttery)	ADAM & THE ANTS ....Liverpool, Eric's
BETTE BRIGHT &	SOFT BOYS ....London, Rock Garden
THE ILLUMINATIONS.................Glasgow, Strathclyde University	PIRANHAS ....London, The Swan
DAMNED ....Glasgow, Queen Margaret Union	THE CURE.............................London, Marquee

28th - Sunday..

"You see the rock business needs rock n' roll cliches, it's what it survives on."
— Mark Perry in *Temporary Hoarding* #7

"Rock n' roll is about cocks and jiving, and the odd bloody nose...and about people like us talking seriously about the social order." — J.J. Burnel of the Stranglers in this week's *NME*

"He (Johnny Rotten) will see who'll sell the most records when this trial is over and it won't be him. I'm the only one of the Sex Pistols left. I was always more famous than any of them. They just didn't have any bottle." — Sid Vicious in this week's *NME*

RADIATORS/VALVES ....London, Hope & Anchor	YOUNG BUCKS/PORTRAITS .London, Marquee

29th - Monday...

STIFF LITTLE FINGERS are readying themselves for an extensive UK tour with Essential Logic and Robert Rental. Fans are surprised that original drummer Brian Faloon has been replaced by Jim Reilly. Faloon had been playing with SLF guitarist Jack Burns since they were both fifteen. It's not known what the reasons were for the split, although they will probably cited as "musical difference." The new line-up make their debut in Bournemouth this Friday.

JOE JACKSON has his debut album out on A&M Records this week. It's called "Look Sharp" and is a crisp, sharp, new pop album. The

JANUARY 1979

JOE JACKSON

LOOK SHARP!

cover is a simple black and white photo of Jackson's fashionable feet. That obsession with style is central to the album. It features the title track "Look Sharp" as well as his attack on the tabloids "Sunday Papers," and personal problems, "Is She Really Going Out With Him?," "Fools In Love" and "Happy Loving Couples." Jackson is backed up by Graham Maby on bass, Gary Sanford on guitar and Dave Houghton on drums. Joe is out front with vocals and plays piano and harmonica. The shoes on the cover are side-lace Denson Winklepickers and are generally priced less than sixteen pounds. Joe is currently showing off these shoes (and his new album material) on his "Be There And Spiv" tour. "I was a slightly odd teenager" — Joe Jackson in *NME*.

THE TOURISTS are onstage tonight at the Hope & Anchor in their newest stage clothes, cherry red cabaret jackets and pink Beatle boots. Among the crowd are more than a few A&R men, toes tapping in the back row and sweaty hands on checkbooks.

Pursey's Package with
ANGELIC UPSTARTS/
INVADERS ....Birmingham, Barbarella's
BETTE BRIGHT &
THE ILLUMINATIONS/
HEADBOYS/JOE JACKSON..........Edinburgh, Tiffany's

TOURISTS.............................London, Hope & Anchor
CUDDLY TOYS/CRASS ....London, Moonlight Club
PATRIK FITZGERALD/
MOLESTERS/THE WALL
NICKY & THE DOTS/CRASS ....London, Music Machine

30th - Tuesday...

BUZZCOCKS Although there are rumors that The Buzzcocks are splitting up, it isn't true. There is a grain of truth to the stories though. Buzzcock drummer John Maher is currently working with Patrik Fitzgerald on the poet's debut album. Also, Steve Garvey and Pete Shelley are both reportedly working on solo singles. The group recorded a new single just days ago and will re-group for a few dates in March.

JOE JACKSON ....Glasgow, Tiffany's
PORTRAITS ....London, Brecknock
ELVIS COSTELLO/
RICHARD HELL/
JOHN COOPER CLARKE..............London, Hammersmith Palais
PRESS/NEON HEARTS ....London, Moonlight

LIVE TONIGHT!

TOURISTS.............................London, Hope & Anchor
RANDOM HOLD ....London, Rock Garden
ELECTROTUNES......................London, Stapleton
VIRGINIA WOLF/
VIBRANT THIGH.....................Manchester, Band On The Wall
WRECKLESS ERIC/SOFTIES.........Sheffield, Limit Club

31st - Wednesday..

SHAM 69 "A lot of people over the last months have slagged us, blaming us for everything. Because of those people, this is the last gig that Sham 69 are ever gonna play." Those were the words that stilled a capacity crowd at Friar's in Aylesbury tonight just two songs into a venomous set by Sham 69. The problems reached a peak at last Friday's gig in Hendon. Pursey is quitting! It's said that he had to be coaxed to do this gig as well. After telling the crowd that this was Sham's last live appearance, Pursey launched into "Cockney Kids Are Innocent" altering the lyrics to "Sham 69 Are Innocent." The set was littered with Sham classics and some revealing covers. During their version of the Beatles' song "Day Tripper" Jimmy stretched out the line "…it took me soooooo long to find out." The gig came to a thunderous conclusion, the band giving all they had into a final, frenetic moment. Afterwards they were asked back in the future by the Friar's promoter. The band declined the offer. Sham as a live band have been stilled by the actions of a few unruly, inconsiderate fans.

MEMBERS ....London, Hope & Anchor
PUNISHMENT OF LUXURY/
BITCH..................................London, Music Machine

RECORDS ....London, Marquee
ABC ....London, Nelson's Club
PIRANHAS ....London, Windsor Castle

February 1st - Thursday.....................................

THE LEYTON BUZZARDS got the attention of Chrysalis Records in a competition called Band Of Hope And Glory staged by *The Sun* and Radio One. The goal was to find the latest and greatest unsigned bands. The Leyton Buzzards sent in a tape, were narrowed down to the final fifty bands and eventually won the contest at the finals in the London Palladium. The prize was a recording contract with Chrysalis. Their first 45 for the label is released today is "Saturday Night Beneath The Plastic Palm Trees," b/w "Through With You." The sessions were produced by Steve Lillywhite are the band's follow up to last summer's "19 And Mad" single on Small Wonder Records.

B-52's Kate and Cindy, are pictured in the T-Zers section of this week's *NME* posed against someone's garage door in their hometown of Athens, Georgia. The caption reads, "Allow T-Zers to introduce you to Kate and Cindy, two all-American ladies from all-American band the B-52's, the biggest thing to come out of Athens, Georgia since…well, actually we don't know of anything else…but we know that US record company men are currently stubbing their cigars out in each other's faces to sign them."

SID VICIOUS The fight that Sid got himself into on December 9th at Hurrah's has kept Sid in Riker's detox for almost seven weeks. Sid was clean, free from heroin and got to have his hearing. James Merberg is a persuasive enough attorney to get Sid released immediately. Leaving Rikers, he's greeted by some of his junkie friend's from the Chelsea and his mother, who had already purchased more heroin for her detoxed son. The group went back to a friends apartment in Greenwich Village to celebrate his release. Backsliding from the seven weeks of detox he painfully endured, Sid immediately jumped back into heroin. The dose wasn't very potent, and he argued that he needed more. His mother obliges him. Twenty minutes later Sid's collapsed on a bed and the friends talk about whether to take him to the hospital, but Sid says he's all right. Sometime past midnight, Sid awakes and finds the rest of the heroin in his mother's purse, he uses it

FEBRUARY 1979

and drifts off, permanently.

Afterwards a note is found and kept by Sid's mother, Anne Beverley, that reads, "We had a death pact. I have to keep my half of the bargain. Please bury me next to my baby in my leather jacket, jeans and motorcycle boots. Goodbye." It's believed by everyone that Sid's death was accidental but this note throws new light on it.

U2 ....Dublin, Trinity College (The Buttery)	CHELSEA/UK SUBS/
LAURA LOGIC/	CUDDLY TOYS.........................London, Music Machine
DOUBLE EXPOSURE ....High Wycombe, Nag's Head	MEMBERS/LOCAL OPERATOR .....London, Nashville
JOE JACKSON ....London, Dingwalls	ALIEN TINT/THE STOPOUTS.........Manchester, Pip's

2nd - Friday...

LENE LOVICH is jump-starting her career by re-releasing her single "Lucky Number." Originally out back in July as Stiff #35, she's re-recorded the song and Stiff issues it again with a new number, Stiff #42. The flip side is new as well, another original titled "Home." The re-recorded song will turn the trick, and in two weeks the song will hit #3 in the UK.

THE PRETENDERS' show tonight at the Moonlight club, is only about the fifth the band has played, and already there is a huge buzz about the band being the next big thing. Fronted by American vocalist Chrissie Hynde, she wows the audience of new fans, journalists and envious rival record company men. *NME's* Nick Kent is impressed and describes the band as one who can "whip most other outfits- new wave or otherwise to a frazzle… Chrissie Hynde is the kind of talent that (gender be damned) appears only once in a blue moon. A treacherously powerful vocalist, adept rhythm guitarist, fiery stage presence and often startlingly effective songwriter, her talents are perfectly complemented by her band."

RAMONES "I was surprised, very much so, when Jeffrey (aka Joey Ramone) and the band started putting out records…The first coupla times I saw the group play, I must say I didn't like them, but I got used to it- although it took some time…Still, I think they oughta put more different things in their music, 'n complicate it up a bit, if they wanna get high up on the whattaycallit- the list, the charts? I dunno, I'm an old square." — Joey Ramones' father Noel Hyman in *Sounds*

ELVIS COSTELLO 's new single is "Oliver's Army," a track from Armed Forces. It's flipped with the non-LP standard "My Funny Valentine" just in time for obligatory radio play next week. Whether it's the "A" side, or the musical greeting card on the reverse, the 45 turns into Elvis' first real hit, climbing to #2 in the UK.

BETTE BRIGHT &	ADAM & THE ANTS ....High Wycombe, Town Hall
THE ILLUMINATIONS.................Birmingham, Barbarella's	PASSIONS/THE RAINCOATS/
DED BYRDS/MALCHIX/	DISTRIBUTORS ....London, Acklam Hall
ORCHESTRAL MANOEUVRES/	PRETENDERS/CANNIBALS ....London, Moonlight Club
TEARDROP EXPLODES...............Liverpool, Eric's	SOFT BOYS/E.F. BAND...............London, Nashville
UK SUBS ....High Wycombe, Bucks College	

3rd - Saturday...

STIFF LITTLE FINGERS' debut album hits the shops this week. The album is titled "Inflammable Material" and contains new, hotter mixes of the Belfast band's two 45s of "Alternative Ulster" and "Suspect Device." There's also other biting political songs like "State Of Emergency," "Barbed Wire Love," "Breakout," "Law And Order" and "Johnny Was." The LP was produced by Geoff Travis and Mayo Thompson at Spaceward Studios in Cambridge. The song "Rough Trade" would appear to be an attack on Rough Trade Records. It's actually about Island Records. SLF were brought into London with promises and the prospect to be on Island, and the hopeful lads all quit their day jobs and moved into a hotel residency in the big city. When label boss Chris Blackwell returned he dismissed them as no longer desirable. The group ended up leaving Belfast, but have become determined to do things THEIR WAY.

THE SOFT BOYS have left Radar Records on the eve of the release of their debut album when Radar decided that the recording for "The Day They Ate Brick" was too bad to release. Their single "Anglepoise Lamp," was out last May, but their album will have to wait until they get their own record company, Two Crabs Music, together next month.

HUMAN LEAGUE ....Liverpool, Eric's (2 shows)	SPLIT RIVITT / DYAKS ....London, Moonlight Club
DED BYRDS.........................Liverpool, University	PRETENDERS.........................London, E. London Poly.
BETTE BRIGHT &	DAMNED ....Manchester, Factory
THE ILLUMINATIONS.................London, Music Machine	

4th - Sunday...

TONTRIX begin distributing copies of their self-financed debut single around Liverpool. It's on their own Townton label and combines "Shell-shocked," with "Slipping Into Life." The group have been playing around Merseyside for a few months and comprise Hambi Haralambous on vocals and rhythm guitar, Steve Lovell on lead guitar, future Flock Of Seagulls member Mike Score on bass, Ian Johnstone on drums and Bobby Carr on keyboards. *Sounds* magazine reviews the 45 as a, "…strange blend of new music and pomp rock, with a certain brittle charm, but they haven't quite worked it out yet."

ESSENTIAL LOGIC "Punk was supposed to break down the barriers, but since punk established itself, there have been even more barriers than before. Like you have to dress in a certain way, play in a certain style." — Laura Logic in this week's *NME*

THIS HEAT ....London, Film Co-Op	LEYTON BUZZARDS ....London, Pegasus

FEBRUARY 1979

5th - Monday..

THE DISTRACTIONS are the subject of the second TMJ Release in as many months. It's a four track, 12" EP titled "You're Not Going Out Dressed Like That!" Songs include "Doesn't Bother Me," "Nothing," "Maybe It's Love" and "Too Young." The Manchester-based group is comprised of Adrian Wright and Steve Perrin-Brown on guitar, Mike Finney on vocals, Alec on drums, and Pipnichollls on bass.

FAST PRODUCT, the same people who recently brought you records by the Gang Of Four and the Human League, now bring you "The Quality Of Life (Sexex)." It's a send up, or a serious attempt perhaps at the sort of Warholian art mongering that's festering in the punk community. It's not a record, just a baggie filled with stuff that inferences about life, love, the matter of the universe, et al. are to be made of. Inside you'll find a dozen xeroxed sheets, an empty soup package, a piece of orange peel and a brief introductory blurb, "...information can only be disseminated via packaging...the initial idea has to moulded into a package. Fast Product, realizing that the packager/ marketer makes as important a contribution to the communication as everybody else, decided this was a good thing, since it means more people can get in on the act." The special limited edition package is only 75p at selected outlets.

LIVE TONIGHT!

FASHION	Birmingham, Barrel Organ	MEMBERS/Q.T.'s	London, Moonlight Club
X-FILMS/CLERKS/		STRANGEWAYS/	
THE JUVIES	London, Dingwalls	PSYCHEDELIC FURS/	
WRECKLESS ERIC/SOFTIES	London, Marquee	STRANGEWAYS	London, Pegasus
ADDIX	London, Fulham Golden Lion		

6th - Tuesday..

THE ONLY ONES have their new single "You've Got To Pay" out today on CBS in the UK. It's flipped with "This Ain't All (It's Made Out To Be)." Both are new tracks, not included on their debut album.

THE WASPS, one of the bands that used to frequent the Vortex in London, have been signed by RCA in the UK and have their single "Rubber Cars" and "This Time" released. They are a London-based quartet consisting of Jesse Lynn-Dean on vocals and guitar, Neil Fitch on lead guitar, David Owen on bass and Tiam Grant behind the drums. They've also recorded a session for the John Peel radio program and will have it aired on the 13th.

THE ONLY ONES
new single YOU'VE GOT TO PAY

THE CURE's 45 of "Killing An Arab," which was pressed up by Small Wonder Records at the end of December last year, has been re-released by a new label set up through Polydor. The new company is called Fiction Records and is run by the Cure's manager, ex-Polydor A&R director Chris Parry. There was an initial run of 15,000 on Small Wonder, and as those sell out the new Fiction label copies will appear. The first exclusive Fiction release is the forthcoming single from the Associates, tentatively titled "Double Hipness." In an *NME* review by Tony Parsons he not only gave the disc "single of the week" status but reviewed it with these words, "Cymbals crash, once, twice, three times. A guitar full of eerie promises, slithering like the sprog of some belly-dancer and a poisonous reptile. Pause. Compact guitar motif, descending guitar motif, descending alone. Then those vocals- taut, terse, tense intonation, very much wired and emotional."

REMA REMA/THE PLANETS	London, Moonlight Club	I.Q. ZERO/F.T. INDEX/	
		NOT SENSIBLES	Manchester, Band On The Wall

7th - Wednesday..

THE SEX PISTOLS Trial commences in Court #37 with John Lydon squaring off against Malcolm McLaren. Lydon wants to have a third party sort out the Sex Pistols financial quandary, and also to keep McLaren from using the name the Sex Pistols other than in connection with the members of the now split band. Among the things that Johnny is trying to stop is his being included in the upcoming Sex Pistols film the *Great Rock & Roll Swindle*. He's also seeking damages for the prevention of the Sex Pistols playing live gigs. Lydon's statement to the court said, "McLaren hoped our record sales would be enhanced if the public were under the impression that we were banned from playing. That was certainly untrue. Some halls wouldn't have us, but others applied to Glitterbest for gigs during 1977 and were either refused or received no replies."

Meanwhile back in New York, the remains of John Simon Ritchie (aka Sid Vicious), are cremated. His last wish was to be buried by Nancy, but the her family won't tell where she's buried. Some time later, Sid's mother will find the cemetery in Philadelphia and scatter Sid's ashes on her grave.

STIFF LITTLE FINGERS/		C GAS 5/ACK ACK	London, Moonlight Club
NORMALS/ROBERT RENTAL/		STADIUM DOGS/PHYSICALS	London, Music Machine
ESSENTIAL LOGIC	London, Acklam Hall		

8th - Thursday..

THE SKIDS offer their fans a peek at the new LP they have planned for later on this month. It's a new 45 titled "Into The Valley." It's going to be the band's biggest UK hit, eventually rising to #10 on *Top Of The Pops*. On the flipside is "T.V. Stars" as recorded live at the Marquee in London on November 1st of last year. Initial pressings of this UK single are on white vinyl and complete with picture sleeve. Mixing sessions for the new LP have hit a bit of a snag. Lead guitar player Stuart Adamson has had a disagreement with producer David Batchelor. It's enough of a fight that Stuart's left the studio and has gone back to Scotland, leaving the producer to bring in session man Chris Jenkins to play on the album.

FEBRUARY 1979

THE PRETENDERS Real Records releases the debut 45 from The Pretenders. That's the group fronted by American ex-journalist Chrissie Hynde. She's played around with a variety of groups in the last five years and set up a distribution deal with Real Records last summer. The single features a cover of the Kinks song "Stop Your Sobbing," b/w a Pretenders original, "The Wait." Both songs were produced by Nick Lowe. The single will become the band's first hit, reaching a teasing #34 on the UK Top 40. The Pretenders are Chrissie Hynde on guitar and vocals, James Honeyman-Scott on guitar, Martin Chambers on drums, and Pete Farndon on bass.

XTC are in the BBC studios tonight recording "Life Is Good In The Greenhouse," "Spinning Top," "Instant Tunes," and "Heatwave" for the BBC Radio 1. These are the first recordings with their new temporary guitarist Dave Gregory since Barry Andrews left. The results will be broadcast in two weeks. Dave is still a member of Dean Gabber and the Gabardines and will play his last official gig with them on the 21st.

JOE JACKSON	High Wycombe, Nag's Head	SKIDS	London, Marquee
DED BYRDS	Liverpool, The Bluebell	TOYAH	London, Mayhem
LEYTON BUZZARDS/		PRESSURE SHOCKS/	
MISPRINTS	Liverpool, Eric's	UK SUBS/MONITORS	London, Albany Empire
THE JAGS	London, Golden Lion	JOHN THE POSTMAN	Manchester, Factory

9th - Friday....................................

RED NOISE follow up their debut 45 two weeks ago with the release of their debut album. Nelson has drastically changed his sound from his previous recordings with Be Bop Deluxe. There is far less reliance on guitars and more emphasis on electronics. The LP is titled "Sound On Sound" and features Nelson's single "Furniture Music" as well as "Revolt Into Style," "The Atom Age," "Don't Touch Me (I'm Electric)," "Stop/Go/Stop" and "Stay Young." From the graphics on the album it is clear that Nelson is the leader, the star of this production. The others who played on the album receive small billing and include Andy Clark on keyboards, Ian Nelson (Bill's brother) on sax, Rick Ford on bass, and Dave Mattacks on drums

O LEVEL are said to be friends of the Television Personalities. There's also the good possibility that O Level are actually Edward Ball and Daniel Treacy, who are the driving force behind the Television Personalities. Their quirky pop style does little to hide a wry disrespect for authority. Their new disc is a four track EP on their own Kings Road Records label. Tracks include "Leave Me," "Everybody's On Revolver Tonight," "Stairway To Boredom" and the first song appreciative of Sex Pistols manager Malcolm McLaren, "We Love Malcolm." O Level are listed as being Paddy O'Level on lead vocals and guitar, Mick O'Level on bass, Brendan O'Level on guitar and Joe O'Level on drums. Are they really the TV Personalities?

HUMAN LEAGUE/SCARS The Human League's concert scheduled tonight at Leicester Square's Notre Dame Hall has been cancelled when the vicar of the church next door complained about the gig on moral grounds. The Scars, who had just driven down from Edinburgh, all crammed into one van, heard the pious pronouncement just two hours before showtime and had to turn back and drive it home. The Human League's set these days features a mix of originals and unusual covers. Originals like "Being Boiled," "Circus Of Death" and "Treatment," are juxtaposed with a straight faced cover of the Righteous Brothers chestnut "You've Lost That Lovin' Feeling" and Iggy Pop's "Nightclubbing." All the while slides of *Stingray*, *The Man From U.N.C.L.E.*, other TV goldies adorn the rear wall.

VALVES/THE IDOLS/		THE CURE/THE PRESS	London, Nashville
INVADERS	London, Acklam Hall	HUMAN LEAGUE/SCARS/	
POLICE/RESISTANCE/		TRANSMITTERS	London, Notre Dame Hall
FASHION	London, King's College	GANG OF FOUR/DELTA 5	Manchester, The Factory
JOE JACKSON	London, Marquee	CURBS/SLOW GUNS/	
EXTRAS/VEINS/		MILITANT FRANK	Manchester, Partington Comm.Centre
NEON HEARTS	London, Moonlight Club		

LIVE TONIGHT!

10th - Saturday....................

THE DICKIES have their debut album out this week on A&M Records. "The Incredible Shrinking Dickies," like so many other records these days, is pressed up in four different colors, yellow, orange, blue and traditional black vinyl. The album features their 45s of "Paranoid," "Eve Of Destruction" and "Give It Back." New originals include "Poodle Party," "Waterslide," "Walk Like An Egg" and "Shake & Bake." There is also a cover of the 60s Monkee's song "She."

CASH PUSSIES Sid Vicious is hardly dead a week and already there's a record out on the subject. It's by a studio group calling themselves The Cash Pussies. Their single's A side is "99% Shit," a song that features actual voice quotes from Sidney. The flipside is "Cash Flow" The 45 was produced by ex-Pistols producer Dave Goodman for his label, The Label. It features ex-Alternative TV guitarist Alex Fergusson, Alan Gruner on bass, Ray Weston on drums, Mark Farley on percussion and vocalist Diana Rich. The sound bites of Sid are from the tapes that Pistols biographers Fred and Judy Vermorel acquired while working on their book and a possible movie titled *Millions Like Us*.

LENE LOVICH	Glasgow, University
POLICE/GANG OF FOUR	Liverpool, Eric's
PSYCHEDELIC FURS	London, Windsor Castle

JOHN COOPER CLARKE/EXODUS ..Manchester, University

FEBRUARY 1979

13th - Tuesday.....................................

ELECTRIC CHAIRS There is a bit of closet cleaning at Step Forward/Illegal Records these days. The latest result is the release of a "new" Wayne County single, "Thunder When She Walks," and "What You Got." Neither track is new, far from it. They both date from the band's sessions back in 1977.

PUBLIC IMAGE There's a change in the line up of Public Image. Drummer Jim Walker is reportedly being replaced by Vivian Jackson, a ex-member of Linton Kweski Johnson's band. Former drummer Jim Walker has packed his bag and has told everyone he's off for Israel.

LIVE TONIGHT!

CURE.............................Birmingham, Barbarella's	MEKONS/FASHION ....London, Nashville
SUBSTITUTE/	PUNISHMENT OF LUXURY ....London, Marquee
PSYCHEDELIC FURS................London, Moonlight Club	CRISPY AMBULANCE/
	A CERTAIN RATIO/STAFF 9..........Manchester, Band On The Wall

14th - Wednesday.................................

THE SEX PISTOLS/Glitterbest suit is at least partly settled. The judge gavels out his verdict finding that of the £880,000 that the Sex Pistols earned, they were indeed entitled to a reasonable chunk of money which McLaren has apparently already spent. The only expedient way to raise the money would be to get the *Great Rock & Roll Swindle* soundtrack out as soon as possible with all the monies to go to the band against their earnings. "OK McLaren, you got your corpse, now sell it." — Geoff in *Teenage Depression Magazine*.

DEXY'S MIDNIGHT RUNNERS ......Birmingham, All Saints Hospital	TICKETS/PURPLE HEARTS ....London, Bridge House
LENE LOVICH/	VALVES/KHz ....London, Rock Garden
FINGERPRINTZ.......................Liverpool, Tiffany's	USERS/CRISIS ....London, South Band Poly.

15th - Thursday.................................

PINK MILITARY STAND ALONE is a new group headed up by Jayne Casey, the former lead singer for Liverpool-based Big In Japan. Her new venture is more serious and less theatrical. This new group is making it's live debut tonight as part of a Manchester Hospital fund raiser with The Nives and The Dogmen Of Albuquerque. Ian Wood from the *NME* is on hand to catch the evening was impressed with Pink Military stating that "Jayne dominates visually, but the current persona is sinister and doom laden, meshing with the stark angularity of her band, Pink Military are surreal and abstract...and will have to suffer comparisons with the Banshees and Ludus, but they will not be ignored." Among the original songs evident in their set are "Clone Sound," "Radio Soundcheck," "Solid Ground" and "Degenerated Man."

DANGEROUS GIRLS/SURPRISES/	HUMAN LEAGUE/SCARS.............London, Nashville
THE DENIZENS ....Birmingham, Bournebrook Hotel	IDOLS/PIRANHAS...................London, Windsor Castle
UK SUBS/THE PACK/	PINK MILITARY STAND ALONE/
THE LOU'S ....London, Brixton Town Hall	THE NIVES/
SCANDAL/MODELS ....London, Pegasus	DOGMEN OF ALBUQUERQUE ....Manchester, Factory
RADIATORS..........................London, Ronnie Scott's	JOE JACKSON ....Sheffield, The Limit

16th - Friday.....................................

U2 are a band that play infrequently, but superbly when they do appear. They are having one of those rare live shows at the Dublin Project Arts Center, as part of the Dark Space Festival. It's a twenty-four hour rock extravaganza featuring Sheffield band, the Mekons, as well as other Dublin groups. Radio DJ John Peel was on hand and was most impressed with Protex ("certainly very good indeed!"), The Virgin Prunes ("a band to keep under observation, despite their silly name") and U2 ("a little old fashioned, a little uninvolving after Rudi, but enjoyed a considerable local reputation.") The Festival featured locals like The Atrix, an Irish reggae band called Zebra, and Rocky de Valera and the Gravediggers, a sort of rockabilly cum blues band. Protex, then Rudi came on next, followed by Dublin's own Virgin Prunes and at 3:30am by U2. PiL never made it there as they planned, and Throbbing Gristle were stuck somewhere on the road to Dublin.

DEXY'S MIDNIGHT RUNNERS ......Birmingham, St. Chad's School	ABC ....London, Dublin Castle
MEKONS/ATTRIX/ZEBRA/	LENE LOVICH/FINGERPRINTZ ......London, Bedford College
ROCKY de VALERA &	PASSIONS/THE NIPS/
THE GRAVEDIGGERS/	DISTRIBUTORS ....London, Moonlight Club
RUDI/PROTEX/U2/	PRETENDERS.........................London, N London Poly.
VIRGIN PRUNES ....Dublin, Project Arts Centre	HUMAN LEAGUE/SCARS.............London, Nashville
GENERATION X......................Edinburgh, University	STIFF LITTLE FINGERS/
JOY DIVISION/	THE NORMAL/
CABARET VOLTAIRE/	ROBERT RENTAL/
JOHN DOWIE ....Liverpool, Eric's	ESSENTIAL LOGIC ....Manchester, The Factory
MONOCHROME SET/	THE JAM ....Reading, University
NEON HEARTS/DATA PANIK ....London, Acklam Hall	

17th - Saturday.................................

BEST OF 1978 The *New Musical Express* reader's poll for 1978 appears this week. Best male singer goes to David Bowie (just beating John Lydon, Elvis Costello and Bob Geldof); best female singer goes to Debbie Harry with follow up by Siouxsie Sioux and Kate Bush. The

FEBRUARY 1979

top albums of the year are, #1 "All Mod Cons" by the Jam, #2 "Give Em Enough Rope" by the Clash, #3 "Live & Dangerous" by Thin Lizzy, #4 "The Scream" by Siouxsie & The Banshees, and #5 "This Years Model" by Elvis Costello. Top 45 of the year goes to the Clash with "White Man In Hammersmith Palais," followed by "Public Image" by Public Image, and "Rat Trap" by the Boomtown Rats. Elvis Costello was voted number one songwriter of the year, much to the chagrin of Paul Weller at number two. The "best group" of 1978 was won by the Clash, followed close behind by The Jam and The Boomtown Rats. Best new groups were as follows: #1 Public Image, #2 Stiff Little Fingers, #3 Siouxsie & The Banshees, #4 Dire Straits, #5 The Cars, #6 The Undertones, #7 Boomtown Rats, #8 John Cooper Clarke, #9 Magazine, and #10 Van Halen. Sid Vicious was posthumously awarded the prize of being "Most Wonderful Human Being" while John Travolta was #1 "Creep Of The Year."

STIFF LITTLE FINGERS/		ELECTRIC CHAIRS/	
NORMALS/ROBERT RENTAL/		LEYTON BUZZARDS	London, N.E.Poly.
ESSENTIAL LOGIC	Liverpool, Eric's	THE EDGE/MOLESTERS	London, Nashville

21st - Wednesday...............................

ADAM & THE ANTS have left Decca Records. They had one single on the label late last year and have been working on their debut album. Some changes in the company have left the band unsettled and they've now parted company with the label. They are currently looking for interest in other companies with their half-finished LP project.

THE STRANGLERS' live album features concert recordings from the last two years and captures the raw energy of the group onstage. Tracks cover the length of the band's recorded career, from "Grip" to "Curfew," and stopping off at "I Feel Like A Wog," "5 Minutes," "Dead Ringer," and several others along the way. The only thing that seems to missing with this take-it-home Stranglers live show is the strippers. Keeping in line with the band's reputation and stage show, the album is titled "The Stranglers: Live X Cert."

PSYCHEDELIC FURS	London, Brecknock	VIPERS/PHYSICALS	London, Music Machine
PRAG VEC	London, Moonlight Club	CABARET VOLTAIRE	Sheffield, University

23rd - Friday...............................

THE CLASH's single of "English Civil War" is released. It's flipped with the Clash's version of "Pressure Drop," which is a classic Toots & The Maytals reggae track.

JOHN COOPER CLARKE appears in the record shops again after five months of dormancy with an odd shaped disc. The 45 is pressed in orange vinyl and has five sides! Two of the sides are "Gimmix, Play Loud!" and "I Married A Monster From Outer Space." The triangular record is a limited edition.

SEX PISTOLS The latest from the Sex Pistols is a taste from the forthcoming soundtrack to the *Great R&R Swindle*. It's Sid's version of the Eddie Cochran song "Somethin' Else," flipped with Steve Jones singing the bawdy sea chanty "Friggin' In The Riggin'."

THE SKIDS' debut album is out. They've only recently released the single "Into The Valley." It's taken from the debut LP "Scared To Dance." Also included on the disc are "Hope & Glory," "Of One Skin," "Melancholy Soldiers" and two older tracks, "Charles," from their debut EP and "The Saints Are Coming." The LP version of "Charles" is a new recording of the 1977 song. A limited number of the first UK LP's will be pressed up in blue vinyl.

RADIATORS	London, Roundhouse	PUBLIC IMAGE/	
THE EDGE/		THE POP GROUP/MERGER	
PSYCHEDELIC FURS	London, Windsor Castle	LINTON KWESKI JOHNSON	Manchester, Bell Vue Centre
GENERATION X/		HUMAN LEAGUE	Sheffield, Poly.
BERNIE TORME	Manchester, The Mayflower		

24th - Saturday...............................

SEX PISTOLS The new album is out faster than anticipated because of the gentle prodding that only a court of law can provide, and a scramble to collect money owed the members of the band. The long-awaited soundtrack to the film *Great Rock & Roll Swindle* is a double album of odds and ends from the Pistols' vaults plus new recordings since the split-up. Virgin is anxious to get it in UK stores quickly to stem the potential flood of French copies coming into the UK from Barclay Records, who hold licensing for Sex Pistols' material on the continent. Ten thousand copies of the album were pressed up by Virgin UK last month and then rejected when the album's running order and song selection changed. Virgin was planning to scrap these rejects but have now decided to put them in the shops to compete with the French issues. These original albums feature a demo track, a cover of the Small Faces' 1965 hit "Whatcha Gonna Do About It?" The "new" version of the soundtrack drops this track and adds "I Wanna Be Me," as well as "Who Killed Bambi." It also features a different version of "God Save The Queen." There are slight differences in cover art as well. The album is a soundtrack, and as such is a conglomeration of sounds designed to fit visual images. The fact that it is proceeding the film makes some of the songs and their interpretations by various others (besides the Pistols) somewhat confusing. Sex Pistols preformed tracks include a furiously bad demo of the Chuck Berry song "Johnny B. Goode," and a similar treatment of Jonathan Richman's "Road Runner," and the Monkee's song "Stepping Stone." Some of the demos are from sessions that Dave Goodman did with the Pistols in July of '76 before they were signed, and

FEBRUARY 1979

have been tarted up with new guitar overdubs added. Songs involved in this refurbishing are "Anarchy In The UK," as well as "No Lip," and the Who's song "Substitute."

Sid had turned in vocal performances on two Eddie Cochran classics, "Somethin' Else," and "C'mon Everybody," as well as his version of "My Way." Guitarist Steve Jones is featured as vocalist on a strangely orchestrated version of "E.M.I." and "Lonely Boy." Drummer Paul Cook is the vocalist for "Silly Thing." Manager Malcolm McLaren sings the Max Bygraves standard "You Need Hands," a French street singer Jerzimy turns in a continental version of "L'Anarchy por le UK," and a dance group called the Black Arabs play a disco version of "God Save The Queen." Ronnie Biggs appears on the LP on "Cosh The Driver" and another version of "Belsen Was A Gas."

GENERATION X/BERNI TORME	.....Birmingham, Barbarella's	WRECKLESS ERIC &	
STIFF LITTLE FINGERS/		FOUR ROUGH MEN/SOFTIES	.......London, Chelsea College
TEARDROP EXPLODES/		GANG OF FOUR/RAINCOATS	........London, Nashville
PRAG VEC	..............................Liverpool, Eric's	RADIATORS	...........................London, Roundhouse
THE POP GROUP/		MONOCHROME SET	..................Manchester, Mayflower
LINTON KWESKI JOHNSON/		JOE JACKSON	........................Manchester, Russell Club
MANICURED NOISE	..................Liverpool, University	LENE LOVICH/ FINGERPRINTZ	......Sheffield, University
UK SUBS	................................London, Electric Ballroom		

LIVE TONIGHT!

26th - Monday.....................................

THE TEARDROPS are the group bassist Steve Garvey started when he left the Buzzcocks. They've just signed a deal with local TJM Records and are working on a three-track EP which is slated for an April release. With Steve in the band is ex-Fall drummer Carl Burns and ex-Passage guitarist Tony Friel.

ANOTHER PRETTY FACE is a new Edinburgh band built on the ruins of several others. The protagonists are ex-*Jungleland* fanzine writer Mike Scott and John Caldwell. They've been playing together since 1975, when they were only fifteen in a band called Karma. The duo drifted apart with John joining a band called AAARGH!, and Mike fronting a punk band called White Heat. They got back together in a new group called D.N.V., and moved to Ayr to attend college and find a bass and drum player. That got them through '78 until things fell apart. For the vacancies in the new group, ex-D.N.V. drummer Ian Walter Craig (Crigg) and Jim Geddes on bass were brought back. They're writing new material and hope to start playing gigs soon.

THE FLYS/		RADIATORS	...........................London, Roundhouse
PSYCHEDELIC FURS	.................London, Music Machine		

March 1st - Thursday.............................

SQUIRE are a four-piece mod band from Woking (the same hometown as the Jam). Their pop sensibilities haven't gone unnoticed, and they're the latest signing to Rok Records who release their debut single next week. In an unusual cost-cutting measure, they share the 45 with another band. Squire's side is "Get Ready To Go" and is flipped with "Doing The Flail" by Coming Shortly. It's part of Rok Records plan to expose a number of heretofore unknown groups. Others singles include Just Frank (from Leeds) singing "You" flipped with The Split Screens (Oxford) playing "Just Don't Try." Other bands signed up include Urban Disturbance (of Swindon), The VIP's (from Clapham), Hazard (Cambridge), The Clerks (Birmingham), Blue Movies, The Noise, and others.

GOOD VIBRATIONS RECORDS has just released a double single, four group "battle of the bands" package. Two 45s are wrapped in the usual Good Vibrations style poster sleeve. One 45 is "Overcome By Fumes" by Rudi flipped with The Idiots' song "Parents." The other single is The Spiders' track "Dancing In The Street" and The Outcasts with "The Cops Are Coming." The double pack is a special limited edition of 2,500.

LENE LOVICH/FINGERPRINTZ ......London, Kings College

2nd - Friday.....................................

THE JAM return to the record racks after successful tours of both Europe and the UK. The vehicle is a single called "Strange Town." The 45 is produced by Vic Coppersmith-Heaven and is flipped with a touching ballad, "The Butterfly Collector."

TEARDROP EXPLODES & THOSE NAUGHTY LUMPS are two new bands with records on the Liverpool indie label, Zoo Records. Those Naughty Lumps are a Liverpool quintet that have been playing frequently at the Havana Club. Their debut is "Iggy Pop's Jacket" b/w "Pure And Innocent." The group are Kevin Wilkinson on drums, Tony Mitchell, P.M. Hart on vocals, Martin Armadillo, and Peter "Kid" Younger. Ex-Big In Japan member Bill Drummond and David Balfe also helped on the session. The second of this week's Zoo releases is by the Teardrop Explodes. The three track EP couples "Sleeping Gas" with "Camera Camera," and "Kirby Workers Dream Fades." The Liverpool four-piece is comprised of Michael Finkler on guitar, Paul Simpson on organ, Gary Dwyer on drums and Julian Cope on vocals. Julian had previously played in a front-room group called the Crucial Three and a short lived club band called The Mystery Girls. When talking with the *NME*, Julian Cope described "Sleeping Gas" as being, "...for other people to interpret. It's about a relationship that's got to a certain point, and it's just like a habit. The chorus line goes 'You can watch *Rafferty* turn into a serial,' as *Rafferty* went out first as a pilot TV show and then it became a serial. So it's about allowing things to go on without you doing anything about them...A lot of the time we act in a stupidly obscure way, that's the way we act as people in any case."

MISTY/UK SUBS/		CARPETTES	...........................London, Windsor Castle
SNEEKY FEELINGS	..................London, Fulham Town Hall	UNDERTONES/THE SQUARES	.......Manchester, Factory

MARCH 1979

3rd - Saturday...

FISH TURNED HUMAN Here's another product of Cambridge reaching the London indie shops. They're Fish Turned Human and their debut EP features "The International," "Porky's Minion," "Here Come The Nuns" and "24 Hour Shop." It's pressed up on the group's own Sequel Records. F.T.H. is Philip Furei on vocals, Adrian Cole on piano, Julian Treasure on drums, Michael Ikon on guitar, and Andy Metcalfe (on loan from the Soft Boys) playing bass. The band were formerly known as The Woodentops.

THE ELECTRIC EELS Rough Trade releases another enigmatic track. The quartet are The Electric Eels and their single features "Cyclotron," and "Agitated." They are Dave E on vocals, John Morton on lead guitar, Brian McMahon on rhythm guitar and Nick Knox on drums. This 45 is extremely raw and distorted and is in reality one of the first punk records ever. It was actually recorded in May of 1975, and is extremely rare. They were based in Cleveland and described their music as "art terrorism." Even in 1974, they were wearing safety pins, and ripped T-shirts with rude slogans on them.

LIVE TONIGHT!

THE POP GROUP/	UNDERTONES/THE SQUARES ......Liverpool, Eric's
ALTERNATIVE TELEVISION/	CARPETTES............................London, Rock Garden
LINTON KWESKI JOHNSON ....Edinburgh, University	LENE LOVICH/ FINGERPRINTZ......Manchester, University
ONLY ONES ....Glasgow, Queen Margaret Union	

5th - Monday..

GARY NUMAN and Tubeway Army have released a new single of "Down In The Park" and "Do You Need The Service." The 12" maxi single has an extra track, titled "I Nearly Married A Human (2)." The lead track is a bit of a sci-fi story about a future where machines rule the world and killing- raping machines are lurking on beneath every streetlight and in every public park.

THE JAGS are a couple of Scarborough lads. Nick Watkinson and John Alder had known each other since they were about fifteen. They got together a group in early 1977. They were both big fans of groups like Brinsley Schwartz and Ducks Deluxe. They recruited drummer Alex Baird from Bournemouth and bassist Steve Prudence from London to fill out the group and rehearsed in a secluded cottage in Wales. Coming to London a few months ago, they've been gigging at local pubs. Now they're the latest signing to Island Records and their debut 45 is in the works.

XTC'S new guitarist Dave Gregory gets to quit his day job at White Arrow Parcels and become a full time musician. He's just formally joined XTC, although he's been playing with them for about four weeks.

6th - Tuesday...

PATRIK FITZGERALD There's a new Patrik Fitzgerald single out this week on Polydor Records in the UK. It's "All Sewn Up," b/w "Hammersmith Odeons." For the sessions, Patrik was joined by John Maher of the Buzzcocks.

THE POP GROUP have been planning to release a record for a year and a half, now it's here. Songs are "She Is Beyond Good And Evil" b/w "3:38." They are currently on tour with ATV and Linton Kweski Johnson and plan to have their album out on Radar very soon.

PURPLE HEARTS leader Robert Manton told the *NME* this week that the band aren't that easy to categorize, "Obviously we think of ourselves as mods, and that's like a state of mind, but it don't mean we gotta sleep in our mohair suits. We don't wanna be tied down by an image. We'd rather be thought of as a group for teenagers, for anybody."

UNDERTONES/THE SQUARES.......Sheffield, The Limit

7th - Wednesday...

BUZZCOCKS Just in time to waylay any rumors that the Buzzcocks are on the rocks, come as new single from the Manchester quartet. This time it's "Everybody's Happy Nowadays," b/w "Why Can't I Touch It?" United Artist Records plans to celebrate this, the band's seventh single release by re-releasing the first six UA 45s in their original picture sleeves.

SQUEEZE The latest from Squeeze is their new single and album titled "Cool For Cats." The "Cool For Cats" 45 is flipped with the non-LP track "Model," both from the prolific pens of Difford and Tillbrook. The album of the same title features songs like "Slap & Tickle," "It's Not Cricket," "It's So Dirty," "Slightly Drunk," "Up The Junction," "Revue" and their previous single "Goodbye Girl." This is the band's second album, and will sell thousands when the single hits #2 on *Top Of The Pops* in the UK.

BILL NELSON'S RED NOISE.........Birmingham, Odeon

9th - Friday...

TOM ROBINSON BAND's second album and a companion 45 are out this weekend. The single is "Bully For You" flipped with his recording of the theme song to the BBC TV show *Our People*, the seven-hour documentary about the origins of the human race that aired in January. LP tracks are the single "A" side "Bully For You," also "Alright, All Night," "Let My People Free," "Law & Order," "Days Of Rage" and another song on the subject of the Liddle Towers murder, "Blue Murder." This second album was produced by Todd Rundgren

MARCH 1979

during mid-December last year and features sit-in drummer Preston Heyman, the temporary replacement for Dolphin Taylor who left the group just prior to the sessions. Against the wishes of the EMI board, Robinson provides a sort of mini-directory of activist groups on the inner sleeve of the LP.

THE ONLY ONES have their second album released by CBS Records in the UK. It's titled "Even Serpents Shine" and features songs such as "Flaming Torch," "No Solution," "Inbetweens," "Someone Who Cares," and their current single "You've Got To Pay."

LIVE TONIGHT!

SKIDS	Birmingham, Barbarella's	ABC	London, Dublin Castle
THE POP GROUP/		RUTS	London, Central Poly.
ALTERNATIVE TELEVISION/		LIGHTNING RAIDERS/	
LINTON KWESKI JOHNSON	Birmingham, Town Hall	BANK OF DRESDEN/	
JOE JACKSON	Liverpool, Eric's	PSYCHEDELIC FURS/	
EDDIE & THE HOT RODS	Liverpool, University	TESCO BOMBERS	London, Africa Centre
REACTION	London, Moonlight	PRETENDERS/STRANGEWAYS	London, Nashville
EL 360/BLANCMANGE	London, The Basement	CURE/SAMARITANS	London, Isleworth College

10th - Saturday...

MENACE Here's an odd one. Menace released their debut 45 of "Insane Society" in the autumn of 1977. They quickly followed it up with "GLC" in the spring of 1978. There is now a release of a third appearance on vinyl in the guise of ""I Need Nothing" and "Electrocutioner." Strangely enough, the single was recorded back in 1977 and produced by John Cale. It has sat around for over a year and a half and is only now released on Illegal Records. Is it better late than never or is it simply too late?

SKIDS' guitarist Stuart Adamson is angered by the record company hype he sees surrounding the Skids, and is talking about leaving the group. He apparently hates the wheeling and dealing, the "business" of rock. He's staying in the band to support the album and his mates, but whether he'll remain after that is unclear. Writing an open letter to the *Record Mirror* he said, "Music only exists in the free meals and handouts of high-powered business executives, I don't need it." In the summer of '81, Stuart reaches his limit and leaves to start his own band called Big Country. This new group will far surpass the Skids and knock back four top ten songs in it's first three years. Even in America, where the Skids had no impact, Big Country hits the top 20 with "In A Big Country."

ALTERNATIVE T.V. released it's second full album. It's under the title "Vibing Up The Senile Man (Part 1)." It's out on Deptford Fun City Records and features all new material such as "Release The Natives," "Poor Association," "Facing Up To The Facts," "Graves Of Deluxe Green" and "Smile In The Day." ATV is basically Mark Perry and Dennis Burns, although Genesis P-Orridge from Throbbing Gristle guest on the LP along with Mick Leinhan and Steve Jameson.

EDDIE & THE HOT RODS	Glasgow, Strathclyde Univ.	SINCEROS	London, Hope & Anchor
BILL NELSON'S RED NOISE	Liverpool, Empire Theatre	SOFT BOYS	London, Rock Garden
TONTRIX	Liverpool, The Masonic	"free fuck off tour"	London, Westbourne Park
BLACK SLATE/FLYS/		THE POP GROUP/	
PRETENDERS	London, School Of Economics	ALTERNATIVE TELEVISION/	
STIFF LITTLE FINGERS/		MANICURED NOISE/	
ESSENTIAL LOGIC/		LINTON KWESKI JOHNSON	Manchester, Poly.
ROBERT RENTAL/		MEKONS/BLANK STUDENTS	Manchester, The Factory
THE NORMAL	London, Electric Ballroom	JAGS	Sheffield, General Club

12th - Monday...

VAULTAGE 78 News from Brighton. There's life on the beaches and it's been captured on vinyl. The best of Brighton's underground groups are assembled in a single volume titled "Vaultage 78: Two sides of Brighton." The album covers seven of the brightest and the best of the beachside community. Starting off side one are Nicky And The Dots with three tracks, "Girl Gets Nervous," "I Find That Really Surprises Me," and "Wrong Street." Next follow the Dodgems with "I Don't Care," and The Devil's Dykes with "Fruitless" and "Plastic Flowers." The side closes with Peter And The Test Tube Babies and "Elvis Is Dead." Side two begins with The Parrots with "Larger Than Life," and "Vicious Circles." This is followed by The Vitamins with "Newtown" and another Dodgems track, "Lord Lucan Is Missing." The Piranhas close off the LP with three songs, "Tension," "Virginity," and "I Don't Want My Body."

GANG OF FOUR There's rumors flying about that the Gang Of Four are going to be signed soon. Speculation is that CBS is the winner with EMI and Polydor strong contenders.

CHELSEA	London, Marquee	FLEXIBLE DUSTBINS	London, Paddington
ANGELIC UPSTARTS/		VALVES/PINPOINT	London, Nashville
INDICATORS	London, Moonlight Club	THE JAGS	London, Rock Garden
STRANGEWAYS/L7	London, Pegasus	THE OUT	Manchester, Band On The Wall

13th - Tuesday..

SWELL MAPS It's been over a year since the release of the Swell Maps' debut 45, "Read About Seymour" and their follow up reveals that the Maps haven't been spending much time in the studio working on new songs. The three track EP features "Dresden Style," (recorded in January of '76), flipped with "Ammunition Train (from December of last year) and "Full Moon" (from September of 1977). Is it so hard to book studio time or do the creative juices flow that slowly?

SPIZZOIL's second single is "Cold City," and "Red & Black" flipped with "Solarisation" and "Platform 3." The group is one of the more

MARCH 1979

unusual signings of Rough Trade Records and feature the duet of Spizz on voice, harmonies, kazoo and percussion, with Pete Petroleum on guitar.

DEXY'S MIDNIGHT RUNNERS	......Birmingham, Aston University	BILL NELSON'S RED NOISE	.........Sheffield, City Hall
JOY DIVISION/FIREPLACE	..........Manchester, Band On The Wall	JOE JACKSON	.........................Sheffield, Limit Club

14th - Wednesday.....................................

SHAM 69 have a new chant-along single "Questions And Answers." It's flipped with two live tracks, "I Gotta Survive," and an off-key (with belches) version of The Beatles' "With A Little Help From My Friends." If you're wondering what happened to Jimmy's voice on the latter, stop worrying. Sham's drummer Dodie sings on it, not Pursey. The self-imposed ban on playing live again for Sham 69 could be ending. There has been a bit of talk that they intend to continue playing live shortly and only needed a rest since the riot six weeks ago.

PLASMATICS The outrageous New York quartet, The Plasmatics, have released their debut 45 on their own Vice Squad label. It's a three track EP combining "Butcher Baby" with "Fast Food Service" and "Concrete Shoes." This limited edition is packaged in a full color, hard cover 7" packet, like a mini-LP. The Plasmatics are fronted by ex-porn screen actress Wendy Williams, who not only sings but plays a mean chainsaw as well. She's backed by Richard Stotts on guitar, Osao Chosei Funahara on bass and Stu Deutsch on drums.

THE SPECIALS' set tonight at the Moonlight club is witnessed by at least one reporter, Dave McCullough of *Sounds* magazine. He's caught up in the "good time thunder" of the evening. He reminds the readers that this is the same band that opened some dates for the Clash recently, but have just struggled free from Clash manager Bernard Rhodes control and management who kept them out of the public eye for almost half a year. Dave writes, "…the songs vary between short, sympathetic adaptations of early reggae favorites to the band's own statements…The Specials can knock the shit out of the many great pretenders around…the songs, the power, the sense of a strong image, everything that counts is there. But is the timing right? The divide between greatness and mere success is often elastic. The important thing is simply that The Specials are here."

LIVE TONIGHT!

UNDERTONES/SQUARES	............London, Marquee	PSYCHEDELIC FURS	.................London, Windsor Castle
SPECIALS/KHz	........................London, Moonlight Club	ARTERY/STUNT KITES	..............Sheffield, University

15th - Thursday....................................

ELVIS COSTELLO finds that America can be a cold and lonely place when you're a foreigner with bad press. Elvis has been getting into bits of trouble from time to time on his US tour. On the 6th in St Louis, an offhanded remark at a concert about the sponsoring station into the song "Radio Radio," had all Elvis' music pulled from the air immediately. The worst incident so far is a barroom brawl that involved Elvis, Steven Stills, Bonnie Bramlett and some of Stills entourage. There are many mixed reports of what actually happened, so here's one beer soaked version. Apparently Elvis was baited by members of the Stills entourage who intimated that Elvis stole his licks from Ray Charles and James Brown. Elvis became abusive, and referred to Stills as "old tin nose" and then launched into the unfortunate diatribe about Ray Charles, James Brown, etc. Things escalated, and Bonnie Bramlett took a swing at Elvis which was met in kind from Stills men. A fight erupted, bottles were broken and the whole mess was pulled apart with Elvis and his sideman Bruce Thomas coming out on the short end. Elvis commented about Bonnie Bramlett, "That woman has made one reputation off one E.C. (referring to Eric Clapton, who helped make Delaney & Bonnie famous in the early '70s), and she's fucking well not going to get more publicity off of another one!"

X-RAY SPEX have a new single the shops. It's "Highly Inflammable" and "Warrior In Woolworth's." Both tracks are originals and come in a special color sleeve.

THE FALL do things in their own peculiar way and their new LP "Live At The Witch Trials," is a great example. It was recorded on December 15th of last year at the Camden Sound Suite and is out this week on Step Forward Records. The LP, the band's first, features all new material. Among the songs are "Frightened," "Rebellious Jukebox," "Various Times," "Underground Medicine" "Futures And Pasts," and "Music Scene."

ONLY ONES	............................Edinburgh, Astoria	PHANTOM/SPECIAL AKA	............London, University College
THOSE NAUGHTY LUMPS	...........Liverpool, Eric's	BOWLES BROTHERS/	
PIRANHAS Q.T's	.......................London, Windsor Castle	THE JAGS	...............................London, Nashville
TRANSITION/PASSIONS/		STRAITS/ SQUARES	.................Manchester, The Factory
ODOUR 7	.............................London, Acklam Hall	SKIDS	........................Sheffield, The Limit Club (2 shows)
RED BEANS & RICE	...................London, Hope & Anchor		

18th - Sunday...

MADNESS/THE SPECIALS Suggs McPherson of the London-based ska band Madness sees the Specials at a Rock Against Racism gig at the Hope & Anchor. He's astounded that there's another band in England traveling the same musical road as his group. They've swapped addresses and Madness have been invited to open for the Specials at their next gig at the Nashville.

FANZINES There's a huge crop of fanzines littering the doorways and racks of independent record shops these days. They cover the gamut from self xeroxed two page missives to elaborate, slick typeset magazines that appear with alarming regularity. Most are priced from ten to twenty-five pence, and will give you great, street level insight into over the top fan enthusiasm. Titles these days include *Jamming, My*

MARCH 1979

Whip, Short Circuit, In The City, Alternative Ulster, Dayglow, Life In A Void, The Next Big Thing, Ripped and Torn, It Ticked and Exploded, Kingdom Come, White Stuff, Heat, The Quality Of Life, Sniffing Flowers, Self Abuse, Widows and P.P. Orphans, Cle, New Diseases, Flicks and *Negative Reaction.*

PATRIK FITZGERALD/		BILL NELSON'S RED NOISE/	
MOLESTERS	Birmingham, Barbarella's	FINGERPRINTZ	London, Drury Lane Royal Theatre
TONTRIX	Liverpool, The Bluebell	THE CURE/LOCAL OPERATOR	London, The Marquee
SPECIALS	London, Hope & Anchor	LENE LOVICH/SQUEEZE/	
ALTERNATIVE TV/		THE YACHTS	London, Lyceum
FASHION/		JAGS	London, John Bull
THE TRANSMITTERS	London, Greenwich Theatre	FINGERPRINTZ	London, Theatre Royal

19th - Monday.........

"M" release their second single today, the follow up to "Moderne Man." The new song "Pop Music" is available on a rather odd 12" pressing that weaves "Pop Music" together with "M-Squad." The two tracks run in parallel grooves on the same side of the record, making it a 50-50 chance which will come up when the needle is dropped. This pressing is limited to the first 10,000 copies and the flipside is a no frills version of "Pop Music" without the gimmick. "M" is actually Robin Scott, who is no newcomer to the music business. He was briefly the manager of Roogalator, and has worked with several bands in France. "M" the group is a cast including Bridgit Vinchon on vocals, Gary on sax, Wally Babarou on synth, Philip Gould on drums and John Lewis doing the electronic programming, and Robin handling the lead vocal. Robin described the song "Pop Music" to *Sounds* magazine as, "...meant to sound like a current pop record. There's nothing dangerous about it. It's a glorified jingle. It was meant to be a Song For Europe, taking what is happening at the moment and taking the most impersonal approach to constructing a record." It will eventually top the US charts, and come in a close #2 in the UK.

EDDIE & THE HOT RODS/		SPECIALS	London, Hope & Anchor
MEMBERS/MAGNETS	Birmingham, Barbarella's	SQUIRE	London, Cockney's
SKIDS	Edinburgh, Tiffany's	PINPOINT/THE VALVES	London, Nashville
TONTRIX	Liverpool, Kirkland's Bar	PIRANHAS/BOBBY HENRY	London, Pegasus
ELECTROTUNES/SOULYARD/		MONOCHROME SET/	
NEUROSIS	London, Dingwalls	CARPETTES	London, Rock Garden

LIVE TONIGHT!

20th - Tuesday.........

THE SCARS have their debut 45 released this week by Fast Records. It combines two of their live favorites "Adult/ery" and "Horrorshow." The Scars were part of the Human League tour that swept through England last month. The Edinburgh quartet is Paul Research on guitar, Calumn Mackay on drums, Bobby King on vocals and John Mackie on bass. All are between eighteen and twenty years old and still have their day jobs. They first started being serious about being a band around Christmas of '77, and were discovered by Fast Record's Bob Last in the spring of '78. They've built up quite a set of originals with titles like "Obsessions," "Romance By Mail," "Your Attention Please," "Screaming Obscenities" and a version of Cockney Rebel's "Psychomodo." Stylistically they're somewhere between The Fall and Pere Ubu. "We are a pop band!" Paul shouts, "because all our songs are pop melodies."

COWBOYS INTERNATIONAL Ever wonder what happened to Terry Chimes (aka Tory Crimes) after he left the Clash two years back? Here he is again, banging the skins for Cowboys International. The group also included Jimmy Hughes on bass, Evan Charles on piano, Rick Jacks on guitar and Ken Lickie on vocals. The single of "Aftermath" is the public's introduction and it's a pop one, with surf overtones.

PRETENDERS	Birmingham, Barbarella's	RARE DEVICE/ MEDIATORS/	
SKIDS	Glasgow, College Of Art	FT INDEX	Manchester, Band On The Wall

21st - Wednesday.........

THE REZILLOS, who split up their group just before last Christmas, are regrouping and looking to the future. The band's vocalists Faye Fifi and Eugene Reynolds, have gotten back together with their old guitarist Hi-Fi Harris in Edinburgh, and have added two new backup singers, Jane and Trish. They're still auditioning drummers and bass players while working on new songs in rehearsals. They still haven't decided whether they shall continue as the Rezillos or take up a new name with the new material.

THE GLAXO BABIES' minimalist 12" EP is out this week. The four songs are all originals, "This Is Your Life," "Stay Awake," "Because Of You" and "Who Killed Bruce Lee." This Bristol-based quartet is Geoff Alsopp on drums, Dan Catsis on guitar and vocals, Rob Chapman on vocals and Tom Nichols on bass. The press hand out claims that the unusual name "originates from some experiments they (the band members) were conducting with baby food names at art school."

JAGS/STICKERS	London, Bridge House	ABC/LOCAL HEROES	London, Pegasus
RAINCOATS/		PATRIK FITZGERALD	Manchester, The Factory
SCRITTI POLITTI	London, Moonlight Club	ONLY ONES	Sheffield, Poly.
PSYCHEDELIC FURS	London, Windsor Castle		

22nd - Thursday.........

THE MEMBERS follow up the success of "Sound Of The Suburbs" with a new 45 today. It's "Offshore Banking Business" and is "an exposé of the cash laundering going on in the Caribbean." It's flipped with a new recording of "Solitary Confinement," which they cut last

MARCH 1979

year for their Stiff debut. The Members will have their debut album out shortly on Virgin Records in the UK.

THE LEYTON BUZZARDS are in Shepherd's Bush today to mime their appearance on *Top Of The Pops*. The musician unions rules for the show require that a band be able to recreate their recording the studio within the ridiculous three hour time limit in order to demonstrate that they are in fact the band that made the recording. Then, to add insult to injury, the band are not allowed to play the song live on *Top Of The Pops*, but instead are required to mime to the recorded hit version. The Buzzards are doing their best to mime their song "Saturday Night Beneath The Plastic Palm Trees" then have to jump into their TR6 and shoot up to Sheffield where they're scheduled to play in a Rock Against Racism show.

PINK MILITARY STAND ALONE	.....Liverpool, Eric's	VALVES/NECROMATS	...............London, Rock Garden
FUTURE BODIES	......................London, The Green Man	BARRY FORDE BAND/	
RED BEANS & RICE	...................London, Hope & Anchor	LEYTON BUZZARDS/	
YACHTS	................................London, Lyceum	PIRANHAS	..............................Sheffield, Poly.

23rd - Friday...

SIOUXSIE & THE BANSHEES have their second single "Staircase" released by Polydor. It's flipped with their version of the T Rex song "20th Century Boy." The band aren't planning to be touring for a while, but they are headlining a giant fund raiser for Mentally Handicapped Children (MENCAP) on April 7th at the Roundhouse.

GENERATION X have their new single "Valley Of The Dolls" released today. The initial pressing is on the ugliest of brown vinyls, with a special picture sleeve. The flipside is their version of the Johnny Kidd classic "Shakin' All Over" recorded for a BBC session.

GENERATION X / VALLEY OF THE DOLLS
c/w SHAKIN' ALL OVER
NEW SINGLE LIMITED EDITION ON MULTI-COLOURED VINYL

THE PSYCHEDELIC FURS play what they boast as their fourteenth gig, and get a favorable review in *Sounds* from Nick Tester. The group is Richard Butler on vocals, his brother Tim Butler on bass. Duncan Kilburn lends sax to the group and the guitars are played by John Ashton and Roger Morris. Paul Wilson plays drums. Veterans in the group are Paul and John who were once members of the Unwanted. Nick Tester wrote, "While psychedelia is an influence (especially leaning on the Velvet Underground), they don't simply return to the form but return it with their own updated colors and character…fast, assertive and rumbling rhythms dart deep beneath the strains of Duncan's sobbing, weeping sax, and Richard's yearning vocals. The snaking throb is borne out by another excellent song, 'Imitation Of Christ' with its cartwheeling chorus outstanding." Other highlights in the set are "Pulse," "Chaos," "Blacks," and "Shoes." The band is currently unsigned but with more reviews like this, it won't last long.

LIVE TONIGHT!

BARRY FORDE BAND/		PSYCHEDELIC FURS/	
PATRIK FITZGERALD/		REDS/VEINS	...........................London, Moonlight Club
ED BANGER/MOLESTERS	............Liverpool, Eric's	CROOKS/CARPETTES	................London, Pegasus
PORTRAITS	....................London, City University	RADIO STARS/	
UK SUBS	.....................London, Kingsway College	BOBBY HENRY/SHRINK	..............London, School Of Printing
ABC	.............................London, Dublin Castle	BUZZCOCKS	.........................Manchester, Belle Vue
C GAS 5/RESISTERS	...................London, Windsor Castle	SKIDS	.........................Manchester, Russell Club
CURE/POISON	..........................London, N.E.London Poly.	EDDIE & THE HOT RODS/	
FASHION	..............................London, Music Machine	MEMBERS/MAGNETS	................Sheffield, Top Rank

24th - Saturday...

ALTERED IMAGES There's a new band springing to life in Glasgow, Scotland. Altered Images is a group put together by school friends Tony McDaid on bass, John McElhone on guitar, and Michael Anderson on drums. In early rehearsals they've also invited Jim McIven (ex-Berlin Blondes keyboards) and vocalist Clare Grogan to join up.

TOM ROBINSON BAND/		SPLITT RIVITT	........................London, Moonlight
STRAITS	...............................Belfast, Ulster Hall	CARPETTES	...........................London, Nashville
DANGEROUS GIRLS	.................Birmingham, Bogart's	PUNISHMENT OF LUXURY	..........London, Thames Poly.
PRETENDERS	.........................Liverpool, Eric's	EDDIE & THE HOT RODS/	
SOFT BOYS	...........................London, Hope & Anchor	MEMBERS/MAGNETS	................Manchester, Apollo

25th - Sunday..

THE TEARDROP EXPLODES are riding high. Just two weeks ago they were the featured band on Granada TV's *What's On* program, and now the attention has spread to the music magazines. Members of the group must be buying dozens of copies of both the new *NME* and *Sounds* to pass out to all of their friends. Caught in Manchester, playing their fifth gig (the first outside of their native Liverpool), a favorable review of the new band is submitted by Ian Wood for the *NME*. He describes the band as having, "…a melodic vision of their own. Julian Cope not only obtaining a fluid lubricous tonality which nears pure Motown but also handling vocal chores with winning charm…(The band) have an understated alliance, based on minimal variation upon a densely layered foundation…I think A Teardrop Explodes are the proof I've been awaiting that a new dawn has broken on the Liverpool scene." *Sounds* magazine Mick Middles wrote, "Suddenly out of the depths of obscurity the Teardrop Explodes have become the most talked about new band in the North West…(They) show all signs of becoming an original and exciting force on the modern music scene. They experimented with melody and power and

MARCH 1979

produces an utterly danceable noise that reminded me of the days of the early Fall."

THE CLASH are reportedly almost finished with their movie. It's as yet untitled, but bassist Paul Simonon has leaked that the soundtrack is finished. The story supposedly revolves around a roadie of the band and what it's like to be on the road with the "real" Clash.

LIVE TONIGHT!

HUMAN LEAGUE/FALL/	PORTRAITS ....London, Rock Garden
GANG OF FOUR	BRAM TCHAIKOVSKY/
STIFF LITTLE FINGERS/	CARPETTES ....London, Nashville
MEKONS ....London, Lyceum	EDDIE & THE HOT RODS/
THE CURE/SCARS ....London, The Marquee	MEMBERS ....Sheffield, Top Rank
SINCEROS ....London, Hope & Anchor	

26th - Monday...

"THE NEW MERSEYBEAT" In this week's *Sounds* magazine, Andy Courtney gets the double page center spread to rave about the "New Merseybeat." Four bands are selected as the best contenders to be the next big thing. The Teardrop Explodes, detail some of the band's past. They expound on the names the band has appeared under, including The Nova Mob, The Crucial Three, Industrial Domestic, The Mystery Girls and the Silly Hats. Their single of "Sleeping Gas" was supposedly ordered in triplicate by BBC DJ John Peel and they are reportedly being considered to be included in the forthcoming Open Eye Records Liverpool sampler titled "World Shut Your Mouth (Don't Be A Twat Sunday.)" Echo And The Bunnymen are a promising trio of Will Sergeant (lead and rhythm guitar), Ian McCulloch (vocals), and Les Pattinson (bass). There's no drummer, only a drum machine known as "echo." Will and Ian got together back in September of '78 and Les arrived in November. They're playing around Liverpool a bit and have a song called "Monkeys" they boast lasts nine minutes. Orchestral Manoeuvres In The Dark are based around two nineteen-year-old neighbors, Andy McCluskey and Paul Humphreys. They were formerly in a band called the Id but split that up last October. Since then they've been working on more songs and have two ready for inclusion on the proposed Liverpool compilation. One is "Almost" and the other "Electricity" were recorded in their friend's home studio. The name came from a song that Andy McCluskey wrote when he was about sixteen. Pink Military Stand Alone will supposedly have an EP out soon and brag that their set has expanded to a list of thirteen songs.

ADAM & THE ANTS are invited back for their third BBC John Peel session. Tonight they record four more new songs, "Ligotage," "Tabletalk," "Animals & Men" and "Never Trust A Man (With Egg On His Face.)"

FASHION ....Birmingham, Barrel Organ	UK SUBS/
NEON HEARTS.........................Birmingham, Barbarella's	DAVE GOODMAN & FRIENDS/
THE WALL/CRASS/	SKUNKS/THE OUTSIDERS ....London, Music Machine
POISON GIRLS ....London, Acklam Hall	VALVES/PINPOINT....................London, Nashville
NICKY & THE DOTS....................London, Goldsmith's College	

28th - Wednesday...

ANGELIC UPSTARTS Trouble follows Jimmy Pursey, even when he has little to do with it. His proteges The Angelic Upstarts were to be signed to Polydor, just as Pursey's band Sham 69 is, but with recent Sham problems, interest in Angelic Upstarts has evaporated. So in step Warner Bros. Records who sign up the Upstarts for an immediate release of their Pursey produced single "I'm An Upstart" b/w "Leave Me Alone." The 45 will hit the streets next week in a special sleeve and the Upstarts album is to follow soon.

THE COM-SAT ANGELS have their debut 45 out this week on their own Junta Records. "Red Planet" is coupled with "I Get Excited" and "Specimen No.2." As with every third record these days, the run of singles is pressed up on red vinyl, with a special black & white picture sleeve. The band is enigmatically credited as Even Steven on guitar, The Jazz Orange on keyboards, Dresden on bass and Michael Spencer-Farquahar on drums.

PATRIK FITZGERALD ....Belfast, The Pound	PSYCHEDELIC FURS ....London, Windsor Castle
SKIDS....................................London, Marquee	

30th - Friday...

MAGAZINE's second album "Secondhand Daylight" is released today in England. This album contains tracks with intriguing titles like "Permafrost," "The Thin Air," "Cut-Out Shapes" "Feed The Enemy," and "I Wanted Your Heart." A 45 from the album of "Rhythm Of Cruelty" is also out today. The single is flipped with the non-LP track "T.V. Baby."

SEX PISTOLS are the subject of another posthumous single from the *Great Rock & Roll Swindle* soundtrack. The track "Silly Thing" features vocalist Paul Cook and "Who Killed Bambi" has ex-C Gas 5 vocalist Ten Pole Tudor out front. As usual it's in a special limited edition picture bag that makes this record product look more like movie product. That is to say the sleeve look just like a movie popcorn box. Blatant cash-in that this record is, it still is driven up the UK charts to reach #6, making it a "hit" on a par with "Pretty Vacant" and "Holidays In The Sun."

FALL ....Liverpool, Eric's	ABC ....London, Dublin Castle
RED CRAYOLA/	EDDIE & THE HOT RODS/
ESSENTIAL LOGIC/	MEMBERS ....London, Rainbow
SCRITTI POLITTI ....London, Acklam Hall	REMA REMA ....London, Screen On The Green
PATRIK FITZGERALD.................London, Hope & Anchor	JOY DIVISION/SX ....London, Walthamstow Youth Centre
SQUEEZE/LONELY GUYS ....London, Nashville	

MARCH 1979

31st - Saturday..

THE BEAT make their public debut at The Mattador Club in Birmingham. The Beat is Dave Wakeling, Andy Cox, David Steele, and Everett Morton. The headline act is a punk band called the Dum Dum Boyz. They are Paul on vocals, another Paul on guitar, Mick on bass and Ranking Roger on vocals and drums. The Dum Dum Boyz and the Beat have both been playing only about six months. Tonight's concert was only days after the Three Mile Island nuclear disaster, and The Beat were introduced as, "...the hottest thing since the Pennsylvania meltdown." In the near future, Ranking Roger would quit his band to join the Beat, giving them their distinctive white soul-toasting beat sound that would push them time and time into the charts.

THE PASSIONS are one of those bands that are destined for that descriptive middle ground between Siouxsie and Penetration. Lead by Barbara Gogan, the quintet turn in "Needles and Pills," and "Body And Soul" as their debut 45. It's out this week on Soho Records. Barbara is backed by Mitch Barker on vocals, Clive Timperley (ex-101'ers) on guitar, Claire Black on bass and Richard Williams on drums. Passions founders Claire and Mitch got together about a year ago. Then they were joined by Clive, Richard and Barbara. Richard had a musical past with a group called the Derelicts, the other two-thirds of which are now calling themselves Prag Vec.

THE HUMAN LEAGUE are politely out of touch when it comes to electronic pop muisc. Ian Marsh from the group told the *NME*, "Y'know I'd really like for us to appear on *Top Of The Pops*. Us appearing on *Top Of The Pops* like we do on stage would be quite something. I can't think of anyone who's like us, with just synthesizers."

THE MISFITS, the UK version, are a not-quite-super group of four "name" musicians backing a heretofore unknown vocalist. Keyboards are Mark Ambler (ex Tom Robinson Band), John Brown is on bass (Wreckless Eric's band), and Rich Kids members Rusty Egan and Midge Ure provide the needed guitar. They play a few originals and lots of covers. The group is temporary, only a few dates are planned before the lot disband and go back to their respective employers. This group is in no way connected with the "shock / horror" group the Misfits that frequent the NYC clubs.

DUM DUM BOYZ/THE BEAT ....Birmingham, Matador Club	PATRIK FITZGERALD
ONLY ONES ....Birmingham, Barbarella's	(under 18 matinee)...................London, Hope & Anchor
CURE......................................Liverpool, Eric's	SQUEEZE/
MISFITS ....London, Bridge House	MARK ANDREWS & GENTS ....London, Nashville
BUZZCOCKS/	RED CRAYOLA/
PATRIK FITZGERALD/	ESSENTIAL LOGIC/
MOLESTERS ....London, Hammersmith Odeon	SCRITTI POLITTI ....Manchester, The Factory
UK SUBS ....Manchester, The Mayflower	

April 1st - Sunday..

RED NOISE have their new single, "Revolt Into Style" released this weekend. The track is taken from the LP "Sound On Sound" and is coupled with "Out Of Touch" recorded live in Leicester just four weeks ago. As with almost every other new single these days, the initial pressings are in a limited edition picture sleeve and blue vinyl disc. A limited 12" version also includes the track "Stay Young."

THE BANK OF DRESDEN are going to have to find another new bass player. Jane Crockford has been thinking that the group was getting far too serious. She's putting together her own group and calling it the Bomberettes. Jane met guitarist Kate Korris on the set of the *Great Rock & Roll Swindle*, and also found June Miles-Kingston, the perfect drummer. Their new vocalist is from Switzerland, she's Ramona Carlier. She met the band at a Vincent Units gig.

           WINNERS/DANGEROUS GIRLS .....Birmingham, Barbarella's

3rd - Tuesday.................

THE THE Matt Johnson has an advert in this week's *NME* looking for musicians to put together a new band with. He's currently living above the King's Head pub in Ongar. Responding to the listing are many unusual musicians, the three that intrigue Matt the most being Keith Laws, fiddle player Peter Fenton-Jones, and a girl drummer called Janis.

THE ONLY ONES take a "Out There In The Night" from their latest album "Even Serpents Shine" and back it with both songs from their 1977 indie debut 45, "Lovers Of Today" and "Peter & The Pets." It's also available on blue vinyl 12."

FALL/LEW LEWIS REFORMER ......Birmingham, Barbarella's	PROPERTY OF/
RED CRAYOLA/	SPHERICAL OBJECTS
SCRITTI POLITTI/	MANCHESTER MEKONS ....Manchester, Band On The Wall
ESSENTIAL LOGIC ....Birmingham, Festival Rooms	ONLY ONES/
PRETENDERS..........................London, Marquee	ANGELIC UPSTARTS/
THE EDGE/	ASWAD/TONTRIX ....Manchester, Poly.
PSYCHEDELIC FURS ....London, Moonlight Club	

5th - Thursday..

THE PIRANHAS first burst onto the scene back on Jubilee Weekend in June of '77. They were part of a "Sod The Jubilee" mini-concert in Brighton. Since then, the original quartet grew by two members and they began playing outside their hometown. As for the rest of

APRIL 1979

England, they first heard about the Piranhas when they were featured on the "Vaultage '78" compilation, a collection of Brighton-based bands. The same label that spilled out that musical cornucopia from Brighton has issued the first proper Piranhas single. Two originals, "Jilly" and "Coloured Music" are the single. Both songs are new to record buyers and come in a psych bag whose reverse is a parody of music instrument adverts. The Piranhas are Al Hambra on keyboards, Johnny Helmer on guitar, Dick Slexia on drums, Reggie Hornsbury on bass, Bob Grover on guitar and Zoot Alors on sax.

SPECIALS "If people want to be racists that's their problem. They've got to make up their own minds. As far as we're concerned, racism isn't an issue. Racism as far as we're concerned is like some kind of mental illness, like fear of spiders." — Terry Hall of The Specials in *Sounds*

LIVE TONIGHT!

DED BYRDS	Liverpool, Eric's	PSYCHEDELIC FURS	London, Albany Empire
RED CRAYOLA/		NICKY & THE DOTS	London, Hope & Anchor
SCRITTI POLITTI/		FLEXIBLE DUSTBINS	London, Western Counties
ESSENTIAL LOGIC	London, Action Space		

6th - Friday...

THE MEMBERS now have something besides a handful of 45s to put their name to. Their debut LP "At The Chelsea Nightclub" hits the streets today. It's eleven tracks that weave in their debut single for Stiff, Solitary Confinement, in a re-recorded version, as well as the single "Sound Of The Suburbs." For some reason their latest, "Offshore Banking Business," is absent. The title track "Chelsea Nightclub" was recorded live at the Hammersmith Odeon last December when the band was opening up for Devo. The Members are Nicky Tesco on lead vocals, J.C. on guitar, Chris Payne on bass, Nigel Bennett on lead guitar, and Adrian Lillywhite on drums. Steve "Rudi" Thompson is the guest sax player, a loan from X-Ray Spex.

J.J. BRUNEL, the Stranglers outspoken bassist has his solo album in the shops today. "Euroman Cometh" is a concept album and features J.J. in the role of writer, vocalist and bassist. Brian James of the Damned plays guitar on the disc and harmonica player extrodinaire Lew Lewis does his best. The front cover shows J.J. dwarfed by the pipes and vents that decorate the exterior of the Pompidou Center in Paris. J.J. Brunel's opening date for his solo tour of England has been cancelled by the owners of London' Theatre Royal in Dreary Lane learned that Burnel is a member of the Stranglers. They take a dim view of "punk" music and consider Burnel dangerous territory. Hundred of tickets have already been sold.

CATCH THE POLICE ON TV ROCK GOES TO COLLEGE THIS FRIDAY AT 11-40 BBC 2 A&M

TEENBEATS It's a perfectly natural thing that the mod revival growing in England is centered on the South coast of England. Hastings has it's own scene brewing and one of the top mod bands to come from there is the Teen Beats. Tonight they've driven up to London and make their debut in the big city at the Music Machine opening for the Young Bucks.

PASSIONS	London, Archway Tavern	ABC	London, Dublin Castle
MOLESTERS	London, Hope & Anchor	EDDIE & THE HOT RODS	London, Moonlight
PURPLE HEARTS	London, Top Alex	YOUNG BUCKS/TEENBEATS	London, Music Machine
WHIRLWIND/BEAST	London, Nashville	ANY TROUBLE	Manchester, Commercial Hotel

7th - Saturday...

SIOUXSIE & THE BANSHEES headline a charity gig for the MENCAP, a charity for the Mentally Handicapped. They felt that since they had "made it," it was time to put something back. They're against the idea of jumping on the now popular Rock Against Racism bandwagon, so a benefit for the truly helpless was an attractive idea. Opening the show are The Human League from Sheffield, and Rema Rema, which is their old friend Marco Pirroni's new group. The Banshees closed the show playing live favorites like "Hong Kong Garden," "Love In A Void," "Overground" and the new 45 "Staircase (Mystery)." Before ending the show, they also unveiled a new song called "Premature Burial." Over-exuberant fans caused enough damage to the Rainbow, that after the band settled with management to cover costs, little was left for MENCAP.

ECHO & THE BUNNYMEN *Sounds* reports that the trio Echo & The Bunnymen, who only a few weeks ago were featured in an exposé of the "New Merseybeat" have now been signed to Zoo Records in Liverpool. They are currently working on tracks for their debut single. There is sort of competition going in Liverpool to come up with the funniest names. Pink Military Stand Alone has a fine entry, while Teardrop Explodes is top notch too. Before settling on Echo & The Bunnymen, other names supposedly considered included Glicerol and The Fan Extractors, Mona Lisa and the Grease Guns, and Something And The Daz Man.

TOM ROBINSON BAND/		PRESS/PURPLE HEARTS	London, Moonlight Club
STRAITS	London, Lewisham Odeon	V1/THE REPTILES	London, Windsor Castle
SIOUXSIE & THE BANSHEES/		DAMNED/THE RUTS	Manchester, The Factory
HUMAN LEAGUE/REMA REMA	London, Rainbow		

10th - Tuesday...

THE DAMNED's latest single is released today on Chiswick. It's a three track EP of "Love Song" coupled with "Suicide" and "Noise Noise Noise." Despite the "historically significant" single releases that have already come and gone, this is the Damned's first "hit" single in the UK, creeping up to #20, and to date is their second biggest song. The track "Love Song" was available to fans at a few special concerts at the first of the year.

APRIL 1979

DAMNED/THE RUTS ....Birmingham, Barbarella's	NECROMATS/MOLESTERS ....London, Moonlight Club
NIK TURNER'S SPHINX/	THE THING/58th VARIETY/
GEISHA GIRLS.........................Liverpool, Mr. Pickwick's	RED ....Manchester, Band On The Wall
LEW LEWIS REFORMER/	
PURPLE HEARTS ....London, Marquee	

12th - Thursday.......................................

THE REZILLOS are finished concluded with their past and move into the future. "Mission Accomplished" is their final vinyl, a live album released today on Sire. Advance orders of over 15,000 show that the public isn't quite finished with their love affair with the Rezillos. It's classic stuff, with the live favorites of "Top Of The Pops," "Good Sculptures," and "Destination Venus," being played with the same vigor accorded to quirky covers like "Thunderbirds Are Go!," "Land Of 1,000 Dances," "Ballroom Blitz" and "Somebody's Gonna Get Their Head Kicked In Tonight." Several songs are new to those who only know the band from their records when Jo Callis contributes "Culture Shock," and "Teenbeat." One song "Cold Wars" has been paired up with two live tracks not included on the album, "Flying Saucer Attack," and "Shout." This "new" 45 will be out next Friday. The live recording was the last show the band ever played at the Glasgow Apollo two days before last Christmas. Ex-Rezillos Faye and Eugene have a new group, but are not going to use their old name. The most recent addition is a new drummer, Robo Rhythm (actually Eugene's brother), and Troy Tate on guitar. They expect to be out and playing new material soon. Jo Callis, Simon Templar, and Angel Paterson are also putting together a band, as yet unnamed. Even so, they claim they'll have out an EP by the end of the month.

JAPAN have their new single "Life In Tokyo (parts 1 & 2)" released just in time to capitalizes on the last date of their world tour. The new single is available in the usual color vinyl formats in 7" and 12" varieties, and include special psych sleeves. The band plays tonight at the Rainbow.

LOU REED.............................Dublin, National Stadium	POLICE/FAMOUS PLAYERS ....London, Nashville
RUTS / EXODUS/	JAPAN/REGGAE REGULAR ....London, Rainbow
SATELLITES ....London, Acton Town Hall	NEWTOWN NEUROTICS/
PSYCHEDELIC FURS/	VEINS ....London, Windsor Castle
LEOPARDS.............................London, Dublin Castle	ZYKLON B ....Manchester, Russell Club
ADDIX..................................London, Rock Garden	THE PASSAGE ....Manchester, Bowden Vale Club

13th - Friday.......................................

J.J. BURNEL, bassist for the Stranglers, follows the release of his solo LP with a the single "Freddie Laker (Concorde & Eurobus)." It's flipped with the non-LP track "Ozymandias" supposedly inspired by a Shelley poem. Burnel is currently on the road touring his new album. Opening up the show is Blood Donor and ex-Vibrator John Ellis' band Rapid Eye Movement, the latter sounding like a cross between Gong and the Tubes. His London show Drury Lane Theatre Royal has now been rescheduled for the Hammersmith Odeon on May 1st.

PINK MILITARY STAND ALONE It was only two months ago that P.M.S.A. were making their live debut and already they have a 45 out. That's immediacy. The four track EP "Buddha Waking- Disney Sleeping," is on the band's own Last Trumpet Records label. It contains "Degenerated Man," "Sanjo Kantara," "(Dead Lady Of) Clown Town," and "Heaven/Hell." The songs were recorded last December 7th during a live gig at Eric's in Liverpool. *NME* writer Paul Morley describes the EP as, "...four dangerous doodles. Untamed and fluid noise fronted by the diabolical moaning of ex-Big In Japan delinquent Jayne. A thoroughly unpolite record." The sleeve is a hard cardboard fold-out job that has several photos of the band inside.

THE CURE's debut single is already being deleted. It seems improbable but true. After only ten weeks, Fiction Records is already pulling the Cure's single of "Killing An Arab." Always looking ahead, the band are back in the studio working on their debut album, scheduled for release in May.

LIVE TONIGHT!

SCARS/THE FREEZE/	TOT & THE GIRLS
PRATS/DISINTEGRATORS/	IN ROOM 419/
ETTES/THURSDAY ....Edinburgh, Transport Halls	BANK OF DRESDEN..................London, Moonlight Club
CRASS/POISON GIRLS...............Liverpool, Eric's	PSYCHEDELIC FURS/
WARM JETS/PROTEX ....London, Bridge House	OUT PATIENTS ....London, Windsor Castle
ABC ....London, Dublin Castle	TOYAH/DOLL BY DOLL..............Manchester, Russell Club

16th - Monday.......................................

THE CARPETTES are the latest band to be signed to the Beggars Banquet stable of stars. They're playing a few dates around Southern England, beginning with a show at the Windsor Castle tomorrow night, before jumping in the studio to get to work.

THE HUMAN LEAGUE are Sheffield's most prominent, and perhaps only electronic band. Their second record released this week is a 12" single called "The Dignity Of Labour." I has nothing to do with the upcoming general election. The band felt that they never have a chance to play instrumentals on stage, so how about a record of them? Here's four of 'em, parts one through four. There is also an amusing addition to the 12" EP. It's a flexi disc of the Human League discussing what to put on the flexi disc. They prattle on and on and no definitive decision must have been reached because the argument IS the flexi disc! Well, at least it's free.

ALTERNATIVE T.V., which began almost exactly two years ago as an extension of writer Mark Perry's imagination, has split up. Perry has become so confounded by his audiences wanting him to "play the hits" and nothing new, that he's packing it in, ready to start under a new name. Under consideration is the moniker "The Good Missionaries." There is one more single due from the band called "The Force

APRIL 1979

Is Blind" and ""Lost In Room." After that ATV is history.

MOHICANS!? *Sounds* magazine, ever the fount of info on the latest thing offered this caption to a quarter-page photo. "We brought you punks, we brought you skins, we brought you mods, and now laydeez and gene'lmen we bring you the Mohicans. Above Birmingham punks Mork Egan, Roy Rat, Johnny Belfast and Paul Guinness model the latest thing in teen coiffure fashion." The photo shows four teens with unusual haircuts. Two have almost shaved heads with two-inch wide, three-inch long blonde stripe running fore to aft across their scalps. The third has partitioned his head into four parallel strips of one inch each and the fourth, a black lad, has simply applied a white stripe down the top of his hair.

TOYAH/RECORDS.....................Edinburgh, Tiffany's	J.J. BURNEL/
STAA MAX/ACK ACK/	CHORDS/SECRET AFFAIR ....London, Bridge House
GLAXO BABIES	RAPID EYE MOVEMENT/
LITTLE BO BITCH ....London, Noise Factory	BLOOD DONOR........................Manchester, Apollo

18th - Wednesday...

THE TOURISTS have just signed a long term deal with Logo Records. It's unclear whether this is a contract renewal from when three of the Tourists were on Logo as "The Catch," or if it is a new deal for a new band. The five-piece band have been one of those A&R favorites around town, just waiting for the right deal. They are led by Annie Lennox, who hasn't recorded since '77 when she and bandmates Dave Stewart and Pete Coombes had a minor hit in Holland as The Catch. The Tourists are currently in Germany working on their debut album with producer Conny Plank, who had worked with Bowie, and the Talking Heads. They've also been invited to be the support for Roxy Music on their English tour next month.

NOT SENSIBLES are a new group from Burnley, just twenty miles North of Manchester. With tongues firmly planted in their collective cheeks, the Not Sensibles are adamant about dance music. Jumping on the bandwagon trying to overrun the *Saturday Night Fever* crowd, their new 45 is "Death To Disco." The single is credited to Haggis on lead vocals, Sage Hartley on guitar, R.C. Rowlinson on keyboards and bass, and Klever Hemingway on drums. Besides the title track, you also get "The Coronation Street Hustle," and the ultimate tribute to slackers "Lying On The Sofa."

LIVE TONIGHT!

VALVES/CUBAN HEELS ....Edinburgh, Astoria	DEXY'S MIDNIGHT RUNNERS ......London, Windsor Castle
DAMNED ....High Wycombe, Town Hall	THE PASSAGE ....Manchester, Bowden Vale Club
GIRLSCHOOL/PIRANHAS ....London, Moonlight Club	MAGAZINE/SIMPLE MINDS ....Sheffield, Top Rank
FLYS/PSYCHEDELIC FURS ....London, Music Machine	

19th - Thursday...

SIMPLE MINDS must be celebrating in Glasgow. Their debut album is released this weekend. "Life In A Day" is stylistically at least a thousand miles away from where the band was two years ago when they were calling themselves Johnny & The Self Abusers. The LP features all original material like "Chelsea Girl," "All For You," "Destiny," "Pleasantly Disturbed," and the title track/current single "Life In A Day." A 45 is also available to those who don't have the four pounds for the album. It's the title track "Life In A Day" coupled with the non LP track "Special View."

THE SLITS are on the BBC 2 TV program *Grapevine*. They aren't the guest, they sing the theme song! They've recorded their own version of the Marvin Gaye song "I Heard It Thru The Grapevine" exclusively for the beeb. The Slits are also celebrating their signing to Island Records. They'll be heading into the studios soon with Dennis Bovell of Matumbi to start on their debut LP.

TOYAH/BARRY ANDREWS...........Birmingham, Barbarella's	SPHERICAL OBJECTS/
XTC.....................................Liverpool, Eric's	VIBRANT THIGH/
MEDIUM MEDIUM/GAFFA	RARE DEVICE/PROPERTY OF ....Manchester, The Factory
ART FAILURE ....London, Acklam Hall	MEMBERS/PINPOINT.................Sheffield, Limit Club

20th - Friday...

SPECIAL AKA are the Coventry-based ska group that were the standouts on the recent "Clash On Parole" across the UK. After some bad experiences working with Clash manager Bernard Rhodes, the Special AKA have decided to do it themselves. They've started their own label, with pressing and distribution handled through Rough Trade in London, and call the company Two Tone. It takes it's name from the two tone (black & white) suits worn by mods and skinheads a decade before. Jerry Dammers from the group has designed the black and white checked logo and has come up with a cartoon rude boy known as "Walt Jabsco," to be hallmark of the label. The 45 itself has the Special AKA on the "A" side doing "Gangsters," a remake of a 1964 Prince Buster ska classic called "Al Capone," even sampling the car screech at the front of the original to start their version. The flipside is an instrumental called "The Selecter" by The Selecter. In truth, the Selecter is actually Specials' friend Neol Davies along with Dammer's roommate John Bradbury. They recorded this instrumental on an old two track Revox deck. Barry Jones, a local session musician, was called in to provide the trombone part. Even though the band is billed as the Selecter, there is no band to speak of yet, just an idea. Dammers has had 5,000 copies pressed up, and the band themselves rubber stamped the plain sleeves. He hopes that that's not too many; he doesn't want to be stuck with 'em.

APRIL 1979

THE DICKIES' latest 45 is a song that they recorded as more of a joke than a serious attempt at a hit. It's an amphetamine soaked version of the kiddie TV show theme "Banana Splits." Flipped with the children's anthem are "Hideous" and "Got It At The Store." In keeping with most other A&M singles these days, it's pressed on banana yellow vinyl. The joke will pay off big as this most unlikely song will capture the ears of England and become the Dickies' biggest hit going to #7.

PENETRATION's newest single is "Danger Signs" and "Stone Heroes" and is released today by Virgin Records. The Newcastle band gives buyers of the 12" single an additional track "Vision."

LIVE TONIGHT!

J.J. BURNEL/		POISON GIRLS/CRASS	London, Film Co-Operative
RAPID EYE MOVEMENT/		ABC	London, Dublin Castle
BLOOD DONOR	Birmingham, Digbeth Civic Hall	PUNISHMENT OF LUXURY/	
FASHION	Birmingham, Barbarellas	RESISTANCE	London, Nashville
MAGAZINE/SIMPLE MINDS	Edinburgh, Clouds	SAD AMONG STRANGERS	London, The Windmill
B-52's	Liverpool, Eric's	IGGY POP/THE ZONES	Manchester, The Factory
RUTS/AGAIN AGAIN	London, Archway Tavern	PASSAGE	Manchester, Middletown Civic Hall

21st - Saturday......................................

THE UNDERTONES' third 45 is "Jimmy Jimmy" flipped with "Mars Bars." Like so many these days, it's first pressing is released today on clear green vinyl with a see-through special pic sleeve.

THE POP GROUP, without doubt, are a challenging group. Outside the mainstream of what is commercially viable, they strain the boundaries once more with the release of their debut album "Y". The cover is a provocative photograph of tribesmen prepared for ceremony in mud masks. Songs include "Thief Of Fire," "Snowgirl," "Blood Money," "Savage Sea," We Are Time," "Words Disobey Me," "Don't Call Me Pain," "The Boys From Brazil" and "Don't Sell Your Dreams." Ever looking forward, the Pop Group have not included their last single on this album. Inside the package, early buyers will get a provocative 20" x 48" color poster, a photo montage of the ugly side of humanity with song lyrics superimposed over top. The quintet is made up of Mark Stewart on vocals, Simon Underwood on bass, Gareth Sager and John Waddington on guitar and Bruce Smith on drums.

MINNY POPS Now here's a odd one. The Minny Pops find refuge somewhere between the Normal ("T.V.O.D.") and Devo. Fractured melodies with very unusual vocals. Their single begins with "Footsteps" and "Nervous" before concluding with the unusual "Kojak," where the lead vocalist does an amusing Kojak impersonation over the squeaks and squanks of the backing track.

XTC/D.C. NEIN	Dublin, University College	PUNISHMENT OF LUXURY/	
IGGY POP/THE ZONES	Liverpool, Eric's	RESISTANCE	London, Nashville
SCRITTI POLITTI	London, Fairfield Play Centre	TOYAH/	
NIPS/MIRRORS	London, Moonlight Club	DEXY'S MIDNIGHT RUNNERS/	
NEO/SATELLITES	London, Windsor Castle	MARTIN'S MIGHTY MOUSE	London, Music Machine
SAD AMONG STRANGERS	London, Plumstead Green Man	THE PASSAGE	Manchester, The Squat (ANL Benefit)

24th - Tuesday......................................

THE SOFT BOYS celebrate the release of 2,500 copies of their debut album "A Can Of Bees." It's a collection of eight studio tracks and three live recordings. Robyn Hitchcock has written a group of unlikely titles, such as "Leppo And The Jooves," "Sandra's Having Her Brain Out," "The Rats Prayer," "Do The Chisel" and "The Pigworker." The live tracks include a cover of Lennon's "Cold Turkey." The album is a re-recorded version of the album rejected by Radar a few months ago. Before settling on "Can Of Bees" the LP was briefly called "Heat Me Up, And Tell Me You're Happy." A major tour follows today's release.

THE SPECIALS' (or Special AKA) show at the Music Machine tonight didn't go unnoticed. They're riding high on the release of their debut single "Gangsters" and a mountain of new press catching up with the growing excitement surrounding this new group. Mark Ellen reviewing tonight's concert for the *NME*, described the band as, "...vocalist Terry Hall, who I'd loosely term as a pacifist skinhead, flanked by two black singers, Linval Golding of the sharp, reggae rhythm guitar and Neville Staples of the frenzied dub voice over and manic maracas...It's the stuff that turns legs to rubber and plays pinball with your brain. They strike a near perfect balance between accessibility and sentiment; as a dance band the Specials are truly something else."

MEMBERS/PINPOINT	Birmingham, Barbarella's	SPECIALS/RED LIGHTS	London, Music Machine
ROBERT & THE REMOULDS/		SQUIRE	London, Upstairs At Ronnie Scott's
ARROGANT	London, Middlesex Poly.	TUNES/VIBRANT THIGH/	
SOFT BOYS/LA STARZA	London, Moonlight Club	RARE DEVICE	Manchester, Band On The Wall
DIRECTIONS/VIP's	London, Bridge House		

25th - Wednesday......................................

J.J. BURNEL is the subject of an unusual tale in the pages of the *NME*. It centers around *Record Mirror* writer Ronnie Gurr and Stranglers bassist J.J. Burnel. There was a falling out between the pop star and the journalist at some time, even though the two were at one time congenial. After repeatedly refusing requests from Gurr for an interview Burnel extended an invitation to meet him at the White Lion in Covent Garden. When Gurr arrived, he supposedly was met not by Burnel, but by a few of his burly friends who bundled Gurr up in a coach and headed off for Burnel who was playing in Hemel Hempstead. Arriving at the gig, Gurr was tied up and locked in a backstage room at the Pavilion. He managed to escape, running across the stage while opening act Blood Donor was on, trailing the toughs that abducted him in the first place. Then Gurr found his way to the local constabulary at about 8:30 PM. He explained his situation, and how

APRIL 1979

he was abducted by a pop group. The local police felt the story a little suspect, even though they did accompany him back to the gig to retrieve his tape recorder and scarf. Unable to make a charge against Burnel he left for London, taking with him an odd message on his tape deck, presumably left by Burnel while he was running from the hall. Gurr isn't revealing what the message says. Is this a true story? Neither Burnel or Gurr will say much about it.

THE RAMONES' foray into the world of "B" movies, *Rock And Roll High School* is debuted in Los Angeles. The story revolves around the life of the ultimate Ramones fan's desire to get into a concert while her school is trying to ban the group. The Ramones appear in the film as themselves. While in Los Angeles, the Ramones will start on the recording sessions for their next album with the legendary Phil Spector. He was the groundbreaking producer who created the "Wall Of Sound" that made hits for the Crystals, Ronettes, and the Righteous Brothers. Phil's wall of sound will have to deal with the Ramones' wall of sound. The two couldn't be more dissimilar. The Ramones usually record "instantly" with little or no overdubs. Phil takes months in the studio working on the smallest of details. The sessions start on May 1st. One can only guess when they'll finish.

PA/FLICKNIFE/L.S.D.	Belfast, Hillhead Youth Club	EXODUS/DISTRACTIONS/	
IGGY POP/THE ZONES	London, Music Machine	PRIVATE SECTOR	Manchester, Bowden Vale Club
INTERVIEW	London, Hope & Anchor	SWELL MAPS/FIREPLACE	Manchester, The Factory
ABC	London, Wimbledon Football Club	THROBBING GRISTLE/	
		COUNTERDANCE	Sheffield, University

26th - Thursday.....................................

STIFF LITTLE FINGERS' new single is "Gotta Getaway" b/w "Bloody Sunday." The "A" side was debuted at their Lyceum show four weeks ago. It's a collaboration between their own Ireland-based Rigid Digits label and Rough Trade Records, which seems to be a relatively permanent relationship even though they're being enticed with offers from the majors.

HUMAN LEAGUE have announced that they've switched from Fast Records to Virgin Records. The Human League will begin working on their new release for Virgin, and will be going out on UK tour as support to Iggy Pop.

BLONDIE's new single is "Sunday Girl" and "I Know But I Don't Know." Both songs are from the new LP "Parallel Lines." If you have the extra money to get the 12" single you'll be rewarded with a third song, the non-LP version of "Sunday Girl" sung in French. Following on the heels of "Heart Of Glass" the public is Blondie crazy, and easily push the song up the UK charts to #1. It never makes the chart at all in America.

DICKIES	Birmingham, Barbarellas	CROOKS/CHORDS	London, Pegasus
PRAG VEC	Liverpool, Eric's	FISHER Z/MEDIUM MEDIUM	London, Nashville
MANICURED NOISE/		VEINS/NEWTOWN NEUROTICS	London, Windsor Castle
REMA REMA/		JILTED JOHN	
SNEAKY FEELINS'	London, Acklam Hall	ANGELIC UPSTARTS	Manchester, The Factory
PURPLE HEARTS/CHORDS	London, Cambridge Hotel	FALL	Sheffield, Limit Club

27th - Friday.....................

Patti Smith Group
Wave

New Album
Album SPART 1086
Cassette TCART 1086
Includes the New Single
FREDERICK 6437 84
Produced by Todd Rundgren
ARISTA

PATTI SMITH's third album "Wave" has arrived. Already a critic's favorite, the LP has to live up to the legacy of "Radio Ethiopia" and "Horses." On the surface, it's the most commercial of the three albums, being produced by Todd Rundgren. The song "Frederick" will probably be the push for radio, but there are more intriguing and subtler moments on the album. Most notably is a song called "Dancing Barefoot," and unexpected whimsy is a cover of the Byrds' song "So You Want To Be (A Rock & Roll Star)."

ULTRAVOX returns from some dates in the US, and lead singer John Foxx quits. He was a founder member and had fronted the band since 1973 when they were called Tiger Lily. Remaining members of the group claim that Foxx had become increasingly difficult to work with. They'll begin a search for a new vocalist immediately, although some members of the band have had offers to work on side projects in the meantime.

THE PACK are a new group put together by Kirk Brandon and ex-Public Image drummer Jim Walker. The Public Image link is the one that's getting them any attention in the music press. Their debut single is a "Brave New Soldiers" and "Heathen." The Pack is Jim Walker on drums, Kirk Brandon on vocals, Simon Wenner on guitar, and John Wenner on bass. They're writing new material and are currently talking with Rough Trade about a possible release.

Since Jim Walker has left Public Image, they've had to find a new drummer and did for a while have in Vivian Jackson, a ex-member of Linton Kweski Johnson's band. Now it appears that Vivian is out and the seat is filled with Richard Dudanski, ex-member of the Raincoats, and if you go back far enough, you'll find him in the pre-Clash group, The 101'ers, five years ago. Most recently he had been in a now defunct group called the Bank Of Dresden.

SPECIALS	Birmingham, Aston University	PASSIONS	London, Architectural Assn.
MAGAZINE/SIMPLE MINDS	Birmingham, Odeon	ROBERT & THE REMOULDS/	
J.J. BURNEL/		ARROGANT	London, Chiswick John Bull
RAPID EYE MOVEMENT/		CLEANERS/TONTRIX	London, Dingwalls
BLOOD DONOR	Edinburgh, Odeon	YACHTS	London, Marquee
PENETRATION/		ELECTRIC CHAIRS	London, Music Machine
COWBOYS INTL.	Liverpool, Mountford Hall	WALL/THE DIALS	London, Windsor Castle
ABC	London, Dublin Castle		

LIVE TONIGHT!

APRIL 1979

28th - Saturday...

THE TOURISTS' concert tonight, is the last before they leave to go on the road opening for Roxy Music. Elissa Van Poznak, writing for the *NME* reviewed the event, describing lead singer Annie Lennox as the, "…reason for delirium. Having now abandoned her flute and only occasionally moving on to keyboards, she concentrates on projecting stage center. Her expressive vocals are packed with a power that belies her sylph-like physique. Totally bewitching, she throws punches in mid air, flaps her hands in imaginary sign language, grabs the mike and her voice soars out over a greedy audience, her eyes blazing like searchlights." Most memorable songs this evening are "The Loneliest Man In The World," "Blind Among The Flowers" "The Golden Lamp," and "Useless Duration Of Time." Although British audiences are beginning to take note of Annie Lennox's talents, it'll be four years until America wakes up and discovers her fronting the Eurythmics.

SPECIALS	Liverpool, Eric's	TOURISTS/CLEANERS	London, Music Machine
PIRANHAS	London, Hope & Anchor	ONLY ONES	London, Rainbow
LOCAL OPERATOR/		XTC	Manchester, Poly.
SOUL BOYS	London, Moonlight Club	ANY TROUBLE	Manchester, Spread Eagle
DICKIES/BRAM TCHAIKOVSKY/		THE POP GROUP/	
HOLLY & THE ITALIANS	London, Nashville	GOOD MISSIONARIES/DAMBALA	Sheffield, University

May 1st - Tuesday..

THE RAINCOATS' debut single for Rough Trade Records is the label's thirteenth. The shop must be fairly certain that they want to be a more than just another outlet to distribute and sell indie singles. The Raincoats are a group that began in earnest back in October of last year when Palmolive, drummer for the Slits, left the band to do her own thing. Since then the Raincoats have been playing, writing and apparently recording as well. The debut single is "Fairytale In The Supermarket" flipped with "In Love" and "Adventures Close To Home." The Raincoats are Vicky on violin, guitar and vocals, Ana on guitar and vocals, Gina on bass and vocals, and Palmolive on drums. The whole effort is very D.I.Y. with labels that appear to be handwritten, a xeroxed insert and low budget sleeve.

ELECTRIC CHAIRS	Birmingham, Barbarella's	STRANGEWAYS/PIRANHAS	London, Pegasus
IGGY POP/THE ZONES	Glasgow, Apollo	SEVENTH ANGEL/	
THE MEMBERS/KAMERAS	London, Moonlight Club	NOT SENSIBLES	Manchester, Band On The Wall

2nd - Wednesday...

EARCOM is a new concept album by Bob Last and Fast Records. This Edinburgh-based label has been responsible for bringing to the world such bands as The Mekons, 2.3, Gang Of Four, The Human League and the Scars. Now, Bob Last has this idea about an "ear comic" or "earcom" for short. It's a chance to go one step earlier than a band's debut 45. He feels that there's a lot of pressure on a band the first time out, so why not release that pressure by releasing a collection of their early rehearsals, first attempts and such. Besides the bands, there's also room for a free poster and a mystery gift. Earcom #1 features four bands. The Prats (a pre-teen band from Inverness, average age fourteen), an "astringent" rock band called The Flowers (from Edinburgh), the Blank Students (a trio from Preston), and Graph (an electronic quartet from Sheffield). The recordings are VERY raw and VERY amateurish. Truly first impressions of bands. The last track on the collection is ex-Rezillo reading "Good Sculptures" over an electronic backing. Rather like the Normal's "TVOD." Inside the jacket is a free green and black poster with photos of the four bands and a little information. The free gift inside is a 7" cardboard disc embossed with the Fast Product logo and "Flesh." It is, of course, flesh colored and is another concept piece from Fast along the lines of "Sexex."

ANGELIC UPSTARTS	Edinburgh, Heriot Watt Univ.	SINCEROS	London, Wimbledon Football Club
SPECIALS/PASSIONS/		MAGAZINE/SIMPLE MINDS	London, Theatre Royal
RED LIGHTS	London, Moonlight Club	UNDERTONES	Sheffield, Top Rank

3rd - Thursday...

THE LEYTON BUZZARDS have their third single released today. A special edition for early buyers comes on florescent green vinyl. The single is "Hanging Around" and is flipped with the tracks "I Don't Want To Go To Art School" and "No Dry Ice Or Flying Pigs." They've just started a tour of English dates opening up for the Only Ones.

JOY DIVISION's show in Liverpool is caught by *NME* reviewer Ian Wood. He's impressed with the band, noting that their "withering grey abstractions of industrial malaise" are deadly accurate and understandable for a band from Manchester. Songs heard during the set included Wilderness," "Not Afraid," "Digital," Glass" and "Atmosphere." Wood continues, focusing in on the band's singer, Ian Curtis, "A slight, thin figure, he moves deftly and delicately, his voice surprisingly strong, in his eyes and face a look of humility and fear. If this sounds like a mere stage play on paper, in reality Curtis' transparent humanity- that of a loser caught in a world only partially understood- is totally credible…Joy Division are, without any exaggeration, an Important Band."

JOY DIVISION/PASSAGE/		HEARTDROPS/	
FIREPLACE	Liverpool, Eric's	PLAGUE OF HEAVEN	London, Canterbury Hotel
PURPLE HEARTS/CHORDS/		MADNESS	London, Hope & Anchor
BACK TO ZERO	London, Acklam Hall	SPECIALS	London, Dingwalls
THE VOID NEW DEVICES	London, Kings Head (Deptford)	BRIAN JAMES' BRAINS/	
PORTRAITS	London, Brecknock	FASHION	London, Music Machine

MAY 1979

4th - Friday..

ELVIS COSTELLO's latest 45 has a new gimmick attached to it's release. The 45 is available in two different sleeves, the majority of which appear to have been manufactured inside-out, with the graphics on the inside of the cover and a plain white outside. The single "Accidents Will Happen" is flipped with "Talking In The Dark" and "Wednesday Week." These two songs were previously available only as a freebie single to those people who attended the Dominion concerts around Christmas in London.

LENE LOVICH Lene has another new release today. This time it's "Say When" and "One Lonely Heart." The 12" single features a bonus track "Big Bird." The tracks are taken from her Stiff LP "Stateless."

XTC "Life Begins At The Hop" is released as XTC's latest 45. The first 30,000 come in a special clear picture sleeve that gives the image that the record is actually on an old dansette record player. The single is flipped with an unusual instrumental called "Homo Safari." The song was re-recorded for this single when the band felt that the album version lacked the punch it needed to make it on the charts.

MEKONS	Belfast, Harp Bar	PURPLE HEARTS/	
ROXY MUSIC/TOURISTS	Birmingham, Odeon	MOLESTERS/	
IGGY POP/THE ZONE	Birmingham, Barbarellas	SPEEDBALLS	London, Moonlight Club
ELECTRIC CHAIRS	Liverpool, Eric's	SORE THROAT/MADNESS	London, Nashville
THE POP GROUP/		CROOKS/BACK TO ZERO	London, Pegasus
GOOD MISSIONARIES/		MEMBERS	Manchester, The Factory
DAMBALA	Liverpool, University	JAM/THE RECORDS	Sheffield, University
ABC	London, Dublin Castle		

LIVE TONIGHT!

5th - Saturday..

ECHO & THE BUNNYMEN debut with a haunting single. The trio were covered in a *Sounds* perspective on Liverpool three months ago, signed by Liverpool-based Zoo Records in April and here's the result. The single is "Pictures On My Wall," and "I've Read It In Books." The 45 was recorded last March at August Studios. The "A" side is a Bunnymen song, while the flipside is a song that lead singer Ian McCulloch wrote with his friend Julian Cope in their Pre-Bunnyman days together. An initial pressing of 4,000 have a color sleeve with a grey and green label on the distinctive disc. The *NME* has selected the 45 as "Single Of The Week," being described as a "rich, new and welcome sound." The single also has scribed into the vinyl the cryptic message "The Revenge Of VooDoo Billy."

THE UNDERTONES become one the first new rock band from Derry that have made it to LP. This 12" long play debut is simply titled "The Undertones" and is a collection of thirteen tracks that the band have been pounding to dust while on the road recently. The current single "Jimmy Jimmy" is there, as well as "Family Entertainment," "Male Model," "Jump Boys," "True Confessions," and "Here Comes The Summer."

WAYNE COUNTY & ELECTRIC CHAIRS have out their third LP today, and it's packaged in what is supposed to be the world's first "washable album cover." It's "Things Your Mother Never Told You." The notable transvestite describes the album as being, "...an exercise in getting the band to do what they wanted to do, instead of making them do what is expected of them." The cover of the LP is a color photo of the band in a bedroom, with Mr/Ms County lounging on the bed in net stockings, go-go boots and a short black dress (fetching!). Songs include "Wonder Woman," "Un-Con-Troll-Able," "Boy With The Stolen Face" and "Berlin." The group these days is Wayne County on vocals, Eliot Michaels on guitar, ex-Police guitarist Henry Padovani, Val Haller on bass and J.J. Johnson on drums. The LP is on Safari Records in the UK only.

MEKONS	Belfast, Harp Bar	THE POP GROUP/	
REVOLVER/U2/VIRGIN PRUNES	Dublin, Liberty Hall (1pm)	GOOD MISSIONARIES/	
MEMBERS	Liverpool, Eric's	DAMBALA	Manchester, University
MODS/SQUIRE	London, Plumstead Green Man	UNDERTONES	Manchester, The Factory
THE SPECIALS	London, Hope & Anchor	JAM/THE RECORDS	Sheffield, University

6th - Sunday..

TUBEWAY ARMY's Gary Numan has out his newest 45, "Are Friends Electric?" and "We Are So Fragile." The "A" side is from the forthcoming album Replicas but the flip is non-LP. "Are Friends Electric" will be the song that will change Gary Numan's life. It's his first chart record, and it will reach #1 in the UK. It's a big beginning and a tough act to follow. Tubeway Army is Gary Numan on vocals, keyboards and guitars, Paul Gardiner on bass and Jess Lidyard on drums. Early pressings are on a limited edition picture disc.

XTC/LADYKILLERS	High Wycombe, Town Hall	CRAMPS/STICKERS/JAGS	London, Marquee
MAGAZINE/SIMPLE MINDS	Liverpool, University	IGGY POP/THE ZONES	London, Pavilion
SOFTIES	London, Hope & Anchor	ROXY MUSIC/TOURISTS	Manchester, Apollo
ELECTRIC CHAIRS/		PENETRATION/	
UK SUBS/SPIZZ ENERGI	London, Lyceum	COWBOYS INTL.	Sheffield, Top Rank

MAY 1979

7th - Monday..

THE FALL have been hit with several personnel changes recently, and here's another one. When the band lost guitarist Martin Bramah because he wanted to do his own material, they brought in two new members. One is replacement guitarist Craig Scanlan. The other is bassist Steve Hanley, who will take over Marc Riley's position as Marc slides over to guitar. They're rushing through their rehearsals and plan to debut the new line-up in Edinburgh on Thursday.

JOE JACKSON's newest 45 is another track taken from his debut LP "Look Sharp." The single is "One More Time" flipped with the non LP track "Don't Ask Me."

LIVE TONIGHT!

MEKONS/MOSIAH/	THE POP GROUP/
AU PAIRS ....Birmingham, Digbeth Town Hall	GOOD MISSIONARIES/
MEMBERS ....Edinburgh, Tiffany's	MATUMBI/DAMBALA ....London, Empire Ballroom
SECRET AFFAIR/THE MODS	BACK TO ZERO/CHORDS/
BEGGAR/SMALL HOURS/	PURPLE HEARTS/SCOOTERS ....London, Music Machine
SQUIRE/MERTON PARKAS ....London, Bridge House	ROXY MUSIC/TOURISTS.............Manchester, Apollo
PUNISHMENT OF LUXURY ....London, Marquee	

10th - Thursday..............................

THE CURE's debut album "Three Imaginary Boys" is released on Fiction Records in the UK. It contains both sides of their debut 45 from last year as well as "Accuracy." "Grinding Halt," "Object," "Fire In Cairo," "It's Not You," "Meathook," and "So What." It's most amusing moment is the inclusion of a shattered version of Hendrix's "Foxy Lady," rendering the song almost unrecognizable. The recordings are the result of a brief, two-day recording session with a little polish, and capture the Cure perfectly. The cover photo of the floor lamp, hoover and fridge mortified the band. Since it was unveiled, Lol has claimed that he's the hoover, Robert's the floor lamp and Michael's the fridge. There are no song titles on the labels of the disc or on the jacket. There are pictures however. You can work out most of the titles by carefully listening to the lyrics and looking at the pictures. There were plans to include a sticker with the song titles and band roster, but few copies include it. Perhaps we're all supposed to make our own track listings and title the songs as we see fit.

THE SPECIALS' debut single is reviewed in the *NME* by Ian Penman. He describes it as, "...a tweety, bouncy interpretation of Prince Buster's 'Al Capone' rhythm, proficient but only pretty , the production isn't at all hard enough. Still, preferable to the like of yer Members and Clash Xerox reggae attempts." Terry Hall, vocalist of the band explained the Specials in the *NME* this way, "It's not that we're just trying to revive ska. It's using those old elements to try forming something new. In a way, it's all still part of punk. We're not trying to get away from punk. We're just trying to show some other direction. You've got to go back to go forward."

SPIZZ ENERGI are Spizz Oil with a new name. It's part of the Spizz idea of the punk ideal. Starting all over every year. From Spizz 77 to Spizz Oil and now Spizz Energi. They make their first appearance under this name tonight at the Lyceum on the Wayne County & Electric Chairs show. The basic difference in the group is the new drummer, Hero Shima (replacing Brian Benzine), and new guitarist Scott (replacing Pete Petroleum). They're a last minute addition to the Rough Trade package show that plays tonight in London. Cabaret Voltaire was originally supposed to be on the bill but pulled out just two days ago! Spizz Energi have their new 45 released just in time for the tour. The lead song is "Where's Captain Kirk?," coupled with "Amnesia."

KLEENEX, the Swiss all-girl band that's been sweeping the UK's indie shops with their single "Ain't You" now have another one out on Rough Trade Records The songs are listed as the "friendly side" as song called "You" and the angry side with a song called "U." Kleenex are Regula Sing on vocals, Klaudia Schiff on bass, Marlene Marder on guitar, and Lisolt Ha on drums. Regula explain their relief of coming to England to the *NME* that, "We aren't accepted (in Zurich, Switzerland) because we're women and because punk isn't taken seriously. There is one hour a day of mixed music on the radio but it's all yodeling and disco. The only places for us to play are the Club Hae and restaurants. Even the police stop you at 11 PM."

XTC.....................................Birmingham, Barbarella's	FASHION ....London, Marquee
FALL ....Edinburgh, Astoria	CHELSEA/COLUMN 88/
KLEENEX/RAINCOAT/	USERS/FOURTH REICH ....London, Music Machine
SPIZZ ENERGI ....London, Acklam Hall	JAM/THE RECORDS ....London, Rainbow
PORTRAITS ....London, Brecknock	SQUEEZE/
PIRANHAS ....London, Hope & Anchor	BRIAN JAMES' BRAINS ....Sheffield, Limit Club
MODS.................................London, Jingles	JAGS.....................................Sheffield, Northern General

11th - Friday.................................

THE CLASH have their new "Cost Of Living EP" on the streets of England today. It's a four-song package that features their version of the Bobby Fuller hit "I Fought The Law," which has been a huge live favorite. There's also "Gates Of The West," and "Groovy Times," which were recorded during the "Rope" sessions but were not included with the LP. Track four is a newly recorded version of "Capitol Radio," which up until now was only available as an *NME* Freebie disc two years ago! A bonus fifth track is a mock commercial for the EP that closes out side two. The whole package is in a special color gatefold sleeve and retails at £1.49. The label was supposed to have the image

MAY 1979

of a £20 note but the Bank Of England denied permission for the image.

THE JAM's concerts at the Rainbow are a pair of rousing successes. They play their two nights to a sold out house of parkas, rude boys and a scattering of punks. The set begins with "In The Street Today," cruises through "This Is The Modern World," "Billy Hunt," and "It's Too Bad," before Weller slows the pace for "Mr Clean," "Butterfly Collector," and "Away From The Numbers." The action starts again, with "All Mod Cons," "To Be Someone," "The Place I Love," and "Strange Town," winding the crowd to a fever pitch. Bruce Foxton stepped forward to sing "News Of The World." Weller takes the lead again for "Down In The Tube Station At Midnight" and concludes with "A Bomb In Wardor Street." The Rainbow erupts as if on cue, enough so that the Jam are lured back onstage to play "Standards," "David Watts," the Martha & The Vandellas 60s classic "Heatwave" and the campy "Batman."

THE UNDERTONES' album is discussed on the *Roundtable* radio program. It's a sort of rate-a-records show that features guest as well as the host Kid Jensen. Just as things begin looking grim, Nick Lowe chimes in with his opinion of the Undertones. "I think they're great!…Love the singer, I think he.. delivers a song from the heart. He seems in such intense pain when he sings, and he's got a voice that sounds like a cross between Roger Chapman and Steve Marriott. I love that little sort of bleat he's got in his voice, very distinctive."

TUBES/SQUEEZE	Glasgow, Apollo
SCRITTI POLITTI/	
PRAG VEC/THE THE	London, Africa Centre
MODS	London, Jingles
ABC	London, Dublin Castle
CRASS/POISON GIRLS/CHARGE	London, N London Poly
STREETBAND/	
MODERN ENGLISH	London, Nashville
JAM/THE RECORDS	London, Rainbow
JOY DIVISION/JOHN DOWIE/	
A CERTAIN RATIO/	
ORCHESTRAL MANOEUVRES/	
JOHN DOWIE	Manchester, The Factory
JAGS	Sheffield, Limit Club

LIVE TONIGHT!

12th - Saturday.........

U2 are an inventive band. They want their fans to see them, but the under eighteens can't get into McGonagles when they play. Instead of disappointing their fans, they're taking their show outdoors. U2 are now playing the first of a series of outdoor concerts at the Dandelion Market, right next door to the Gaiety Green flea market in Dublin. As a result of these shows, their fan base grows dramatically.

THE CHORDS are one of dozens of mod bands that have been gathering in what is being called the "mod revival." It's a resurgence of music based in the American "Motown" sound, but brought to UK ears by groups like the Who. Spurred by the success of the Jam, dozens of bands have built the bandwagon that everyone else is hanging off of. The second tier of the mod groups, The Chords, The Purple Hearts, and Back To Zero have been playing gigs and drawing parka wearing, scooter riding fans since late last year. Others in the growing pack include The Fixations, The Detours, The Points, The Vespas, The Crooks, The Low Numbers, Secret Affair, The Cobras, Merton Parkas, The Scooters, Long Tall Shorty, Captain Scarlet & The Mysterions, The Chicane, Teen Beats and The Estimators. Now the Chords have gotten a foothold on success by being signed up to Jimmy Pursey's (Sham 69) J.P. Productions roster. They're already in the studio and working on their debut single to be out this summer, presumably on Polydor Records.

PATRIK FITZGERALD's newest album has been released today by Polydor Records in England, under an arrangement with Small Wonder Records. The seventeen-song LP is titled "Grubby Stories" and covers familiar material as well as new compositions. The LP features "Suicidal Wreck," "Parentgames," "Nothing To Do" and "As Ugly As You." There's even a minor guest appearance as Buzzcocks drummer John Maher was borrowed for the sessions early in February. Patrik is about to embark on an extensive UK tour where he plays two different sets, an acoustic solo set, and one with a band assembled for the tour. Support acts will play between the sets.

DENIZENS/AU PAIRS	Birmingham, Festival Suite	MONOCHROME SET	London, Film Co-Op
TUBES/SQUEEZE	Edinburgh, Odeon	SECRET AFFAIR/TEENBEATS	London, Marquee
THE POP GROUP/		XTC	London, School Of Economics
GOOD MISSIONARIES/		VOID/CATCH 22/	
DAMBALA	Glasgow, Queen Margaret Union	NEW DEVICES/COME ONS	London, St. Mark's Hall
ROXY MUSIC/TOURISTS	Liverpool, Empire Theatre	DICKIES/	
UNDERTONES	Liverpool, Eric's	HOLLY & THE ITALIANS	Manchester, The Factory
SOFTIES/THE ACT	London, Dingwalls	JAGS	Manchester, University

13th - Sunday......................................

GOOD MISSIONARIES' leader Mark Perry (ex-Alternative TV, ex-*Sniffing Glue* editor) is interviewed in this week's *NME* and has a good- natured way of describing his new band and his goals. He told Danny Baker, "Once I used to believe there was a street truth, but not any more. Because all the people that I used to regard as suss have since fell to bits and become drips. So now I just try to live and do what I think good. Mind you, I've got it easy, I am free from the pressure of commercial success. If my records bomb out I can always do another one. Even so, I still like mucking people about so maybe they'll consider less obvious forms of music."

LENE LOVICH & NINA HAGEN are reportedly in Amsterdam appearing in a movie in the making called *Cha Cha* with Dutch rock star Herman Brood. East Germany's Nina Hagen shocked music fans with an announcement that she was not only leaving her band to go solo, but was also planning to marry Herman Brood!

MAY 1979

SLAUGHTER & THE DOGS have one more record out before they split up in June. Four songs remain from one of the earliest of Manchester's punk bands, "It's Alright," "Twist & Turn," "Edgar Allen Poe," and "U.F.O." The EP is on TJM Records from Manchester.

JOLT/TRADITION	London, Hope & Anchor	JAGS	London, Marquee
IGGY POP/ZONES	London, Lyceum		

14th - Monday.....................

ANOTHER PRETTY FACE have their new single "All The Boys Love Carrie" b/w "That's Not Enough," given "Single Of The Week" status by the *NME* with Julie Burchill saying, "…the song holds hints of a literary talent somewhere between F. Scott Fitzgerald and Springsteen…a great little record." The 45 has been selling briskly, it's first 1,000 copies going almost immediately, and a quick repress of 5,000 more. The instant success has made getting bookings for the band so much easier. Suddenly, Another Pretty Face is in demand! Lead singer Mike Scott told Trouser Press that, "It's caused quit a bit of resentment around Edinburgh 'cos other bands thought we'd had it easy- but that isn't valid 'cos if the single hadn't stood up that wouldn't have happened. We both (Mike and John) had to get jobs as laborers for about six months…to buy guitars and amplifiers and to pay the recording costs." Another Pretty Face is future Waterboys leader Mike Scott on vocals and rhythm guitar, Jim Geddes on bass, Crigg on drums and John Caldwell on lead guitar. Both songs are APF originals and can be found on their own New Pleasures Records, based out of their native Edinburgh, Scotland.

THE RUTS have an invitation extended to them to record some songs for the John Peel Radio 1 program. They'll take the opportunity tonight to record some new songs like "Sus," "Society," "You're Just A…," "It Was Cold" and "Something That I Said." These sessions can be heard on Peel's show on the evening of May 21st.

FASHION	Birmingham, Barrel Organ	PORTRAITS/SECRET AFFAIR/	
KLEENEX/RAINCOATS/		BOZOS	London, Dingwalls
CABARET VOLTAIRE	Birmingham, Digbeth Civic Hall	IGGY POP/TRADITION/	
THE POP GROUP/		THE ZONES	London, Lyceum
GOOD MISSIONARIES/		PURPLE HEARTS/	
DAMBALA	Edinburgh, Tiffany's	LITTLE ROOSTERS/	
CHORDS/SCOOTERS	London, Bridge House	THE COBRAS	London, Notre Dame Hall

16th - Wednesday.......................

PATTI SMITH laid out her plans to stay in Detroit with her new beau Fred Smith, ex-MC5 member, in the *New York Daily News*. She's involved in building up a scene in Detroit and feels that she's gone as far as she could over the last twelve years in her spiritual home of New York City. Most revealing was her feeling for the music movement with which she is so connected. "I really have no patience at all for so much of the crap in the punk rock scene. New Wave is romantically political, but all this shit sticking safety pins in cheeks and all the fucking violence, I feel, is just a style and fad. I came into rock as a purist with a motivation to communicate, something I see as man's greatest gift. If the kids could remember their motivation, where they come from, then the positive aspects could be developed."

PENETRATION/		JAM/THE RECORDS	Liverpool, University
COWBOYS INTL.	Birmingham, Top Rank	ROXY MUSIC/TOURISTS	London, Hammersmith Odeon

17th - Thursday........................

THE SKIDS' new single is "Masquerade" b/w "Out Of Town." Early purchasers can get it as part of a special two record set that also includes "Another Emotion" and "Aftermath Dub." All of the tracks except Masquerade are non-LP.

FATAL MICROBES/POISON GIRLS Small Wonder Records has one 45 released featuring two groups that are related to each other, literally. One is the Fatal Microbes. They're led by fourteen year old Honey Bane (Donna Boyle) and also feature a ten year old drummer and twelve year old guitarist. Honey Bane has had a difficult childhood and has spent the last three years in the St. Charles Home. She was tagged by the Eppin place as a "problem girl." Even though one of the songs was called "Beautiful Pictures," the release of this record was supposedly slowed up because the social services who overlooked her well being weren't so sure about one of their own making a record called "Violence Grows." The other band is the Poison Girls. Their lead singer, Vi Squad (aka Perversa), has been of great help to Honey Bane in working out recording while being in the child center. The Poison Girls have been together about two years, growing from trio to a quartet that now also includes Richard Famous, Lance D'Boyle, and Bernhardt Rebours. The Poison Girls tracks on the EP are "Closed Shop" and "Piano Lessons." Look for the package as "Fatal Microbes Meet The Poison Girls." Both bands plan solo releases soon.

LIVE TONIGHT!

DICKIES/		JOY DIVISION/	
HOLLY & THE ITALIANS	Birmingham, Barbarella's	A CERTAIN RATIO/	
LEYTON BUZZARDS	Edinburgh, Astoria	ORCHESTRAL MANOEUVRES/	
ANGELIC UPSTARTS	Edinburgh, Heriot Watt Univ.	JOHN DOWIE	London, Acklam Hall
JAM/THE RECORDS	Glasgow, Strathclyde Univ.	SQUEEZE/	
JAGS	London, Golden Lion	BRIAN JAMES' BRAINS	Manchester, U.M.I.S.T.
SINCEROS	London, Dingwalls	PUNISHMENT OF LUXURY	Sheffield, Limit Club
PATRIK FITZGERALD	London, N London Poly.		

18th - Friday.......................

THE LURKERS' newest single is an advance track from their album "God's Lonely Men." The lead track "Out In The Dark" is flipped with "Suzie Is A Floozie." Early purchasers get an additional two tracks on the 7" single, "Cyanide" and "Cyanide (pub version)." The

MAY 1979

Lurkers are Howard Wall on vocals, Pete Stride on guitar, Nigel Moore on bass, Esso on drums, and Plug on harmonica.

ESSENTIAL LOGIC have waited exactly a year since their last record, and now Lora Logic is a Virgin Records artist. The 7" single is actually a four track EP featuring "Wake Up," and "Eagle Bird," flipped with "Quality Crayon Wax OK" and "Bod's Message." Lora's band is Will Bennett and Phil Lip on guitar, drummer Rich Tea (AKA Rich Thompson, ex X-Ray Spex), Dave Flash on second sax and Mark Turner on bass. She auditioned over a hundred prospective members in selecting her band. Essential Logic made their debut last September at the Marquee opening for Sore Throat. By now they have eleven originals including "Alkaline Loaf," "Rat Alley" (a song about the Roxy Club), and a revamped "Aerosol Burns."

IAN DURY & BLOCKHEADS have their second LP released this weekend. It's called "Do It Yourself" and finds Stiff Records with another trick to help sell multiple albums to 45 fans. Stiff Records has long tried to come up with various gimmicks to move products. They've released limited edition picture discs, colored vinyl in a rainbow of hues, and special picture sleeves. This time, the album artwork has the appearance of a colored wallpaper with the letters over the top. There are ten different Crown wallpapers to choose from. The album itself features ten songs including "Inbetweenies," "Quiet," "Sink My Boats," "Uneasy Sunny Day For Hotsy Totsy," and "Waiting For Your Taxi." Production for "Do It Yourself" was by blockhead Chaz Jankel. The label bears the message, "Any resemblance to characters living or dead is not meant to be unkind to men in syrups. Plus love to TRB (Tom Robinson Band) TAJ, Clash and everybody else." The group will begin their massive UK tour next month under the banner "Slam And Segue And Break A Leg." Opening all the dates will be American oddity Root Boy Slim & The Sex Change Band.

LIVE TONIGHT!

SQUEEZE/			CROOKS/BACK TO ZERO	London, Pegasus
BRIAN JAMES' BRAINS	Birmingham, Univ.		ABC	London, Dublin Castle
JAM/THE RECORDS	Glasgow, Strathclyde Univ.		PASSENGERS/PRIME MOVERS	London, Chippenham
JAGS	London, City Poly.		PENETRATION/FALL/	
PIRANHAS/MOLESTERS/			COWBOYS INTL.	Manchester, Apollo
NICKY & THE DOTS	London, Moonlight Club		ELECTRIC CHAIRS	Manchester, The Factory
YOUNG BUCKS/PORTRAITS	London, Music Machine			

21st - Monday.....................................

THE RADIATORS' fourth single is out today. It's their original song, "Let's Talk About The Weather," and two old covers, "The Hucklebuck," and "Try And Stop Me." This Chiswick single bears the secret message "Anomic Catholics Ltd." on the "A" side, and "Songs Our Fathers Loved" on the "B" side. The tracks were produced by veteran producer Tony Visconti.

ORCHESTRAL MANOEUVRES & A CERTAIN RATIO both have singles out on Manchester's Factory Records. A Certain Ratio is a quartet of Jeremy Kerr on bass, Simon Topping on lead vocals, Peter Terrell on guitar and Martin Moscrop on guitar. Five thousand copies of their debut single are out. It's "All Night Party" b/w "The Thin Boys." In a strange design mood, the limited edition 45 sleeve features a picture of comedian Lenny Bruce, dead on the floor of his Hollywood home. Orchestral Manoeuvres In The Dark are the electronic Liverpool trio that have played a few gigs at Eric's and The Factory in Manchester. Their debut single is "Electricity" b/w "Almost." Everything about the band spells something different. The group is one of the rare duos that play music in this "new wave" genre. Their electronic sounds are unlike Gary Numan in that they're upbeat and hopeful. Melodies twist through each other playfully and vocal ride prominently on top. Although the song sounds like it was recorded on a synthesizer, the band insist that it's a bass and an electric piano and loads of tape trickery. OMD's 45 comes in a subtle sleeve designed by Peter Saville. It's solid black with raised black letters. The only way to read the sleeve is to tilt it in the light or read it with your fingers.

STIFF LITTLE FINGERS/			PURPLE HEARTS/	
STARJETS	Belfast, Ulster Hall		STA-PREST	London, Bridge House
SPECIALS	Birmingham, Barbarella's		VIRUS/VOID	London, Thames Poly.
ANGELIC UPSTARTS	Birmingham, Digbeth Civic Hall		DISTRIBUTORS/	
SIMPLE MINDS	Edinburgh, Tiffany's		OXY & THE MORONS	London, Moonlight
SINCEROS/CROOKS	London, Nashville		TUBES/SQUEEZE	London, Hammersmith Odeon

23rd - Wednesday.....................................

PROTEX make their major label debut today with the single "I Can't Cope" b/w "Popularity." They were initially discovered in Belfast by Irish impresario Terry Hooley and signed up for his Good Vibrations label. The young band got together just a year and a half ago and retain their original line-up of David McMaster on guitar and vocals, Paul Maxwell on bass, Adrian Murtagh on guitar and Owen McFadden behind the drums.

FASHION/RESISTANCE	London, Albany Empire		TUBES/SQUEEZE	London, Hammersmith Odeon
SQUIRE/STA-PREST/			DICKIES/	
DETAILS	London, Dublin Castle (Coal Bin)		HOLLY & THE ITALIANS	Sheffield, Top Rank

24th - Thursday.....................................

BARRY ANDREWS already has a single out on his own since quitting XTC. It's a four track EP called "Town & Country" that features "Me And My Mate Can Sing," "Bring On The Alligators," "Mousetrap" and "Sargasso Bar." Some of these are songs that XTC had rehearsed but never recorded. On the EP Andrews is aided by David Marx on guitar, Rob Wilford on drums and borrowed XTC bassist Colin Moulding. Barry would resurface in the '80s as the leader of a group called Shreikback.

NICK LOWE's "Labor Of Lust" is just out. It's his follow up to last year's LP, "Jesus Of Cool" (aka "Pure Pop For Now People.") The song "Cruel To Be Kind" starts the album, although it's a not the version that was on the flipside of last year's 45 of "Little Hitler." It's been

MAY 1979

slowed down, and the swirling carnival keyboard on the original is missing from this acoustic heavy remake. The album them moves through "Cracking Up," "Big Kick, Plain Scrap" and careens into the newest single "American Squirm." Also included are "Switchboard Susan," "Skin Deep," and a nod to the Everly Brothers called "Without Love."

Musicians on the album are Rockpile, the band that Dave Edmunds and Nick Lowe now share. Billy Bremner and Dave Edmunds both play guitar on the record, Nick on bass and Terry Williams on drums. Ex-Brinsley Schwartz Bob Andrews is on synth and American Huey Lewis is borrowed from Clover to cut some harmonica parts.

TUBES/SQUEEZE	London, Hammersmith Odeon	DOLE/ OUTPATIENTS	London, Windsor Castle
LEYTON BUZZARDS	London, Music Machine	LURKERS	Sheffield, Limit Club

25th - Friday.................................

WAYNE COUNTRY & ELECTRIC CHAIRS are having trouble at their Sussex University gig tonight in Brighton. It all started when the Electric Chairs were playing three weeks ago at the Lyceum. During the show, they were pelted with beer cans (some half full) by irritated fans of the UK Subs. One of the cans hit Wayne, who picked it up and threw it back. His aim was a bit off, and it struck a girl in the audience, who was cut. An ambulance was called in, the parents filed a complaint with the police, and the chase was on. That was three weeks ago. At the end of tonight's gig, Brighton police showed up to block every exit, with police dogs on the grounds sniffing what police dogs sniff, and plain clothes men looking out of place among the usual Electric Chairs audience. The band saw what was happening but didn't connect it to the earlier incident. Fearing that something was fishy they tried to smuggle Wayne / Jayne out of the venue stuffed into a flight case. It didn't work. Caught before reaching the truck, he/she was taken into custody, taken to the police station where he/she plead guilty, paid a £50 fine, £50 damages and managed to escape.

DICKIES/		THE POP GROUP/SLITS/	
HOLLY & THE ITALIANS	Edinburgh, Clouds	GOOD MISSIONARIES	London, College of Printing
KLEENEX/RAINCOATS/		PSYCHEDELIC FURS/	
SPIZZ ENERGI	Liverpool, Eric's	OUTPATIENTS	London, Windsor Castle
TUBES/SQUEEZE	London, Hammersmith Odeon		

26th - Saturday.................................

RIFF RAFF Remember them? They're the combo fronted by Billy Bragg that had the "I Want To Be A Cosmonaut" EP out on Chiswick last summer. Since then they moved to Peterborough and have become quite big on the local scene. Now they're looking for a way out. They're tired of playing the small halls and gay pubs like the Lion's Den, birthday parties, a dog show, and the American Air Force base. A wistful notice appeared in today's *NME* in the classifieds under Special Notices. It reads, "MANAGER REQUIRED for London band currently exiled in darkest Peterborough, (Talented but disorganized!) Track record includes plenty of London gigs + one EP released; current activities mainly gigging in Midlands. More London gigs urgently required, so if you have plenty of drive, ambition, audacity, organizational ability, etc, apply TODAY. Seriously thou'…write RIFF RAFF, 15 North St, Oundle, Peterborough, or ring Oundle (08322) 2298."

R.T. and HELTER SKELTER present
SATURDAY, MAY 26 at 8 pm

THROBBING GRISTLE & BAUHAUS 1919

at the GUILDHALL,
TOWN CENTRE, NORTHAMPTON

Advance tickets only £1.50 from
Spinadisc Records, 19A Abington Square, Northampton, telephone 31144 and
Acme Clothing Company, Wellingborough Road, Northampton.

LIVE TONIGHT!

ONLY ONES/U2	Cork, Downtown Kampus	THE POPGROUP/	
GANG OF FOUR	Liverpool, Eric's	GOOD MISSIONARIES/	
SQUIRE/THE MODS	London, Ealing Old Hat	DAMBALA	London, School Of Economics
TUBES/SQUEEZE	London, Hammersmith Odeon	KLEENEX/RAINCOATS/	
SECRET AFFAIR	London, Marquee	SPIZZ ENERGI	Manchester, The Factory
PSYCHEDELIC FURS	London, Windsor Castle	THROBBING GRISTLE/	
CRASS/POISON GIRLS	London, Conway Hall	BAUHAUS 1919	Northampton, The Guildhall

27th - Sunday.................................

LOCH LOMOND ROCK FESTIVAL (DAY 2) The Loch Lomond festival is not only the first festival of the year, it's the biggest festival ever staged in Scotland. The festival site is Cameron Bear Park, normally a drive-through wildlife reserve, just thirty-five minutes outside of Glasgow. It's the second day and attendance has grown to thirty-five thousand. After sitting through a day and a half of mostly average bands, with sets from the Stranglers and Buzzcocks thrown in, it clear that the best band was saved for last. The Boomtown Rats, just returned from their three month US tour, put on the show of their career. The Boomtown Rats started off their set with their new song "I Don't Like Mondays." This was not a the usual way to start a set. An open stage with Bob Geldof accompanied by a solo piano. Quiet, simple, and effective. The crowd loved it. They launched into their set, which went without a hitch, until "I Never Loved Eva Braun." In the middle of the song, a Scottish bagpipe band was to come onstage and play a little bit before the band finished the song. Instead they stayed and stayed and stayed. They played "Scotland The Brave" and the audience began singing football songs. The Boomtown Rats finally got the band to leave after three songs. During "She's So Modern" some of the concert organizers thought it would be amusing to have people dressed up as bears (since it was being held at a Bear Reserve) come onstage and dance around. Geldof kicked them offstage. All in all the show was seen as a great success and the band's reviews tagged them as the next big thing for the '80s.

FASHION follow up their March single release with another new one. Released under their own Fashion Music banner, the 45 is "Citinite," and "Wastelife."

MAY 1979

PSYCHEDELIC FURS/
CUDDLY TOYS.........................London, Billy's Club
TUBES/SQUEEZE ....London, Hammersmith Odeon

GANG OF FOUR/SPECIALS/
MEKONS ....London, Lyceum
JAGS ....London, Marquee

28th - Monday..

THE SINCEROS have their debut single released by Epic, only a dozen weeks after signing with the giant. The songs are "Take Me To Your Leader" and "Quick, Quick, Slow." Both tracks were written by vocalist Mark Kjeldsen. Early copies of the disc are being pressed up on a hopefully eye-catching green vinyl.

THE STUDIO SWEETHEARTS are no newcomers to the music business. The new group is made up of Mike Rossi on guitar and Howard Bates on bass who are two ex-members of Slaughter and the Dogs. Phil Rowland on drums came from Eater and Billy Duffy on rhythm guitar was in the Nosebleeds. Their debut single, "I Believe," is on DJM. The band have been together for some time and expect to be playing live very soon. Of the group, Billy Duffy has the brightest future, not with the Studio Sweethearts but with another band called The Cult that will come along in a few years.

THEY'RE NOW STUDIO SWEETHEARTS AND THEIR DEBUT SINGLE 'I BELIEVE' IS OUT NOW! (DJS 10915)
Studio Sweethearts
LIMITED EDITION IN SPECIAL COLOUR B

PORTRAITS ....London, Brecknock
SECRET AFFAIR/THE MODS.....London, Bridge House
VAPORS ....London, East Ham Ruskin Arms
UK SUBS/SECURITY RISK/
MODERN ENGLISH ....London, Music Machine

PURPLE HEARTS/THE MODS/
BACK TO ZERO/
SQUIRE ....London, Notre Dame Hall
STIFF LITTLE FINGERS/
STARJETS ....Manchester, Apollo

29th - Tuesday..

THE TOURISTS make their vinyl debut with both an album and a 45 for Logo Records. Live favorite "Blind Among The Flowers" and "He Who Laughs Last, Laughs Longest," have been tapped for the single. Early purchasers will get a special double pack 7" with an additional free single with two songs that are not on their debut album. They are "The Golden Lamp," and "Wrecked." The album is imaginatively titled "The Tourists" and has an odd sleeve with two different front covers, one group pose on the front and another on the reverse, allowing the album to appear to have two different sleeves while having only one jacket. Tracks on the album include "Save Me," "Fools Paradise," "Can't Stop Laughing," "Another English Day," "Deadly Kiss," "Ain't No Room," and four others. All of the Tourists' songs were written by Pete Coombes. The Tourists are Annie Lennox, Dave Stewart, Jim 'Do It' Toomey, Peet Coombes, and Eddie Chin.

THE SPECIALS join that special group of performers who have a Radio One session broadcast by John Peel. The four songs chosen were their current 45 "Gangsters," and three new songs, "Too Much, Too Young," "Concrete Jungle" and the Maytals song "Monkey Man."

EDDIE & THE HOT RODS are fighting back rumors about a split. Talk of a breakup was fueled by the band being dropped by Island Records. Their manager, Roger Harding explained that the band is maintaining a low profile while they work up new songs and new stage routines. Currently, Rods bassist Paul Gray is touring with the members and Barrie Masters and Steve Nicol are playing in a temporary group called "Plus Support." It's uncertain if the Rods are really through or just in a holding pattern. What is clear is that in five short years, the world surrounding them has changed dramatically and they might not be able to compete as Eddie & The Hot Rods.

LIVE TONIGHT!

ELECTRIC CHAIRS ....London, Dingwalls
PSYCHEDELIC FURS/
BUMPERS ....London, Music Machine

BRAINIAC 5 ....London, Rock Garden
RUTS ....London, Moonlight Club
CURE ....Sheffield, Limit Club

31st - Thursday..

KIRSTY MacCOLL is the talented nineteen-year-old daughter of folk singer Ewan MacColl. She's just recently been added to the Stiff Records roster and is the subject of their 47th release. The single "They Don't Know" comes perilously close to being a Lesley Gore song, eerily capturing the sound of early 60s pop. The first 10,000 copies are in a special picture sleeve. The 45 is flipped with "Motor On." Both songs are Kirsty's own compositions. Prior to going solo, Kirsty was in a few bands, her first was when she was only sixteen called Rat Alley. Next was a brief stay with the Drug Addix, where she actually got on their "Make A Record" EP under the name Mandy Doubt.

SHAKE is the new spin-off from the split up of the Rezillos last year. The group is three ex-Rezillos: Angel Paterson, John Callis and Simon Templar. They're joined by Troy Tate, an ex-member to Cheltenham-based band The Index. Their debut EP is a 10" special pressing of four songs, "Culture Shock," "Glass House," "Dream On" and "(But) Not Mine." Special early issues come with a free comic book.

SHAKE ....Edinburgh, Astoria
POLICE/CRAMPS.....................Glasgow, Apollo
NINE NINE NINE/
PINPOINT ....London, Marquee
DOLLY BY DOLL/MERGER/
S.P.G/PSYCHEDELIC FURS ....London, Venue

SIMPLE MINDS/
BRUCE WOOLEY &
THE CAMERA CLUB...................London, Music Machine
JAGS ....London, Rock Garden
PIRANHAS / THE NAME ....London, Windsor Castle

June 1st - Friday..

DEVO's latest single is at least partially taken from their new LP "Duty Now For The Future." The "A" side features "The Day My Baby Gave

JUNE 1979

Me A Surprise." The flip is the non-LP "Penetration In The Centerfold."

THE ANGELIC UPSTARTS' gig in Wolverhampton results in nearly half a dozen people injured. The trouble started when fifty or so National Front supporters attacked the stage of the Lafayette Club while shouting Nazi salutes "Sieg Heil" and "NF." This all during the band's first song! The group stopped in mid-song trying to maintain order. The band's manager was stabbed in the stomach. Club management refused to call in the police thinking their bouncers could handle it. They couldn't. The fight spread from wall to wall and when police did arrive no arrests were made. The Upstarts still have no idea what provoked the NF supporters. Upstarts lead guitarist Mond told the *NME*, "It was definitely an organized thing. We could see these guys pushing their way forward. They weren't punks or skinheads or anything like that; they were all wearing flared jeans and T-shirts, just ordinary guys."

LIVE TONIGHT!

FASHION	Birmingham, Barbarella's	PROTEX/LA STARZA	London, Moonlight Club
LURKERS	Edinburgh, Clouds	MERTON PARKAS	London, Two Brewers
POLICE/CRAMPS	Edinburgh, Odeon	SIMPLE MINDS	Manchester, The Factory
SECRET AFFAIR/		RUTS	Manchester, Middletown Civic Hall
BACK TO ZERO	London, City Poly.	THE CURE/DEAD CERT/	
NINE NINE NINE/		THE ASSETS/PARKERS	Surrey, Carshalton Carnival
PINPOINT	London, Marquee		

2nd - Saturday...

THE RAMONES are in the midst of their new album sessions with Phil Spector, while they have two new albums released at the same time. One for the UK and another for the US market. In England Sire Records release "It's Alive," a two LP set of the quintessential live Ramones concert recorded at the Rainbow in London on December 31, 1977. The twenty-eight songs are the band's best material to date, delivered in a top notch performance. They cover the range of the Ramones emotions, from the up tempo "Rockaway Beach," and "Gimmie Gimmie Shock Treatment" to the up tempo "Sheena Is A Punk Rocker" and "Surfin' Bird." Then they move on to the up tempo "California Sun," "Do You Wanna Dance" and the uptempo "Suzy Is A Headbanger." All in all, an up tempo set. The adverts in England state that twenty-eight tracks for only £4.99, works out to 17.821428 pence per song. What a bargain!

The Ramones live album isn't released in the US, but the soundtrack for the new movie *Rock & Roll High School* is. The compilation includes the title track, as well as "I Want You Around," "Come Let's Go," and a Ramones medley recorded live at the Roxy in Los Angeles of "Blitzkrieg Bop," "Teenage Lobotomy," "California Sun," "Pinhead" and "She's The One." Other tracks on the album include songs from Devo, Eddie & The Hot Rods, Eno, Brownsville Station, Todd Rundgren, Alice Cooper, Chuck Berry and Nick Lowe.

SQUEEZE have another 45 out today, and it's taken from their album "Cool For Cats." The single pairs album tracks "Up The Junction" with "It's So Dirty." Early copies are in a special picture sleeve and are pressed in translucent purple vinyl. It'll become the band's second single to reach #2 in England.

WIRE have their new single, their fifth, out this weekend. The lead track is "A Question Of Degree." It was written by Graham Lewis while he was in America last year. It's flipped with "Former Airline," a song that gets it's name from the chord structure of the song, B-E-A.

POLICE/THE CRAMPS	Liverpool, Empire Theatre	SOFT BOYS/VOLUNTEERS	London, Nashville
THE POP GROUP/		BLOOD DONOR/	
GOOD MISSIONARIES	Liverpool, Univ.	NIK TURNER'S SPHINX	London, Dingwalls
NINE NINE NINE/		OXY & THE MORONS	London, City Poly.
PINPOIN	London, Marquee	SOFT BOYS/ESCALATORS/	
MERGER/PHOTOS	London, Music Machine	GUY JACKSON	London, Southbank Poly.

3rd - Sunday...

THE FRESHIES are one of the latest exports from Manchester, and they sound more gleeful than the rest. Their sound is straight forward pop, frequently naive and joyfully underdone. They've got their own Razz Records label going and that's where you'll find their EP "Straight In At Number 2." The four tracks on it are "Johnny Radar," "Skid Room," "U-Boat" and "Last." To try to help with radio play, there is a "radio request slip" included right in the sleeve for you to fill in and send to your favorite disc jockey. The limited edition is numbered and all of the labels are hand-drawn with colored felt tip pens. The Freshies are Lyn Oakey on guitar, Steve Hopkins on keyboards, Paul Burgess on drums and Chris Sievy on vocals, guitar and bass.

SHAM 69 have been beset with trouble time and time again in their short two years as a band. Just when it looked like the band was indeed split and the members could go their separate ways, they won't be allowed to start afresh because they owe another two albums to their label. Vocalist Jimmy Pursey and bassist Dave Treganna have supposedly been working with Cook and Jones from the Sex Pistols (also still under contract). The new group will have to keep a low profile until the lawyers define who owes who what. It's still not clear what this new will call themselves, if they do appear in public. Speculation is rampant with the "Sham Pistols" or the "New Sex Pistols" as top favorites. In the *NME* "Thrills" article this week, Shares Bono speculates about ex-Pistol Steve Jones solo projects conjuring up an, "...homage to Phil Spector LP, utilizing Spectors 'Wall Of Sound' technique on a fearsome remake of The Ronettes' 'Do You Love Me;' wherein Steve duets delightfully with the splendid Mr Chrissie Hynde (A Pretender late of this parish)."

U2	Dublin, McGonagles	PSYCHEDELIC FURS	London, Billy's Club
KLEENEX/RAINCOATS/		NINE NINE NINE	London, Marquee
SPIZZ ENERGI	London, Dalston Rio Cinema	LEYTON BUZZARDS/	
DEXY'S MIDNIGHT RUNNERS	London, Hope & Anchor	MODERN MAN	London, Nashville
SKIDS/THE EDGE/		STIFF LITTLE FINGERS/	
ANGELIC UPSTARTS	London, Lyceum	STARJETS	Sheffield, Top Rank

JUNE 1979

5th - Tuesday...

THE RUTS' new 45 is out this week on Virgin Records. The galloping "Babylon's Burning" is flipped with "Society." The song is destined to become the Ruts' top hit, climbing to #7 in the UK. The Ruts are currently on tour with the Damned.

NICK LOWE confessed to *Feature* magazine that, "As a producer, my biggest break came during working on 'Watching The Detectives' (for Elvis Costello), and I discovered where the echo button was on the tape machine."

MENACE The farewell single from Menace is released this week on Small Wonder Records. It's "Last Year's Youth" and "Carry No Banners" The songs were recorded last October in the band's last session before splitting up. Menace were Morgan Webster on vocals, Steve Tannett on guitar, Charlie Casey on bass and Noel Martin on drums.

CRASS is the musician's collective that releases broadsides/records of their views. Their newest is "Reality Asylum" and "Shaved Women." Both sides of the single features Eve Libertine on vocals with the usual cast of Gem Stone, N.A. Palmer, Pete Wright, Penny Rimbaud, and Phil Free playing along. This Crass release comes in a 14" x 21" fold up sleeve.

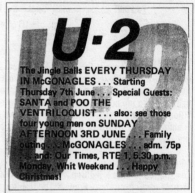

The Jingle Balls EVERY THURSDAY IN McGONAGLES . . . Starting Thursday 7th June . . . Special Guests: SANTA and POO THE VENTRILOQUIST . . . also: see those four young men on SUNDAY AFTERNOON 3RD JUNE . . . Family outing . . . McGONAGLES . . . adm. 75p . . . and: Our Times, RTE 1, 6.30 p.m. Monday, Whit Weekend . . . Happy Christmas!

LIVE TONIGHT!

SOFT BOYS	Birmingham, Barbarella's
KLEENEX/RAINCOATS/ SPIZZ ENERGI	London, Albany Empire
CRAMPS/BOBBY HENRY/ STICKERS	London, Marquee
PURPLE HEARTS	London, Leicester Sq. Empire
JAGS	Sheffield, Totley College

7th - Thursday...

U2 are staging a Christmas event in the middle of the summer. It's designed to get them noticed and it works. It's called the "Jingle Ball" and is during their Thursday night residency at McGonagles in Dublin, and is more than a showcase for U2. The evening also features Poo the Ventriloquist and an appearance from Santa himself. Although the band is playing in front of a plastic palm tree, the postage stamp- sized stage is decked out in Christmas decorations that make it Christmas in June.

THE GANG OF FOUR follow up their startling debut last October with an equally original single for EMI. The song "At Home He's A Tourist," is coupled with "It's Her Factory." The lead track has been the focal point of the band's live sets for the last several months. The driving backing track rages against the anti-solos of Andy Gill. It's tagged "Single of the Holiday Season" by Adrian Thrills in today's *NME*.

UK SUBS had their dreams come true only a few weeks ago when they signed a record deal with Gem Records after releasing a very successful indie 45. Today their first single is being rush released on red vinyl. The "A" side features "Stranglehold," and is flipped with "World War" and "Rockers."

SOFT BOYS	High Wycombe, Nag's Head	ESSENTIAL LOGIC	London, Hope & Anchor
CURE	Liverpool, Eric's	TOURISTS	Sheffield, Limit Club

9th - Saturday...

THE SOFT BOYS are back home in Cambridge tonight, playing at the College Of Art & Technology. They've set up to record the concert, just as they did in London last Saturday. The band hopes to get some good recordings to include on their next album planned for release in the fall. It's tentatively titled "That's My Fish You're Holding." More immediately, they've set the wheels in motion for the release of their next single, "Rock & Roll Toilet," for release sometime next month.

GARY NUMAN & TUBEWAY ARMY have a new album called "Replicas," which expands on the stories of the "Macmen," aliens and other tales of quiet desperation. Gary controls all aspects of his career. He wrote all the songs, produced the album, came up with the cover concept, and when he's ready, he might even play live. In the last few weeks his life has dramatically changed. The single of "Are Friends Electric?" sits at #20 in the UK. He's being bombarded with requests for interviews from *Record Mirror, Smash Hits, Melody Maker, Sounds* and the *NME*. He's already appeared on both *Top Of The Pops* and *The Old Grey Whistle Test*. Not bad for someone who doesn't see music as his chosen lifestyle. Gary Numan's dream isn't pop fame. He's an avid flyer and sees himself in the cockpit of a Dakota painted in '40s war colors flying formation over France and Germany. It's an odd dream but Gary Numan IS an unusual person. He told the *NME*, "I'm over-the-top paranoid. I'm very intolerant and I get fed up with people easily."

OXY & THE MORONS/ CHARGE	Belfast, Beachmount Leisure Ctr	BRIAN JAMES & THE BRAINS VERMILION	London, Nashville
SKIDS/THE EDGE	Liverpool, Eric's	CURE	Manchester, Poly.
ANOTHER PRETTY FACE	Liverpool, Edgehill College		

10th - Sunday...

THE FRANTIC ELEVATORS are the Manchester quartet that centers around the vocals of eighteen-year old Mick Hucknall. His group was one of several signed up by TJM Records recently, and their debut 45 is beginning to appear in the shops. "Voice In The Dark" is flipped with two pop songs, "Passion" and "Every Day I Die." Sadly, after several singles the Frantic Elevators won't find fame, but Mick will when he begins another band in '84 called Simply Red.

JUNE 1979

U2	Dublin, McGonangles	POLICE/BOBBY HENRY	London, Lyceum
STIFF LITTLE FINGERS/		FABULOUS POODLES	London, Nashville
STRAITS	Glasgow, Apollo	VIP's	London, Two Brewers

11th - Monday...

THE YACHTS' debut album is just out on Radar Records. It's simply called "The Yachts" and contains their previous 45s "Look Back In Love (Not Anger)," "I Can't Stay Long," "Yachting Type" and "Love You, Love You." Also included are "Semaphore Love," "Tantamount To Bribery" and "Mantovani's Hits." Early copies of the album will include a free picture-sleeved single with a live version of their Stiff single "Suffice To Say" and "On And On" recorded at the Nashville in London on November 2nd of last year. The Yachts are Martin Watson on guitar and vocals, Henry Preistman on keyboards, Martin Dempsy on bass and Bob Bellis on drums.

SKIDS	Birmingham, Digbeth Civic Hall	CROOKS/CHORDS	London, Nashville
JOHN COOPER CLARKE	Edinburgh, Tiffany's	HEADBOYS/SMALL HOURS	London, Moonlight
015	Liverpool, Kirklands	DAMNED/RUTS/	
PURPLE HEARTS/		LOCAL HEROES	Sheffield, Top Rank
BACK TO ZERO	London, Bridge House		

12th - Tuesday...

NINA HAGEN has been the subject of much hype and expectation since her appearance on the scene a year ago. Now there's something to compare the stories against, a full length album. CBS Germany has just put out the LP "The Nina Hagen Band." It begins with her version of the Tubes' "White Punks On Dope," retitled as "TV-Glotzer," then spins through "Rangehn," "Heiss," "Auf'm Friedhof" and seven other original songs. All are performed in German.

BRIAN JAMES Ex-Damned guitarist, has another go at a recording career with a solo 45 on Faulty Products. Only a year after going solo, he's already abandoned the Tanz Der Youth project and is putting out singles under his own name. The 45 is "Ain't That A Shame," b/w "Living In Sin" and "I Can Make You Cry." All three are James originals. There are some copies floating about that incorrectly list the flipside as "Living In The Sun."

ESSENTIAL LOGIC	Birmingham, Barbarella's	JAGS	London, Music Machine
CLOSE RIVALS/DEADLY TOYS	Birmingham, Elizabethan Days	HEADBOYS	London, Marquee
HUMAN LEAGUE/SCARS/		PURPLE HEARTS	London, Hope & Anchor
AU PAIRS	Birmingham, Digbeth Civic Hall	TOURISTS	London, Marquee
DAMNED/RUTS/		YACHTS	Sheffield, Univ.
LOCAL HEROES	Edinburgh, Tiffany's	RECORDS / LOCAL HEROS	Sheffield, The Limit

14th - Thursday...

JOY DIVISION's ground breaking debut LP is out this week. It's called "Unknown Pleasures" and is as different from the current ideas in the "new wave," as the punk scene was from the disco scene it buried. The LP's cover is stark black with a graphic that Bernard suggested as the intergalactic scream of a dying star. First copies came in a richly textured sleeve with a simple black & white cover. On the record itself, the sides are labeled "inside" and "outside." In the run-off groove there are the messages "Atrocity Exhibition" and "I've Been Looking For A Guide" scratched in. The running order of the LP is "Disorder," "Day Of The Lords," "Candidate," "Insight" and "New Dawn Fades." Side two features "She's Lost Control," "Shadowplay," "Wilderness," "Interzone" and concludes with "I Remember Nothing." The LP was financed by Tony Wilson, presenter of the Granada TV program *So It Goes*. He's fronted the 8,500 pounds needed to press up the 10,000 copies of "Unknown Pleasures." The mournful sound of the album marks it as something different. It's dark, brooding and instantly accessible. The band is augmented with sound effects and eerie production. Joy Division is currently looking for a major label to work with. This album with Manchester's Factory Records was just to see how things work out with indie labels.

THE THE appear again, much different than the four-piece that played at the Africa Centre last month. The The has been trimmed to a duo of Matt Johnson and Keith Laws. They're playing tonight at the Acklam Hall in London.

CABARET VOLTAIRE played their first gig in Sheffield four years ago. You would think in all that time they would have a handful of 45s and albums out. Not so. So far the Cab's only have two, the newest is "Nag Nag Nag" and "Is That Me (Finding Someone At The Door Again?)." It's out on Rough Trade Records and comes in a sleeve with pictures of the band live in Paris.

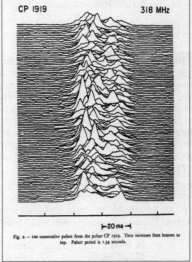

CP 1919   318 MHz

|←20 ms→|

Fig. 2. – 100 consecutive pulses from the pulsar CP 1919. Time increases from bottom to top. Pulsar period is 1.34 seconds.

Original astronomy illustration used for "Unknown Pleasures" album art.

TOURISTS	Birmingham, Barbarella's	SAD AMONG STRANGERS	London, Hammersmith Swan
U2	Dublin, McGonangles	MERTON PARKAS	London, The Fountain (New Malden)
HUMAN LEAGUE/FLOWERS	Edinburgh, Astoria	SKIDS	Manchester, Apollo

LIVE TONIGHT!

JUNE 1979

PLAIN CHARACTERS/	LURKERS ....Manchester, Ardri Cinema
THE THE ....London, Acklam Hall	ARTERY/TV PRODUCTS.............Sheffield, Poly.

15th - Friday...

JOHN COOPER CLARKE and Epic Records have come up with the perfect concert souvenir; a live 10" LP of Clarke's best spoken word bits called "Walking Back To Happiness." Included on the mini-LP are "Gabardine Angus, Majorca," "Bronze Adonis," "Split Beans," "Twat," "The Pest," "Nothing," "Limbo," "Who Stole The Marble Index" and a version of "Gimmix Play Loud" with the Invisible Girls backing. The LP is slightly under a half hour long and comes in clear vinyl, in a clear poly bag.

THE LURKERS get the bad news. Just as they are starting to make some money, they have to spend it all on new gear before setting out on their American adventure on Monday. Last night, on the way back from the West Coast, their equipment van collided with a brick truck and exploded into matchwood. The two roadies and a lighting man escaped without damage but the instruments were a total loss. The band are cancelling their gig at Barbarella's tonight, they're not an acapella act. The good news is that their second album "God's Lonely Men" is out. It features their current single "Out In The Dark" as well as "Bad Times," "Non-Contender," "Seven O'Clock Someday," "Whatever Happened To Mary" and "She Knows."

THE ADVERTS have a new single out on RCA this weekend. It's "My Place" b/w a live recording of "New Church." The band have recently completed their new LP for RCA and will be setting up a full length tour to promote it when it comes out later this month. The Adverts remain Gaye Advert on bass, TV Smith on vocals, Howard Pickup on lead guitar and Rod Latter on drums.

ANOTHER PRETTY FACE...........Edinburgh, Pollock Hall	MERTON PARKAS ....London, Two Brewers
ROCKPILE (with Nick Lowe)/	HUMAN LEAGUE/
JOHN COOPER CLARKE ....Liverpool, Eric's	ESSENTIAL LOGIC ....Manchester, The Factory
CHORDS/THE MODS/	POLICE/BOBBY HENRY ....Sheffield, Top Rank
SQUIRE................................London, Marquee (Mod Festival)	

LIVE TONIGHT!

17th - Sunday...

GENERATION X add another single to their stack this weekend, and the band won't be around to promote it in the UK. The single "Fridays Angels" is the band's hint of their third LP, and was produced by Ian Hunter. The single is flipped with "Trying For Kicks" and "This Heat," both Idol-James originals. Early buyers of the 45 will get it on snappy red vinyl and in a special picture bag. Generation X will play a few dates around London to promote the 45 before heading for Japan. Upon returning they plan to finish their next LP.

RICH KIDS split! It's official! The Rich Kids have quit. Glen Matlock, Midge Ure, and Rusty Egan are all working on other projects. There is no plan for a farewell tour or record.

BEARS ....London, Brecknock	JOHN COOPER CLARKE/
POLICE/CRAMPS/	JOY DIVISION ....London, Royalty Theatre
BOBBY HENRY ....London, Lyceum	ROBERT & THE REMOULDS/
CHORDS/BACK TO ZERO/	BETWEEN PICTURES ....London, Windsor Castle
KILLERMETERS ....London, Marquee (Mod Festival)	

18th - Monday...

THE MERTON PARKAS are from Merton Park. One would wonder where they got their name from. They started out a year and a half ago as a pop band called The Sneakers playing the clubs south of the Thames. Since those times, they have bought parkas, scooters and cropped their hair in the mod fashion. They're in a celebratory mood since they are the latest band to be signed to Beggars Banquet Records. They're regulars around the Two Brewers Pub, The Bridge House and the Wellington. The group is Danny Talbot on guitar and vocals, his older brother Michael Talbot on keyboards and guitar, Neil Hurrell on bass and Simon Smith on drums. Their concert last night at the Wellington was reviewed in the *NME* by Adele-Marie Cherreson who wrote, "It was a pleasant surprise to actually hear what was being sung and to understand the lucid lyrics of writer/manage/vocalist/guitarist Danny Talbot. The keyboards of Mick Talbot effectively embellished the rhythm lines…" Mick explained that he, "…never got into the punk thing at all. I know it sounds a bit strange to you, but it's true. I liked the energy but I just couldn't take the non-musicality of it all."

SECRET AFFAIR's gig at the Bridge House is reviewed for *Sounds* by Gary Bushell, and he's head over heels in love with the band. Evident in his opening paragraph, is the revelation he's had seeing the band live, and ignoring what the press has said about them. "The 400 plus kids down the Bridge this Monday don't need any telling 'cos they know. They know that despite the lies and twisted cynicism of envious gub-grumble has-beens, something is happening here, and the pompous pampered press don't know what it is. That something belongs to these kids and it's called Secret Affair."

SECRET AFFAIR/	BRAM TCHAIKOVSKY/
THE CROOKS ....London, Bridge House	CARPETTES ....London, Nashville
MEDIUM MEDIUM ....London, Windsor Castle	

20th - Wednesday..

THE GANG OF FOUR have dared to "bite the hand that feeds" of Auntie Beeb. They were invited to perform their song "At Home He's A Tourist" on the BBC TV program *Top Of The Pops*. They had been through all the preliminary steps, which began abruptly when they had to interrupt their rehearsals to come down to London just yesterday morning. When it came to showtime, the BBC insisted that the lyric

JUNE 1979

"They make their profit from the things they sell. To help you cob off, and the *rubbers* you hide in your pocket…" The word "rubbers" in the song was considered offensive to some viewers, it would have to be changed. The group refused. They had considered changing it to "packets," which still carried the meaning of the lyric, but even that was unacceptable. Taking it right to the wall, the Gang Of Four flatly refused to budge, as did the BBC on their position. So, the Gang Of Four weren't seen by the fourteen million viewers that tuned in to see presenter Dave Lee Travis count down the top songs like "Go West" by the Village People, and "Dance Away" by Roxy Music. With a record at #58 in the UK charts, the TV appearance would almost certainly have pushed it even higher. The Gang Of Four would rather have it remain at #58 instead of bowing to the pressures of the censoring forces of the BBC.

THE XDREAMYSTS have their first 45 for Polydor Records released. It should do well back in Belfast, since their debut single six months ago is now considered a "collectable." The Polydor release couples "Bad News" with "Money Talks."

COWBOYS INTERNATIONAL have their second single released by Virgin. It's "Nothing Doing" b/w "Millions." To make the package more interesting, the group also include a clear flexi of "Many Times" in the sleeve.

THE CRAMPS' first 12" outing is a gathering together of their previous releases in one package. Under the banner "Gravest Hits," the LP takes in both sides of their debut single "Surfin' Bird" and "The Way I Walk," as well as both tracks on their second indie "Human Fly," and "Domino." An additional, heretofore unreleased song, "Lonesome Town," is the only new material included. All five songs were recorded in Memphis back in October of '77 with Alex Chilton producing. The Cramps are Nick Knox on drums, Bryan Gregory on lead guitar, Lux Interior on vocals and Ivy Rorschach on rhythm guitar.

MUSIC CLUB/BLANCMANGE ....London, Moonlight Club	MODS........................London, Dublin Castle (Coal Bin)
GENERATION X/	SECRET AFFAIR/
PRIVATE VICES........................London, Marquee	MERTON PARKAS/SQUIRE ....London, Music Machine

22nd - Friday.......................................

THE POLICE try and try again. Their single of "Can't Stand Losing You" didn't do as well as planned when it was released last September, but when the subsequent LP "Outlands d'Amour" started selling, their record company felt that a re-release is in order. So today's new Police is the old Police single. The re-release nets the band a #2 hit single in the UK.

THE SEX PISTOLS have another 45 to their credit, even though the band went their separate ways over six months ago. Virgin has just issued Sid's version of the Eddie Cochran '50s rocker "C'mon Everybody," coupled with "God Save The Queen (Symphony)" and "Whatcha Gonna Do About It." The latter is actually an early demo recording of the band from the dawn of their career. At the time, they had several Small Faces songs in their set before they had written much material and this is one of the few covers that they've recorded.

ARTERY are one of the newest Sheffield bands. They make their vinyl debut with a three track EP today on their manager's Limited Edition Records. The songs are "Mother Moon," "Pretends" and "Heinz." The group is Toyce Ashley on vocals and rhythm guitar, Mark Gouldthorpe on guitar, Neil MacKenzie on bass, and Gary Wilson on drums. Roots of Artery can be traced back to a punk band simply called "The."

ESSENTIAL LOGIC/MIRRORS ....Birmingham, Barbarella's	CRAMPS/
YACHTS/THE EDGE ....Liverpool, Eric's	VERMILION & THE ACES ....London, Nashville
JAGS ....Liverpool, Poly.	CHORDS/THE MODS/
PIRANHAS ....London, Hope & Anchor	MERTON PARKAS/
HUMAN LEAGUE/	SMALL HOURS........................London, Notre Dame Hall
SPIZZ ENERGI ....London, Marquee	BEARS ....London, Windsor Castle
SQUIRE ....London, Moonlight Club	PETER & TEST TUBE BABIES/
SAD AMONG STRANGERS...........London, The Windmill	MEKONS ....Manchester, The Factory

LIVE TONIGHT!

23rd - Saturday.......................................

THE CURE's new single is "Boys Don't Cry" b/w "Plastic Passion." Both tracks are new and were not part of the band's LP "Three Imaginary Boys." Carved into the matrix on the side with "Boys Don't Cry" is "But Bill Does." On the reverse is the message "From The Land of 1,000 Microphones." Early purchasers will be rewarded with a limited color picture sleeve. Even though this song today is one of the band's best known numbers, it never was a hit in it's own time, failing to even get into the top 100. In 1986, a re-issue and heavy UK airplay will push it to a respectable #22.

TELEVISION fans in England are rejoicing. Back in '75, Television released their debut single, the critically acclaimed "Little Johnny Jewel." Since then, the band's following has grown despite their split, and the 45 had become increasingly sought after, a badge of hipness for anyone lucky enough to have a copy. Now, this long deleted single has been reissued in 12" format, complete with a color pic sleeve and a live version of "Little Johnny Jewel" on the flipside.

ORIGINAL MIRRORS/MEKONS .....Liverpool, Eric's	SQUIRE ....London, Plumstead Green Man
ADVERTS/QT'S/	WIRE ....Manchester, The Factory
OUTPATIENTS ....London, Music Machine	

24th - Sunday.......................................

THE CRAMPS play at the Factory in Manchester, counting among their fans Steven Morrissey, who is so inspired by this band, he immediately writes letters to the music dailies. The *Record Mirror* received a missive asking, "Who are the Cramps? They are the most beautiful, yes beautiful group I've ever seen. The fact that they exists is enough. Meanwhile Manchester will never be the same again (Thank God.)" A letter sent to *Sounds* said, "The Cramps are worth their weight in gold for making the Police seem like a great big sloppy

JUNE 1979

bowl of mush. The Police, hardly dabbling in degrees of the unexpected, presented a farcical imitation of their *Rock Goes To College* thing- several people clapped, but then, I suppose someone has to. The Cramps were enough to restore faith in the most spiritless." Another note, sent to *NME* stated simply, "I've just seen the Cramps and they're at that funny stage. This is the kind of group that start revolutionary outrages and all that. Steven Morrissey, Kings Road- Manchester." His *NME* letter is followed by a Cheshire lad, "You can edit this to 'I think The Cramps are crap' if you like, signed Scrubber."

THE MADNESS gig at the Hope & Anchor tonight is reviewed by Adrian Thrills for the *NME*. He described Madness as "strictly a 'renewal' rather than a revival band." Before the show, Suggs was onstage handing out free records to prize winners in the front rows. The group does a variety of covers in the show, beginning the set with the Prince Buster instrumental "One Step Beyond." (Their original songs) about a dozen in all, range from the autobiographical "Nutty Theme" to the heavily ironic borstal song "Land Of Hope And Glory," to "Stepping Into Line," a song about fashion. By the time they encored with Smokey Robinson's "Shop Around," and the straighter rock and roll of Bazooka Joe's "Rockin' In A Flat," the cramped cloisters of the Upper Street basement were converted."

LURKERS/THE CHORDS/
BACK TO ZERO ....London, Lyceum
SPIZZ ENERGI/
PSYCHEDELIC FURS ....London, Nashville

MADNESS..............................London, Hope & Anchor
SQUIRE ....London, Two Brewers
CRAMPS ....Manchester, The Factory

26th - Tuesday.......................................

SIMPLE MINDS release their new 45 this week, in conjunction with their tour to support the LP "Life In A Day." The new 45 has the song "Chelsea Girl," as well as the non-LP song "Garden Of Hate." Their three-week tour starts Saturday in Birmingham.

CHELSEA have imaginatively titled their debut album "Chelsea." It gathers the band's newest unrecorded material like "I'm On Fire" "Free The Fighters," "Government," "Twelve Men," "Trouble Is The Day" and "Decide." There is even a cover of the Jimmy Cliff scorcher "Many Rivers To Cross." The album is out now on Step Forward Records and has "I Only Followed Orders" inscribed on the matrix near the label. Chelsea are Gene October on vocals, Dave Martin on guitar and vocals, James Stevenson on lead guitar and vocals, Geoff Myles on bass and Chris Bashford on drums and vocals.

TOURISTS ....Glasgow, Queen's Hall
CRAMPS ....London, Dingwalls
CHORDS...............................London, Hope & Anchor
MEMBERS ....Sheffield, Top Rank

FRANTIC ELEVATORS/
PRIVATE SECTOR/V2/
DISTRACTIONS/ALTIFITS ....Manchester, Russell Club

27th - Wednesday.......................................

THE PRETENDERS, still riding high on the success of their debut single "Stop Your Sobbing" have a second released this week by Real Records. "Kid" and "Tattooed Love Boys" make up the single, which is being supported by an extensive UK tour. The band plays tonight in Scarborough and will conclude their month-long tour on the 4th in Manchester. When the band get off the road they will finish their debut album, currently in the works with producer Chris Thomas, who offers up this bit of prophesy on the picture sleeve, "Covent Garden London, Spring 1979. A new sound is taking the British pop scene by surprise, with their second offering the Pretenders have finally arrived! The Pretenders will be around for a long time even if I'm not!" *NME* reviewer Steve Clarke agrees, "If they split up or are ignored by the record buyers of the West it will be a tragedy, but it seems that The Pretenders have enough perspective and are down to earth enough to survive…Without a doubt, The Pretenders are a real band for the '80s."

YACHTS/THE EDGE ....Edinburgh, Clouds
UK SUBS ....High Wycombe, Town Hall

JAGS ....London, Marquee

28th - Thursday.......................................

PUBLIC IMAGE LTD. unleash their second 45 today. It's got the startling title "Death Disco," and is flipped with "No Birds Do Sing." There is also a 15,000 copy limited edition of the lead track in the "1/2 Mix" and "Megga Mix" varieties. Public Image at this writing are John Lydon on vocals, Keith Levine on guitar, Jah Wobble on bass and new drummer Richard Dudanski.

NICK LOWE, Britian's top new music producer, is dissapointed in the new crop of bands. He confessed to the *NME*, "I haven't seen a good group for ages. Everything seems so stagnant. It seems to be like '76 still, and the punk thing is being replaced by this awful arty farty shit…like hippy music with thin ties or something. It's exactly the same old cobblers I can remember when the pub rock thing started."

THEY MUST BE RUSSIANS is one of the more unusual names for a band, but the quirky moniker is a perfect fit for this Sheffield combo. The name supposedly came from a London newspaper's response to the Sex Pistol's song "God Save The Queen." They Must Be Russians have just released their four track debut EP. Perhaps the most unusual aspect of the EP is the revved up version of the children's song "Nellie The Elephant." Other songs include "Nagasaki's Children," "Circus" and "I Want To Hold You Now." The EP is produced by their friends in Cabaret Voltaire.

CRAMPS ....Birmingham, Barbarella's

PATRIK FITZGERALD/
TEARDROP EXPLODES..............Birmingham, Festival Suite

JUNE 1979

TOURISTS.....................Liverpool, Eric's	SPECIALS ....London, The Nashville
PIRANHAS/ENCHANTERS............London, Albany Empire	SQUIRE ....London, The Wellington
PRAG VEC.....................London, Hope & Anchor	JOE JACKSON ....Sheffield, Limit Club

29th - Friday..................

SHAM 69 were thought to have packed it in after a disastrous gig in Hendon back in January. Now they're back having one more moment in the spotlight, one more farewell show. Tonight's gig at the Glasgow Apollo was a rumor only a week ago, and now it's reality. The classic line up of Sham played, Jimmy Pursey, Dave Parsons, Dave Treggana and Mark Cain. Lately, Jimmy Pursey has been working with various bands in his production deal with Polydor Records, as well as appearing from time to time with ex-Pistols Cook and Jones. It seems that this is indeed the end of Sham 69. Opening the show are a local band, The Valves, as well as a set by the UK Subs.

YACHTS/THE EDGE ....Birmingham, Barbarella's	
SHAM 69/VALVES/ UK SUBS........Glasgow, Apollo	
JOE JACKSON ....Liverpool, Eric's	
SQUIRE.............................London, The Marquee	
BARRACUDAS ....London, The Chippenham	
PATRIK FITZGERALD/	
TEARDROP EXPLODES..............Manchester, The Factory	

30th - Saturday..................

SIOUXSIE & THE BANSHEES have two singles released on the same day, but each single is unique to each issuing country. In England, Siouxsie's new 45 is "Playground Twist" b/w "Pulled To Bits." However over in Germany, there's a simultaneous release of a German vocal version of "Metal Postcard" titled "Mittageisen." It's backed with the English version of "Love In A Void." The German 45 will not be released in the UK, however it will be available as an import. While the picture sleeve of "Playground Twist" is what appears to be a child's painting, "Mittageisen" is an odd '30s photo cover of a family eating a bicycle!

THE SWELL MAPS' second album "A Trip To Marineville," is released by Rough Trade Records. It contains seventeen songs, some incredibly short, some epics. Titles include "Midget Submarines," "H.S. art," "Vertical Sum," "Adventuring Into Basketry," and "Harmony In Your Bathroom." Looking over the copious notes on the inner sleeve you'll see that this is the result of years of recordings. Some sessions date back to July of '77! The Swell Maps are Nikki Mattress, Epic Soundtracks, Phones B. Sportsman, Jowe Head, Biggles Books, and Golden Cockrill. A note on the sleeve encourages buyers to, "Try it at 16 rpm, 33 rpm, 45 rpm and 78 rpm! It is probably funniest at 33!! and most musical at 16!!" As an added bonus, all early copies of the album come with a free four track EP with a special picture sleeve. Some of these are autographed by the band.

JOHN LYDON appears as the special guest on the BBC rate-a-record show *Jukebox Jury*. His job, along with three other guests, is to determine if a record is a "hit" or a "miss." Host Noel Edmunds has on as other guests Joan Collins, Elaine Page and Alan Freeman. Of the records played here is a brief rundown of Johnny's comments. Showaddywaddy "rubbish," Donna Summer "horrible," Abba "it's nothing." When asked what kind of music he DID like, he replied "my music." With the playing of the Monks "I Ain't Getting Any" more complaints from Lydon were forthcoming prompting guest Alan Freeman to say "Shut up, will you?" During the closing the host hopes that, "...it wasn't too exciting for Mr. Lydon" and Johnny walks off the set. At least he wasn't asked to say anything naughty. That's one lesson Bill Grundy taught the BBC.

SIMPLE MINDS ....Birmingham, Barbarella's	CARPETTES..........................London, Moonlight Club
CRAMPS/	YACHTS ....London, Music Machine
PINK MILITARY STAND ALONE.....Liverpool, Eric's	CHELSEA ....Manchester, Factory
RECORDS/SQUIRE ....Liverpool, Oscar's	JOE JACKSON ....Manchester, Poly.

July 1st - Sunday..................

THE CURE headline at the London Lyceum tonight on a bill alongside the Ruts and the Purple Hearts. Mark Ellen, writing for the *NME*, reviews the concert. "(The Cure are) vastly misconstrued by some as the trailblazers for the '80s, they trade more on their acutely sensitive rearrangement of rock music's components than actually create a new and positive context...What comes over strongest in their set is their marvellous ability to color all the space they've cleared for themselves. With a sound so close to their albums that it's uncanny, and some powerfully contrasting lights, they trace every song with sparse, understated details, giving them, on one level a clear definition, and on another, a very vague and alluring haziness." The Cure's set includes Jimi Hendrix's "Foxy Lady," most of their debut album "Three Imaginary Boys" and a satirical song about their first label called "Do The Hansa."

DEVO's latest album is "Duty Now For The Future." This second album takes up the slack in the live material that everyone has been clamoring for to be on album. It starts with the Devo Corporate Anthem, works it way through " S.I.B," "Wiggly World," "Triumph Of The Will," "Pink Pussycat" and a strange remake of the Johnny Rivers' classic "Secret Agent Man."

PROTEX ....London, Hope & Anchor	CURE/THE RUTS/
MEKONS ....London, Nashville	PURPLE HEARTS ....London, Lyceum

2nd - Monday..................

THE JAGS have a rare talent. On their debut EP, they have a song that sounds just like an Elvis Costello outtake, and another that's a dead

JULY 1979

ringer for Nick Lowe. The Island EP contains "Back of My Hand" (the Costello one), and "Double Vision" (the Lowe sound-alike). Other tracks are "Single Vision" and "What Can I Do." Addressing the Costello soundalike bit in *Sounds* magazine, lead vocalist Nick Watkinson claims that, "I'm no cheapskate Elvis Costello. I've never tried to impersonate him. For a start, we're more humorous, more tongue in cheek than him. He's much more bitchy and venomous. Like a middle aged child! In any case, that Costello style of vocal all came from the Brinsleys. Both Costello and Parker have just exaggerated and extended Nick Lowe's Brinsley vocal style. And that's all I've done."

MEMBERS	Birmingham, Digbeth Civic Hall		MEDIUM MEDIUM	London, Hope & Anchor
SPECIALS	Edinburgh, Tiffany's		LEYTON BUZZARDS/	
COWBOYS INTL./ DEFENDANTS	London, Nashville		STRANGEWAYS	London, Notre Dame Hall

4th - Wednesday....................................

THE BUZZCOCKS' latest single is "Harmony In My Head" b/w "Something's Gone Wrong Again." This is the second time that the "A" side was a Steve Diggle song, rather than the usual Pete Shelley track. The flip features Pete Shelley on piano.

PRAG VEC/PRIME MOVERS	London, Rock Garden	MODS/LOW NUMBERS	London, Dublin Castle (Coal Bin)

5th - Thursday....................................

THE HEARTBREAKERS' sorta-new album is finding its way to shops this weekend. It's "Live At Max's Kansas City," and was recorded in November of last year when Johnny Thunders teamed up with the members of the Heartbreakers for two last shows. The LP covers a variety of oldies with nothing new. Uninspired versions of "London," "Chinese Rocks," "Let Go," "All By Myself," "One Track Mind" and "Take A Chance" fill the LP. There is also "Chatterbox" which is also known as "Leave Me Alone," appearing on the LP under the title "Milk Me." It's not a new song but it's repackaged so you'd think it was. The LP on Beggars Banquet in the UK, is released with a companion 45 of "Get Off The Phone," and "I Wanna Be Loved." Both of these tracks are also on the album, and come in a limited edition with a free Heartbreakers patch. The *NME's* Danny Baker was unimpressed with the song when reviewing the new singles and described it with, "I never like to use the word 'dated' but this record positively walks with a stick."

NEWTOWN NEUROTICS are another pub band that have climbed to the next level. They've just had their debut single released by the Harlow-based No Wonder Records label. It's two originals, "Hypocrite" b/w "You Said No."

CURE	Birmingham, Barbarella's	
CLASH/MODETTES/		
LOW NUMBERS	London, Notre Dame Hall	
BARRACUDAS/		
PRIME MOVERS	London, Acklam Hall	
SIMPLE MINDS	London, Marquee	
JOY DIVISION/BETTE BRIGHT &		
THE ILLUMINATIONS	Sheffield, Limit Club	

LIVE TONIGHT!

6th - Friday....................................

THE B-52's move beyond singles with a full length album. Following in the wake of comic rock like the Monks and the Rezillos, the B-52's make music that's not to be taken seriously. The album includes eight originals like "Planet Claire," "Dance This Mess Around," "Lava" and "6060-842." There are new re-recorded versions of the songs that they had on their debut single, "Rock Lobster" and "52 Girls." The LP closes out with a cover of Petula Clark's "Downtown." The LP was recorded at Compass Point studios in the Bahamas with Island chief Chris Blackwell producing. A special limited number of the first albums will come with a free copy of their Island debut 45 "Rock Lobster" stuck inside.

WRECKLESS ERIC has a new stiffie. It's "Hit And Miss Judy," a song inspired by a Spanish waitress he met one time that couldn't get much correct, "…she was rather hit & miss," flipped with "Let's Go To The Pictures." A limited edition 12" single comes pressed up on orange vinyl with the additional track "I Need A Situation."

ADAM & THE ANTS release their first indie single since parting ways with major label Decca. Since the departure, Adam & The Ants have signed a new agency deal to get booked throughout England, and have also cut a deal with indie Do-It Records, to release their newest songs. The debut for Do-It are the tracks "Zerox" and "Whip In My Valise." Both are live favorites and are out this week in a limited edition picture sleeve single.

YELLOW MAGIC ORCHESTRA They've been described by outsiders as "Sergio Mendes meets *Star Trek*," but they refer to their own sound as "Technopops." They're no doubt something new in music. Yellow Magic Orchestra are the Tokyo-based all-electronic band that's just released their debut album in the western world. The group is Haruomi (Harry) Hosono and Ryuichi Sakamoto on keyboards, and Yukihiro Takahashi on drums. Their album "Yellow Magic Orchestra" is on A&M Records.

BETTE BRIGHT &		SCRITTI POLITTI/	
THE ILLUMINATIONS/		ACME SEWAGE	London, Hitching College
SECRET AFFAIR	Birmingham, Barbarella's	CLASH/MODETTES/	
FALL	Liverpool, Eric's	LOW NUMBERS	London, Notre Dame Hall

JULY 1979

LITTLE ROOSTERS	....................London, Hope & Anchor	SHAKE/BASCZAX	......................London, Nashville
LEYTON BUZZARDS/		CURE	....Manchester, The Factory
TICKETS/39 STEPPES	................London, Acklam Hall	COWBOYS INTL.	.......................Sheffield, Limit Club

7th - Saturday.................................

THE MERTON PARKAS, who were only signed up by Beggars Banquet three weeks ago, have their debut 45 rush released. The tracks selected are "You Need Wheels," and "I Don't Want To Know You." Early copies of the single come with a Merton Parkas sew-on patch, presumably to sew onto your Merton parka. The band was recently captured on film for a proposed short subject called *Comin' Out*. It's an hour long "B" film about London youth. The trouble began when the Merton Parkas were filming outdoors on their scooters. They were following a red convertible that was filming them riding through Battersea when they were stopped for not having helmets, insurance and a proper license. The film is planned for a September release nationwide.

LIVE TONIGHT!

WIRE	.............................Liverpool, Eric's	SIMPLE MINDS/SUSSEX	.............London, Nashville
THE ACT/HEARTBREAKERS	.........London, Dingwalls	PASSIONS	..............................London, St. Marks's
VALVES	................................London, Hope & Anchor	CHRIS SIEVEY & FRESHIES/	
CARPETTES	..........................London, Marquee	UNITS/C.P. LEE & FRIENDS/	
MODS/SMALL HOURS	.............London, Moonlight Club	GORDON THE MORON	..............Manchester, Poly.
JOE JACKSON/LIVE WIRE	..........London, Music Machine	COM-SAT ANGELS	..................Sheffield, Broadfield Hotel

8th - Sunday....................................

WIRE's Graham Lewis isn't fooled by fashion. He is disappointed that the changes in the music industry that punk promised haven't happened. Interviewed in this week's *NME*, he said, "People say things (the music scene) are healthier than they've ever been. But I think what's happened has just replaced what was there before. Maybe it is better, but it hasn't changed as much as people would like to think, because the whole thing's done back to the same hierarchy, the same ego battles, getting involved in all that show biz shit."

THE B-52's are onstage in London playing for their largest audience ever. Their set began with "Planet Claire," throbbed through "52 Girls," "There's A Moon In The Sky," "6060-842," "Dance This Mess Around," "Hero Worship" and a new unrecorded song called "Devil In My Car." Then followed "Lava" and "Rock Lobster." The group were rapturously received and encored with two more new songs, "Strobe Light" and "Private Idaho." *NME's* Nick Kent reviewed tonight's show. He wrote, "...these jesters probably believe that theirs is the music of the future. Unfortunately for them, fashion will be the first to go in the much mooted slashing away of chaff from the wheat that the 1980's threatens to be takes place. It would merely be far too easy but downright irresponsible to juxtapose the phoney filigrees of fashion against the ingenious pulsebeat of the B-52's to show how America's hot bands are trashing out native talent...They provide a beat so fearsomely gorgeous that if your feet fail to respond, then you're dead." The reporter was also confronted at the concert by five guys who were in a London-based band called the B-52's who split up some months ago. They had regrouped, just to "show these damn Yankees who were the real B-52's."

IAN DURY & THE BLOCKHEADS/		B-52's/FASHION/	
ROOT BOY SLIM &		DELTA 5	..............................London, Lyceum
SEX CHANGE BAND	..................Birmingham, Odeon	DUFFO/CARPETTES	.................London, Nashville
R.D.B./RIFF RAFF	....................London, Bridge House	TUNES/DONKEYS/C.P. LEE/	
MADNESS	............................London, Hope & Anchor	GORDON THE MORON	..............Sheffield, Limit Club
SECRET AFFAIR	......................London, Marquee		

10th - Tuesday..................................

MONOCHROME SET, PRAG VEC & MANICURED NOISE are the three Rough Trade bands that are on a packaged tour that embarks on a ten-day jaunt across England. The bands all take turns in the headlining slot. To tie in with the tour, two of the three bands have new singles released. Monochrome Set's new 45 is "Eine Symphonie Des Grauens," b/w "Lester Leaps In." Lester refers to lead guitarist Lester Square. Prag Vec release their second 45 "Expert" and "The Follower" on their own Spec Records label. The tracks on the 45 aren't listed as side "A" and "B." Instead, they're track "G" and "P."

THE UNDERTONES are only a little late with this new single, it's the middle of July and they're singing "Here Comes The Summer." The 45 is flipped with two bonus songs, "One Way Love" and "Top Twenty." This is the band's fourth single.

NICKY & THE DOTS/		MERTON PARKAS	...................London, Hope & Anchor
PIRANHAS/EXECUTIVES	.............London, The Venue		

11th - Wednesday...............................

HUMAN LEAGUE release a puzzler. The Human League have just recently signed to Virgin Records, and on their debut for the label, they're masquerading as The Men. The 12" dance track is "I Don't Depend On You" b/w "Cruel (instrumental)." There's a woman dressed as a man on the cover and no hint as to who the group are unless you read the fine print under the songwriting credits. What an odd way to debut on a major label!

FOREIGN PRESS are a new Manchester band making their debut on vinyl this week. Their single "Downpour" is reviewed favorable in the *NME*, with Paul Morley describing the 45 as, "...choppy, spiralling, edgy and well rinsed with guitars. Although Foreign Press stop

JULY 1979

short of achieving the channelled psychotic blitzkrieg thrust of the very great Joy Division, they manager a fluctuating fortified sort of '79 psychedelia that makes them 'A Group To Look Out For.' The comparison to Joy Division was not a long stretch since the single was co-produced by Joy Division manager Bob Gretton. The single is available in Manchester on Streets Ahead Records.

CHORDS ....London, Dingwalls   PURE HELL ....London, Moonlight Club

13th - Friday...

BOOMTOWN RATS' powerful and anthemic "I Don't Like Mondays" is released by Ensign Records in England. It was inspired by a January shooting in San Diego, when schoolgirl Brenda Spencer shot and killed several of her schoolmates. It was debuted in May at the Loch Lomond Festival when Geldof and Johnny Fingers alone began the Rats set with it, just vocals and keyboards. The 45 is flipped with "It's All The Rage." Those shocked by the change in the Rats demonstrated by this new sound will rest easy as the song turns into one of the band's biggest hits, their second #1. Presently, the Rats are rehearsing new material and will start recording their third album soon, for release sometime late in the year.

TEARDROP EXPLODES follow up "Sleeping Gas" released on Liverpool's Zoo Records with "Bouncing Babies" and "All I Am Is Loving You." The Teardrop Explodes are beginning to play outside their native soil and have gigs as far away now as Birmingham.

JOE JACKSON/VALVES...............Birmingham, Digbeth Civic Hall		PASSIONS/JOHNNY G/	
CHELSEA/		MOD-ETTES............................London, Moonlight Club	
VERMILION & THE ACES ....Liverpool, Eric's		PETE TOWNSEND/RUTS/	
LAST WORDS/SWELL MAPS/		THE POP GROUP/MISTY ....London, Rainbow	
GLASS TORPEDOES ....London, Albany Empire		SW 1/THE MODS......................London, Windsor Castle	
PURPLE HEARTS ....London, Marquee		JOY DIVISION ....Manchester, The Factory	
PASSION KILLERS/		PRETENDERS/INTERVIEW...........Sheffield, Univ.	
S-HATERS/VITZKRONIKUAK ....London, Mayhem Club			

LIVE TONIGHT!

14th - Saturday.......................................

U2 Still two years away from having a hit single, U2 are featured in an article this week titled "Cassettes and Drugs and Rock And Roll." It's an overview of demo tapes from new bands that have been received by *Sounds* magazine. Gary Bushell writes, "U2, the Dublin band featured on his playlist as 'another great undiscovered Irish Band,' and for good reason. On the strength of this cassette U2 are of a poppy Television bent, boasting nice atmospheric sounds with floating dreamy vocals. Watch out for a McCullough feature soon."

COWBOYS INTL. ....Birmingham, Barbarella's
ADAM & THE ANTS/PROTEX ....Birmingham, Digbeth Civic Hall
SPECIALS ....Liverpool, Eric's
CRASS/POISON GIRLS...............London, Hope & Anchor
THE LAST WORDS....................London, Moonlight Club
DUFFO/CARPETTES ....London, Music Machine
CROOKS/THE MODS/
SMALL HOURS ....London, Albany Empire
CLASH/ASWAD/MEMBERS/
SWELL MAPS/
GLASS TORPEDOES/
BONGO DANNY.......................London, Rainbow

15th - Sunday.............

THE UK SUBS' concert tonight at the Lyceum is being filmed for use as a twenty minute documentary that will run as a companion piece to *Scum*, the BBC short film about Borstal. Besides the film cameras, there is a twenty-four track mobile sound truck there to record the concert. The thought is that the 'Subs could use the live material for a full length album in the future.

THE RUTS' lead vocalist Malcolm Owen was interviewed by Steve Clarke for this week's *NME*. He expressed his views on lyrics and swaying the views of his fans, especially about using heroin, "...take the song 'H-Eyes,' about the smack right? It's not saying naughty, naughty, you mustn't ever take smack. It's an observation of a guy I knew who died from smack. I've taken it before. I wouldn't write it otherwise- it's just: 'you're so young / you take smack for fun / it's gonna screw your head / you're gonna wind up dead.' You know? It's not saying you mustn't do it...but let's face it, it's no good for you. It's nice when you take it, but it's going to fucking kill you if you get well into it. That's all. I'm just trying to put my own experiences over, a lot of people are impressionable." The irony about the statement is that Malcolm Owen would overdose on heroin himself in a year. "Do as I say, not as I do."

THE MOD-ETTES are reviewed in the *NME* with a kind ear. They're compared to early Raincoats or the Slits. Songs in their set include "Dark Park Creeping," "White Mice," "Masochistic Opposites," "Favorite Things," and a version of the 60s chestnut "Twist & Shout." The Mod-ettes are Ramona Carlier on vocals, Jane Crockford on bass, Kate Korris on guitar, and June Miles-Kingston on drums. They started out together back in March as the Bomberettes. They've been added to the Rough Trade tour, replacing Manicured Noise.

MONOCHROME SET/PRAG VEC/
THE MOD-ETTES ....London, Albany Empire
THE WALL/
COCKNEY REJECTS..................London, Hope & Anchor

UK SUBS ....London, The Lyceum
SECRET AFFAIR/
BACK TO ZERO ....London, Marquee

JULY 1979

16th - Monday...

DALEK I is the Liverpool band Dalek I Love You after withering down to it's two primary members, Alan Gill and David Hughes. The group began some time ago, when Alan Gill and Dave Balfe left Radio Blank, and teamed up with Andy McCluskey from The Id. Also brought into the group were Kenny, The Worm, and Max. By the time that they'd recorded a demo for local label Eric's, the group had already started to shrink. By the time that Phonogram signed the group, there were only two members left. Balfe had joined up with Big In Japan and McCluskey had rejoined Paul Humphries in Orchestral Manoeuvres. Their debut 45 is "Freedom Fighters" b/w "Two Chameleons" and is out this week. Alan Gill and David Hughes play all the instruments and provide all the vocals on this electronic-based pop recording which is very much along a Human League frame yet not so threatening.

THE SINCEROS' debut album "The Sound Of Sunbathing" is released on Epic Records. On the LP is both sides of their current hit single "Take Me To Your Leader" plus others like "My Little Letter," "Little White Lie," Worlds Apart" and "Hanging On Too Long." The Sinceros are guitar and vocalist Mark Kjeldsen, Don Snow on keyboards, Ron Francois on bass and Bobbi Irwin on drums.

TEENBEATS ....London, Bridge House	SECRET AFFAIR/BACK TO ZERO/
BRAINIAC 5 ....London, Hope & Anchor	LITTLE ROOSTERS ....London, Vespa's
CHORDS/57 MEN ....London, Marquee	MERTON PARKAS/REFUGE ....London, Windsor Castle
EXTRAS/THE WALL.................London, Moonlight Club	

17th - Tuesday...

THE OUTCASTS aspire to be Belfast's most popular band, and their debut LP "Self-Conscious Over You" is just out on local Good Vibrations Records. The quartet are the second best selling band on Good Vibrations, just behind the Undertones, but then that only leaves Protex and Rudi. They've previously released two singles, one of "You're A Disease" that sold an amazing 5,000 or so copies in Ireland! Their second was "Just Another Teenage Rebel" on Good Vibrations. You can also find "Cops Are Coming" on the Good Vibrations "battle of the band's" EP. Tracks on the LP include "Love Is For Sops," "Spiteful Sue," "Clinical Love," and "Cyborg." The Outcasts are the three brothers, Marty Cowan on guitar, Greg Cowan on bass, Colin Cowan on drums and non-brother Getty on guitar.

JOHN COOPER CLARKE in the *NME* on modern rock, "My relationship to rock and roll is like Lenny Bruce's with modern jazz. I like the clothes and attitude."

LIVE TONIGHT!

BRIAN JAMES' BRAINS/	PURPLE HEARTS/
DEADLY TOURISTS ....Liverpool, Number 1 Club	BACK TO ZERO/MODS................London, Music Machine
LES ELITE ....London, Hope & Anchor	MERTON PARKAS/
PSYCHEDELIC FURS/	SMALL HOURS ....London, Shades
LONESOME NO MORE................London, Moonlight Club	CLOCK DVA/STUNT KITES ....Sheffield, The Marples

18th - Wednesday...

THE POP GROUP are staging a "Bankruptcy Benefit" for themselves tonight at the Notre Dame Hall in London's Leicester Square. The group are burdened with massive debts and hope the concert will raise the funds to get their heads above water. Tickets are only £1.20. In a few weeks the Pop Group will have another record out, this time a 12" EP consisting of various demos and songs recorded for the John Peel radio program.

FAD GADGET are the newest Mute Records signing and make their live debut tonight at the Moonlight Club in West Hampstead. Their debut single is due out in about four weeks. Fad Gadget are not a group per se, they are actually Frank Tovey and his rampant imagination, the finished product sounding somewhat like the Human League meets the Flying Lizards.

TICKETS/COCKNEY REJECTS ....London, Bridge House	TOYAH..................................London, Riverside Studios
LAMBRETTAS/TEENBEATS ....London, Dublin Castle	PIRANHAS ....London, Rock Garden
CHELSEA/ARTHUR'S DILEMMA ....London, Marquee	THE POP GROUP.....................London, Notre Dame Hall
MONOCHROME SET/	SAD AMONG STRANGERS ....London, The Castle (Tooting)
FAD GADGET/	ACCELERATORS/
MANICURED NOISE ....London, Moonlight Club	THOSE NAUGHTY LUMPS ....Manchester, Russell Club

19th - Thursday...

THE TOURISTS have another 45 taken from their debut album this week, at least in spirit. The "A" side, "The Loneliest Man In The World" has been totally re-recorded and vastly improved. It's flipped with "Don't Get Left Behind," also an album track. The newest Englishman in the group is now Eddie Chin. The Malaysian-born bassist has applied for and received his British citizenship. No sense in getting deported just when the band is beginning to make noise.

TOYAH Wilcox is the flamboyant singer chosen as the newest signing for indie Safari Records. Toyah's single is "Victims Of The Riddle (Vivisection) Parts 1 & 2." Toyah is not only a singer, but an actress as well. She's appeared in Derek Jarman's films "The Tempest" and "Jubilee" as well as a small role in *Quadrophenia*.

THE FLYING LIZARDS are really a one-man band of David Cunningham. He plays practically everything on the disc, with the exception being the exceptional vocals from Deborah Evans. His last single "Summertime Blues" was a reasonable success and now the followup is a reworking of another 50s song. Barret Strong would never have guessed his original hit of "Money" could be so twisted, churned and mutated into this version. The song will quickly climb to #5 in the UK and be a summertime novelty always associated with 1979.

JULY 1979

MERTON PARKAS ....High Wycombe, Nag's Head	DYNAMITE/POLECATS ....London, Southgate Royalty Ballroom
LEOPARDS/X-FILMS/	IAN DURY & THE BLOCKHEADS/
VIRUS.....................................London, Albany Empire	ROOT BOY SLIM &
RUTS ....London, Marquee	SEX CHANGE BAND ....Sheffield, City Hall
WIRE/VICE VERSA/THE THE.........London, Notre Dame Hall	

20th - Friday..

IAN DURY has a new one out today. It's called "Reasons To Be Cheerful, Part 3". Curious title as no one can remember parts one and two. The single coincides with his current and extensive tour of England. Neither the "A" side or the flip, "Common As Muck," is included on the LP "Do It Yourself." "Reasons To Be Cheerful, Part 3" will be Dury's third time into the UK Top Ten and will find itself peaking at #3.

CRASS/POISON GIRLS/	MERTON PARKAS/
AU PAIRS ....Birmingham, Festival Suite	SNEEKY FEELINS' ....London, Albany Empire
ADAM & THE ANTS/PROTEX ....Edinburgh, Clouds	WIRE/VICE VERSA/THE THE.........London, Notre Dame Hall
PRETENDERS/INTERVIEW ....Liverpool, Eric's	FALL ....Manchester, Factory
INMATES/SCANDAL ....London, Nashville	ANY TROUBLE...........................Manchester, Spread Eagle

21st - Saturday..

THE TWO TONE CONCERT is the special event to re-open The Electric Ballroom. The event features The Specials, Selecter, Dexy's Midnight Runners, and Madness. Huge crowds packed the dance floor and a line stretched far down the Camden High Road waiting to get in. The Selecter were making their live debut tonight and went on first, followed by Madness. Dexy's Midnight Runners were unable to make the gig and the Specials went on last bringing the evening to a roaring climax. The Specials were joined at concert's end by Madness for a encore of the Pioneer's ska classic "Long Shot Kick De Bucket." Madness will have a single out next month of "The Prince" on the Specials' Two Tone label. The Specials are the real surprise. Only three months ago there was no Selecter, just Neol Davies and an idea. He latched onto an all-black Coventry-based reggae band called Hard Top 22. Neol took a back seat and vocalist Pauline came to the front. The Selecter are planning an album for October, and have their debut single out at almost any time.

THE SLITS are going to have to find another drummer. One time Big In Japan drummer Budgie, who joined the Slits last October, has left the group. It's not said why, but it's certainly not because he can't beat the skins off a set of drums. Last chance to hear him as a member of the Slits will be on their album that is set for release next month.

ANGELIC UPSTARTS/BEEZ ....High Wycombe, Town Hall	IAN DURY & BLOCKHEADS/
B-52's....................................Liverpool, Eric's	ROOT BOY SLIM &
SPECIALS/MADNESS/	SEX CHANGE BAND ....Manchester, Apollo
SELECTER..............................London, Electric Ballroom	ADAM & THE ANTS/PROTEX ....Manchester, The Factory

22nd - Sunday..

ECHO & THE BUNNYMEN are featured in the *NME* on the heels of their eighth gig. It took place in Liverpool at the Everyman Theatre and staff writer Paul Du Noyer was intrigued at the band's lack of a drummer. Lead singer Ian McCulloch "a pair of huge eyes and an elaborate quiff" explained, "Er' that's 'cos we've never found a drummer. They're always either drunk or not reliable enough. There's this thing between us, we do think that, like, we are Bunnymen and another member, a drummer, might not be a Bunnyman." The real Bunnymen are Ian McCulloch, Will Sergeant and Les Pattinson.

B-52's ....Birmingham, Digbeth Civic Hall	SPIZZ ENERGI ....London, Nashville
PRIVATE VICES/SELECTER/	IAN DURY & THE BLOCKHEADS/
TEMPORARY TITLE...................London, Acklam Hall	ROOT BOY SLIM &
SECRET AFFAIR/SQUIRE ....London, Marquee	SEX CHANGE BAND ....Manchester, Apollo

23rd - Monday..

THE TOM ROBINSON BAND are splitting up! It was quite a shock, but the TRB have officially announced that they are going their separate ways only four months after the release of their last LP "TRB2." Lead singer Tom Robinson had been feeling that the magic had gone out of the group since founder member Mark Ambler on keyboards and Dolphin Taylor on drums had left the group. Tom is working on writing some new material and planning a solo project. The others are taking in some studio work as they can. Danny Kustow, guitarist for the group hasn't wasted a minute getting his new group together. He's calling it the "Jimmy Norton Explosion." As a bit of a parting shot, EMI has released a single with two of the last Tom Robinson Band songs that remain unissued. The "A" side is "Never Gonna Fall In Love (Again)" which is credited as Tom Robinson with the Voice Squad. The overall sound is almost a dance club single with a synth backing, marking a totally new sound for Tom. It's flipped with "Getting Tighter" a normal sort of TRB song.

B-52's/FASHION ....Birmingham, Digbeth Civic Hall	BRAINIAC 5 ....London, Rock Garden
PRETENDERS/INTERVIEW..........Edinburgh, Tiffany's	MERTON PARKAS/MOD-ETTES/
SMALL HOURS/VAPORS.............London, Bridge House	FIXATIONS/TEENBEATS.............London, Global Village, (Vespa's)
SECRET AFFAIR/	SQUIRE ....London, Windsor Castle
MERTON PARKAS/THE MODS ......London, Nashville	UK SUBS ....Sheffield, Penthouse

JULY 1979

24th - Tuesday.......................................

PATTI SMITH's newest single is perhaps her strongest yet. The original song "Dancing Barefoot" is taken from the LP "Wave." The non-LP flipside is a cover of Manfred Man's "5-4-3-2-1" recorded live in New York last May.

THE POLECATS Ever since Robert Gordon became the cool new thing in New York, it was inevitable that rockabilly fever would eventually spread across the Atlantic where teds have kept the '50s alive since the '60s. The latest English proponents are London-based revivalists The Polecats, who have their debut single out this week on the new Nervous Records label. They started out under the name Cult Heroes, soon changed their name to the Polecats and are now Phil Bloomberg, Chris Hawkes, Martin (Boz) Boorer and Tim Worman. Tracks are "Rockabilly Guy" and "Chicken Shack." Both songs are Polecats' originals. Secret messages scratched in the wax are "Chester's Been Fed" and "Mill Hillbillies," the latter probably referring to the neighborhood near South Acton. The Polecats have a long wait for fame, and it's fleeting at that. In the summer of '81 they'll briefly make it into the UK Top 40 three times with covers of songs like "Jeepster," and "John I'm Only Dancing."

PROTEX/THE URGE/		BRAINIAC 5	London, Music Machine
DIGITAL DANCE	London, Albany Empire	MODS/LITTLE ROOSTERS	London, Shades
PURPLE HEARTS/SQUIRE	London, Marquee	B-52's	Sheffield, Limit Club

25th - Wednesday.......................................

SHAM 69 have another new farewell single out this week. It's the sing-along "Hersham Boys" coupled with live songs from their London Roundhouse concert in February of last year. On the 12" version you get four extra tracks including "I Don't Wanna," "Tell Us The Truth," "Rip Off" and "I'm A Man, I'm A Boy."

THE RADIATORS' debut album is in the shops this week. It's titled "Ghostown" and includes their previous single "Let's Talk About The Weather," as well as "Johnny Jukebox," "Kitty Ricketts," "Million Dollar Hero," "Confidential" and five others. All songs are originals and were recorded earlier this year at Good Earth Studios with veteran producer Tony Visconti. The Radiators are Phillip Chevron on lead vocals and lead guitar, Jimmy Crashe on drums, Mark Megaray on bass and Peter Holiday on rhythm guitar. Messages in the inner groove wax include (Boredom In Brackets) and {Paralysis in Parentheses}.

MODS/THE JUMP	London, Dublin Castle	SMALL HOURS	London, Upstairs At Ronnie Scott's
PIRANHAS	London, Moonlight Club		

26th - Thursday.......................................

STUDIO SWEETHEARTS When Slaughter & The Dogs split up late last year, Mike Rossi on guitar and Howard Bates on bass teamed up with one ex-Eater and one ex-Nosebleed as the Studio Sweethearts. They cut a single, "I Believe," and then got stuck. Nobody wanted to book the band. They did however, always ask about Slaughter & The Dogs. In order to meet market demand, Mike Rossi and Howard Bates have rejoined Wayne Barrett and Muffet Grantham as the new Slaughter & The Dogs. Rossi told the *NME* that, "…there were no suitable gigs for a new band, though plenty of venues were prepared to book Slaughter. We couldn't continue to subsidize Sweethearts. It was a matter of survival." The new "Slaughter" have already been signed by DJM Records and make their debut in Nottingham on Saturday.

ANGELIC UPSTARTS have their debut album out this week. "Teenage Warning" features their debut single "A" side of 'Liddle Towers," as well as both sides of their prior 45 "I'm An Upstart" and "Leave Me Alone." New tracks include "Student Power," "We Are The People" and "Youth Leader." A single has been taken from the album of "Teenage Warning" and "Young Ones." The songs were produced by Jimmy Pursey. Paul Morley reviewing it for the *NME* described it as, "…cheaply packaged, excruciatingly but proudly designed, it contains five pulp gems that place it many rungs higher than the Eater or Dogs bursts, and only just below the Damned debut. The ultimate masters of the genre, Clash and Sex Pistols are credited as 'inspiration,' along with the Northubria Police." The Angelic Upstarts are Mensi (aka Tommy Mensforth) on lead vocals, Mond on lead guitar, Ronnie Wooden on bass and Decca on drums, and come from Newcastle.

ADAM & THE ANTS/PROTEX	Liverpool, Eric's	PIRANHAS	London, Hope & Anchor
SAD AMONG STRANGERS/		VAPORS	London, Duke Of Lancaster
RED TAPE/EL SEVEN/		CROOKS/SMALL HOURS	London, Windsor Castle
CUBAN HEELS	London, Albany Empire	SIMPLE MINDS	Sheffield, Limit Club

LIVE TONIGHT!

27th - Friday.......................................

THE SEX PISTOLS' vault is plundered again! Virgin calls this one "Some Product: Carri On." The LP is a cobbled together collection of interviews, the infamous Bill Grundy interview, radio adverts for their records, and even a bit from the Sex Pistols penultimate day together recorded off the radio in California. The LP cover has no end of phoney Sex Pistols products in the photo. There's "Fatty Jones" chocolates, a "Rotten Bar," "Sex Pistols Pop Corn," a "Vicious Burger" and even some "Gob Ale." Capitalizing on Sid, there's even a "Sid Action Doll" in a little coffin. How tasteful!

X-DREAMYSTS	Belfast, Harp Bar	BARRACUDAS	London, Acklam Hall
SPECIALS	Birmingham, Barbarella's	PIRANHAS	London, Hope & Anchor
SIMPLE MINDS	Liverpool, Eric's	WRITZ/VAPORS	London, Music Machine
TEENBEATS/LESS ELITE/		CRASS/POISON GIRLS/	
SQUIRE	London, Moonlight Club	PILGRIM	London, Colombo St. Comm. Ctr.

JULY 1979

28th - Saturday...

SHAM 69 "We're not playing anymore and we really mean it this time." That's probably what Jimmy Pursey and Sham 69 were thinking when they agreed to do one more concert. The on again/off again nature of this band has been driving their fans nuts. Tonight's farewell at the London Rainbow Theatre should not be confused with the first "farewell concert" on January 31st at Friar's in Aylesbury, or the second "farewell concert" on June 29th at the Glasgow Apollo.

It was no surprise that the concert was a fiasco. The skinheads who have claimed this band as their own, (even though Jimmy Pursey denies them), were there in force. The concert began with "I Don't Wanna," followed by hard, driving, punked out versions of "What Have We Got," "Red London" and "That's Life." By the time they began "Angels With Dirty Faces," trouble erupted in the audience. The band was forced offstage as the crowd surged on it and the curtain was hastily brought down. The crowd is coaxed offstage and the band comes out again to start "Angels With Dirty Faces" leading into the rousing "Borstal Breakout." Midway through the song a skinhead tried to re-take the stage and a fight erupted again in the seething audience. Jimmy stops the show sending his microphone to the floor. He heaves the bass drum after that, shouts something about having enough and storms offstage. The concert is finished, a shambles after only twenty minutes. Sham 69 is over.

The evening started calmly enough. Beforehand, Jimmy was on BBC-1 TV, as a guest record rater on *Juke Box Jury*. Looking down the road, Jimmy Pursey plans to continue working with ex-Pistols Steve Jones and Paul Cook, probably under the name "Sex Pistols." There's new songs already written like "Money," and "Cold Blue In The Night," which were originally penned for inclusion in the soundtrack to Quadrophenia. A ten minute version of "Borstal Breakout" has been cut, as well as a driving version of the Beatles' chestnut "Day Tripper."

LIVE TONIGHT!

CRAMPS	Birmingham, Barbarella's	SHAM 69 (farewell show)	
STIFF LITTLE FINGERS	Liverpool, Eric's	LOW NUMBERS/	
DELTA 5/GANG OF FOUR/		LITTLE ROOSTERS	London, Rainbow
SPOILSPORT	London, Electric Ballroom	SQUIRE	London, The Wellington
JOLT/PRETTY BRITISH	London, Fulham Greyhound	B-52's	Manchester, The Factory
LITTLE ROOSTERS	London, Hope & Anchor	FALL/JOY DIVISION/	
BRIAN JAMES'S BRAINS/		HAMPSTERS/THE WALL	
QT's	London, Nashville	GORDON THE MORON/	
DISTRIBUTORS/		DISTRACTIONS/LUDUS	
MEDIUM MEDIUM	London, Windsor Castle	FRANTIC ELEVATORS	Manchester, Mayflower
BURN/LO/BAD MANNERS	London, Bethnal Green Weavers Field		

29th - Sunday...

THE (LEYTON) BUZZARDS have dropped "Leyton" from their name. Knowing that the average American consumer would not understand the significance of a name like Leyton Buzzards, they've elected to just shorten it. Their label is about to start a massive push behind the band as they increase their marketing to include America. Their new single is "We Make A Noise," b/w "Disco Romeo." The sleeve was designed by Terry Gilliam of Monty Python fame and features a colorful pic of a man whose head is exploding.

IAN DURY & THE BLOCKHEADS/ ...		PRETENDERS/MADNESS/	
ROOT BOY SLIM &		INTERVIEW	London, Lyceum
SEX CHANGE BAND	Edinburgh, Odeon	FALL	London, Marquee
YACHTS/RUTS/MISTY/		SQUIRE	London, Two Brewers
THE POP GROUP	London, Gladstone Park	ANY TROUBLE	Manchester, Commercial Hotel
PIRANHAS	London, Nashville		

30th - Monday...

MIDGE URE, former member of the Rich Kids, is currently on tour with Thin Lizzy while denying rumors he's joining the band full time. He's just filling in the hole left from the departure of Gary Moore. Midge is currently on tour in the US and will continue with Thin Lizzy through dates in Japan and Australia. His real future was revealed in a phone call to the *NME* where he revealed that, "It's really not my sort of music, in fact I'm joining Ultravox on November 1st. I was due to join them as guitarist and singer in September but they've agreed to wait until I've finished my dates with Lizzy." Ultravox are currently looking for a new label, after being dropped from Island Records after three disappointingly slow selling albums.

THE OUT	Birmingham, Railway Hotel	THE NAME/TEENBEATS/	
IAN DURY & THE BLOCKHEADS/		SQUIRE/SPEEDBALL/	
ROOT BOY SLIM &		SMALL HOURS	London, Global Village (Vespa's)
SEX CHANGE BAND	Edinburgh, Odeon	CHORDS/DONKEYS	London, Marquee
SECRET AFFAIR/SQUIRE	London, Bridge House	SIMPLE MINDS/PICTURES	London, Music Machine
BAD MANNERS/BURN/LO	London, Dingwalls	SAD AMONG STRANGERS	London, Pegasus
REACTION/THE SHAPES	London, Dublin Castle (Coal Bin)	CARPETTES	London, Rock Garden

31st - Tuesday...

WAYNE/JAYNE COUNTY has been kicked out of his own band! Or at least, that's what his band is saying. When Wayne began undergoing his sex change operation, he understandably became wrapped up in his new identity and arranging his transformation. The rest of the band tired of waiting for him to contribute anything to the band. Trying to set the record straight about the split, Wayne/Jayne

JULY 1979

County wrote an open letter to *Sounds*. In the text he/she claims he/she intended to go solo for a long time and that the rest of the band were just looking for a little publicity. Wayne/Jayne goes on to claim that, "Safari Records told me that they would pay for my entire sex-change operation. Then only half way held up to the promise. They would not give me the rest of the money to finish my operations until I got commercial enough to sell more records…I have been stabbed in the back and treated like an animal, with no regards to my feelings or artistic opinions." Wayne/Jayne has returned to New York to find another way to pull together the money needed for the final cosmetic surgery he/she wants. The Electric Chairs are moving ahead, recording a new album with Dave Cunningham (Flying Lizards) producing.

SQUIRE/THE V.I.P's ....London, Hope & Anchor	BACK TO ZERO/LEPERS..............London, Shades
MERTON PARKAS/	MEDIUM MEDIM ....London, Rock Garden
SMALL HOURS ....London, Marquee	MADNESS/THE EFFECT ....London, The Number 1 Club
UK SUBS ....London, Notre Dame Hall	ANY TROUBLE.........................Manchester, Birch Hotel

August 1st – Wednesday.....................

MADNESS are the North London band that have appeared occasionally with the Specials and the Selecter. They're considered part of the growing ska/bluebeat boom that sweeping England. Their debut single is a tribute to one of ska's first stars back in the early 60s, Prince Buster. The song, "The Prince" is flipped with "Madness," a theme song of sorts. The record is released today on the Special's Two Tone Record label. A secret message scratched in the vinyl reads, "Chas says that nutty sound." The song will reach #16 in the UK, and while that's a great start, it's only a modest precursor to a string of over a dozen top ten hits over the next four years for Madness.

THE COCKNEY REJECTS originally tossed their demo into the box with the fifteen or so other tapes that arrive at Small Wonder's offices every day. But something was different. Something exciting. The Cockney Rejects were offered the usual, limited contract with Small Wonder (1 record), and here's the result. The single is "Flares and Slippers" b/w "Police Car" and "I Wanna Be A Star." They've pressed up an optimistic 5,000 copies.

NO CITY FUN Everything connected with Factory Records gets a number. Not only records but a short film, done by an amateur film maker about some Factory bands. The eight-minute, 16mm film is called *No City Fun* and is composed of blurred snatches of shots from cars and busses, shots from tops of deteriorating buildings, all woven together with Joy Division's music. The film has been given Factory inventory number #9.

LIVE TONIGHT!

LAMBRETTAS ....London, Dublin Castle	MERTON PARKAS/SQUIRE/
PHOTOS ....London, Hope & Anchor	LAMBRETTAS ....London, Music Machine
UNDERTONES/DONKEYS ....London, Marquee	

3rd – Friday..

DEVO have a single from their newest album "Duty Now For The Future" in the shops this weekend. The 1966 Johnny Rivers' cover "Secret Agent Man" is flipped with the non-LP "Soo-Bawlz." Early copies come in a suitably futuristic picture sleeve.

TOYAH had her first record out on Safari only a few weeks ago, and already she's followed it up with a 7" mini album. There are six tracks on this extended single totalling up to more than twenty minutes of music, fully half an album. To make it the true self-described "Safari alternative play record," it spins at 33 1/3 RPM and comes in a full color sleeve. It's titled "Sheep Farming In Barnet." Toyah has more than a recording career to mind. She's also just landed a part in the BBC TV play *Shoestring* which will air later in the year.

JIMMY NORTON EXPLOSION ....London, Music Machine	UNDERTONES/DONKEYS ....London, Marquee
THROBBING GRISTLE/	PIRANHAS ....Manchester, West Indian Center
CABARET VOLTAIRE/	SPECIALS ....Sheffield, Limit Club
REMA REMA ....London, Prince Of Wales	

5th – Sunday..

STIFF LITTLE FINGERS After being turned down by several major labels a year ago, Stiff Little Fingers have become the hottest new rock band available. Offers from Virgin, Pye, and CBS have been offered and refused. Chrysalis Records was the only one among them that offered Stiff Little Fingers the total control that they demanded. The group has had three major indie single hits and a brisk selling album. Their "Rigid Digits Productions" company has been taken under the Chrysalis banner and S.L.F. will begin recording immediately. Could it be they got the attention because their LP "Highly Inflammable" has topped the 80,000 sales mark? It's a rare feat among bands of this ilk. While most of London's attention is turned to Ian Dury's concerts down at the Hammersmith Odeon, Stiff Little Fingers are playing at the Hammersmith Palais. For £3, you could see three bands. S.L.F. plus Starjets and The Vapors. The strains of "Land Of Hope And Glory" filled the theatre as the band came onstage. The immediately launched into "Suspect Device," followed by "Alternative Ulster." A small contingent of skinheads down front started "sieg heiling" bringing lead singer Jake Burns to say, "They're not going to ruin this gig like they did Sham 69!" The band played their full set, including "Closed Groove," "Breakout," "State Of Emergency," "Gotta Getaway," "Law And Order" and Bob Marley's "Johnny Was." Some new number also surfaced, "Wait And See," and "Strong Boys." During their encore of pop group Mud's "Tiger Feet," they had to stop to help a member of the audience being terrorized by the skinheads who had gathered down front. The band, disgusted with the rabble, tossed instruments aside and left the stage. Robbi Millar, writing for *Sounds*, "SLF are very, very, clever and totally committed. They're a four man crusade to right wrongs. And they state their case through their music. But I wonder how many of the frantically leaping bondaged adolescents were really there to listen to the words."

AUGUST 1979

SWELL MAPS' member Nikki Mattress confessed to the *NME* this week, "It took me two years to learn two chords. I can't ever see ourselves becoming polished, not perfect and all that. We hardly ever rehearse- about once every six months. We do about half an hour, then we get bored, have a cup of coffee and watch TV."

IAN DURY & THE BLOCKHEADS/	PIRANHAS ....Birmingham, Barbarellas
ROOT BOY SLIM &	
SEX CHANGE BAND..................London, Hammersmith Odeon	

7th - Tuesday.....................................

X-RAY SPEX have called it quits. It all happened about the time that X-Ray Spex were playing in Paris and lead vocalist Poly Styrene began wanting to play more and more acoustic slow numbers. The remaining four members wanted to find someone to replace Poly. They tried a few replacement singers out in auditions but nothing was working. So here they are headed their separate directions, with different groups in the works. Guitarist Jak Airport and drummer B.P. Hurding have started up a new group they're calling Classic Nouveaux. They've recruited a vocalist (Sal Solo) and a bass player (Mik Sweeney) from a band called the News. They've already played a low profile gig at Bedford to gage the reaction and were encouraged. It's still uncertain what will happen to Spex bassist Paul Dean. Sax player Rudi Thompson has been thinking of joining the Members. He was a guest on their last LP "Chelsea Nightclub."

IAN DURY & THE BLOCKHEADS/	THE CRASS ....London, The Pied Bull
ROOT BOY SLIM &	
SEX CHANGE BAND..................London, Hammersmith Odeon	

10th - Friday.....................................

STRANGLERS have let almost exactly a year slip by since their last single "Walk On By" was released. In that time, we've seen Hugh Cornwell and J.J. Burnel take on solo careers to varying degrees of success. The new Stranglers single is "Dutchess" b/w "Fools Rush Out." It's taken from their forthcoming LP "The Raven," due out next month. The Stranglers will be part of the Who's concert at London's Wembley Arena, along with AC/DC and Nils Lofgren. After that they'll be hitting the road for an extensive UK tour.

MARCH OF THE MODS isn't a new horror movie, it's an ambitious tour gathering together three of the hottest new mod bands on a country wide tour. Secret Affair, recently signed up to Arista Records, will headline the bill that also includes the Purple Hearts and Back To Zero. The seventeen date tour begins tonight at the Scarborough Penthouse and will conclude the first of September in Liverpool. The Purple Hearts and Back To Zero should have their debut singles out by that time. Originally the Roosters were to be on the bill but they were taken off at the last minute in favor of Back To Zero. It's more that the usual disappointment because the members of the Roosters had just all quit their day jobs and a month's worth of bookings so they could go on the tour. Needless to say, they're a little peeved.

THE DANGEROUS GIRLS are not girls at all. It's all a name. They are in fact Michael Robert Cooper on vocals, Rob Peters on drums, Rob Rampton on bass and Chris Ames on guitar. Their debut single is "Dangerous Girls" b/w "I Don't Want To Eat (With The Family.)" The single is on their own Happy Face Records label, based in their home turf of Worcester, just south of Birmingham.

ORCHESTRAL MANOEUVRES ....Liverpool, Eric's	OUTSIDERS/SCISSORS FIT ....London, Norbiton Grove Tavern
IAN DURY & THE BLOCKHEADS/	SLAUGHTER & THE DOGS/
ROOT BOY SLIM &	VICTIM................................Manchester, The Factory
SEX CHANGE BAND ....London, Hammersmith Odeon	SPECIALS/PRIVATE SECTOR........Manchester, Mayflower
SORE THROAT/RIFF RAFF...........London, Nashville	

LIVE TONIGHT!

11th - Saturday.....................................

THE BUZZCOCKS' third album is out this weekend in British shops. It's called "A Different Kind Of Tension" and is 100% new material. Among the dozen songs are "You Say You Don't Love Me," "I Believe," "Mad Mad Judy," "Hollow Inside" and "Radio Nine." The Buzzcocks will be showing off this new material live in a free concert in Hyde Park next Saturday.

ORCHESTRAL MANOEUVRES IN THE DARK are in the midst of arranging the licensing of their indie single "Electricity" to a larger, more profitable label. Lead singer Andy McCluskey is looking forward to finally quitting his day job as an executive officer in the Customs and Excise department. He told *Sounds* magazine that, "…at the moment we're penniless. We're licensing "Electricity" so we can buy two more synthesizers. Because half of the instruments we've got are on their last legs, and half of them are dead cheap anyway." Although "Electricity" doesn't turn into a big hit, it does set the stage for a string of top ten UK hits like "Enola Gay," "Souvenir," "Joan Of Arc" and "Maid Of Orleans" begining next fall.

TOYAH.........................Birmingham, Barbarella's	YOUNG ONES.........................London, Bridge House
JOY DIVISION/SWELL MAPS........Liverpool, Eric's	TEENBEATS ....London, Fulham Greyhound
ESSENTIAL LOGIC/	PHYSICALS ....London, Hope & Anchor
PRAG VEC/	PIRANHAS ....London, Marquee
MONOCHROME SET ....London, Vespa's	RUTS ....London, Nashville

AUGUST 1979

IAN DURY & THE BLOCKHEADS/	
ROOT BOY SLIM &	
SEX CHANGE BAND ....London, Hammersmith Odeon	

| SQUIRE ....London, The Wellington |
| SLAUGHTER & THE DOGS...........Manchester, The Factory |

13th - Monday.......................................

THE REZILLOS are the subject of an amusing miss-pressing of their debut single. Sensible Records, who pressed up their debut single "I Can't Stand My Baby" back in August of '77, recently re-issued the single. Somehow, instead of the flipside being "I Wanna Be Your Man" a rare early demo of the Rezillos playing "(My Baby Does) Good Sculptures" appears instead. The pressing in error is limited to about 4,000 copies and looks just like the non-error version. The labels read one thing, the record plays another. The easy way to tell is that the secret message scratched near the label should read "Come Back John Lennon." On the mistaken copies it reads "De-Sire-able Product" instead.

THE FALL have just released their fourth single, "Rowche Rumble," a song about "valium and speed." It's flipped with "In My Area." As all other releases, it's on Step Forward Records and comes in a deluxe black and white picture sleeve. The Fall, an everchanging and mercurial bunch, are at this time Mark E Smith on vocals, Marc Riley on guitar, Craig Scanlan on guitar, Steve Hanley on bass, Yvonne Paylett on piano and Mike Leigh on drums. This could be one of their most stable lineups, holding steady for almost six months now.

STA-PREST ....London, Bridge House	
MODS/ LAMBRETTAS/	
6 MORE PROPHETS/	
THE SPIDERS.........................London, Vespa's	

| RUTS.....................................London, Marquee |
| JOY DIVISION/ |
| ORCHESTRAL MANOEUVRES/ |
| A CERTAIN RATIO....................London, Nashville |

14th - Tuesday.......................................

NICK LOWE gets lucky the second time around. His newest single is a re-recorded version of a song from over a year ago. He's taken "Cruel To Be Kind," which was released as a single in May of '78, slowed the tempo, gotten rid of the carnival organ and added tambourine and strummy acoustic guitars. The single is taken from Nick's LP "Labour Of Lust" released ten weeks ago. Revamped, the song climbs to #12 in the UK and is offered up paired with a new track called "Endless Gray Ribbon."

MADNESS have been invited to record a session for the BBC Radio 1 John Peel show. The excitement has totally built on their live shows. The session tonight includes "Bed And Breakfast Man," "Land Of Hope & Glory," "Stepping Into Line" and a version of their debut single "The Prince." The actual recording won't be on the Peel program until the 27th.

JAGS' vocalist John Alder told *Sounds* magazine about his disappointment with some of the bands around today, "Man, we saw the UK Subs play the other week, and their singer, who must have been about thirty-five said, "Vis is a song about be-in on ver dole." And it was pathetic. The kids didn't want to cheer that. I can't believe they did. We've been on the dole, and it's not something to write songs about.

SCARS/FLOWERS.....................Edinburgh, Aquarius	
IAN DURY & THE BLOCKHEADS/	
ROOT BOY SLIM &	
SEX CHANGE BAND...................London, Ilford Odeon	

| PIRANHAS ....London, Dingwalls |
| RUTS.....................................London, Marquee |
| THE WALL/SUSPECTS ....London, Number 1 Club |

15th - Wednesday.......................................

THE BUZZCOCKS' debut EP, one of the first indie punk records ever, has been steadily increasing in value as the years roll by. Originally issued in January of '77, it sold through 16,000 copies before going out of print. Now, with increased demand for this artifact, and increasing interest in the Buzzcocks' former vocalist Howard Devoto, the single is being re-issued. It will be in an almost identical sleeve with the exception of a Devoto vocal credit on the front of the sleeve. Also, the labels on the re-issue will be paper, not the pressed and raised plastic of the original.

LORI & THE CHAMELEONS are a studio band, not a touring/gigging band. They want to remain a mystery but here's the secret. Lori is seventeen-year-old Lori Lartey, a student at Liverpool Art College. She's backed by Bill Drummond (ex-Big In Japan) and David Balfe (Teardrop Explodes). The single is a cute, vaguely oriental love song called "Touch" b/w "Love On The Ganges." The "group" are from the Allerton district of Liverpool and haven't played a single gig yet, and perhaps never will considering the contrived nature of the "band."

ECHO & THE BUNNYMEN are becoming one of the more talked-about new bands to emerge from Liverpool in the last five years. Their debut single "Pictures On My Wall" has sold out it's initial pressing and is being played regularly on John Peel's BBC program. He's invited the band to record special sessions for the show tonight and they're in the studio. They're re-recording a version of "Read It In Books," (the flipside of their single) as well as three new songs, "I Bagsy Yours," "Villiers Terrace" and "Stars Are Stars."

GOOD MISSIONARIES/	
BLANK SPACE/DICK HELEY/	
ZOUNDS/SELLOUTS/	
GOOD FOR NUFFINKS................London, Acklam Hall	
TEENBEATS ....London, Dublin Castle	
MADNESS/RUDE BOYS ....London, Rock Garden	

| IAN DURY & THE BLOCKHEADS/ |
| ROOT BOY SLIM & |
| SEX CHANGE BAND...................London, Ilford Odeon |
| ROBERT & REMOULDS/ |
| CHALET................................London, Windsor Castle |

16th - Thursday.......................................

SECRET AFFAIR have just been signed to Arista Records. The debut single will be distributed by Arista, but will be under their own label

AUGUST 1979

imprint, the I Spy Records label. It's titled "Time For Action" b/w "Soho Strut." Secret Affair are Ian Page (aka Ian Paine) on lead vocals and trumpet, David Cairns on guitars and backing vocals, both of whom were in The New Hearts until last October. The rest of Secret Affair is Dennis Smith (ex-Advertising) on bass and Seb Shelton on drums. They produced the single themselves. The first song that Secret Affair wrote together was a mod anthem called "Glory Boys." It's dedicated to the East End mods that make up the band's] sturdy following.

SECRET AFFAIR/	SPIZZ ENERGI/
BACK TO ZERO/	LAST WORDS..........................London, Nashville
PURPLE HEARTS ....Birmingham, Barbarella's	TOYAH.................................Sheffield, Limit Club

17th - Friday...

ANGELIC UPSTARTS/COCKNEY REJECTS Referring to the earlier trouble with skinheads at concerts, Glenn Gibson headlined his review of tonight's Angelic Upstarts gig with "I wonder if I can type a review with broken fingers?" He needn't worry, the concert was rough but didn't get shut down by authorities. The Cockney Rejects started the evening off, "…screaming abuse into a thrashing tangle of fists, tattoos, yells and mis-shapen shaved skulls." Glenn observes that, "The (Cockney) Rejects are no worse than most, within their limited ambitions, but there's nothing inventive in the music, no imagination in the clothes and more. It all seems very drab now, a very narrow view amongst so many subjective definitions of punk." The Low Numbers are in the middle slot, providing the crowd with Jam-style mod-rock. A fight erupts in the middle of the hall and is quickly extinguished. On come the Angelic Upstarts. "At the front it's like the Hong Kong rush hour during an attack of flying scorpions. Mensi dances some kind of deranged, dry land variation of the Australian crawl; roars bent forward in classical Pursey-pose, eyes burning as if in blood-lust frenzy; or hangs from the microphone gathering strength for further excesses." At one point the fighting in the crowd reaches proportions that cause Mensi to throw his mic stand across the stage and storm off, but that would only make things worse. He returns and finishes the set, worried that the skinheads that pushed Sham 69 into oblivion might have sights set on them, ready to smother the thing they love with mindless aggression that repulses the object of affection.

XTC's new album is "Drums & Wires," which is probably a more fitting title that it's working name "Boom-Dada-Boom." It's out today on Virgin Records. It features "Roads Girdle The Globe," "Ten Feet Tall" and "When You're Near Me I Have Difficulty," plus eight others. A single of "Making Plans For Nigel" is cut from the album. It is paired up with two non-LP tracks, "Bushman President" and "Pulsing Pulsing." First copies come in an elaborate sleeve that folds out into a 20" x 20" gameboard based roughly on "chutes and ladders." One player is Nigel's parents, the other is Nigel. Whoever reached square 70 first wins. There is a cardboard cutout pair of markers and a spinner included.

PENETRATION's newest single is out this weekend. It's Come Into The Open" b/w "Lifeline." The single is their fifth for Virgin and is from their much-anticipated second album is scheduled for next month. Both tracks were produced by Steve Lillywhite.

RUTS/	TOYAH/AGONY COLUMN ....London, Music Machine
LINTON KWESKI JOHNSON ....Edinburgh, Clouds	SECRET AFFAIR/
ANGELIC UPSTARTS/	BACK TO ZERO/
LOW NUMBERS/	PURPLE HEARTS ....Manchester, The Factory
COCKNEY REJECTS...................London, Electric Ballroom	SQUIRE.................................London, Duke Of Wellington

18th - Saturday...

THE BUZZCOCKS' proposed free concert in Hyde Park today has been cancelled at the last minute. Their record company was unable to come up with the support to stage the concert. This is the second time that the Buzzcocks have been thwarted in a proposed free Hyde Park concert.

THE RAMONES' newest single is a sample from their forthcoming film. It's "Rock & Roll High School" flipped with two oldies "Rockaway Beach" and "Sheena Is A Punk Rocker."

THE TEENBEATS are part of the growing Mod movement, all parkas, Vespa scooters and short hair. Their debut single is out this weekend on Safari Records. It's a cover of the Trogg's '60s song "I Can't Control Myself," flipped with "I'll Never Win."

THE BUZZARDS/THE BEEZ	WHO/THE STRANGLERS/
T.V. SURF BOYS/	AC-DC/NILS LOFGREN ....London, Wembley Arena
ATOMIC ROCKERS...................High Wycombe, Town Hall	RIFF RAFF ....London, Windsor Castle
ADVERTS/LOCAL OPERATOR ....Liverpool, Eric's	SELECTER.............................Manchester, The Factory
UK SUBS/THE PACK/	DISTRACTIONS/
LAST WORDS..........................London Electric Ballroom	ARMED FORCE/HAMSTER...........Manchester, The Funhouse
TEENBEATS/	YACHTS ....London, Nashville
LITTLE ROOSTERS/	JAGS ....London, Marquee
STA-PREST ....London, Global Village (Vespa's)	

19th - Sunday...

"STREET TO STREET" is a new compilation album on the streets in Liverpool that captures the sound of '79 wonderfully and features a

AUGUST 1979

dozen of examples of Liverpudlian new music. Side one starts off with the instrumental "Match Of The Day" from the sadly defunct Big In Japan. Track two is "Julia's Song" by the Id, an early incarnation of Orchestral Manoeuvres, and a song that they still do from time to time live. Jaqui & Jeanette is the result of a late night "all star" session at Open Eye Studios, bringing together Ian Broudie, drummer Budgie (ex-Slits), Dave Balfe on keyboards, Ambrose (ex-Ded Byrds) on bass, and Steve Lindsey (ex-Deaf School) and Gary Dwyer (of the Teardrop Explodes) on backing vocals. Finishing up the side are Modern Eon, Activity Minimal and Dead Trout.

Side two starts with Tontrix, who've just broken up after recording this song "Clear On Radar." Then the Accelerators, Malchix and Fun. The latter having now mutated into another band called the Victims Of Romance. The Moderates are also in a state of flux, and closing the album are newcomers Echo & The Bunnymen. Their debut single still warm from the presses shows how far the band has come since this demo recording of "Monkeys." All tracks were recorded at Open Eye Studios in Liverpool over the last year.

SQUIRE	London, 101 Club	ADVERTS/THE DIKS/	
CHORDS/VAPORS	London, Marquee	ARTERY/THE NEGATIVES	Sheffield, Top Rank
YACHTS	London, Nashville		

20th - Monday...

FASHION is Birmingham's latest claim to album fame. They were regulars at the Barrel Organ and Barbarella's in Birmingham until they started coming south early this year. Now they've left two singles behind them and are celebrating the release of their debut album "Product Perfect." It's a dozen new songs (with the exception of "Citinite") all originals, produced by Fashion. Titles include "Technofascist," "Hanoi Annoys Me," "Die In The West" and the title track "Product Perfect." The band possessing only one name each: Luke on guitar and vocals, Dik on drums and vocals, and Mulligan on bass and synth.

THE OUT	Birmingham, Railway Hotel	MADNESS	London, Hope & Anchor
MERTON PARKAS/		LOCAL OPERATOR/	
ANOTHER PRETTY FACE	Edinburgh, Tiffany's	COWBOYS INTL./	
JOE JACKSON	Edinburgh, Clouds	FINGERPRINTZ	London, Nashville
SMALL HOURS/THE FACE	London, Bridge House	BUZZARDS/AMBRA/	
TEENBEATS/BEGGAR/		TOUR DeFORCE	London, Walthamstow Central
ROMANTIX	London, Vespa's		

21st - Tuesday...

THE BARRACUDAS are heavily into mid '60s American surf and pop. They have taken their name from a hip mid '60s American car, and their sound isn't far removed from music of that same locale and vintage. Their debut single "I Want My Woody Back" b/w "Subway Surfin'" should have been a clue. The single is on their own Cells Records label with the sides comically labeled "Sell Out One A" and "Sell Out One B." The secret message "Dick Dale is God!" is scratched in the vinyl near the center. Dick Dale was the consummate US surf guitarist. The Barracudas are a multi-national group with Canadian Jeremy Gluck on vocals, bassist David Buckley is from Boston, and English members Nick Turner on drums and Robin Wills on guitar. In this week's *Sounds*, Jeremy describes the Barracudas as, "Surf & Destroy… all the fun of the Stooges and non of the mess, the illusion of danger with the reality of milk toast."

DUBLIN is featured in this weeks *Sounds*. Dave McCullough treks to Dublin to check up on the burgeoning rock scene there. Top of his list to check out is U2. He heard their demo tape earlier this year and had to see them to believe his ears. The band plays tonight at the Baggot Inn. It's the first time that they've had a "new wave" type band in there. He's very impressed with the show. The club is packed. Dave is riveted as he watches the band go through their set. "You follow Bono with your eyes as he counts on his fingers or runs across the stage or spontaneously mimes something that is impenetrable but opposite to the moody, fat rolling sound…And the songs are splendid, inspired impressions of that big sound the band seek, from the Skidsian raunch of "Out Of Control," the analytical power of "Twilight," and "Stories For Boys," or the speedy pop of "Boy Girl." It's just a thought but somebody suggested that if the Boomtown Rats were the John The Baptists of Irish r'n'r, then U2 must be…"

The Virgin Prunes are lauded with the statement that they're "probably closer to the genius of the (true) Sex Pistols than any band in Britain today." Lead singer Gavin Friday claims that he's out to shock the audience. "If they can't stand what we're doing then we tell them to fuck off, we don't want them near us. Sometimes we go transvestite on stage. Sometime we wear suits. We shock." Songs in the band's current set include "Caucasian Walk," "Grey Light" and "Art Fuck."

The Atrix are the first of the Dublin crowd to actually have released a single. The tiny Dublin label Mulligan Records recently released "The Moon Is Puce" b/w "Wendy's In Amsterdam." They're more theatrical than most, hence the name-pun, and are similar in some ways to XTC.

D.C. Nein are doing something almost unknown in Ireland. They're taking matters in their own hands and are trying to put out their own record, on their own label. They're cumulative record collections will reveal discs by the Human League, Kraftwerk and Gang Of Four. Little wonder that their music is so dark and foreboding. They're starting to get some respect in town and have the opening slot for the AC/DC concert in Dublin.

U2/THE BLADES	Dublin, The Baggot Inn	SELECTER	London, Hammersmith Palais
DANGEROUS GIRLS/		MADNESS	London, Hope & Anchor
ANDROIDS OF MU/		BUZZARDS	London, Marquee
VINCE PIE & THE CRUMBS/		VAPORS	London, Moonlight Club
THE Q 12/THE MOB/		LOCAL OPERATOR/	
ASTRONAUTS	London, Acklam Hall	COWBOYS INTL./	
V.I.P's/SQUIRE	London, Fulham Greyhound	FINGERPRINTZ	London, Nashville
		MERTON PARKAS	Sheffield, Limit Club

LIVE TONIGHT!

AUGUST 1979

22nd - Wednesday.....

GARY NUMAN tells a bleak tale of not trusting the outside world, and wanting to remain on the leatherette, behind the wheel, in control, locked in. That's the feel of the new one from Gary Numan. It's "Cars," a new single taken from the forthcoming LP "Pleasure Principle." The 45 is flipped with the non-LP track "Asylum." This new song "Cars" is destined to be Numan's biggest hit worldwide, eventually reaching #9 in the US and becoming his second #1 in England.

MERTON PARKAS/SQUIRE	High Wycombe, Nag's Head	ROBERT & THE REMOULDS	London, Windsor Castle
DRONES	London, Marquee		

23rd - Thursday.....

THE JAM have their eighth single released. The lead track is a Paul Weller song titled "When You're Young," it's flipped with Bruce Foxton's "Smithers-Jones." Early copies come in the usual color picture sleeve.

CLASSIX NOUVEAUX have barely been together three weeks and are making their live debut tonight at the Music Machine. The band is made up from remnants of X-Ray Spex and The News. They will build their identy partially around their rather blitzish sound and partially around Sal Solo's striking bald head. In 1981 they'll find a little success, with their only real hit being "Is It A Dream" in the spring of '82.

MOD'S MAYDAY The tapes from the Mod's Mayday concert on May 7th at the Bridge House have been sifted through, sorted, assembled into an album and released to the mod population. The "first mod album of 1979" features five of the six bands that played at the festival. Each group is given three songs to stretch out in, only the Merton Parkas being left out because of contractual ties to another record company since the tapes were made. The live tracks include "Time For Action," "Let Your Heart Dance" and "I'm Not Free (But I'm Cheap)" from Secret Affair. Squire turns in live versions of "B-A-B-Y Baby Love," "Walking Down Kings Road" and "Live Without Her Love." The Mod's contributions are "Tonights The Night," "Let Me Be The One" "and "Love Only Me." Beggar play "Don't Throw Your Life Away," "Broadway Show" and "All Night." Small Hours tracks are "End Of The Night," "Midnight To Six" and "Hanging In The Balance."

TOYAH	Liverpool, Eric's	CLASSIX NOUVEAUX/	
SCISSORS FIT/DIALS	London, Adam & Eve (opening nite)	OPPOSITION	London, Music Machine
PUNISHMENT OF LUXURY	London, Marquee	THE PACK	London, Forester Hall
JAGS	London, Nashville	SQUIRE	London, White Hart

24th - Friday.....

TALKING HEADS "Fear Of Music" is the title of their new LP. It's the band's third long player and doesn't overly stray from the well worn path the Talking Heads have cut over the last two years. Among the tracks on the LP are "Paper," "Cities," "Memories Can't Wait," "Drugs" "I Zimbra" and the knockout "Life During Wartime." Brian Eno produced the LP and early reviews are using the word "masterpiece" a lot. The Talking Heads are the subject of a intriguing little bootleg. Usually, bootleggers stick to live concert recordings. Inept audience tapes from mics hidden deep in pockets somewhere on the 2,000th row next to the guy who shouts "Rock And Roll" every five minutes. This time, it's a 7" EP of some of the Talking Heads demo sessions from way back in '75. Song uncovered are the ultimate primitive version of "Psycho Killer," followed by "First Week/Last Week... Carefree" and "Artists Only." A bonus track is a crude live recording of their version of the '60s bubble-gum classic "1-2-3 Red Light." To make things more interesting, the picture label features a picture of Tina Weymouth as a high school cheerleader on one side.

MADNESS	Liverpool, Eric's	YACHTS/LOCAL OPERATORS	Manchester, The Factory
BARRACUDAS/BABY PATROL/		FALL/LIGGERS/	
NUMBER 1's/57 MEN/		GLASS ANIMALS	Manchester, The Funhouse
PRIME MOVERS		POLICE/TOURISTS/	
THE PASSENGERS	London, Acklam Hall	THE CURE/	
POISON GIRLS	London, Conway Hall (Holborn)	WILKO JOHNSON &	
CUDDLY TOYS/MOD-ETTES/		THE SOLID SENDERS/	
PRETTY BRITISH	London, Vespa's	DOLL BY DOLL/THE JAGS	
STA-PREST	London, Klook's Kleek	PUNISHMENT OF LUXURY/	
MEMBERS/DECORATORS	London, Nashville	MOTORHEAD	Reading Rock Festival

LIVE TONIGHT!

26th - Sunday.....

SPECIALS = Style. It's in the music, the setting, and the wardrobe. Singer Terry Hall of the Specials told the *NME* this week, "The clothes are almost as important as the music as far as I'm concerned. They are really important to the whole thing. I always class ourselves as being on the edge of the Mod thing. We're not specifically a mod band or a skinhead band. It's more a mixture of both. The rude boy thing is a real mixture and there's also elements of punk in what we do."

THE PSYCHEDELIC FURS are playing tonight at the Nashville. They're still unsigned but are getting more and more attention these days because of their rapidly growing following. Their set tonight is reviewed by Steve May for *Sounds* magazine. It began, "The fleshy moat around the Nashville is a graphic indication of the Psychedelic Furs rapidly growing audience. A multi-hued crowd come to bear witness to perhaps the most uniquely exciting band to emerge during this year. There was a combo playing as the Psychedelic Furs some two years ago down in the depths of the Roxy, although they bear little resemblance to the troupe of today, who solidified in November '78 and have

AUGUST 1979

evolved into quite possibly the most important crooners to surface in these six months past." The Psychedelic Furs set list is a solid one consisting of "Sister Europe," "We Love You," "Fall," "Pulse," "Imitation Of Christ," "Flowers" and a dozen others. Steve concluded, "The Psychedelic Furs are something very special indeed." After nearly endless auditions, have found a permanent drummer. He's Vince Ely, a former member of the Photons. Look for him behind his kit when the Psychedelic Furs open for Toyah and the Only Ones at the Lyceum on the 2nd.

SECRET AFFAIR/	PETER GABRIEL/
BACK TO ZERO/MADNESS	WHITESNAKE/
PURPLE HEARTS ....London, Lyceum	CLIMAX BLUES BAND/
PSYCHEDELIC FURS/	SPEEDOMETERS/
REACTION..............................London, Nashville	AFTER THE FIRE/MEMBERS/
	WILD HORSES/ZANE GRIFF.........Reading Rock Festival

27th - Monday............................

SQUIRE have reportedly recorded their debut single "I Spy" and are readying it for release on their own Twist & Shout Records label. Squire are Tony Meynell on vocals and guitar, Enzo on bass and a new drummer, Kevin Meynell (Tony's brother.) They've been together about a year and are all around twenty-years old. They've has some interest from some labels but still haven't signed up with anyone. They're all keeping their day jobs to be on the safe side. If there's any similarity between Squire and the Jam, Tony says it's because he and the Jam's Paul Weller sat next to him in school. They both come from the same place, geographically and musically.

PURPLE HEARTS' guitarist Simon Stebbing denies the punk tag some people lay on them. In this week's *NME* he said, "If we were a punk band, then the early Who were a punk band, 'cos we play the same harmonies and beat as them. When you talk about punk, you're talking about 4/4 rhythm, fuzzy guitars, simplistic bass, screaming vocals and major chords. We'll we've got complicated chord changes and jangly guitars, and that's not punk!"

BEGGAR/LONG TALL SHORTY .....London, Bridge House	PIRANHAS/THE BATS/
FLOWERS.............................London, Hope & Anchor	BETWEEN PICTURES ....London, Music Machine
SATELLITES ....London, Klook's Kleek	SHAKE ....London, Nashville

28th - Tuesday............................

NIGHTMARES IN WAX are a new Liverpool band that have just signed with Eric's Records. They're fronted by flamboyant Pete Burns and expect to be recording soon. They get a big break opening for the Damned in Manchester tonight at the Factory (Russell Club.) After numbereous changes in personnel, Nightmares In Wax will become Dead Or Alive by May of 1980, and go all the way to #1 in England with "You Spin Me Round," in March of '85.

EDDIE & THE HOT RODS Once top of the heap, Eddie & The Hot Rods are now trying to get back in the game and compete with the bands that have left them in the dust of what's hip and happening. The Hot Rods have been signed to EMI following four months of label shopping after being dropped from Island Records.

COWBOYS INTL. ....London, Dingwalls	SECRET AFFAIR/
DAMNED/	BACK TO ZERO/
NIGHTMARES IN WAX ....Manchester, The Factory	PURPLE HEARTS ....Sheffield, Limit Club

29th - Wednesday............................

THE MEKONS, the Leeds group that distinguished themselves "Never Been In A Riot" and "Where Were You?" last year, have just signed to Virgin Records. They're in the studio preparing two singles for release in the next few months and also plan to have an album out by January.

MODERN ENGLISH are part of the Do It Yourself school of music. They haven't waited to be gobbled up by a record company, they've started their own. The new label, Limp Records, proudly announces the release of their debut single "Drowning Man" and "Silent World." Modern English are Robert Grey on vocals, Gary McDowell on guitar, Steve Walker on keyboards, Mick Conroy on bass, and Dick Brown on drums.

U2 Irish band U2 get one of their first mentions in the music weeklies this week. It's in *Sounds* magazine, under the heading "Sounds Playlist," where various writers list what they're excited about listening to. Dave McCullough has listed "Out Of Control" and "Shadows And Tall Trees" from "Bono's tape of U2." The band has only rarely played outside of Ireland and have no records available to the public.

VAPORS ....London, Klook's Kleek	CHELSEA/THE WIMPS ....London, Marquee

30th - Thursday............................

SIOUXSIE & BANSHEES and THE CURE's concert tonight in Aylesbury is reviewed in the *NME* by Deanne Pearson. It's a warmup gig for their national tour that's to start in less than a week. The impression left with the reviewer was not a positive one. Deanne wrote about the Cure that, "...they came over as a good, heavy rock band with a seriousness and depth to their music that suggests they have the

AUGUST 1979

technical know-how but lack imagination…Theirs is a bare, basic sound, void of excitement or real feeling." Siouxsie and the Banshees can't get the crowd to react, at one point provoking Siouxsie to sarcastically ask, "Why don't you dance? I'm sure one of the bouncers will dance with you." New songs were mixed with the old, and almost nothing was acknowledged. All in all, it was described as a lackluster way to prepare for a major tour.

TOM VERLAINE's solo album after the demise of Television is a quiet record. Elektra is keeping a low profile on this one, as is Tom himself. The LP is simply called "Tom Verlaine," and exhibits touches of blues, frivolous pop, and straight ahead rock. "Souvenir From A Dream," "Kingdom Come," "Last Night," "Mr Bingo" and "Yonki Time." On the touching "Breakin' In My Heart," B 52's guitarist Ricky Wilson provides the driving rhythm behind the track. Tom's also enlisted Fred "Sonic" Smith on bass, Jay Dee Daugherty on drums, while Tom plays guitar, keyboard and sings.

THE UK SUBS' follow up "Stranglehold" with a new single called "Tomorrow's Girls." It's on Gem Records and is available in a limited edition with a picture sleeve and blue vinyl. The single is flipped with two new songs, "Scum Of The Earth" and "Telephone Numbers."

THE SILICON TEENS are not what they seem. Looking at the sleeve notes, you'd be led to believe that they are a quartet of Darrly, Jacki, Paul and Diane. Nothing of the sort! The Silicon Teens are Daniel Miller, end of story, period. Daniel Miller is the synthesizer player who brought us "T.V.O.D." by the Normal in April of '78. His new "group" is more friendly, more commercial, and does lots and lots of covers songs from the '60s. The first offering is a single of Chuck Berry's "Memphis Tennessee," and Chris Montez' "Let's Dance." This release is released today on Daniel's Mute Records as it's third single.

AU PAIRS	Birmingham, Golden Eagle	TEARDROP EXPLODES/	
SUBTERRANEANS/LEOPARDS/		ECHO & THE BUNNYMEN............	London, Nashville
THE RED TAPE	London, Acklam Hall	SHAKE	Sheffield, Limit Club
FIRE EXIT/THE SCARS	London, Adam & Eve		

31st - Friday...

SIOUXSIE & THE BANSHEES have their second LP released by Polydor. It's called "Join Hands" and captures a more organized version of their infamous version of "The Lords Prayer." It was the first song they played in public back in September of 1976 at the 100 Club Punk Festival. The only previously released track on the album is "Playground Twist," everything else is new, including "Icon," "Regal Zone," and "Placebo Effect."

SQUEEZE have their new single "Slap & Tickle" released today. The "A" side is taken from their last album "Cool For Cats" but the flipside "All's Well" is not on any album. Squeeze will be one of the dozen or so bands to play on the "Big Day Out" concert in Edinburgh Scotland tomorrow. Squeeze has just returned from a tour in the US where they were billed with The Tubes. When not on the road, Squeeze are in the studio working on their next album.

THE RUTS' newest single is "Something That I Said" and a song recorded by the BBC for one of their radio sessions, "Give Youth A Chance." It's the band's third release. Their debut album is expected in stores sometime next month.

THE GLAXO BABIES make a noise with their new single. It's "Christine Keeler" and "Nova Bossanova." The group have had a few changes over the last six months, retaining only the group's leader. Rob Chapman remains the chief songwriter and vocalist, but new in the group are Charles Llewelyn on drums, Melancholy Baby on guitar and synth, Wrafter on tenor sax, and Slow Death on bass.

LIVE TONIGHT!

JOY DIVISION/		MADNESS/WORKING BOYS/	
MONOCHROME SET/		VAPORS	London, Nashville
SCRITTI POLITTI/		TEARDROP EXPLODES/	
A CERTAIN RATIO.....................	London, Electric Ballroom	ECHO & THE BUNNYMEN............	Manchester, The Factory
		MERTON PARKAS	Manchester, New Century Halls

September 1st - Saturday............................

INXS make their live debut at the Ocean View Hotel in Toukley, Australia. They had begun as the Farriss Brothers in Sydney, then changed their name to INXS, partly in homage, and partly inspired by XTC. INXS won't have any impact outside of Australia for over six years, when their third album "Shabooh Shoobah" is released in the UK and America. Even then, fame on a grand scale won't touch INXS until 1988.

THE PLASMATICS are the subject of a lot of talk in New York. They're said to be so outrageous, but few people have actually had the chance to see them. They're not the sort of band that's likely to get on *Rock Goes To College* or *The Old Grey Whistle Test*. In fact, they make the Sex Pistols look positively tame. They include a mohawk haircut guy in a nurse's uniform, an oriental bassist wearing shock treatment headgear, and a lead singer who's toplessness is only hidden behind a pair of two inch strips of electricians tape. The group has pyrotechnics onstage and even chainsaw a guitar in half during the show. This act makes total sense, when you consider how many people are enthralled with the movie *Rocky Horror Picture Show*. The band has one single, "Butcher Baby," to their credit and are regulars in the underground clubs in New York. Jim Farber, writing for *Sounds*, wasn't impressed with their stage show. "Lead singer/ex-porn star/current weight lifter Wendy Orleans Williams (W.O.W. for short) spends most of the Plasmatics' show fondling her family size breasts, scratching her sweaty snatch and eating the drum kit, among other playful events. For people who like doo-doo and pee-pee jokes, this is a hot night on the town."

THE DISTRACTIONS don't conform to the sonic guidelines set down by Joy Division, Buzzcocks and The Nosebleeds. A second release for the Distractions catches the band growing fast in the field of pop song writing. The new 45 is "Time Goes By So Slow," and "Pillow Fight." It's their first for Tony Wilson's Factory Records and wins this weeks "NME Disk To Risk" award.

SPIZZ ENERGI	Birmingham, L.S.D. Club	SWELL MAPS/RED CRAYOLA/	
VAPORS	London, Marquee	BARRACUDAS	London, Nashville

SEPTEMBER 1979

SECRET AFFAIR/BACK TO ZERO/	SQUIRE ....London, The Wellington
PURPLE HEARTS ....Liverpool, Eric's	MADNESS ....Manchester, The Factory

2nd - Sunday...

THE SKIDS' lead guitarist Stuart Adamson, is unlike other musicians who deny the "punk" label. He welcomes it. Stuart told *Sounds* magazine, "I think we're a punk band. We're a fucking punk rock band, man. We're young and honest, playing music we believe in. That's what punk rock was about getting up on stage and saying 'fuck you, this is what we're about.' That what we wanna do. That is not giving a fuck about Led Zeppelin, or the New Barbarians. I don't want number ones. I want to write classic singles. Singles like 'Down In The Tube Station,' like 'White Man In Hammersmith Palais,' like 'Borstal Breakout,' 'Shot By Both Sides,' 'Here Comes The Summer.' Like 'Boredom,' like 'Anarchy,' like 'Neat Neat Neat,' like 'Alison.' There's literally been a hundred classic singles in the last three years and I'm really glad to be a part of it. I tell you, it's still happening. There couldn't be a better time for being alive."

STIFF LITTLE FINGERS/	JOHN COOPER CLARKE..............Edinburgh, Old Chaplin
OX EYES/	SELECTER.............................London, Brixton Carnival
SPOILSPORTS........................London, Brixton, Brockwell Park	ONLY ONES ....London, Lyceum

3rd - Monday.........................

NIGHTS IN WHITE SATIN **THE DICKIES**

THE DICKIES' newest single is somewhat familiar to most people. They've done another one of their patented, 150 mph versions of the Moody Blues classic "Nights In White Satin." The song is reviewed in the *NME* with only one line, "Far superior to the Moody Blues original." It's flipped with a Dickies original, "Waterslide," and anticipates the release of their next, as yet untitled album.

THE REVILLOS, one of the two groups to rise out of the split of the Rezillos, make their live debut tonight in Edinburgh. The group was put together by former Rezillos vocalists Fay Fifi and Eugene Reynolds. Along with them are Robo Rhythm on drums, Felix on bass, Hi Fi Harris on lead guitar, and Cherri and Babs handling the backing vocals. Their debut single "Where's the Boy For Me" b/w "The Fiend" is out this Friday as the first release on the new Din Disc label.

PASSAGE/CONTACT/I.Q. ZERO Manchester-based Object Music Records has three single releases. The label burst on the scene back in May of '77 when they released the Spherical Object's LP "Past & Parcel." The company is run by the Spherical Objects leader, Steve Solomar, who originally intended to only confine releases to his band's recordings. Since then there have been singles and albums, introducing England to Mancunian bands like Warriors, Alternomen Unlimited, Grow Up, Steve Treatment, The Passage and others.

The Passage, a subject of a prior single, have a new one out called "About Time." It's a four track 7" EP with "Sixteen Hours," "Time Delay," "Taking My Time" and "Clock Paradox." The Passage are headed by Tony Friel on bass, guitar and vocals, along with Lorraine Hilton on organ, and Dick Witts on drums.

Contact are a new Object band, and they too have a four track EP to their name this week. It's under the title "Contact:Future/Contact:Past" that we find four songs, "Fascinated By Time," "Constant Beat," "Nite Time" and "Someone Like You." The sleeve gives little information about the band, but appears to be a side project from The Passage for bassist Tony Friel and his friend Duncan Prestbury.

I.Q. Zero made their debut on the Manchester Collective LP out earlier this year. Their debut single is "Insects," and bears more than a little resemblance to XTC.

REVILLOS (debut gig)................Edinburgh, Tiffany's	CROOKS/THE MODS.................London, Bridge House
JOHN COOPER CLARKE ....Edinburgh, Old Chaplin	SLAUGHTER & THE DOGS...........London, Marquee

4th - Tuesday..

THE VAPORS are not a mod band! That's the message that the band's management company has been blanketing the music press with this week. Not wanting to get caught up in the possibly fleeting nature of the mod trend, the Vapors have distanced themselves, at least in the press from mod. They've still not changed their sound, which is to the average listener, totally mod. They'll find their own identity in less than six months with a song they've written called "Turning Japanese."

THE SWELL MAPS dig more songs out of their archives for their latest single. It's strange that the Swell Maps, a group that exists in the here and now, persists in releasing singles that feature tracks from two years ago! Todays 45 is "English Verse," recorded in July of '77, flipped with the January '77 song "Monologues," and "Real Shocks" from April of this year. What an odd thing. Are they really so hard up for new material?

ANOTHER PRETTY FACE.............Edinburgh, The Aquarius	SHAKE ....London, Marquee
JOHN COOPER CLARKE.............Edinburgh, Old Chaplin	MERTON PARKAS ....London, Nashville
SEVENTEEN...........................Flint, Raven Hotel	SMALL HOURS ....Sheffield, Limit Club

5th - Wednesday..

THE SLITS' eye-catching cover of their first album "Cut" has the band looking for all the world like *National Geographic* refugees.

SEPTEMBER 1979

They're outdoors in a rose garden, trapped out in loincloths, topless and covered chin to toe in sticky brown mud. They've been playing two and a half years, and have only one single to tell the tale. Songs on the album include "Instant Hit," "So Tough," "Spend, Spend, Spend," "Adventures Close To Home" and their debut single "Typical Girls." The drawings on the inner sleeve of the album showing the Slits being attacked by bugs was apparently done by one of the band's roadies, depicting how the Slits were beset with fleas in the studio while working on "Cut."

THE MEMBERS' newest single is out this weekend. Its "Killing Time" b/w "GLC." Early copies of the Virgin 45 come in a special sleeve that is printed to look like a washing machine. The labels, visible through the machine window, portray a news presenter and a shark.

THE POISON GIRLS are difficult to understand and difficult to tolerate. At times they grate, but always they challenge with their recorded tantrums and observations. Their new EP is called "Hex" and features eight of the band's newest songs. They are "Old Tart's Song," "Crisis," "Ideologically Unsound," "Bremen Song," "Political Song," "Jump, Mama, Jump," "Under The Doctor" and "Reality Attack."

SIOUXSIE & THE BANSHEES/		SQUIRE/V.I.P.'s/	
THE CURE	Belfast, Ulster Hall	THE LEGEND	London, Music Machine
JOHN COOPER CLARKE	Edinburgh, Old Chaplin	PATTI SMITH GROUP	London, Wembley Arena
MADNESS	London, Dingwalls	PROPERTY OF	
MERTON PARKAS	London, Marquee	RARE DEVICE/GOD'S GIFT	Manchester, The Factory
TENPOLE TUDOR	London, Moonlight Club	TOYAH	Sheffield, The Penthouse

6th – Thursday...

FOUR BE TWO Here's a sort-of spin off from Public Image Ltd. It's Johnny Lydon's little brother Jimmy. The band is Four Be Two and is twenty-two year-old Jimmy Lydon, and 18 year-old bassist Martin "Youth" Glover (also in Killing Joke). There's also two mystery names, a Dreary O'Hoodlum on guitar and Paddy O'Reilly on drums. On the sleeve itself no picture is shown. Tracks are "One Of The Lads" and a piss take on the Skids called "Ummbaba." Jimmy Lydon described the record to *Sounds* as, "…a mix between every record you've ever 'eard. It's disco-Paddy, that there it all comes from, the big Irish crack, music from the building sites." Jimmy reckons that there will be loads of people who buy the record just because of his brother and not because it's necessarily any good, but "I like the color of money, don't you? You've got to give the kids something for their money, and I think we do that."

THE MONOCHROME SET are getting a reputation for being a singles machine. Their third single this year is out, and it's imaginatively titled "The Monochrome Set." It's a theme song of sorts, whose lyric goes "Set, monochrome set, monochrome set, monochrome se-e-e-et!" It's flipped with the rhythmically alluring "Mr Bizarro." The Monochrome Set is led by guitarist and vocalist Bid, Lester Square on guitar, J.D. Haney on drums, Jeremy Harrington on bass and the newest addition Tony Potts on the "visual media."

ANOTHER PRETTY FACE have come all the way down from Edinburgh to London to open for their friends The Revillos. They play well, but the moment is lost when a great deal of their gear is stolen after the show. The group has been smitten lately with troubles. Original bassist Jim Geddes left and was replaced with Ray Taylor. On the bright side, their past is being publicly plundered by their manager with the release of single of Mike's previous band D.N.V. The group split up late in '78 when Mike moved back from Ayr after dismissing college as a waste of time. Tracks discovered in the vaults include "Death In Venice," "Mafia" and "Goodbye 1970's." The three track single with poster sleeve is on their own New Pleasures label. D.N.V. was Mike Scott on guitar and vocals, Allan McConnel on lead guitar, Wart Clogg (aka Norman Roger, later of TV21) on bass and Crigg (Ian Walter Craig) on drums. The last song, "Goodbye 1970's" would be re-recorded for the flip of Another Pretty Face's single for Virgin in February of '80.

LIVE TONIGHT!

JOHN COOPER CLARKE	Edinburgh, Old Chaplin	PIRANHAS	London, Dingwalls
NOT SENSIBLES/		LAMBRETTAS	London, Fulham Greyhound
VIBRANT THIGH/		BUZZARDS/	
PROPERTY OF../		ROGER RUSKIN SPEAR/	
MANCHESTER MEKONS	Liverpool, Eric's	KINETIC WARDROBE	London, Music Machine
SMALL HOURS SQUIRE	London, Adam & Eve	REVILLOS/	
LEOPARDS/THE RED TAPE/		ANOTHER PRETTY FACE	London, Notre Dame Hall
SHOOT STRAIGHT AT		PROTEX/BALLOONS	London, Rock Garden
RIGHT ANGLES/		TOYAH	Manchester, The Factory
SUBTERRANEANS	London, Albany Empire		

7th – Friday...

GARY NUMAN's follow-up to chart topping LP "Are Friends Electric" is "The Pleasure Principle," More music from a mechanized world. Tracks like "Metal," "Complex," "Tracks," "Films" and "Cars" bespeak of a future that's not user-friendly.

SPIZZ ENERGI are becoming one of the more prolific singles bands around today. Another new single springs forth from their association with Rough Trade Records. The latest is "Soldier Soldier." It's backed with a suitably mutated version of Roxy Music's '72 oldie "Virginia Plain."

THE SKIDS headline tonight at the Edinburgh Odeon as part of the last night of the Edinburgh Rock Festival. They've got a new single just out as well. It's "Charade" and "Grey Paradise." Both songs are new and are from the sessions they've had recently with ex-Be Bop Deluxe/current Red Noise member Bill Nelson. The Skids have a temporary drummer tonight in Edinburgh. Tom Kellichan left the group unexpectedly, and is being replaced, albeit temporarily, by ex-Rich Kid Rusty Egan.

PURPLE HEARTS If you're a mod, pull on your parka, hop on your scooter, and rush down to W.H. Smiths to buy this next one. It's the debut release from the Purple Hearts, self-proclaimed leaders of the new mod explosion sweeping London. They've been signed up to Fiction Records who have just released "Millions Like Us" and "Beat That!!" The band are regulars onstage at the Bridge House, Music Machine and the Marquee.

SEPTEMBER 1979

SIOUXSIE & THE BANSHEES Just as their important tour is beginning, it's beset with troubles. Shortly before tonight's gig in Aberdeen, guitarist John McKay and drummer Kenny Morris left town. The show opened with The Scars playing followed by the Cure. Backstage there were signs of trouble. With a crowd waiting for the Banshees, the Cure played and played and played. At last, an announcement over the sound system, "Attention. Your attention please. Owing to the disappearance of two members of the Banshees, the gig will not take place. If you would stay in your seats, arrangements will be made to refund your tickets." Then Siouxsie appeared onstage, along side her fellow Banshee Steve Severin. Siouxsie spoke, "Two original members of the band are here tonight. Two art college students fucked off out of it...All I can say is we will be back here with some friends who have got some roots. If you've got one percent of the aggression we feel towards them, if you ever see them, you have my blessings to beat the shit out of them." The two left the stage to cheers from the audience and back onstage walked the Cure.

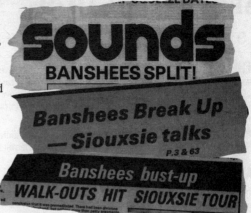

They began playing "The Lords Prayer" and all was right again. That song is an important one for the band. It not only was the first one the band ever played in public, but it also served as the final song for almost every gig over the last two years. It is fifteen minutes of intense, primal Banshees.

Apparently the problem began earlier in the day when the group were in a record shop signing autographs. John and Kenny wouldn't have anything to do with it, insisted on playing the new Slits album instead of letting the band's own album finish, and gave the store owner a difficult time because he was selling promotional copies of the album when his normal stock ran out. And these were promos that he was sold by Siouxsie to cover the stock deficit! A blow up between Siouxsie and the pair was inevitable and they left the store, and left town as well. Manager Nils Stevenson found the pair getting in a cab and was left in a cloud of dust. He chased them to a town twenty miles distant in the band's tour bus and lost the pair at the rail station. Pulling out of several dates and having to pay travel expenses and lose deposits on venues will cost the Banshees upwards of £50,000. *Sounds* writer Phil Sutcliffe was present for an event that told just how deep the rift is. He wrote, "I went down to the bus to drive back to the hotel with the remnants of the band and for some minutes Siouxie sat in the open door signing autographs. One fan was asking for a badge and they hadn't got any left but then Nils noticed John McKays guitar lying beside his seat. He picked it up and told the lad, 'Here, take this. A souvenir.'" All concert dates on the tour have been cancelled through the 24th, where they'll pick up again with new musicians. It is ironic that the band's new LP is titled "Join Hands" just as they are going their separate ways.

THE SOFT BOYS' debut their new line-up. Bassist Andy Metcalfe left to join Telephone Bill & The Smooth Operators, eventually joining Squeeze. He is replaced by ex-Bruce Wooley Band member Matthew Seligman. Drummer Jim Melton left to start his own band and is having his duties heaped on drummer Morris Windsor. The Soft Boys are again a four-piece group.

LIVE TONIGHT!

POISON GIRLS/AU PAIRS ....Birmingham, Bournebrook Hotel	COBRAS ....London, Howard Hall
SKIDS/BERLIN BLONDES ....Edinburgh, Odeon	PHOTOS/TOUR DE FORCE ....London, Music Machine
JOHN COOPER CLARKE..............Edinburgh, Univ.	PROTEX/ INNOCEN ....London, Nashville
SCHOOL BULLIES/	SOFT BOYS/ SCISSORS FIT ....London, Rock Garden
COCKNEY REJECTS...................London, Bridge House	SHAKE ....Manchester, The Factory

9th - Sunday.....................................

SHEFFIELD (The Scene) This week's *NME* features a article exploring the new music scene in Sheffield. The Northern city is known primarily for its industrial products, not its music, and perhaps the only band that readily comes to mind when mentioning Sheffield is The Human League. That would be a disservice to the lesser known, and less commercial Cabaret Voltaire. Bands given a name check in the article include Clock DVA, Cabaret Voltaire spin offs They Must Be Russians, Xero, punky band The Stunt Kites, Deaf Aids, and electronic trio Vice Versa.

The Com-sat Angels are first up in the piece. Their previous single "Red Planet" is touched on, but counted as dated material when put up against their new demos of "Independence Day," "Missing In Action," "Monkey Pilot" and "Baby." The quartet began more on the jazz rock side of things before drifting into the pop arena under the name Radio Earth. They changed their name as the style shifted, flirted with a Radar Records deal and moved on to make their own music, under their own terms. They are one of the more complex, and potentially commercial of the new crop of bands in Sheffield.

Salon Graph were first heard earlier this year on the Earcom 2 collection as "Graph." The former trio is now a quartet and consider themselves "experimentalists" influenced by all other forms of art in their quest for the ultimate non-pop song. Salon Graph are Martin Rootes, Ian Burdon, Ian Elliott and Nik Allday.

Artery are another band that have but one single to mark their time on the scene. They're also on the experimental side of things, based around fuzz guitar washes and unusual, somewhat nasal vocals. Their debut single "Mother Moon" is to followed soon by a second called "The Slide." They're experimenting with recording only vocals and percussion on that one.

I'm So Hollow are the fourth band in the series. At this time they're still unrecorded, and are prepared to wait for the right moment. They came up through the last three years in the punk movement, beginning in a group called V4. This mutated into I'm So Hollow, an the sound has gravitated away from the '76 style punk riff to one more closely associated with Siouxsie & The Banshees and Wire. The group is built about guitarist Rod Leigh, Joe Sawicki on drums, Gary Marsden on bass, and vocalist Jane Wilson.

PIRANHAS ....London, Hope & Anchor	NINA HAGEN/THE PACK/
MADNESS/BEATTY ....London, Nashville	MO-DETTES...........................London, Lyceum

SEPTEMBER 1979

10th - Monday.....................................

PENETRATION It's been almost a year since Penetration have made their album debut. A second LP from the Newcastle group is released this week on Virgin. It's "Coming Up For Air" and includes both sides of the band's newest single "Come Into The Open" and "Lifeline." All the songs are originals, among them "Shout Above The Noise," "Killed In The Rush," "On Reflection" and "She Is The Slave." Penetration are Pauline Murray on lead vocals, Fred Purser on lead guitar, Neal Floyd on rhythm guitar, Robert Blamire on bass and Gary Smallman on drums.

PATTI SMITH is playing the biggest concert of her career tonight in Forence, Italy. She's onstage for the last time at the Stadium Communale. After this show she's retiring (at age 32) to Detroit to begin a new life with guitarist Fred "Sonic" Smith. What a last hurrah too. There's 85,000 at the stadium tonight.

FAD GADGET is one man, Frank Tovey. His debut single is just out on Mute Records. It's "The Box" b/w "Back To Nature." The sparse recording is electronically based and quite haunting.

SQUIRE/SW 1	London, Bridge House	CHORDS	London, Marquee
PIRANHAS	London, Hope & Anchor	SHAKE	London, Nashville

11th - Tuesday.....................................

EX-SQUEEZE bassist Harry Kakoulli is being erased from Squeeze. Harry was fired from the band two months ago, and if that wasn't enough, now their current LP "Cool For Cats" has been reissued with a photo of the group on the back without Harry! Even worse, is that the photo that's now on the LP included new addition John Bently, who is credited as playing bass on the LP! Harry is being written off in the most literal manner.

THE RADIATORS have another single taken from their new LP "Ghost Town." The single of "Kitty Rickets," is flipped with the non-LP track "Ballad Of The Faithful Departed."

VICE VERSA are an experimental electronic Sheffield group who have just burst on the scene with their debut EP "Vice Versa Music 4." It's a four song EP of "Riot Squad," "Camille," "New Girls/Neutrons" and "Science - Fact." The trio are Stephen Singleton, David Sydenham and Mark White. The single is on the band's own Neutron Records and comes in a poster sleeve that unfolds to a full 21" x 14" size. In a few months Vice Versa will be interviewed by Martin Fry for a fanzine called *Modern Drugs*. He's intrigued by the band and teams up with Stephen and Mark to form a new band called ABC that will have hits of "Poison Arrow" and "The Look Of Love" in 1982.

LIVE TONIGHT!

SHAKE	London, Marquee	CHORDS	Sheffield, Limit Club
XTC/YACHTS/DAZZLERS	Manchester, The Apollo		

12th - Wednesday.....................................

JOHNNY THUNDERS split up the Heartbreakers last year and it seemed he would just take his chances going solo, but after only a few shows, and almost nine months, Thunders is back in a band again. The new aggregation is called Gang War. Johnny's teamed up with several other grizzled veterans, namely ex-MC5 Wayne Kramer, ex-Detroit Wheels Ron Cooke and John Morgan. This potentially explosive line-up are currently on tour on America's east coast.

PHOTOS	London, Hope & Anchor	ANY TROUBLE	Manchester, Birch Hotel
MERTON PARKAS/		XTC/THE YACHTS/	
SMALL HOURS	London, Marquee	DAZZLERS	Sheffield, Top Rank

13th - Thursday.....................................

SHAM 69 have a new twist, a punkish album with a western cover. No, seriously, the jacket to the latest Sham 69 album looks like a still from a Clint Eastwood movie. It's serapes, cowboy hats and six guns blazing. The album's "The Adventure Of The Hersham Boys." It's Sham's farewell to their fans. The album contains their previous singles "Questions And Answers" and "Hersham Boys," as well as "Joey's On The Street," "Voices," and the live favorite "What Have We Got?" There's also an obscure Manfred Mann cover of "You're A Better Man Than I." As a bonus to early buyers, the album is packaged with a 12" single of extended versions of "Borstal Breakout" and "If The Kids Are United." Jimmy Pursey would tell the *NME*, "Sham gives the punters their money's worth. Who else has given away 23,000 records? Who else stuck in a free record with their album? It don't matter if people think the record's crap. The fact that we're giving it away is what counts, right!"…The line notes, however brief, close with a somewhat cryptic message from Jimmy Pursey, "We could mention many names. We could start all over again, but would it be the same. No legend my friend. Sham 69 was a name."

THIS HEAT The adverts have been running in the music papers for weeks. What did they all mean? The answer is revealed as the LP from experimentalists This Heat. It's out on their own Piano Records and catches the band not too distant from their roots. To explain, This Heat began in 1976 when ex-Gong member Charles Hayward, got together with Charles Bullen and Gareth Williams. The group blended art-rock with jazz-fusion and came into their own as a very unusual amalgam of styles. This Heat's debut album is actually a catch-you-up on two year's

SEPTEMBER 1979

worth of recordings. Some of the songs are challenging, such as "Testcard," but the real rewards are "Horizontal Hold," "Not Waving," The Fall Of Saigon" and "24 Track Loop." It's not your average pop record, unless you're from somewhere besides planet Earth.

POLICE ....Birmingham, The Odeon	PHOTOS/CLONES ....London, Bridge House
PROTEX/THE DRILLS ....Liverpool, Eric's	ADVERTS ....London, Dingwalls
CARDIAC ARREST/	COWBOYS INTL. ....London, Marquee
DANGEROUS GIRLS...................London, Acklam Hall	

14th - Friday.......................................

THE CHORDS have a single out at last! They've been having trouble after trouble getting their debut single out. They started out as part of Jimmy Pursey's productions but shook loose a while back. They found a new producer, Peter Wilson, and re-cut the sessions for their single "Now It's Gone" and "Don't Go Back." The Chords are in the midst of their first ever tour covering seventeen dates over the course of the month. Tonight they play at the Factory in Manchester.

THE VIBRATORS have been out of the picture for almost a year. It was back in October of last year that lead vocalist Knox quit to go solo. Their tour was cancelled and the future was uncertain. Now, drummer Jon Edwards and guitarist Greg Van Cook debut with their new, re-vamped version of The Vibrators. They're joined by ex-Electric Chair guitarist Elliot "Brooklyn" Michaels, and ex-Eater bassist Ian Woodcock. On vocals is "Kip." They've been rehearsing for the last three months and plan not only UK dates, but a trip to America as well. The other former Vibrators are scattered throughout several bands. John Ellis put together a group called Rapid Eye Movement, Don Snow is now a member of the Sinceros, and Gary Tibbs is with Roxy Music.

MADNESS have signed a deal with Stiff Records. Their current single "The Prince" is available on Two Tone Records and is rapidly climbing the UK charts. Plans for a follow up are already under way. The North London dance group have been together almost two years.

VIBRATORS (return)/	X-DREAMYSTS/PHOTOS.............London, Moonlight Club
THE DARK................................London, Nashville	CHORDS/THE CHEATERS ....Manchester, The Factory

15th - Saturday......................................

THE POLICE have their latest single released. It's "Message In A Bottle." Over 20,000 people had a preview when the song was featured in the group's set at the Reading Festival. It's flipped with a track called "Landlord" that will not be included on their next album. The song will become the band's first #1 hit in the UK, and although it's a familar song to most Americans, it never even touches the US Top 40.

LIVE TONIGHT!

TEARDROP EXPLODES/	VAPORS ....London, Marquee
ECHO & THE BUNNYMEN ....Liverpool, Eric's	X-DREAMYSTS...........................London, Moonlight Club
POISON GIRLS/	FALL/SCRITTI POLITTI ....London, Prince Of Wales
RUBELLA BALLET....................London, Conway Hall (Holborn)	PHOTOS ....London, Windsor Castle

16th - Sunday...

THE JAM are in the studio working on their next album. Some fragments from the session are revealed in this week's *NME* by Nick Kent. He visited the band and was shown lyric fragments of songs with titled of "Little Boy Soldiers," "Meet Me On The Wasteland," "Burning Sky," "The Eaton Rifles" and "Thick As Thieves." Lead singer Paul Weller describes the album as being set in Britain in the 1980's, "...about three close mates, who get split up when the civil war occurs, one joins the left, one veers off to the right while the third one doesn't feel any particular affiliation whatsoever. He's the abstainer. After the war's conclusion, three splintered ex-comrades plan to meet up again." The album is as yet untitled.

UB40 receive a great plug in this week's *Sounds* magazine. Stephen Gordon writes, "I saw UB40 and was transfixed! I heard UB40's demo tape and was astounded! Loaves-and-fishing with a mere four tracks, yet their achievement was something contemporary and forward...at last! They've arrived at a very special sound, one that admitted only distant relation to the rather staid, often maudlin, English outfits of this man's exsistence." There is talk that UB40 will have a tribute to Martin Luther King, Jr. called "King" out on 45. It'll be the launching pad for UB40 and go top 5 in the UK, beginning a long string of UK top ten hits that are still continuing to this day.

VAPORS ....London, Fulham Greyhound	CLASSIX NOUVEAUX ....London, Nashville

17th - Monday..

THE SIOUXSIE & BANSHEES tour thrown off the rails ten days ago when half of the band quit, gets back on track tonight. The rest of the tour will go on as planned, with the missed dates slotted in where possible. As replacement for the guitar and bass gone walking will be ex-Slits drummer Budgie, and Robert Smith of the Cure on guitar. That means that Smith will be pulling double duty, playing in his own band for the opening set, and again with Siouxsie. There were hundreds of offers to fill in as replacements, and these two were chosen as fill-ins until permanent members can be found. Robert Smith told *NME* reporter Deanne Pearson about the day of the disaster. "We were all shattered when it happened. We just sat around after the Aberdeen gig and talked, and drank, and kept on drinking until eight o'clock in the morning. I just felt that as long as we sat there we could keep the whole thing going, and if I went to bed then that'd be it, then end of the tour. Siouxsie and Steve said not to worry, they had lots of friends who would fill in, and they'd start auditioning right away, and I said if they couldn't get a guitarist then I'd play and the Fatman (Lol Tolhurst, the Cure's drummer) even said he would play drums if it came to that. Then a few days later Siouxsie rang me up and said would I come down and audition, and before I knew it I was the Banshees guitarist."

LITTLE ROOSTERS/	XTC/THE YACHTS/
THE FACE ....London, Bridge House	DAZZLERS ....London, Rainbow

SEPTEMBER 1979

SHAKE ....London, Marquee	SINCERE AMERICANS/
HEADBOYS/RIFF RAFF ....London, Rock Garden	FATAL CHARM ....Sheffield, Penthouse Basement

18th - Tuesday.....................................

THE PATTI SMITH GROUP is associated with great songwriting. Most of her albums are considered instant classics in record reviews, and musicians watch for each new offering with great interest. How unusual, then, that the latest single from Patti Smith is a cover of the '60s Byrds' hit "So You Wanna Be (A Rock n' Roll Star.)" The song was recorded live in New York on May 23rd, the same concert that generated a track for the flipside, Manfred Man's "5-4-3-2-1." There is also a studio track of "Fire Of Unknown Origin."

THE PSYCHEDELIC FURS have just signed a recording deal with CBS Records! They've been around for almost two years, and have lately been playing out frequently and gathering quite large crowds. They've got a different sound than most. The moody vocals of Richard Butler are set off with a mournful sax from Duncan Kilburn. That's not to say they're in a similar frame of reference to Joy Division. They're more accessible than that. Their first single will either be "Fall" or "We Love You." Vocalist Richard Butler told the *NME* that the Psychedelic Furs are a constantly changing band. "There was a time when I used to go on with lots of make-up and that was just being silly. At that time we didn't really know what we were doing, but now we've got much more workmanlike. We are basically trying to say something, and something which is positive. We're trying to do something that we haven't heard before, and it requires much more work. But it doesn't freeze. We're never gonna play it the same two nights running. This band will never be like that, and CBS might hate the fact but I don't care."

PHYSICALS ....London, Bridge House

19th - Wednesday...................................

STIFF LITTLE FINGERS have their first release on Chrysalis. It's a single of "Straw Dogs" and "You Can't Say Crap On The Radio." The group will be on the road most of next month, and plan to start on their new album in November.

PERE UBU have a new album out this week. It's part of a new mid-line series that Chrysalis is starting up to introduce new groups to buyers at a bargain price. The disc is "New Picnic Time" and was recorded this summer. The always intriguing song titles have among them "Have Shoes, Will Walk," "49 Guitars And One Girl," "A Small Dark Cloud," "All The Dogs Are Barking" and "The Voice Of The Sand." The group at this time are Tom Herman, Scott Krauss, Tony Maimone, Allen Ravenstine and David Thomas.

LIVE TONIGHT!

SLITS/DON CHERRY/	MERTON PARKAS ....:.....London, Marquee
PRINCE HAMMER.....................Birmingham, Digbeth Civic Hall	PHOTOS/TEENBEATS................London, Rock Garden
SIOUXSIE & THE BANSHEES/	ART FAILURE/THE OUT/
THE CURE ....Birmingham, The Odeon	GORDON THE MORON ....Sheffield, The Penthouse
MEDIUM MEDIUM ....London, Hope & Anchor	

20th - Thursday....................................

GARY NUMAN is the central figure of his band and prides himself on non-dependence on others to perform his music, he has however gathered together a band to play live. The tour starts tonight in Glasgow. Onstage with Gary is Paul Gardiner on bass, Chris Payne and Billy Currie on keyboards, and Ced Sharpley on drums. A huge stage set has been constructed that includes two twenty foot towers, laser guns, remote controlled robots and unusual lighting. Some say that the backdrop with musicians perched in squares arranged in a two up, two across fashion look like the TV set for "Celebrity Squares (aka Hollywood Squares)." The set list for the show is as follows: "Airline," "Me I Disconnect From You," "Cars," "M.E.," "You Are In My Vision," "Something In The House," "Random," "Every Day I Die," "Conversation," "We're So Fragile," "Bombers," "Remember I Was Vapor," "On Broadway," "Dream Police," "Films," "Metal," "Down In The Park," "My Shadow In Veil," "Are Friends Electric" and "Tracks."

THE UK SUBS' debut album is "Another Kind Of Blues," but the only thing blue about the album, is the album itself. It's in a blue sleeve with blue lettering, a blue inner sleeve with a blue vinyl record that has a blue label on it. There's little on it that isn't the color blue! The album has all the songs from their first two singles. The tracks from their debut single include "C.I.D." I Live In A Car" and "B.I.C.," and are here in re-recorded form. The second single "Stranglehold," "World War," "Rockers" are the same session and there's also the lead track from their new single "Tomorrow's Girls."

BLONDIE's fans get a taste of something new today with the release of the single "Dreaming" b/w "Sound A-Sleep." Both tracks are from their new LP "Eat To The Beat" that will be released next week. "Dreaming" has a brief eight-week run on the UK charts, quickly rising up to, and falling from, the #2 slot.

PINK MILITARY have another 12" EP out in Liverpool. This one's under the title "Blood & Lipstick." It included the title track plus "Spellbound" and "I Cry." There's also another version of "Clowntown," that was on their previous EP "Buddha Waking." It comes in a special 12" sleeve. Pink Military are Jayne Casey, Pete, Nicky, Roy, Steve Tordh and Tim Whittaker.

XTC/THE YACHTS/	RELUCTANT STEREOTYPES.........London, 101 Club
DAZZLERS ....Edinburgh, The Odeon	SQUIRE...................................London, Hope & Anchor
GARY NUMAN ....Glasgow, Apollo	MEMBERS ....London, Marquee

SEPTEMBER 1979

ASTRONAUTS/THE MOB/
ZOUNDS/ANDROIDS OF MU ....Liverpool, Eric's

X-DREAMYSTS ....London, Moonlight Club

21st - Friday...

THE STRANGLERS' newest release is "The Raven." The group have mellowed just a bit, and there's not much of the frenetic energy found on their previous albums. They have however developed their talents at writing and playing hypnotic, interlocking riffs. Their new single "Dutchess" is there, as well as "Longships," "Baroque Bordello," "Don't Bring Harry," "Genetix" and "Nuclear Device." The track "Meninblack" is related to one of their new pet theories that aliens actually prey on humans on a regular basis. "Shah Shah A Go Go" is about the civil war now raging in Iran. The first 20,000 copies feature a 3-D image of a Raven on the cover, an effect that takes up nearly the entire cover. The Stranglers always brings some of their own experience into songs. From the lyrics, there is apparently no love lost between the band and the town Los Angeles. Hugh Cornwell described one of the instances that made a bad first impression. "Los Angeles is the only town that I've ever been to where I've been stopped by the police for walking on the sidewalk. I was just walking, dressed the way I dress, and a police car stopped, put me up against the police car, frisked me, and they asked me what I was doing. I said I was taking a Sunday afternoon stroll, and they said, "...haven't you noticed no one else is? They said I was looking suspicious, just walking in Los Angeles." Check out the song that resulted, "Dead Loss Angeles."

THE BOOMTOWN RATS' single "I Don't Like Mondays" is going to finally be released in the US. It's not that they've had Monday lovers lobbying to keep it off the shelves, it's that their corporate attorneys were concerned it might prejudice jurors in the Brenda Spencer trial. She's the schoolgirl who allegedly shot up the playground in San Diego back in January, and was the inspiration for the song. There is also no concern, no matter how ironic, about the song's potential to enter the charts "with a bullet," meaning it will move quickly to the top as it did in England and Europe.

TEENAGE FILMSTARS are the subject of rumors that they're actually the Television Personalities under a different name. There's something to that. This "new" group is actually Edward Ball and Daniel Treacy, who are the driving force behind the Television Personalties. This isn't the first time that they've masqueraded under a different name. Remember the O Level record "We Love Malcolm" back in February? The Teenage Filmstars' single is "There's A Cloud Over Liverpool" and "Sometime Good Guys Don't Follow Trends," and is released today on the Clockwork Records label.

ASTRONAUTS/THE MOB/	SQUIRE.................................London, White Lion
ZOUNDS/ANDROIDS OF MU ....Birmingham, Bournebrook Hotel	TEENBEATS/
CHORDS.................................Liverpool, Eric's	LONG TALL SHORTY ....London, Windsor Castle
THE PACK ....London, Brixton Town Hall	SIOUXSIE & BANSHEES/
MEMBERS ....London, Marquee	THE CURE..........................Manchester, Apollo
PSYCHEDELIC FURS ....London, Nashville	REVILLOS ....Manchester, The Factory

22nd - Saturday...

THE SWELL MAPS/LUDUS' gig in Manchester tonight is being spied upon by Mick Middles for *Sounds* magazine. It's hard to tell from his review whether he loved the band or loathed them. Of the Swell Maps he wrote, "The very sloppy Swell Maps are presently attempting to conquer the art of turning badness into madness. Their jokey, half-formulated view of rock n' roll is intriguing to watch, but unfortunately fairly painful to listen to. They wander around the stage, they whistle, they laugh, they talk to each other during songs in fact Swell Maps are the most professional unprofessional band I've ever had the (mis)fortune to witness." His opinion on Ludus was more favorable, although the band described seems to be one from another planet, "The voice of Linder (the lead singer) has amazingly evolved into a classy off-key vehicle for the band's bleak and meaningless lyrics. She has learned to use her voice more as an instrument and less of a means of chanting the lyrical message. Beneath her voice, the band stray into areas verging on the absurd. It lacks any sense of humor but it sparkles with vitality."

RIFF RAFF has another single out. Well, perhaps it's best described as half a single. The "A" side is by ex-Bees Make Honey bassist Ruan O'Lochlainn singing "Sweet Narcissus." He's currently the bassist for Riff Raff who back him on this side. On the "B" side is "Barking Park Lake." The single can just barely be found on Albion Records.

REVILLOS ....Liverpool, Eric's	JOY DIVISION/
SHATTERED DOLLS ....Liverpool, The Masonic	DISTRACTIONS......................London, Nashville
SOFT BOYS ....London, 101 Club	DEXY'S MIDNIGHT RUNNERS/
TEENBEATS/DIRECTION/	LUDUS/THE SWELL MAPS ....Manchester, The Factory
EDDIE STEADY GO ....London, Fulham Greyhound	THE MOB ....Manchester, The Funhouse
POLICE/FASHION ....London, Hammersmith Odeon	ASTRONAUTS/THE MOB/
LAMBRETTAS ....London, Marquee	ZOUNDS/
SQUIRE.................................London, The Wellington	ANDROIDS OF MU ....Manchester, Mayflower

LIVE TONIGHT!

23rd - Sunday...

WIRE sees the release of their third album this weekend. The fact that they're up to their third album puts them in a class of a select few. Up to now, less than ten "new wave" bands have been able to release three albums worth of material. This new one from Wire not only covers a full LP worth of material but also spills out onto a free four track EP within the LP. You'll hear much more synthesizers and studio "jiggerypokery" going on. The band is moving off in a different direction than their previous tracks. The title "154" refers to a running count that Robert Gotobed kept in his diary of how many gigs that Wire had done up to the point of naming the album. By the time that the LP is hitting the stores, it would be more accurately titled "188." There are thirteen original tracks on "154" including, "2 People In A

SEPTEMBER 1979

Room," "The Other Window," "On Returning," "Blessed State," "Map Ref. 41 North 93 West" and "40 Versions." The first 20,000 copies of "154" come with a freebie EP. There are four songs, one from each member of the group. "Song 1," by Gotobed, "Get Down" by Newman, "Let's Panic Later" by Lewis, and "Small Electric Piece" by Gilbert.

THE COCKNEY REJECTS supposedly ran into Jimmy Pursey of Sham 69 over the weekend, got inspired and went into the studio to record a pair of tracks with him. The two songs, "Ain't Got Nothing" and "East End," could be their next single. There's talk going around that the Rejects are moments away from a deal with Warner Brothers.

POLICE	London, Hammersmith Odeon	JOHN COOPER CLARKE	London, St. Paul's Church
SELECTER/THE BEAT	London, Nashville	TEENBEATS	London, The Wellington

24th - Monday.....................................

BAUHAUS, formerly known as Bauhaus 1919, are from Walthamstow and have been taken up by Small Wonder Records as a new band worthy of a deal. They get the customary one single handshake arrangement and their debut is "Bela Lugosi's Dead," b/w "Boys." The release is only the second 12" single that Small Wonder has done, mandatory for this recording since Bela covers almost nine and a half minutes! This could be the longest "new wave" record ever. Bauhaus will linger in 20s to 50s on the UK charts and ultimately have a greater affect on music as an influence over dozens of others who follow in their Gothic footsteps. The individual members will split the group in '83 with Peter Murphy pursuing a solo career, the other forming Love And Rockets.

THE FEELIES are the latest band that have been signed to Stiff Records. The New York band are in the studio recording something new for release in October. Meanwhile, Rough Trade Records announces that the Feelies debut single "Fa Ce La" will be out on Rough Trade next month.

LIVE TONIGHT!

SLITS/DON CHERRY/		VAPORS	London, Fulham Greyhound
PRINCE HAMMER	Edinburgh, Astoria	DR. MIX & THE REMIX	London, Hope & Anchor
PHOTOS	London, 101 Club	SELECTER	London, Rock Garden
SPEEDBALL/LAMBRETTAS	London, Bridge House	XERO	Sheffield, Penthouse Basement

25th - Tuesday.....................................

THE SELECTOR, cohorts of the Specials, Madness and closely associated with the Ska revival, have their debut single out on the Specials' Two Tone Records. It's Two Tone's fourth release and couples two live favorites "On My Radio," with "Too Much Pressure." The Selecter are currently on their first headline tour, concluding with a concert in London at the Electric Ballroom on the 13th. When the Selecter made their debut on the flipside of the Specials single some months back, there was no proper band, only Specials friend Neol Davies. In July, a full band emerged onstage under the Selecter name, including Compton Amanor, Desmond Brown, Pauline Black, Arthur Hendrickson, Charley Anderson and Charley Bembridge.

JOE JACKSON's dapper new single is "I'm The Man." It's a the title track from his next LP, due out in another few weeks. The single is flipped a cover of a Chuck Berry song called "Come On" that will not be a part of the album.

THE FRESHIES' third D.I.Y. release is out this week on their own Razz Records label. The limited edition, numbered single features "Amoco Cadiz," a love song to the oil freighter that spilled it guts on the English seaside recently. It's flipped with "Children Of The World" and "Octopus." The three track EP is under the title "The Men From Banana Island Whose Stupid Ideas Never Caught On In The Western World As We Know It." The Freshies are about to be signed up to a major label, and the fate of Razz Records isn't known. They're hoping that they will be able to continue putting out special limited edition singles and sell them by mail order. With that notion in mind, included in this single is a special coupon offer. Chris writes a note saying, "...when we recorded this EP, there were eleven tracks in all finished on tape, plus a few odds and ends, so we have put them onto a stereo cassette under the title "The Girls From Banana Island Who's Stupid, Etc." It is a limited edition of 1,000 copies and you can get it by filling in the form below and sending in £2 to..." Deadline is December 15th, 1979. Sorry if you missed out. The Freshies are Chris Sievey on vocals, guitars and keyboards, Rick Maunder on bass, Barry Spencer on guitar and Bob Dixon on drums.

GARY NUMAN	Liverpool, The Empire	SLITS/DON CHERRY/	
PHOTOS	London, Dingwalls	PRINCE HAMMER	Manchester, Apollo
CHORDS	London, Marquee	SELECTER	Sheffield, Limit Club
PIRANHAS/REACTION	London, Music Machine		

26th - Wednesday.....................................

NINE NINE NINE's seventh release finds the band on their third label since 1977. They're one of the recent signings to Radar Records and their newest is "Found Out Too Late," b/w "Lie, Lie, Lie." On the single, drummer Ed Case, who filled in for the injured Pablo Labritian back in the spring, appears as drummer with Pablo listed as percussion. Could it be there are two drummers in one band?

BACK TO ZERO are the second London mod band to be signed to Fiction Records, the other was the Purple Hearts. Back To Zero are making their debut with "Your Side Of Heaven" and "Back To Back." They've only been together since last Christmas, and draw lots of inspiration from vocalist Brian's extensive '60s record collection. They insist that they're not revivalists, they're renewing music, not resurrecting it. The group have just come off of the March Of The Mods tour with lablemates The Purple Hearts and Secret Affair. They're ready now to start playing shows with Back To Zero at the top of the bill. Back To Zero are Brian Betteridge on vocals, Sam Burnett on guitar, and Mal on bass. Drummer Andy Moore has just quit the band and is being replaced with eighteen-year old Nigel Wolff.

SLITS/DON CHERRY/		MEDIUM MEDIUM	London, Hope & Anchor
PRINCE HAMMER	Glasgow, City Hall	GARY NUMAN	Manchester, Apollo

SEPTEMBER 1979

TEENBEATS ....High Wycombe, Nag's Head	DEAD AIRMEN/
DESTROY ALL MONSTERS ....London, Dingwalls	VOX PHANTOMS ....Sheffield, The Penthouse

27th - Thursday..

BLONDIE has a new album in stores in England this weekend. It's called "Eat To The Beat" The album features a dozen new originals including "The Hardest Part," "Union City Blue," "Accidents Never Happen," "Die Young, Stay Pretty" and "The Hardest Part." The album also contains the single track "Dreaming," not "Creaming" as was reported in *Sounds* magazine. American songwriter Ellie Greenwich provides backing vocals on "Dreaming" and "Atomic." "Eat To The Beat" was recorded this summer at three different studios, Power Station, Media Sound and Jimi Hendrix's Electric Ladyland. Debbie's also working on *Union City Blue*. It started out as an amateur movie and has grown and grown. There's talk now that it's about to be picked up for UK distribution on the hopes it will be finished soon. Debbie's past success and future promise give way to talk that there might be a movie career for her if she wants it.

THE POLICE's second album from the Police is just out. It's "Regatta de Blanc" and features the new smash hit single "Message In A Bottle," as well as potential hits like "Walking On The Moon" and "The Bed's Too Big Without You." Other tracks are "Deathwish," "It's Alright For You," "No Time This Time" and "Bring On The Night." The album picks up right where "Outlandos" left off. More pseudo-reggae, jazz riffing on pop songs.

SQUIRE have their second mod single out today, "Walking Down Kings Road" b/w "It's A Mod Mod World." The band have recently been signed to Secret Affair's I Spy record label.

UK SUBS/PLASTIC PEOPLE/	GARY NUMAN ....London, Hammersmith Odeon
LOST PROPERTY ....High Wycombe, Town Hall	PHOTOS ....London, Hope & Anchor
BOOMTOWN RATS/PROTEX ....Liverpool, Empire	MERTON PARKAS ....London, Marquee
SLITS/DON CHERRY/	COWBOYS INTL. ....London, Nashville
PRINCE HAMMER.....................Liverpool, Eric's	RUTS/FLYS ....Sheffield, Limit Club

28th - Friday..

BUZZCOCKS have a colourful new single out today of "You Say You Don't Love Me" and "Raison D'etre." Both tracks are from their current album "A Different Kind Of Tension." The Buzzcocks are about to begin an extensive UK tour with Joy Division opening up the dates.

LENE LOVICH is in Europe on tour but is preparing to take on England once again. To pave the way for her next country-wide tour, a new album is being prepared and her new single is out today on Stiff Records. It's "Bird Song" b/w "Trixi". The 12" version includes an additional track "Too Tender To Touch," taken from her previous album "Stateless."

THE UNDERTONES' newest single (their fifth) is "You've Got My Number (Why Don't You Use It!?)" It's paired with a cover of the 1967 Chocolate Watch Band psychedelic raver "Let's Talk About Girls." One can only wonder where nice Irish lads ever heard this obscure California oldie. The Undertones next LP is scheduled for release in about a week.

LIVE TONIGHT!

ART FAILURE/THE OUT/	PUNISHMENT OF LUXURY ....London, Nashville
GORDON THE MORON ....Liverpool, C.F. Mott College	SLITS/DON CHERRY/
BOOMTOWN RATS/PROTEX.........Liverpool, Empire	PRINCE HAMMER.....................London, Rainbow
ADAM & THE ANTS/	PHOTOS ....London, Southbank Poly.
CLASSIX NOUVEAUX/	JOY DIVISION/
A CERTAIN RATIO/	TEARDROP EXPLODES/
MANICURED NOISE ....London, Electric Ballroom	FOREIGN PRESS ....Manchester, The Factory
GARY NUMAN ....London, Hammersmith Odeon	STRESS/ALIEN TINT/
CARPETTES...........................London, Hope & Anchor	JOHN DOWIE ....Manchester, Middletown Civic Hall

29th - Saturday.....................

ORCHESTRAL MANOEUVRES IN THE DARK's single of "Electricity," which was released by Factory Records four months ago, is re-mixed and re-issued on the new Din Disc label. The sleeve has changed from the raised black on black sleeve to a simple white on black design that's infinitely easier to read and reproduce.

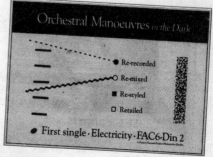

Orchestral Manoeuvres in the Dark
● Re-recorded
○ Re-mixed
■ Re-styled
□ Retailed
● First single · Electricity · FAC6-Din 2

THE RUTS make it to the album racks with "The Crack," their debut long player. Single tracks like "Babylon's Burning" and "Something That I Said," stand toe to toe with new classics like "Jah War," "Dope For Guns" and "Criminal Mind." The album has the band augmented with a full horn section and presents a much more polished sound for the Ruts than their live shows. The Ruts are Malcolm Owen on vocals, Paul Fox on guitars and organ, John "Segs" Jennings on bass, and Dave Ruffy on drums.

RUTS/THE FLYS.......................Liverpool, Eric's	ADAM & THE ANTS/
ART FAILURE/THE OUT/	CLASSIX NOUVEAUX
GORDON THE MORON ....Liverpool, Oscar's	A CERTAIN RATIO/
JOHN COOPER CLARKE/	MANICURED NOISE ....London, Electric Ballroom
THE PHOTOS ....London, City Poly.	BOOMTOWN RATS/PROTEX.........Manchester, Apollo
PUNISHMENT OF LUXURY ....London, Nashville	BUZZARDS/ARTERY ....Sheffield, Poly.

OCTOBER 1979

October 1st - Monday................................

THE PHOTOS are the perfect vehicle for the talents of nineteen-year old vocalist Wendy Wu. This Evesham quartet have just been signed to a record contract with CBS. They're in the studio now working on their debut single. Wendy became acquainted with the trio when they were playing under the name Satan's Rats.

THE NIPS have their third single released today. They've signed up with Soho Records, who've pressed up two more Shane McGowan originals, "Gabrielle" and "Vengeance." There has also been a distribution deal struck with Chiswick Records so that their future singles will have wider reach. The Nips are Shane MacGowan, Shanne Bradley, and new members Gavin Douglas and Stan Brennan. Shane will find wider fame in the '80s as the lead singer of the over-the-top Irish band The Pogues.

FELT is actually an individual "Lawrence," from Birmingham and has his debut single out on his own Shanghai Records. Tracks are "Index" and "Break It." A cryptic paragraph on the homemade sleeve says, "A distant voice pleaded for silence in a disused language." Reviewing the single for *NME*, Danny Baker wrote, "It's just a solo guitar being strummed like when you or I pick one up at a mate's house and whack away to everyone's earache until told to belt up or clear off or both. Just a guitar being strummed for three minutes, that's all…this (is a) major step forward for British rubbish." Copies of the single are only one pound each and can be ordered from Felt at 3 Albion Cottages, Birmingham Road, Water Orton, Birmingham B46.

THE AU PAIRS aren't prepared to take care of you, but they are ready to entertain. Their debut single is now out on 021 Records. It features "You," "Domestic Departure" and "Kerb Crawler." The Au Pairs are Lesley Woods on vocals and guitar, Paul Foad on vocals and guitar, Jane Munroe on bass and Pete Hammond on drums. Secret messages scratched in the vinyl are "sink into his arms" and "arms in his sink."

LIVE TONIGHT!

BUZZARDS/ SHEENIE & THE GOYS/ NEGATIVES ....Birmingham, Digbeth Civic Hall	DIALS ....London, Hope & Anchor
TEENBEATS/V.I.P.'s..................London, Bridge House	NINE NINE NINE.......................London, Marquee
VAPORS ....London, Fulham Greyhound	QUADS/DANGEROUS GIRLS ....London, Nashville
	DESTROY ALL MONSTERS ....Sheffield, Penthouse Basement

2nd - Tuesday..................................

DALEK I (formerly Dalek I Love You) are in name alone connected with Dr. Who. They could be traced more directly to the family tree which begat Orchestral Manoeuvres. That perhaps explains the common electrical ground they share. Like their friends in OMID, Dalek I are a duo. It's the combined talents of Alan Gill and Dave Hughes who wrote, played and produced their new Phonogram single "The World" and "We're All Actors."

DOLLY MIXTURE have been around about a year and a half and are still in the pre-recording stage of their career, not looking for a major to sweep them up, just the chance to do a single or two. They got together in Cambridge when Hester and Debsey were at school together. They wanted to start a band although they didn't play anything. So start they did, enlisting the help of Ratchel, who lived down the street. Among their songs are a odd covers of "Honky Honda," "Fatsticks," Tommy Roe's "Dizzy," and The Osmond Brothers' "All Fall Down." They've already recorded a BBC session for John Peel's show and are hoping to get a demo session with Nick Lowe. They've played publicly about thirty times and will play again tonight at the Music Machine in London. Dolly Mixture is Debsey on bass, Ratchel on guitar, and Hester on drums.

BUZZCOCKS/JOY DIVISION ....Liverpool, Mountford Hall	PENETRATION/ LOCALOPERATOR ....Manchester, Russell Club
NINE NINE NINE ....London, Marquee	TEENBEATS ....Sheffield, Limit Club
V.I.P.'s/BARRACUDAS/ DOLLY MIXTURE ....London, Music Machine	

3rd - Wednesday..................................

THE STRANGLERS have a single released from their LP "The Raven" this week. It's the politically inspired "Nuclear Device." Hugh Cornwell describes the song as being about, "…an ongoing situation in Queensland (Australia), it's been going on just over ten years. The guy's remained in power with only 17% of the vote, he's managed this by various ruses, i.e. gerrymandering, changing the electoral boundaries to suit his party, which happens to be the country party. Ninety percent of Australia lives in urban communities on the coast, however John Bjelke Peterson, the fascist dictator in question, has managed to make the vote of his constituents, all the large ranch owners, worth twice the vote of a city person. He's killing off all the Abo (Aboriginies) so he can get the uranium out of their land, and sold a big stretch of coastline to Japan to build a resort without telling the rest of Australia. And he's not even Australian! He's a Swede! He tried to get into England about twelve years ago and they wouldn't let him in, so he went to Australia." The single is flipped with the non-LP track "Yellowcake UF-6."

The Stranglers are also still compiling film footage for their proposed feature length movie. Recently they shot some satirical film in Portugal to go along with the new single "Nuclear Device." They've been adding to it for almost two years, tucking in a bit of live footage here, a comedy routine there. Already there is four hours waiting editing.

STRANGLERS ....Dublin, Chariot Inn	CUDDLY TOYS/TRENDIES ....London, Moonlight Club
CARPETTES............................London, 101 Club	VAPORS/ARTHUR'S DILEMMA .....London, Music Machine
MEDIUM MEDIUM ....London, Hope & Anchor	MANCHESTER MEKON/ STEVE MIRO & THE EYES ....Manchester, The Factory
NINE NINE NINE.......................London, Marquee	

OCTOBER 1979

4th - Thursday...

PUBLIC IMAGE LTD. has a new single called "Memories." It's an advance track from the new LP "Metal Box." The single is flipped with "Another," a non-LP track. In an open letter to the *NME*, PiL drummer Richard Dudanski revealed that, "In the absence of any statement from PiL, I would like to inform you, that as from our Leeds gig (September 8th) I have ceased to be a member of that group. My disagreements and inability to work with certain members of the group in particular, resulted in mutual satisfaction at my exit." Public Image are currently searching for a new drummer.

COWBOYS INTERNATIONAL have nothing to do with western music. They're a pretty straight ahead electro-pop band that just happens to have ex-Clash drummer Terry Chimes as one of its members. Their full length album is just out in a very odd package from Virgin. "The Original Sin" comes in clear red plastic sleeve with the usual inner sleeve. The red sleeve filters the graphics so only the band name and personnel show through. Their previous single "Aftermath" and "Thrash" are both here, as well as nine new songs, among them "Pointy Shoes," "Part Of Steel," Hands" and "The (No) Tune." Cowboys International are Terry Chimes on drums, Jimmy Hughes on bass, Evan Charles on pianos, Ken Locke on vocals and Rick Jacks on aquarium guitars. Keith Levine from PiL guests on "Wish."

SEX PISTOLS have another single released. Can you believe it? Talk about milking a dead cow. The latest are two more tracks from *The Great Rock & Roll Swindle* soundtrack. On the topside is the theme song from the movie, "The Great Rock & Roll Swindle," and its flip is the '55 oldie "Rock Around The Clock" with Ten Pole Tudor on vocals. The picture sleeve is black with a credit card in color. The only subtle difference is that American Express is replaced by "Sex Pistols."

STRANGLERS	Belfast, Ulster Hall	PATRIK FITZGERALD/	
AU PAIRS	Birmingham, Golden Eagle	THE METHOD	London, Rock Garden
NINE NINE NINE	London, Marquee	PIRANHAS	London, School Of Economics
DESTROY ALL MONSTERS	London, Music Machine		

5th - Friday...

THE UNDERTONES are the subject of a most unusual reissue. Their debut album "The Undertones" has been repackaged. As of today, the original version goes out of print and a new version of the LP hits the shops. On the new version are additional tracks not on the original. They are the original indie versions of "Teenage Kicks" and "Get Over You," as well as the superior 45 version of the song "Here Comes The Summer." The jacket itself changes from the black and white photo of the band on a wall in Derry to an overhead shot in full color. A more appealing cover overall.

JOE JACKSON's second album is "I'm The Man." It's only ten tracks but what it looses in length, it makes up in substance. Pop songs with a point, and pointing at everyone but himself. Titles include "On Your Radio," "Don't Wanna Be Like That," "Amateur Hour," "It's Different For Girls" and "Geraldine And John." Lyrically you'd guess that Joe was a little unhappy in life before finding fame. Joe's band are Gary Sanford on guitar, Dave Houghton on drums and Graham Maby on bass.

THE MEKONS' third single, (their first since signing to Virgin) is out this weekend. It's "Work All Week," b/w "Unknown Wrecks." The review in the *NME* downplays the amateur abandon they launch into their music with. "The Mekons keep falling and there are too many groups doing this sort of amateur rumble for real for them to be given the laurels of yore. The track is a shambles and unlovable with it."

LIVE TONIGHT!

RUTS/THE FLYS	Birmingham, Aston Univ.	TOYAH/VOID QUARTET	London, Nashville
REVILLOS	Birmingham, Digbeth Civic Hall	NINE NINE NINE	London, Marquee
BOOMTOWN RATS/PROTEX	Edinburgh, Odeon	CHORDS	London, City Poly.
PENETRATION/LOCAL OPERATOR	Edinburgh, Univ.	SOFT BOYS/DOLLY MIXTURE	London, Rock Garden
BUZZCOCKS/JOY DIVISION	Glasgow, Apollo Centre	THE MEKONS	London, N. London Poly.
PIRANHAS	Liverpool, Poly.	TEN POLE TUDOR	London, Moonlight Club
ADVERTS/COWBOYS INTL./		JAGS	London, Queen Elizabeth College
CUDDLY TOYS	London, Electric Ballroom	BUZZARDS/FAST CARS	
SQUIRE	London, Goldsmith's College	SHEENY & THE GOYS	Manchester, The Funhouse

6th - Saturday...

ECHO & THE BUNNYMEN have good changes coming their way. First, the group has been fielding offers from various labels and has decided on the indie Korova Records, who has distribution through Warner Brothers. Second, would be the sacking (or is it packing?) of their original drum machine drummer (Echo) and replacing with a live flesh and blood human named Pete de Freitas.

THE CARPETTES have made the leap from singles band to album band. Their debut long-player is "Frustration Paradise." The trio turn in a dozen original songs, including "Reach The Bottom," "Lost Love," "I Don't Mean It," "Johnny Won't Hurt You," "Indo-China" and "Cruel Honesty." The Carpettes are Neil Thompson on vocals and guitar, Tim Wilder on drums and George Maddison on vocals and bass.

THE OUT will have the last record on Manchester-based Rabid Records. The company has been responsible for records by Slaughter & The Dogs, The Nosebleeds, Ed Banger, Jilted John and Gordon The Moron. This final single is a limited edition single by The Out of "No One Is Innocent" b/w "Linda's Just A Statue." The Out are Jo Roberts on vocals, George Borowski on guitar, Chris Daniels on bass, Dave Bassnet on keyboards and Lyndsey Frost on drums.

OCTOBER 1979

LIVE TONIGHT!

BEAT ....Birmingham, Aston Univ.	SECRET AFFAIR/SQUIRE ....London, Music Machine
BUZZCOCKS/JOY DIVISION ....Edinburgh, Odeon	TEARDROP EXPLODES/
MODERATTES/DARK HEARTS/	ECHO & THE BUNNYMEN............London, Nashville
THE PROFUNDOS/	CHELSEA ....London, Rock Garden
THE PASSAGE/	PATRIK FITZGERALD ....London, University College
ACTIVITY MINIMAL ....Liverpool, Walton Park Hall	UNDERTONES ....Manchester, Apollo
CUDDLY TOYS.........................London, Bridge House	THE OUT/ART FAILURE/
TEENBEATS ....London, Fulham Greyhound	GORDON THE MORON/
VAPORS/THE NEWS ....London, Marquee	GERRY & HOLOGRAMS..............Manchester, Poly.

7th - Sunday..

ONE GANG LOGIC describe themselves as "Scunthorpe's answer to Cabaret Voltaire." It makes sense that a North Midlands industrial town would generate a rather industrial band. They've just released their debut EP, a four-song affair containing "Alienate (Kafka Laughs)," "Queue Here," "Repeat Action" and "Who Killed Sex?" The numbered limited edition is on their own Stark Products label. One Gang Logic are Chris Leaning, Paul Singleton and Mick Clark.

PUBLIC IMAGE LTD. are starting to be the butt of jokes about their upcoming release of "Metal Box" that will be sold in a metal box. In this week's *Sounds*, under the heading "Brutal Sarcasm" this missive appears on the letters page, "Is it true that the next Public Image single will contain twenty seconds of music, come complete with a four-bedroom house in Surrey to keep it in, and will be limited to an edition of five and sell for only £35,000? TV, Luton."

UK SUBS/THE SECRET ....Dumfermline, Cinema	FALL ....London, School Of Economics
STRANGLERS ....Glasgow, Apollo Centre	DEVO.....................................Manchester, Odeon

8th - Monday..

B-52's The newest single from the B-52's simply pairs off two songs from their album, "6060-842" and "Hero Worship." It does come in a nice pink sleeve though that's identical to the album jacket except for the color.

THE GANG OF FOUR get to stretch out over an album. It's called "Entertainment!" The situationist style cover had a trio of pictures of a cowboy and Indian shaking hands with a matching trio of inscriptions, "The Indian smiles, he thinks the cowboy is his friend. The cowboy smiles, he is glad the Indian is fooled. Now he can exploit him." This triptych easily describes Gang Of Four's relationship with EMI as they see it. They feel their role as educators and shapers of society are wrapped up in their music. Tracks on the album of note are "Natural's Not In It," "Guns Before Butter," "Glass," "Essence Rare," "Not Great Men," and the prior single "Damaged Goods." Tight, sparse playing and driving rhythms mark this Leeds group as one to watch in the future.

THE SLITS' new single is something old, something new. The something new is "Typical Girls," taken from their album "Cut." On the flipside is their version of the Marvin Gaye song "I Heard It Through The Grapevine." This oldie was recorded for the BBC 2 *Grapevine* program back in April.

THE FEELIES, a New Jersey quartet that share more than a few ideas with the Talking Heads and Television, have their first UK single released. The group is incredibly low key and play live only occasionally. Their debut single is "Fa Ce La" and "Raised Eyebrows." An earlier version of "Fa Ce La" was released two years ago in the states. This one's out on Rough Trade as the labels twenty-fourth release. The Feelies are Bill Million on guitar and vocals, Glenn Mercer on guitar and vocals, Keith DeNuncio on bass and vocals, and Anton Fier (aka Andy Fisher) on drums. They've recently signed with Stiff Records who will have their product from now on. In the '80s and '90s, Anton Fier will distinguish himself in a group called the Golden Palominos.

PENETRATION/	VAPORS ....London, Fulham Greyhound
LOCAL OPERATOR...................Birmingham, Digbeth Civic Hall	PIRANHAS/
DEVO....................................Birmingham, Odeon	THE PRIME MOVERS ....London, Rock Garden (benefit)
FALL ....Liverpool, Eric's	DESTROY ALL MONSTERS ....Manchester, The Factory
SQUIRE ....London, 101 Club	GARY NUMAN ....Sheffield, City Hall

9th - Tuesday..

THE SPECIALS, who are about to embark on a major tour with Madness and the Selecter, have a new single out today. The "A" side is a cover of the 1967 Dandy Livingstone (aka Robert Thompson) ska track "Rudy, A Message To You." The Specials have re-arranged the title but not the song. It's almost note for note like the original including frequent guest Rico on trombone, who played on the 1967 Jamaican original! It's flipped with the original song "Nite Klub." The songs were produced by Specials admirer Elvis Costello.

IGGY POP is having trouble at Rockfield Studios where he's recording his next album. Longtime friend James Williamson, who Iggy has worked with for a decade, has been fired from his role as producer. The argument was over the general direction of the sessions. With all the basic tracks and vocals recorded, Iggy felt that the sessions were straying from the uncompromising rock and roll vision he held.

OCTOBER 1979

Williamson was under a great deal of pressure from Arista to produce an album that had a hit or two. He had assembled a talented group of musicians, including Glen Matlock and Steve New from the Rich Kids, and Barry Andrews from XTC. One of the new songs called "Play It Safe," features a guest vocal by David Bowie, and members of the Simple Minds who were working on their album at Rockfield as well. It remains to be seen what will happen with the thirteen tracks on the unfinished, unmixed tape.

MEKONS	London, Marquee		JAGS	London, Nashville
TOURISTS	London, Middlesex Poly.		DEVO	London, Rainbow
FIXATIONS/KILLERMETERS/			MADNESS	Sheffield, Limit Club
SEVENTEEN	London, Music Machine			

10th - Wednesday.....................................

THE HUMAN LEAGUE, Sheffield's best known electronic export, are now officially an album band. Their LP "Reproduction" has just hit the streets. It's ten tracks paint a bleak and sometime chilled picture of the future, without delving into science fiction like Gary Numan. Most are new songs, the exception being a re-recorded version of "Circus Of Death." Tracks featured include "Almost Medieval," "The Path Of Least Resistance," "Empire State Human," "Zero As A Limit," and an eerie version of the Righteous Brothers song "You've Lost That Loving Feeling."

THE TOURISTS release and album for the second time in only six months. The new one is "Reality Effect." Its cover portrays the band, all in white in a white room, photographed from above while streamers of paint falling from on high. Does this all mean something? The real gem on the album is a version of Dusty Springfield's "I Only Want To Be With You." There's originals too, "So Good To Be Back Home," "Nothing To Do" and "Everywhere You Look."

THE ADVERTS are back with their first release since "My Place" this past summer. They come forward with an album titled "Cast Of Thousands." Although the band now has Paul Martinez (ex-Stretch) instead of Howard Pickup, the LP was recorded before the switch. On vinyl are the previous single "My Place," plus new songs "Male Assault," "Television's Over," "I Looked At The Sun," and a song called "The Adverts." In a move possibly unique in the movement, the Adverts have a Bible quote on their album reverse of 1 John 2.15.

PERE UBU's new single "The Fabulous Sequel," is taken from the LP "New Picnic Time." It's flipped with two non-LP "B" sides. One is "Humor Me" recorded live in London, the other is "The Book Is On The Table." The *NME* describes this as a, "...fairly hilarious bit of uproar."

LIVE TONIGHT!

STIFF LITTLE FINGERS/			SOFT BOYS/BOOKS/	
DONKEYS	Birmingham, Digbeth Civic Hall		THE ACT	London, Music Machine
BOOMTOWN RATS/PROTEX	Glasgow, Apollo Centre		PIRANHAS	London, Nelson's
ADVERTS	Glasgow, College Of Technology		CLOCK DVA	Manchester, The Factory
CARPETTES	London, 101 Club		UK SUBS	Manchester, Univ.

11th - Thursday.....................................

THE DAMNED's newest single couples a new song with an old one. The "A" side is "Smash It Up," and is a sample from their next LP tentatively titled "New World Symphony." It's flipped with "Burglar," a song that found its way into a few hundred people's hands as a freebie disc back in January. All early copies are in a special color picture sleeve. Secret messages in the wax read "daylight robbery" and "now buy the album!"

THE KILLERMETERS are a Northern mod band that began their life as the usual bash and trash punk group in mid '77. They split up by the end of their year and saw the error of their ways. By October of '78 they were back together and were changing direction. They've become the top Northern mod band and draw crowds from Birmingham to Yorkshire. RCA subsidiary Gem Records have jumped on the Mod bandwagon (or is that Mod scooter?) and have signed up The Killermeters, who have their second single released today. It's "Twisted Wheel," and a tribute to the primo pre '68 scooter "SX 225." The Huddersfield band's members are Vic Vespa on vocals (is he the Szczesmowicz in the credits?), Mick Moore on guitar, Graham "Jez" Jessop on drums, and Sid & Tony Ruttle on support guitars.

GERRY & THE HOLOGRAMS are another Absurd Records band that is shrouded in mystery. No clues to their identity can be found anywhere on the sleeve. All that can be told is that the tracks are "Gerry & The Holograms" and "Increased Resistance." The group sound somewhat like a budget version of Devo. It's perhaps in that frame of mind that Absurd Records also released Gerry & The Holograms second single "The Emperors New Music." It's a novel statement about new music and trendies. The single is painted and glued into the sleeve. It is totally unplayable. It is fashion. It could be the next big thing.

AU PAIRS	Birmingham, Golden Eagle		PHOTOS/INMATES	London, Nashville
ADVERTS	Edinburgh, Astoria		KILLERMETERS/FIXATIONS/	
BOOMTOWN RATS/PROTEX	Glasgow, Apollo Centre		SEVENTEEN	Manchester, The Factory
DESTROY ALL MONSTERS	Liverpool, Eric's		STRESS/JOHN DOWIE/ALIEN TINT	Manchester, Poly.
RELUCTANT STEREOTYPES/3D5	London, 101 Club		JAGS	Sheffield, Limit Club

12th - Friday.....................................

THE SKIDS' new album "Days In Europa" bears a cover strikingly different from most albums in this musical genre. Borrowing heavily from Eastern European poster art from the '20s, the image of an olympian being crowned adorns the front of this proud album. Their single "Charade" is here, and so are nine others that will vye for your attention. Tops among them is "Working For The Yankee Dollar," followed by "A Day In Europa," "Thantos," "Animation" and "Home Of The Saved." Instead of remaining in the studio behind the console, former Be Bop Deluxe singer Bill Nelson played the keyboards required for these sessions. The most puzzling part of the album is the

OCTOBER 1979

cryptic note from the band, "Two down and six to go. Dedicated to the ghosts of futility."

"IS THE WAR OVER?" Cardiff is the capitol of Wales, located in the farthest West of England on the Bristol Channel. It's also apparently the home of a bristling new music scene. A compilation called "Is The War Over" captures sounds from eight new groups. The effort is on Z-Block Records and was recorded entirely on location at the Grass Roots Coffee Bar at 58 Charles Street in Cardiff. Side one starts with Addiction, a quartet that turn in three songs, "Stampede," "Seek and Search" and "Violence." Mad Dog likewise play a trio of songs. Test To Destruction is the experimental entry with only one track "Passive" on the disc. The Riotous Brothers must be Riotous but they're named Webb, Davies and Williams. Their two songs are "Airey Neave" and "No Justice. On side two we meet the Reptile Ranch, who had a single out this past May. The New Form turn in an unusual version of "Mack The Knife" and an original called "Kleptomania." The most unusual tracks are by the Young Marble Giants. This trio of Phil and Stuart Moxham, along with Alison Stratton play "Ode To Booker T" and "Searching For Mr. Right." Sort of a stripped down, nearly acoustic Flying Lizards groove. The LP bears a note that is so true to the D.I.Y. punk ethic that's becoming more rare these days. It says "It Was Easy, It Was Cheap. Your Turn Next."

SELECTER	Birmingham, Digbeth Civic Hall	MADNESS/	
DANGEROUS GIRLS/		ECHO & THE BUNNYMEN/	
DENIZENS	Liverpool, College Of Food	BAD MANNERS	London, Electric Ballroom
MEKONS	Liverpool, Eric's	PIRANHAS/THE PARROTS	London, Nashville
SQUIRE/BACK NUMBERS	London, Moonlight Club	LENE LOVICH/ JAINE AIRE/	
TOYAH/ONE EYED JACKS	London, Music Machine	METEORS	Sheffield, Poly.

13th - Saturday......................................

THE CURE are in London opening for the Siouxsie and Banshees tour. They're much tighter for it and their set is improving. In an article headlined "No Image, No Style, No Bullshit" Deanne Pearson captured some intriguing comments from band leader Robert Smith. "I think people are disappointed because we have no image. There's nothing for them to identify with, and imitate, like there is with the Clash, or The Ramones, or the Banshees. I wear the same clothes onstage as I do off stage- and that's nobody's idea of a pop star. I used to wear posey gear though, whatever was the 'in' thing to wear at the time, but those sort of clothes are always either too baggy or too tight, and I just like to wear clothes I'm comfortable in."

THE MERTON PARKAS' album is "Face In The Crowd," and is just out on Beggars Banquet Records. Twelve songs in all, there are two covers, "Tears Of A Clown" and "Stepping Stone." The other ten include a re-recorded version of both "You Need Wheels" and "Plastic Smile." There's also "I Don't Want To Know You," "Give It To Me Now" and "Empty Room." It captures nearly all of the band's live crowd pleasers.

LIVE TONIGHT!

PENETRATION/		SIOUXSIE & THE BANSHEES/	
LOCAL OPERATOR	Glasgow, Strathclyde Univ.	THE CURE	London, Lewisham Odeon
SLAUGHTER & THE DOGS	Liverpool, Eric's	PIRANHAS/NICKY & THE DOTS/	
SELECTER/MO-DETTES/		PETER & THE	
THE BEAT	London, Electric Ballroom	TEST TUBE BABIES	London, Thames Poly
PHOTOS	London, Moonlight Club	GANG OF FOUR	London, Univ.
ESSENTIAL LOGIC/		PASSAGE/MEDIATORS/	
SWELL MAPS/FAD GADGET	London, Nashville	GROW UP	Manchester, The Funhouse

14th - Sunday......................................

Ex-PISTOLS Steve Jones and Paul Cook refuse to just sit back and live on their semi-legendary status as the two least known members of the Sex Pistols. They're in rehearsals with a new group, and they've even latched onto a new manager, Fachtna O'Kelly, manager for the Boomtown Rats. The new trio, as yet unnamed, is Paul on drums, Steve on guitar and vocals, as well Andy Arthurs (from the Lightning Raiders) on bass. They're currently in the studio working on what they hope will be their debut album. Songs in the session are several original titles, "Rockin' Mick," "Madhouse," "Skull And Crossbones," "Another Dream" and "Kamikaze," and a few odd covers.

THE TALKING HEADS' newest single is "Life During Wartime" and "Electric Guitar." Both tracks are from the new LP "Fear Of Music." The band will be touring to support the new LP and haven't played a UK tour since '77. They start the dates at the end of November.

PENETRATION announce their splitting up onstage in their hometown of Newcastle! Pauline Murray told the *NME*, "I never wanted to be in Penetration and to be worrying all the time. I wanted it to be fun, not to be always thinking of hit singles and cracking America and writing for the next LP." After three years of touring and recording it's all become too routine. The band feel that they've lost sight of their initial goal and are weary of the record game. Tonight's hometown farewell gig was recorded by Virgin's Manor Mobile studio. They've got only a few more concerts in them, most notably the gig at London's Electric Ballroom on November 3rd. It's uncertain what the members will do apart from the band afterwards.

RANDOM HOLD	London, Marquee	ORIGINAL MIRRORS/	
STRANGLERS	Sheffield, Top Rank	PENETRATION	Newcastle, City Hall

15th - Monday......................................

SPLODGENESSABOUNDS are the South-East London band that is nervous their concerts will start being cancelled on a regular basis. They're a large group (eight members) who are rather theatrical in their presentation. Their act and song lyrics have had management and councilmen close down gigs in Chiselhurst, Geckenham Park, Bromley and Deptford. The general objection is a song called "Michael Booth's Talking Bum," where Max Splodge drops his trousers so he can talk out of his bum. They'll try to play tonight at the 101 Club in liberal Clapham.

OCTOBER 1979

THE HUMAN LEAGUE are preparing for their national tour to support the release of their album "Reproduction." They've added some films to the familiar slide show that normally accompanies them on the road, projecting them onto a 14' x 21' screen. To further focus attention on the album, Virgin Records has released a single of "Empire State Human" b/w the non-LP song "Introducing." Secret messages in the vinyl are "bloody witty, that was."

SEX PISTOLS cause trouble, even when they aren't together any more. It only took a little over a week for them to become the target of a legal action by American Express over the sleeve to their latest single whose sleeve bears a parody of the American Express card. The image stuck too close to home for the company who have won a temporary court injunction to halt the sales of the single in the offensive sleeve. Virgin has been charged with Breach of Copyright, Trade Marketing Infringement, and Trade Libel.

STRANGLERS	Birmingham, Top Rank	SPLODGENESSABOUNDS	London, 101 Club
MEKONS/GANG OF FOUR	Edinburgh, Tiffany's	UK SUBS/STUNT KITES	Sheffield, Penthouse Basement
LITTLE ROOSTERS/ THE MODS	Liverpool, Eric's		

16th - Tuesday.......................................

COWBOYS INTERNATIONAL The new single from Cowboys International takes "Thrash," a track from their new LP and couples it with the non-LP "Many Times (Revised)." The flipside was originally handed out as a flexi disc with their last single "Nothin Doing." This is a different version of that freebie.

YELLOW MAGIC ORCHESTRA have been described as a Japanese version of Gary Numan, who is in all fairness the English version of German band Kraftwerk. The group began as a trio when they recorded their LP, but have since grown to twice that size (just like in the monster movies!) and land on the Venue's stage in London as a six-piece band ready to play. Their next LP "Solid State Survivor" is finished and will have material featured in tonight's show.

PSYCHEDELIC FURS have been getting headlines lately about long lines, packed shows and electrifying sets of original music. Today, they've made the next big step to fame. The Psychedelic Furs debut single for Epic Records is out. It's "We Love You," b/w "Pulse." The London-based group is Richard Butler on vocals, his brother Tim Butler on bass. Duncan Kilburn lends sax to the group and the guitars are played by John Ashton and Roger Morris. Vince Ely plays drums.

ASTRONAUTS/THE MOB/		PIRANHAS	London, Dingwalls
THE ANDROIDS OF MU	London, Acklam Hall	UK SUBS/THE URGE	London, Marquee
CUDDLY TOYS/		STIFF LITTLE FINGERS/	
PRETTY BRITISH	London, Bridge House	DONKEYS	Manchester, Poly.
YELLO MAGIC ORCHESTRA	London, The Venue	MEKONS	Sheffield, Limit Club

17th -Wednesday..

THE SPECIALS' self-titled skanking debut album is out on Two Tone Records. The LP was produced by Elvis Costello and is an excellent document of the Specials live favorites. The album covers several covers like "Monkey Man," "You're Wondering Now," "Do The Dog" and "Too Hot." Originals include "It's Up To You," "Concrete Jungle," "Blank Expression," and the show stopping admonition "Too Much, Too Young." Even Chrissie Hynde gets in on the backing vocals on "Night Klub." The Specials are Jerry Dammers on keyboards, Horace Panter on bass, John Bradbury on drums, Roddy Radiation (aka Roddy Byers) on guitar, and the trio of Lynval Golding, Neville Staples and Terry Hall on vocals.

THE VAPORS, proteges of the Jam, have laid another career milestone. Their single "Prisoners" and "Sunstroke" is just released on United Artists Records. The Gilford quartet are Steve Smith on bass, Howard Smith on drums, Dave Fenton on guitar and vocals and Edward Bazalgette on guitar. They're on the road with the Jam throughout November and will play a few solo gigs before hitching their wagon to the superstars.

GANG OF FOUR	Glasgow, Technical College	TENPOLE TUDOR	London, Moonlight Club
BATS/CAR CRASH	London, 101 Club	DOGEMS/CHEFS	London, Thames Poly.
SCARS	London, Hope & Anchor	BOOMTOWN RATS/PROTEX	Sheffield, City Hall
UK SUBS/THE URGE	London, Marquee		

LIVE TONIGHT!

18th - Thursday.......................................

THE ASSOCIATES had a big enough hit with their debut single in their hometown of Edinburgh, that MCA Records has purchased it, remixed it and rush-released it. Their cover of Bowie's "Boys Keep Swinging" was previously out on their own Double Hip record label. The Associates are Billy Mackenzie, and Alan Rankine. Although the song won't be a hit for MCA, the Associates will hit the UK Top 40 three times in 1982 with dance oriented songs like "Party Fears Two," "Club Country" and "18 Carat Love Affair."

SHAM 69 have a single taken from the newest Sham 69 LP on the streets this week. The track "You A Better Man Than I," is flipped with the non-LP song "Give The Dog A Bone." Early copies come in a special picture sleeve.

PROTEX are still at work on their debut album for Polydor, tentatively titled "Strange Obsessions." They do however, have a new single out. It's "I Can Only Dream" and "Heartache." The sessions are being produced by Hendrix producer Chas Chandler.

SHAM 69/DRONES	Birmingham, Bingley Hall	UK SUBS/THE URGE	London, Marquee
DESTROY ALL MONSTERS	London, Dingwalls	TOURISTS	Manchester, U.M.I.S.T.
POISON GIRLS/THE CRASS	London, Electric Ballroom	REVILLOS	Sheffield, Limit Club

OCTOBER 1979

...DON'T WATCH THAT • WATCH THIS

MADNESS

ONE STEP BEYOND...

19th - Friday.....................

MADNESS have both a single and album out! The 45 is a cover of the Prince Buster classic "One Step Beyond" and is flipped with "Mistakes." The 12" version of the single comes with the extra track "Nutty Theme." "One Step Beyond" will become the band's theme song for the next decade when it hits the UK #2 and remains on the charts for an amazing seventy-eight weeks. It's only the begining of an amazing string of fifteen top 10 singles over four years. The album "One Step Beyond" includes a re-recorded version of their debut hit "The Prince," as well as "My Girl," "Land Of Hope & Glory," "Tarzan's Nuts," "Bed & Breakfast Man," "In The Middle Of The Night," "Madness" and a version of "Swan Lake!" Since Chas Smash's contribution is mainly visual in a live concert, he's on the LP in a photo series on the back doing that "nutty dance" in a pattern that some will mistake for instructions to copy the dance.

SHAM 69 Tonight's the return/farewell of Sham 69, and the special concert is scheduled at the same venue that they played their second farewell concert last June 29th. Vocalist Jimmy Pursey and bassist Dave "Kermit" Treganna have joined with Dave Parsons and Ricky Goldstein. This is positively the last time that Sham 69 will have a farewell concert (until the next time.) Apart from Sham 69, Jimmy Pursey has been busy in the role of producer for Warner Brothers Records. His latest projects include singles by Bob A Lewie, Jimmy Edwards, Long Tall Shorty, Kids Next Door and The Low Numbers.

THE ANGELIC UPSTARTS have a new single in the shops this weekend of "Never 'Ad Nothin'" It's a new song recorded since their album release this past summer. The song is based on the story of eighteen-year old Paul Howe who held a man hostage at gunpoint at the Castle Pub in Essex. In the end he tried to run and was shot dead by the police. The Castle's management is trying to get the single banned because they feel it is making money out of a local tragedy. The single is flipped with "Nowhere Left To Hide." The group are currently on tour in England throughout the month.

THE CLASH "I don't want to see punk as another slavish attitude and image and everything is pre-planned and pre-thought out for you to slip in comfortably. Like, say, mod is. Let's all put on mod suits and feel less nervous. I vote for the weirdo. I vote for the loonies. I vote for the people off the left wall. I vote for the individuals." —Joe Strummer of the Clash in this week's *NME*.

LIVE TONIGHT!

DANGEROUS GIRLS	Birmingham, New Inn	RUTS/THE PACK	London, Electric Ballroom
BOOMTOWN RATS/PROTEX	Birmingham, The Odeon	CLASSIX NOUVEAUX/	
CHORDS	Birmingham, The Underworld	LIMITED EDITION	London, Music Machine
SHAM 69 (return)/		ANGELIC UPSTARTS/	
THE DRONES	Glasgow, Apollo	THE WALL	London, The Nashville
SKIDS/FINGERPRINTZ	Liverpool, Mountford Hall	STRANGLERS	London, Rainbow

20th - Saturday.....................

THE NOT SENSIBLES' approach to music that would best be described as the total antithesis to the Sex Pistols. The single "I'm In Love With Margaret Thatcher" is the band's second single. Their boundless enthusiasm for Thatcher is tempered with the sarcastic delivery that makes the message clear they're not serious. It's coupled with "Little Boxes" and "Garry Bushell's Band Of The Week." This homemade single is on Redball Records in a limited pressing of one thousand. The band is from Burnely in Lancashire, and is Haggis on silly vocals, Sage on guitar, Cliff H on bass, Kev on drums and R. C. Rawlinson on keyboards. Talking to Mick Middles from *Sounds*, vocalist Haggis said "All we want to do is make silly records and play silly gigs. We've got loads of material as well, hundreds of them."

MARTIN CHAMBERS BIG STICK is the name that The Pretenders are using to hide under for a warm-up gig prior to their next tour. Using their drummer's name for the group, hundreds sus out the ill-hid mystery and turn out for the show. Police arrive, hoping to quell the trouble that began brewing there at last night's Angelic Upstarts concert. The concert was stopped at 11pm, despite the venue having the proper permits to remain open til midnight.

ANOTHER PRETTY FACE have a basic goal met. They've been signed to Virgin Records. It was a tough road. Over the last year the band has had its good times. Their debut single "All The Boys Love Carrie" was named the *NME* "Single Of The Week." It sold phenomenally well. On the other hand A.P.F. have had their gear stolen on their first trip to London, and have had a hard time keeping the group together. They have a new rhythm section with Willie Kirkwood the new bassist and Steve McLaughlin the new drummer. This new band is in rehearsals, writing new material. The proposed single could be either "Whatever Happened To The West?" or "The Kids Are Back."

BOOMTOWN RATS/PROTEX	Birmingham, Odeon	PURPLE HEARTS/SQUIRE/	
DANGEROUS GIRLS	Birmingham, The Underworld	DOLLY MIXTURE/	
MERTON PARKAS/		TEENBEATS	London, Electric Ballroom
THE CROOKS	Glasgow, Univ.	PATRIK FITZGERALD	London, Hope & Anchor
RED CRAYOLA/SWELL MAPS/		BACK TO ZERO	London, Marquee
SPIZZ ENERGI	Liverpool, Eric's	PRIVATE VICES/	
		MARTIN CHAMBER'S BIG STICK	London, The Nashville

OCTOBER 1979

21st - Sunday.....................................

ELVIS COSTELLO is appearing in a comedy film called *Americathon*. The film is set 200 years in the future when America goes bankrupt and has a TV telethon to bail itself out. It's stars are John Ritter as the President, Harvey Korman, Fred Willard and Chief Dan George. Music for the film included one old song, "I Don't Want To Go To Chelsea," and one new song "Crawling To The U.S.A.," where Elvis actually appears singing it. The rest of the soundtrack brings together Eddie Money, The Beach Boys, and Nick Lowe ("Without Love").

WIRE's new single is taken from the LP "154." It's "Map Ref. 41 N 93 W." My stuttering geography makes me think that's the coordinates for Sullivan County, Missouri. The flip is the non-LP "Go Ahead." Not allowing the grass to grow under their feet, Wire have reportedly recorded a fifteen-minute epic called "Crazy About Love." The song is the result of their latest John Peel session. Not being told what to record, they were given fifteen minutes of time, to make of it what they would. Instead of recording four different songs, as they had twice in the past, they thought they'd offer up something different. One long song.

BOOMTOWN RATS/PROTEX	........Birmingham, Odeon	TOYAH/VITUS DANCE	................London, Marquee
REVILLOS	...............................Glasgow, Pavilion	BUZZCOCKS/JOY DIVISION	.........Sheffield, Top Rank
X-DREAMYSTS	........................London, Hope & Anchor		

22nd - Monday.....................................

SIOUXSIE & THE BANSHEES' lead singer Siouxsie collapsed after the Hammersmith Odeon show tonight. Rushed to the hospital, she was diagnosed as suffering from hepatitis and ordered to take a two-month rest from touring. She was in this same condition only two weeks ago, but without a solid diagnosis, kept on the road pushing herself. Now she's been ordered to stay home. Everything else on the tour has been cancelled except perhaps a TV spot on the *Something Else* program next month. It's not said how she got hepatitis, but the habit of fans gobbing on bands is an easy way to acquire it.

THE CARPETTES, Newcastle's fifth best known band, have their newest release on the streets. It's a single of "I Don't Mean It" b/w "Easy Way Out." While the "A" side if from their album "Frustration Paradise," the flip is a non-LP track.

FASHION	................................Birmingham, Barrel Organ	SIOUXSIE & THE BANSHEES/	
LENE LOVICH/JANE AIRE/		THE CURE	...............................London, Hammersmith Odeon
METEORS	...............................Birmingham, Odeon	PRETENDERS	.........................London, Marquee
BACK TO ZERO/STA-PREST	.........Liverpool, Eric's	SPIZZ ENERGI/	
UNDERTONES/TENPOLE TUDOR	...Liverpool, Mountford Hall	DR. MIX & REMIX	...................London, Nashville
STRANGLERS	..........................Liverpool, Romeo & Juliet	MO-DETTES/DELTA 5	................London, Notre Dame Hall
QUADS/DANGEROUS GIRLS	........London, Hope & Anchor	SHAM 69/THE DRONES	.............Manchester, The Apollo

23rd - Tuesday.....................................

CABARET VOLTAIRE release the first of a long string of LP's. This debut is called "Mix-Up." It's nine unusual snapshots of a most unusual band. Starting off with "Kirlian Photograph," the LP wanders through the Seed's '60s psychedelic song "No Escape," into originals like "Fourth Shot" "Heaven And Hell," "Eyeless Sight," "Phototopia," "On Every Other Street," "Expect Nothing" concluding with "Capsules." Recorded this last summer, the LP covers new territories in music, if not in sound alone, in arrangement too. You see, Cabs are a drumerless synth trio. The *NME's* Andy Gill describes the album as, "...emotional soundscaping, offering several alternatives to the pure noise, pure pop furrows endlessly ploughed by Latter-day synthesizer bands...the 'Cabs display a hitherto unrivalled ability to slowly, inexorably increase tension, the subliminal turn of the screw operates to good effect throughout the album."

SECRET AFFAIR's newest single is "Let Your Heart Dance" and "Sorry, Wrong Number." The group has also added to its number, Dave Winthrop, who's been playing sax with Secret Affair on their records and at a few live dates is now an official member of the group.

THE TEENBEATS follow their August debut single with another called "Strength Of The Nation." It's paired with "I'm Gone Tomorrow." The Hastings mod band have a growing following at the Windsor Castle, Bridge House and Fulham Greyhound. The Teenbeats are Eddie, Huggy, Dave, Ken and Paul.

UK SUBS/THE URGE	.................Birmingham, Digbeth Civic Hall	ADVERTS/DECOYS	...................London, Marquee
UNDERTONES/TENPOLE TUDOR	...Birmingham, Odeon	CLASSIX NOUVEAUX/	
PIRANHAS	...........................London, Dingwalls	VITUS DANCE	.........................London, Nashville
YELLOW MAGIC ORCHESTRA	......London, The Venue	SKIDS/FINGERPRINTZ	...............Manchester, Apollo

24th - Wednesday.....................................

THE BOOMTOWN RATS' album "The Fine Art Of Surfacing" has surfaced in UK record shops. It's the album that wraps together the mega hit single "I Don't Like Mondays" with new tracks like "Diamond Smiles," "Having My Picture Taken," "Someone's Looking At You" and "When The Night Comes." Press reviews are beginning to mention lead singer Bob Geldof as "the next Mick Jagger." Mainstream buyers have pushed advance orders of the album to the highest ever for the band. However, the jaded music press dismiss the album. In this week's *NME* appears, "The Rats' sound is so busy and bright that you barely have time to place it before it's off again on some other tacky tangent. It doesn't demand close attention, it just makes a lot of noisy fuss. Scrutinize it, and it tends to collapse under the weight of its many influences. You could call it clever but you can't really admire it for anything other than sheer crass nerve. You could excuse it as fun but it's so contrived that it isn't."

THE DICKIES' second album is "Dawn Of The Dickies." It had originally been titled "Nightmare Alley" but emerged with a new name, and a cover that parodies a scene out of *Dawn of The Dead*. The Dickies gained a great deal of their fame by singing covers, but only one

OCTOBER 1979

is on this album, the previously released "Nights In White Satin." The rest are originals with titled like "Fan Mail," "Attack Of The Mole Men," "I'm Stuck In A Pagoda (With Tricia Toyota)" and a song about Sammy Davis, Jr. called "Where Did His Eye Go?"

LIVE TONIGHT!

BUZZCOCKS/JOY DIVISION .... Birmingham, Odeon	YELLOW MAGIC ORCHESTRA ...... London, The Venue
PSYCHEDELIC FURS .... High Wycombe, Town Hall	ADVERTS/DECOYS .... London, Marquee
LENE LOVICH/JANE AIRE/	GAFFA/ARTERY .... London, Rock Garden
METEORS .... Liverpool, Univ.	SKIDS/FINGERPRINTZ .... Sheffield, Top Rank
LAMBRETTAS .... London, Hope & Anchor	THE FALL .... Sheffield, Penthouse Basement

25th - Thursday..

THE TOURISTS' newest single could be their strongest to date. It's a cover of the Dusty Springfield '60s hit "I Only Want To Be With You" flipped with "Summers Night." The band was so close to success with their last single, but even two appearances on *Top Of The Pops* failed to push it into the top 30. Hopes for this one to be their biggest yet are realized when the song reaches #4 on *Top Of The Pops* in England.

THE FALL's second album is "Dragnet." It was carefully crafted over three days last August with the Fall producing. Needless to say, it's by no means slick and predictable, but the Fall seldom are. Unusual titles abound including "Psykick Dancehall," "Dice Man," "Muzorewi's Daughter," "Spectre vs. Rector," "Choc-Stock" and "Flat Of Angles." The mercurial lineup of the Fall in this snapshot are Mark E. Smith on vocals, Mike Leigh on drums, Marc Riley on guitars, Craig Scanlan on electric guitar and Steve Hanley on bass.

HUGH CORNWELL, vocalist for the Stranglers, has a record all his own. It's a sample from the forthcoming solo LP "Nosferatu." It's a rather straight up read of the Cream classic "White Room," flipped with an instrumental version of "Losers In A Lost Land."

ESSENTIAL LOGIC's first full length album is cumbersomely titled "Waddle Ya Play? Beat Rhythm News." The Rough Trade LP contains previously released tracks like "Quality Crayon Wax OK," "World Friction" and "Wake Up." New songs are "The Order Form (I want to order a pelican)," "Shabby Abbott," "Albert," "Alkaline Loaf (in the area)," "Collectors Dust" and "Popcorn Boy." *Sounds* magazine describes the album as, "…a real surprise. Like X-Ray Spex on heat, whole swirling fairgrounds of saxes wail, powerful bass and meathook guitars spread themselves gloriously round Lora's rich expressive voice, the whole album makes for a brilliant revelation."

SKIDS/FINGERPRINTZ .... Birmingham, Odeon	BOOMTOWN RATS/PROTEX .... London, Hammersmith Odeon
JAGS .... Edinburgh, Astoria	CHRIS SIEVEY & FRESHIES/
HOLLY & THE ITALIANS/	THE ACT .... London, Kings College
KEVIN ARMSTRONG'S	ANGELIC UPSTARTS/
LOCAL HEROS .... London, 101 Club	THE WALL .... London, Nashville
LAUGHING GAS/FAN CLUB .... London, Acklam Hall	STRANGLERS .... Manchester, The Apollo

26th - Friday..

THE CURE's new single is a song about following other people's fashions called "Jumping Someone Else's Train." It's backed with "I'm Cold." Robert describes it as being, "…about kids latching onto the passing bandwagon. Whether it's the latest music or newest fashion, trading in their clothes and their records for todays flavor. You know, like all the kids trading in their leathers and bondage trousers for mod suits and pork pie hats." Both tracks are new recordings. The Cure have just finished a successful tour with Siouxsie & The Banshees, putting them in front of more people in one month than they've probably played to since they got together. There have also gone through some changes in the band, bringing in two new members. Michael Dempsey, who was in the band from the beginning has left the group and is being replaced with two new people. One is ex-Lockjaw bassist Simon Gallup, an old friend of Robert's. The other is Matthieu Hartley who joins in on keyboards. Both Simon and Matthieu were in a group called the Mag Spies while holding down jobs in a plastic factory (Simon) and at a hairdressers (Matthieu). This new line-up of the Cure will make their debut at Eric's in Liverpool on the 16th.

Concerning his departure from the group, Dempsey phoned *Sounds* magazine with his side of the story. "First off, Robert (Smith) rang up to say we wouldn't be rehearsing again. Then Chris Parry phoned to say Robert didn't want to work with me any more. There were no internal problems that I know of. Never any blazing rows or anything like that. I always thought I got on well with Lol and had a working relationship with Robert. But when I rang them up both insisted the split was purely for personal reasons. There was no musical differences involved."

COCKNEY REJECTS were close to doing a deal with Warner Brothers, and now it's announced that they have signed with EMI instead. Their debut on the label is a single of "I'm Not A Fool" and "East End" to be followed soon by an album produced by Jimmy Pursey. The Cockney Rejects are Micky Lard Geggus on lead guitar, Stinky Turner on vocals, Andy Scott on drums and Vince Riordan on bass. EMI's promotional clout, and a solid boot-boy fan base, pushes the single to #65 in the UK, and most of their future singles don't fare any better.

KILLING JOKE CONFIRM YOUR WORST FEARS
ask your dealer

KILLING JOKE make their debut with a 10", three song EP. "Are You Receiving," is coupled with "Turn To Red" and "Nervous System." It's on the Malicious Damage record label and the record sleeve is stuffed with a paper insert and four small cards. Killing Joke are Martin "Youth" Glover on bass, Jaz Coleman on vocals and keyboards, Geordie (aka K. Walker) on guitar and Paul Ferguson on drums. The roots of the group go back to late '78 when Jaz and Paul met. At the time Paul was a member of the Matt Stagger Band and Jaz joined him briefly on keyboards. The two eventually wanted to do their own thing, quit, placed adverts in the music papers and found their band members. The group is based in the Notting Hill Gate area of London and possibly took their name from a Monty Python sketch about a lethal joke developed during WWI by the British. Their sound is somewhat similar to the Stranglers, without the gothic keyboards.

OCTOBER 1979

LIVE TONIGHT!

MERTON PARKAS ....Birmingham, The Underworld	LEOPARDS/AU PAIRS/
LENE LOVICH/JANE AIRE/	POISON GIRLS/PRAG VEC...........London, Goldsmith's College
METEORS ....Glasgow, Apollo Centre	VAPORS/THE NIPS ....London, Music Machine
THE ACT ....London, Chelsea Art College	TEA SET/LITTLE ROOSTERS/
SQUIRE ....London, Crystal Palace Hotel	BODIES ....London, Notre Dame Hall
JOY DIVISION/	ENGLISH SUBTITLES ....London, Windsor Castle
A CERTAIN RATIO/	PSYCHEDELIC FURS ....Manchester, The Factory (closed?)
THE DISTRACTIONS ....London, Electric Ballroom	SLAUGHTER & THE DOGS...........Sheffield, Limit Club
BOOMTOWN RATS/PROTEX.........London, Hammersmith Odeon	

27th - Saturday...

ADAM & THE ANTS set a sarcastic mention in *Sounds*. Jaws reported, "Termites Fall Out (Millions Rejoice). Rumour has it that Adam and The Ants have split up. Yep, hand out the flag music lovers, the terrible termites have packed it in at long bleeding last. Uh-oh, should have read on, seems Adam's gonna go solo and tour round as Adam Ant with a backing band. Drat." From the tenor of the notice you shouldn't expect any positive reviews in *Sounds* anytime soon of the new group. The reality is that guitarist Matthew Ashman and bassist Andy Warren have left, leaving Adam and drummer Dave Barbe. Their debut album is slated for release early next month.

THE ADVERTS are no more! They play their last-ever gig tonight at Slough College. They felt that they were all moving in different directions after four years and, with no great upheaval or fight, have packed it in. Vocalist TV Smith will remain with RCA Records and is putting together a new band with keyboardist Tim Cross, a late addition to the Adverts. Vocalist Gay Advert is planning a anti-vivisection single on her own and is considering putting together another group.

U2 get another encouraging mention in this week's *Sounds* magazine. Dave McCullough lists U2's Irish debut single among his three favorite new discs. He had seen the band in Dublin in August and listed "Out Of Control" and "Shadows & Tall Trees" among his favorites from a cassette given him by Bono. Now there's a real record out, an Irish CBS release titled "U2-Three." Three songs make up the EP, "Out Of Control," "Stories For Boys" and "Boy/Girl." U2 is Adam Clayton on bass, Larry Mullen on drums, Bono (Paul Hewson) on vocals, and The Edge (Dave Evans) on guitar. All three of the songs will remain unique to the EP. "Out Of Control" and "Stories For Boys" will both be re-recorded in a slower, more produced version for their debut album. "Boy/Girl" will appear as a live recording on the flipside of the single "I Will Follow." The initial Irish release is as a 12" single, with each of the 1,000 copies individually numbered. Further copies come in a black, white and red pic sleeve.

THE PORTRAITS are a London-based band that have their debut single just out on Ariola Records. The tracks are "Little Women" and "Hazard In The Home." They've been playing around town since late '78. The group is Cy Curnin on lead vocals, Adam Woods on drums and Rupert Greenall on synths. They're regulars on the live scene playing at the Bridge House, Brecknock, and the Marquee. They will eventually mutate into The Fixx and in 1982 have hits like "Stand Or Fall" and "Red Skies."

MERTON PARKAS/CROOKS ....Birmingham, The Underworld	CABARET VOLTAIRE/
PINK MILITARY ....Liverpool, Eric's	THE PASSAGE/
SOFT BOYS/THE LIMOS ....London, 101 Club	THE TILLER BOYS ....London, Tottenham Court YMCA
BOOMTOWN RATS/PROTEX.........London, Hammersmith Odeon	ANGELTRAX/AU PAIRS/
ECHO & THE BUNNYMEN/	MO-DETTES...........................London, University Union
TEARDROP EXPLODES/	BUZZCOCKS/JOY DIVISION ....Manchester, Apollo
EXPELAIRES ....London, Thames Poly.	

28th - Sunday...

THE NEW YORK BLONDES is the name on a quasi-legal record that's just appeared in Europe. The original version was supposed to be released last year, but in nowhere near the way it's finally come out. Here's the story. Rodney Bingenheimer, a Los Angeles DJ, was to be the lead vocalist on a version of the '60s car song "Little G.T.O." A cast of musicians was assembled to help cut the backing tracks, with Debbie Harry of Blondie on scratch vocals. That means, a vocal track that Rodney was to sing with to get the meter and pitch of the song. It was intended to be mixed out leaving only Rodney coached along in the headphones by the phantom vocals that the public would never know were there. Wrong! A single has just surfaced on Decca/London Records. It's under the group name "The New York Blondes" and is the track "Little G.T.O." with Debbie Harry singing. Rodney has been mixed out, not Debbie. There's little doubt that most people perceive this as a new Blondie record even though it's technically a bootleg! The song is near and dear to Debbie Harry's heart and was frequently a part of the band's set back in '77.

PLASMATICS have a second single released on their own Vice Squad Records label. The shock-rockers turn in an unlikely cover of the Bobby Darin chestnut "Dream Lover," flipped with two originals "Corruption" and "Want You Baby." The single comes in clear yellow vinyl and a 7" hard cardboard color jacket.

NIPS' vocalist Shane O'Holligan (aka Shane McGowan) addresses the changing trends in music in this week's *NME*. "The way I see it is that we're coming up to the '80s and somebody's got to save rock 'n' roll from all those prats with synthesizers and a university education. And it might as well be me!"

MERTON PARKAS/CROOKS ....High Wycombe, Town Hall	TEENBEATS ....London, Rock Garden

OCTOBER 1979

RANDOM HOLD ....London, Marquee	RUBELLA BALLET/
ORIGINAL MIRRORS/	POISON GIRLS ....London, Stratford Theatre Royal
THE ACT ....London, Nashville	BUZZCOCKS/JOY DIVISION ....Manchester, Apollo

29th - Monday...

JIMMY PURSEY of Sham 69 has been asked to sit in for vacationing Radio One DJ Mike Read. He'll be playing the frisky disks and stacks o' wax through Thursday. In this week's *NME*, Jimmy is interviewed by Nick Kent who gets an excitable response from him when asked about his views on the Sex Pistols, Sid and Virgin Records. "Look at the way they exploited poor old Sid Vicious! People reckon I'm a bleedin' Wally and that the Pistols are so cool, but Christ I'd rather be a Wally, who's alive and healthy, instead of some so-called rock 'n' roll hero who's dead, or some basket case causality with his brain cells and blood spurting all over the walls and ceiling. But that's what they call fashionable. That's bleedin' fashion for yer! One thing Sham 69 are absolutely not about is fashion."

THE BUZZARDS have their recorded history compressed into forty minutes on an LP called "Jellied Eels and Record Deals." The LP covers the band's career from their debut single "19 & Mad," through John Peel sessions of "Sharp Young Me" and "British Justice," up to their latest single "We Make A Noise." The band writes on the back of the album, "Having completed their trial flights, The Buzzards mark the occasion with this clutch of songs. This album records their history to date, and includes unreleased demo material hatched in the brooding wilderness of Leyton and captured here in its raw state, together with their better know work. The band now intend to make significant changes of direction, but before they wander forever from Leyton, leave you with the fruits (and Veg) of the last two years."

LIVE TONIGHT!

SPECIALS/MADNESS/	TEN POLE TUDOR....................London, Hope & Anchor
SELECTER...........................Birmingham, Top Rank	MONOCHROME SET/TEA SET
LENE LOVICH/JANE AIRE/	THE NORMALS/FAD GADGET/ ......London, Notre Dame Hall
METEORS ....Edinburgh, Tiffany's	THE PRETENDERS ....London, Marquee
SMALL HOURS/LAMBRETTAS ......London, Bridge House	UK SUBS/THE URGE ....Sheffield, Penthouse

30th - Tuesday...............................

ADAM & THE ANTS are no longer simply a singles band! Their debut album is now out on Do-It Records. It's called "Dirk Wears White Sox" and catches you up on their best tracks. The only previously released track is "Car Trouble," which kicks the album off. It's followed by "Digital Tenderness," "Nine Plan Failed," "Day I Met God," "Tabletalk," "Cleopatra," "Never Trust A Man (With Egg On His Face)," "Animals And Men," "Family Of Nose" and "The Idea." The album was recorded last month in London with Adam doing the producing himself. The newest addition to the Ants is Lee Gorman who has just joined on bass filling the spot left by Andy Warren and ex-Pistols manager Malcolm McLaren enters the scene as the Ants new manager.

THE DANGEROUS GIRLS are ready to conquer the world! Or at least a little part of it. The Worcester band release their second record, an EP called "Taaga." The four song 7" features "Safety In Numbers," "Jump Up And Down," "Down On The File" and "Sex." Like last time, it's on their own Happy Face Records label.

GANG OF FOUR ....Birmingham, Digbeth Civic Hall	BARRACUDAS/
DANGEROUS GIRLS/	PRIVATE VICES.......................London, Moonlight Club
A.B.O.W./	UNDERTONES/
ANDROIDS OF MU ....Birmingham, Univ.	TENPOLE TUDOR ....London, Rainbow
COWBOYS INTL. ....London, Dingwalls	PATRIK FITZGERALD ....London, Wessex St. Youth Club
PIRANHAS ....London, Marquee	MERTON PARKAS/CROOKS ....Sheffield, Limit Club

31st - Wednesday..

THE RUTS are riding high with the success of their debut album "The Crack," that currently sits at #16 on the UK album charts. Their new single is "Jah War," b/w the non-LP song "I Ain't Sofisticated."

THE EXPELAIRES are another Liverpool band to be caught in Zoo Records' net. Their single "To See You" and "Frequency" is the seventh release for the indie label. The Expelaires are Grape on vocals, Carl Harper on drums, Mark Copson on bass, Dave Wolfenden on guitar and Craig Adams on keyboards.

TOURISTS..........................Birmingham, Poly.	TEA SET ....London, Upstairs At Ronnie Scott's
DRONES/THE LIMOS ....London, Music Machine	RUTS/FLYS ....Sheffield, Poly.
THE ACT ....London, Shepherds Bush Trafalgar	

November 1st - Thursday.................................

THE PURPLE HEARTS were the first mod band to be signed by Fiction Records, and today they follow up their debut single with a second called "Frustration." The single is flipped with "Extraordinary Sensations."

THE POLICE, SHAM 69 and **SQUEEZE** have skeletons rattled out of their closets today. Due to public demand, all three of the band's debut singles have been reissued. The Police's "Fall Out" and "Nothing Achieving" single features the original line-up before Andy Summers joined the band. The single is on the Illegal Records label as #001. The sleeve of the single, which was originally a black and white photo, is now in color with a checkerboard pattern added behind the band on the cover. Sham 69's debut single "Ulster" comes in a color sleeve that is totally different from the original black and white photo. It was originally issued in September of '77 on Step Forward

NOVEMBER 1979

Records. Squeeze's debut single, the "Packet Of Three" was originally out in July of '77 on Deptford Fun City Records. Now it's been re-packaged in a color sleeve and is available again. All three of the songs on the EP have been out of print for almost two years.

THE MOONDOGS are a mod band from Belfast. Tracks are "She's Nineteen" and "Ya Don't Do Ya?" The group are on the mod-pop side of things and are being touted as the next big thing from Ireland since the Undertones. One of the best things about records on Belfast's Good Vibrations label is that the sleeve almost always fold out into these great 16" x 12" posters. The Moondogs debut single is no different. The Moondogs are Jackie Hamilton on bass and vocals, Austin Barrett on drums, and Gerry McCandless on guitar and vocals.

PATRIK FITZGERALD	Edinburgh, Astoria	PHOTOS/DECOYS	London, Nashville
RELUCTANT STEREOTYPES	London, 101 Club	BRAINIAC 5	London, Rock Garden
LITTLE ROOSTERS/		ROBERT & THE REMOULDS	London, Windsor Castle
DOLLY MIXTURE	London, Bridge House	SPECIALS/SELECTER/	
COWBOYS INTL./		DEXY'S MIDNIGHT RUNNERS	Manchester, Apollo
JOE PUBLIC	London, King's College		

2nd - Friday.........................

THE JAM's gig tonight at the Marquee was billed as "John's Boys." Word must have leaked out that "John's Boys" were in reality the Jam because the club was packed. The Jam haven't played a venue the size of the Marquee in London since early last year. Tickets sold at a record pace for this gig which turned out to be one of the worst kept secrets of the year. Shane McGowans' band The Nips opened up the show, invited on the bill as special guests of the Jam. Then on came John Weller, Jam lead singer Paul Weller's dad, to introduce "John's Boys." Outside, a sizeable crowd gathered and troubles with a few skinheads and a few bouncers escalated into a full scale, brick-throwing, glass-shattering mob. They stormed and destroyed the Marquee's front doors with bricks, boards and boots. The rioters were skinheads who were refused admittance to the concert because the management felt they were troublemakers. The Jam's new single "Eton Rifles" is climbing the charts on it's way to #3 in the UK. It's flipped with the non-LP track "See-Saw."

JOHN COOPER CLARKE's playing another joke on the public, and this time it's not one of his in between poem puns, it's a vinyl trick. His new single has the confusing title "Splat/Twat." The two titles because there are two pieces and it's a fifty-fifty chance if you can play the one you want. The single has the appearance of having only one selection on it, however the double groove lets you play either reading depending on where your needle happens to land. One is a clean version of his "insult poem," the other is the familiar filthy one. Take a chance! "Twat" was recorded live at the Marquee, the parallel track "Splat" is a studio recording. It's flipped with a song from his forthcoming LP called "Sleepwalk" with help from the Invisible Girls backing him. Cooper's about to hit the road on a full length UK tour with the Freshies opening up.

TOYAH	Birmingham, The Underworld	DIALS/SCISSORS FIT/	
SPECIAL BRANCH/		DETAILS	London, Moonlight Club
WASTED YOUTH	London, Bridge House	V.I.P.'s/THE MODS/	
PIRANHAS/THE ACT	London, Camberwell Art College	LAMBRETTAS/BEGGAR	London, Notre Dame Hall
REVILLOS/THE CROOKS/		ORCHESTRAL MANOEUVRES	
PHOTOS	London, Electric Ballroom	IN THE DARK	London, Queen Mary College
DISTRACTIONS	London, Hope & Anchor	SKIDS/FINGERPRINTZ	London, Rainbow
JOHN'S BOYS/THE NIPS	London, Marquee	DANGEROUS GIRLS	Manchester, The Funhouse
SOFT BOYS/FUNBOY 5	London, Rock Garden		

3rd - Saturday.........................

VISAGE are the latest group to sign to the Radar Records roster, already bulging with talent from Nick Lowe, Elvis Costello, Soft Boys, 999 and the Yachts. Their single is "Tar" and "Frequency 7." The "superstar group" is lead by Steve Strange (aka Steve Harrington) and features ex-Rich Kids Rusty Egan, and Ultravox's Midge Ure and Billy Currie, and Magazine members John McGeogh, Dave Formula and Barry Adamson. The music is electronic, dancy and something totally different. You might say it's new and romantic. By this time next year, Visage will have a top ten single called "Fade To Grey" and will have influenced hundreds of young men to dress up in frilly shirts, blousey pants, lipstick and funny ladies hats.

MARTHA & THE MUFFINS, by their nature, will have to forever endure being described as Toronto's answer to the B 52's. Just because they have an amusing femme lead singer, and an even more unusual choice of song topics. Their debut single is out in the UK on the new DinDisc label. It's "Insect Love" and "Cheesies and Gum." See what I mean? Martha & The Muffins are lead by Martha Johnson with Mark Gane on guitar and synth, Carl Finkle on bass, Tim Gane on drums, Andy Haas on sax and Martha Lady on Ace Tone organ and backing vocals. It will take a trip to Echo Beach to provide the band with the inspiration for their one and only hit record.

UB40/VITUS DANCE	Birmingham, The Underworld	PENETRATION	
RUTS/THE FLYS	Glasgow, Strathclyde Univ.	ORCHESTRAL MANOEUVRES/	
CHARLIE AINLEY/		LOCAL OPERATOR	London, Electric Ballroom
WASTED YOUTH	London, Bridge House	PHOTOS	London, School Of Economics
BOOKS/BAUHAUS	London, Marquee	COWBOYS INTL.	Manchester, Poly.
EATON RIFLES/THE NIPS	London, Nashville		

NOVEMBER 1979

4th - Sunday.............................

ANOTHER PRETTY FACE & THE EXPLOITED are mentioned in a *Sounds* magazine article titled "Scotland Uber Alles" as the bands to watch from the North. Garry Bushell wrote that Another Pretty Face were, "…something of a cross between The Clash and Springsteen, they loom large as a well tasty bait. And the description is not as ear shattering as it suggests. An Edinburgh band formed in March by songwriters John Caldwell and Mike Scott, they recorded one impressive single 'All The Boys Love Carrie' on New Pleasures and proffer a powerful epic rock approach which has got several record companies sniffing and I'm sure will conquer America someday soon."

Garry also writes about the Exploited as a band where "eternal UK Subs support gigs" seem assured. They wear real bondage pants and thrash out songs in the '76 punk mode. Other bands worth watching for in the article include PS, The Freeze, Switch, Metropak, Flowers, AVO-8, Prats, Josef K, The Fakes, The Alleged, Zips and Friction.

PIRANHAS	London, 101 Club	BOOMTOWN RATS/PROTEX	London, Hammersmith Odeon
TOURISTS/THE MONOS/		SPECIALS/MADNESS/	
DOLLY MIXTURE/THE JAGS	London, Lyceum	SELECTER	Sheffield, Top Rank

6th - Tuesday.............................

THE BOOMTOWN RATS have a single of "Diamond Smiles" taken from their top ten album "The Fine Art Of Surfacing." It's flipped with the non-LP track "Late Last Night."

THE PACK have their second single out today. It's "King Of Kings" and "Number 12." The Rough Trade single comes in a special picture sleeve that appears to be hand drawn by the band themselves. The Pack is Jim Walker on drums, Kirk Brandon on vocals, Simon Wenner on guitar, and John Wenner on bass. In the early '80s Kirk Brandon will find minor fame fronting a band called Theatre Of Hate.

THE POP GROUP release another cheerful slice of vinyl today, via Rough Trade, called "We Are All Prostitutes." The plain black sleeve is covered with typed slogans like, "Capitalism is the most barbaric of all religions. Department stores are our new cathedrals…At this moment despair ends and tactics begin." On a financial note, it was only four months ago that the Pop Group were having a "Bankruptcy Benefit" for themselves. The flipside of this toe-tapper is "Our Children Shall Rise Up Against Us." It takes its text from the Amnesty International report on British Army torture of Irish prisoners. All proceeds from the single are supposed to go to the Cambodia Fund.

PORTRAITS	London, Bridge House	MERTON PARKAS	London, Nashville
LENE LOVICH/JANE AIRE/		BOOMTOWN RATS/PROTEX	London, Rainbow
METEORS	London, Hammersmith Palais		

7th - Wednesday.............................

THE DAMNED's new album is "Machine Gun Etiquette." The LP features the band's current smash hit "Love Song." Others are "Plan 9 Channel 7," "Noise Noise Noise," "Liar," "I Just Can't Be Happy Today," "Antipope" and a version of "Smash It Up" that comes with a snappy instrumental intro. Rat Scabie's interim group the White Cats, have their song "Second Time Around" re-worked and re-titled as "Machine Gun Etiquette." The album starts with a short intro that sounds a little like Alfred Hitchcock and slams through the eleven songs in under forty minutes. The inside sleeve has a instructional cartoon by "Mr God Awful Ugly, the famous pig rustler" to teach you the chords to play "Smash It Up." *Sounds* reviewer Pete Silverton called the album, "…a bewildering mix of genius, garbage, taste, idiocy, noise, misjudgment, alcohol, aggression, wind-ups, grotesqueness, psychosis and awful clothes."

THE LURKERS have a new single out of "New Guitar In Town" b/w the oldie "Little Old Wine Drinker Me." The band has just started a series of Wednesday night gigs at the Marquee throughout the month of November beginning tonight. The group has been joined by Honest John Plain who was formerly with the Boys and short-lived group the Rowdies.

THE LAMBRETTAS are the latest from the Mod contingent to get signed by a label. This time Rocket Records steps in and releases the Lambrettas debut disc "Go Steady," b/w "Cortina" and "Listen, Listen, Listen." The Lambrettas are Jez Bird on vocals and guitar, Doug Sanders on guitar, Mark Ellis on bass and Paul Wincer on drums. They take their mod moniker from a make of motor scooter.

SQUIRE	Glasgow, Technical College	THE ACT	London, Shepherds Bush Trafalgar
THE PACK	London, 101 Club	TEENBEATS	Manchester, Univ.
LURKERS/CARPETTES	London, Marquee	TEARDROP EXPLODES/	
PIRANHAS	London, Music Machine	ECHO & THE BUNNYMEN	Sheffield, Univ.
FALL	London, School Of Economics		

LIVE TONIGHT!

8th - Thursday.............................

SLAUGHTER & THE DOGS are back! After five months of gigs, the new Slaughter & The Dogs, almost indistinguishable from the old Slaughter & The Dogs, have a new single out. It's a cover of an old Four Seasons' song "You're Ready Now." What a way to plot your comeback; instant credibility problems. The single is flipped with "Runaway" and prompts *NME's* Charles Shaar Murray to describe it as a "crappy record." On the other hand, *Sounds* magazine's Giovanni Dadomo reviews it glowingly with,"Great Fun. I never realized they were quite this good."

THE DICKIES newest single is "Manny, Moe & Jack" and "She Loves Me Not." The songs are tracks from their LP "Dawn Of The Dickies." The group is planning an extensive UK tour to begin the end of this month.

THE CHORDS are the butt of a cruel letter. It seems that when ever a band finds a little success, there's someone just around the corner to drag a skeleton out of the closet and rattle the bones. In this week's *NME*, Debbie H. writes to reveal the not-so-mod past of The Chords,

NOVEMBER 1979

"I knew the Chords when they were Orgasmic Peroxide and played classics like "Nights In White Satin," "Something" (by the Beatles), and "Sweet Home Alabama" (Allman Brothers). One drummer they had was the only musician in the group."

CHELSEA ....Birmingham, The Underworld	BUZZCOCKS/THE PHOTOS ....London, Marquee
FALL ....Liverpool, Eric's	LURKERS/THE CARPETTES ....London, Nashville
HOLLY & THE ITALIANS ....London, 101 Club	BEAT/TALKOVER ....London, Rock Garden
SOFT BOYS ....London, Hope & Anchor	

9th - Friday...

THE STRANGLERS' Christmas present to their fans is a new EP that gathers together four diverse and rare tracks in one package. The lead track is "Don't Bring Harry," a song included on their new LP "The Raven." It's followed by "Wired" from lead singer Hugh Cornwell's solo LP. On the flip are two live tracks! One is J.J. Burnel's "Crabs" recorded at the Hemel Hempstead show in April '79 and "In The Shadows" recorded live by the Stranglers back in '77 at the Hope & Anchor. The limited edition single comes in a special picture sleeve with a dead turkey on the front.

THE LINES made their entry on the scene last summer with "White Night" and now follow it up over a year later with a second single. Their latest is "On The Air" coupled with "Through Windows" and "Dance For A Drop Of Blood." The Lines are Richard Conning on vocals and guitar, Joe Forty on bass, and Nicholas Cash on drums.

SCRITTI POLITTI have a new EP out. They've teamed up with Rough Trade Records for their new release, a 12" single under the title "4 A Sides, The Cost Of Meaning." On it are "Confidence," "P.A.s," "Bibbly-o-tek" and "Doubt Beat."

LIVE TONIGHT!

SKIDS/FINGERPRINTZ ....Glasgow, Apollo	BUZZCOCKS/JOY DIVISION ....London, Rainbow
PSYCHEDELIC FURS ....Liverpool, Eric's	THE METHOD/ DOLLY MIXTURE....London, Rock Garden
WIRE ("People In A Room")........London, Cochran Theatre	PIRANHAS/MONITORS...............London, Southbank Poly.
CHELSEA/	THE ACT ....London, Univ.
SLAUGHTER & THE DOGS...........London, Electric Ballroom	TEENBEATS ....Manchester, Mayflower
SQUEEZE ....London, Hammersmith Odeon	TOURISTS/THE MONOS..............Sheffield, Poly.
JAGS ....London, Marquee	

10th - Saturday..

BUZZCOCKS/JOY DIVISION concert last night and tonight at the Rainbow is the place to be. The Buzzcocks are reaching heights of popularity that they probably never imagined and Joy Division are one of the top new buzz bands to emerge from Manchester over the last year. Joy Division are reviewed in the *NME* by Mark Ellen who describes the decision to use them at the concert, "...a brave but appalling choice." He continues, "There was a dance that was popular a while back in more lunatic circles known as the Dead Fly. Devotees could be found lying on their backs and flailing their arms and legs in the air as if there were no tomorrow. Ian Curtis, singer of Joy Division, can do the Dead Fly standing up, as if he's walking on a tightrope. He flings himself into the most gnarled contortions- limbs buckling at all angles- which makes an apt focus for the band's disarming, profoundly depressing soundtrack. Close up, Joy Division are quite intriguing;

from a distance they're oppressive as hell." Another viewpoint, that of Robbie Millar is, "The Rainbow is virtually motionless. Mute faces stare at the crazed bundle of energy that is Joy Division's vocalist onstage. Stare and sit very still as he throws himself into epileptic contortions in an attempt to entertain the not very full stalls." The Buzzcocks are better received by Mark, being called, "...magnificent, warm and exhilarating." They run through their hit-laden set which takes in "Ever Fallen In Love," "Mad Mad Judy," "You Say You Don't Love Me," "I Believe," "Money," "Promises" and "I Don't Know What To Do With My Life." The two night concert at the Rainbow were the last two dates of the month long tour with the two groups.

THE LEMON KITTENS are an experimental band from Richmond, Surrey that are striving to stretch the boundaries with their debut EP for Step Forward. The EP is actually more of a 7" mini album, with seven songs covering over seventeen minutes. Tracks are some of the most primitive on record with vocals sounding like they were recorded down a telephone wire (and a faulty one at that!). The EP is called "Spoonfed + Writhing" and features "This Kind Of Dying," "Morbotalk," "Bookburner," "Whom Do I Have To Ask," "Chalet d'Amour," and a bizarre version of "Shaking All Over." The Lemon Kittens have a fluid line-up (so casual) and on this LP are Karl Blake, G. Thatcher, Mylmus, Danielle Dax and N. Mercer. A decade from now, Danielle Dax will capture the imagination of the underground dance generation.

WIRE ("People In A Room")........London, Cochran Theatre	BACK TO ZERO/THE MODS/
PSYCHEDELIC FURS/	SPEEDBALL/LES ELITE...............London, Notre Dame Hall
MONOCHROME SET/	UK SUBS/LAST WORDS..............London, Queen Mary College
PRAG VEC/LUDUS '.................London, Electric Ballroom	BUZZCOCKS/JOY DIVISION ....London, Rainbow
SLAUGHTER & THE DOGS/	SQUIRE/SEVENTEEN/
CHORDS.................................London, Marquee	FIXATIONS ....Rhyl, Town Hall

NOVEMBER 1979

11th - Sunday...

THE HUMAN LEAGUE are going through some changes. They're making their last appearance onstage tonight with Ian Marsh and Martin Ware. These two co-founders of the group are splitting off to do their own new band "The British Electric Foundation," which will eventually become Heaven 17. Phil Oakey and Adrian Wright are left with the band name "Human League." The trade is acceptable yet somehow one-sided. While Marsh and Ware were the instrumental portion of the band, Oakey was the voice. Wright supplies the group with its slides, films and live imagery. A new bassist Ian Burden has been brought in from a Sheffield band called Graf, and two seventeen-year old girls who will provide backing vocals and dance onstage are brought in. They are Joanne Catherall and Suzanne Sulley. They were both cocktail waitresses at a Sheffield bar that Oakey frequented. They will write a song called "Don't You Want Me Baby" about finding the girls and it will become the band's first major US hit in 1981. The Human League as such, have had to cancel many of their UK dates to break in the new band. They hope to be on line soon enough to join the Talking Heads when they visit Britain.

LIVE TONIGHT!

TOURISTS	Birmingham, Repertory Theatre	TEENBEATS	London, Fulham Greyhound
SQUEEZE	Birmingham, Odeon	HUMAN LEAGUE/	
SPECIALS/MADNESS/		TEARDROP EXPLODES/	
SELECTER	Glasgow, Tiffany's	THE BEAT/FLOWERS	London, Lyceum
WIRE ("People In A Room")	London, Cochran Theatre	CHORDS	London, Marquee

12th - Monday...

THE PRETENDERS' third single is released by indie Real Records. It's "Brass In Pocket" flipped with "Nervous But Shy" and an instrumental called "Swinging London." Chrissie got the inspiration for "Brass In Pocket" at their first gig when they were the support group another Real Records band called Strangeways. One of the guys in the other band asked, "Did you take my trousers to the dry cleaners?" "Yeah," the other says. "Was there any brass in pocket?" That casual expression for looking for loose change tossed off backstage will eventually become the seed for The Pretenders' first #1 hit song.

LABELS UNLIMITED is the title of another intriguing compilation on Cherry Red Records, a companion to last years "Business Unusual" collection. It's titled "Labels Unlimited" and gathers together sixteen indie bands from sixteen different indie labels into one package. Some of these recordings were on such small labels with such limited pressings it would be almost impossible to find all of them. The groups on side one are Rudi, Girlschool, Those Naughty Lumps, Spizz Oil, Llygod Ffyrning, Newtown Neurotics, Crisis, and Scissor Fits. Side two begins with The Shapes and Piranhas, and works it's way through Staa Marx, Glaxo Babies, Poison Girls, I Jog & The Tracksuits, AK Process and Second Layer. David Marlow's liner notes conclude with this observation, "You don't need to study the intestines of a goat or gaze into a crystal ball to realize that contrary to the predictions of some mealy-mouthed industry observers the small labels aren't going to fade away. The plebes outside are calling the tunes while the arthritic conglomerates scrabble about in their boardrooms tutting and clucking over their red rimmed balance sheets. The boot is on the other foot, why not learn how to tie your own laces?"

CULT HERO is the newest single from Fiction Records. It sounds remarkably like the Cure, if they had a different vocalist, and for good reason! It is the Cure with a different vocalist, Frank Bell. The story goes something like this. Before Simon joined the band, Robert would occasionally go out drinking with Simon and his mates. One night in the pub, someone suggested that they ought to take the local Horley postman, who had a t-shirt saying "I'm A Cult Hero," into the studio and turn him into a disco star. It was a great joke. Robert, Lol, Simon, Porl and Robert's sister Janet all were in on the gag. Two songs were recorded at Morgan Studios, "Cult Hero" and "I Dig You." You'll see Frank on the single picture sleeve.

DANGEROUS GIRLS	Birmingham, Aston Univ.	BEAT/GRADUATE	London, Bridge House
SPECIALS/MADNESS/		WIRE ("People In A Room")	London, Cochran Theatre (Holborn)
SELECTER	Edinburgh, Tiffany's	PRETENDERS/THE MICE	London, Marquee

14th - Wednesday...

PUBLIC IMAGE LTD. new album "Metal Box" is one of the most ambitious album packages that any record company would tackle. It was Public Images' idea that the album actually be in a metal box. Some 12" tins with the PiL logo embossed on the lid were just perfect. Well almost. The tin is such a tight fit that the three 12" singles inside have to be tipped out carefully, or perhaps pried out from the center. The records are separated by thin paper layers but are not in sleeves. It's a self-destruct sort of package. It's a strictly limited edition of fifty thousand copies with a retail price of £7.50, nearly twice the price of a normal release. With the cost overruns in production, the lyric sheet which was to be included in the album was scrapped. To make them available to the public, Johnny has insisted that a full page advert in the *NME* be taken out that includes all the lyrics. Tear it out and stuff it in the can. The three discs present a little over sixty minutes of music and all run at 45 rpm. The songs on disc one are "Albatross," "Memories" and "Swanlake;" disc two, "Poptones," "Careering," "No Birds" and "Graveyard;" disc three, "The Suit," "Bad Baby" and "Socialist Chant Radio 4." The insert card has been hastily changed to reveal that PiL are John Lydon, Keith Levine, Jah Wobble, Jeannette Lee and Dave Crowe. No mention of Richard Dudanski who quit the band only four weeks ago.

THE DAMNED's new 45 is "I Just Can't Be Happy Today." It's out on Chiswick in a colorful sleeve with a dayglow Beethoven in a Viking helmet on the sleeve. It's paired with a cover of Sweet's "Ballroom Blitz" and a strange little ditty about getting a turkey (and a rhino!) out of the house. Guest bass on Blitz is provided by Lemmy from Motorhead. Rat Scabies says, "It's NOISE. In the final analysis, it's all noise."

DANGEROUS GIRLS	Glasgow, Strathclyde Univ.	TEA SET	London, Music Machine
MO-DETTES	London, Hope & Anchor	THE ACT	London, Shepherds Bush Trafalgar
LURKERS/CARPETTES	London, Marquee	MEDIUM MEDIUM	London, Windsor Castle
CAPITAL X EFFECT	London, Moonlight Club	DRONES/COM-SAT ANGELS	Sheffield, Broadfield Hotel

NOVEMBER 1979

15th - Thursday.....

HUGH CORNWELL, Stranglers' vocalist, is getting the chance to stretch out on his own on a record. It's hoped that the release of his LP "Nosferatu" will be more of a success than his solo tour this last summer. The album sessions took place at the first of the year in California pairing Cornwell with Beefheart drummer Robert Williams. The sparse rhythms that set the timbre on Capt. Beefheart's albums is clearly evident. Guests on the sessions included members of Devo and Ian Dury. Songs on the LP cover some unusual territory with titles like "Irate Caterpillar," "Rhythmic Itch," "Mothra," "Big Bug" and "Wrong Way Round."

GARY NUMAN's newest single "Complex" is from his LP "The Pleasure Principle." It's flipped with a live version of the positively ancient song "Bombers." Gary originally recorded it back in August of last year. The live recording and photo on the reverse of the sleeve is from his September concert at the Hammersmith Odeon. The single will become almost as big a hit as "Cars," climbing to #6 in the UK.

MEDIUM MEDIUM are a quintet from Nottingham that operate in the artistic space between the The Police and The Gang Of Four. Their debut single "Them Or Me" and "Freeze" is out now on Apt Records. The group are John Lewis on sax and vocals, Andy Ryder on guitar, Graham Spink on "sound," Alan Turton on bass and Nigel Stone on drums.

LITTLE BO BITCH	Edinburgh, Astoria	B-52s/TROGGS/VIPs	London, Electric Ballroom
CHEETAHS/THE PRATS	Edinburgh, Heriot Watt Univ.	THE CARPETTES	London, Hope & Anchor
DANGEROUS GIRLS	Edinburgh, University	COWBOYS INTL.	Sheffield, Limit Club

16th - Friday.....

THE JAM's newest LP is "Setting Sons," and can almost be described as a concept album. Loads of songs with war imagery, and titles like "Burning Sky," "Private Hell," Wasteland" "and Little Boy Soldiers." There's also lighter moments like their cover of the '60s classic "Heat Wave." Other less than heavy moments are the almost comic "Girl On The Phone" and an orchestrated version of "Smithers - Jones" which was given the full band treatment as a single flipside to "Eaton Rifles."

THE SKIDS bring out a double pack single to help promote their new album "Days In Europa." The track "Working For The Yankee Dollar" is flipped with the non-LP "Vanguard's Crusade." In a special limited edition of 5,000 singles, there's a second 45 included free of "Hymns From A Haunted Ballroom," recorded as a John Peel radio session, and a cover of the David Bowie song "All The Young Dudes" originally recorded for the Kid Jensen radio show.

THE PHOTOS, who were signed to CBS only five weeks ago, have their debut single out. It's the narcissistic "I'm So Attractive" and "Guitar Hero." The Photos are Wendy Wu on lead vocals, Steve Eagles on guitar, Dave Sparrow on bass and Ollie Harrison on drums.

PSYCHEDELIC FURS	Birmingham, Univ.	POP GROUP/SCRITTI POLITTI	London, Univ.
CURE/PASSIONS/ASSOCIATES	Liverpool, Eric's	LAMBRETTAS	Manchester, Mayflower
MADNESS/RED BEANS & RICE/		JOHN COOPER CLARKE/	
BAD MANNERS	London, Electric Ballroom	THE OUT/THE FRESHIES	Sheffield, Polytechnic
COWBOYS INTL./VICE VERSA	London, Marquee		

17th - Saturday.....

JOY DIVISION's new single is "Transmission" and "Novelty." The single comes in a star photo sleeve with a look as if it's printed on canvas. "Transmission" is one of the songs that the band featured on their *Something Else* TV appearance back in September. During the sessions three other songs were recorded, "Dead Souls," "Something Must Break" and a demo for a new song called "She's Lost Control."

A CERTAIN RATIO are another Factory band with a record release today. "The Graveyard And The Ballroom" is a special thirteen-track cassette release that comes in a clear orange, blue, green or red colored plastic pouch. It's the Manchester band's second release.

SPANDAU BALLET invite all fifty of their friends to come by an Islington studio to hear their new songs. The members of the group are regulars at the Soho night clubs like The Blitz, Billy's Le Kilt, and Le Beate Route. Their material is unlike the punk scene that surrounds them, drawing more from David Bowie and dance music from the gay underground. By December of next year, Spandau Ballet, their kilts and their followers will be spreading the news of the "new romantic" movement with chart hits like "To Cut A Long Story Short," "The Freeze" and "Musclebound."

LIVE TONIGHT!

SQUEEZE/PHOTOS/		PISS ARTISTS (Lurkers)	London, Fulham Greyhound
WAZMO NARIZ	Dublin, Univ.	BEAT	London, Hope & Anchor
SIMPLE MINDS	Glasgow, Queen Margaret Union	YACHTS/BIG BOXES	London, Music Machine
GANG OF FOUR/AU PAIRS	Liverpool, Eric's	CURE/ PASSIONS/ ASSOCIATES	London, School Of Economics
MADNESS/RED BEANS & RICE/			
BAD MANNERS	London, Electric Ballroom		

19th - Monday.....

THE BEAT are the latest signing to the successful Two-Tone Records label. They're a combo with mixed mod and ska roots from Birmingham, and have been playing together for a little over six months. The "A" side of their debut is a cover of the Miracle's "Tears Of A Clown." It's backed with "Ranking Full Stop." As a debut single, it'll be a lot to live up to when it makes it to #6 on the UK top forty. The Beat is Ranking Roger on vocals and toasting, Dave Wakeling on vocals and guitar, Andy Cox on bass, David Steele on bass, and Everett Morton on drums. Forty-nine year old Jamaican sax player "Saxa" has joined the band for the recording session. In the mid '80s Ranking Roger and Dave Wakeling will put another band together called General Public.

NOVEMBER 1979

THE COMSAT ANGELS are the latest Sheffield band to be signed to a multi-record contract. They had a bit of success with their indie release of "Red Planet" back in the spring, and have a load of new songs in demo form ready to polish. They still live in Sheffield and say they have no intentions of moving to London. In a few weeks time, they'll start work on their new release for Polydor Records.

"499-2139" The phone number in the classified ads was prefaced by this advert, "We are a young, successful record company and we want to record the sound of today and get it out next week. If you think your band's got that sound, ring 499-2139 NOW." Bands called the number, loads of them. The young record company was Rocket Records. Home to Elton John, Kiki Dee and Neil Sedaka. The bands that would up winning the competition were, for the most part, mod and pop. From the scene around London came Escalator, Reafer, Les Elite, The Wardens, The Classics, Wolfboys! and The Act. On the South coast The Lambrettas represent the mod scene in Brighton while Malcolm Practice are from Portsmouth. Out of the North, Sinister call Liverpool home, the Brick Wall Band hail from Grantham in the North Midlands, and the Vye come in from Leeds.

KIDS NEXT DOOR/LOW NUMBERS/	SIMPLE MINDS.........................Edinburgh, Tiffany's
JIMMY EDWARDS/	RIFF RAFF/TRANZISTORS...........London, Rock Garden
LONG TALL SHORTY ....London, Moonlight Club	

20th - Tuesday.........................

SECRET AFFAIRS's publicist must be proud of their work. The group has scored the rare coup of making the covers of both *Sounds* and *NME* in the same week, the very week that their debut LP is in the shops. The remarkable debut is "Glory Boys." It contains the band's singles "Time For Action" and "Let Your Heart Dance" as well as "Shake & Shout," "One Way World," "Don't Look Down," the title track "Glory Boys," and a cover of the Miracle's song "Going To A Go-Go." They appear on TV tonight on the *Old Grey Whistle Test* and will embark on an extensive UK tour to support the LP release.

DEUTCH AMERIKANISCHE FREUNDSCHAFT are a German band shrouded in mystery. Their UK debut is tonight in Norwich where they're beginning their tour with The Fall. The group is supposedly from Dusseldorf, Germany and centers around the talents of Robert Gorl, along with Wolfgang Spelmanns, Ludwig Hass, Gabi Delgado-Lopez and Micheal Kemner. A full length LP called "Produkt Der D.A.F." is out in Germany on Warning Records. It's similar to early efforts of Throbbing Gristle in its strained industrial sounds prompting *Sounds* to write, "If 'D.A.F.' has an onstage duel with Throbbing Gristle, there would be no-one left alive at the end to announce the winner."

LIVE TONIGHT!

FALL/	MALCOLM PRACTICE/
DEUTCH AMERIKANISCHE	THE ACT/LAMBRETTAS ....London, Nashville
FREUNDSCHAFT ....London, Marquee	JAM/THE VAPORS ....Manchester, The Apollo
KIDS NEXT DOOR/	GANG OF FOUR ....Manchester, Poly.
LOW NUMBERS/	SQUEEZE/PHOTOS/
JIMMY EDWARDS/	WAZMO NARIZ ....Sheffield, Limit
LONG TALL SHORTY ....London, Moonlight Club	
SMALL HOURS/THE SAFE/	
THE ACT ....London, Music Machine	

21st - Wednesday..................

ESSENTIAL LOGIC don't do things like everyone else. Usually bands put out a single to promote the current album. Not Essential Logic. Expect the unexpected with them. Their new single follows on the heels of their debut LP by only four weeks. The "A" side of the single is a new song called "Flora Force," not found on the LP. It's coupled with "Popcorn Boy (Waddle Ya Do)?," which is on the album.

UK SUBS are punk stalwarts and keeper of the flame. Their new single is an unusual choice of songs to sing though. The "A" side is cover of the '60s Zombies' hit "She's Not There" and an original called "Kicks." It's flipped with two more originals, "Victim" and "The Same Thing." Early copies of the single are available in green vinyl and a full color sleeve.

ELVIS COSTELLO is the subject of an unusual contest from the *NME*. They're having a contest where if you correctly answer eight difficult Costello trivia questions, you could win a mega-rare Costello cassette. The tape is a recording of the sessions that Elvis cut for the "Honky Tonk" radio show back in August of '76 under the name D.P. Costello. The cassette called "Elvis At Home" features solo acoustic versions of "Blame It On Cain," "Lip Service," "Mystery Dance," and three unreleased songs, "Poison Moon," "Wave A White Flag" and "Jump Up." I sure hope Elvis' manager knows about this.

SPECIALS/SELECTER/	MEDIUM MEDIUM ....London, Windsor Castle
DEXY'S MIDNIGHT RUNNERS ......Liverpool, Mountford Hall	JAM/VAPORS.........................Manchester, Apollo
LURKERS/CARPETTES ....London, Marquee	CURE/PASSIONS/
JETS/THE DIALS ....London, Moonlight Club	ASSOCIATES ....Manchester, Univ.
PORTRAITS/TRENDIES...............London, Music Machine	

23rd - Friday...............................

THE POLICE cut another single from their album "Regatta de Blanc. It's "Walking On The Moon" and the non-LP flip of "Visions Of The Night." The Police will begin an extensive UK tour beginning December 10 in Leeds.

SIMPLE MINDS have their second album "Reel To Reel Cacophony" released today on Zoom Records. This new LP features

NOVEMBER 1979

"Premonition," "Changeling," "Film Theme," "Reel To Reel" and eight other originals. The dark blue textured sleeve is virtually featureless except for the band name and title at the top.

BLONDIE's newest single is "Union City Blue" and "Living In The Real World" lifted straight off the LP, "Eat To The Beat."

LIVE TONIGHT!

SPECIALS/DR. FEELGOOD	Belfast, Univ.	GANG OF FOUR/	
COWBOYS INTL.	Birmingham, The Underworld	RED CRAYOLA/AU PAIRS	London, Electric Ballroom
SIMPLE MINDS/PORTRAITS	Birmingham, Univ.	SQUEEZE/PHOTOS/	
REVILLOS	Liverpool, Poly.	WAZMO NARIZ	Manchester, Apollo

24th - Saturday...

THE DAMNED & THE MISFITS surprise each other. With only forty-eight hours before the start of their UK tour, NY doom-rockers the Misfits show up on lead singer Dave Vanian's doorstep. They're ready to hit the road together, even though they weren't invited or expected! When the Damned played at Hurrah's in New York, the Misfits opened for them. They got chummy and talked about going on tour together in the UK. So now the Misfits have bought their own tickets to England and are here ready to go, and go they will. Showing initiative, they're taken on and will appear on the upcoming Damned's tour.

THE BODYSNATCHERS are another new two-tone styled band on the scene. They're an all-girl ska type band and make their debut tonight at the Windsor Castle in London. They've only been together about eight weeks. In their set, which was mostly covers, were versions of "007," "Monkey Spanner" and "Double Barrel." Within two years the Bodysnatchers will break up, with four of the girls moving on to become a new group The Bell Stars, who will hit the UK Top 40 a few times between '82 and '83.

XTC/RANDOM HOLD	Birmingham, Univ.	HERE & NOW/	
GANG OF FOUR/		SPLODGENESSABOUNDS	London, Queen Elizabeth College
THE POP GROUP/ DELTA 5	London, Lyceum	QUADS/THE NAME	London, Rock Garden
TEARDROP EXPLODES/		BODYSNATCHERS	London, Windsor Castle
HOLLY & THE ITALIANS	London, Nashville	SECRET AFFAIR/SQUIRE	Manchester, Univ.

25th - Sunday...

PETE SHELLEY, lead singer of the Buzzcocks, has been looking for ways to express himself in music for a long time, longer than the Buzzcocks have been around. Back in the spring of '74, when Pete was still a student, he recorded an electronic composition called "Sky Yen." It rambled on for what seemed like an hour and was a simplistic noise composition without vocals or other instruments besides his "purpose built oscillator." There must be some inordinate interest in Pete's past that has prompted the release of this bit of noise as a 12" single in a limited edition of one thousand. Look for it on Groovy Records.

JAM/THE VAPORS	Birmingham, Bingley Hall	JOHN COOPER CLARKE/	
HERE & NOW/		THE OUT/	
SPLODGENESSABOUNDS	High Wycombe, Nag's Head	CHRIS SIEVEY &	
SPECIALS/SELECTER		THE FRESHIES	London, Venue
DEXY'S MIDNIGHT RUNNERS	London, Lyceum	PIRANHAS	London, Finchely Torrington

26th - Monday...

THE MEKONS join the growing ranks of bands that are "serious" enough to make it to the stage of putting together a full length album of their material. The Mekons LP debut is called "The Quality Of Mercy Is Not Strnen." It's a wordplay on the notion of the hundred monkeys in the room with typewriters creating the works of Shakespeare. On the LP are all new songs, no single sides revisited. Tracks on side one are "Like Spoons No More," "Join Us In The Countryside," "Rosanne," "Trevira Trousers," "After Six" and "What Are We Going To Do Tonight?" Side two features "What," "Watch The Film," "Beetroot," "I Saw You Dance," "Lonely And Wet" and "Dan Dare." On the back cover of the album is a small photo tribute to their former labelmates the Gang Of Four.

JOY DIVISION are certainly on their way to big things. Their single of "Transmission" is a regular on John Peel's show, as were tracks from the album "Unknown Pleasures," and the singles before that. They've been invited back for their second session at the BBC studios tonight, recording four more new songs for John Peel. Selected for the session are "Love Will Tear Us Apart," "24 Hours," "Colony" and "The Sound Of Music."

NICE MEN/WAH HEAT	Liverpool, The Everyman	MONEY/KILLING JOKE	London, Rock Garden
DANGEROUS GIRLS	London, Acklam Hall	THE ACT	London, Shepherd's Bush Trafalgar
ESSENTIAL LOGIC/		TEENBEATS	Manchester, Pip's
SCRITTI POLITTI		DAMNED/VICTIM/	
DELTA 5/DOOR & THE WINDOW	London, Notre Dame Hall	MISFITS	Sheffield, Top Rank

27th - Tuesday...

THE BOYS had disappeaerd over a year and a half ago! Boys members Honest John Plain and Matt Dangerfield flirted briefly with a group called the Rowdies, when they were not writing new material or recording in Norway. Now the band is back in full force with a new record company and an album and single as well. The LP is "To Hell With The Boys" and is on Safari Records. The title refers to the place where they recorded, Hell, Norway. On the disc, it's all new material stretching from "Lonely Cowboy," "Waiting For The Lady" and "Independent Girl" to "Terminal Love," "Rue Morgue" and "You Can't Hurt A Memory." There's even a rave-up of the classical song "Saber Dance"

NOVEMBER 1979

rather like Dave Edmunds did it ten years ago. A single from the LP of "Kamikaze" is out with "Bad Day" on the flip. Both sides are on the LP. As a bonus to early buyers, the band has included a free songbook of Boys' songs. The Boys are Jack Black on drums, Kid Reid on bass, Matt Dangerfield on lead guitar and vocals, Casino Steel on keyboards and Honest John Plain on guitar and vocals.

LIVE TONIGHT!

JOE JACKSON/		MERTON PARKAS/V.I.P.'s	London, Nashville
ORIGINAL MIRRORS	Birmingham, Top Rank	GANG OF FOUR	Sheffield, Limit Club
MEDIUM MEDIUM/		CURE/PASSIONS/	
LONG TALL SHORTY	London, Rock Garden	ASSOCIATES	Sheffield, Univ.

28th - Wednesday.....................

SEVENTEEN are a Welsh band from the far North in Rhyl, almost across the Mersey from Liverpool. Their debut single is on the new Red Rose label of "Don't Let Go" and "Bank Holiday Weekend." The band are cut in a rather mod mode these days, far from their former existence as "The Toilets" in punkier times. Seventeen are Mike Peters on lead vocals and bass, Eddie MacDonald on guitar and keyboards, Dave Sharp on guitar and Nigel Buckle on drums. The single is from a planned, but never released LP called "Best Of British." Wanting to find a new sound, Seventeen will change their name to the Alarm in 1981, and rise to prominence in the UK scene in the mid '80s.

THE POLICE kept a promise they made back in October of '77 to Eberhard Schoener. Before they had made it, and were living from gig to gig, they agreed to play the role of backing band for German electronic musician Eberhard Schoener. The sessions went well and Eberhard invited them back for a second year next year. They needed the money and did the job. The results of these sessions came out in Germany as Eberhard Schoener albums and disappeared into the musical swamp of cut-outs and returns. Now those sessions have risen up to haunt the Police on their home turf. The Schoener album "Video Flashback" will give you an idea of what the Police would sound like without their songwriting and an additional member. Songs from the '77 session include "Signs Of Emotion" and "Frame Of Mind" while from the '78 recordings come "Video Magic," "Speech Behind Speech," "Trans Am," "Only The Wind," "Koan," "Octogon" and "Code Word Elvis." The Police are augmented by an avant garde orchestra and Sting handles all the vocals. Odd to say the least.

CURE/PASSIONS/		HERE & NOW/	
ASSOCIATES	Birmingham, Univ.	SPLODGENESSABOUNDS	London, Goldsmith's College
SECRET AFFAIR	Liverpool, Univ.	LURKERS/CARPETTES	London, Marquee
HOLLY & THE ITALIANS/		PIRANHAS/SECOND NATURE	London, Moonlight Club
LUCY'S/NINE BELOW ZERO	London, Albany Empire	THE ACT	London, Shepherds Bush Trafalgar
WASTED YOUTH/ INDUSTRIALS	London, Bridge House	XTC/RANDOM HOLD	Manchester, Univ.
UB40	London, Fulham Golden Lion		

30th - Friday...........................

SQUEEZE have a new single out just in time for the Christmas season. It's the instant seasonal classic "Christmas Day," the updated Mary and Joseph story complete with pool, cable TV and free phone. The single is coupled with "Going Crazy." Both tracks are unique to the single and will not be on any or their albums. The single comes in a limited edition pic sleeve and snow white vinyl.

THE PIRANHAS know a good thing when they see it, and they jump right in with both feet. They've found a way to capitalize on the video game "Space Invaders" that's sucking the coins out of today's kids' pockets. Their new single is "Space Invaders" and addresses the video addiction that arises from having to keep killing the advancing aliens! It's flipped with a live recording of "Cheap N' Nasty," the point in the band's set where the band members are introduced to the crowd. The track was recorded at their Marquee concert last July.

THE LEATHER NUN are Swedish friends of Throbbing Gristle, and have been given a single release on Industrial Records. Their "Slow Death EP" features "No Rule" and "Death Threats," coupled with "Slow Death" and "Endam I Natt." "Death Threats" was recorded a year ago in Sweden, while the other three are new songs. The tasteful picture sleeve is a newspaper pic of a man with third degree burns after a firebomb attack on a neo-nazi rally.

CHORDS/ORPHAN/PIRANHAS	Birmingham, Univ.	PSYCHEDELIC FURS/	
SIMPLE MINDS/PORTRAITS	Liverpool, Eric's	SOULBOYS	London, Nashville
MEKONS/OXY & THE MORONS	London, Chat's Palace	REVILLOS	London, Queen Mary College
COWBOYS INTL.	London, Dingwalls	DAMNED/VICTIMS/MISFITS	London, Rainbow
WILKO JOHNSON/		PROTEX	London, Rock Garden
HOLLY & THE ITALIANS	London, Music Machine	DICKIES/CHELSEA	Sheffield, Poly.

December 1st - Saturday.................

THE GREEDIES have their holiday single rushed out today by Polygram. They're a loose group of friends that occasionally play together more for the fun of it than anything else. The seasonal single is "A Merry Jingle" and "A Merry Jangle." The Greedies are ex-Pistols Steve Jones and Paul Cook, Thin Lizzy's Phil Lynott and Brian Downey and Scott Gorham. A Christmas charity concert on behalf of London orphans is being planned for the 24th. It will basically be a jam session with the Greedies and special guests like Billy Idol and Tony James of Generation X, Richard Jobson of the Skids, Mick Jones from the Clash, as well as member of the Psychedelic Furs, and the Banshees. Support acts on the bill as rumored to be Killing Joke and Four Be Two.

DECEMBER 1979

U2 are in London for the first time. Their manager Paul McGuiness has set up a series of ten appearances over the next two weeks for the Irish imports. He's got high hopes that the right record company people will hear about the band and be there to witness the live show, U2's strength. They've had to scrape together £3,000 out of friends and family to make the long trek. Their big break will be playing on the Talking Heads bill at the Hammersmith Palais in London on the 7th and 8th. Their concert tonight at the Moonlight club is as the opener for Dolly Mixture. *Sounds* writer Dave McCullough, a long time fan of the band, reviews the band. He describes them this way, "U2 are about four people. Their music has minimum distortion and, free of fad or image associations, their songs reflect the strength of the four individuals. Imagine that strange quality that everybody used to aimlessly tag to Penetration, that weird thing called "honesty," and you come close to the U2 vibe. There's a kind of naive, young, rushing feeling about their music, flickering at times between the Skids, Penetration, The Doors, The Fall, and the Swell Maps." Paul Morley, writing for the *NME*, "U2 are still young and free of any kind of bizzy contradictions, so I can have my fun with no guilt. And if the wild wit and serious rave of U2 won't turn you on, they look so cute. Pretty drummer, odd bassist, tense guitarist, and to deliver their jittery balance of amiability and aggression, a lead singer who could well grow to be something of a nuisance when U2 are *Top Of The Pops* regulars…Like naughty Mork, the unpredictable alien, he's irrepressible, irritating and accidentally, incidentally and purposefully incisive."

THE MODS	Birmingham, Golden Eagle		WHIRLWIND	London, Music Machine
THE POP GROUP/			SPIZZ ENERGI/UK DECAY	London, Nashville
SCRITTI POLITTI	Liverpool, Eric's		TALKING HEADS/	
SPECIALS/SELECTER/			A CERTAIN RATIO	Manchester, Free Trade Hall
DEXY'S MIDNIGHT RUNNERS	London, Lewisham Odeon		SIMPLE MINDS/	
DOLLY MIXTURE/U2	London, Moonlight Club		PORTRAITS	Manchester, Poly.

2nd - Sunday...

SIOUXSIE & THE BANSHEES have announced that fill-in drummer Budgie is now full-time drummer Budgie. He first sat in behind the kit when Kenny Morris walked off the tour back in September. He's a former member of the Slits. Meanwhile, the Banshees are still looking for a replacement guitarist. Interested parties are to contact radio personality John Peel who will pass on the resumes and tapes. The band are currently taking time off the road, giving Siouxsie rest to fully recover before trying any more live dates.

DELTA 5 are further proof that something around Leeds encourages bands to pursue the slightly funk, slightly punk style that has been so established by the Gang Of Four. The latest release from the Leeds funk/punk scene is from Delta 5. They've been signed up to Rough Trade and have their single "Mind Your Own Business" released this weekend. It's flipped with "Now That You're Gone." Delta 5 are Bethan on bass and vocals, Roc on bass, Julz on guitar, Alan on guitar and Kelvin on drums. The group got together in September of last year, Roz being the only veteran, having spent time in the Mekons.

TALKING HEADS/			SPECIALS/SELECTER/	
A CERTAIN RATIO	Birmingham, Odeon		DEXY'S MIDNIGHT RUNNERS	London, Lyceum
JOE JACKSON/			FASHION/U2	London, Nashville
ORIGINAL MIRRORS	Edinburgh, Usher Hall		JAM/THE VAPORS	London, Rainbow
SECRET AFFAIR/SQUIRE	Glasgow, Tiffany's			

3rd - Monday...

HOLLY & THE ITALIANS are new transplants from Los Angeles to London. Their debut single of "Tell That Girl To Shut Up" is out today on Oval Records in the UK. The single is flipped with a cover of the 1964 Dixie Cups' classic "Chapel Of Love." The release is in conjunction with their visit to the UK which begins on the 6th with a concert at the 101 Club in Clapham. Holly is a former member of LA band Backstage Pass. She quit that group and put together her own about a year ago. Holly & The Italians are Holly Vincent on guitar and vocals, Mark Henry on bass and Steve Young on drums.

THE HUMAN LEAGUE have been dropped from their upcoming opening slot on the Talking Heads tour. This was going to be a big break for the League and they were going to try something totally new and different for the tour. Their new idea was called "remotely controlled entertainment" and would entail even more use of films, slides and special lighting than ever before used. Films of the group playing would be augmented with tapes and loops. This unique concept would allow the band to watch their own show from the audience. It's all on tape! The Talking Heads management and the concert promoters felt that concert patrons will balk at the idea of a pre-recorded band. Off the Heads tour, the Human League plan to take their experimental new concept on the road after the new year.

SECRET AFFAIR/SQUIRE	Edinburgh, Tiffany's		JOHN COOPER CLARKE/THE OUT/	
JOE JACKSON/			CHRIS SIEVEY & THE FRESHIES	London, King's College
ORIGINAL MIRRORS	Glasgow, Apollo Centre		THE MODS/RUN 229	London, Bridge House
UB40/WIDE BOYS/DENIZENS	London, Dingwalls		DISLOCATION DANCE/	
U2	London, 101 Club		IMMEDIATES	Manchester, Cyprus Tavern
JAM/VAPORS	London, Rainbow			

LIVE TONIGHT!

DECEMBER 1979

4th - Tuesday...

BLONDIE a.k.a THE NEW YORK BLONDES cover of "Little G.T.O.," the thinly-veiled Blondie vocal track is being withdrawn from sale by Decca/London Records. Chrysalis has been granted an injunction just four weeks after the record hit stores. Chrysalis claims that the marketing for the single intrudes on their contract with Blondie, and that Bomp Records (who provided the master tapes that were remixed to bring Debbie's scratch vocal forward) were not cleared by Chrysalis. The group themselves stand behind Chrysalis as this single was never intended to be released this way.

U2 are new to London, and tonight is only their fourth gig here. Some of the gigs are going great and other not so great. Tonight's "concert" at the Hope & Anchor is before a curious yet indifferent crowd of nine.

SQUIRE have their third mod single out today. It's "The Face Of Youth Today" and "I Know A Girl." It's on Secret Affair's I Spy Records label and is produced by that band as well. The group narrowly missed disaster a week ago when a lighting tower onstage fell and struck drummer Kevin Maynell. He was rushed to the hospital and is in full recovery.

DAMNED/VICTIM/MISFITS	Glasgow, Apollo Centre	THE BOYS/THE DRILL	London, Nashville
DICKIES	London, Marquee	JAM/THE VAPORS	London, Rainbow
MODERN ENGLISH	London, Fulham Greyhound	KNOX	London, Rock Garden
TALKING HEADS/		JOE JACKSON/	
A CERTAIN RATIO	London, Hammersmith Palais	ORIGINAL MIRRORS	Manchester, Apollo
U2	London, Hope & Anchor	PHOTOS	Sheffield, Limit Club

5th - Wednesday...

THE RAINCOATS' LP cover is a joyous crayon cartoon of forty-three Chinese children singing in a choir with one accordion. Perhaps that will mislead some, but the Raincoats are that different. "The Raincoats" advances music into the '80s just as the Gang Of Four's or the Slits' LP did. The album is somewhat pop, somewhere near the Velvet's and somewhat unearthly. Perhaps it's the violin. Songs include the previously released single tracks "In Love" and "Adventures Close To Home." There's also the unusual cover of the Kink's "Lola" and a load of new originals like "The Void," "Off Duty Trip," "No Looking" and "You're A Million." The Raincoats are Vicky Aspinall on violin, guitar and vocals, Ana da Silva on guitar and vocals, Gina Birch on bass and vocals, and Palmolive on drums.

PULP are along the same lines as Robert Rental and Throbbing Gristle. It's a duo of Paul Burwell and Anne Bean. Their debut is a strictly D.I.Y. single of "Low Flying Aircraft" b/w "Something Just Behind My Back" and "So Lo." Each of the singles has a bare plastic area where the label should be with a white pen numbering (up to #2,000) and a hole burned through. The sleeves are plain white with the signatures of both Anne and Paul on them. The *NME* describes the single as, "...a hilarious intense mix of Burwell's manic precision percussion and Bean's vocal yelps, grunts and screams, leavened with distortion and feedback."

LIVE TONIGHT!

JOHN COOPER CLARKE/		THE ACT	London, 101 Club
THE OUT/CHRIS SIEVEY &		DOLLY MIXTURE/U2	London, Rock Garden
THE FRESHIES	Liverpool, Poly.	SECRET AFFAIR/SQUIRE	Sheffield, Poly.

6th - Thursday...

SID VICIOUS exploited! If you thought that the LP "Sex Pistols Carri On" was scrapping the bottom of the barrel for material, wait till you hear this one. It's "Sid Sings" and it's just out on Virgin Records. It's been almost a year since Sid assumed room temperature, and he's back again with his touching low-fidelity live versions of some Sex Pistols material, some oldies and some live trash. Side one begins with a live version of the Johnny Thunder's song "Born To Lose" followed by the Stooges' "I Wanna Be Your Dog," the New York Doll's "Take A Chance On Me," and the Monkees' "Stepping Stone." The final track is the Frank Sinatra song "My Way" that also appeared on the *Great Rock & Roll Swindle*. This LP version is the vocal and some guitar tracks from the original session, without the copious guitar and string overdubs. Side two begins with Sid's version of "Belsen Was A Gas," a song that Johnny sang on the soundtrack of the *Great Rock & Roll Swindle*. Then his cover of the Eddie Cochran song "Something Else." Thunders' song "Chatterbox" is up next leading into the Stooges' "Search And Destroy." The Johnny Thunders & Heartbreakers' hit "Chinese Rocks" follows with "I Killed The Cat," a shattered version of "My Way" ends the LP. The album is from live recordings made in New York at the end of last year, and are barely above bootleg quality.

ANOTHER PRETTY FACE	Edinburgh, Univ.	SPIZZ ENERGI	London, Middlesex Poly.
HOLLY & THE ITALIANS	London, 101 Club	BACK TO ZERO/	
ELECTROTUNES	London, Hope & Anchor	DOUBLE VISION	London, Rock Garden
CURE/PASSIONS/		KILLERMETERS/SEVENTEEN	Manchester, Osbourne Club
ASSOCIATES	London, Music Machine	SIMPLE MINDS/PORTRAITS	Sheffield, Limit Club

7th - Friday...

THE CLASH have waited just a little over a year since the release of "Give 'Em Enough Rope," and they've already got a new double album in the shops. Their new one is "London Calling." Its packaging of a black and white live shot of Paul Simonon smashing his bass onstage with pink and green lettering is a direct parody/tribute to Elvis Presley's debut album. The photo on the cover comes from the Clash's appearance in New York this last November. The double album covers nineteen songs, among them the title track "London Calling," as well as "Lost In The Supermarket," "Guns Of Brixton," "Clampdown," "Lovers Rock," and the '59 Vince Taylor song "Brand New Cadillac." There's a sort of reggaefied version of "Stagger Lee" under the title "Wrong 'Em Boyo," and a cover of Jackie Edwards "Revolution Rock." There's also the song "Train In Vain" added at the bottom of side four. It was a last minute addition and was originally intended to be an *NME* freebie flexi disc but didn't work out. It arrived at the pressing plant after the jackets were made, but has still been

DECEMBER 1979

The Clash new double album

included. Sometimes mistakes work out to your benefit that way. A single to support the album is also out. It couples "London Calling" with the newly recorded reggae cover "Armagiddeon Time." Just as the album sleeve uses a '50s image as its base, the single sleeve takes 1950s Columbia and HMV 78rpm sleeves and works The Clash's name into it. The single will be the most successful single ever for the Clash reaching #11 in the UK. Despite their influence on the scene, the Clash never have a top ten record in their own country. In a strange turnabout though, they will go top ten in America, the country that refused to release their first album when it came out in England.

In other Clash news, the film they've been working on for well over a year with director Jack Hazan might just get scrapped. The band is unhappy with the cut that has been presented for their approval. The movie follows the day to day life of a Clash roadie and includes behind-the-scenes footage as well as concert clips.

THE PLASTICS beg the question, "What if Devo had grown up in Tokyo instead of Akron. What would they sound like?" Probably just like the Plastics. They're a mixed quintet that borders on the electronic side of silly. Their first Western single is "Copy" and "Robot." This Japanese group are Chica on vocals, Toshi on guitar, Hajime on guitar, Ma-Chang on electronics, and Shima-Chang on rhythm box.

JOHN COOPER CLARKE/			TALKING HEADS/	
THE OUT/CHRIS SIEVEY &			ORCHESTRAL MANOUEVRES/ U2	
THE FRESHIES	Birmingham, Poly.		IN THE DARK	London, Electric Ballroom
PURPLE HEARTS	Birmingham, The Underworld		MERTON PARKAS	London, Marquee
ANOTHER PRETTY FACE	Edinburgh, Napier College		GIRLSCHOOL/	
DICKIES/CHELSEA	Edinburgh, Odeon		PATRIK FITZGERALD/	
MO-DETTES/WAH HEAT	Liverpool, Eric's		AU PAIRS/MISSTAKES	London, Poly.
BAUHAUS/THE URGE	London, 101 Club			

8th - Saturday..............................

NICK LOWE is the subject of a riotously wonderful competition in the *New Musical Express*. The cover reads, "Win Nick Lowe For The Weekend; Would you let Britain's best loved producer mix your masterpiece?" The contest will allow one band to have Nick Lowe, body and soul, for the weekend as their producer. Two songs, a singles worth. Nick spelled out some of the reasons, "It'll be much more enjoyable than producing something like Blue Oyster Cult's next album. The thought of discovering someone with a good song and having some fun in the studio turning it into a finished job could prove quite stimulating." Who needn't apply? "None of your artsy-fartsy types, and none of those groups still furiously thrashing away trying to sound like the Sex Pistols three years too late, or modding it up by re-doing the Who's first album yet again." The contest runs for the next three weeks. Cut out the competition voucher in all three *NME* issues, and send in a cassette with one original song. Then sit back and wait for the phone to ring. In reality, the contest is Jake Riveria looking for talent for his new F-Beat Records label, who has Nick Lowe already signed up.

Although Harry & The Atoms won the contest, the runner up was a band called White Dice. They've only been together a few weeks and are Rob Allman on vocals, John Maher (later Johnny Marr of the Smiths) on guitar, and Paul Whittall (ex-Freshies) on keyboards. Two of Maher's friends from a previous band called The Paris Valentinos are brought in as a rhythm section. They are Bobby Durkin on drums and Andy Rourke (also a future Smiths member) on bass. Nick Lowe really likes the White Dice and arranges for some studio time in April for the group to flesh out their ideas. Demos cut included original songs "You Made Me Cry," "Makes No Sense," "The Hold," "Somebody Waved Goodbye," "On The Beach" and the Tom Petty song "American Girl." No formal White Dice record ever came out though. It would be a few years before John Maher (renamed Johnny Marr) and Andy Rourke would team up with the band the Smiths.

DANGEROUS GIRLS/QUADS	Birmingham, Univ.		MERTON PARKAS	London, Marquee
ANOTHER PRETTY FACE/			MO-DETTES	London, Nashville
SKAS/VISITORS/			SECRET	AFFAIR/SQUIRE/
JOSEF K	Edinburgh, George Sq. Theatre		DOLLY MIXTURE	London, Rainbow
JAM/THE VAPORS	Glasgow, Apollo Centre		DONKEYS/THE TREND	London, Rock Garden
JOY DIVISION/SECTION 25	Liverpool, Eric's		PIRANHAS	London, School Of Economics
SMALL HOURS	London, 101 Club		PETER & TEST TUBE BABIES	London, Thames Poly.
TALKING HEADS/U2			SLAUGHTER & THE DOGS	Manchester, Funhouse
ORCHESTRAL MANOEUVRES	London, Hammersmith Palais		PHOTOS	Manchester, Poly.

LIVE TONIGHT!

9th - Sunday..............................

THE BEAT is a melding of two different music styles. Lead singer Dave Wakeling told the *NME* that the choice wasn't an accident either. "I liked music that was exciting but for dancing, like punk, but punk was starting to disappear and something was going very wrong with pop. There was just nothing happening, and I wanted to create a totally distinct type of music. I was listening to two very distinct types of music, rock and reggae, and watching at parties. They used to work really well together. Rock'd get people up and dancing, reggae'd keep them moving, so I brought my two favorite kinds of music together."

DEXY'S MIDNIGHT RUNNERS' debut 45 is declared the *Sounds* "single of the week" within days of its release, and described as, "...the next porkpie-hatters to break through after the Specials, Madness etc. This is a big, fat brassy sound with enough poke and front to make in tin the current mohair mode." The Oddball Records single is "Dance Stance" and "I'm Just Looking." Dexy's is fronted by ex-Killjoys singer Kevin Rowland or Carlo Rolan as he's now called. He's joined by Al Archer on rhythm guitar, Pete Williams on bass, J.B. on

DECEMBER 1979

tenor sax, Big Jim Patterson on trombone, Steve Spooner on alto sax, Pete Saunders on piano and Bobby Junior on drums. They've been together since September of last year.

JOE JACKSON/	
ORIGINAL MIRRORS ....London, Empire Ballroom	
KILLING JOKE ....London, Hope & Anchor	
SLAUGHTER & THE DOGS..........London, Marquee	

SELECTER/THE BEAT/	
UB40 ....London, Lyceum	
TEENBEATS/	
MISSING PERSONS ....London, Nashville	

10th – Monday...............................

THROBBING GRISTLE's latest album is titled "20 Jazz Funk Greats." It's a great title, carrying on the joke of playing up the band as something mass appeal when quite the opposite is the truth. The group appears in nice Abba-eque type dress in a field of flowers. Very nicey-nice. Titles include "Beachy Head," "Still Walking," "Hot On The Heels Of Love" and "Six Six Sixes." The whole package does nothing to betray what lies within. It's electronic experimental pop tinges songs with a dark edge. Throbbing Gristle have been recording now for only a little over two years, and already they have three albums to their credit. They are Genesis P-Orridge, Cosey Fanni Tutti, Peter Christopherson and Chris Carter. The *Daily Mail* has described the band, "These people are the wreckers of civilization."

PUBLIC IMAGE LTD. have a new drummer, their fourth in just over a year and a half. He's Martin Atkins, an unknown in the music world whose career up to this time amounts to "not a lot."

JAM/THE VAPORS ....Edinburgh, Odeon	
JOHN COOPER CLARKE/	
THE OUT/THE FRESHIES ....Edinburgh, Tiffany's	
POSITIVE NOISE ....Glasgow, Doune Castle	

SLAUGHTER & THE DOGS..........London, Marquee	
KILLING JOKE/HARDWARE..........London, Music Machine	
CARPETTES/STATISTICS ....London, Rio Cinema	
THE ACT ....London, Shepherds Bush Trafalgar	
DAMNED/VICTIM/MISFITS ....Manchester, Apollo	

11th – Tuesday...............................

XTC's Andy Partridge has completed a solo album called "Take Away- The Lure Of Salvage." It's a full length album of shattered remixes of previously recorded XTC songs. Some of the versions are so far removed from the originals in form and sound that they might as well be new songs. It will be released next month as part of Virgin's budget line albums.

THE YOBS can't be a mystery any more. Certainly by this time, everyone's figured out that the Yobs are the alter egos of the Boys. For the third year in a row, the Boys submit a Sham-like reading of a Christmas song. This year's offering is "Rub-A-Dum-Dum" (aka "The Little Drummer Boy") flipped with "Another Christmas." This could be a Christmas single that wasn't intended for the whole family, and what about that sleeve? German uniforms and swastikas!

U2 is lucky to have *Sounds* magazine's Garry Bushell as their self-appointed London-based cheerleader. He reviewed tonight's date at the Bridgehouse writing, "U2 themselves are a quality delicacy with few peers, their rich tapestry of sparkling pop, a swirling kaleidoscope of tempos and ethereal melodies laced with neat searing guitar and Bono's sweet vocals. The wee man nipped in and out of his fellows like the proverbial Ronnie Biggs, gesticulating all over the stage, smiling, winking…a latter day Walt Disney wizard. U2 are a pop force for the future stamped with an indefinable Irish quality, an aching beauty and a wistful innocence. Such cheerfulness is catching. Such inventiveness will be rewarded."

U2/IDIOT DANCER ....London, Bridge House	
THE ACT ....London, Univ. College	
ARFUR & THE ADVERBS.............London, 101 Club	

VIVA/	
HOLLY & THE ITALIANS ....London, Rock Garden	
PURPLE HEARTS ....Sheffield, Limit Club	

12th – Wednesday...............................

NAZIS AGAINST FACISM How's that for a name? Nazis Against Fascism is actually Ben Brierly, a former member of the Vibrators and the '60s group The Ivy League. His cohort in the Nazis is Heathcote Williams. The single is released today on Truth Records and is "Sid Did It (Intelligible)" and "Sid Did It (Radio Version)." More Sex Pistols cash-in months too late.

SPLODGENESSABOUNDS are making waves. They've been described as "the most juvenile band in England" and "lewd eccentrics." Their stage set includes originals like "I Fell In Love With A Female Plumber From Harlesden NW10," a mod anthem called "Snot" and "Michael Booth's Talking Bum," which features Jamaican DJ-style farting on demand. Splodge's highpoint is "Blown Away Like A Fart In A Thunderstorm" where Max Splodge gets a blowjob onstage from his female singing partner. It's understandable that police frequently attend these gigs, not as fans, but as enforcers of the public decency, and as such have carried Max off to jail on several occasions. They play tonight at the Woolwich Tramshed.

LIVE TONIGHT!

POLICE ....Glasgow, Apollo Centre	
JOHN COOPER CLARKE/	
THE OUT/THE FRESHIES............Glasgow, Technical College	
THE ACT/BILLY KARLOFF............London, 101 Club	

WAYSTED YOUTH/	
IN CAMERA ....London, Bridge House	
HOLLY & THE ITALIANS ....London, Hope & Anchor	
SPLODGENESSABOUNDS ....London, Woolwich Tramshed	

14th – Friday...............................

THE CLASH's LP "London Calling" gets two stars in its review by *Sounds* writer Garry Bushell. That rates it "★★ BORING." He thinks the Clash have no credibility left and are only occasionally relevant, "Aside from sporadic spurts of brilliance (like one every six months). The

DECEMBER 1979

Clash seriously dried up well early on, losing their perspective and momentum. Unable to go forward they've clutched at straws, ending up retrogressing via Strummer's R&B past and Jones' Keith Richards fascination, to the outlaw imagery of the Stones and tired old rock cliches…just think what they could have been." There are loads of comparisons to the Rolling Stones. Bushell is the lone dissenting voice in a forest of praise. Across the street at the *NME* Charles Shaar Murray writes, "'London Calling' is the first of The Clash's albums that is truly equal in stature to their legend." In 1990, Rolling Stone Magazine readers voted the LP their "#1 album of the decade" of the '80s.

NINE NINE NINE have just signed with Polydor Records and plan to have a new album out on January 1st. They'll be starting the new year with the album "The Biggest Prize In Sport."

THE MOD-ETTES are joining the ranks of fledgling bands on Rough Trade Records. Their debut release is "White Mice" and "Masochistic Opposite." The group has been together about eight months, tracing their genesis to the split up of the Bank Of Dresden. From the name the Mod-ettes you would almost assume that they're a mod band, but not so. They actually are a pop group along the lines of Lene Lovich.

EDDIE & THE HOT RODS	Glasgow, Strathclyde Univ.	STRAIGHT 8/U2	London, Dingwalls
SPIZZ ENERGI/SWELL MAPS	London, Camberwell Art College	SIMPLE MINDS/PORTRAITS	London, Marquee

16th - Sunday....................................

THE CURE's lead singer Robert Smith has barely started his career, and already has a clear vision of where he wants to take the Cure. He stated in an interview this week in *Sounds* magazine, "This is an admittance, that I would rather play songs that bring out the blacker side of life. It seems to stir your emotions a lot more. Bleaking out. It's a very modern desire. I don't believe in catering for your audience. The audience should come to you on your own terms, because otherwise what you are doing is looking for a gap in the market. If we did that we'd have to call ourselves the Illness, or the Malignant Growth."

U2 completed their first London tour with a gig at the Windsor Castle last night. Today they climb into their van with their manager and begin the long trip back to Dublin. They had several great shows, a few disasters. The Edge's cut hand from the auto accident just before leaving Dublin didn't make things any easier. Strange as it seems, U2 is returning just as they'd left Dublin two weeks ago, unsigned and practically broke. They were seen by some influential people though and won't have long to wait before the world opens up for them.

HOLLY & THE ITALIANS	London, 100 Club

18th - Tuesday...................................

BERLIN aren't a German band. If fact their music isn't even vaguely European. Berlin are a Los Angeles combo that have been active for quite a while, making their debut on Renegade Records. It's two originals "It's A Matter Of Time" and "Renegade," with the sides labeled not "A" and "B," instead they've opted for "East" and "West." Geddit? Berlin is Virgin MacAlino on vocals, John Crawford on bass, Jo Julian on synth, Chris Velasco on guitar and Dan Van Patten on drums. It will take a few years before Berlin find success with songs like "Sex (I'm A…)" and "The Metro" in the early '80s. This single is at least a jillion miles away from "You Take My Breath Away," their chart smash song from the '86 movie *Top Gun*."

LIVE TONIGHT!

JOE JACKSON/		POLICE	London, Hammersmith Odeon
ORIGINAL MIRRORS	Dublin, Olympic Ballroom	KILLING JOKE/HARDWARE	London, Moonlight Club
PIRANHAS	London, 101 Club	WRECKLESS ERIC	London, Nashville
MO-DETTES/INDUSTRIALS	London, Bridge House	BAD MANNERS	London, Windsor Castle

19th - Wednesday...............

JOHN FOXX, the former lead singer for Ultravox, is back with a new sound. He quit the group back in April and has been putting together his own Metal Beat Records label. His first release will be his own single "Underpass" on January 4th. That will be followed by a full length album he's already finished. He's also looking for bands to sign on a one-off basis to record and produce.

U2 and other Irish bands are featured on a sampler called "Just For Kicks." It's on Kick Records and is a celebration of new bands churning around Dublin, Ireland. It's also a great vehicle for an unsigned band to be heard. The LP starts off with local heroes U2 and "Stories For Boys." This is the same version of the song from their EP "U2-Three-Four." It's followed by Berlin, D.C. Nein, Rocky de Valera & The Gravediggers, Pesistors, Sacre Bleu, The Atrix, New Versions, The Teen Commandments, Zebra, Jaroc, and Square Meal. In the album's liner notes, Irish Radio personality Dave Fanning wrote "Now that Dublin has proved to be as important a city on the international rock map as almost any other in Europe, the local scene has clearly benefitted in every way. The success of Thin Lizzy and the Boomtown Rats, the availability of pirate radio, the consolidation of Hot Press as the authoritative rock journal, and this year's huge success of FTE Radio 2, have all combined to create a firm base to take us through the Eighties. From the Baggot to the Crofton, and McGonagles, to the Dandelion, all of these bands have helped to keep the music (a)live."

BEAT/GOD'S TOY	Liverpool, Eric's	OUT/LIPSTICK/ART FAILURES	London, Moonlight Club
V.I.P.'S/THE ACT	London, 101 Club	PIRANHAS	London, College Of Printing
YACHTS	London, Nashville	BOYS	London, Marquee

DECEMBER 1979

PISS ARTISTS (Lurkers) ....London, Fulham Greyhound   POLICE ....London, Rainbow

21st - Friday...

MADNESS have a new single, their second for Stiff Records out today. It's called "My Girl" and is flipped with "Stepping Into Line." While the "A" side is from their album "One Step Beyond," the flip is a new, non-LP track.

THE BEAT, who are riding high with their debut single "Tears Of A Clown," have signed with Arista Records. They'll have their own imprint called "Go Feet Records" and will be able to suggest other groups for the label.

Their patrons, The Specials, have had a great year in '79 as well. Their Two Tone Records label had five single released this year and all five were hits. They're planning a live EP after the first of the year that included "Too Much Too Young," "Guns Of Navarone," "Skinhead Moonstomp," "Liquidator" and "Longshot Kick The Bucket." They're also to be featured in a documentary on the label as part of the BBC 2's *Arena* TV series. It's scheduled to be aired in March.

LIVE TONIGHT!

STIFF LITTLE FINGERS/	TEARDROP EXPLODES/
MEMBERS ....Belfast, Ulster Hall	ECHO & THE BUNNYMEN/
SPECIALS ....Edinburgh, Tiffany's	SCRITTI POLITTI/
SQUIRE..................................London, Acklam Hall	THE EXPELAIRES ....London, Electric Ballroom
THE ACT ....London, Dingwalls	TRADITION/
FLOCK OF SEAGULLS ....London, Electric Ballroom	BODY SNATCHERS ....London, Music Machine
MEDIUM MEDIUM ....London, Hope & Anchor	XTC/RANDOM HOLD ....London, Nashville

22nd - Saturday...

THE TOURISTS' gig at the Nashville tonight is being recorded for a possible live album. Their live dates are usually sell out events and everyone seems excited about the shows, except the music press. Perhaps that's why they're hitting the road after the first of the year under the headline "The Last Laugh Tour." The Tourists are currently #6 in the UK with their single "I Only Want To Be With You."

SQUEEZE & THE POLICE are getting in the holiday spirit, by teaming up to do a charity concert. The double bill is under the heading "Regatta de Cats," taking in a portion of both of the band's current album titles. Admission is granted by donating a toy for Dr. Barnado's Homes. Only 2,500 tickets are available and will be administered by the Capitol Radio staff. Squeeze will be leaving on a month-long tour covering the UK in February and will have their next LP "Argy Bargy" out in March, after which they head for the States.

THE PRETENDERS' debut album is almost ready for release. It's called "The Pretenders" and will include a new version of "The Wait" as well as "Brass In Pocket" the Kinks' song "Stop Your Sobbing" and "Private Lives." It's out on January 4th. The Pretenders play the second of two special Christmas shows tonight at the Marquee.

PROTEX ....Glasgow, The Bungalow	DAMNED/SECURITY RISK/
TEARDROP EXPLODES/	SATELLITES ....London, Electric Ballroom
ECHO & THE BUNNYMEN............Liverpool, Eric's	DOLLY MIXTURE/KICKS ....London, Moonlight Club
PRETENDERS...........................London, Marquee	TOURISTS................................London, Nashville

26th - Wednesday...

THE BOOMTOWN RATS are the subject of a two-hour Radio 1 Special called "The Year Of The Rats." It's an interview and music program that features Bob Geldof talking about the band's rise to success from obscurity in Ireland. Rare, never before released, early recordings will be included in the broadcast tonight from 6-8pm.

JOY DIVISION are featured on a new Earcom collection from Fast Records. Each band gets a pair of new songs. Joy Division contribute "Auto Suggestion" and "From Safety To Where...?" Both are leftover tracks from the sessions that produced their LP "Unknown Pleasures." The tracks are dark, haunting and some of the band's best.

THE BODYSNATCHERS are featured in *Sounds* this week in a full page article titled "Invasion Of The Bodysnatchers." The seven-piece all-girl band got their beginnings only three months ago when Nicky took out a newspaper advert looking for "rude girls," reggae slang for girls inclined to the ska lifestyle. By September the group was coming together. Nicky took up the bass, "S.J." (aka Sarah Jane Owens) on guitar, Miranda Joyce on sax, Stella Barker on rhythm guitar, Pennie Leyton on keyboards, Jane Summers on drums, and Rhoda Dakar on vocals. They play mostly covers but have two originals. One is "The Ghost Of The Vox Continental" and the other is "The Old Boiler."

THE CLASH ....London, Acklam Hall   SAD AMONG STRANGERS ....London, Two Brewers

28th - Friday...

THE THOMPSON TWINS have just finished recording their debut single "Brave" and plan to have it out in a few weeks on Manchester-based Rhesus Records. The group are from Chesterfield. Just starting to "pay their dues" in the business, the Thompson Twins will help define 1983 with songs like "Love On Your Side," "Hold Me Now" and "We Are Detective," but from a 1979 perspective, that's a long way off.

PORK DUKES are, without doubt, the crudest punk band. Now they've graced us all with an album's worth of their own juvenile sordid sex songs. The LP contains the "hit" singles "Bend & Flush," "Melody Makers" and "Tight Pussy," but wait there's more! Also on the album are "Stuck Up," "Big Tits," "Penicillin Princess," "Soho Girls" and "Sick Of Sex." The album is pressed up on the cheapest of pink vinyl

DECEMBER 1979

and comes in a plain white sleeve with stickers identifying the band and a photo sticker of a pig in red boots. Low budget, low brow.

CRASS anarchists celebrate! The Crass have another LP out and it's a double one for less than £3! The "Stations Of The Crass" is almost forty tracks carefully recorded over a period of twenty-four hours. Three of the sides are studio material, one is a live set from last August. Sing-along anarchistic tracks include "White Punks On Hope," "Crutch Of Society," "I Ain't Thick, It's Just A Trick" and "Chairman Of The Bored." This special release comes in a 3' x 2' fold out poster with all the words copiously typed out and photo montages on the reverse.

LIVE TONIGHT!

PROTEX ....Dublin, McGonnagles	MADNESS/BAD MANNERS
ORCHESTRAL MANOEUVRES	V.I.P.'s/BODYSNATCHERS/.........London, Lyceum
IN THE DARK/DALEK I ....Liverpool, Eric's	LAMBRETTAS/
HAWKWIND/	MALCOLM PRACTICE ....London, Music Machine
PSYCHEDELIC FURS ....London, Electric Ballroom	HOLLY & THE ITALIANS ....London, Nashville
THE WHO/SPECIALS ....London, Hammersmith Odeon	

29th - Saturday.....................................

ANOTHER PRETTY FACE are on the cover of the new *Sounds* magazine. Inside, Garry Bushell describes the Scottish band as, "...working in orthodox rock areas, their best numbers topical feel of most of 'Give 'Em Enough Rope' or later Springsteen songs. Their music is CONTINENT size, large and sinewy building to ecstatic pinnacles on the broad-shoulders of twin ace men Mike Scott and John Caldwell." Their debut single of "Whatever Happened To The West" and "Goodbye 70s" is scheduled to be released at the end of January. Other songs in their set are Lightning That Strikes Twice," "That's Not Enough," "Witness," "Soul To Soul" and "Graduation Day."

SCRITTI POLITTI have a new single out, a little over a month since their last EP, and now Scritti Politti have out a new record, their third for the year. The EP is "Peel Session," which is exactly what it is, four songs recorded for BBC broadcast by John Peel. He had played their previous record on his evening radio program and invited the band to do a session. They recorded "Scritlocks Door," "OPEC-Immac," "Messthetics" and "Hegemony." These four songs are now available on a 7" EP on St Pancras/Rough Trade Records. Its "sleeve" is actually two xeroxed squares that detail record pressing costs, as usual with this D.I.Y. band.

ELVIS COSTELLO is part of a huge Christmas concert tonight. On the bill is Paul McCartney & Wings, Rockpile, and Elvis Costello. Tape decks are rolling and a new track called "The Imposter" by Elvis is captured. It will eventually appear on the "Concerts for Kampuchea" double album. Elvis had hoped he would have his new album out by now. It's already recorded, but the collapse of Radar five months ago has tied it up in legal claims. Elvis hopes that at least a single can be released soon. There are plans for a 45 with a cover of the Sam & Dave song "I Can't Stand Up For Falling Down" b/w Dave Edmunds' song "Girl Talk" to come out on Two Tone Records in a few weeks. If the lawyers can work it out. Meanwhile, Elvis does appear on the new George Jones album "My Very Special Friends." The country superstar sings duets with guests like Emmylou Harris, Waylon Jennings, Johnny Paycheck, Tammy Wynette and Elvis Costello. The duo go through "Stranger In The House."

HAWKWIND/	LEW LEWIS/BAD ....MANNERS Liverpool, Eric's
PSYCHEDELIC FURS ....London, Electric Ballroom	

31st - Monday.........................

TOM ROBINSON has been out of the scene since he split up the TRB in July. His new group is in rehearsals and is about to debut. They call themselves S-27, short for Sector 27. It's as neutral a name as they could come up with. S-27 is Tom Robinson on vocals and rhythm guitar, Jo Burt on bass, Derek The Menace on drums and Stevie B on lead guitar. Robinson told the *NME* that, "The most important thing is to wipe the slate completely clean, so that the new thing stands or falls in its own right. We won't be singing '2-4-6-8 Motorway' again, we won't be trading on the reputation of the previous band."

BLONDIE ....Glasgow, Apollo Centre	MEMBERS ....London, Music Machine
SELECTER.............................London, Dingwalls	BAD MANNERS/RACQUETS ....London, Windsor Castle
ADAM & THE ANTS/	ANY TROUBLE........................Manchester, Commercial Hotel
BLACK ARABS/CYANIDE/	JOY DIVISION
ENGLISH SUBTITLES ....London, Electric Ballroom	(private party) ....Manchester, Picadilly Gardens

"Forget about music and concentrate
on generating, generation gaps.
Terrorize, threaten and insult your own
useless generation."

— Malcolm McLaren, 1978, *The Great Rock & Roll Swindle*

BRITISH ISLES

ABERDEEN ●

SCOTLAND

● GLASGOW

● EDINBURGH

N. IRELAND

● BELFAST

NEWCASTLE ●

IRELAND

● DUBLIN

BLACKPOOL ●

● LEEDS

LIVERPOOL ●

● MANCHESTER

● SHEFFIELD

● NOTTINGHAM

WALES

● WOLVERHAMPTON

● BIRMINGHAM

● COVENTRY

ENGLAND

CARDIFF ●

● BRISTOL

● CAMBRIDGE

● SWINDON

HIGH WYCOMBE ●

READING ●

● PLYMOUTH

GUILDFORD ●

● LONDON

● CROYDON

● BRIGHTON

N

To use index: Find entry, then seek out date in Diary. All entries arranged by date.

ABOUT THE AUTHOR..................

It would be difficult to find anyone more in touch with the punk music than George Gimarc. Early in 1977, he originated one of America's first new wave radio programs, The Rock & Roll Alternative. It ran continuously for fourteen years and was heard on various stations in England, Ireland, Belgium, Italy, Australia and New Zealand, as well as at home in Texas. Since hitting the air in 1975, George has remained on the forefront of music, discovering new talent and breaking cutting edge sounds. He's interviewed hundreds of the scene's movers & shakers, making careers and setting trends. He was the driving force behind KDGE radio in Dallas; one of the nation's leading new rock stations with an audience in the hundreds of thousands. Always looking for the next big thing, he now runs an independent record company that releases CD's twice a year of unsigned bands from around America. His passion for music explains his collecting some 65,000 records, and knowing something about each and every one of them. There are few that can put a work like this together working from real life experience and their own resources.

George first started writing "PUNK DIARY: 1970-79" because he needed a reference book on the period and there wasn't one to be found. Even now, a decade later, there is little except "England's Dreaming" which takes an accurate and detailed look at the entirety of the punk boom. "Punk Diary" changes all that. Not only accurate with the resources used to compile it, it has also been fact checked by many of the major musicians of the period, each giving it a resounding thumbs up.

A 70 minute compact disc interview companion to Punk Diary is available from George Gimarc, price £3.50. If you want one, please send a money order to George Gimarc, Box 280173, Dallas, Texas 75228, USA and it will be shipped immediately by air. The contents are listed below.

PUNK DIARY - CD